Secret History

OF THE AMERICAN REVOLUTION

BOOKS BY CARL VAN DOREN

AUTOBIOGRAPHY

Three Worlds

BIOGRAPHY

Benjamin Franklin   ·   Swift   ·   Thomas Love Peacock
James Branch Cabell   ·   Sinclair Lewis
Jane Mecom

FICTION

Other Provinces   ·   The Ninth Wave

LITERARY HISTORY AND CRITICISM

The American Novel   ·   Contemporary American Novelists
The Roving Critic   ·   Many Minds
American and British Literature Since 1890
(with Mark Van Doren)

What Is American Literature?

HISTORY

The Great Rehearsal   ·   Mutiny in January

EDITED

The Cambridge History of American Literature
Modern American Prose   ·   An Anthology of World Prose
The Letters of Benjamin Franklin and Jane Mecom

SECRET HISTORY

of the

American Revolution

○ ○ ○

An Account
of the Conspiracies of Benedict Arnold and Numerous Others
drawn from the Secret Service Papers of the British Head-
quarters in North America now for the first time examined
and made public

○ ○ ○

By Carl Van Doren

THE VIKING PRESS : NEW YORK

Viking Compass Edition
Issued in 1968 by The Viking Press, Inc.
625 Madison Avenue, New York, N.Y. 10022

Distributed in Canada by
The Macmillan Company of Canada Limited

Library of Congress catalog card number: 41-24478
Printed in U.S.A.

PREFACE

HERE for the first time the story of Benedict Arnold's treason is fully told. This was not possible before the complete Arnold-André correspondence recently came to light in the British Headquarters files preserved among the Clinton Papers now in the William L. Clements Library at the University of Michigan. That correspondence—including Arnold's letters and copies of André's—at last furnishes a detailed record of the beginnings of the treachery, of the intricate negotiations, of the confederates, emissaries, and messengers, of the schemes leading to the famous catastrophe. The treason, long so mystifying, now appears as the downright transaction it was. Traditional guesses about Arnold, either that he was a villain out of melodrama or that he was a disillusioned hero honestly converted to the enemy, give way to facts which show him to have been bold, crafty, unscrupulous, unrepentant: the Iago of traitors.

The Arnold-André correspondence led naturally and irresistibly to hundreds of unpublished letters to or from Arnold, on public or private business, in the Library of Congress among the Washington Papers or the Papers of the Continental Congress. In them Arnold contrived to seem a patriotic American throughout the sixteen months in which he was bargaining with the British. These letters led still further to the earlier records of Arnold's accounts with Congress and of his greedy dealings while in command at Philadelphia, and of his later self-justifications and claims and rewards. Unknown or neglected sources, all of them cited in the General Bibliography and Chapter References at the end of this volume, add so much to the old story as to make it virtually new. The Appendix, with its exact text of the Arnold-André correspondence, must rank at once with the most striking and revealing Revolutionary documents published in the past hundred years.

What began as a special study of Arnold and his treason had to be enlarged to a general history of such transactions during the Revolution. For Arnold was only one of many rebels who thought of changing sides or were urged to do it. The war had its rise in a political controversy, and it remained a civil conflict in America after it had become a struggle between the United States and Great Britain. Loyalist partisans and British officials always believed that the patriot party might at any time collapse and that individual patriots might give up the hopeless cause if they were offered a safe and profitable chance to make peace with their former government. Advances were made, as this history displays, to Israel Putnam, John Sullivan, Philip Schuyler, Ethan Allen, Samuel Holden Parsons, and in Paris to Silas Deane and even to Franklin. Along with the operations of the armed forces went the less visible designs of the British secret service with its loyalist intermediaries, always ready to treat with discontented rebels.

There were more than a few such rebels. Benjamin Church, director of the first American army hospital, was a paid informer of General Gage in Boston. Metcalf Bowler, chief justice of Rhode Island, was in treacherous correspondence with Sir Henry Clinton. William Heron, a member of the Connecticut assembly, was a double-dealer who for more than a year served the British and got favours from them. Edward Fox of Maryland, a clerk in the Continental treasury at Philadelphia, offered to procure information for the British and received an encouraging payment. William Rankin, colonel of militia in York county, Pennsylvania, assured the British that he had organized 7000 Americans on that frontier and in Delaware and Maryland who would rise against Congress if Clinton would support them. Samuel Wallis, of Muncy Manor on the Susquehanna, was Arnold's agent and Clinton's correspondent though so stealthy in his movements that he has not hitherto been detected. And there were numerous others, outwardly patriots, who gave the British clandestine aid in a desire to stand well with the victors, whoever they should be.

Some of these traitors or double-dealers have already been exposed. Their stories are now fitted into the secret history of which they are a part. The secret history is presented only as a part of the whole history of the Revolution. Yet that whole history turns out to have been affected and coloured by the constant hope of the British and loyalists that they might win wavering patriots over and by the fear of the firmer patriots that this could be done.

Beneath the open war there was a hidden war, more dangerous to the Americans than has ever been realized.

Though innumerable printed sources have been consulted for this book, its principal sources are manuscripts. Acknowledgments are due, and gratefully rendered, to the William L. Clements Library, the Library of Congress, the New York Public Library, the New York Historical Society, the Historical Society of Pennsylvania, the Fort Ticonderoga Museum, the Harvard College Library, and the Yale University School of the Fine Arts for permission to read, photograph, or reproduce manuscripts in their possession. The study was suggested by Julian P. Boyd, librarian of Princeton University, and made possible by Randolph G. Adams, director of the Clements Library, who granted the freest, easiest access to the most precious papers in that incomparable collection. Howard Peckham, who transcribed and collated the documents in the Appendix, and Lloyd A. Brown, curators at the Clements Library, lent valued technical assistance. And generous help on particular points came from Katharine W. Bennet, Weldon A. Brown, Bernhard Knollenberg, Ida M. Mellen, and T. Kenneth Wood—not to mention dozens of correspondents who answered inquiring letters.

Though the characters and events of this narrative sound like fiction, nothing in *Secret History* has been invented. Every statement is based on a document, and every conjecture. Actual men or women did or thought or wrote these things in actual places at actual times, and the record wherever possible is in their actual words. The story is as close to history as it could get. At that distance history is the next thing to experience.

CONTENTS

ILLUSTRATIONS

Before Arnold

Shifting Loyalties

EARLY in October 1777, when Lieutenant General John
Burgoyne with his British army of invasion from Canada
still hoped that in spite of the swarming rebel levies he might
reach Albany, command the Hudson, and cut the American rebellion in two, Lieutenant General Sir Henry Clinton, commanding the British forces in occupied New York, moved suddenly up
the river, took Forts Montgomery and Clinton in the Highlands
below West Point, and sent an expedition to burn Kingston, then
the temporary capital of the state. Not satisfied with this public
defeat of Major General Israel Putnam, American commander in
the Highlands department, Clinton took occasion also to make
secret overtures to Putnam who might, Clinton hoped, now think
it prudent to give up the unpromising rebel cause and return for
safety to his old allegiance.

Putnam, the valiant, peppery folk-hero of the subsequent Revolutionary tradition, has come to seem one of the last Americans
whom any British general would then have chosen to approach
with such a purpose. But ten months earlier it had been reported[1]
from New York to the Earl of Dartmouth, late secretary of state
for the colonies, that Putnam thought the American cause was
"nearly ruined"; and Clinton may have heard through some informer that Putnam, in the Highlands command since May, appeared to be obstinate and unenterprising—or discontented and
discouraged? Putnam's grievance might be Clinton's chance. Fur-
thermore, Clinton had an emissary who could go to Putnam on
the pretext of an innocent errand.

This was Colonel Beverley Robinson, who had recently distinguished himself at the storming of Fort Montgomery. Robinson,
whose father had been an acting governor of Virginia under the

Crown and whose brother a treasurer of that province, had himself been a friend of George Washington in their youth. Beverley Robinson in 1746 raised a Virginia company for the expedition against Canada on which William Franklin, son of the great Franklin, went with the Pennsylvania troops. In New York Robinson met and married Susanna, daughter of Frederick Philipse of Philipse Manor. An early legend which is still cherished along the Hudson insists that Washington, visiting New York after Braddock's defeat, met and courted Mary Philipse, sister of Susanna Robinson and also an heiress of the great Philipse estate in Westchester and Dutchess counties. There have been guesses as to what might have happened if Washington through Mary Philipse had become a landowner in New York instead of becoming, partly through Martha Dandridge Custis, a landowner in Virginia.

Robinson, capably managing his wife's fortune and thoroughly assimilated to the New York gentry, could not bring himself to side with his rebel countrymen after the Declaration of Independence, though till February 1777 he lived quietly at his manor house in Dutchess county, Then, when John Jay told him that he must choose[2] but that the Americans "should be exceeding happy to have you with us," Robinson finally refused to take the oath of allegiance to the new state and was obliged to leave his house for refuge in New York inside the British lines. Shut up in the crowded town, he raised a regiment called the Loyal Americans, chiefly among his tenants and neighbours in the country, and busied himself with collecting information for Clinton about American activities along the Hudson. Robinson's house, on the east side of the river a little below West Point, was occupied by the Americans and used variously as headquarters and hospital for the Highlands district. Putnam—or at least his family—was there when Clinton took the Highlands forts. Robinson, so close to his house, could seem to be going to it on private business and nobody else but Clinton and Putnam need know what his actual intention was.

In a letter[3] to Clinton, preserved in the British Headquarters files, Robinson told the story. "As you mentioned to me that you would be very glad to sound the old man and to try if he could

SIR
HENRY
CLINTON

not be brought over, when I was in my house in the Highlands
I waited on Mrs. Putnam in her room." She was then confined to
the bed in which she died on October 13. "After the first compliments were over I desired everybody to leave the room. I then
told her I really had a regard for the general and should be
happy could it ever be in my power to serve him; that I had so
good an opinion of his principles that they could not differ a
great deal from my own, which was to wish for and endeavour to
restore peace and legal government to our poor country. And
therefore if he had the least inclination to make his own peace
(and put an end to the rebellion) that I was convinced it was in
his power to do it upon honourable terms. And if he wished to
take that step I should be glad to have a conference with him and
did not doubt but it would be in my power to make him such
offers as would be agreeable; and I desired her to make this
known to him. But whether she did or not I could never know."

Whether or not Putnam received this message, he did not re-
spond directly to it or confer with Robinson. But Robinson remained for some time in the neighbourhood, sent a letter under
a flag of truce to Putnam, and got a civil letter (now missing)
from his son and aide, Major Daniel Putnam. "I answered that
letter as civil as I could," Robinson reported to Clinton, "and
pressed to have a conference with him or his father." This was
on October 24, after both Robinson and Putnam had heard of
Burgoyne's surrender at Saratoga, and the rebel cause looked
promising once more. Daniel Putnam on November 11 wrote to
Robinson appointing a time and place for a conference.

Of course Putnam's invalid wife may not have told her husband of Robinson's inquiring overtures, and Daniel Putnam may
have thought this conference was to be solely about the household
goods Robinson had left for Putnam's use. In any case, there is
not a sign in the son's letter that either he or his father felt outraged or dishonoured by whatever proposals had reached them.
Daniel Putnam was sorry, he wrote, that Robinson's request of
the 24th had been "through some mistake . . . not delivered to
me till after you had gone down the river. I should have been
particularly happy in a conference with a person so universally
esteemed as Colonel Robinson; and the disappointment gave me

not a little uneasiness. But if you have still an inclination and will come with a flag to Williams's on Friday next the 14th instant at twelve o'clock, I will meet you there, and you may depend on safe protection and liberty to return when you think proper." He had delayed answering, he explained, only because he had been ill. His father, "as commanding officer of the post, thinks it rather improper for him, otherwise he would have waited on you himself. He desires his compliments to yourself and family."

Robinson, forwarding the letter to Clinton, said he would gladly go out if Clinton approved and would "give me a lesson what to say." But here the documents of the episode end, and do not show whether Clinton consented or Robinson went to the meeting which General Putnam had agreed to. If there was a meeting, of course nothing came of it such as Robinson had in mind. Neither of the Putnams ever appeared to waver in loyalty to the United States. Yet the Robinson-Putnam correspondence strikingly illuminates those complex times. Robinson could assume that Putnam might think the war had gone on long enough and might be ready to make a private peace with the British if he could do it honourably—and safely. Putnam through his son could use a language of compliment and courtesy, as if Robinson were not so much a dangerous enemy as a member of a rival political party.

II

To make such attitudes intelligible it is necessary to reconsider the two years and more before Burgoyne's invasion and defeat. The American Revolution had begun as a political controversy which no remembered American—except possibly Samuel Adams—looked upon as a revolution that might lead to independence. Many American Tories opposed the American policy of the British ministry and approved of the firm though loyal protests sent to the king by the First Continental Congress in 1774. The American Whigs believed that in their resistance to specific acts of the British government they were defending the general rights of Englishmen. Benjamin Franklin, agent in London for Georgia, Pennsylvania, New Jersey, Massachusetts, and virtual ambassador from America, had been regularly consulted by the British Whigs. The Earl of Chatham, greatest of Whigs, had trusted the American's judgment on American affairs, Chatham told Franklin, "as men set their watches by a regulator." Franklin in July 1773 had written to John Winthrop at Harvard that "as between friends every affront is not worth a duel, between nations every injury not worth a war, so between governed and the government every mistake in government, every encroachment on rights, is not worth a rebellion." In October 1774 the peace-loving philosopher was still in "perpetual anxiety . . . lest an accidental quarrel, a personal insult, an imprudent order, an insolent execution of even a prudent one"—in Massachusetts to which British troops had been sent to quiet the rebels—"or twenty other things may produce a tumult, unforeseen and therefore impossible to be prevented, in which such a carnage may ensue as to make a breach that can never afterwards be healed."[4]

The battles of Lexington and Concord six months later produced just such a tumult as Franklin had foreseen and dreaded. But even Thomas Jefferson, who was to draft the Declaration of Independence, could on August 25, 1775[5] write that he was still "looking with fondness towards a reconciliation with Great Britain. . . . I . . . would rather be in dependence on Great Britain, properly limited, than on any nation on earth, or on no nation." John Adams, who with Franklin was the next year to help revise the Declaration, on October 4 wrote[6] from Philadelphia, where he was sitting as a delegate to the Second Continental Congress, that reconciliation was still possible. "We cannot in this country conceive that there are men in England so infatuated as seriously to suspect the Congress, or people here, of a wish to erect ourselves into an independent state. If such an idea really obtains amongst those at the helm of affairs, one hour's residence in America would eradicate it. I never met one individual so inclined, but it is universally disavowed." Jefferson's letter, to John Randolph in London, found its way to Dartmouth. Adams's, to William Lee, was intercepted by the British post office. Both were presumably read by officials who did not take too much stock in the rebels' insistence that they would yield no further unless the ministry yielded first.

And yet there was frequent talk about American independence in England, where the idea flourished. Alexander Wedderburn, the king's solicitor general, had in January 1774 viciously sneered at Franklin before the Privy Council for favouring, if not plotting, a "Great American Republic." Josiah Tucker, dean of Gloucester, had in a pamphlet[7] the same year gravely argued that both England and America would profit if they were to become separate nations though still allied by treaty. It was a common English retort to American demands for a larger measure of self-government that these could end only in independence and therefore must not be granted. A process familiar to many public and private histories was at work. The English by prophesying phantoms were creating realities.

A similar process was at work across the Atlantic. In the bitter vituperations that went on during 1775, between the American Whigs who believed that only armed force could uphold the rights of Englishmen in America, and the American Tories, who persisted in thinking that peaceful constitutional measures would do the same thing better, the Tories insulted the Whigs by saying they aimed at independence, and the Whigs indignantly denied it. Congress, after it had chosen Washington to be commander-in-chief of "the army of the United Colonies, of all the forces raised or to be raised by them, and of all others who shall voluntarily offer their services and join the said army for the defence of American liberty and for repelling every hostile invasion thereof," drew up a final petition as from "your Majesty's faithful subjects" hoping for "happy and permanent reconciliation." The petition reached Dartmouth too late to be presented to the king, who had on August 23 proclaimed that the Americans were in "open and avowed rebellion." Not only, according to the proclamation, were the civil and military officers to exert "their utmost endeavours" to suppress it, but "all our subjects of this realm, and the dominions thereunto belonging, are bound by law to be aiding and assisting in the suppression of such rebellion, and to disclose and make known to us all traitorous conspiracies and attempts against us."[8] Americans, organizing an army to resist the British government, might have expected that the government would think and call them rebels. But they resented both the name and the consequences. Heretofore it had been the British and American Tories who talked of independence. Now the idea began to be accepted by those who had been accused of it.

After the burning of Falmouth (Portland) by the British in October some unknown friend of liberty on November 21 distributed a printed broadside[9] among Washington's officers and men at Cambridge and Roxbury, telling them "we expect soon to break off all kind of connexion with Great Britain, and form into a Grand Republic of the American United Colonies." In the *Virginia Gazette* on January 5, 1776, after the burning of Norfolk, an American deplored "that childish fondness for Britain, and that foolish, tame dependence on her." Five days later the English-born Thomas Paine in Philadelphia published *Common Sense*, the pamphlet which became a war-cry.

The Americans had heard such words before, but never set to such ringing tunes. "Society in every state is a blessing, but government even in its best state is but a necessary evil; in its worst state an intolerable one. . . . Government, like dress, is the badge of lost innocence; the palaces of kings are built upon the ruins of the bowers of paradise. . . . To the evil of monarchy we have added that of hereditary succession; and as the first is a degradation and lessening of ourselves, so the second, claimed as a matter of right, is an insult and imposition on posterity." As to the present conflict between America and England: "The sun never shined on a cause of greater worth. 'Tis not the affair of a city, a county, a province, or a kingdom, but of a continent—of at least one eighth part of the habitable globe. . . . All plans, proposals, etc. prior to the nineteenth of April [the day of Lexington and Concord] . . . are like the almanacs of last year, which though proper then are superseded and useless now. . . . Everything that is right or reasonable pleads for separation. The blood of the slain, the weeping voice of nature, cries: ' 'Tis time to part.' . . . Nature hath deserted the connexion, and art cannot supply her place. . . . In no instance hath nature made the satellite larger than its primary planet; and as England and America, with respect to each other, reverse the common order of nature, it is evident they belong to different systems: England to Europe, America to itself." The true king of America "reigns above, and doth not make havoc of mankind like the Royal Brute of Great Britain. . . . O ye that love mankind! Ye that dare oppose not only the tyranny but the tyrant! Stand forth! Every spot of the old world is overrun with oppression. Freedom hath been hunted round the globe. Asia and Africa hath long expelled her. Europe regards her like a stranger, and England hath given her warning to depart. O receive the fugitive, and prepare in time an asylum for mankind."

To one contemporary[10] *Common Sense* seemed "completely calculated for the meridian of North America. The author introduces a new system of politics, as widely different from the old as the Copernican system is from the Ptolemaic. . . . This animated piece dispels . . . the prejudice of the mind against the doctrine of independence and pours in upon it . . . an inundation of light and truth. . . . The ineffable delight with which it is perused, and its doctrines imbibed, is a demonstration that the seeds of independence, though imported with the troops from Britain, will grow surprisingly with proper cultivation in the fields of America." Yet while the sentiment of independence grew so rapidly that Congress on July 4 could adopt its famous Declaration, there were still in every part of the country many honest men who were as passionately opposed to it as ever. Parliament had prohibited all trade and intercourse with the colonies and had declared an absolute blockade. But Parliament had also, the Americans heard, appointed commissioners to bring what the king—borrowing a term from Congress—liked to call the Olive Branch of peace.

The commissioners were Sir William Howe, already commander-in-chief of the British land forces in North America, and Richard, Earl Howe, admiral of the British fleet which was to blockade the American ports. Conciliation was to go hand in hand with coercion. The loyalists (Tories) did not object to this. They regarded the Second Continental Congress as a usurping body, and they were as anxious as king or Parliament to see it overthrown. The Howe brothers were known to be friends to America. Through them, the loyalists had no doubt, the conflict might be settled on friendly terms. It was a pity that Lord Howe did not arrive in New York harbour till the week after independence was declared. Still, Congress might rescind its illegal act rather than go on with the mad war, and the colonies might be restored to a happier place and share in the British Empire. It turned out that the Howes had authority only to accept submission and issue pardons to repentant rebels, after which British rule in America might be reorganized with considerable reference to American dissatisfactions and demands. Congress refused to yield to the British commissioners, who did not recognize the right of Congress to speak for America, and the majority of Americans took the side of Congress.

The commissioners, offering to treat separately with colonies, districts, towns, or individuals that had never joined the common cause or that might be willing to desert it, intensified the division between the loyalists and the patriots (Whigs). What had been a political controversy became increasingly a civil war. The king's proclamation, ordering all faithful subjects to aid and assist in putting down the rebellion, gave the loyalists a legal sanction for resistance to the rebel usurpers. An unnamed loyalist recruiting officer in a speech on Long Island in September 1776[11] told his hearers that Congress, along with other rebel committees and conventions, had deluded the populace, betrayed their trust, forfeited the confidence of the public, and ruined the country. "Not to oppose them and their measures were criminal." So long as the quarrel was merely politics, all shades of opinion had been possible, from extreme conservatism to extreme radicalism, with many intermediate variations. When independence became the essential issue, and the country was definitely in a state of war, the number of opinions had—or seemed to have—to be reduced to two. Men must, the patriots declared, be either for or against the liberties of America; or must, according to the loyalists, be either for or against the lawful government. Both sides had excuses for the violent measures they took against each other.

They had excuses, too, for certain secret measures which were far more numerous than any history of the Revolution has ever made known. The hard line drawn between the parties to the conflict found persons who were not clearly, unchangeably on either side, but who might, converted or resentful, under pressure or influence, shift loyalties. From the loyalist point of view, all American officials and soldiers were conspirators, mutineers, deserters from their true allegiance. Of the twelve generals besides Washington who were appointed by Congress in June 1775 all but one—Nathanael Greene of Rhode Island—had held commissions under the Crown, if only in the colonial militia; and three of them—Charles Lee, Horatio Gates, and Richard Montgomery—had been born in England and had served in the British army. No loyalist, any more than any British commander or his agent, saw anything wrong in trying to win the deserters back. They could not, strictly speaking, be traitors to a state which had no constitutional right to exist, and which therefore did not exist. To coax or urge or bribe them to come over was only to make an effort to restore them to their lawful duty.

The patriots had another point of view. They believed they had set up a legitimate government founded on natural human rights. Before July 1776 revolutionary committees had nagged and bullied Tories, and wherever possible disarmed them. Mobs had grossly abused and humiliated them. After the Declaration the new states passed laws against the loyalists as traitors. Living in America, they adhered to a European government which by its laws might, if it suppressed what it still called a rebellion of its colonies, hang the rebels and confiscate their property. The patriots, who moved more rapidly than the loyalists and formed an American government while the loyalists were waiting for the British government to act, struck first with such fines, imprisonments, banishments, confiscations, and—later—even death sentences against loyalists as the patriots themselves might expect if they should be defeated. The loyalists, outnumbered and outmanœuvred, could turn only to the British armed forces for protection.

Hundreds of refugees from various parts of New England found shelter with General Gage in Boston in 1775, and 1124, according to official lists, left with General Howe for Halifax in March 1776.[12] When the Howes took New York in October nearly 1000 New Yorkers signed their names to a loyal address[13] declaring: "that we bear true allegiance to our rightful sovereign George the Third as well as warm affection to his sacred person, crown, and dignity." During General Howe's occupation of Philadelphia from September 1777 to June 1778 so many Pennsylvanians committed themselves to the king's side, and so incurred American hostility, that something like 3000 loyalists accompanied the British on their return to New York. Till the end of the war New York was the stronghold of loyalist refugees, who from all parts of the United States came to live there in swarming desperation. There most of the loyalist regiments were raised to fight against the rebel Americans. And there most of the secret loyalist or British measures against the rebels were undertaken and managed.

III

New York had seen plots before the British occupation. On June 15, 1776, when Washington was in Manhattan and the royal governor William Tryon on one of the king's ships in the harbour where he had spent the past eight months, two Continental soldiers came before the provincial congress on the charge of attempting to pass counterfeit currency. One of them, Thomas Hickey, was a member of Washington's guard. Locked up in the City Hall, they both in the hearing of other prisoners "cursed and swore a great deal and damned themselves if they would ever fight any more for America." They were, they bragged, enlisted with others on the island who were to turn against the Americans as soon as the expected British came. The names of 700 were already "on board the man-of-war." Two days later the provincial congress decided that the New York courts, "being as yet held by authority derived from the Crown of Great Britain," were incompetent to try Continental soldiers; and so turned the accused men over to Washington to be dealt with by court martial. At the trial of Hickey on the 26th it was testified that he had enlisted men for the conspiracy, promising each of them a dollar "by way of encouragement." Hickey in his own defence said "he engaged in the scheme at first for the sake of cheating the Tories, and getting some money from them, and afterwards consented to have his name sent on board the man-of-war, in order that, if the enemy should arrive and defeat the army here, and he should be taken prisoner, he might be safe." The court found him guilty of mutiny and sedition, "and of treacherously corresponding with, enlisting among, and receiving pay from the enemies of the United American Colonies." On the 28th he was hanged in a field "near the Bowery Lane, in the presence of near 20,000 spectators."[14]

Rumour had already magnified the conspirators. It was said they planned to murder the staff officers, blow up the magazines, and secure the passes of the town. Mobs attacked Tories in the streets. The provincial congress, through a committee headed by John Jay, examined many suspected persons. The tangled, conflicting evidence seemed to point to Gilbert Forbes, a gunsmith of Broadway, as the principal recruiting agent. He had, he admitted at Hickey's trial, received over £100 for that service from the mayor of New York, David Mathews. Mathews, seized at Flatbush and brought before the committee on June 23, said that on a permitted official errand to Tryon's ship he had been asked by the governor to carry money to Forbes. Supposing Forbes was selling guns to the enemy, Mathews "told him he would be hanged if he was found out," and doubled his warning when it appeared that Forbes had recruited men for the king. After that, Mathews claimed, he had avoided any further part in the scheme. Since the royal governor could not be reached or questioned, the inquiry ended here. There was no proof that, as some convicted counterfeiters swore, Tryon was having counterfeit money made on shipboard; or that, as the gossip in taverns went, Tryon had promised 200 acres to any man who would enlist, with 100 for his wife and 50 for each child.[15]

Hickey was the only conspirator tried or put to death, but thirteen others, including Mathews and Forbes, were bundled off to prison in Connecticut, safely away from the seat of war. The mayor, as a man of rank, got some consideration. At first committed to the common jail at Hartford, he was within a week removed to Litchfield, where on August 12 he was living at the house of the sheriff of the county, "who, together with his wife, have behaved in the most genteel, kind manner. . . . They have nothing of the Yankee about them."[16] Connecticut in general, however, distrusted and disliked the New York conspirators.

Mathews and the twelve escaped or were sent back late in the year, and never had a hearing. While the mayor always denied the charges against him, he remained a loyalist official, prospered under British military rule, in October 1779 was attainted of treason by the state, and at the end of the war took flight to Cape Breton.[17] Patriot New York would not forget that he had had a hand in one of Tryon's undertakings, and was willing to believe that he had plotted assassination, even of Washington. The Hickey plot, as magnified—and falsified, blackened the reputation of the loyalists throughout the country.

Herman Zedwitz, lieutenant colonel in the 1st New York regiment of the Continental army, did not wait for temptation to come to him, but made his own advances to Tryon. Formerly an officer in the Prussian and, for a few months, in the British service, Zedwitz had entered the American with the indifference of a professional. He had been ruptured by a fall from a precipice at the attack on Quebec in December 1775 and had been recommended to Congress, which voted him $255.60 for the cure of his wound and his expenses from Quebec to Philadelphia. Disabled from active service, he brooded in New York. What he heard about the money Gilbert Forbes was said to have received from Tryon suggested to Zedwitz another scheme. The arrival of Hessian troops at Staten Island in August gave him an occasion.

Congress on the 14th—acting on the report of a committee which included Jefferson and Franklin—resolved to offer immediate rewards to Hessians who might "choose to accept of lands, liberty, safety, and a communion of good laws and mild government in a country where many of their friends and relations are already happily settled, rather than continue exposed to the toils and dangers of a long and bloody war waged against a people guilty of no other crime than that of refusing to exchange freedom for slavery." Hessians, or other foreigners, if they would desert from the British army would be accepted as American citizens "and be invested with the rights, privileges, and immunities of natives." Moreover, Congress would provide "for every such person fifty acres of unappropriated lands in some of these states, to be held by him and his heirs in absolute property." Washington on the 19th had been sent translated copies of the offer and wanted more to distribute among the dangerous—but possibly purchasable—mercenaries.[18]

Zedwitz on the 24th wrote a preposterous letter to Tryon, "to bag Your Eccilency humly to Explain the Contents of this broke English To the Admiral"—Howe who had brought the Hessians. Washington, Zedwitz untruthfully said, had asked him to translate the Hessian offer "in god Hy german": an offer, according to Zedwitz, of "200 Akers of land and a Horse & a Kow, and if he has no mynd to Serve he shall receve the sam and go to thake possession of these plantations." Tryon must remember that he himself had consented to Zedwitz's joining the Americans, "to do all in my power for his Majesty." And Tryon would know that Zedwitz, "Forced to accepd or be a Ruined Men," had "luked on me self as a forced men of a Rebellion Mopp." (There is no evidence that Tryon had any reason to remember or know anything of the kind, though Zedwitz at his subsequent hearing testified that he had come to America in 1773 with a letter to Tryon from Lord North.) Besides this untruthful and belated information about the Hessian offer, Zedwitz had a wild story of Washington's intention to poison "the Watering place." The chief news in Zedwitz's letter was that "a gentelman wich is allways near the general and has the opportunity" was willing to furnish Tryon an "Accurat State of the Armee" every week till December, for £4000 to be paid beforehand and in hard money to Zedwitz, who thought it might be managed at half that figure. Zedwitz concluded with the boast that Washington was assigning him to the command of three forts in the Highlands.

Augustus Stein, chosen to carry this letter to Tryon, was suspicious. He turned it over to Alexander Hamilton, Washington's aide, who delivered it to Washington. Zedwitz was arrested and tried by court martial at Headquarters the next day. His defence was as confused as his letter. While in the service of the British, he said, he had made friends with the Marquis of Granby, his commander. Granby had contracted with him to recruit 1000 riflemen in Germany. He had enlisted twenty and transported them to London. Within nine or ten days after Zedwitz submitted his accounts, Granby died, and neither his father the

Duke of Rutland nor the government would repay the money Zedwitz had spent. His offer to Tryon, Zedwitz insisted, was merely a scheme to recover what the British had cheated him out of. His falsehoods had been intentional deceptions. He had hoped that Tryon might dine with him, to arrange for the surrender of the Highland forts. He would then have taken Tryon prisoner. The court martial could see that Zedwitz was a fool, but they thought he had meant little more mischief than he now said. Instead of being hanged he was cashiered, rendered incapable of ever holding a commission in the service of the United States, and confined to various prisons from which he wrote persistent letters to Washington. In May 1779 Zedwitz escaped from Lancaster and was captured, dressed as a woman, at Morristown, on his way back to New York.[19]

There was nothing complex in the treachery of William Demont, adjutant to Colonel Robert Magaw of the 5th Pennsylvania regiment. Magaw was at the beginning of November 1776 in command at Fort Washington, the last stand of the Americans on Manhattan before the British who had driven Washington's main army north to White Plains and beyond. Demont, English by birth, appointed adjutant early in the year by the Pennsylvania committee of safety, and according to Alexander Graydon "intelligent in point of duty," deserted on the night of the 2nd and went over to the camp of Earl Percy at McGowan's Pass. As the deserter later[20] put it: "I sacrificed all I was worth in the world . . . and brought in with [me] the plans of Fort Washington, by which plans that fortress was taken by his Majesty's troops the 16th instant, together with 2700 prisoners and stores and ammunition to the amount of £1800. At the same time I may with justice affirm, from my knowledge of the works I saved the lives of many of his Majesty's subjects."

Captain Graydon, one of the prisoners taken, thought the British "must have had a perfect knowledge of the ground we occupied"; and he suspected Demont.[21] The assault on Fort Washington was undertaken and carried out with great exactness, probably with full benefit of the plans brought in by the deserting adjutant who knew as well as the fort's commander what were the weakest points of defence and the best approaches.

It is possible that Demont's treachery affected General Howe's decision to turn back from the pursuit of Washington northward, which might be successful, to the storming of Fort Washington, which was certain to be. It is also possible that the loss of the fort, heavy as it was, cost the Americans in the long run less than they might have lost if Howe had not—to their mystification—changed his plans. The loyalists thought so, and bitterly complained of Howe. Thomas Jones, a justice of the New York supreme court who was then an angry prisoner in Connecticut, insisted that the Americans captured at Fort Washington should all have been put to the sword.[22] "The most rigid severity at the first," he argued, "would have been the greatest mercy and lenity in the end."

Demont, whatever service he had rendered, did not profit much by it. He seems to have gone with Howe the next year to Philadelphia and to have remained with the British till 1780 when he returned to England. But in 1792 he was still claiming[23] that the British government owed him £182 10s 3d, part of which he had paid out of his own pocket for engaging guides, getting intelligence, and paying clerks. He had, he complained, "studied the interest of my country and neglected my own. Or, in the language of Cardinal Wolsey, had I have served my God as I have done my king, he would not thus have forsaken me." In less lofty language, he had failed to get his pay in advance of his treason and had afterwards, like other traitors of his or any time, found it hard to collect. The British government finally allowed him £60.

IV

Conspiracy, informing, and desertion were of course not peculiar to New York. Before the British established themselves there in September–November 1776, to remain throughout the war, and while the line between patriot and loyalist was still unfixed or uncertain, there was lively plotting all the way from New Hampshire to Georgia. The royal governors wherever they could kept up a show of power in the face of the new revolutionary governments. To the governors the patriots seemed to be engaged in a general conspiracy. Since they were outlaws it was a duty to use any weapon against them. To conspire against conspiracy, the loyalists felt, was merely to fight fire with fire. Countless minor instances might be given. A few outstanding ones will be enough to show the motives at work and the methods used.

When Thomas Gage, British commander-in-chief and governor of Massachusetts, on the night of April 18, 1775 sent troops from Boston with orders to capture the American stores at Concord, he was acting on information sent him by one of the leaders of the patriots. This was Benjamin Church, a member of the provincial congress of Massachusetts and of the committee of safety. Church was a Boston physician and minor poet, looked upon as extravagant and here and there suspected of divided loyalties. But in days when many men were divided as to what was the best course to take, Church had the confidence of the chief Boston patriots and ranked among them close to John and Samuel Adams, John Hancock, and Joseph Warren. Nobody guessed that Church was a paid informer of Gage, or that for six weeks before the battle of Lexington he had been sending Gage letters, two of them for some reason in bad French, which gave the enemy the most hidden military and political secrets of the Americans— secrets some of them unknown to history till Church's letters were recently found among Gage's papers.[24]

Church always claimed that "a regard to place, popularity, or the more detestable motive of avarice never influenced his conduct in public life. The sole object of his pursuit, the first wish of his heart, was ever the salvation of his country." Not too much trust can be put in the story of "a gentleman who studied with Church" and who told Paul Revere, according to Revere's later recollection, that before Lexington Church "was much drove for money; then all at once he had several hundred new British guineas." But there can be no mistake about the meaning of a sentence in one of Church's letters to Gage: "The 25th of this month finishes a quarter." It was a plain reminder that on April 25 (or some later month, since the letter is undated) a quarter's wages would be due. Church's motive seems to have been mainly a desire for money.[25]

The British retreated from Lexington, and the Americans laid siege to Boston. Church was allowed to go in from Cambridge on

April 22, as if on medical affairs. Though he was questioned by the British, and said he was watched during his stay, he seems to have had a private conference with Gage and may have arranged a mode for sending further letters. On May 13 Church wrote Gage that the Americans meant to fortify Bunker Hill—more than a month before the British, on the morning of June 17, found it fortified. In a letter which Gage received on May 24 Church wrote that the provincial congress had voted to apply for advice and help from the Continental Congress which had just met at Philadelphia. Since Hancock and the Adamses had gone, Church was nearly the first man among the Massachusetts patriots. He was, he told Gage, "appointed to my vexation to carry the dispatches . . . and must set out tomorrow, which will prevent my writing for some time unless an opportunity should be found from thence by water."

Church went by way of Providence, to visit his mother, and on June 2 appeared before the Continental Congress. As to advice, Congress recommended that Massachusetts choose a new assembly to act "until a governor, of his Majesty's appointment, will consent to govern the colony according to its charter." As to help, Congress proceeded to organize a Continental army, including the troops outside Boston, with Washington as commander-in-chief. "I mingled freely and frequently with the members of the Continental Congress," Church said.[26] They thought so well of him that on July 27, after his return to Cambridge, he was made director and chief physician of the first American army hospital. He may then have been too busy to continue his letters to Gage, or may have considered it too difficult or dangerous. But late in July he mysteriously involved himself in what turned out to be a fatal blunder.

A refugee from Boston brought Church a letter—in cipher—from his brother-in-law John Fleming, a loyalist printer, who told him that the British were "determined to crush this rebellion. . . . For God's sake, Doctor, come to town directly. I'll engage to procure your pardon. Your sister is unhappy, under the apprehension of your being taken and hanged for a rebel. . . . We know well that you [the patriots] are divided; that your people are discouraged; that you want discipline, artillery, and ammunition." If Church could not pass the lines, he might come by way of Rhode Island in a British warship. At least he could write by that channel, directing his letter to Major Cane, who was Gage's aide. Church admitted that his fears, for himself and his cause, were "greatly excited. . . . A week, perhaps, or ten days after I had received this letter I was confined to my lodgings by a stormy day, contemplating our disagreeable situation." It occurred to him that he might write a letter which would give a favourable account of the patriots' readiness to go on with the war, in the hope that this might make the British readier with moves toward peace. Since it happened that "a young woman in the same house was to set off for Newport the next morning," he hastily wrote his letter—also in cipher—and sent it with her.

Or so Church afterwards explained his actions.[27] The letter itself, perhaps because of haste, was confused, part of the time straightforward, part of the time melodramatic. Its high talk about American preparedness and its plea for a change in British policy must have been intended for more influential eyes than Fleming's—probably Gage's. "For the sake of the miserable convulsed empire, solicit peace, repeal the acts, or Britain is undone. This advice is the result of warm affection to my king and to the realm. Remember I never deceived you; every article here sent you is sacredly true." Since there were falsehoods in the letter, Church was now trying to deceive Gage, if the letter was meant for Gage. Perhaps the conspirator was withdrawing from the plot and wanted to offset the help he had given Gage before. Perhaps Church genuinely believed that matters had got to a point where any stratagem for peace was justified.

The young woman who took the letter to Newport was unable to get it into the hands of any British or loyalist official. She left it with a patriot acquaintance who thought there must be something wrong, tried to read it but could not make out the cipher, and kept it till he got an anxious inquiry from the girl in Cambridge. If she knew it had not reached Boston, he reasoned, she or somebody must have learned this through the lines. The suspicious cipher original was hurried off to Washington in the last week of September. "I immediately secured the woman," Washington wrote to Congress on October 5, "but for a long time she was proof against every threat and persuasion to discover the author." Washington understood she was Church's mistress. Finally she confessed. Washington arrested Church and seized his papers. "But it appeared, on inquiry, that a confidant had been among the papers before my messenger arrived." (This unidentified confidant may have been Benjamin Thompson,[28] afterwards the famous scientist known as Count Rumford, who was already suspected of disaffection to America, who seems to have aided Church in sending information to Gage, and who certainly left Woburn on October 13 to go on board a British warship at Newport and begin his career as an avowed loyalist.)

Though Church "made many protestations of the purity of his intentions," he was brought before a council of war on October 3–4. The officers unanimously agreed that he had carried on a "criminal correspondence" with the enemy. As the articles of the Continental army had no penalty for such an offence, the case was referred to Congress and Church imprisoned in Cambridge.[29] Congress, first providing the death penalty thereafter "or such other punishment as a general court martial shall think proper" for cases of the sort, resolved on November 7 that Church "be close confined in some secure jail in the colony of Connecticut, without the use of pen, ink, and paper, and that no person be allowed to converse with him except in the presence and hearing of a magistrate of the town or the sheriff of the county where he shall be confined, and in the English language, until further orders from this or a future Congress."[30]

Meanwhile Church had had his principal hearing before the Massachusetts legislature, meeting on October 27 in the church at Watertown, where the accused stood at an improvised bar in the aisle. He defended himself angrily and resentfully. "I have been led from Caiaphas to Herod, and from Herod to Pontius Pilate." He went through the intercepted letter paragraph by paragraph, with intricate explanations. The legislature did not accept them as to the letter they knew he had tried to send, and they thought there was a "violent presumption that before that time he had secretly communicated intelligence to the said enemy"—as he had. The intercepted letter, which may have been only an imprudence, brought him the punishment he deserved for his earlier treachery. The legislature on November 2 "utterly expelled" him. On the 22nd he arrived under guard at Lebanon, Connecticut, and was assigned by the governor and council to the jail in Norwich, which had to be partly rebuilt for so important a prisoner.[31]

In May, after the British had evacuated Boston, Congress returned him to Massachusetts, to be set free if surety were given that he would appear in court whenever called for trial, and if he were put on parole to have no communication with the British and not to leave the "said colony." "I fear the people will kill him if at large," James Warren wrote to John Adams on June 5. "The night before last he went to lodge at Waltham, was saved by the interposition of the selectmen but by jumping out of a chamber window and flying." Church seems to have been kept in jail till the latter part of 1777, when he was allowed to leave—it is said for the West Indies—in a schooner which was never heard of again. His wife went to England. The British government gave her a pension of £150 a year on account of "certain services" her husband had performed. General Gage, she said in her petition, would know what they were.[32]

The most grandiose conspiracy against the conspiring patriots was planned by Lord Dunmore, royal governor of Virginia, and Dr. John Connolly of Pennsylvania. In April 1775 Connolly was captain and commandant of the Virginia militia at the post on the Ohio which the Pennsylvanians called Fort Pitt and the Virginians Fort Dunmore. Both provinces claimed the territory. Connolly, a speculator who hoped to make a fortune out of land granted him by Virginia, sided against his native province. After Lexington the patriotic excitement in Pittsburgh obliged him to leave, and in August he joined Dunmore on a king's ship lying off Portsmouth. Two weeks later Connolly set out for Boston with dispatches to Gage, Dunmore's commander-in-chief. After ten days in Boston Connolly returned, with Gage's instructions to Dunmore which authorized him to undertake what Connolly had proposed. This was that Connolly, as lieutenant colonel, should return to the back country, raise a regiment to be called the Queen's Royal Rangers, equip an expedition at Detroit, capture Pittsburgh, proceed through Virginia to Alexandria, and there join the loyalist forces to be gathered by Dunmore. "Alexandria was to be strongly fortified, as a place of arms, and the communication between the southern and northern parts of the continent thereby cut off."[33]

Connolly's new commission was signed on November 5 by Dunmore, who at Norfolk two days later proclaimed martial law in Virginia. He called upon all persons capable of bearing arms to "resort to his Majesty's standard" or else to be looked upon as traitors and "thereby become liable to the penalty the law inflicts upon such offenders: such as forfeiture of life, confiscation of lands, etc., etc." Moreover: "I do hereby further declare all indented servants, Negroes, or others (appertaining to rebels) free, that are able and willing to bear arms, they joining his Majesty's troops as soon as may be." This move of Dunmore's to free and arm the slaves seemed to the Virginia patriots an unforgivable extremity—and to most of the remaining loyalists. At about the same time Connolly and two other conspirators left Norfolk for the West where the Ohio Indians, Connolly had told Gage, were by direction of Dunmore prepared to act with the loyalists against the rebels.[34]

The three were to go by boat up the Chesapeake and the Potomac to a point from which Connolly and Allan Cameron would take the shortest route to Detroit and John Smith (J. F. D. Smyth) would travel by way of Pittsburgh. They carried eighteen sheets of instructions from Dunmore "in a secret manner invented by, and executed under the inspection of, his lordship. All these papers were concealed in the mail pillion-sticks on which the servant carried his portmanteau, they being made hollow for that purpose and covered with tin plates, and then canvas glued thereon as usual."[35]

Another servant had informed against Connolly. The conspirators were taken up in Frederick county, Maryland, and examined on the 23rd. Thanks to Dunmore's ingenuity, the hidden instructions were not found. But "an old torn piece of paper . . . discovered some part of our design; and then Colonel Connolly, to prevent our falling immediate sacrifices to a frantic mob, acknowledged our commissions." The Maryland authorities notified Congress and were told to send the conspirators to

Philadelphia. Before this could be done, Smyth escaped from their Maryland jail with letters from Connolly which incriminated him when Smyth was recaptured. Connolly and Cameron reached Philadelphia by January 3 and Smyth fifteen days later.[36]

The disclosure of their plans came at a bad time for them. Dunmore, who could not expect early help from the back country, had gone on with his little war against the rebels, been sharply defeated at Great Bridge on December 9, and on January 1 vengefully bombarded and burned Norfolk. Connolly, with Dunmore's commission, seemed to the patriots a criminal accomplice in a wicked plot. Nor did he clear himself by the defence he offered.[37] "My difference in political opinion," he wrote to Congress on February 8, "and the causes instigating me to action, however criminal they may appear, I can with the integrity of a man of honour assert arose from a sense of duty [to the king] and gratitude [to Dunmore] too powerful to be combated by any contrary arguments." His countrymen insisted on believing he would have turned the Indians loose on the frontiers. "I assure you that a design so inhuman never entered my breast." In carrying out his duty as a soldier he would have done no more than was "consistent with humanity and the law of arms." Unlike Church, Connolly had always been a loyalist and could not be charged with conspiring with the enemy while in the Continental service. But he was too dangerous a conspirator to be paroled or released.

His wife was permitted to visit him, but not to go back to their only child in Pittsburgh for fear she might take information to the enemy. The committee of safety made her an allowance of twenty-five shillings a week. On that she could not afford separate lodgings and had to live in the jail. On November 25, 1776 she informed the committee that her husband was planning to escape. The committee found she was consequently "so ill used by him as makes it impossible to live with him but on the worst terms"; and recommended that she be allowed to go home. Connolly was sent to another prison in Baltimore.[38] Finally exchanged in October 1780, he went first to New York and early the next year to Virginia with Benedict Arnold. He was again captured by the Americans and in December 1781 was in prison in Philadelphia. He went afterwards to England where the government finally allowed him £793 of his claim for losses of £6849 13s.[39]

The British ministers in London were convinced that the southern colonies were less rebellious than the northern and might be separated from them, and that the southern back country might be turned against the Tidewater. Josiah Martin, governor of North Carolina, established—like Dunmore—headquarters on a warship, and there formulated a plan for the subjugation of all the colonies south of Virginia. He promised to raise 10,000 American loyalists if the king would send as many British soldiers. While this plan was being considered and adopted by the ministry, Martin was active. In July 1775, about the time he took to his ship, he secretly conferred with Farquard Campbell of the inland county Cumberland and gave him "the encouragements I was authorized to hold out to his Majesty's loyal subjects in this colony." Campbell, who had earlier served as captain in Martin's campaign against the regulators, seemed to be loyal to the Crown, and said he abhorred the violence of the present "leaders of sedition," though he promised only to consult with them and report to the governor.

As a member of the committee of safety and of the provincial congress, and at the same time a confidant of Martin, Campbell may have intended to play a double part, but neither side was satisfied. The provincial congress on September 5 first accused Campbell of being too friendly with Martin and then exonerated him. Martin on October 16 wrote to Dartmouth that Campbell had apparently held "all the American popular principles and prejudices" and had—the governor was told—cleared himself before the congress by divulging Martin's secrets. With or without help from Campbell the governor raised a force, chiefly of the Scottish settlers among whom Campbell had great influence, to put down the rebels. The loyalists were overwhelmed by the patriot militia at Moore's Creek on February 27, 1776. Campbell, arrested by the Americans, was sent in April with the captured loyalist officers to Philadelphia. Called a "spy and confidential emissary" of Martin, he there joined Dunmore's emissary Connolly, and was kept there for two years.[40] The British reinforcements from Boston and from Ireland found no loyalist support in North Carolina in May and were beaten off when they went further south and attacked Charleston and its patriots in June.

In South Carolina the governor, Lord William Campbell, during the summer of 1775 carried on a correspondence which he assured the patriots he was not carrying on with the up country districts where an apparent majority disliked the Tidewater planters and merchants more than the British ministry. Moses Kirkland, a captain in the patriot militia, went over to the loyalists and was made a colonel. A patriot captain in September tricked the governor by pretending to be a messenger from Kirkland, and obtained proof of Campbell's dealings with the loyalist enemy. Moreover, Campbell had encouraged John Stuart, royal commissioner for the southern Indians, to turn the Catawba and Cherokee nations against the rebels. Stuart thought "an indiscriminate attack by Indians" on the civil population was not called for and "might do much harm; but I shall dispose them to join in executing any concerted plan, and to act with and assist their well-disposed neighbours"—the white loyalists—against patriots actually in arms.

Governor Campbell hurried aboard a king's ship, Stuart and Kirkland got away to St. Augustine in loyalist Florida. Stuart in October sent Kirkland off to Boston with dispatches for Gage. The vessel was taken by the Americans, and Washington on December 18 forwarded a whole packet of intercepted letters to the Continental Congress.[41] They brought Congress full information not only from South Carolina and Florida but also from Virginia, where the ship had stopped on its way north. Kirkland was sent to Philadelphia, to join Connolly in January before Farquard Campbell came in April.

Washington thought Kirkland "a much more illiterate and simple man than his strong recommendation"—from John Stuart —"bespake him." But he was enterprising enough to escape in May: "a stout corpulent man, between fifty and sixty years of age, about five feet ten inches high, of a swarthy complexion, fresh coloured, and wears his own grey hair tied behind. He had on a green coat faced with blue velvet, a blue velvet waistcoat, and brown velvet breeches."[42] Kirkland managed to reach the Chesapeake and take refuge on shipboard with Dunmore, who sent him to St. Augustine. There he acted as deputy commissioner to the Seminole and helped keep them on the British side. He served valiantly at Savannah and at Ninety Six, went to Jamaica, and was drowned at sea on his way to England in December 1782. His widow was allowed £4000 by the commission on loyalist claims.[43]

The summer of the Declaration saw the end of the royal governors. In New England, Gage of Massachusetts and the Americans John Wentworth of New Hampshire and Joseph Wanton of Rhode Island had all left their posts by October 1775. Sir James Wright, governor and native of Georgia, gave up hope in February 1776 and sailed from Halifax in May. William Franklin of New Jersey was in June ordered, by Congress, to confinement in Connecticut. That same month John Penn of Pennsylvania made no special protest when the old colonial assembly ceased to act, or Robert Eden of Maryland when he was peaceably required to quit the province. In June, also, Campbell of South Carolina was wounded in the siege of Charleston, and soon returned to England with his American wife. In August, Martin of North Carolina had retired to his father-in-law's estate on Long Island, and Dunmore was in or near New York, to cross the Atlantic before the end of the year. Only Tryon remained, and he had no civil power in a New York which was under military rule. He at first busied himself with taking loyalist oaths of allegiance to the Crown, and in 1777 became an active commander of loyalist forces sent out from New York against the rebels, particularly in Connecticut. From Nova Scotia to Florida there was after November 1776 no British authority except that of the army and the fleet.

2

Three Generals and a Chaplain

O N DECEMBER 13, 1776 a party of British dragoons at Basking Ridge, New Jersey, captured Major General Charles Lee, who was second in command in the American army and had no doubt he should be first. Only that morning he had written to General Gates that Washington was "most damnably deficient." Lee, after Magaw's loss of Fort Washington a month before, had been ordered to join the main army, but had delayingly preferred to harass the flank of Howe who was pursuing Washington in his retreat from New York towards Philadelphia. American troops, Lee insisted, could not face the British in pitched battles and should stick to guerrilla fighting. In his separate command he had, he apparently thought, a chance to make himself conspicuous by some dramatic stroke for which he would get all the credit. Instead he was humiliatingly taken prisoner at a tavern four miles from his lines, and was carried, tied on a horse, bareheaded and without a greatcoat, to Brunswick, where the more hilarious among his captors are said to have celebrated by making his horse drunk.[1]

Lee's whole career had been spectacular. Born in England, no relation to the patriotic Virginia Lees, he had come to America with Braddock, survived the defeat, and later been adopted by the Mohawk and briefly married to a Seneca woman. Returning to Europe, he served under Burgoyne in Portugal, was put on a colonel's half pay at the end of that war, and went as a soldier of fortune to Poland and southeastern Europe. In England he wrote violently against the Tories till 1773. After that he wrote violently against them in America, which on May 6, 1774[2] he called liberty's "last and only asylum"—nearly two years before Paine said almost the same thing in *Common Sense*. From New

York to Virginia Lee consorted with the patriot leaders, hoping to command the American army which he urged them to raise. In May he was buying an estate in Berkeley county, Virginia (West Virginia), with the specific motive of recommending himself, as a landowner, to the Continental Congress.[3] On June 7 he wrote from Philadelphia to Burgoyne in Boston, abusing the king and the ministry.[4] "Of all courts I am persuaded that ours is the most corrupt and hostile to the rights of humanity." Congress was pleased by such thoroughgoing language, and Washington valued Lee as a professional soldier. Self-confident and articulate, he impressed, and continued to impress, many Americans.

At the same time, he looked out for himself. When on June 17 he was appointed one of the four major generals he did not accept till Congress on the 19th resolved to indemnify him "for any loss of property he might sustain." Not till the 22nd did he write to denounce his half pay as a British colonel, now that he was an American general.[5] Though he resented being less than commander-in-chief, he caused little trouble in New England or New York, or in the south during the summer of 1776. On his return in October he so represented his private affairs to Congress that they advanced him $30,000 to repay the money he had borrowed to buy his plantation.[6] Encouraged by this substantial tribute, and by agreeable praise for his defence of South Carolina, Lee felt more sure of himself than ever, and more dissatisfied with Washington, whose recent "manœuvre of Fort Washington," Lee said in his letter to Gates of December 13, "has completely unhinged the goodly fabric we have been building."

For a month after his capture Lee was held in New Jersey while Washington, joined by Lee's army, crossed and recrossed the Delaware, captured a whole command of Hessians, broke the British line at Princeton, and forced Howe to draw back to Brunswick. In New York, Lee found himself regarded not as a prisoner of war subject to exchange but as a deserter from the British army. Yet though he was confined in the City Hall, with a sentry at his door, he had one of the largest and best rooms, had his table "very handsomely kept by the General," and was allowed to entertain guests every day at dinner.[7] One of his early callers was Henry Strachey, secretary to the Howe brothers' peace commission, who called at least twice before February 9.[8] Whether at Strachey's suggestion or of his own accord, Lee on the 9th wrote a letter to Washington enclosing a letter to Congress. He had, he informed Congress, important proposals to make. Would they send a committee to him, on General Howe's guarantee they would be safe?

Congress thought Lee insolent, for supposing they might meet such a demand, and unlikely to be of any use, now he had carelessly let himself be captured and lost to the American army. What he then had in mind is not clear. He later said he had discovered Howe's plan of campaign for the year 1777 and would have revealed it to the committee, even though this meant violating the confidence Howe had hospitably placed in him.[9] Having received no answer from Congress, Lee on March 19 wrote again to Washington. This brought an answer, dated April 1, saying that Congress could not send a committee but would try to arrange for Lee's exchange. Lee had before that, on March 29, drawn up a plan[10] to be followed by the Howes if they desired an early triumph.

He felt sure, he said, that Great Britain must win. But since this could be only after heavy losses on both sides, "I think myself not only justifiable but bound in conscience to furnish all the lights I can to enable 'em [the Howes] to bring matters to a conclusion." In his opinion nothing was to be gained by taking Philadelphia. Congress, expecting this, had arranged to continue the rebel government elsewhere. It would be better to send a British expedition to Alexandria and Annapolis and there proclaim a general pardon to all rebels who would surrender on a given day. This would reduce Maryland and intimidate Virginia and Pennsylvania. "I am so confident of the event that I will venture to assert with the penalty of my life, if the plan is fully carried out and no accidents (such as a rupture betwixt the powers of Europe) intervenes, that in less than two months from the date of the proclamation not a spark of this desolating war remains unextinguished in any part of the continent."

"Mr. Lee's Plan 29th March 1777," endorsed in Strachey's handwriting, presumably reached the Howes, but they made small use of it, if they made any. While they did send an expedition to and up the Chesapeake, it was only as a route to Philadelphia, which

Lee had advised them not to bother with. The Howes had more influential American advisers than Lee.

Joseph Galloway, member of the First Continental Congress, ablest of all the Pennsylvania loyalists, arrived in New York before Lee, and was introduced to Lord Howe on January 21. Galloway believed that "the power of the rebellion is pretty well broken, and that, though 'tis probable that the colonies may make some further efforts, those efforts will be only feeble and ineffectual. . . . Pennsylvania itself (which certainly could subsist better alone than any other province) was in extreme distress for clothing, salt, dry goods, and all other importable necessities; and . . . if the fleet constantly blocked up the ports during the next summer the business might be concluded, almost without the intervention of the army." By February 18 Galloway was laying plans to raise a loyalist militia in Pennsylvania, seize Congress, and destroy the bridge of boats which Washington had thrown across the Schuylkill for a possible retreat from Philadelphia. On March 17 Galloway said 100 loyalists were sworn together in the scheme for taking Congress. On April 4 he was worried because a spy he had sent to Philadelphia, to find pilots who might assist the British in getting past the American defences in the Delaware, had been captured and might be hanged—as James Molesworth had been.[11] The move against Philadelphia was already settled upon by the Howes, possibly with some reference to Galloway's advice, certainly against Lee's.

Lee emerges from the record as a busybody, willing to side with either party as the chance offered, in the arrogant assumption that if only he were given a free hand he could bring about a reasonable, conclusive peace. Having failed in his application—almost an order—to Congress, he fraternized in New York with British officers who were his old friends but none of whom, it appears, took him very seriously. In June he was confined for a time on the *Centurion*. The British government ruled against holding him as a deserter, and on December 27 he was given his liberty on parole, though not to go outside the city limits. He informed Washington, who in January sent Elias Boudinot, American commissary general of prisoners, under a flag to New York to see if Lee could be exchanged. Lee had a new proposal for the

Americans. Since they could not, he still insisted, hope to stand up to British soldiers, they should build a great fortress at Pittsburgh, send their money, old men, women, and children to it, and prepare an escape for Congress down the Mississippi to Spanish territory. Boudinot, who had given the British his word not to carry messages out of New York, was shocked at Lee's willingness to deceive Howe, who knew nothing, Lee said, of this proposal. And Boudinot wondered how Lee could be so reckless—or so unregarded?—as to carry the scheme written out in his pocket.

Washington, who according to Lee "was not fit to command a sergeant's guard," still thought he needed Lee in the American army. There were delays in the exchange. Lee hated the sea, and persuaded the British not to send him to Philadelphia by ship but to let him travel through New Jersey. On April 5 he was "enlarged" on parole, acknowledging himself a prisoner of the king's army and pledging his "faith and sacred honour that I will not directly or indirectly do anything contrary to the interest of his Majesty or his government." Yet he went promptly to Congress at York, where he told President Laurens that Washington, "considering how he is surrounded, cannot do without me"; and on the 13th wrote to Washington, at Valley Forge, sending him a plan for the complete reorganization of the American army. At York it was arranged that the Americans would give up General Prescott, captured in Rhode Island, for Lee.

About the end of the month he arrived at Valley Forge, to be welcomed like a hero. Washington rode out four miles to meet him, dismounted, and greeted Lee "as if it had been his brother." The general officers waited for them two miles from camp. Lines of soldiers were drawn up all the way to Headquarters. There was an "elegant dinner," with music. "A room was assigned to him back of Mrs. Washington's sitting room, and all his baggage was stored in it. The next morning he lay very late, and breakfast was detained for him."[12]

At once Lee was again a busybody, and a double-dealer. At his last meeting with Howe, Lee told Boudinot, Howe thought independence a crazy idea, Lee thought it a shrewd one. Since America had nothing but the independence it claimed, it could at least offer to yield that in a treaty with the British government, and might get something in exchange. Howe granted that independence might have value as a strategic pretext. On May 3—or perhaps a few days before—Lee wrote a letter to General James Robertson, of the British army, who turned it over to Clinton, Howe's recent successor as commander-in-chief. (The letter survives among the Clinton papers.) If more confidence had been placed in Lee the past year, he said, he might have ended the war. He supposed he had been denied the opportunity on the ground that he was in danger of being tried for desertion, and so may have offered his services to avoid punishment. In his present safe situation he might be listened to. His advice was that Great Britain should pass an act of indemnity without exceptions and renounce any right to tax the colonies. America should forget independence and promise to obey the navigation acts. All that remained was to give Lee authority to take the first step with these proposals, and he would "at the risk of my popularity divulge them."

And on June 4, after Lee had been for two weeks with the American army, he sent friendly communications to both Lord Howe and Clinton. The first was through a British officer whom Lee met at an exchange of prisoners on that day.[13] He took him "aside for a moment and told him that he was very unhappy in and very adverse to the present course of affairs, and that he might assure Lord Howe that he had acted entirely as he had promised him and wished for nothing so much as to promote every idea of peace." The second was a letter which Lee wrote that day to Clinton, to congratulate him on his promotion to succeed Howe. "General Lee presents his most sincere and humble respects to Sir Henry Clinton. He wishes him all possible happiness and health and begs, whatever may be the event of the present unfortunate contest, that he will believe General Lee to be his most respectful and obliged humble servant." This was twenty-four days before the battle of Monmouth.

Lee, who had sat on the board that tried Benjamin Church, knew perfectly well that correspondence like this with Howe and Clinton was forbidden by army regulations and would be impossible to explain away if found out. He swore on June 9 that he acknowledged the independence of the United States and would to the utmost of his power support, maintain, and defend it against the king and his successors, abetters, assistants, and adherents. Yet Lee certainly did not let himself think of his secret correspondences as treason. He persisted in seeing the conflict as essentially a political one, between two parties who had taken to arms. A compromise peace would be good for both of them, and good for the Empire. He was the man to engineer the compromise. Men have been hanged for slighter misjudgments than Lee's. Vanity, envy, and frustration had brought him to a point where all his thoughts and words were violent. He scolded Congress for promoting other generals while he was a prisoner. He wrote with almost intolerable arrogance to Washington, who tolerated it.

When Lee resumed his military duties on May 20 the Americans were sure the British would soon evacuate Philadelphia, and Washington at Valley Forge was making ready to follow them, attacking from the flank or rear. If they set out for New York, Washington's left would encounter them first. Lee was assigned to that post of honour, but declined. The British, he thought as late as June 15, would go in the other direction, to Delaware or Maryland. If he actually knew the British intentions, and hoped to keep Washington from strengthening his left, this was of course plain treason. But it is not at all likely that Lee, whom the British never valued or trusted, had been told what the British meant to do; and it is very likely that he was positive they would go south because he had himself advised it the year before. On the 18th they started north across New Jersey, and the Americans followed. Lafayette led the advance corps in the pursuit. When he was ordered to attack at Monmouth, Lee jealously asserted his right to take command. Lafayette, who though a major general was not yet twenty-one, gracefully yielded to the experienced soldier. In the battle on the 28th Lee retreated with the main body of his forces, and the army was in a headless confusion when Washington came up and took command himself. This again might look more like treason in Lee if his retreat had not been in keeping with his fixed theory that American troops were no match for British except in guerrilla skirmishes. But an American general so anxious as Lee to please British generals was bound to lack spontaneity and fire in attacking British soldiers. Lee's fraternizing had made him indecisive, and his indecision at Monmouth was, in effect, treachery.

Denying any guilt, he demanded a court martial. The court on August 12 after a long and complicated trial found him guilty of disobedience to orders, misbehaviour before the enemy, and disrespect to the commander-in-chief, and suspended him from the army for twelve months. He never returned to it, and had no further dangerous opportunity for his overbearing, underhanded mischief.

I I

General Howe asked his government to send him 15,000 new men for the campaign of 1777. Lord George Germain, secretary of state for the colonies, finding it impossible to recruit any such number in Great Britain or to obtain them from Germany or Russia as Howe had hoped, sent 2500. He supposed Howe could more or less make up the difference by enlisting loyalists in the Provincial regiments which were to be used against the Continentals. The loyalists in London never stopped assuring the ministers that the majority of Americans were devoted to the Crown and many would join the king's forces if they were properly encouraged. The loyalists advising the Howes in America were of the same opinion. The day after General Howe landed on Long Island on August 22, 1776 he proclaimed[14] that "all those who choose to take up arms for the restoration of order and good government within this island shall be disposed of in the best manner and have every encouragement that can be expected." He was less specific than Congress, which four days later offered to foreigners, including Hessians, who would leave the British service, rewards in land according to rank: 1000 acres to a colonel, 800 to a lieutenant colonel, 600 to a major, 400 to a captain, 300 to a lieutenant, 200 to an ensign (sublieutenant), 100 to a noncommissioned officer or private. There must have been desertions —though not of officers—for on September 30 Howe promised pardon to deserters who would return at once.[15]

In September 1777, when he had taken Philadelphia, he offered land to all who would join the Provincials: 200 acres to each noncommissioned officer, 50 to each private.[16] His recruiting offers for the Pennsylvania Loyalists regiment were addressed to "intrepid, able-bodied heroes" who were desirous not only of saving the country from the rebels but also of "acquiring the polite accomplishments of a soldier. . . . Such spirited fellows who are willing to engage will be rewarded at the end of the war, besides their laurels, with fifty acres of land, where every gallant hero may retire and enjoy his bottle and lass." On enlistment they would get $5 bounty in hard money.[17] The bounty in cash down, during that winter of currency depression and of hardship at Valley Forge, perhaps had more effect than any talk of land and ease after the war. By March 25, according to Galloway's tabulation, 1488 deserters had come in from the rebel army and fleet. The international complexion of the Continental army appears from the nationality of these deserters: 275 born in England, 78 in Scotland, 649 in Ireland, 104 in Germany, 20 in France, 4 in Canada, 358 in the United States.[18] And in both armies, throughout the war, there were thousands of the rank and file who deserted from Americans to British or from British to Americans, restive, resentful, tempted, indifferent. The balance in this trade lay on the side of the British, who had more to offer.

Joseph Galloway had been Franklin's close friend and colleague in Pennsylvania up to Lexington, and they had shared a large, far-sighted vision of the British Empire that might be founded on equal justice to both England and America. Franklin, disgusted with the ministry after many years in London, had given up hope and taken his seat in the Second Continental Congress. Galloway, refusing to be a delegate, continued his arguments in favour of imperial union. The imperial government paid no attention to him, and the Americans hated him as an apostate. Finding he could not remain neutral, he joined General Howe late in 1776 and from November 1 was made an allowance of £200 a year "for his support until he could be otherwise provided for."[19] He was otherwise provided for in Philadelphia, after the British occupation, by being made superintendent of the police (at a salary the same as his earlier allowance) and of the port (with an extra twenty shillings a day).[20]

Useful as Galloway was, he seems to have been little more considered by Howe than Washington had been by Braddock. British generals did not listen much to civilians, certainly not to civilians who were Americans. Nothing came of Galloway's active correspondence with the 300 American "gentlemen of weight and influence"[11] who by the next June were "ready to engage, and will immediately do so, if Washington's army be defeated, dispersed, or removed over the Susquehanna, or to the north of the Delaware, and the people can be assured of the continuance of the British troops to support them in pressing after the main force of the rebellion." Galloway had a list of their names—now apparently lost—and of the twenty-two counties where they lived in New Jersey, Pennsylvania, Delaware, Maryland, and Virginia. "Several of the counties would raise 1000 men, none under 500, so that we may safely count upon 500 on an average in each, making in the whole 10,000 men."[21]

Galloway and other loyalists always blamed Howe for not putting down the rebellion in the first two years with a vigorous employment of the British army and of the loyal Americans. But Galloway's scheme for his army—on paper—shows how far the loyalists were themselves responsible. At a time when they had every reason to be desperate, they were still looking to the British commander-in-chief for their support and prepared to act only when the way should have been made clear for them. The patriots had organized their government and their armed forces in spite of the royal officials and in the face of Great Britain's immense military and naval superiority. Either the loyalists were not as numerous as they claimed or they were decidedly less prompt and capable than the patriots, for whom the loyalists had a contempt as fatal as their confidence in the British government.

This contempt often took the particular form of ridicule for the low social status of the rebels: Washington, a paltry colonel of militia; Franklin, a printer who had worked with his hands. In April 1777 Galloway and some loyalist friends laughed and wondered together, at a country house on Long Island, over a story they heard about Jonathan Trumbull, the patriot governor of Connecticut.[22] "The common barber's shop of the town where he resides is the Governor's resort for shaving. He has too little salary to keep a proper servant for that purpose; and the barber is too high to wait upon him in any other place than in the public shop. Here the governor comes constantly, stands among the rest, and among them takes his turn in the chair. . . . Were he to assume any state or precedence upon the occasion, his affectation of superiority as a man would be instantly marked, and at the year's end he would probably lose his distinction as a magistrate, which he annually obtains by the suffrages of the people, and which, it is said, so far as public authority is concerned, they are not backward to support." Laughing at this homespun anecdote, the loyalists were laughing at the American future, when it would be remembered that Trumbull, elected by his people, was the only governor who survived the outbreak—and the end—of the Revolution; when few Americans would see anything undignified in Trumbull's taking his turn in the barber shop or would wonder that he was no less respected as governor because he had good manners as a man.

The most egregious instance of loyalist snobbism was the famous, foolish attempt of the Rev. Jacob Duché, former chaplain of the Continental Congress, to persuade Washington to give up the rebellion because there were so few rebels he could feel, Duché assumed, like inviting to dinner.

Duché, rector of Christ Church and St. Peter's in Philadelphia, had been an excited patriot in September 1774 when the First Continental Congress asked him to open its third session with prayer, and again in July 1775 when the Second Continental Congress came in a body to hear him preach on the day of humiliation, fasting, and prayer which was being observed throughout the country. In August he sent Washington a sermon dedicated to him, "which I lately preached to the First Battalion of our city. . . . My prayers are continually for you, and the brave troops under your command."[23] On July 9, 1776 Duché was appointed chaplain of Congress, for his "uniform and zealous attachment to the rights of America," and officiated every morning at nine till the middle of October, when he resigned asking that the $150 voted him be used for the relief of widows and children of Pennsylvania officers.[24] "Look down in mercy, we beseech Thee," he prayed, "on these our American States, who have fled to Thee from the rod of the oppressor, and thrown themselves on Thy gracious protection, desiring to be henceforth dependent only on Thee."[25] Though a minister of the Church of England, Duché after the

Declaration dropped the prayers for the royal family from his services. But while praying for the American States that desired to be dependent only on God, Duché was, he later said, always against the independence on England which the United States had declared. On the first Sunday after the British occupied Philadelphia, in September 1777, Duché prayed for the royal family.

Leaving his church he was arrested and taken off to jail because of his late association with the Congress that had got away to York. Nothing is known of what happened except that he was released after one day and on October 8 wrote at formal length to Washington.[26] "Be assured, Sir, that I write not this under the eye of any British officer, or person connected with the British army or ministry." For himself, he said, he had always been opposed to violence and independence. He was convinced that this must have been true also of Washington. "You risked everything that was dear to you. You abandoned all those sweets of domestic life of which your affluent fortune gave you an uninterrupted enjoyment. But had you, could you have had, the least idea of matters being carried to such a dangerous extremity? Your most intimate friends shuddered at the thought of a separation from the mother country; and I took it for granted that your sentiments coincided with theirs."

But now, Duché went on, "the most respectable characters have withdrawn" from the contest, "and are succeeded by a great majority of illiberal and violent men. Take an impartial view of the present Congress. What can you expect of them? Your feelings must be greatly hurt by the representation of your native province. You have no longer a Randolph, a Bland, or a Braxton," but men "whose minds can never mingle with your own." These included Richard Henry Lee and Francis Lightfoot Lee. "As to those of my own province, some of them are so obscure that their very names have never met my ears before, and others have only been distinguished for the weakness of their understandings and the violence of their tempers. . . . From the New England provinces can you find one that, as a gentleman, you could wish to associate with, unless the soft and mild address of Mr. Hancock can atone for the want of every other qualification necessary for the seat he fills? Bankrupts, attorneys, and men of desperate fortunes are his colleagues." These included John and Samuel Adams of Massachusetts, and Oliver Ellsworth and Roger Sherman of Connecticut. "Are the dregs of a Congress, then, still to influence a mind like yours? . . . Most of them were chosen by a little, low faction, and the few gentlemen that are among them now well known to be on the balance, and looking up to your hand alone to move the beam."

The army, Duché thought, was no better than Congress. "Have you, can you have, the least confidence in a set of undisciplined men and officers, many of whom have been taken from the lowest of the people, without principle, without courage? Take away those that surround your person, how very few are there that you can ask to sit at your table!" Without Washington the army would be nothing. He had no fleet and no resources. Nor was there the slightest reason to expect help from France. "Believe me, from the best authority, 'twas a fiction from the first." Duché had talked with a Frenchman in Philadelphia, and knew the truth, which was very different from the misleading news that Franklin sent back to Congress. England was prosperous and united. "All orders and ranks of men in Great Britain are now unanimous, and determined to risk their all in the contest." In America: "How unequal the contest now! How fruitless the expense of blood! Humanity itself (and sure I am humanity is no stranger to your breast) calls upon you to desist. . . . 'Tis to you, and you alone, your bleeding country looks, and calls aloud for this sacrifice. . . .

"Your penetrating eye needs not more explicit language to discern my meaning. With that prudence and delicacy, therefore, of which I know you to be possessed, represent to Congress the indispensable necessity of rescinding the hasty and ill-advised declaration of independency. . . . Recommend, and you have an undoubted right to recommend, an immediate cessation of hostilities. . . . Whatever censures may be thrown out by mean, illiberal minds, your character will rise in the estimation of the virtuous and noble. . . . Your interposition and advice, I am confident, would meet with a favourable reception from the authority under which you act. If it should not, you have one infallible recourse still left. Negotiate for America at the head of your army."

It was five days before Duché found a means of sending his letter

rough the lines, by the poet Elizabeth Graeme Ferguson who
as one of his parishioners. Washington had lately permitted her
o come from her house in the country to Germantown to meet her
Scottish husband, who had arrived in Philadelphia with Howe.[27]
Henry Hugh Ferguson, who was then not connected in any way
with the British army or government but the next month became
Howe's commissary of prisoners, may have had something to do
with the writing of the Duché letter. He certainly arranged for
his wife to be the bearer of it and assumed she would be happy to
"serve so esteemed a friend" as Duché.[28] It is even possible that
Ferguson deceived his wife as to the nature of the letter she was
to carry. She was eleven years older than he, unhappy over his
separation from her, and hopeful of winning him to the patriot
side, to which she was strongly attached.[29]

"I have delivered my sentiments to you upon the present state
of our unhappy contest without reserve," Duché said in a note to
Washington on the 13th, "and with full confidence in your
honour." He seems actually to have believed that the incor-
ruptible, punctilious Washington could or would keep secret a
letter which abused his associates and urged him, giving up the
idea of independence, to override Congress by force if it would
not give up the idea too. Washington sent the letter at once to
Congress. "Notwithstanding the author's assertion," he wrote on
the 16th, "I cannot but suspect that the measure did not originate
with him; and that he was induced to it by the hope of establishing his interest and peace more effectually with the enemy."
Congress believed that Duché had been influenced by the British,
and resented his opinions no less than his attempt on Washington.
The original letter, now in the Library of Congress, shows much
handling and was frequently copied. It was first printed in Rivington's *Royal Gazette* in New York on November 29.

In the storm that followed Duché left for England late the next
month. Ambrose Serle, secretary to Lord Howe, reported to Dartmouth[30] that Duché had done "a great deal of harm. He is thought
to be a tolerable sample of American confidence and duplicity."
This may only refer to Duché's early faith in Congress and his
subsequent straddling; or it may hint at calculated double-dealing.
Serle unquestionably looked upon Duché after his blunder as a

recruit to the British government, even if not a valuable one. "He may perhaps be usefully employed upon some occasions, but never confidentially trusted." Pennsylvania confiscated all Duché's property except enough money to send his wife and children after him. In England he was rewarded by being made chaplain of the Asylum for Female Orphans at Lambeth. Always homesick for Philadelphia, he was allowed to come back in 1792, and in the last years of his life what had once been hated as his treachery was thought of rather as his folly.

III

While Burgoyne in the early summer of 1777 was still in Montreal preparing his expedition toward Albany, Peter Livius, chief justice of the province of Quebec, on June 2 wrote a letter from Montreal to Major General John Sullivan of the Continental army.[31] Livius, a banished loyalist, had been chief justice of New Hampshire, and Sullivan the first New Hampshire soldier to be made a Continental general. It must have been known to Livius that Sullivan, taken prisoner by the British on Long Island the past August, had gone on parole to Philadelphia as the bearer of an oral message from Lord Howe to Congress, which Howe could not recognize in writing. And it may have been thought by Livius, as it unjustly was by some Americans, that Sullivan, willing to act as Howe's messenger, had perhaps become less patriotic during his few days' captivity. Burgoyne's move from Canada seemed to Livius—and no doubt to Burgoyne as well—to furnish an opportunity for trying to win over a northern general who, they believed, was in command at Fort Ticonderoga.

He had long wished, Livius said, to write to Sullivan, but correspondence had been impossible till he hit upon the present messenger. Sullivan could not now fail to see that ruin faced the Americans. Hopelessly inferior to the British on land and sea, they talked of a foreign alliance only to "keep up the spirits of the deluded common people." The contest was sure to be ended by Burgoyne in a few months. "You was the first man in active rebellion, and drew with you the province you live in." Livius here referred to December 1774 when Paul Revere came to Portsmouth with a warning and Sullivan led the party of rebels who removed 100 barrels of gunpowder from the royal fortress in the harbour to the cellar of a meeting house. "What hope, what expectation can you have?" He was sure to be "one of the first sacrifices to the resentment and justice of government. . . . Now, Sullivan, I have a method to propose to you, if you have resolution and courage for it, that will save you, and your family and estate, from this imminent destruction. It is, in plain English, to tread back the steps you have already taken," and, "for a real essential service to your king and country," to assist in bringing about tranquillity and legal order.

"You know I will not deceive you. Every one of you who will exert himself for government will be received, and I do assure you firmly, upon my honour, I am empowered to engage particularly with you, that it shall be the case with you, if you will sincerely endeavour to deserve your pardon." It was not necessary for Sullivan to declare himself at once, "nor indeed to declare yourself at all, until you can dispose matters so as to bring the province with you." Working by stealth, he might get difficult men out of New Hampshire and keep worthy men at home. He could send useful information to Livius—or to Burgoyne: "and by your using my name he will know whom it comes from, without your mentioning your own name." Such conduct was "not only prudent, safe, and necessary," but right and honourable. Livius promised that Sullivan, besides being pardoned, would save his property from confiscation, and "be further amply rewarded."

Livius's messenger, William Amsbury, was captured by an American scouting party on the Onion river and taken to Ticonderoga, commanded not by Sullivan but by Major General Arthur St. Clair. Because Amsbury had a British pass and an unusual amount of money, and carried letters from Montreal to various Americans, St. Clair decided the messenger must be a spy. He was sent on the 15th to Saratoga to be questioned by Major General Philip Schuyler, commanding the northern department of the American army. Schuyler not only found out more about Burgoyne's plan of campaign than the Americans yet knew but also made Amsbury confess that he had come on a secret errand. In a canteen with a false bottom which he had left with an adjutant at Fort George, he said, there was something his searchers had not found. Schuyler at once sent an aide to get the canteen and carry it, unopened and under strong escort, to Fort Edward. There on the 16th Schuyler took out Livius's letter in the presence of several officers who signed their names as witnesses.[82]

Dispatching the letter the same day to Washington, Schuyler laid a plan to make use of it. "I shall," he told the commander-in-chief,[33] "consulting with the general officers at Ticonderoga, try to send an answer to Mr. Livius's letter, as from General Sullivan, in which I shall leave him to suppose (what I do not by any means believe) that General Sullivan has entered into his views. Your Excellency will please to mention my intention to General Sullivan" —who was then in New Jersey near Washington—"and to assure him that my only view is to serve the public." Without waiting to hear from Washington or Sullivan, Schuyler showed a draft of his letter to the Ticonderoga officers on the 20th and got their approval of the scheme. The letter, which he sent to Congress to lie till now unnoted in their files, was dated at Albany the 17th.[84]

"I am much obliged," Schuyler made Sullivan seem to say, "by the anxiety you express for me, and am happy that an opportunity is given me to evince my duty to my king and country." It was true he had taken an early and active part in the conflict from principle. But as soon as he learned that Parliament "no longer insisted on the right of internal taxation, my resentment ceased. I was however and still am under the disagreeable necessity of putting on the appearance of being warmly attached to the measures carrying on by the Americans, which (especially since the Declaration of Independence) I abhor from my soul. But should I give the least reason for the Congress to suspect that I do not approve their proceedings, my life would be in danger. I agree with you, my dear Sir, that what you recommend to me is right and honourable. My heart has long since returned to its duty to the best of kings, and I hope to give striking proofs of my sincerity by not only attempting to carry into execution what you recommend, but by doing, as soon as ever I can, everything which his Majesty's servants may please to direct; and I shall therefore with great pleasure receive General Burgoyne's orders for that purpose, to whom I entreat you earnestly to recommend me." (Orders from Burgoyne to Sullivan, read by Schuyler, might give the northern army some hints as to British designs for the campaign.)

With involved caution, the letter then spoke of Sullivan, in the third person, as having just arrived at Albany to take command of Ticonderoga as soon as he recovered from "a defluxion which has fell upon his eyes" and made him unable to write. This would explain to Livius why the letter was not in Sullivan's handwriting. "It has been hinted to me that he [Sullivan] is not altogether in sentiment with the rebels, and may perhaps be brought to render a capital service to his Majesty." Livius would understand that the letter, if taken by the Americans, must not appear to be from Sullivan. But perhaps Livius—or Burgoyne—would not realize that the figures given him, in detail, about the forces with Washington in New Jersey, with Putnam in the Highlands, and with Schuyler in the north, were much exaggerated.

To complicate the deception still more, the Sullivan who was not to appear to be Sullivan reported on Schuyler whose name (by Schuyler himself) was spelled Skyler. "Skyler has declared that he receives intelligence regularly from Montreal of all that is doing there." Here followed some circumstantial news that Schuyler had actually had by spies from Montreal, and that Livius would recognize as fact. "I think it would be worth while to try to make him quit the American cause. I believe if assurances were given him, not only of pardon but of ample rewards, that he would." (Only a man with a clear conscience could have written this about himself and then sent a copy of it to Congress.) To round out the measure, Schuyler as a disguised Sullivan said that this letter would be carried from Albany to Ticonderoga "by —— to whom you gave forty dollars at one time and twenty-four at another at Quebec, when he was prisoner there. You will know who I mean; and although he is a major in the American army he is nevertheless a well-wisher to his Majesty and will embrace the first favourable opportunity to return openly to his duty. Any letters intended for me should be sent to him enclosed, if possible, in the manner yours was." The well-wishing major was Henry Dearborn, who as one of the officers at Ticonderoga read and approved the letter to Livius.

On the 25th Schuyler, sending the Sullivan-Livius letter to Congress, explained that the statements in it about Dearborn were of course true only as to the money he had received, which Livius would remember. The rest was a ruse to encourage Livius. Getting the letter to Montreal called for another ruse. This was done, Schuyler told Congress, "by a soldier of ours who was to have corporal punishment inflicted for attempting to desert to the enemy." Since he did not yet know what his sentence was, "I employed a trusty officer in the character of a Tory to make him entertain a belief that his punishment would be capital, and to advise him to escape and aid him in it. Which was effected in such a manner that we have every reason to believe the fellow does not entertain a thought that we had any agency in it." If the enemy did not suspect a trick, a valuable correspondence might be opened.[35]

Washington, whose reply of the 20th did not reach Schuyler till after the guileful letter had gone by the duped deserter, said he drew "a very favourable omen from the intercepted letter to General Sullivan. It shows that they despair of carrying their schemes by force and are reduced to the necessity of having recourse to the arts of flattery, bribery, and intimidation." He had written to Sullivan, who was at another post, but was not yet sure how he would feel about Schuyler's use of his name. "If your letter has not gone you had better wait for his concurrence, for it is a delicate matter."[36]

Sullivan on the 21st had just read the letter "from (The Infamous) Mr. Livius. . . . I conclude it to be his handwriting, with which I have been long acquainted. But if I doubted his handwriting, the extravagant ideas of my carrying a whole province in my pocket and transporting with [at] pleasure such part of them as I did not like to any part of the globe, are so much his own that I am sure they could flow from no other fountain. Besides I know not a villain upon earth more capable of making such a dirty attempt. . . . I am exceeding sorry General Schuyler attempted to answer the letter, as Mr. Livius has been for near ten years acquainted with my handwriting. He was judge of the court when I was at the bar and saw my writing almost every day. . . . Though I feel a great aversion to acting a deceitful part with any man, yet to deceive a traitor is at least excusable. If therefore General Schuyler's letter can be stopped I will consent to answer his letter when I can be more acquainted with the manner of the messenger's being sent and a manner in which I may convey a letter without raising the suspicions of Mr. Livius too much."[37]

Learning, presumably, that Schuyler's letter had left Ticonderoga, Sullivan seems to have taken no deceitful steps. Nothing is known of the fate of the letter itself. Going off with the deserter, it went out of history. Sullivan decided to expose Livius, and on August 6 wrote to Samuel Loudon, printer of the *New York Packet* at Fishkill, asking him to publish Livius's offer. "Indeed, I could wish it to be published in all the states, that the people may see that every measure is adopted by our enemies to accomplish their tyrannical purposes. Nothing is left unattempted which they think may promote their hellish designs. They are so far lost to all sense of natural honour and honesty that by their own feelings they judge it a right matter for a person to sacrifice his honour and conscience by betraying the trust reposed in him by his country, and assisting them to establish despotism upon the ruins of freedom."

The Livius letter probably appeared in the *Packet* for August 14, though no copy of that issue is known, and the date given is the one ascribed by the loyalist *New York Gazette* which reprinted the letter on September 1 for a larger circulation than the patriot *Packet* had. But St. Clair on September 30 had apparently seen the *Packet* with Sullivan's communication. On that date St. Clair sent an aide to Sullivan with a pointed letter inquiring about Sullivan's final paragraph to Loudon.[38] "This letter [Livius's]," Sullivan had said, "was directed to me as commander at Ticonderoga; therefore how great the importance of having the command of our frontier posts in the hands of those who have the greatest attachment and the strongest ties to bind them to the cause of their country." That remark, St. Clair said, had "been generally supposed to contain an insinuation that the officer to whom the defence of Ticonderoga was committed was not trustworthy, and intended to convey that idea. I would not wish to misunderstand it, nor to put a forced construction upon it. It is therefore left to yourself to explain, and that explanation, whatever it is, I expect you will be good enough to send me by the bearer." St. Clair, as the officer in charge when Ticonderoga was lost to the British, could tolerate no hint of aspersion on his good faith. In times so touchy, with Burgoyne still so perilous a threat, slander from a friend was worse than from an enemy. Sullivan probably explained to St. Clair's satisfaction, for there is no record of any further difficulty between them on this count.

I V

Burgoyne, in a conference with his Indian auxiliaries at the Bouquet river above Fort Ticonderoga on June 21, commanded them to attack only men in arms, to spare women, children, and prisoners, and in no case to go beyond the orders of the king's officers. But in a proclamation eight days later he threatened savage warfare against all rebels who would not return to their duty, as he offered them this opportunity to do. If they persisted they could not escape him. "I have but to give stretch to the Indian forces under my direction, and they amount to thousands [actually about 400], to overtake the hardened enemies of Great Britain and [the true interests of] America; I consider them the same wherever they lurk." This threat—out of character in the humane Burgoyne—did perhaps more than anything else to rouse the border, which had an old experience of Indian methods and dreaded them. Yet the border militia were widely scattered and slow in gathering, and Burgoyne with his British and German troops, loyalists, and Indians expertly forced the evacuation of Ticonderoga on July 6, and the next day dispersed the flying patriots. Ticonderoga had been thought so strong that a preposterous story sprang up to account for its surrender.[39] This was that Schuyler and St. Clair had "acted the part of traitors to their country; and that they were paid for their treason by the enemy in silver balls, shot from Burgoyne's guns into our camp; and that they were collected by order of General St. Clair and divided between him and General Schuyler."

Though Philip Skene, Burgoyne's favourite loyalist adviser, knew how preposterous the story was, he knew also that Schuyler, as a Yorker, was unpopular with the Yankees in the northern army and had earlier in the year been fitfully mistreated by Congress, which would doubtless blame him for the loss of Ticonderoga. This seemed to Skene a likely moment to make an attempt on

Schuyler, against whose loyalty there had been persistent but unsupported charges.[40]

They had fought together against the French at Ticonderoga in 1758. Schuyler, related by blood to one of the powerful Albany families and by marriage to another, settled down to the management of the estates he inherited on the Hudson and the Mohawk. Skene, a British major, acquired by royal patent a tract of 34,000 acres around the southernmost point of Lake Champlain and founded a settlement called Skenesborough (Whitehall), where he built a stone manor house and a barn big enough for a garrison. Part of his domain lay in Vermont, then known as the Hampshire grants and claimed by both New Hampshire and New York. In the controversy, which amounted to a local war, Skene like Schuyler sided with their province, which was supported by the Crown. Skene, who became postmaster of Skenesborough in 1771, went later to England and in January 1775 got himself appointed lieutenant governor of Crown Point and Ticonderoga. This was to be a new government set up, by the authorities in England, to embrace the disputed territory and end the conflict. Ethan Allen and Benedict Arnold, hurrying to take Ticonderoga for the Continental Congress in May 1775, spared men to take possession of Skene's house and boats, along with his son and daughters.

When Philip Skene returned to Philadelphia in June he was suspected by Congress of being a "dangerous partisan of administration" and was sent to internment in Connecticut, where he remained till October of the next year. Learning of Burgoyne's expedition, Skene joined it at Lake Champlain, intending to assume his duties as governor of the district. Burgoyne, who paid Skene his year's salary of £200, kept him with the army. Other loyalists resented Skene's influence. They blamed him for Burgoyne's decision to go from Ticonderoga to Skenesborough, where he fixed his temporary headquarters at Skene's house, and then through the wooded country to Fort Edward on the Hudson, instead of by water through Lake George. There was not so much to choose between the two routes as they thought. But they believed Skene had urged his choice for the sake of the military road that had to be built through his land, much to its improvement.[41]

On July 10 Burgoyne at Skenesborough summoned the people

of the neighbouring townships—not less than ten from each township—to assemble at Castleton, Vermont, on the 15th and there affirm their allegiance to the Crown, "under pain of military execution." Skene would represent the Crown and give them guarantees of safety. Schuyler at Fort Edward on the 13th answered with a proclamation declaring that all who accepted protection from the enemy would be traitors and would be "apprehended."[42] The people, in a cross-fire of orders, were confused and divided. The British, an American officer noted on the 17th,[43] "begin to dispense their protections in great numbers. Those who take them, and are discovered, we send immediately to jail." There was no conflict in Skene between his public principles and his private interests. Some of these people were his tenants. If he could hold them to their duty he might advance the king's cause. If the king's forces won, Skene would be a triumphant landlord and governor. Schuyler, it must have seemed to Skene, was in nearly the same position. The two landlords might come to some reasonable understanding.

At Skenesborough on the 19th Skene wrote to Schuyler. He desired, he said, to contribute his mite toward establishing constitutional government on a solid and permanent footing. Burgoyne had commissioned him "to grant protections to those who wish to see themselves once more united to that country from whence they derived their existence. . . . From my own feelings I am inclined to believe that the prosperity and not the destruction of your country is the ultimate object of your wishes. Our former knowledge [acquaintance] and the present distracted state of independency makes me extremely desirous to converse with you upon matters of the highest consequence. As I have nothing to propose that I flatter myself you will not wish to hear or that will not be fully performed, I shall be glad to hear this offer of mine will meet your approbation." It was of course a hint to Schuyler that he might have the British protection which he had publicly declared only traitorous Americans would accept. Since the letter was brought, under a flag, by a released American prisoner, Skene had unmistakably acted with the permission of Burgoyne.

Schuyler's cold answer the next day was to both of them. "As his Excellency Lieutenant General Burgoyne commands the British troops and is at the place where your letter was dated, I cannot consent to open a correspondence except with him, or officer commanding in his absence, to whose flags I shall always pay that respect which is due from one military commander to another. And if a correspondence is desired and an officer appointed in the part of General Burgoyne, one of mine of equal rank will meet him." This was a rejection on technical, though proper, grounds. But Schuyler the same day took pains to send copies of the correspondence to General Nixon of the Continental army and General Fellows of the Massachusetts militia, and on the day after to Washington.[44] Far from making the least response to Skene's attempt, Schuyler by instantly revealing it cleared himself of any possible suspicion in the matter. Skene—or Burgoyne—sent copies of the letters to Germain.[45]

The loss of Ticonderoga cost Schuyler his command, and he was succeeded by Gates on August 19. Before that Schuyler had reassembled his forces with energy and skill; on the 12th dispatched Arnold on his successful march against the reinforcements for Burgoyne who were turned back at Fort Schuyler on the Mohawk; and on the 19th learned of the defeat of a British-German-loyalist-Indian detachment at Bennington by the New England militia three days before. Skene had urged the Bennington expedition on Burgoyne, confident that this would bring many loyalists to the British camp. The effect, rather, was to encourage the patriot militia to join with Gates and his Continentals. In the fighting which culminated at Saratoga the official credit went to Gates, the personal renown to Arnold. Schuyler, whose manor house and mills at Schuylerville were burned by order of Burgoyne, behaved with chivalrous decency both to the Americans who had eclipsed him and to the captured British officers, Burgoyne among them, who were for a week Schuyler's guests at Albany. Skene, a prisoner or on parole throughout the war, lost Skenesborough by confiscation, though the British treasury eventually paid him the salary of his paper office as governor from his first appointment to the treaty of peace, and allowed him £20,350 for his losses.[46] Schuyler, while he showed no bitterness over being superseded, was impatient for a hearing upon his conduct. A court martial was a court of honour. He was put off till October 1778, when he was honourably acquitted of any guilt in the evacuation of Ticonderoga.

Not a word or act that can be positively traced to Schuyler indicates that in his natural depressions during the last months of 1777 he for a time lost faith in the American cause. But January of the next year saw a mysterious episode in his history.

Among the British officers with Burgoyne was Major John Dyke Acland, whose wife (daughter of Lord Ilchester) had accompanied him and become the captivating heroine of the expedition. She was no less popular with the Americans after the surrender. Gates, in a letter on October 17, called her "the most amiable, delicate little piece of quality you ever beheld. Her husband is one of the prettiest fellows I have seen, learned, sensible, and an Englishman to all intents and purposes; has been a most confounded Tory, but I hope to make him as good a Whig as myself before he and I separate."[47] Badly wounded at Stillwater on the 7th, and already a prisoner when Burgoyne capitulated, Acland was not sent with the Convention troops to Cambridge but was moved to Albany for medical treatment. Schuyler's papers made no mention of Acland for the rest of the year, and no other record of their acquaintance has come to light. But at the end of December, when Acland had been exchanged, Schuyler sent him to New York in the charge of Lieutenant Henry Brockholst Livingston, Schuyler's nephew and aide, who was to look out also for certain goods which Schuyler on December 27 ordered from New York, where the shops were better than in Albany. On January 3 Livingston reported from Young's House, fifteen miles above Kingsbridge.

"Agreeable to your request I escorted Major and Lady Harriet Acland to Fishkill, but, not finding General Putnam at that place, and hearing there were some of his guards on the road, I proceeded at Major Acland's request to Colonel Philipse's house" at Phillipsburgh (Tarrytown). As there was no snow below the Highlands, and no wagons to be hired, the travellers had been obliged to go dragging on in the sleighs in which they had left Albany. If Frederick Philipse, brother-in-law of Beverley Robinson, was then at the manor instead of in Manhattan, he was on strict parole to the patriots. But Livingston was able to get a chaise at Phillipsburgh and send the Aclands to the British outpost at Kingsbridge, beyond which Schuyler's coachman was permitted to take them to New York. The goods he was to bring back cost nearly £200. When the gold coins to pay for them turned out to be short in weight, Acland promised to pay the difference. Livingston, waiting for the goods to come out of town, was captured by a loyalist party but set free when he proved that he was under a flag of truce. After six days at Young's he started north again. Though on the 12th he was still afraid that "Tories and plunderers from both armies" might rob the coachman on the road, Livingston wrote that he would try to protect the goods as far as Rhinebeck, to which Schuyler would have to send fresh horses.[48]

Acland went promptly to Clinton, commanding in New York, and told him that Schuyler was opposed to independence. This was a high matter, to be dealt with by the commissioners. General Howe was in Philadelphia and Lord Howe at Rhode Island. Presumably under Clinton's direction, Acland on the 8th wrote Lord Howe a letter which has been lately whispered about in various quarters but never before published.

"As I am well convinced that every information which in the remotest degree may lead to the reconnexion of the Empire, the establishment of general tranquillity, and the vindication of British honour, will be most acceptable to your Lordship from whomsoever it may come, I should think myself inexcusable if I did not take the earliest opportunity of transmitting to your Lordship the report of a conversation that passed between me and ———, whose interest and connexions in the counties of Albany and Tryon give him a very prevailing influence in the province of New York. He desired a private conversation and opened it by saying that it was with the greatest sorrow he perceived that those men who had now the direction of Continental affairs had entirely quitted first principles and totally changed the ground of the contest; that for his part, at every period of the dispute he should have been shocked at the idea of independence; that his aversion to it had been daily increasing, by the conduct of those in power, which power was rapidly devolving to the lowest and most desperate of the people; that he considered American independence and American slavery as synonymous terms; that he had repeatedly refused taking the oath to the Congress, and had three times desired leave to retire from their service as an officer and had as often been refused.

"He assured me that many of his friends and relations (naming them, and they were of the first influence) felt as he did, and were ready to stand forth in the support of the following plan, viz.: That at the election of representatives in March for this province the people who are much discontented should be induced, as he asserts they may be, to instruct their representatives to order their delegates to move the Congress for the opening a treaty with the commissioners, and as a preliminary step to rescind the act of independence. He thinks that to enable him and his friends to carry this point with the people it would be of the utmost importance that some means may be devised by which they might have it in their power to deface from the minds of the people the idea impressed on them by the agents of the Congress, that unconditional submission previous to treaty is required by Great Britain. Such instructions given to the representatives of this province, —— supposes it would be a center to which all those who were averse to independence would gravitate. He was sanguine that the number would be great, but drew the clear inference that the strength of the party would be at least tried."

This plan, Acland ventured to suggest, did not seem "altogether absurd, if it be directed by that discretion, management, and secrecy which has so lately marked the conduct of the friends of government in America." He hoped to God that the talk with Schuyler would "become the foundation of a correspondence in the province of New York which under the influence of your Lordship's abilities might be improved to the general advantage of Great Britain."

Acland's letter, which is the original source of knowledge as to Schuyler's wavering, is only Acland's report of a conversation. Nothing in the letter indicates that Acland had been authorized to treat for Schuyler, or that Schuyler had even hinted at treacherous intentions. All he had in mind—if Acland reported him correctly —was an open constitutional effort to restore the union which independence had disrupted. This effort could succeed, he held, only if the British government made it clear to the Americans that "unconditional submission previous to treaty" would not be required of them.

If the affair is very differently represented in a memorandum written by Clinton seven years later, this need not mean that Acland had told Clinton more than he cared to write to Howe. It may rather mean that Clinton's views of the affair had enlarged his recollection. "Among others of the Saratoga Convention army who came in to me was Major Acland, who informed me that he had had many conversations with Philip Schuyler; that he was certain he was a staunch friend to government; and that he was authorized by him to open a correspondence between us; that he wished me to settle a cipher and said he had his authority to declare if the commissioners would promise on their part that taxation would be given up and unconditional submission not insisted upon, he would join government with all his force."

Here almost every clause has details that never reached Howe, who as responsible commissioner should certainly have been told them. Eight years after this memorandum Clinton wrote another, with erratic speculations. "General Schuyler was the person. His motives were interested. In the first place, till Ticonderoga was taken Burgoyne could not advance. It was the wish of Schuyler that he might, because the Vermonters, his [Schuyler's] bitter enemies and who claim the greatest part of his estates, would in that case be obliged to disclose themselves. If they joined the king's troops, Schuyler would have been hearty with the Americans. If on the contrary they should oppose the king's troops Schuyler would certainly take the opposite side, for reasons in both cases very obvious. The Vermonters had acquired so much credit with the Americans by their spirited exertions against Burgoyne's army that Schuyler was decided in the part he was to take, and thence his proposal to me through Major Acland."[49] The Vermonters did not claim Schuyler's estates, nor did he ever show the slightest sign of wishing to lose Ticonderoga.

In the letters of Lord Howe at the time there is little to support Clinton's later enlargements and speculations. On the day after Acland's letter of January 8 Clinton sent it off to Howe. Howe on the 18th replied that he could not tell from Acland's "information" how Schuyler "wished to have the assurances of the fact which he wants to have ascertained." This indicates that Howe had heard of only one "fact"—unconditional submission—and had apparently heard nothing of a correspondence to be opened. Would Clinton please "obtain from Major Acland such further lights as he can furnish upon the matter"? The next surviving word from Howe is an extract from a letter to Acland on February 17, copied out in Clinton's hand. Howe had, he said, asked Clinton to convey a few lines to Schuyler if it could be done with safety. "The inquirer will then be informed that neither unconditional submission—nor, I have thought expedient to add, Parliamentary taxation—would have been claimed by the commissioners, but such terms of reconciliation proposed as no candid American would disapprove. Furnished with that declaration I should hope he will esteem himself qualified to proceed upon the plan he suggested to you." This was simply Schuyler's political plan for the coming elections. But Howe did imply that he now understood a cipher had been settled upon with Schuyler. If the communication had to go by a messenger, not some safe friend, the messenger might convince Schuyler of the genuineness of the communication by "using the catchwords of the cipher in the manner of a countersign."

Howe wrote out for Clinton the few lines that were to be conveyed: "Neither unconditional submission nor Parliamentary taxation would have been claimed by the commissioners. But such terms of reconciliation proposed as no candid American would disapprove." Clinton's secretary made a tiny copy of the message on tissue paper, as if to be carried by a spy. On April 6 Clinton wrote Howe: "I have with difficulty prevailed on a proper person to carry the message to our northern friend, with the cipher word as a token, without the bearer's suspecting it to be such." As Clinton recalled it fifteen years later, the message was "sent out by duplicates and triplicates." But if any copy ever reached Schuyler, no answer ever came to Clinton. If Schuyler had in December preferred reunion to independence, and had made inquiries of the British which he did not tell Washington or Congress about as he had told them about his letters to Livius and Skene, at least he went on without any visible break in his career as a patriot. In May or June he presumably took the oath of allegiance, now required of all American officers, to the free, sovereign, and independent United States, and renounced, refused, and abjured any allegiance or obedience to George III.

Schuyler's letter to Livius may have reached Burgoyne, and Schuyler's feigned suspicion of Skyler may have been the basis of a hope which Burgoyne turned over to Acland. It is even thinkable that Schuyler, who had tried through Livius to trick military information out of Burgoyne, may have tried through Acland to trick political information out of Howe or Clinton. Whatever Schuyler's intentions were, Clinton went on believing that Schuyler might be influenced, as this record will later show. And news of Schuyler crossed the ocean to the king, who on February 24 wrote to Lord North: "The letter transmitted to you by Major Acland, enclosing the copy of the one he had wrote to Lord Howe, is highly important, as it contains the seeds of great heart-burnings in the rebellious colonies, which I am persuaded would have greatly encouraged the idea of such a proposition"—for conciliation—"as has been made, if it had arrived before you had taken that step."

3

Designs for Peace

THOUGH the king and his first minister had taken a step toward conciliation, they had first tried the experiment of sending a spy across the Channel to find out what effect the American victory had had, or was likely to have, in Paris, where the American commissioners from Congress—Benjamin Franklin of Pennsylvania, Arthur Lee of Virginia, and Silas Deane of Connecticut—were known to be working for an alliance between France and the revolted provinces of her ancient enemy.

The British secret service on the Continent was then managed by William Eden, an alert, ambitious under-secretary of state who still after Saratoga hated and dreaded the idea of imperial disunion as thoroughly as many Americans were later to dread the idea of secession still after Bull Run. Eden could not believe that the rebels, even if independent of England, could expect to be independent of all Europe. Some "qualified control," he took it for granted, "should rest somewhere" across the Atlantic.[1] Surely Britain had a better and more natural sovereignty to offer than France or Spain. It was to the interests of the Americans to return to a place in the British Empire, now on easier terms. While the British ministry could not at present treat openly with the rebel commissioners, it was willing to listen to any proposals except for absolute independence, and required only to be told how the commissioners would like matters of independence and peace to be negotiated.

To carry this apparently candid message Eden chose the loyalist Paul Wentworth, formerly a member of the New Hampshire council and agent for New Hampshire in London. Wentworth while agent had become a double-dealer by an agreement with Lord North,[2] and had presumably shared the colony's secrets with the minister. Born an American, Wentworth considered himself a cosmopolitan, and was a stock-jobber in London, Amsterdam, and Paris. He lived comfortably and gallantly, cared little for the £200 a year he got for his secret services, and desired nothing so much as an established if modest position in the compact society of England: office-holder, member of Parliament, and baronet. For the sake of these pleasant rewards he was willing to be a spy though intensely unwilling to be suspected of being one. He hoped the rebellion would fail, for otherwise he as a loyalist would lose his New Hampshire estates. And he had no compunction about trying to assist the failure.

Wentworth genuinely believed that most of the rebels were actuated primarily by envy, ambition, or interest, and that many of them would change sides if it were made worth their while or if they faced no penalty for rebellion. "The highest degree of political profligacy already prevails," he had lately written, "and perhaps a well-timed offer of indemnity and impunity to these Cromwells and Barebones may serve, like a strong alkali, to reduce the effervescence in the mass of the people, or turn their fury on their misleaders."[3]

There is no evidence that Eden instructed or encouraged Wentworth to promise personal rewards to the commissioners; neither is there any evidence that Eden disapproved of the offers Wentworth did make. Such matters were then taken for granted, and seldom set down in words that might later prove inconvenient. Bribery and corruption were transacted under George III in a language elegantly bristling with subtle points of decorum. The king, fountain both of honour and of profit to his dutiful servants, did not expect that they would serve him without their share of both. The substantial, dependable bloc that supported his American policy in his two houses of Parliament was known simply as the king's friends. Whigs and moralists protested on either side of the Atlantic. Franklin, whom the king looked upon as the arch-rebel, had three years before written from London, in a letter which may have been opened and read if it passed through the mails, that "if America would save for three or four years the money she spends in fashions and fineries and fopperies of this country, she might buy the whole Parliament, minister and all."[4]

Plenty of British officials and American loyalists believed that Congress, if the officials and loyalists could get at its members, would be as amenable as Franklin said Parliament was. The ministry had been able to hire Americans—such as Wentworth—for secret agents in England and France. Edward Bancroft of Massachusetts, friend and confidant of Franklin in Paris, was a British spy, paid to watch the commissioners. John Vardill of New York spied on Americans in London—on the promise that he would be regius professor of divinity in King's (Columbia) College as soon as British order should be restored in his native province. The king's commander-in-chief in America had hired Americans to oblige him with services and information, sometimes publicly joining the British, sometimes acting in secret within the rebel lines. The king, North, Eden, Wentworth: no one of them would have been astonished if they had found even Franklin corruptible.

Franklin, as it turned out, refused to meet Wentworth at all unless he would first promise that there was to be no mention of rewards "in any part of the conversation."[5] The meeting did not take place till January 6, nearly four weeks after Wentworth arrived in Paris. Eden, in a letter which Wentworth was allowed to show Franklin with the assurance that it was from somebody close to the British government, had said that England was ready to go on fighting ten years to prevent independence; Franklin said America was ready to fight fifty years to win it, and that the two countries would be better off politically separate and bound together only by peaceful, equal trade.[6] Nothing could be done with Franklin, Wentworth had to conclude.

He did not realize that his coming to France, far from hindering the Franco-American alliance, had accelerated it. The French foreign minister, the Comte de Vergennes, used Wentworth as an argument to the French and Spanish kings that the Americans might be making peace with Great Britain. This, Vergennes was sure, would be bad for France and Spain. "The power which first recognizes the independence of the Americans," he wrote to the French minister at Madrid, the day after Wentworth reached Paris, "will be the one to gather all the fruits of this war."[7] And on the day after Wentworth saw Franklin, Louis XVI at last consented to a treaty between France and the United States without waiting longer for the co-operation of Spain, which still held off. Thanks in part to Wentworth and other emissaries sent from London to Paris, and to Franklin's masterly handling of them, the American commissioners who for a year before Saratoga had been asking France for an alliance, after Saratoga were asked by France to become allies without further delay.

But Wentworth, though he had less than no luck with the sage Franklin and none with the irascible Arthur Lee, was apparently not altogether wrong in his cynical conviction that most men could be influenced. At one of his earliest conferences, with Deane alone, he offered Deane "the honour of [first] pointing out the mode and means of salvation to his country," with the "dignity and emolument" which that would bring him.[8] In refined political language, Wentworth was hinting at a bribe. Deane did not touch the bait that day. But at some later meeting he seems to have listened to Wentworth's large talk about the advantages to Americans "which Great Britain only can give permanently." These would include "honours and emoluments to the leaders, governors general, privy seals, great seals, treasurers, secretaries, councillors in the general governments, local barons, and knights."[9] This was a standard theme for loyalists, especially in Europe, where they liked to think of the lucrative offices which might spring up in America if the English system of government could be extended to that frugal country.

Deane may not have wanted a title or an office in America under the Crown, but he was carrying on private business while acting as commissioner, and was possibly trading on the London stock market with the benefit of political information in advance.[10] Wentworth, leaving Paris on January 10 with secretive hints at "three partners . . . at the fountain head," may already have come to some preliminary understanding with Deane.[11]

Three weeks later Lord North wrote to the king about certain goods which were to be purchased by Wentworth in London and sent to New York for the profit of "Mr. D." and about "Mr. D.'s proposals, to which are added some pieces of intelligence Mr. W. received from him."[12] Skimpy as the proof is, it is enough to testify that Deane, before he heard that Congress in December had recalled him and appointed John Adams in his place, had listened to

Wentworth's temptations, furnished him information, made him some kind of proposals, and was to be rewarded through the round-about channel of clandestine trade. George III had stubbornly re-fused to credit Wentworth's news about the French alliance, be-cause Wentworth was a stock-jobber and might be scheming to affect the price of stocks. But on February 3 the king wrote North that "undoubtedly if the intelligence sent by Benson is founded, France has taken her part and a war with Great Britain must soon follow." Since the British seem to have had no informer in Paris named Benson, and since Deane was known by the British to have used the name Benson in his correspondence,[13] this Benson of the king's letter was probably Deane and the intelligence was probably that communicated through Wentworth.

Here at last was an American the king was willing to put con-fidence in. Deane's return to Philadelphia seemed, the king wrote on March 9, "a very fortunate event" which, along with the concili-ation bills, "I should naturally conclude may bring America to a state of tranquillity."[14]

II

Lord North brought his conciliation bills before the House of Commons on February 17. David Hartley, member for Hull, sent them at once to his old friend Franklin in Paris. Franklin, replying on the 26th, saw in them the ministry's "little arts and schemes of amusing and dividing us." Parliament might now intend not to exercise its right to tax the colonies—a right the Americans did not acknowledge—but might change its mind another session. The commissioners who were to be sent to America might proclaim a truce, and then revoke their proclamation as soon as the militia had gone home. "Indeed, Sir, your ministers do not yet know us. We may not be quite so cunning as they; but we really have more sense as well as more courage than they have ever been willing to give us credit for; and I am persuaded these acts will rather ob-struct peace than promote it and that they will not in America answer the mischievous and malevolent ends for which they were intended. In England they may indeed amuse the public creditors, give hopes and expectations that shall be of some present use, and continue the mismanagers a little longer in their places. *Voilà tout.*"[15]

Franklin had not needed to read the letter in which North on January 29 explained his intentions to the king. "The anxiety of his mind for the last two months," the minister wrote, "has deprived Lord North of his memory and understanding." As matters stood, he felt an effort must be made "to draw some of the colonies from their claim and plan of independency." This might be done by promising that any colony which would renounce its claim should be exempt from Parliamentary taxation. It would be an economical promise. "To give up the levying of positive taxes here is to give up in effect nothing, as it is pretty certain that none will for the future be ever levied by the British Parliament." But it would be difficult, North saw, to declare against the right to tax in such a way as not to make trouble on one side or the other. The friends of the ministry would resent being asked to back down on "the first subject of the quarrel, though in the end they are convinced it must end in this or worse." And the Americans would hesitate to take any step on the mere promise that Parliament would reward them. "No colony would quit the confederacy for this advantage, if the enjoyment of it were to depend upon terms to be settled after they should have quitted their friends and consequently put themselves at the mercy of Great Britain." The best avowable scheme North had been able to think of was to repeal the tea duty and the Massachusetts charter bill, and to leave other points of controversy to be settled by the commissioners. He sent the king a preliminary sketch of his proposal. As always in such times of stress, North was willing to retire from his office if the king should wish it.[16]

The king thought North's letter so serious that he waited a day before answering it on the 31st. "I should have been greatly hurt at the inclination expressed by you to retire, had I not known that however you may now and then be inclined to despond, yet that you have too much personal affection for me, and sense of honour, to allow such a thought to take any hold on your mind." North would remember that the king had before the Parliamentary recess been opposed to the minister's binding himself to make a move toward conciliation: "not from any absurd ideas of unconditional submission, [which] my mind never harboured, but from foreseeing that whatever can be proposed will be liable not to bring America back to a sense of attachment to the mother country, yet to dissatisfy this country, which has in the most handsome manner cheerfully carried on the contest and therefore has a right to have the struggle continued until convinced that it is in vain." But that same day the king heard through Wentworth from Silas Deane (Benson), and by February 9 was urging North not to delay his "American proposition."[17]

North's offers of February 17 would conceivably have ended the rebellion if they had been made three years before, when the Americans had asked no more than this and had hardly thought of independence. But now the sentiment of independence had become a fixed principle of the chief American leaders and perhaps —North could not be sure of this—of a majority of the people. The king was as determined as ever not to yield on so essential a point, and the majority of Englishmen were still with him, though an increasing number had come to be willing to let the colonies go. It seemed impossible to frame conciliatory proposals which could promise enough, short of independence, to interest the Americans, and yet not too much for the English to accept. Any conciliation must be a compromise. Moreover, there was the threatening alliance of the rebel colonies with France. To avoid a war with France it would be worth while to make large concessions to the Americans, but to do that might be to stimulate the French to still more vigorous aid to their allies. No time could be wasted. The conciliatory bills, not yet passed by Parliament, were hurried off on the 20th by the warship *Andromeda,* in the hope that they would reach America and affect opinion before news came from France. The ministry could not wait to see how the race would come out. Military and naval plans for the year must go on, in case the Americans should reject the proposals and the war continue. Conciliation could be only one of several efforts in a complex undertaking.

Sending the king the first draft of his proposals, North spoke of the zealous and laborious help he had received from the attorney general, Edward Thurlow, and the solicitor general, Alexander Wedderburn. But the surviving documents show that William

Eden was as energetic in the matter of conciliation and the commission as he had been in the secret service before the Franco-American treaty.

He drew up one of the two earliest plans—Wedderburn the other—and busied himself with every detail of the process. He was the centre of correspondence from others working on the same problem. Wedderburn sent to Eden a "brother projector" who had a project for "an accommodation with the Americans which he proposes to sell upon very reasonable terms. You have got mine gratis, and I wish you would return it me if plans bear any price."[18] (While he was about it, Wedderburn put in a more serious application in behalf of an old "governor and servant" of his who had grown "very deaf and stupid. . . . If the patent of king's stationer should happen to be vacant I should be really much obliged to you to cut me out a slice of it for him.") On February 22 the Earl of Carlisle, close friend of Eden at Eton, was appointed head of the commission, and the next day Eden "agreed to go if certain persons whom I named could not be induced to go, or if the commission were filled up by those whom I should like."[19] On March 3 the king had carefully read Eden's reports and consented to his having £1000 "to fit himself" for the enterprise.[20] Two days later Eden accepted, and on the 7th the attorney general wrote him: "I am very glad, for the public, that the business is to be put into your hands. A more important trust was never put in any hands, or on a more delicate occasion."[21]

Carlisle, heading the commission, brought to it the prestige of high rank and great wealth. Not yet quite thirty, he was a man of fashion, a wit, and a minor poet who had published an *Ode* on another Eton poet, Thomas Gray (and was twenty years later to become chancery guardian of his difficult cousin Lord Byron). Admiral Byron, soon to reinforce Admiral Howe in America, was Carlisle's uncle. From a youthful career of spectacular gambling Carlisle had lately turned to politics and been made treasurer of the king's household and privy councillor. Personally agreeable to the king, the young nobleman had since Eton been intimate with his fellow-gambler Charles James Fox, who was brilliant in the opposition to the king's American policy. Carlisle, whose friendship with Fox would please the Americans, had already proposed to cross the Atlantic as "the bearer of such offers of peace to America as the interests of both countries required . . . previous to any intimation I had received that the appointment of commissioners for the purpose of treating with America was in contemplation."

He stipulated that he "be joined by men whose character, rank in life, and abilities might restore that importance and weight to the commission that it might lose by my youth and inexperience" and that "no powers should be denied us to bring the business to a quick termination. . . . I was soon informed that my offer was acceptable, that the king had received it as a testimony of my affection to his person and as a proof of my zeal to serve my country in the moment of difficulty and distress. . . . On the 25th [of February] Mr. Eden called upon me to acquaint me that it had been proposed to him to be joined with me in the commission, a proposal that he seemed willing to accept. The intimacy I had always lived with him, the experience I had had of his honour and understanding, rendered his nomination to the employment very satisfactory to me. Soon after this Mr. Jackson was mentioned to me by Mr. Eden to complete the number of those who were to compose the commission. I bent to the persuasion that his accurate knowledge of the country to which we were to repair and his long and familiar acquaintance with her interests would outbalance the insignificance of his situation and the obscurity of his name."[22]

Richard Jackson (now remembered as the Omniscient Jackson of Charles Lamb's *Old Benchers of the Inner Temple*) had been a correspondent of Franklin as early as 1753 and later Franklin's colleague in the agency for Pennsylvania, and was supposed to know as much about America as any Englishman. On the 28th he wrote to Eden that he would serve if he were appointed, and though he hoped to be back in London by Christmas, he would cheerfully stay ten years in America "or even on the Gold Coast" if there were any prospect of success. "The commencement of the American war always appeared to me an impolitic measure; the continuance of it cannot be less than ruin to this empire." While he was not sure that the conciliatory bills would have the effect the ministry hoped for, he believed the commission might do some good if the instructions were "full and precise."[23] But on March 1 he was still in doubt as to the instructions, and on the 3rd Eden urged

Wedderburn to make them "palatable to Jackson, and that without delay." On the 13th France through its ambassador to London announced the treaty with America, and that evening Carlisle, Eden, and Jackson met for the first time at Lord North's.[24]

The commission, which was to include also the former commissioners, the Howes in America, seemed to be complete, though many eminent persons had refused to serve on it. But Jackson was still uncertain. On the 30th Eden wrote Wedderburn: "After you . . . went away last night"—from Lord North's again—"Jackson gave to every person in the world to understand that he had no intention to proceed in the commission. He said it was idle and ruinous to go to war with France . . . that we should proceed immediately to give independence to the colonies . . . that it did not signify when they [the commissioners] arrived [in America], and was of no consequence except to satisfy the people of this country . . . 'and such a deal of skimble-skamble stuff.' Upon the whole he has convinced us that he does not mean to go, and also that he ought not to go. Lord North has now written to him that the commissioners must positively leave London on or before the 12th April, to which of course he will reply that he cannot go."[25]

Eden was nearly in despair. All his efforts might come to nothing. Of possible substitutes for Jackson the most likely man, he thought, was George Johnstone, Scottish post captain who had been governor of West Florida and was known in Parliament as a partisan for America. Wedderburn spoke to Johnstone and found him eager to be chosen. North wrote to the king on April 1 that Johnstone "will go in Mr. Jackson's place, and his friends will, in that case, be better inclined to side with administration." The king at 11:49 that day thought that "Johnstone, if made palatable to Lord Carlisle, which I should think Eden might easily manage, would not be an improper person."[26]

Eden would have been more despairing than he was if he had been fully trusted with the secrets of the king and his ministry. The commissioners knew that they must be supported by the armed forces if their offer of peace was to seem to the Americans an attractive alternative to war. On March 7 Germain showed Eden the instructions going the next day to Clinton, the new commander-in-chief in America, for the year's campaign. The king hoped, Germain said, that the commission would be able to bring about a lasting peace. Yet while that was pending the army and navy must be as active as ever. Reinforcements in large numbers would probably be sent. It might be better not to risk a decisive engagement with Washington, but ships and troops were to strike at the seaports from New York to Nova Scotia. Philadelphia was to be held unless Clinton should think it wiser to withdraw the forces there for the general attack along the coast. With this Eden was content. Neither he nor any of the commissioners was told that on the 21st Germain sent Clinton secret instructions, signed and sealed by the king himself, to evacuate Philadelphia and if need be New York; to keep Rhode Island if possible and certainly Halifax; to send troops to hold Florida and an expedition to take the French island of St. Lucia in the West Indies; but not to undertake any offensive operations on the continent.[27]

The change of plans was forced by the changed situation with regard to France. Yet North was intolerably lax—or disingenuous —with the commissioners whom he kept in ignorance. As if he had lost faith in their venture, he was remote and hard to see. Carlisle at the meeting on March 13 was "not a little shocked at the slovenly manner" in which the affair was handled. Eden at his final meeting with North on April 12, the day before the commissioners left London, felt that the minister treated the long farewell "in the style of a common acquaintance who is stepping from your room to the water closet and means to return in five minutes."[28]

III

The conciliatory acts, passed in both houses of Parliament and officially dispatched to America on March 16, offered the rebels everything but independence. Though the commissioners were empowered to treat with Congress and Washington as if their country were independent for the time being, and were instructed not to insist on a formal revocation of the Declaration and other "votes, orders, and resolutions" of Congress, this was on the ground that they, "not being legal acts, will be in effect rescinded by the conclusion of the treaty." But the commissioners' instructions looked beyond a possible refusal of Congress and Washington to treat. In that case, the commissioners might deal directly with any province that desired "to revert to the ancient form of government" under a governor to be appointed by the commission. In doing this they were cautioned not "to give umbrage or jealousy to the powers with which you are publicly treating. . . . But such caution is not to prevent you, or any three of you, from entering into any correspondence or treaty with particular colonies, bodies of men, or individual persons, to answer the purposes of the commission."[29] As North had explained to the king in January, and Franklin had seen in February when he read the conciliatory acts, the British government intended—though only if outright and public measures failed—to divide the United States and deal with them separately if it could.

While the commission was being organized, efforts toward some kind of adjustment went on in London and Paris. Franklin, who believed that Great Britain by acknowledging the independence of the United States might avoid a war with France, and genuinely wished that this might happen, hoped to see the Whig opposition come into power and undo the damage done by the Tory ministers. Lord Chatham and Lord Camden had in December, even after the news of Saratoga, sent him their best compliments; and he managed to keep more or less in touch with the opposition leader Lord Shelburne. In February Franklin sent Jonathan Loring Austin, who had brought Paris the first word of Burgoyne's surrender, secretly to London to carry messages to the Whigs. Nothing came of it. The king was, as he wrote to North a month later, incorrigibly resolved not to "stoop to opposition. . . . Whilst any ten men in the kingdom will stand by me I will not give myself up into bondage. My dear lord, I will rather risk my crown than do what I think personally disgraceful. And whilst I have no wish but for the good and prosperity of my country, it is impossible that the nation shall not stand by me. If they will not, they shall have another king."[30]

In March the ministry sent William Pulteney, member for Shrewsbury and pamphleteer, twice to Franklin in a final attempt at negotiation before the commission left for America. It is a tangled story. As to their first meeting Franklin was perfectly explicit. "When I first had the honour of conversing with you on the subject of peace, I mentioned it as my opinion that every proposition which implied our voluntarily agreeing to return to a dependence on Britain was now become impossible; that a peace on equal terms undoubtedly might be made; and that though we [the American commissioners in Paris] had no particular powers to treat of peace with England, we had general powers to make treaties of peace, amity, and commerce with any state in Europe, by which I thought we might be authorized to treat with Britain; who, if sincerely disposed to peace, might save time and much bloodshed by treating with us directly. I also gave it as my opinion that, in the treaty to be made, Britain should endeavour by the fairness and generosity of the terms she offered to recover the esteem, confidence, and affection of America, without which the peace could not be so beneficial, as it was not likely to be lasting. In this I had the pleasure to find you of my opinion."[31]

Pulteney, back in London with his report, was more hopeful than North, writing to the king on the 25th, thought there was much reason to be. The king, replying the next day, suspected that Franklin out of a constant "hatred to this country" had encouraged Pulteney in order to postpone or hinder the departure of the commission to America, or to get further information about British policy. Still, the king thought it "proper to keep open the channel of intercourse with that insidious man" in Paris. There must be another interview of "the agents employed in this dangerous business" and something put down in writing. Pulteney was furnished with a draft of a letter, drawn by North and approved by the king, which Franklin was to be asked to write and sign before the negotiations could begin. "If Franklin is not sincere (and Lord North has no opinion of his sincerity) he will not write such a letter."[32] Besides this Pulteney carried also a set of proposals approved by the ministry, which it is reasonable to guess were about the same as those embodied in the instructions then being prepared for the commissioners going to America.

Pulteney, once more in France under the name of Williams, on the 29th sent a note to Franklin. "Mr. Williams returned this morning to Paris and will be glad to see Dr. Franklin, whenever it is convenient for the Doctor, at the Hôtel Frasilière, rue Tournon. It is near the hotel where he lodged when the Doctor saw him a fortnight ago. He does not propose to go abroad [out], and therefore the Doctor will find him at any hour."[33]

That same day or the next Franklin saw Pulteney in the presence of their friend William Alexander, a Scot who lived near Paris and whose daughter the next year married Franklin's grand-nephew Jonathan Williams. The ministry's proposals proved to Franklin, as he wrote on the 30th, "that the ministers cannot yet divest themselves of the idea that the power of Parliament over us is constitutionally absolute and unlimited; and that the limitations they may be willing now to put to it by treaty are so many favours, or so many benefits, for which we are to make compensation." He did not believe any treaty between the two countries could be made on any such terms, and he knew the American commissioners had no authority to make one. They had no authority to "make even the declaration specified in the proposed letter." But, though he himself did not approve of the proposals or think they had a chance of being accepted in America, he reminded Pulteney that there were two other commissioners in Paris. " 'I will, if you please, show your propositions to them, and you will hear their opinions. I will also show them to the [French] ministry here, without whose knowledge and concurrence we can take no step in such affairs.' 'No,' said he, 'as you do not approve of them it can answer no purpose to show them to anybody else; the reasons that weigh with you will weigh with them; therefore I now pray that no mention may be made of my having been here or my business.' To which I agreed."[34]

Apparently before he had made this promise, or in spite of it, Franklin gave a copy of the proposals to Silas Deane, who on the 31st set out for Toulon on his way to America in company with Conrad Alexandre Gérard, the first French minister to the United States. But on the 7th Franklin sent a letter after Deane. "The negotiator is gone back, apparently much chagrined at his little success. I have promised him faithfully that since his propositions could not be accepted they should be buried in oblivion. I therefore earnestly desire that you would put that paper immediately into the fire on receipt of this, without taking or suffering to be taken any copy of it, or communicating its contents."[35] The spy Bancroft in Paris had too hastily written to the spy Wentworth in

London that Pulteney's first "hints for a negotiation are adopted."[36] And by the 16th Bancroft had heard, or said he had heard, from somebody in England that Pulteney was supposed to have gone back with Franklin's approval. "I wish you would assure our friend," Franklin wrote to Bancroft, "that Dr. Franklin never gave any such expectations to Mr. Pulteney. On the contrary, he told him that the [British] commissioners could not succeed in their mission whether they went to recover the dependence or divide."[37]

Pulteney afterwards insisted he had authorized nobody "to hold the language which has been imputed to him on that subject." But Pulteney seems to have given Johnstone a memorandum of the discussions in Paris,[38] and Johnstone in Philadelphia claimed that Franklin had approved of the Pulteney proposals. Though the connexion between Pulteney and Johnstone has been overlooked by all the historians of the episode, it was a natural one. Pulteney was Johnstone's elder brother who had changed his surname on his marriage to an heiress of the great Pulteney estate.

George Johnstone was to be a trouble-maker for the commission. Sympathetic toward the colonists since his three years in Florida, he had during ten years in Parliament generally defended America against the ministry, in a language often extreme enough for the most passionate Americans. If there was not much in his speeches except the common rant in favour of liberty, neither was there much in his lively reputation as a duellist, though he was known to be ready and adroit with a pistol, and he had forced a bloodless duel on Germain. But Johnstone was used to acting promptly, and he promptly wrote a flattering, insinuating letter to an American whom he hoped to influence. This was Colonel Joseph Reed, formerly adjutant general of the Continental army, Washington's friend, and a member of Congress. Johnstone had no acquaintance with Reed, but Reed had an English wife, and Johnstone knew her brother.

"Your pen and your sword," Johnstone wrote Reed on April 11, "have both been used with glory and advantage in vindicating the rights of mankind and of that community of which you was a part. . . . During the contest, I am free to confess, my wishes have ever been that America might so far prevail as to oblige this country to see their error. . . . It has pleased God, in His justice, so to dispose of events that this kingdom is at last convinced of her folly and her faults. . . . Nothing could surpass the glory you [the Americans] have acquired in arms except the generous magnanimity of meeting on the terms of justice and equality, after demonstrating to the world that the fear of force could have no influence in that decision. The man who can be instrumental in bringing us all to act once more in harmony, and to unite together the various powers which this contest has drawn forth, will deserve more from the king and the people, from patriotism, humanity, friendship, and all the tender ties that are affected by the quarrel and reconciliation, than ever yet was bestowed on human kind."[39]

There was nothing clearly suspicious in this letter except that Johnstone did not know Reed and had something besides friendship for a motive. Many Englishmen were writing the sincerest letters to American friends, urging them to listen to the commission and help end the tragic war. Others were perhaps more mixed in their intentions. Sir Robert Eden, who as governor of Maryland had known Washington and his family, wrote to him "that should the commissioners, by whom I have the honour of sending this, be fortunate enough to accomplish a reconciliation it will give me the highest pleasure. When I inform your Excellency that my brother, William Eden, whom I have a very great regard for, is one of them, I have no doubt of his meeting with all such civilities as you in your station can offer or he, in his, desire. You may believe me when I assure you that he heartily wishes success to his undertaking, and that you will find as much candour and probity as you could desire in a person you will probably have to treat with. He will assure you that I have endeavoured at all times to do justice to your character, and that I shall be happy in meeting your Excellency again on the same free and friendly terms we formerly lived."[40]

IV

Governor Eden may or may not have known that his brother had taken advice from his spies Vardill and Wentworth as to less direct methods of dealing with influential Americans.

Vardill at William Eden's request wrote out, on April 11,

Sketches and Hints for the use of the commissioners.[41] "To secure the respect of the people in general, especially in the middle and eastern provinces," the clergyman in Vardill warned, "you will find it prudent to maintain a gravity in your deportment, to join as little as possible in convivial parties and public diversions." The loyalist in him warned them against having a great deal to do with other loyalists, who were "too much under the impulse of passion and prejudice to be relied on for information, and too obnoxious to the leading rebels to be of any service in conciliating their affections. You will therefore be difficult of access to them on your arrival, as it will save you the necessity of disobliging them and the pain of perpetual applications for assistance and favours." The commission would be wise to avoid any "apparent attachment or connexion with any" of the conspicuous loyalist families in New York. As to New Yorkers "in the Congress cause," Vardill thought it most important to win over William Smith, a member of the council, "who has more influence over the rebels in the province than any other person. . . . He is subtle, cool, and persuasive. . . . He may be secured by an application to his ambition." Vardill did not know that Smith had already refused to take the oath of allegiance to the new state, lost his former influence, and been put on parole at Livingston Manor; nor, of course, that he was soon to join the British in New York and be appointed chief justice under the Crown.

Next to Smith on Vardill's list of persons to be courted stood John Jay, chief justice under the state constitution which he had drafted, and member of Congress. Jay was, Vardill thought, "possessed of a strong understanding though much perverted by the study of the law joined to a temper naturally controversial. You can sooner gain him to your opinion by submitting to be confuted by him than by a direct attempt to convince him. . . . A prospect of keeping his present office of chief justice would probably weigh much with him, as he before the war solicited, with Mr. Robert Livingston, through me to be appointed a puisne judge." Here Vardill somewhat distorted the facts. He and Jay had been friends at King's College. Early in 1774, when Jay in New York was developing into a patriot, and Vardill in London into a loyalist, Vardill had persuaded the British government to offer Jay a minor post, perhaps to check his growing patriotism. Jay, who supposed that Vardill's share in this was purely out of friendship, had declined the post in question but had admitted that he and Livingston would like to be visiting judges in the county courts of common pleas. Perhaps Vardill's friendship might be of service with the authorities in London. Hostilities had put an end to the project. Not till years later did Jay know that Vardill had been a British agent.[42] Far from influencing Jay, Eden did not even have a chance to approach him, though Vardill had furnished letters of introduction to Jay and other New York patriots.

Vardill assumed that influence might have effect on any of the men he named in New York, New Jersey, or Pennsylvania, but he thought "the great end of your commission" could hardly be achieved "unless Dr. Franklin has privately approved of the plan. . . . Some of the Congress are friends to independency from principle, and others will not readily agree to measures which will sink them to their primitive obscurity." The people at large, though probably for peace, would be "awed into silence and acquiescence" by Congress and the army. Nothing could be of more consequence than "to make it the interest of the Congress and army to close with you. From the many conversations I have had with the ambitious in America, and from the nature of the thing itself," Vardill believed that there should be an American Parliament of two houses: the lower made up of delegates from the different assemblies, and the upper "an order of nobles or patricians." The chance of becoming some kind of peer—though only an American peer—would bring almost any ambitious American, Vardill was almost certain, back to his old allegiance. The army, officers and soldiers, might be "continued in their rank and pay and employed in the service of the Empire, against our common enemies," which meant France, until it should be convenient to disband them.

Wentworth in his Minutes and Sketches[43] insisted that the rebel provinces must be thought of as three districts actually more distinct in character than "the three districts of the realm in Europe." The United States, so called, was an incongruous federation of the Eastern Republic of New England, the Middle Republic from the Hudson to the Potomac, and the Southern Republic. Each of them had its local leaders, but the influence of Franklin was general, and that of Washington was rising. "I believe Washington is really jealous of the New England actors, though he moves and appears to confide in them. . . . He is very jealous of Dr. Franklin and those who are governed by republican principles, from which he is very averse."

Believing that, Wentworth could believe anything, such as his recommendation about Samuel Adams: "An unprincipled man in his morals; steady to one point in his politics. Independency was his constant prayer. Of great talents, particularly adapted to the management of popular assemblies. Fertile in expedients, dexterous in applying them. Subtle and unaffected, he can embrace an advantage or sacrifice it to the wishes of an indifferent friend. Cool in deliberation, impetuous in the execution. His similes are bold and striking; his arguments naturally deduced, close yet seem familiar. His conclusions are forcibly drawn and his language though not always chaste is often beautiful. He is diffuse both in speaking and writing, yet he does both with great energy and persuasion. He has acquired these talents by dint of labour. Twenty years ago he was not distinguished from the crowd of very middling characters. He is, I should think, an impracticable man, but certainly worth gaining to act the double part, for which he is well qualified." This seems an especially bad guess about a patriot who would have been as hard to wheedle as a porcupine.

Wentworth thought that James Lovell of Massachusetts, the most active member of Congress's committee for foreign affairs, might be "practised upon." Like Vardill, Wentworth pointed hopefully to William Smith: "ambitious and avaricious; would prefer certain gratifications [from the British] to speculative pursuits [with the Americans]; few men are so able, if he could be trusted." The Rev. John Witherspoon, president of the College of New Jersey (Princeton), was "a zealot, a republican, but prone to the love of power and riches," and so should not be overlooked. Nor should Thomas Paine in Philadelphia, who was "naturally indolent and led by his passions." John Rutledge of South Carolina was according to Wentworth "very artful, sensible, ambitious, and a man of business; may be practised upon."

Commenting on the rebel leaders, Wentworth particularly noted their wealth or lack of it. "R means rich; M mediocrity; S small fortune; E embarrassed; RR, rank and riches from this rebellion." He took it for granted that such information would be valuable. Rich rebels might be anxious not to lose their fortunes by confiscation to the Crown, and poor rebels eager to prosper from so opulent a source. Carlisle, copying the names from Wentworth's list, made no notation on Lovell, and left Paine out altogether, but he heavily starred the names of Samuel Adams, Smith of New York, Witherspoon, and John Rutledge (along with several others about whom Wentworth had been less positive).[44]

There can be no doubt that Eden, as manager of the commission, meant to work openly and honestly as far as he could. Neither can there be any doubt that the commission was equipped for corruption if that should be necessary. At the end of Eden's preliminary budget of expenses he added: "Some arrangement should be settled as to the power of drawing for contingent secret service money, which should be vested in the three civil commissioners upon their unanimous agreement according to the circumstances which may arise." North arranged the matter by a letter to the commander-in-chief in America, "desiring him to furnish you [the commissioners] with secret service money out of the army contingencies. . . . As peace is the first object of the military force employed in America, and as the power given to you over the army money is among the most efficacious methods of restoring peace, I do not think that any person who wishes to see a happy conclusion of the present trouble will seriously blame me for having sent the enclosed letter to the commander-in-chief, especially as the same power is possessed, and may possibly have been exercised, by Lord and Sir William Howe."[45]

William Lee in Paris had heard as early as February 28 that the British were counting more on the secret service guineas they were to send to America than on the troops; and Arthur Lee by May 10 that the commissioners had taken as many Americans, secretly loyalist, as possible with them to help in the sly negotiations.[46] These were lavish suspicions in the Lee manner. The commission was accompanied—or followed—by only two informal agents who were to do what they could on their own responsibility. One was John Berkenhout, a physician who had known Arthur Lee in London and who had tried to sound him out by letter at about the time Wentworth went over to confer with Franklin and Deane.[47] While the terms of Berkenhout's engagement with the commissioners are not known, Germain on April 18 instructed the Admiralty to receive Berkenhout "and suite" on board the *Lioness*, to sail with John Temple, about whose engagement the most explicit record has survived.[48]

This was that John Temple who had been involved with Franklin in the famous affair of the Hutchinson letters in London in 1773. Born in Boston and married to a Boston woman, Temple had strong family connexions in England. He had been an officer of the customs in America and in London. Opposed like other Whigs to the ministry's American policy, he had since 1774 come to think of his dismissal along with Franklin's as a common sacrifice, and perhaps an equal one. There was the difference that whereas Franklin had admitted getting the letters and sending them to America, Temple had denied any share in the scheme and had fought a duel to prove it; and he was not yet ready to claim in public that he had been a hero as well as a victim of the episode. But Temple, who had remained in England while the war went on in America, thought of himself as an American, and proposed himself as a volunteer assistant to the commissioners. By April 1 he had talked with North, who said he now thought the Americans would be satisfied with nothing less than independence, but who was willing to let Temple try to prove to them that, as Temple claimed to think, independence would be "bad for both countries."[49]

A memorandum in Eden's hand set down Temple's purposes and Temple's price, which seems to have been higher than any so far promised to an American for services to the British government. He was to go as soon as possible to America, in a ship to be named by the minister, and there "faithfully exert his utmost influence in assisting the commissioners now going out to bring about a reconciliation or reunion between those colonies and Great Britain. In consideration of which, and his former faithful services in various employments under the Crown, Mr. Temple is to have £2000 immediately paid to him; is to be authorized to draw on the treasury (provided the said commissioners shall approve his conduct) for £2000 more; is to be made a baronet of Great Britain, the patent for the same to be sent out to America by the commissioners; and, independent of the success of the commission, he is to have a pension for life of £2000 per annum . . . provided the said commissioners now going out shall approve his conduct." Since the terms were prodigal, it was stipulated in an explanatory note added at North's request that Temple's conduct must be "an active exertion of notoriety and weight" which the commissioners could approve in writing. If the commission failed totally, Temple's pension would not be due him. His first payment of £2000 in banknotes came from John Robinson, who handled secret service funds, to Eden "for Mr. Temple as ordered" on April 10.[50]

Temple and Wentworth both looked upon the Declaration of Independence as an opportune move which might now be bargained over like any other advantage on either side. Both saw the American quarrel as a partly justified rebellion to be ended by reasonable satisfactions to the rebels in the interests of the whole Empire. If the two Anglo-Americans served their two countries they were willing to be paid by the one that could best afford it. How much closer Wentworth and Temple were to the old England than to the new America appears in their desire to be baronets. Respect for titles was a mark of loyalists. Vardill in London thought the usurping leaders of America could be bribed with titles, "as their present precarious power would be by this means secured to themselves and handed down to their posterity." Galloway in New York the past year had thought "hereditary honours, *pro loco et quodam modo,* should be introduced, in order to counteract all levelling ideas."[51] Similar opinions were cherished here and there in Great Britain. Sir John Dalrymple proposed that Washington be made a duke, as General Monk had been made Duke of Albemarle for deserting the Commonwealth and joining Charles II.[52] And some mysterious enthusiast, who has never been identified, made a final attempt on the American commissioners in Paris, with a plan for the creation of American peers among whom the principal rebel leaders should be the first chosen.

Nothing but a single curious document can here be added to the familiar story. Toward the end of June, after the British commissioners had left for America, a long letter with two long enclosures was thrown into Franklin's house in Passy. It was dated at Brussels the 16th and signed Charles de Weissenstein.[53] Franklin, to whom it was addressed, showed it to John Adams, who had succeeded Deane. The pseudonymous writer, who said he was an Englishman, blamed England, praised America, and disparaged France. America had been driven to declare its independence, but could never become actually independent. "Our title to the Empire is indisputable, and will be asserted either by ourselves or successors whenever occasion permits. We may stop a while in our pursuit to recover breath, but shall assuredly resume our career again." Since the Americans could not hope to gain their ends by war, and did not trust the ministry, "why not offer some conditions directly to the king himself?" Weissenstein said he would "undertake through a most eligible mediator to transmit into the king's own hands any proposals on your part which are not couched in offensive terms."

Franklin in person was to bring his "preliminaries in writing" to the choir of the Cathedral of Notre Dame between noon and one o'clock on Monday, July 6, or Thursday the 9th and turn them over to a messenger who thought he was assisting in a common intrigue. "You will ascertain my friend by his having a paper in his hand, as if drawing or taking notes. On any one's coming near him, he will either huddle it up precipitately or, folding it up, tear it with an appearance of peevishness, and walk away. At that very altar where he stood, place your packet within reach, or if there is nobody else near, throw it on the ground and walk away instantly. Don't if you can avoid it, let even him see it is you that bring it, much less anybody else. As soon as he sees the coast clear, he will return and look for the packet." The messenger would wear a rose in his hat or in the button-hole of his waistcoat.

In one of the enclosures, called A Project for Allaying the Present Ferments in North America, Weissenstein proposed immediate rewards for Adams, Hancock, Washington, Franklin, etc., who were to have "offices or pensions for life at their option, according to the sums opposite their respective names." The spaces were left blank, as if to be filled out by the beneficiaries. They should be peers as soon as there were American peers, and Washington be at once a British lieutenant general. The second enclosure, Great

Outline of the Future Government in North America, described the Supreme Continental Court of Universal Jurisdiction which should be in effect an American House of Lords. "The members shall be named by the king, and shall never exceed two hundred. Each shall be for life, and they shall either bear titles as peers of America with remainder to their issue or otherwise as shall be decided by his Majesty, but their personal privileges shall be clearly and positively defined and secured to them."

"Dr. Franklin . . . affirmed to me," John Adams later said, "that there were in the letter infallible marks by which he knew that it came from the king, and that it could not have come from any other without the king's knowledge. What these marks were he never explained to me."[54] The Project and Great Outline of Weissenstein are so fantastic, and so far from the proposals which the king had recently approved in the instructions to the British commissioners, that Weissenstein appears to have been rather a private busybody than a royal emissary. But Franklin on July 1 wrote Weissenstein a letter which powerfully summed up the opinion of republican America about "places, pensions, and peerages" and threw them back in the teeth of his former sovereign. It was never sent, though a copy was turned over to Vergennes with the originals from Weissenstein. Franklin and Adams considered the attempt too trifling to be mentioned to Congress. And the report—hitherto unpublished—of the French police throws no light on the mystery.

At the request of Vergennes a police agent went on July 6 to Notre Dame with three men to watch for the messenger. Precisely at noon a foreigner came into the church and went to the grille at the left of the choir, where Weissenstein had said Franklin was to go. "The foreigner took paper and pencil out of his pocket and walked round the choir, seeming to study the chapels, scribbling or writing." At a quarter past one, since nobody had come to him, he left the church and went, through streets which the policeman named, to the Hôtel d'Hambourg. "I learned that this foreigner is M. Jennings who was a captain of the King's Guards in England four or five years ago. His father was minister at some foreign court. He arrived here the 20th of last month from Bordeaux and is to leave tomorrow or Thursday to return to England. He is a very gloomy man and has no callers. He usually goes out in the morning about eight, alone and on foot, comes back to dine, and uses his carriage after dinner. He often goes to the theatre, but after that returns to the hotel and does not go out again. Yesterday he went to the [Théâtre des] Italiens. M. Jennings appears to be thirty-six to forty years old, five feet two inches, hair extremely blond tied *en Cadogan* [clubbed], very thin-faced and tanned. Yesterday he wore a grey coat, blue waistcoat, and black breeches, [illegible] hat, and carried a cane. On his way home from Notre Dame yesterday he stopped at nearly every street corner to read the posters, and seemed to be dreaming."[55] As Adams long afterward remembered the police report, the messenger had called himself "Colonel Fitz-something—an Irish name that I have forgotten." But neither name is more likely to be genuine—or important —than Charles de Weissenstein.

V

Eden, drawing up the schedule of payments for the commissioners,[56] proposed that the three going from England be given the "allowance always made to ambassadors," which would amount to about £1600 for each of them. His salary, at a nominal £100 a week but subject to the usual deductions, would in twelve months come to about £4625. This £6225 (allowance and salary) would have to cover "the whole expense of carrying secretaries, servants, carriages, clothes, wines, many articles of furniture, table furniture, etc., besides the constant expense of housekeeping within the colonies in such a style as may support the dignity of the commission and promote the ends of it." The commissioners would not ask for the £400 a quarter allowed an ambassador "in the name of extraordinaries." Eden supposed that the commissioners already in America, the Howe brothers, were taken care of, since they were "receiving great emoluments in another way upon the spot." To the king, writing to North on April 3, Eden's figures looked "rather exorbitant. He seems to think *éclat* a part of the character of a commissioner; I think business their sole occupation. But I shall certainly consent on that head to whatever you may think reasonable."[57]

North was not disposed to be niggardly with those whom the king favoured. When the commissioners on April 13 set out for Portsmouth, to go on board the man-of-war *Trident,* 64 guns, they went somewhat as if for a parade or a picnic. Besides the two Etonians Carlisle and Eden there was a third, Anthony Morris Storer, known as the best dancer and skater in London. Eden's wife, who had to leave a small child and was four months gone with another, spiritedly accompanied her husband. Johnstone's particular friend was Adam Ferguson, the renowned professor of moral philosophy at Edinburgh, who went as acting secretary of the commission. Nor were the commissioners to have the ship to themselves. Earl Cornwallis was returning to America, to be second in command to Clinton. Commodore John Elliot of the *Trident*, an uncle of Eleanor Eden, hoped he would never again have such a service assigned to him: "for the servants and baggage is past all belief."[58]

On the 16th Eden wrote his farewell letter, to his brother Morton. "We came aboard this morning and have dropped anchor after sailing about six miles." In addition to the commissioners, Cornwallis, and "Mr. Storer who goes as an idle man *pour s'amuser,*" they had "two or three private secretaries, about twenty footmen, and Mrs. Eden with Madame Dumont and another maidservant. We have been received with a prodigious consumption of noise and gunpowder, on a beautiful morning, in the center of thirty-three ships of the line, besides frigates, transports, East Indiamen, etc. We are well accommodated and in an excellent ship with an uncle who is one of the best commanders in the navy . . . and is also a very pleasant man. We have not yet begun to be sick but shall all be so, no doubt, in due time. In all this, which seems almost like a dream to me, Eleanor is perfectly cheerful except only when the recollection of her little girl brings a tear or two. The operation of quitting London was a very arduous one, and I was obliged to surprise her into a post chaise two days before she had any idea of going. The young one is left in the custody of Lady Elliot"—her grandmother. As to the consequences of their mission, "a few months will show. I am given to speculation upon most occasions, but in this it fails me totally. . . . I only know that I am in neither extreme either of confidence or despondency."[59]

Waiting off St. Helen's for a favourable wind, Commodore Elliot learned on the 20th that some enemy or criminal had cut the collar of the mainstay and the inner gammoning of the bowsprit so that in a wind the topmast might come down. Elliot offered 100 guineas reward, but nothing was found out and the saboteur possibly remained on the *Trident*. It was a congenial voyage, though the ship was crowded with 600 persons and there was, Eden wrote, "every possible variety of weather and sea. . . . Mrs. Eden . . . went through the whole with the composure of the Commodore himself. . . . When a wave of an immense size broke in through her cabin windows, cleared all before it, and ducked her completely in her bed, she laughed very heartily and considered it merely as a cold bath which came without being called for."[60] Eden and Storer at first were seasick. Carlisle and Cornwallis were better sailors. When Storer had recovered, he played whist six hours a day and slept twelve. Carlisle and Cornwallis were content with three rubbers an evening. Ferguson seemed to Carlisle a "very plain, mild, and sensible man."

Johnstone at a meeting of the commissioners on May 6 laid before them his Heads of Accommodation which were supposed to be based on the discussions of Franklin and Pulteney. According to an unpublished letter from Eden in the Clinton papers, Johnstone claimed to have received a "secret information" from Franklin saying that an offer to the Americans of seats in Parliament "would be more alluring than any other."[61] But there is no other evidence for this, and Franklin can never have approved a scheme which, while continuing the state governments, gave the king the right to name a governor general, and which, while recognizing Congress, gave the king the right to appoint its president.[62] On June 1, the day before the *Trident* reached Henlopen, Carlisle began a draft of the commissioners' projected letter to Congress. "At the opening of this solemn and important business some explanation must of necessity be required from us of the general purport and intention of our mission. I shall endeavour to lay before this assembly its real object in the plainest and simplest manner in my power."[63] So far as he got, it was a generous and graceful letter, full of goodwill to America, sharply hostile to France. The commissioners wished not only to win the Americans back to the status of colonists but also to bring them over to the status of allies in another European war.

Though the commissioners had on May 27 heard from a passing brig that both the Howes were in Philadelphia, and had accordingly instructed Elliot to take them to Philadelphia instead of to New York, they still did not know that the government behind their backs had planned to evacuate Philadelphia and had thereby seriously damaged the prospects of the commission.

Failure of a Mission

THE British *Andromeda,* carrying the drafts of North's conciliatory bills, and the French *Sensible,* carrying the treaties
already signed by France and the American commissioners in Paris,
raced across the Atlantic. The French dispatches were actually first
to arrive at an American port, on April 13. But to avoid the British
cruisers lying in wait from Philadelphia to Boston the *Sensible* had
gone far north and put in at Casco Bay. Simeon Deane, the bearer,
had to travel overland to Congress at York, Pennsylvania. The
British dispatches came directly and safely to New York on the
14th. Since the Howes were both in Philadelphia, Tryon as royal
governor took charge, published the bills—as drafted though not
yet passed by Parliament—next day, and sent printed copies as
fast as possible in every direction. One of them got by way of
Philadelphia unofficially to Washington at Valley Forge on the
17th. Though he was on the 18th not certain whether "this insidious proceeding is genuine . . . or contrived in Philadelphia," he
agreed with Franklin that it was "meant to poison the minds of the
people and detach the wavering, at least, from our cause." He
hoped Congress would at once investigate the British offer and
"expose in the most striking manner the injustice, delusion, and
fraud it contains."[1]

Two recent forgeries had made him suspicious. One was a set of
Letters from General Washington to Several of his Friends which
he was alleged to have written in June–July 1776, with strong expressions of dislike for independence. The forger was possibly
Vardill, who had been tutor to Washington's stepson at King's
College; or more possibly John Randolph, last royal attorney general of Virginia, who was a refugee in London but knew Washington and his family well enough to make the letters sound circum-

stantial. Originally published in England, they had during the past February–March appeared in newspapers in New York and Philadelphia, and as a pamphlet in New York.[2] The other forgery, printed in the *New York Gazette* for March 9, purported to be two resolutions of Congress ordering that all state troops, no matter for what terms they had enlisted, were to be considered as Continental troops while the war lasted and be punished as deserters if they tried to go home when their lawful terms were up. Both forgeries had annoyed Washington and now made him wonder if the bills too might not be spurious.

Spurious or genuine, the bills were, Washington thought, likely to have a "malignant influence." They authorized the British commissioners to deal with any bodies or assemblies of men or with any person or persons whatsoever, to grant pardons to any number, and to set up royal government in any of the colonies. Such offers would immensely strengthen the hands of Americans who had never desired independence or who had come to feel that it was not worth the heavy cost of a longer conflict. On that point Washington was as firm as Franklin. "Nothing short of independence, it appears to me, can possibly do. A peace on other terms would, if I may be allowed the expression, be a peace of war."[3] He asked if it would not be good policy for Congress to counteract the British offer of pardon to rebels by recommending that the several states offer pardon to loyalists who had adhered to the enemy. Congress on the 23rd voted to recommend this. On the 22nd after a good deal of discussion it unanimously resolved that "the United States cannot with propriety hold any conference or treaty with any commissioners on the part of Great Britain, unless they shall, as a preliminary thereto, either withdraw their fleets and armies or else in positive and express terms acknowledge the independence of the said States." And it was further resolved that, since the drafts of the conciliation bills were being "industriously circulated . . . in a partial and secret manner," they "ought to be forthwith printed"—by the Americans—"for the public information."[4]

That day Washington received a letter from Tryon with copies of the bills and with what Washington called the "extraordinary and impertinent request" that they be communicated to his officers and men. Tryon was asking Washington to spread enemy propaganda through his own army. Washington on the 26th assured Tryon that the bills would be freely circulated among the soldiers, "in whose fidelity to the United States I have the most perfect confidence." He sent a newspaper showing that Congress had resolved to make the bills public, and a few printed copies of the resolution about pardon for loyalists. "I take the liberty . . . to request that you will be instrumental in communicating its contents, so far as it may be in your power, to the persons who are the objects of its operation. The benevolent purpose it is intended to answer will, I persuade myself, sufficiently recommend it to your candour."[5] With this dry irony Washington turned the tables on Tryon. Let them both spread enemy propaganda and see which was the more effective.

A week later Simeon Deane arrived at York, after Congress had adjourned for Sunday. They met during the adjournment, received Deane and his dispatches, and on Monday May 4 ratified the treaties with their new ally. The French had won the transatlantic race. The British commissioners, with a month's voyage still ahead of them, might have turned back if they had been able to know of Congress's resolves and of the completion of the French alliance. Without power to withdraw the British armed forces or to recognize American independence, the commission could have no chance of success, if Washington and Congress had and could keep the support of the people.

II

The British commissioners, proceeding up Delaware bay and river on the *Trident* to New Castle, had reason to be troubled. "We found," Carlisle later wrote, "to our great surprise all the naval armament collected together with evident preparation for the immediate evacuation of Philadelphia by his Majesty's military forces. Every vessel of war was recalled from the coast, and the transports, etc. which we passed, to the amount of near four hundred, were filled with the miserable inhabitants of that city whose attachment to our cause obliged [them] to risk their fortunes with us, or swear allegiance to the Congress."[6] On the 4th the commissioners sent ahead of them to Lord Howe, announcing their arrival. The next day Eden wrote out a brief analysis of their dilemma.[7]

It was only too clear that the commission's overtures to Congress would have little weight if the British army was not to support them in Philadelphia. "It may be very fair, whilst that city remains in our power, to hold out the possibility of our being driven, by a rejection of all terms, to destroy it; upon the principle of its being just to extend the ravages of war in a country which declares itself at all events determined to become an accession to the strength of France. The effect of this implied menace will be lost if previous to treaty we leave Philadelphia without injuring it. And on the other hand, if we commit any devastation there previous to any treaty with the Congress we lose the advantage of putting them in the wrong, and also furnish them with a pretence to say that instead of seeking peace we are blindly forcing forwards the worst extremes of war."

On the 6th, then at New Castle, the commissioners received a note of welcome from Howe. He was sending an armed sloop in which they were to come to Philadelphia. The Delaware would otherwise not be safe. The commissioners were further troubled, as Carlisle wrote, to find that the British did not control the river banks. "The enemy were suffered to act in the most offensive manner under the guns of our ships of war. No boat was permitted by the inhabitants of either side to approach the shore. No fresh provisions were furnished to the sick. And we as we passed . . . were insulted by a party of riflemen who fired several shots at us, which, though striking at too great a distance to occasion the least alarm, yet manifested the malevolence as well as rashness of their intentions."[8] In Philadelphia that evening the commissioners learned that the order to evacuate Philadelphia had been issued while the commissioners were still in London—though it had been "industriously" kept a secret from them—and that Congress had six weeks before taken its rigorous stand on offers from Great Britain.

The commissioners soon learned, or had a chance to learn, many things. The British forces had passed a comfortable winter in Philadelphia, despising but not attacking the cold and hungry Americans at Valley Forge. The most thorough patriots had left the town before the enemy came. The people who remained were already friendly to the British, or became friendly out of interest or liking, or were neutral and quiet. While prices were high, there was plenty of British money, and more than a few Philadelphians prospered. An account of secret service expenditures from January 1 to May 26, preserved among Clinton's papers, shows that only $12,828.12 was given out, some of it presumably for the relief of loyalists in distress. Mary Kearsley, widow of Dr. John Kearsley who had been outrageously treated by the Whigs in 1775, got $214.16; Judge John Potts of Pennsylvania, $948.98; Thomas Robinson, a refugee from Delaware, $628.32; Peter DuBois, a refugee from New York, $428.18. Much of the secret service money was handled by General Howe's aide for purposes not specified. There is nothing to indicate how far it was used to influence wavering patriots.

The winter was gay with dinners and dances and amateur theatricals at which the amiable daughters of Philadelphia revealed no enmity to the agreeable British officers. The season reached its splendid climax on May 18 in the Mischianza, "a regatta, fête champêtre, tilts and tournaments, a procession through triumphal arches, dancing, exhibition of fireworks, music, and feast,"[9] got up as a farewell to General Howe, who was in a few days to sail for England leaving the chief command to Clinton. Captain John André, who took part in the tournament, wrote a friend in England a long and lively account of the celebration which appeared in the *Gentleman's Magazine* for August. André, who had especially busied himself with the dramatic performances of the past winter, was quartered in the house of the rebel Franklin, whose portrait André carried away with him as a souvenir of Philadelphia.

Three days after the Mischianza General Howe clouded the pleasant scene by telling one of the loyalists that the British would probably withdraw and advising him "to make his peace with the states, who, he supposed, would not treat them harshly."[10] The news spread, and with it a general consternation. The British officers felt disgraced and humiliated at surrendering the American capital without a blow at Washington. There began to be numerous desertions from the British ranks. The loyalists were terrified.

Promised full protection, they had sided openly with the British government against their countrymen. Now they must deal with the patriots who regarded them as traitorous renegades. Their predicament was worse than that of the refugees in Boston with Gage two years before. Independence had been declared since then, and civil animosities had grown more furious. Though Congress had recommended pardons to loyalists, it was by no means certain that the states would grant them or would not make exceptions of all the loyalist leaders. Pennsylvania before the evacuation voted to confiscate the property of any loyalist who would not take the oath of allegiance to Congress. There were refugees in Philadelphia from New Jersey, Delaware, and Maryland. Different states might decide on different measures, but all would be harsh.

Galloway, chief of the loyalists in Philadelphia, conspicuous for his services to the Howes, had already been attainted in body and goods by Pennsylvania and could expect no leniency. On the 22nd he heard from General Howe and Clinton of the British plan to evacuate the town, called the loyalist magistrates together, and told them. The next day Lord Howe through his secretary Serle advised Galloway and his loyalist friends to lose no time in their negotiations with the patriot authorities. "The only way seemed to be, to profess candidly to the Congress that it was true he and they had adhered to the old constitution while they thought it possible to live under its protection; but that, being deserted, they would as faithfully adhere to the present establishment."[11] Galloway seems to have agreed to this. He consulted with Lord Howe and Clinton.

Notes of the conference were taken by Clinton's aide and preserved among Clinton's papers. "Mr. Galloway, on the part of the principal persons of the town, asks permission to make terms with Washington." But when Howe, consenting, proposed that Clinton furnish the loyalists with a flag of truce for their errand, the new commander-in-chief refused to give "a sanction to any persons treating on those grounds with declared rebels." Howe proposed sending a private communication. Clinton said he would do his best to prevent it. "It is to be remembered," Clinton said, "that half the garrison of New York are Provincials, who might be certain of gaining what terms they pleased by betraying the post, and may they not be tempted to it if they conceive all our hopes in this city to be over, which an accommodation between these people and Washington would give them just reason to suspect?"

The Philadelphia loyalists were special victims of the total situation. In order to make more energetic war on France in Europe, the London government was relinquishing Philadelphia. The loyalists there might look out for themselves. But Clinton denied them freedom of action, in order to be sure of holding New York. No longer able to protect the loyalists, the British did not trust them. Suppose, no matter what their earlier inclinations had been, they should now think it to their interest to join forces with the rebels. The British could still face a divided people, but not a united nation. Galloway, so long as the British were in Philadelphia, kept up his wasted arguments against the withdrawal and in favour of offensive operations.[12] Lord Howe and Clinton were busy with the problem of how to move all the soldiers and military equipment and all the loyalists and their goods to New York. The fleet and transports could not hold them. It was suggested that, to save room on board, the 5000 army horses should be left behind, with their throats cut. This idea, according to Carlisle, was abandoned because it "would add to other humiliating appearances." By the time the commissioners arrived in Philadelphia the plan of evacuation had been settled. The British army would march across New Jersey, risking an attack by Washington, and the loyalists would go by water. It was their presence on the transports in the Delaware which gave the commissioners their first warning that they were not to find what they had expected.

The commissioners had a long conference with Lord Howe on the 7th. Disappointed that he was not the head of the commission, as North by letter had promised, Howe declined to serve at all, though he was willing to do what he could while he remained in America.[13] General Howe had already sailed, and Clinton, succeeding him as commander, took his place on the commission. Lord Howe, who on May 27 had sent the conciliatory bills, as finally passed by Parliament, to the president of Congress—Henry Laurens—and to Washington, had had a noncommittal acknowledgment from Washington but no answer from Congress. This came on June 9. Laurens, reminding the commissioners that Congress had already published its resolution on the conciliatory bills, added only that "when the king of Great Britain shall be seriously disposed to put an end to the unprovoked and cruel war waged against these United States, Congress will readily attend to such terms of peace as may consist with the honour of independent nations, the interest of their constituents, and the sacred regard they mean to pay to treaties."[14] Lord Howe's secretary exclaimed in his journal: "Small hopes from this of these rebellious tyrants being likely to treat with commissioners!" Serle had no doubt that Congress was primarily concerned with holding on to its usurped powers. "The moment an agreement is made, the demagogues must sink into their former obscurity."[15]

In spite of Laurens's unpromising reply the commissioners that same day addressed a letter to Congress. They could not, as matters stood, count on time for negotiation, and so at once proposed all they had authority to offer, and more. They would consent to an immediate cessation of hostilities by land and sea; restore free intercourse between the parts of the Empire and "every freedom to trade that our respective interests can require"; agree that no military forces should be kept up in America against the wishes of the Americans; concur in measures to discharge American debts and raise the value of the depreciated currency; and arrange for a reciprocal legislative representation, with Americans in Parliament and British agents in the American assemblies. On these terms Britons and Americans might thrive equally "under our common sovereign." The commissioners took this occasion to speak of the "insidious interposition of a power which has from the first settlement of these colonies been actuated with enmity to us both." France had entered into an alliance with America only to prevent a conciliation and prolong the destructive war. Surely America would prefer "a firm and perpetual coalition with the parent state to an insincere and unnatural foreign alliance." A meeting for further discussion might be held wherever Congress chose, though the commissioners admitted they might soon think it best to go to New York. In these circumstances they could make only a conventional threat: that if "the horrors and devastation of war should continue we call God and the world to witness that the evils which must follow are not to be imputed to Great Britain."[16]

Adam Ferguson, now formally appointed secretary of the commission, was chosen to be the bearer of the message to Congress. Clinton sent a note to Washington asking that a passport meet the messenger at the advanced post at Radnor about ten o'clock on the morning of the 10th. He was met instead with a note from Washington saying he could not grant this special passport without instructions from Congress.[17] The commissioners' letter went the next day by ordinary military post and reached Congress at York on Saturday the 13th. Congress broke off a debate to hear the letter read. When the reader came to the passage about France he was interrupted by a motion "not to proceed farther, because of the offensive language." The letter was not read to the end till the 16th, when Congress resolved that it could not "hear any language. reflecting upon the honour of his most Christian Majesty, the good and faithful ally of these states." The next day Congress voted the answer which Laurens was to send. Nothing but an earnest desire to avoid further bloodshed had induced them to read a paper so "disrespectful" to France or to consider offers which assumed that the people of America were subjects of the British Crown. Congress, however disposed to peace, would treat, as it had resolved two months before, only if American independence were acknowledged or the British fleets and armies withdrawn.[18]

The commissioners before they heard from Congress had to leave Philadelphia and return, on the 16th, to the *Trident* still lying at New Castle. Carlisle during his ten-day stay had ridden out one morning with Clinton as far as Germantown: "a place as remarkable, and as much an object of curiosity to those who have any respect for the present times, as Edge Hill or Naseby Field is to those whose veneration is only excited by their great-grandfathers."[19] Eden, too, had come to a new sense of the meaning of America to Great Britain. "It is impossible," he wrote his brother on the 15th, "to give you any adequate idea of the vast scale of this country. I know little more of it than I saw in coming 150 miles up the Delaware; but I know enough to regret most heartily that our rulers instead of making the tour of Europe did not finish their education by a voyage round the coasts and rivers of the western side of the Atlantic."[20]

Possibly without the knowledge of Carlisle and Eden the trouble-making Johnstone in his short stay in Philadelphia involved the commissioners in the most embarrassing of their difficulties.

To Galloway and Serle, at least, Johnstone seemed to be dangerous. He talked about a federal union between England and America which Galloway pointed out could not be formed unless America were equal and therefore independent. Other "strange propositions . . . absurd or contradictory," as Serle thought them, were "said to originate from Governor Johnstone." He had brought letters from England to rebels. "He was very inquisitive about the value of lands and landed security in this country, and expressed his intention of selling what he has in England and sitting down here. . . . His conversation about the town . . . has given great offence to the king's loyal subjects, who speak of him with great reproaches."[21] Before the commissioners left England Eden had called Johnstone "manly and right-headed on the points in question . . . in his whole character active, decisive, and bold." On June 18 Eden, back on the *Trident,* could still say that Johnstone "has hitherto gone on well with us, and I believe is well satisfied so far as we are concerned"; but had to say also that Johnstone's "feelings at present are roused beyond his power to govern them; and though he will wish to go on with us as pleasantly as he has done thus far, I cannot answer for his doing so."[22]

If Johnstone had been an instinctive conspirator he might have acted the part of an over-zealous friend of America for the benefit of the Americans whom he tried to influence. He was probably less a conspirator than a blunderer, who could not believe there was any better way to appeal to members of the stubborn Congress than to hint at the rewards they might expect for helping to bring about a reconciliation on British terms.

The commissioners were certain they had the secret good wishes of many patriots in Congress and in the Continental army. Along with the official letter to Congress the commissioners sent a packet of private letters, some of them from England, to members then at York, and other letters separately in care of members for various constituents who had English friends. Eden and Johnstone both wrote polite compliments to Washington at Valley Forge, recommending the learned Ferguson.[23] Of Johnstone's other letters, only the one he had forehandedly written to Joseph Reed in April was plainly insinuating. But a letter to Laurens on June 10 asked for personal consideration. "If you [Congress] should follow the example of Britain in the hour of her insolence and send us back without a hearing, I shall hope from private friendship that I may be permitted to see the country and the worthy characters she has exhibited to the world."[24] And in a letter the same day to Francis Dana, member from Massachusetts, Johnstone deliberately—or at any rate ignorantly—misrepresented the attitudes of France and Spain and said that Franklin on March 28, "discussing the several articles we wish to make the basis of our treaty, was perfectly satisfied that they were beneficial to North America and such as she should accept."[25]

Washington, transmitting the letters, wrote privately to Laurens to suggest that if there were among them any addressed to "persons with whom you are not acquainted or in whose firmness and attachment you have not an entire confidence, it may not be improper to open them." The commissioners should not be allowed to get past Congress and tamper with the people. Congress was alert, and seems to have particularly suspected Johnstone. Might his letter to Laurens not mean that Johnstone, if the commission as a whole were unsuccessful, desired an unofficial opportunity to influence the worthy characters he spoke about? A Congressional committee was appointed to prepare a resolution on correspondence with the enemy, and the chairman, William Henry Drayton of South Carolina, set himself to collecting materials to display "the governor's good designs." On the 20th Drayton published Johnstone's letter to Laurens, and Laurens's intended answer, in the *Pennsylvania Gazette,* then issued at York.[26] "Until the basis of mutual confidence shall be established," Laurens said, "I believe, Sir, neither former friendship nor any other consideration can influence Congress to consent that even Governor Johnstone, a gentleman who has been so deservedly esteemed by America, shall see the country. I have but one voice and that shall be against it."[27]

Johnstone, unaware in Philadelphia of what was happening, impatient of the tedious delays of public negotiation, and violent over the forced return to the *Trident*, had on his last day— the 16th—in the town taken two further steps which were to ruin his reputation with the Americans. One was a letter to Robert Morris, chairman of the Congressional committee on finance. Morris had voted against the Declaration as premature, though he later signed it, and some Philadelphia loyalists believed—with Duché—that Morris had been dragged reluctantly into the measure and had continued in it from a false idea of honour. Johnstone, who already knew Morris, wished they might work together for reconciliation "with all the prudence and all the means possible and virtuous. I believe the men who have conducted the affairs of America incapable of being influenced by improper motives. But in all such transactions there is risk, and I think whoever ventures should be secured; at the same time, that honour and emoluments should naturally follow the fortune of those who have steered the vessel in the storm and brought her safely to port. I think that Washington and the president [of Congress] have a right to every favour that grateful nations can bestow if they could once more unite our interest and spare the miseries and devastation of war. I wish, above all other things, to see you, and I hope you will so contrive it."[28]

This was, as Washington later remarked, "of a pulse-feeling cast." Such talk about means possible and virtuous and men incapable of being influenced by improper motives went hand-in-hand with talk about honours and emoluments and the favours to be bestowed by grateful nations. If Morris should take offence, Johnstone could claim that all his intentions had been as honourable as some of his words. If Morris should be responsive, here were the discreet preliminaries of what might come to be a serviceable understanding.

Johnstone's overtures to Reed on the 16th appear to have been more blunt than those to Morris. As Johnstone then put nothing in writing, and afterwards denied having made any offer whatever, the episode must be studied in the records of only two of the three persons concerned. But from these records, closely studied, a fairly credible outline of fact seems to emerge: more credible, all things considered, than Johnstone's later denial when the affair had reached the public and he was under fire.

Reed had received Johnstone's April letter at Valley Forge, and on June 14 drafted an answer which he submitted to Washington for his approval. Washington on the 15th, saying he would like to see Reed before the letter was transcribed and sent, hinted that Reed had perhaps been too complimentary. Congress, Washington supposed, was preparing an official answer to the commissioners. If Reed, a member of Congress though then at Headquarters, were not careful he might seem to be in disagreement with his colleagues, and "an unfavourable use, more than probably," might be made of his answer by the British.[29] But Washington permitted Reed to match compliments with Johnstone, who was ranked in the revised letter with Burke, Barré, Chatham, and Camden for friendship to America. The war could be ended, Reed said, only when good and wise men on both sides had persuaded Great Britain to give up "her visionary schemes of conquest and empire for the solid benefits she may yet derive from our amity and commerce. I will ever hope, Sir, for your aid in so good a work. Should the same fatal influence which blasted your former salutary counsels again frustrate your humane and generous purpose, come to America, the future asylum of the brave and virtuous from every quarter of the world. She will think herself honoured to receive into her bosom so illustrious a citizen. His eloquence will not then be spent in vain, nor his eminent worth pass unrewarded."[30]

Reed, holding out counter-prospects of reward to Johnstone, at least assumed that Johnstone was already in favour of independence and need not change his position, only persist in it, to deserve American gratitude. What Johnstone, who did not receive Reed's letter in Philadelphia, persisted in was the attempt on Reed. Serle had heard that Reed was "full of chicane, intrigue, and duplicity," and may have told Johnstone.[31] He may have heard that Reed had once thought Washington inferior to Charles Lee, and so might still be disaffected to the commander-in-chief. But perhaps Johnstone, without too many reasons or too much planning, merely seized the opportunity which came to him in the person of Elizabeth Graeme Ferguson, who had carried Duché's letter to Washington.

It was not by pure accident that Johnstone met her. He had brought her, from England, "Washington's picture in the lid of a snuffbox."[32] Her husband, Hugh Ferguson, was related to Adam Ferguson of the commission. She was related by marriage to the loyalist Charles Stedman in whose house Johnstone was lodged. In spite of the Duché affair she came again, with Washington's permission, through his lines to Philadelphia and herself stopped at Stedman's house. She had come, in grief and terror, to take leave of her husband, who was going to New York with the British. He had been ordered to appear before the Pennsylvania supreme executive council at Lancaster on June 24 to answer to the charge of high treason. Since he was a British subject, who had returned to Scotland in 1775 and come back to Philadelphia only after it was occupied by Howe, she thought the charges were unjust. She spoke in Johnstone's hearing of her intention to go to Lancaster to intercede with the executive council. Johnstone told her he very much wished to see Morris and Reed, especially Reed who she thought was at Lancaster. Their conversation, as she recounted it under oath on February 16, 1779,[33] took place in Stedman's tea room at from ten to eleven o'clock on the morning of June 16, "to the best of my memory."

"I heard, says he [Johnstone], that Reed has a great deal to say with Washington. I believe, Sir, returned I, that [Adjutant] General Reed stands very well with General Washington (for I always made it a point to give our officers their titles immediately when any of the British gentlemen omitted them). I had thoughts, says Johnstone, of applying to both these gentlemen (meaning Mr. Reed and Mr. Morris) for their good offices, but the fewer people one applies to the better. But I should be particularly glad of Mr. Reed's influence in this affair. Mrs. Ferguson, says he, and I think he looked a little confused, if this affair should be settled in the way we wish, we shall have many pretty things in our power, and if Mr. Reed, after well considering the nature of the dispute, can, conformably to his conscience and view of things, exert his influence to settle the contest, he may command 10,000 guineas and the best post in the government, and if you should see him, I could wish you would convey that idea to him. I own I felt hurt and shocked, for I regarded the hint as indelicate, and from that moment Mr. Johnstone appeared to me in a different point of light."

Johnstone started to leave the room, but she stopped him. "Do you not think, Sir, that Mr. Reed will look upon such a mode of obtaining his influence as a bribe? (I really made use of that plain term.) Do you think so, Madam? I really, Sir, should apprehend so. By no means, Madam; this method of proceeding is customary to all negotiations; and one may honourably make it a man's interest to step forth in a cause." She did not believe Reed could be influenced to act against his opinions. Johnstone said "he did not see the matter in the same point of light exactly as I did, and abruptly bade me farewell; and I believe, if his heart had at that moment been seen, he was vexed he had gone so far."

The story is carried on in Reed's account in the *Pennsylvania Packet* on July 21 and in his later pamphlet.[34] Two days after the conversation between Mrs. Ferguson and Johnstone the last of the British soldiers left Philadelphia and the first Americans entered it. Reed came in that same day, and Benedict Arnold a day later to take command of the city. On the 21st Reed, at Arnold's headquarters, received a letter from Mrs. Ferguson addressed to him at Valley Forge where she now thought he was. She must see him in person, she said, "as writing will not do. . . . Be so obliging as to appoint the place; but I could wish to avoid passing through the camp; but any little cottage or farmhouse would be agreeable to me to see you in." Reed, knowing her to be "a lady of family and reputation," called on her that evening.

She talked with him first, much agitated, about her husband's proscription and what was to be done. These matters, it seems, were her overpowering concern, and she later insisted she did not think of herself as an emissary from Johnstone or believe that Reed could be influenced against his judgment. But "from this subject," as Reed told the story, "we imperceptibly slid into that of the British commissioners, their business and characters, when Mrs. Ferguson mentioned Governor Johnstone's [formerly] lodging in that very house with her. . . . Mrs. Ferguson then went on to say that Governor Johnstone expressed great anxiety to see me, and particularly wished to engage my interest to promote the object of their commission: viz, a reunion between the two countries, if it was consistent with my principles and judgment; and in such a case, it could not be deemed improper or unbecoming in [the British] government to take a favourable notice of such conduct; and in this instance I might have £10,000 sterling and any office in the colonies in his Majesty's gift. I found an answer was expected, and gave one: That I was not worth purchasing, but such as I was, the king of England was not rich enough to do it."

Reed did not at once make the offer public, but went off with the army to New Jersey, fought at the battle of Monmouth on the 28th, and returned to his seat in Congress, now in Philadelphia again, on July 15. "In the meantime I was deliberating what steps I ought to pursue. On the one hand, the duty I owed to my country seemed to demand a full disclosure; on the other, a reluctance to expose the lady to a criminal prosecution, or popular resentment, and myself to the imputation of vanity and ostentatious integrity, kept me silent, except to General Washington and two or three other gentlemen." Reed found that Congress had six days before ordered its members to lay before it any letters they had received "from any of the British commissioners or their agents, or from any subject of the king of Great Britain, of a public nature." Robert Morris had already produced his letter from Johnstone. Dana did the same thing on the 16th, Reed on the 18th. All three of them were published in the *Packet* for the 21st with Reed's account of the oral offer made to him, though without the intermediary's name.

With these papers in the *Packet* was what seemed to be further evidence against Johnstone. Silas Deane, who had just arrived in Philadelphia from Paris, authorized the statement that Franklin had not, as Johnstone wrote to Dana, approved the proposals sent to Paris by the "secret negotiator" (Pulteney) in March but told him they could not be accepted and promised they should never be revealed. Congress, ordering these matters to be published, resolved against answering a second letter from the British commissioners, dated July 11, since it agreed neither to the acknowledgment of independence nor to the withdrawal of the British forces.

Johnstone's denials, though much involved in public consequences, may here be given as separately as possible to round out the Reed episode. After Congress on August 11 had voted to have no further dealings with Johnstone as commissioner, Johnstone, resigning from the commission on the 26th with a contemptuous statement, made no mention of the charges against him except to say that he reserved the right before leaving America to issue a justification of his conduct.[35] This appeared in the *New York Gazette* of October 5, shortly after Johnstone had sailed for England. He was leaving behind with Adam Ferguson, he said, "complete, indisputable evidence that no act of mine, by word, writing, message, or conversation with any person whatever, could have been conceived by the member of Congress, Joseph Reed, Esq., previous to the 19th of July last, as an attempt, or having a tendency, in any manner whatsoever to corrupt his integrity." A "regard to the faith of private communications," Johnstone said, "and an attention to the peace and safety of innocent individuals" kept him from making his proofs public.[36]

He never made the proofs public. The only guess at what they were came from Reed. He had written, he said, a note (date not given) to an unnamed acquaintance going to New York, asking her to find out if any letters had come there from his English brother-in-law addressed to any member of Reed's family. She might, Reed told her, apply to Johnstone as a last resort if she had difficulty in getting the letters, and might tell him that Reed had received Johnstone's letter of April 11; but she was not to give Johnstone her note from Reed. Johnstone, according to Reed, heard she was in New York inquiring for the letters, called on her, got possession of the note, and kept it. Reed supposed this was Johnstone's alleged proof that before July 19—possibly the date of Reed's note—Reed did not think he had been offered a bribe. And it does seem incredible—and disagreeable—that Reed, who on the 18th had written the story of the offer and of his grandiloquent reply, could on the 19th, before the story was published, ask even the slightest favour of Johnstone. It is not, however, positive that Reed's note was dated the 19th or that it was the proof Johnstone left behind him.

After his return to England, where he was for the first time in his life received by the king, Johnstone on November 26 denied in the House of Commons that he had made any offer to Reed or that Reed had any reason to believe it. Not that Johnstone wished, before that knowing assembly, to make himself out too virtuous. "I do not mean to disavow I have had transactions where other means besides persuasion have been used. It was necessary; in my situation it can be no reproach." He may have bribed others in his day, but he had not tried Reed. And who was the lady whom Congress failed to name? Reed could, Johnstone told the Commons, have produced no one able to "avow any authority from me."[37] When Johnstone's speech got back to America Mrs. Ferguson in February wrote out her sworn story, and Reed in September published the entire transaction with the documents. He became the hero of the episode, she the victim. Her husband was attainted and his property—by right of marriage to her—confiscated. She never saw him again. Her remaining property too was confiscated. According to the testimony of her loyalist nephew John Young, she was so "much attached" to the rebels that "she would not complain, believing it to be the necessary consequences of the measures they were pursuing."[38] Because the patriot leaders decided she had been merely imprudent rather than guilty, Graeme Park was returned to her in 1781. Johnstone, back in England, was cured of his partiality for the Americans and became a violent supporter of the king's party in Parliament. He was thought by all ranks of people, Wedderburn observed, to have been an offensive bungler.[39]

IV

The British commissioners, secure but helpless on the *Trident,* were bitter at the trick that had been played on them by the ministers and had no faith in the prospects of the mission. "It is impossible," Eden wrote on June 18, "to see even what I have seen of this magnificent country and not to go nearly mad at the long train of misconducts and mischances by which we have lost it."[40] Carlisle, as angry as the others, still took time to note in his letters that America was as hot as Italy and the gnats (mosquitoes) as large as sparrows. "I have armed myself against them by wearing trousers [instead of breeches], which is the constant dress of this country." He bought a raccoon to take home as a curiosity.[41] The *Trident* left the Delaware on the 28th and reached New York two days later. Carlisle was lodged in Walter Franklin's house in Cherry Street, afterwards Washington's first presidential residence; and Eden in the Bowery with his wife's uncle, Andrew Elliot. When the powerful French fleet under Admiral d'Estaing arrived off Sandy Hook on July 11 the commissioners, now somewhat less bitter, were inclined to believe that the sudden evacuation of Philadelphia may have saved the British fleet and army.

Yet they were so tightly shut up in New York that they could deal only at long range, to no real use, with Congress. On July 2 they finally received the letter Laurens had written on June 17. They wrote a second letter on the 11th, but Congress on the 18th resolved that it called for no answer. On August 7 they wrote to Congress about Burgoyne's surrendered army, still held by the Americans. By the terms of the Convention agreed to by Gates at Saratoga the British troops were to be allowed free passage to England on condition they would not serve again in North America during the war. Congress, realizing that their return would free other troops to cross the Atlantic in their place, was unwilling to let them go. But instead of repudiating Gates's action, Congress found various excuses for not turning the Convention troops, as they were called, over to the British command. Now the British commissioners made a peremptory requisition for the release of the captives.[42]

The records of Congress indicate that this letter was received on the 12th, the day after Congress accused Johnstone of trying to corrupt and bribe its members and resolved therefore not to negotiate "in any degree" with the commissioners.[43] But the commissioners held that the requisition had reached Congress first and that the resolution was a shifty device for getting out of an honest answer to a just demand. Whatever the true chronology, Congress and the commission were each bound to put the other in the wrong. The commissioners—Carlisle, Clinton, and Eden only—declared on the 26th that they had not had "any knowledge either directly or indirectly of the letters and conversation" objected to "until they saw them made public in the newspapers. At the same time they do not mean either to imply any assent to the construction put on private letters which the Congress have thought proper to publish, or to intimate a belief that any person could have been authorized to hold the conversation" between Mrs. Ferguson and Reed. "Nor do they on the other hand mean to enter into an explanation of the conduct of a gentleman whose abilities and integrity require no vindication from them." For the rest, they contented themselves with deploring the wicked French alliance, and left it to Johnstone in his accompanying declaration to accuse Congress of making charges against him in order to save its own face.[44]

But the commissioners were still willing to employ secret agents and had already sent John Berkenhout off to Philadelphia. He and John Temple, those two auxiliaries of the commission, had arrived in New York early in August. Eden, writing to Carlisle on the 20th, spoke of the letter of credit from North to Clinton authorizing the commission to draw on army money for secret service expenses. "In the present moment I do not see that it can be used to any beneficial purpose, but I am not so absurd as to oppose any experiment which others think has the slightest probability of doing good." He would not confer officially with Temple. "I . . . have seen very mortifying proofs, since I arrived here, of the inexpediency of trusting to those principles of implied honour and confidence under which it is usual to transact business in Europe." Whereas Europeans made or received offers of influence on the assumption that whether accepted or declined they would be kept from the public, Americans—such as the members of Congress—had other notions and less reserve. Temple would probably be suspected if he stayed longer in New York, but he would have to go to his native Boston without confidences from the commissioners. As to sending Berkenhout to Philadelphia, Eden did not see any possible benefit that could balance the probable mischief.[45] Nevertheless Berkenhout was given "300 or 250" pounds with which to undertake the journey, to be gone about sixteen days and to expect no help from the commissioners if he should be detected. Soldier, physician, man of letters, he seems to have had no American friend but Arthur Lee: they had been students of medicine together at Edinburgh.

A recently discovered journal (sent to Germain) gives Berkenhout's account of his excursion.[46] He left New York on Sunday the 24th with a pass from Clinton, got an American pass "after some hesitation" from Brigadier General William Maxwell at Elizabeth, and travelled across New Jersey by way of Brunswick ("a dismal town, but pleasantly situated") and Princeton ("remarkable for its fine college, which is now an hospital") to Trenton, from which on the 27th he went by sloop down the Delaware to Philadelphia. Talking with everybody he met on the way, and pretending to be an important British agent sent to Congress, Berkenhout came to the conclusion that there was no good reason why Howe should not have routed Washington's army and "marched triumphantly into Philadelphia without let, hindrance, or molestation" in December 1776. Washington, Berkenhout heard and believed, had at that time given up the cause and was ready to disband his army and himself retire to the banks of the Ohio, where he hoped the British would not think it worth their while to follow him.

Arrived at Philadelphia, "I sent General Maxwell's pass, with a card, to Richard Henry Lee, one of the delegates for Virginia. He paid me a visit the next day, accompanied by one of his colleagues. He afterwards introduced me to [Samuel] Adams and to several other members of Congress with whom I frequently conversed, jointly and separately. The subjects of our conversation were chiefly the cause of their Declaration of Independence, their treaty with France, reasons why Britain ought immediately to make peace with America, state of the American army, cause of their success, Governor Johnstone's private letters, his political opinions and conduct, etc."

At first Berkenhout, introducing himself to Lee as his brother's friend, said he had come to the land of liberty intending to settle somewhere as a physician. Soon he was posing as an eager friend of America who thought he might go back to England and present the American cause to the ministry. But Maxwell wrote to Richard Henry Lee warning him against Berkenhout, and Congress learned from a London newspaper quoted in Philadelphia that Berkenhout and Temple were supposed to have come on some kind of ministerial errand. By order of the supreme executive council of Pennsylvania the questionable visitor was on September 3 brought before it.

"This sage council," Berkenhout wrote in his journal, "interrogated me concerning my business in Philadelphia: whether I was sent by the British government or by the commissioners? They said they had received intelligence from Dr. Franklin of my voyage to America. My papers were perused with great attention by two of their members, and before their contents were known my commitment was signed. This executive council was composed of men who, from their appearance and capacity, seemed such a club of tradesmen as commonly assemble in an alehouse in the borough of Southwark." The council (which then included Judge George Bryan, Colonel Joseph Hart, and James Read) found among Berkenhout's papers a letter he had written but not yet sent to Richard Henry Lee asking him to put on paper "the outline of such a treaty of peace and commerce as America would probably approve." He need not sign it. Berkenhout wanted it, he said, only to assist his memory.[47]

Committed to the new jail, Berkenhout was twice visited by Benjamin Rush, "whom I had formerly seen at Arthur Lee's chambers in London. He was lately a member of Congress"—and had the past winter been much dissatisfied with Washington. "Under an American mask of sympathetic feeling for my situation, with uncommon loquacious plausibility, he expected to make some important discovery concerning the nature of my commission." But Berkenhout, who did not suspect Rush of any British leanings, thought he had learned from him "the purport of some of the secret articles of the treaty with France." It was different with Timothy Matlack, secretary of the executive council, who called several times. "His character is that of a deep, shrewd fellow. He affected great openness and ingenuous conversation. He said if I had anything to propose I might safely speak to him without reserve; if I wanted any information he would frankly answer my questions; or if there was any other person, any man of letters with whom I wished to converse, he would be immediately sent to me." When Berkenhout proved to be reticent he was, he thought at Matlack's request, allowed no further visitors. "This Matlack I think might be bribed, and I believe it not impossible to open a secret correspondence with him." There seems to have been nothing in Matlack's career to warrant Berkenhout's suspicion.

On the 14th Berkenhout was released on parole with precautions against his carrying any letters away, taken by Matlack to the Delaware, and seen on board a sloop "loaded with deals [planks] and shingles for building stables at Trenton for Washington's light horse." From Trenton he proceeded in the company of three rebel officers who were all Irish. "These gentlemen, being neither remarkable for wisdom nor sobriety, told me all they knew concerning the former and present state of their army. They unanimously confirmed the accounts I had before received of Washington's perpetual danger, the incredible distress of his army, and his constant inferiority in point of number. . . . On my return to Elizabethtown I waited on General Maxwell with my pass. I sat with him near an hour. We drank grog and talked of General Howe's campaigns. . . . This Maxwell always commands the light troops. By his language he must be a Scotchman or from the north of Ireland." Maxwell, actually born in County Tyrone, Ireland, was called Scotch Willie by his men. "Before the rebellion he was a farmer in New Jersey. He wears an old threadbare blue coat and a still shabbier hat. In England one would take him for an invalided corporal of artillery."

Back in New York on the 19th, Berkenhout wrote out his reflections. As the members of the executive council of Pennsylvania were low and contemptible, so the members of Congress were "in general unpolished, illiterate, poor, and of no character. . . . Washington is doubtless a man of some genius, but he owes his reputation to his opponent's want of abilities, or to something worse": that is, Berkenhout was hinting, to Howe's indolence or even treachery. If Howe had been active, instead of remaining idle in Philadelphia, he might have driven Washington to the south and then remained in full possession of Pennsylvania, New Jersey, and New York. "Most of the Americans with whom I conversed on my journey through the Jerseys and at Philadelphia lamented their separation from the mother country, disapproved the Declaration of Independence, and detest their French alliance."

Berkenhout felt sure that the British government could, by properly supporting its friends in America, raise a Provincial army strong enough to destroy the Continentals in one campaign. "If Washington be ever defeated and resolutely pursued, his troops will disperse and hide themselves in the woods. They are not, as has been represented, a respectable body of yeomanry fighting *pro aris et focis,* but a contemptible band of vagrants, deserters, and thieves," chiefly Irish. As to the insolent demagogues in Congress, they depended entirely upon Washington's reputation as a soldier and yet were jealous of his power and extremely fearful of the people. Parliament had only to be unanimous and ruthless. "When Britain once resolves to conquer America, the business is done. Previous to this (pardon my presumption) I wish that Parliament would resolve not to treat with Congress on any terms whatsoever."

Burgoyne, with more experience than Berkenhout, had after Saratoga written to Germain in a different language. "I should now hold myself unjustifiable if I did not confide to your lordship my opinion, upon a near inspection, of the rebel troops. The standing corps which I have seen are disciplined. I do not hazard the term, but apply it to the great fundamental points of military institution: sobriety, subordination, regularity, and courage. The militia are inferior in method and movement, but not a jot less serviceable in the woods. My conjectures were very different after the affair of Ticonderoga, but I am convinced they were delusive; and it is a duty to the state to confess it. The panic of the rebel troops is confined and of short duration; the enthusiasm is extensive and permanent."[48] But Berkenhout had listened too much to loyalists, accepted their opinions, and echoed their bad advice to the British command.

Nor had he learned anything about the temper and mettle of countless patriots. Once more in England, where for his efforts and sufferings he was given a pension, he wrote on Christmas day to Arthur Lee in Paris. "I hate all your bloody-minded rogues on both sides the question," he said. "Peace, everlasting peace is my hobby-horse. . . . I dreamt last night that you and I met somewhere on the Continent of Europe. Whether it was at Paris, at Spa, at Brussels, or at Aix-la-Chapelle I am not certain. I thought I had ten thousand things to communicate; that we entered deeply into several important disquisitions; that every obstacle vanished before us; that we restored the jarring world to harmony and that emoluments and honours were the rewards of our labours. If you have had any dream of this sort, tell me so, and I will meet thee at Philippi, be that where it may."[49] Lee did not answer the absurd letter, but informed Vergennes of the receipt of it and sent a copy to Congress as evidence of "how much our enemies are distressed and yet how inveterate they are in their persuasion that because everything is venal among themselves therefore it must be so among us."[50]

V

Berkenhout's expedition did less than no good. The day after his arrest Congress resolved in effect not to treat with the British commissioners on the subject of the Convention troops. The commissioners lingered, fretting but futile, in New York till the end of November. They came to feel doubtful about loyalist reports of disaffection among the patriots. "The leaders on the enemy's side are too powerful," Carlisle wrote in a letter to England.[51] "The common people hate us in their hearts, notwithstanding all that is said of their secret attachment to the mother country." But he thought America superb, particularly in autumn. "There are some trees, when touched by the night frosts, have their leaves turned to a bright red which has a very extraordinary effect among the different shades of green and yellow which predominate. . . . Everything is upon a great scale upon this continent. The rivers are immense; the climate violent in heat and cold; the prospects magnificent; the thunder and lightning tremendous."[52] He hardly left Manhattan except to ferry to Long Island to ride in open country. He bought, as a curiosity to take home with him, a horse with an unfamiliar American gait. "A good pacer will pace fourteen and fifteen miles in an hour, but the motion is uneasy." His steward added a grey squirrel, a fish hawk, and other native creatures to the Carlisle museum and thought of buying a little Negro boy for Lady Carlisle.

In September Carlisle planned for a time to go to Rhode Island, to confer with his uncle Admiral Byron about the conduct of the war. Clinton discouraged this. In October Lafayette challenged Carlisle to a duel, holding him personally responsible for the commission's attacks on France in the letters to Congress. Carlisle on the 11th sensibly and not too seriously refused. "You ought to have known," he told Lafayette in his answer, "that I do and ever shall consider myself solely answerable to my country and my king and not to any individual for my public conduct and language."[53] Washington, whose letter of disapproval had reached Lafayette too late to prevent the challenge, wisely foresaw the answer. "The generous spirit of chivalry, exploded by the rest of the world, finds a refuge, my dear friend, in the sensibility of your nation only. But it is in vain to cherish it unless you can find antagonists to support it; and however well adapted it might have been to the times in which it existed, in our days it is to be feared that your opponent, sheltering himself behind modern opinions and under his present public character of commissioner, would turn a virtue of such ancient date into ridicule."[54]

On October 3 the commissioners by a Manifesto and Proclamation undertook to carry their offers over the head of Congress to the American people. They pointed out that Congress had in the beginning asked only for redress of grievances from the British government and had denied any wish to be independent. But now that the Americans were granted all they had asked, Congress had enlarged its demands and insisted on independence or nothing. The commissioners could not believe that Congress had general support for this unreasonable change or for its obstinate refusal to consider any terms of reconciliation. "It has not been, nor is it, our wish to seek the objects which we are commissioned to pursue by fomenting popular divisions and partial cabals; we think such conduct would be ill-suited to the generous nature of the offers made and unbecoming the dignity of the king and the state which make them. But it is both our wish and duty to encourage and support any men or bodies of men in their return of loyalty to our sovereign and of affection to our fellow-subjects."

They urged the assemblies of the various colonies to meet and consider the offers already made to Congress. They told all soldiers in the American armies that they might either return to peaceful occupations or, "if the honours of a military life are become their object," fight for the king in the battles of the "United British Empire against our late mutual and natural enemy." Clergymen were reminded that "the foreign power with which the Congress is endeavouring to connect them has ever been averse to toleration" and that Great Britain was the "best guardian of religious liberty." All the "free inhabitants of this once happy Empire" should bear in mind that they were kept at war by an irresponsible Congress, and that the benevolent policy of the British government could not last forever. If America was to become an ally of France, England might have, for the sake of self-preservation, to do such damage to the colonies as would make them of as "little avail as possible" to their scheming and greedy allies.

There were Americans, the Manifesto said, who persisted in thinking that the commissioners had power to concede independence and might still concede it if Congress held out. "We answer without reserve that we neither possess nor expect powers for that purpose; and that if Great Britain could ever have sunk so low as to adopt such a measure we should not have thought ourselves compellable to be the instruments in making a concession which would in our opinion be calamitous to the colonies for whom it is made and disgraceful as well as calamitous to the country from which it is required." Since independence was not to be hoped for, Americans at large should cease being misled by Congress and should make their own terms. Whatever they might have done before this date would be forgiven them. The commissioners proclaimed full pardon also to all American soldiers or officials who should ask it during the next forty days, from October 3 to November 11, excepting only such persons as might "under the pretext of authority, as judges, jurymen, ministers, or officers of civil justice, be instrumental in executing and putting to death any of his Majesty's subjects" in the colonies after the date of the proclamation.[55]

Copies of the Manifesto and Proclamation, in English and German, were dispatched to the president of Congress and all the members, to Washington and all his generals in command, to the governors of all the provinces and all the provincial assemblies, to the chief justices and the commanders of the armed forces in all the provinces, to ministers of the Gospel, to the commanders of the British army on detachment or at the outposts, and to the British commissaries of prisoners. Congress, learning on the 15th that the copies were going out by a number of British vessels to all parts of the country, recommended the next day to the state authorities everywhere to arrest and imprison the bearers of the "seditious papers," whether they came under the sanction of a flag or otherwise, and to have the papers printed in the "several gazettes, more fully to convince the good people of these states of the insidious designs" of the commissioners.[56] This recommendation was so widely carried out that the commissioners seemed to have run against a wall of American unity as hard as Congress.

Carlisle had his thirtieth birthday on the voyage to America, and Eleanor Eden her second daughter in September at New York. Storer, who had come along to amuse himself, found still a fourth Etonian in Lord Cathcart of the British Legion, and was the first to guess that Cathcart would marry Elizabeth Elliot, the Edens' cousin, as he did the next year. Eden, concerning himself with every aspect of the commission's business, formed a friendship for Clinton and made the acquaintance of several loyalists. One of them, the William Smith whom both Vardill and Wentworth had urged the commissioners to try to win to their cause, was a close neighbour to Andrew Elliot in the Bowery, and saw as much of Eden as he could. Another was William Franklin, royal governor of New Jersey held by the Americans, who was exchanged for John McKinley, American president of Delaware held by the British, and in October came back to New York after two years' detention in Connecticut. He reported that many Americans were in favour of accepting the British offers and opposed to the alliance with France. The commissioners took some comfort from this.[57]

On November 27 the commissioners' party was on board the *Roebuck* ready to sail for England. They landed at Plymouth on December 20 after a "flying passage" of only twenty-two days. Though their mission had been a failure the king and the ministry, having sent them blindfold to America, could not let them go unrewarded for their efforts. Carlisle was the next year made president of the board of trade, and the year after lord lieutenant of Ireland, with Eden as his chief secretary. Johnstone, who had never commanded a ship, was in May 1779 made commodore of a squadron stationed off the Portuguese coast. Much of the time he lived easily on shore at Lisbon while his squadron took prizes for which he got the honours.

Eden was the most difficult of the three to reward. Not only had his footless errand cost him a good post as under-secretary but it had also disgusted him with the administration. He refused in February to go back to his seat in the House of Commons, where he was sure to be pressed with questions, unless "ostensible favours are done to the American commissioners." For his own reward he would prefer that "one of the offices"—at court—"which are or have been usually held by ladies of family may be given to Mrs. Eden" with £600 a year. This, he said, would "preclude me from all farther wishes for favour of this kind to the last hour of my life."[58] After some discussions between North and the king, she was awarded a pension of that amount to run during the king's pleasure.[59] There were always honours and emoluments for faithful servants of the king, as his friends kept telling the recalcitrant Americans.

When the commissioners left America they left John Temple behind them to act the anticlimax of the mission. From New York he had on August 23 written to Samuel Adams in Philadelphia, saying he had after seven years returned to his own country and asking for a passport so he might pay his respects to Congress. Congress, just then wary on account of Berkenhout, told Temple to choose which state he meant to live in and to get that state's permission before applying for a passport. He went to Boston, pleased some of the patriot leaders there by his zeal for America, and travelled to Philadelphia accumulating recommendations to Congress as he went. At his arrival on December 1 Adams took him to call on Laurens, and Temple dined with Congress that evening.

Whatever Temple talked about with the members during his three-week stay, he cannot explicitly have urged the reconciliation he had come to promote for the good of America and for the sake of his promised baronetcy and pension. Anything of the kind would have put him instantly in jail. Cautious as he was, he was suspected. Congress would not forget that he and Berkenhout had in London been supposed to be in the employ of the British government and had crossed the Atlantic together; or that Temple had after a month in New York been permitted by Clinton to try to confer with Congress. Gérard, the French minister, watchfully hinted that Congress might be dealing, without knowing it, with a British emissary. Congress did not want to offend their ally. Temple was prudent enough to leave suddenly on the 20th.[60]

In Boston, where he read accounts of the commissioners' reports in London and Galloway's examination before the House of Commons, Temple resolved that he would go again to England. This time he would tell the ministry that Great Britain could do nothing, as he wrote to General Gates on May 7, "but with the very best grace she can, offer her hand to America upon the very terms that America herself has proposed and from which she will never recede." Seven years in England had kept Temple convinced that reconciliation was still possible. As many months in America had converted him to independence. Before he sailed he told a group of Boston patriots that it was he who obtained the Hutchinson letters for Franklin five years before, though "not in the way apprehended by the British ministry."[61] It now seemed both safe and meritorious to claim the credit where he had formerly denied the blame. But the Americans never quite trusted a man so long so fluid in his loyalties. Temple remained a British subject and after the war returned to spend the rest of his life in America as British consul general.

Bitter Division

THE British peace offers of 1778 intensified the bitter division in America between the patriots and the loyalists. Congress, snubbing the commission, gave the loyalists fresh reasons for their charge that unscrupulous usurpers were tightening their hold on the country as their power increased. Had they not at first protested that they aimed only at redress of grievances and had no wish for separation from Great Britain? Were they not now indifferent and insolent to generous offers of all they had once demanded, and rigidly set on the policy of independence they had long denied? The loyalists, who had stood still while Congress shifted its ground with the development of the conflict, saw Congress as malevolently, guiltily inconsistent.

As it had changed on the point of independence, so had it in the matter of France. In April 1776 Congress had sent commissioners to Canada to win that loyal colony over to the side of the rebels. The Canadians, almost all of them French, were to be told that the Quebec act of 1774 which had guaranteed them French law and the Catholic religion under the British government was a "base, cruel, and insidious" design of Parliament to make them "the mere spoils and prey of conquerors and lords." The presumption was that French law and the Catholic religion were instruments of tyranny. Yet later in that same year, Franklin, head of the Canadian commission, was sent to Paris as head of another commission, which hoped to make a French alliance. And now that the United States had concluded a treaty of friendship with the ancient enemies of the English, France was America's "good and faithful ally" against whom the British and the loyalists might not say a word.

A loyalist calling himself Philarethes in Rivington's *Royal*

Gazette on December 9 said in brief what all loyalists were saying at length. The contrast between the conduct of the British commissioners, "such as deserves the highest encomiums from every friend of truth, virtue, and humanity," and the conduct of Congress, with its "illiberal, indecent, and absurd resolves and acts . . . must convince even the rebels that their rulers are a set of men as destitute of humanity and truth as they are of dignity of character; and that the low sphere of life they formerly moved in" was the one to which they should confine their little talents. Here was the usual loyalist contempt for the patriots. "The Congress surely cannot be serious when they imagine that a union with Great Britain . . . would not be advantageous to them; for were they in full possession of independence, and at peace with all the world, the protection and assistance of Great Britain would be of more consequence to America than any mercenary alliance" with a foreign power. Here was the usual loyalist conviction that America must depend on some country in Europe, and that England was more dependable than France.

Congress had accused the British forces of brutality and cruelty in carrying on the war. Philarethes assured his readers that if the British had made war as Congress said they had, "Congress would not at this time dictate to the continent." The British army had been moderate in its measures, the British government temperate. "It was not the prowess of the Americans, their French alliance, nor their resources that extorted such offers from the mother country." They had been yielded by Great Britain in voluntary magnanimity. "From a kingdom arrived at that pitch of glory, riches, and strength, and whose resources are so inexhaustible, it would be absurd to suppose it proceeded from any motive of fear or distrust." Her army and navy could "scarce be supposed to cringe to a Pandemonium that would bow their heads to the representatives of a Machiavellian court." Hereafter the war must take on a sterner character, and Congress be held accountable. "The colonies are British, and her troops must keep or conquer them. . . . This continent does not belong to the Americans. It is a part of the British Empire and cannot be separated without the violation of the most just and dear ties of society."

The patriots were determined that the continent should belong to the Americans, not to the British or their loyalist partisans. Though Congress in April recommended indemnity to loyalists who would leave the British cause, not many of them seem to have left it. Nor did the states do much to encourage them. Most of the state governments had already disarmed and disfranchised loyalists, laid special taxes upon them, put them under strict restraint, banished many of them, and taken over their property if not confiscated it outright.[1] During 1778 these laws were widely reinforced with others still more stringent. They were concerned less with offering indemnity to any who might have been disaffected than with requiring all persons to take oaths of allegiance and abjuration on penalty of being considered traitors and enemies to America. Naturally the influential, the conspicuous, and the rich came in for more scrutiny than ordinary men. Congress on November 27, 1777 had recommended that the property of obdurate loyalists be confiscated for the benefit of the patriot public. The states, pressed for money, did not hesitate. Neutrals were forced to declare themselves. Those who would not support the rebellion had to see their estates seized and sold for the support of it. Some of these offending victims were put in prison. Others got away to Canada or England. But after the evacuation of Philadelphia, New York, the British stronghold, became the loyalist capital.

On July 25, less than a month after his return there, Clinton wrote Germain that "nothing distresses me so much as the applications I hourly receive from great numbers of refugees who crowd to this place from all quarters, many of whom have been reduced from affluent circumstances to the utmost penury by their attachment to government. To provide for these unfortunate people in the manner they may merit, or perhaps expect, I know is impossible; but humanity and good policy requires that some attention should be paid to them and at least a temporary relief afforded them."[2] He ordered that they be furnished rations at government expense. This would at least keep them from starving. A letter to Clinton from Beverley Robinson on November 11 shows how troubling the situation was. "I should have waited on you myself this morning, but I am so surrounded with refugees that I can't get out of the house, as this is my day for giving them orders for provisions."

Safe only within the British lines, the frustrate loyalists brooded in a wretched leisure over the history of their disappointments and defeats. Despising the patriots, they still underestimated their numbers, their abilities, and their honesty. Loyalist writers, free to publish their opinions in New York, exchanged fierce recriminations with patriot writers everywhere else. As in all such controversies each side accused the other of having been first to offend. The patriots remembered that British governors in the opening year of the struggle had threatened rebels with confiscation. The loyalists could retort that this had been a lawful threat which was not carried out, while the rebel confiscations were the acts of outlaws who had welcomed any excuse for their tyrannical behaviour. Loyalists and patriots alike claimed pure and just intentions in themselves and found atrocious designs in their opponents. The two parties gave credit and currency to stories of inhuman deeds done by either to the other. If the loyalists could argue that the American governments were more oppressive than the British had ever been, the Americans could reply that the British were using German hirelings against free citizens and Indian savages against women and children as well as men.

Actually the Americans had enlisted Indians earlier than the British. There were a few Indian minute-men in Massachusetts before Lexington, and perhaps more of them among the levies that laid siege to Boston. Governor Gage of Massachusetts held that this justified the British use of Indians, and Dunmore of Virginia on May 1 proposed the use of them before—it seems likely—he could have heard of the Indian minute-men. Congress, learning that the British meant to employ Indians as auxiliaries, resolved in July 1775 to treat with the Six Nations in an effort to keep them from taking any part in the "present commotion"; and in the following May resolved to engage Indians in the American service. But in the race for the favour of the Iroquois the Americans were able only to keep the Oneida and the Tuscarora neutral, while the British won the active help of the more powerful Mohawk, Onondaga, Cayuga, and Seneca nations. Since the French and Indian war British officials on the frontier had frequently upheld the rights of the Indians against encroaching American settlers, and the Indians were loyal to the Crown out of genuine gratitude.[3]

Though John Stuart, British superintendent of Indian affairs south of the Ohio, in February 1778 sent deputies to prepare the Cherokee in the mountains and the Seminole in Florida for hostilities against the patriots in Georgia and the Carolinas, and in March established white soldiers and Indian warriors on the lower Mississippi, the southern Indians did little damage that year. The principal attacks by loyalists and Indians were made on the New York-Pennsylvania border fronting the territory of the Six Nations. This, according to the treaty of Fort Stanwix in 1768, had definite boundaries and gave western New York and northwestern Pennsylvania to the Iroquois. Their proud confederation had been used to dealing with the British and colonial governments through Sir William Johnson, the most influential, most dramatic of all the Crown officers in America. Superintendent of the northern Indians from 1756 to his death in July 1774, he lived at Johnson Hall (Johnstown) in manorial state, first with his German-American wife and then in turn with two Mohawk women, by each of whom he had children. He not only had the confidence of the Iroquois but he also dominated the frontier county of Tryon which bordered the Iroquois country and included all the rest of western New York north to the St. Lawrence.

Johnson at his death left a kind of dynasty on the border. His son John Johnson succeeded to the baronetcy, the greater part of the immense estate with Johnson Hall, and the rank of major general of militia. Sir William's son-in-law Guy Johnson, of Guy Park near Amsterdam, became superintendent of Indian affairs. Another son-in-law, Colonel Daniel Claus, and Colonel John Butler of Johnstown had been trusted deputies of Sir William and remained as loyal as he had been. Joseph Brant (Thayendanegea), the Mohawk war chief who was brother to one of Sir William's Indian wives, after his patron's death became secretary to Guy Johnson. Suspected of planning to raise the Six Nations against the patriots, the Johnson dynasty was disarmed by forces under Schuyler and in 1775–76 fled to Canada. Sir John Johnson, whose wife was Schuyler's cousin, and Butler had the special grounds for bitterness that their wives and children were for a time held as hostages at Albany.

But the Tryon county loyalists, unlike the loyalists shut up in

Boston or Philadelphia or New York, had a chance to act. Commissioned by the British governors in Canada, and assisted by their Indian allies, they made deadly raids on the rebel frontier. The centre of their operations was Niagara on Lake Ontario, from which the Johnsons, Butler, and his son Walter led the loyalist raiders, Brant the Indians. The most notorious of all these expeditions came in 1778, when John Butler at the head of Sir John Johnson's loyalist regiment and a party of Indians (without Brant) invaded the Wyoming valley in Pennsylvania in July, and Walter Butler with his father's loyalist troops and Indians headed by Brant struck at Cherry Valley in New York in November. At Wyoming it appears that only rebels in arms were killed by the loyalists and Indians, who gave no quarter. At Cherry Valley there was a general massacre of about fifty persons, less than a third of them soldiers. Walter Butler held some of his captives as hostages till they could be exchanged for his mother and her younger children.

The harsh facts of the border raids became nameless horrors in the stories that spread among the patriots and soon settled into bloody legends. The loyalists might point out that they had only been fighting for the homes that had been taken from them; and that they had as good a right to win the Indians to their side as the Americans to try to win them. But there was still something essentially unequal in the situations of the loyalists and the patriots. The patriots could hardly have used the Indians except against British or loyalist soldiers. The British and loyalists could and did use them against unprotected patriot farms and villages, and could not count on keeping the Indians from the usual practices of savage warfare. Whatever their intentions, and whatever their efforts to control the Indians, the loyalist raiders of 1778 were in the long run far more deadly to the British-loyalist cause than to the American.

II

Sir Henry Clinton as commander-in-chief in North America was in a perpetual predicament. The loss of Burgoyne's army to the Americans in 1777 would normally have called for a vigorous

British campaign the following year. France's entrance into the war not only cost Clinton the fresh troops from England he had hoped for but also deprived him of the 8000 or more men he was ordered to send to Canada and the West Indies. Though the menacing French fleet fought inconclusive actions with the British, and the French-American attack on Rhode Island in August failed to dislodge the British garrison, Clinton was unwilling to take the offensive and except for a brief excursion to Rhode Island stayed safe in the New York islands, which were strongly fortified. For a month or two after Monmouth he outnumbered Washington, who was moving the bulk of his army across the Hudson to hold the country north and east of Manhattan, with brigades in New Jersey to watch the British from that quarter. But Clinton could or would not strike so soon after his successful retreat from Philadelphia. He settled to what amounted to a state of siege, with a few raids into Westchester, Connecticut, or New Jersey for provisions, which otherwise had to come all the way from England.

The British government assumed that Clinton would not greatly miss the reinforcements he had expected. He had only to enlist as many as he wanted of the numberless loyalists who were said to be eager to join the British army. This was easier to suggest than to do. Both the government and the army stood against admitting Americans to equal rank with Englishmen. The Provincials had their own regiments. Clinton was instructed by Germain to be sure, "in the choice of [Provincial] officers, to give the preference to such of his Majesty's subjects as are natives of America, and are of weight and influence, and have property in that country, and of such others [from England] of merit and influence as have settlements [investments] there."[4] In practice Clinton found himself often obliged to give commissions to loyalist gentlemen who had suffered at the hands of the rebels. Such officers—and their men— were so vengefully bent on retaliatory raids that Clinton found it difficult to restrain them, though the Provincials were supposed to operate under strict military rule. Some of them resented their subordination to the British, some of them the regulations which hampered their revenges. Yet on August 15, 1778 the Provincial forces near New York included not only Oliver DeLancey's and Cortlandt Skinner's brigades but also the substantial beginnings of thirteen additional regiments: the New York Volunteers, Queen's Rangers, Orange Rangers, Loyal Americans, Pennsylvania Loyalists, Maryland Loyalists, Roman Catholic Volunteers, West Jersey Volunteers, Chasseurs, Royal Americans Reformees, Volunteers of Ireland, British Legion, Guides and Pioneers.[5]

With or without the help of the loyalists Clinton seems never to have had any confidence that he could put down the rebellion with the forces he had or was likely to get from Great Britain. He had not particularly desired to be commander-in-chief and he offered his resignation once or more a year. His dispatches to Germain were full of complaints and grievances. With fewer soldiers than Howe, Clinton was asked to do what Howe had not been able to do. Washington could not, Clinton was certain, be drawn into a decisive battle, but the rebels were so alert that it was almost impossible to surprise and defeat them piecemeal. To an orthodox professional military man like Clinton there seemed only one course to take. Neglected by his government, he must hold the post assigned to him but must not run the risk of losing it to the enemy.

Outwardly his life in crowded New York was not unendurable. Besides his headquarters in the Archibald Kennedy house at 1 Broadway he had the James Beekman house at Turtle Bay for a country seat and—it is said—five farms on the various islands.[6] He lived as became a grandson of the sixth Earl of Lincoln, a son of an admiral who had been royal governor of New York. But Sir Henry Clinton was not a genial man, had few intimates, and might refuse to see anybody for two or three days at a time. Fat and irritable, he was depressed by his optimistic instructions from London and vexed by the urgent demands of the loyalists gathered in New York. They had not been given the protection promised them by the British. When they tried to help themselves, they were not encouraged. Clinton's inaction condemned them to virtual imprisonment while the rebel captors exulted outside the lines. They insisted that Washington was weaker than Clinton thought he was. They had no doubt that the rebels could be corrupted and won over by favourable offers. But the destitute loyalists looked jealously on favours shown to the less loyal, and contended for favours among themselves. If Clinton took advice from one of them, he might offend the others. If he took none, he offended them all.

In John André, who became Clinton's aide in November, Clinton seems to have found his most comfortable confidant. André was twenty-seven, ambitious, industrious, capable, and engaging. He had come in 1774 to America as lieutenant in the 7th regiment, been taken prisoner in Canada in November 1775, and spent a year on parole in the interior of Pennsylvania. During the British occupation of Philadelphia, having become a captain in the 26th, he served as aide to General Charles Grey, who recommended him to his friend Clinton. In New York André kept up his interest in the theatre and continued to write lively verses which pleased both the British and the loyalists. It was pleasant for Clinton to have so amiable a subaltern near at hand and to know that he was as discreet in his duties as he was gay in society. André was particularly trusted with Clinton's correspondence with his secret agents and with the Americans who sent secret information to British Headquarters, hoping for suitable rewards and perhaps for larger rewards for larger services to come.

III

One of these agents, whom Clinton had engaged before André's arrival from Philadelphia, was Daniel Hammill of the Dutchess county militia who in October 1777 was brigade major to General James Clinton, in command of the Continental forces at Forts Clinton and Montgomery on the Hudson. According to Hammill's later statements,[7] he had been an Irish farmer living peaceably and loyally who was drafted into the rebel militia and did not dare to refuse on account of his wife and children. When Sir Henry Clinton, in an effort to co-operate with Burgoyne, captured the Hudson forts, Hammill was among the prisoners at Montgomery and at once went over to the British. In the following April Clinton sent him, Hammill said, up the river "with proposals from his Excellency to George Clinton, the governor of the state, and his brother James Clinton." These proposals were probably only copies of North's conciliatory bills which had just arrived from London. The matter was discreetly managed. "He was taken from his lodgings in the city of New York and put on board his Majesty's ship *Preston*, when a canoe was provided for him in which it was to be pretended he made his escape." He was accompanied by Samuel Geake, an Irish private captured at the same time, who afterwards testified that he understood they were to win over as many Irish-American deserters as possible and enlist them in the Irish Volunteers, a new regiment being formed by Lord Rawdon, Clinton's adjutant general. Geake expected to be made a lieutenant, Hammill a captain in the Volunteers.

They made their way to Poughkeepsie, from which Geake, again in the American army, was assigned to the frontier Fort Schuyler commanded by Colonel Peter Gansevoort. Hammill had little time in which to carry out his errand. Some anonymous patriot, held prisoner by the British on Long Island, wrote on May 5 to Brigadier General Samuel Holden Parsons at West Point that Hammill had been "frequently sent for incog. to Sir Harry Clinton's" and was believed by the other American prisoners to have been sent out of New York as a British spy.[8] Hammill was arrested and put in the Poughkeepsie jail, and a letter was sent to Gansevoort telling him that Geake must be watched. A sergeant set to watch him got into his confidence and was told that Geake had been instructed by Rawdon (whom Geake called Lord Rodman) to obtain information, persuade men to desert, and spike the fort's guns when they left. Geake, arrested on June 17, was tried by a garrison court martial on July 1 and sentenced to be hanged.[9] But when Gansevoort sent the verdict to Washington for confirmation, Washington ordered on August 13 that Geake be held as witness "until matters are ripe for the prosecution of Major Hammill."[10]

Geake's evidence seems not to have been thought enough, nor the warning letter from the prisoner on Long Island. His information could not be cited, for whatever it might be worth, without danger to him if the British should learn that he had written to Parsons. Hammill remained in jail till August 1779 when he escaped with 19 other loyalists and got back to New York. Destitute himself, he was soon joined by his wife and children who were sent in after him. He supported them on six shillings a day, earned as clerk in the fuel office, for about a year and then emigrated to Nova Scotia. In August 1784 he was in London, where he told the commission on loyalist claims of his services to the king and asked for compensation for losses amounting to £283 10s. He was allowed £79 16s.

Metcalf Bowler was a more secret though not more successful agent for Clinton among the patriots. A London-born merchant and speculator of Newport, Bowler had formerly been speaker of the Rhode Island assembly and chief justice of the state. He had served on the committee of correspondence and signed the state's declaration of independence in July 1776. But after December 8 of that year, when Clinton took Rhode Island to establish a British base in New England, Bowler remained a patriot only four days. "From some peculiar circumstances attending my situation in life," he wrote to Clinton on the 12th, "have been unwarily led from my duty to the king and joined the provincials in their opposition to his Majesty's legal government and accepted of some offices inconsistent with my allegiance to his Majesty. But since the arrival of the British forces on Rhode Island, and having the opportunity of seeing his Majesty's most gracious proclamation, have desisted from acting in any capacity contrary to his Majesty's government and propose to submit myself to his Majesty's clemency as soon as I am able to wait on your Excellency." He was willing, he said, to give up his commission as chief justice if Clinton should think it "incompatible with his Majesty's government."

Bowler's reasons for his sudden loyalty were simple. "As the Hessian troops are quartered on the island, and having committed many outrages and depredations on many of the inhabitants by entering their houses and plundering their effects and even putting them in fear of their lives; as I am situated on the island, should esteem it a favour and indulgence if your Excellency would order, as soon as convenient, a guard to my habitation at Portsmouth that I may be protected from the insults of the Hessians, having put myself under the protection of his Majesty's troops."

Clinton during his expedition to Rhode Island in August 1778 had an interview with Bowler and proposed that he "keep up an epistolary communication with your Excellency at New York," as Bowler put it in his letter of September 15. The informer had soon "come to a determination to do myself that honour, though should it ever come to the knowledge of the provincials, shall run a violent risk of my life and forfeiture of my estate both real and personal. But as you pledged your honour to me my name should never be made mention of nor called into question; my letters perused by no person saving yourself; that I might make use of what signature I pleased; so now I commit my life and fortune into your hands and protection and hereafter shall address you by the signature of [Rusticus]." He was afraid he could, on the island, get little information that would be of use to Clinton. But he would not mind moving with his family to the mainland, "providing your Excellency thought my going . . . might be productive of any essential service to his Majesty's government—and you would be willing to advance me a sum in specie to carry with me."

He thought that if he got to Providence he could count on becoming a member of the rebel council of war and of the assembly again, and perhaps—"with some pecuniary assistance"—delegate to the Continental Congress. The rebels were well disposed to him because of his "grievous complaints (and give me leave to say not without reason)" of his treatment under British rule on the island. "My house and garden on the hill in the town of Newport has been taken out of my possession and converted into a hospital . . . nigh eighteen months ago. My farm whereon I dwell is an entire waste, having had an encampment on it for this two years past." The fences were gone. He had been unable to raise any crops, "saving what sauce my garden produced. My only cow, the support of my children," had been "most wantonly butchered"; his library "plundered of sixty-odd volumes"; his horses and cart claimed for the king's service without compensation. "In short, such is the severe treatment I have met with of late that am almost discouraged."

Clinton sent Bowler a gratuity which enabled him to move first to Newport and then to Providence by the following April. Bowler was dissatisfied. "I am now running the grandest risk possible," he wrote on May 11, "and pledging my life at stake; and for what a paltry pittance that has been more than expended in the transportation of my family and effects; and all promises made me been violated. Without something handsome is done soon to make me compensation and encourage me to persevere, you must not expect to hear further from me." He would promise only to keep himself "a strict neuter until affairs are settled." But after a trip to Boston Bowler on June 5 wrote again. He could not, he said, resist "my strong inclination to serve my friends." The Bostonians were "much divided, every one wishing an end of the contest and depreciating the first authors of their misery." He had heard many former "high Sons of Liberty" say that if a British fleet were to blockade the harbour and a British army lay siege to the town, not a hundred of the inhabitants would rise in defence, "for they had rather submit to British government than be oppressed in the manner they now are."

In Rhode Island "no persons of any consequence seems inclined to interfere in government affairs. Government is at present conducted by a set of low, ignorant, headstrong men. I have been strongly solicited to accept several posts but have declined them, thinking I can at present do much more service in a private station than a public. I keep shop for a livelihood, though had but few goods to sell, every European article being so very scarce here and extravagantly dear; therefore at present confine myself to the West India produce." He still trembled every moment for fear of detection. "However I flatter [myself] I shall not fail of a reward hereafter"—not from heaven, apparently, but from Clinton.

He trembled in letters written in July and September, and seems to have ended the informing series with a last appeal on October 2 for more goods to sell in his shop: "a few pieces of black and tailored ribbons, a few green shoe bindings, a piece or two of black calamancos, one or two dozen more black handkerchiefs, a piece or two of good cambric, a few packs of pins and some coloured and coarse white threads, some black and coloured sewing silks, a small assortment of cutlery ware in buckles, penknives, etc.—and a good case-coat cloak that is camlet lined with bear; then I may be fit in the cold during the winter season to pick up intelligence." Always timid, always needy, Bowler was of little use to Clinton, who paid little attention to him. His information was never first-hand or really valuable. He was a shivering neutral who cut a poor figure between two fires, but who kept his treacherous secret for a century and a half.[11]

Loyalist offers which Clinton thought more promising came to him on December 13, 1778 through Christopher Sower of Pennsylvania.[12] Sower, head of the noted firm of German printers and publishers at Germantown, had joined Howe at Philadelphia and accompanied Clinton to New York. The estate of the Sower family had been confiscated and sold during the past August. In December "an inhabitant of the back parts of Pennsylvania" arrived in New York, bringing with him, Sower reported to Clinton, "the strongest assurances of the loyalty of great numbers of the people in the parts aforesaid and of their good disposition to promote his Majesty's service."

The messenger was Andrew Fürstner, a refugee from Lancaster whose brother-in-law William Rankin was colonel of militia in York county. Fürstner had, he said, been authorized by Rankin and Captain Martin Weaver of the Northumberland county militia "to represent them and their numerous friends as entirely devoted to the service of [the British] government and ready to take the most active part as soon as the commander-in-chief in his wisdom shall think fit to call them forth. . . . They propose to hold their present commissions under the now usurping powers till the moment they shall be ordered to appear in the king's behalf, if his Excellency shall approve of their so doing and will save them harmless from the penalties denounced by the commissioners. The above [Rankin] and [Weaver] act in concert and without being too sanguine engage to furnish a complete battalion." Moreover, an unidentified colonel of the Lancaster militia, while not "acting in concert" with the other two, wished to be represented to Clinton "as having exactly the same good intentions and being equally desirous of receiving his Majesty's commands."

Sir William Erskine, one of Clinton's aides, gave Sower an answer which Sower appears to have written out for Fürstner to take back with him. "The commander-in-chief directs that you will inform the gentlemen named in your representation that his Excellency will save them harmless from all penalties denounced against rebels and request them to continue in their respective posts under the present usurped authority; that it is his pleasure they increase the circle of their acquaintances and furnish him from time to time with all such important intelligence as may come to their knowledge." Erskine gave Sower, at Sower's request, a "watchword or certain sign whereby the parties may be assured of the genuineness of such orders as may hereafter be brought to them on the king's part." Since the watchword was to be spoken only, not written, it does not appear, but for a sign the answer by Fürstner was enclosed in a Continental bill—in this case for $6.

Three months later, when Fürstner got back to New York, Clinton was at Southampton. Sower, on his way there, encountered André at Oyster Bay on March 20 and showed him a letter for Clinton which André thought indiscreet because it mentioned names.[13] André kept the letter and sent Sower on with a mere memorandum which would do no harm if it should happen to fall into rebel hands. Most of what Sower wrote for Clinton was Fürstner's "account by word of mouth." The rebels' principal magazine at Carlisle, he reported, contained large quantities of flour, beef, and pork, between 800 and 900 tons of powder, 1000 stand of arms, several wagonloads of gunlocks, a cannon forge and a number of cannons already made, and "divers other military articles." The patriots were planning an expedition against the Six Nations, to retaliate for the raids against Wyoming and Cherry Valley the past year and to end the Indian menace once for all. In this the loyalists of the back country meant to play a subversive part.

Although the expedition was to be made up chiefly of Continental troops, it was to include a body of militia raised in the frontier counties of Pennsylvania. Rankin of York and the Lancaster colonel were doing their best, Sower told Clinton, "to get the command of these conferred upon a certain [unidentified] Mr. —— of these parts with whom they have a perfect good understanding. If this can be obtained, of which they have the fairest prospects, Colonel Butler will have little to fear." At a time when the frontier patriots were still in daily terror of Butler with his loyalists and Brant with his Indians, there were frontier Americans who hated the usurpers in Congress more than the raiders from Niagara and were willing to sacrifice their rebel neighbours to the savages. "If it shall please his Excellency to direct Colonel Butler to make a descent upon the open town of [Carlisle], the said colonels with their friends will give all possible assistance towards taking and destroying the magazine, by which the king's friends, who are very numerous, would obtain a sufficiency of arms and ammunition.

Colònel [Rankin] will convey any orders from the commander-in-chief to Colonel Butler and, if authorized so to do, open a correspondence with him and act in conjunction."

The loyalists of the back country expected help from Philadelphia. "By means of ——, a member of the supreme executive council who has already been sounded, they hope to come at all the secrets relative to the expedition against Butler and to be warned of any suspicions there may be entertained of themselves in the course of the affair; and therefore humbly beg to be enabled to give such encouragement to the said —— as his Excellency shall think fit." This member of the council has not been identified. As to the secret loyalist who was to lead the frontier militia against Butler there was a letter from Rankin which Sower cited without quoting. Rankin said that "Mr. —— expects a captain's commission in a troop of light horse for his services." Rankin went on to say that "Butler with about 600 men would be sufficient to answer his purpose, and that the destruction of said magazine must greatly tend to finish the war."

Lord Rawdon, the British adjutant general, replied that "——['s] request shall be granted upon the same footing with the Provincial corps, upon his joining the army, as also to such other officers as they may appoint. The General [Clinton] will send a message to Butler, from this place, and approves of the seizure and destruction of the said magazine." But Sower had later to write in his record of the transactions that "some time after Colonel [Rankin] sent a message desiring Mr. Sower to acquaint the General that in consequence of his last letter he sent to Colonel Butler to know when he would approach, and received for answer that he had received no directions for Sir Henry and was not acquainted with anything he mentioned." It was often easier for loyalists to form designs than to get British support for them.

In the winter of 1778–79 Clinton, no matter how promising he thought these frontier schemes, probably reflected that the loyalists forever talked of loyal uprisings but that none of them had so far made any real headway against the rebel governments. He had inherited Howe's secret agents, several from the back counties. There was the Rev. Daniel Battwell, sent in 1774 by the Society for the Propagation of the Gospel to York and Cumberland, where he had loyally opposed the rebels till a party of them threw him into an icy river and banished him to the British lines in Philadelphia. He was with Andrew Fürstner and others in the plot to destroy the magazine at Carlisle, and claimed that after going with the British army to New York he first recommended Rankin to Clinton as a valuable ally in York.[14] There was this same Fürstner, a German farmer who joined the British on their way to occupy Philadelphia and became Galloway's spy. At the evacuation he was sent "with dispatches to the frontiers of Pennsylvania to Colonel Butler" and rejoined the British on the march back to New York. He became one of the most trustworthy of all Clinton's messengers, with the pay (though without the commission) of a Provincial lieutenant.[15] There was Dr. Henry Norris of York whom Battwell called "madly loyal." Norris, who formed an early secret association of 500 loyalists in his county, then or later kept five horses in different places for use in his incessant riding on his loyal business. He was captured three times by rebels, the third time at Valley Forge on his return from Philadelphia in March 1778. He was sentenced on the 25th to a month's hard labour and a fine of £50 "for the use of the sick in camp."[16] On his return to York he united his loyalist followers with those enlisted by Rankin.[17]

Galloway, reporting in June 1778 that there were loyalists in York and Lancaster ready and eager to be embodied in armed forces, undoubtedly knew of Norris's and Rankin's plans. Clinton did not proceed much faster than Howe might have done. But during the winter of 1778–79 Clinton seems to have decided that Norris and Fürstner were excellent messengers, Sower the authorized agent of the united association, and Rankin its actual head.

Rankin, an influential landowner in York, a justice of the court of common pleas and quarter sessions, a representative of his county in the Pennsylvania assembly under the new constitution of 1776, had been a Whig before the Declaration.[18] But, by his own account, "as soon as he found the liberal offers of Great Britain were rejected and that independence was the grand object of Congress, from a sense of duty to his sovereign and love of his country [he] determined at every risk to endeavour to prevent a separation between the two countries. . . . With the approbation and at the request of the friends of government he continued in the command of his regiment of militia, because he might thereby not only have an opportunity of favouring the loyalists but also of rendering essential services to government. . . . In the year 1776 he was ordered by the committee of York to march out with the militia to lay waste the estates and seize the persons of a number of loyalists in the said county. He obeyed the orders in appearance, but in the execution of them pursued such measures as to prevent the intended effect." Instead of harming the loyalists, he began to organize them in 1778. "To each of these associators he administered an oath abjuring the Congress and the rebel states, of secrecy in regard to the association, of fidelity and allegiance to his Majesty, and of enlistment under their respective officers."[19] Though in March 1779 he had made only a beginning, it was a beginning such as Clinton could not disregard.

IV

December 1778 saw a mysterious transaction between Major General William Phillips, then with the Convention troops at Cambridge, and Horatio Gates, victor at Saratoga who had lately come to take command of the American forces at Boston. The two had been acquainted while Gates was still in the British service and had of course met again when Phillips became Gates's prisoner. Congress, resolved to move the Convention troops to Virginia for safe-keeping, had chosen Gates to be in charge of their departure from Massachusetts. When Gates arrived from Hartford and assumed his new command on November 7 or 8 he found Phillips pleased with the arrangement and went to Cambridge to call on him on the 13th.

On the 15th Phillips wrote Gates a letter proposing a new scheme for the settlement of the long quarrel over Burgoyne's surrendered army.[20] An exchange of prisoners on the usual terms might be difficult, since there were captive British officers of higher rank than any American officers held prisoners by the British. Why not fix money values on officers and men of all ranks? This would make it possible to work out equivalent cash totals without contention over the mere number of soldiers involved on either side. "I dare say," Phillips wrote, "you would be very glad to be a happy instrument in effecting any good purpose, and I am sure I should. And I think we might both be useful without committing ourselves to our superiors. . . . This is a public letter, a private letter, or no letter at all, as you shall make it." Phillips insisted, "upon the faith of an old acquaintance," that he had no concealed design in making his proposal.

By the 28th almost all the Convention troops had set out for Virginia, but Phillips remained behind for a few days longer. Within that time he wrote an undated letter enclosing a "private letter" which was "secret to all but my secretary." Phillips said of his private letter: "I most sincerely wish it may become useful. Let me know what you think of it and what you mean to do. . . . I give you my honour I venture this matter at my own instance. I have no doubt of my carrying it into execution on my part, and I really believe it will lay the foundation of a general exchange. It belongs to you. You made the treaty [Convention] and I am sure will be glad to assist in putting an end to all disputes."[21]

The private letter dated December 1, which Gates was to send to Congress if he thought it proper, proposed that "the troops under Convention, from Lieutenant General Burgoyne to the private soldiers included, be rendered back into the full activity of service in every part of the world under a cartel formed upon the plan of the treaty of cartel settled between General Conway and the Marquis de Barail at the beginning of the last war; and that a ransom should be paid by me in specie for every officer and soldier of the troops of Convention according to values which may be settled on each rank by mutual agreement."[22] This would be better for the British, who could afford the ransom money, than to have the Convention troops interned in America, or even shipped back to Great Britain as the Convention had originally provided.

Phillips's confidential aide Lieutenant Campbell carried the letter proposing exchange by ransom to Gates on the evening of the 2nd. Gates the next day, acknowledging "your letters," said that the one "particularly relative to the general exchange of the troops of the Convention shall be sent with my other dispatches to Congress. To gratify your desires on a subject which would do you honour were your proposals published I have, in my own name, requested your letter may be considered as private."[23] Gates's letter that same day to Congress said he had informed Phillips that the request would be made. Gates did not, he told Congress, think that Phillips was "in earnest. But, whatever his views may be, I cannot presume to negotiate with our friends, or our foes, unless I be authorized by those who legally represent the Confederation, of which I never will forget that as an individual I am but one member."[24]

But Gates, sending Phillips's private letter to Congress, did not mention the unwritten answer which it appears he sent back by Lieutenant Campbell on the 3rd. What this answer was is indicated by Phillips's reply later in the day. Gates could be assured, Phillips wrote, that the private letter of the 1st would not go beyond his secretary. "You have opened on the matter with Lieutenant Campbell, of which I am perfectly satisfied, as he is an officer of trust. He informs me that you mean to collect the heads of my letter for the perusal of some members of the American Congress who are your friends, and it is to be so done as not to render my letter public or endanger my situation. And this is perfectly what I wish."[25] Phillips understood that Gates was not only to send the proposal for exchange by ransom to the president of Congress but was also to take the matter up privately with certain friendly members.

A letter from Phillips to Clinton of December 8 seems to offer an unpleasant explanation of the intricate affair. Ransoming the Convention troops, Phillips admitted, would cost money but would probably cost less than sending them back to England and bringing others over in their place. "The plan in general of whatever will be done will in course, if put into execution, be public, but for some particular parts of the plan I refer you to my most secret letter." This was enclosed with a copy of the private letter to Gates of the 1st, or Gates's written answer of the 3rd, and Phillips's reply on the 3rd commenting on Gates's oral message by Campbell. The most secret letter to Clinton had to do with another "part of the transaction" which was for Clinton alone.

"Supposing," Phillips wrote, "I can persuade a certain person to use his interest to forward a negotiation for a general release of the troops of the Convention by ransom, and that a negotiation takes place, I am to make an acknowledgment of 2000 guineas. Supposing upon a negotiation that a general release of the troops of Convention takes place, I am then to make an acknowledgment in value of 6000 guineas.

"I have bound myself under the strictest secrecy never to disclose the name or person to whom I thus engage. I have in the most sacred manner pledged my honour upon it, which I shall most inviolably keep. It is understood to mean in all descriptions of secrecy, so that the fact as well as the person must remain unknown. I have given my positive promise for this for myself and for you.

"It now remains with you, Sir, to determine upon the propriety of this matter as I have stated it. Shall I close in with this offer or must I desist? I desire your orders."

There can be no doubt that this generous "acknowledgment" was a part of the ransom transaction. There can be no doubt that the ransom transaction was between Phillips and Gates. There seems to be no doubt that the "certain person" had himself made the "offer" of his influence to Phillips. If the documents in the case do not mean that Phillips was trying to get 8000 guineas for himself on the pretence of using them for a bribe, they mean that when Phillips proposed his scheme to ransom the prisoners Gates proposed to further the scheme, privately, for a secret reward to be paid by the British for services desirable and valuable to them.

It is difficult to see the episode as less than double-dealing on Gates's part. Though he may have disapproved of Congress's handling of the Convention problem, he was sworn to carry out the orders of Congress and he knew Congress believed that the release of the prisoners would directly or indirectly augment the enemy. He knew himself that it would. He might, of course, have held that the prisoners ought in honour to be allowed the free passage to England which his Convention had granted them. But to allow them to be ransomed was in no sense to fulfil that contract. Gates, if he did encourage this different scheme for their release, was not being punctilious. He was simply willing to ask and take money from the British for helping them win a point over the Americans.

As with so many of the secret plans of these divided years, this one seems to have come to nothing. There is no evidence that Gates sent any private letters to members of Congress or that Clinton ever authorized Phillips to go on with the transaction. Phillips set out from Cambridge on the 13th for Virginia. Congress refused him permission to stop in New York, where he might have conferred with Clinton.[26] The two did not meet till Phillips came back on parole in November. If they ever discussed the scheme for making use of Gates's influence, at least they left no written record of it in the Headquarters papers.

V

Clinton's correspondence during the winter of 1778–79 was full of proposals by or about the loyalists. Germain on September 2 wrote that the king intended to provide for worthy refugees from the rebel provinces by setting aside a tract of land between the Penobscot and the St. Croix and there erecting a new government where each refugee might be granted as much land as he had lost, up to 1000 acres, free of quitrent for ten years. The loyal settlers already there were not to be disturbed.[27] James Chalmers, colonel of the Maryland Loyalists, on the 15th presented a scheme for establishing a loyal refuge between the Delaware and the Chesapeake. Provincial troops from this peninsula could "annoy the most fertile district in the Jerseys and destroy the piratical inlets of Egg Harbor etc., and more especially render useless to Congress the eastern shores of Virginia and Maryland. A government worthy of Great Britain might be established for 175 or 180,000 people possessed of 10,000 or 11,000 square miles of country which at this time might be rendered extremely valuable to Great Britain: a government forming a happy political contrast to the despotic sway of the rebels. A pleasant asylum might here be formed for the friends of government now supported by the king, it is said at considerable expense." Chalmers was sure the enterprise would be easy and successful.[28]

Vermont seemed another possibility. On December 24 Clinton wrote to Eden enclosing an undated letter "from a friend" about the situation of the Hampshire grants. The friend believed that

Ethan Allen, "a man of infamous character" who had been chosen governor of Vermont, might "be easily tempted to throw off any dependence on the tyranny of the Congress and made useful to government by giving him and his adherents the property of all the lands appropriated [granted] to rebels and making that country a separate government dependent on the Crown and the laws of Great Britain. This would not only attach the present riotous crew at present but draw to them numbers from the rebels which would weaken them and make their present expiring rebellion desperate."[29] Eden possibly turned the suggestion over to Germain, who on March 3 wrote to Clinton: "The separation of the inhabitants of the country they call Verdmont from the province in which it was formerly included, is a circumstance of which I should hope much advantage might be made by discreet management. I see no objection to your giving them reason to expect his Majesty will erect their country into a separate province and confirm every occupant that shall give proof of his return to his duty in the possession of the ungranted lands he occupies. . . . I shall therefore only add upon this subject that the restoring that country to the king's obedience would be considered as a very important service, and that I am commanded by his Majesty to recommend it to your attention."[30] The king, ordinarily so firm for strict procedure, was in this emergency willing to support loyal Vermonters in their squatters' rights.

Suggestions came to Clinton from William Franklin, who Tryon thought ought to be placed "in a respectable point of view in contrast to his father's principles and employ."[31] As the rebels had the philosopher, the royal government should make conspicuous use of his son the governor. On November 19 William Franklin through Eden offered Clinton the service of two loyalist writers who had been employed by Howe, did not expect more than £50 a year apiece, and could "keep the paper full of decent, well-meant essays." They were the Rev. Samuel Seabury, a refugee from Connecticut, and the Rev. Jonathan Odell from New Jersey.[32] On January 9 Franklin sent Clinton a plan for "distressing the rebels" by organizing the refugees in companies of 50 each who should choose their own officers and obey the rules of the British army, "military punishment excepted." The association would be managed by subscribers—not named by Franklin—who were to be, in effect, a joint stock company for plunder. "Each subscriber shall have a voice in the election of an agent in whose hands whatever shall be taken by us or any of us shall be deposited in order for him to sell and dispose of in the best manner for the use of us the subscribers." They were in no case to distress friends of government, and were to promise payment for any necessaries that might have to be taken from them. Tryon strongly recommended that Franklin be made head of these Associated Loyalists, as he later was.[33] By a coincidence the British treasury, allowing Franklin £500 a year, fixed on January 9 as the day from which his allowance should be paid.[34]

Franklin's scheme for plunder had to do with retaliation for property plundered (confiscated) from the loyalists by the rebels. On March 27 the more violent John Mason of New York proposed retaliation for loyalist lives lost or threatened. A Warning to Rebels, of which a manuscript copy came to Clinton, was Mason's private proclamation. He warned the rebels not to harm the loyalists then in jail in Poughkeepsie, Goshen, Sussex, and Morristown. "We loyalists do solemnly declare that we will hang six for one, which shall be inflicted on your head men and leaders. And wherever we loyal refugees finds militiamen in arms against us or against any of his Majesty's loyal subjects, we are fully determined to massacre them on the spot. We embody not with the British army but keeps by ourselves in full companies, chooses our own officers. . . . There is some thousand of us from all the provinces on the continent." Now at last they meant to have full revenge for what they had suffered. Mason, a ruffian who a year or so later was under arrest by the British for "inadvertingly plundering some invetrite enemies to government," of course got no countenance from Clinton. But here is a reminder that the loyalists were by no means all high-minded gentlemen afflicted and overwhelmed by rebel riffraff.[35]

Arnold

6

Whirlwind Soldier

BY MAY 1779, when Benedict Arnold made his first overtures to Sir Henry Clinton, the contemporary methods of treachery had all been tried, even standardized, and there was nothing new either in Arnold's offer or in Clinton's reply. Arnold was not the first renegade, as he was not the last. If he stands in history as the supreme and classic traitor of the Revolution, remembered when others are forgotten, it is only because he was the most conspicuous and dangerous of them all, laid the most skilful and most sinister plot, failed with the most tragic consequences, and left behind him the fullest records: the bulk now for the first time revealed to the world.

The secret processes by which he changed from a fearless, tireless, stormy, ardent patriot to a calculating friend of the British government are hard to follow. His situation forced him to be intensely guarded before his treason was found out, and encouraged him afterwards to justify his behaviour with arguments intended to prove to the British that at heart he had never been a rebel. These later arguments contain some incidental information, and must be used. But Arnold was so unscrupulous, or so self-deceived, in his apologetics that his facts as well as his excuses must be tested at every point. Traitors, whether successful or unsuccessful, seldom tell the simple truth. There seldom is any simple truth in treason.

The clearest statement Arnold ever made about his conduct and motives was in a letter he wrote in London on July 18, 1784 to George Johnstone.[1] This was of course nearly four years after the failure of Arnold's plot had brought him utter dishonour in America and little compensating honour in England. The day before the letter Arnold had talked with Johnstone, recently chosen a director of the East India Company. It may have occurred to Arnold that

Johnstone, accused of offering a bribe to an American in 1778, might be considerate toward an American convicted of accepting one in 1780. Johnstone, when Arnold said he too would like a post with the Company, asked for a written account of the Arnold affair which might—presumably—be shown to the other directors. Arnold, sending a copy of his printed self-vindication, added some details found nowhere else.

"My sentiments respecting the war," he wrote, "were well known to Colonel Philip Skene and several other British officers to whom I declared that my only object was to obtain a redress of grievances; and at the same time I disclaimed any idea of independence or a separation from Great Britain. These, Sir, were invariably my sentiments during every period of the war. Nor did I consent to join the British army until I had received the most unequivocal and positive assurances from Sir Henry Clinton that Great Britain had given up every idea of taxing America; that she wished to extend her every right and privilege which she enjoyed before the war; and in return only expected her to acknowledge the sovereignty of Great Britain."

So far as Clinton is concerned Arnold's statement was false. It was Arnold not Clinton who opened the negotiations, and Arnold —as will appear in their correspondence—offered his services without any mention of British taxes and American rights. As to Skene, Arnold met him in 1774,[2] probably on a trading trip between New Haven and Montreal; and he may have talked with him again after Saratoga if Skene, during the few days before he left for Cambridge, was allowed to call on Arnold in the Albany hospital. As to the several other British officers to whom Arnold said he had made known his sentiments, not a confirming word from any of them, any more than from Skene, has come to light.

Johnstone's reply to Arnold three days later analysed Arnold's predicament. While Johnstone, he said, himself thought highly of Arnold's conduct, others might not agree. "The explanations are so interwoven with a complicated detail of circumstances that the great vulgar herd will always be divided in opinion upon them." Only gentlemen and scholars, Johnstone implied, could comprehend this treason. "Under an unsuccessful insurrection all actors are rebels. Crowned with success they become immortal patriots.

A fortunate plot holds you up as a saviour of nations; a premature discovery brings you to the scaffold or brands your fame with dark and doubtful suspicions. My Lord Falkland and General Monk are instances where we may view the best men from the best motives obliged to change sides. It is inglorious in a great mind, who has taken a leading part, to retire until the scene is settled; and in the multiplied difficulties in which the most virtuous may be environed, he must trust his conscience for the rectitude of his conduct and appeal to the honour of his life to prove that the general good was his motive." Johnstone was pointing out, politely but cynically, that Arnold had not succeeded, and so must look to his virtue for his reward. "Although I am satisfied of the purity of your motive, the generality did not think so. While in this case no power in this country could suddenly place you in the situation you aim at under the East India Company."

II

Analysis cannot do justice to Arnold's story. It must be narrated through its zigzag course during the four years before it took its dark turn underground to treachery and catastrophe.

Great-grandson of a Benedict Arnold who had been governor of Rhode Island, the most famous of the many Benedict Arnolds was born in Norwich, Connecticut, on January 14, 1741. Apprenticed at fourteen to a firm of druggists (cousins to his mother), the boy ran away in March 1758 to enlist in a New York company raised against the French, was advertised as a deserter in May 1759, enlisted in another company in March 1760, served for a short term that took him to Albany and the northern lakes,[3] returned to Norwich, and completed his apprenticeship. Since both his pious mother and his respectable but alcoholic father were now dead, Dr. Arnold—as he was then usually called—sold the Norwich homestead for £700 and moved with his sister Hannah to New Haven where he opened a shop for the sale of drugs and books. Rapidly prospering as a merchant, he bought ships and sailed them himself to the West Indies, to which he carried horses, mules, cattle, and provisions. He traded also, particularly for horses, in Quebec and Montreal. Margaret Mansfield, whom he married in 1767 and who had three sons in five years, was a daughter of the high sheriff of the county. Though Arnold was unquestionably a smuggler like many colonial merchants, was more given to grandiose speculation than to solid enterprises, and wrangled with his creditors, he stood well with the less conservative elements in New Haven, had a handsome house in Water Street, and in December 1774 was elected captain of a militia company.

His recorded early comments on public matters were infrequent and elementary. When he heard of the affray of March 1770 known as the Boston Massacre he wrote in June from the West Indies where the news had reached him: "I was very much shocked the other day on hearing the accounts of the most wanton, cruel, and inhuman murders committed in Boston by the soldiers. Good God, are the Americans all asleep, and tamely yielding up their liberties, or are they all turned philosophers, that they do not take immediate vengeance on such miscreants?"[4] John Adams and James Otis, who were on the ground, were willing to defend the accused British soldiers when they were tried. Arnold at a distance was headlong for an instinctive verdict and an immediate vengeance. With the same promptness, as soon as he heard of Lexington he assembled his New Haven company, forced the reluctant selectmen to give them ammunition, and marched off to Cambridge. Before they left, Arnold and the company signed an agreement disavowing "every thought of rebellion to his Majesty as supreme head of the British Empire, or opposition to legal authority." Nothing less than the "last necessity," they declared, had obliged them "to have recourse to arms in defence of our lives and liberties," and only the "suddenness of the occasion" had deprived them of "that legal authority the dictates of which we ever with pleasure obey."[5]

At Cambridge Arnold at once proposed to the Massachusetts committee of safety that a force be sent to capture Fort Ticonderoga and Skenesborough. This would block a British advance by the lakes and would supply the rebels with artillery they much needed in their siege of Boston. On May 3 he was made a Massachusetts colonel and instructed to go at once to "the western parts of this and the neighbouring colonies" and there raise not over 400 men for an attempt on Ticonderoga.[6] As if in prophetic irony his instructions were signed by Benjamin Church, chairman of the committee of safety, who was regularly sending Gage in Boston the innermost secrets of the rebels.

When Arnold with his instructions and an orderly arrived at Castleton on the 9th he ran into a tangle of ambitions and jurisdictions.[7] Connecticut had already sent a committee with £300 and a handful of volunteers on the same errand, and the Berkshire district of Massachusetts a larger number of militiamen. But Castleton was in Vermont which, though it then had no recognized separate government, had contributed three times as many Green Mountain Boys led by Ethan Allen. Arnold, with the most authoritative instructions, had no force to back him. Allen was not a man to yield to a paper authority, and his followers threatened to go home if he were superseded. The Connecticut committee, improvising instructions, put Allen in command.

"I have the inexpressible satisfaction," Allen reported on the 11th, "to acquaint you that at daybreak of the 10th instant, pursuant to my directions from sundry leading gentlemen of Massachusetts Bay and Connecticut, I took the fortress of Ticonderoga with about 130 Green Mountain Boys. Colonel [James] Easton with about 47 valiant soldiers [from Massachusetts] distinguished themselves in the action. Colonel Arnold entered the fortress with me side by side." As Ticonderoga was in New York, where the Connecticut, Massachusetts, and Vermont troops had no legal right to go at all, this report of Allen's was made to the authorities at Albany and brought in further complications.

Outnumbered and overshadowed in a venture which had promised to be glorious primarily for him, Arnold that same day reported to the Massachusetts committee of safety that Allen, "finding he had the ascendancy over his people, positively insisted I should have no command, as I had forbid the soldiers plundering and destroying private property." But on the 14th Arnold had raised about 100 men under his own commission and had seized a small schooner which was the private property of Philip Skene. Having the advantage of being a sailor as well as a soldier, Arnold took a force down the Champlain to St. John's beyond the Canadian end of the lake, where on the 18th they captured a small British garrison, an armed sloop and some bateaux, and military stores. This made Arnold, who returned to Crown Point, in effect commander on water though not on land. By the 29th Allen had given up the contest and the Vermonters had most of them gone back to their farms.[8]

There were fresh complications. The Continental Congress, hearing in Philadelphia that "several inhabitants of the northern colonies" had taken Ticonderoga and Crown Point, earnestly recommended that the cannon be moved to Fort George which might be strongly fortified against an expected British attack from Canada. Massachusetts, which had sent Arnold for the Ticonderoga artillery, thought proper to ask Connecticut's permission to transport it. Connecticut consulted New York, which claimed title to the captured guns. (They did not reach Boston till the following February.) New York, slower than Massachusetts and Connecticut in taking action on the lakes, found itself joined with troops from both those colonies in a common but not congenial defence. On June 1 Massachusetts instructed Arnold to continue in command till further notice; then on the 14th instructed a committee to go to Ticonderoga and put the Massachusetts forces under the command of a chief officer from Connecticut. They were to make themselves "fully acquainted with the spirit, capacity, and conduct of the said Arnold," and if he objected to the change might discharge him and direct him to return and render his accounts.[9]

Arnold, the committee reported, "seemed greatly disconcerted and declared he would not be second in command to any person whomsoever."[10] In a refusal written on the 24th he said that Massachusetts was plainly "dubious of my rectitude or abilities, which is sufficient inducement for me to decline serving them longer." He considered that the change of leaders was "a most disgraceful reflection" on both himself and his troops. Moreover, he had not been sent the money promised him and had had to advance £100 in cash and stake his private credit for more.[11]

The majority of his men accepted the transfer, but some of them sympathized with him to the point of mutiny. The Massachusetts committee thought "the particulars of it too tedious and disagreeable" to report. A Connecticut committeeman, writing to Governor Trumbull, was more explicit. Arnold and his sympathetic minority took to the British sloop and Skene's schooner lying off Crown Point and threatened, the committees understood, "to go to

St. John's and deliver the vessels" to the British. There is no other evidence that this threat was in earnest, if it was made. Peacemakers from Massachusetts, Connecticut, and New York conferred with the mutineers. "We got on board the vessels about eleven o'clock in the morning, and he confined three of us on board each vessel; men sat over us with fixed bayonets, and so kept us till sometime in the evening. . . . We reasoned with the people on board the vessels all the while we were there and convinced some of them of their error, who declared they had been deceived by Colonel Arnold."[12]

Arnold, naturally resentful at being sacrificed for political reasons, emerged from the angry episode with the reputation of a good soldier but a difficult servant of the public. His wife had died while he was on the lakes, his private affairs had suffered. Leaving Crown Point on July 5, to return by way of Albany and New Haven to Cambridge at the end of the month, he found the Massachusetts legislature at Watertown suspicious of his accounts. In the hurry and squabble of the campaign the orders and vouchers had not been kept with ledger regularity. It does not appear that Arnold had been more high-handed with public money than with his own. Though he was fond of money, he wanted it to spend not to hoard. If he had been able to avoid the unavoidable turmoil on the lakes, and to rouse no animosities, he might have been held less strictly accountable. As matters stood, a committee headed by Benjamin Church scrutinized Arnold's orders and vouchers throughout August and the legislature paid the charges in cautious instalments.

In November, after Church had been detected and arrested, and Arnold had gone on his march to Quebec, the committee reported that Arnold had received the payroll for one of his companies but had not turned it over to the captain. Since the captain and his men were said to be in "great want of their money," it was paid again and Washington was notified in order that Arnold might be charged with the amount: £36 5s 5d.[13] For Arnold was now in the Continental service. Congress, which made him a brigadier general on January 10, 1776, on the 22nd allowed him $819 as the belated balance due for his Ticonderoga-Crown Point expenses and ordered that it be paid to Silas Deane. Deane, member of Congress from Connecticut and Arnold's friend, sent the money to Arnold's sister

Hannan, who after the death of his wife cared for his children and his business.

This first chapter of Arnold's Revolutionary history was an epitome of the whole. As a soldier he was original and audacious, quick in forming plans, quick in putting them into vigorous execution. He led his soldiers, not drove them, and won and held the devotion of the rank and file. He had a gift for command when the objective was clear and his imperious will could be fully bent upon it. He could carry out orders when he was assigned to a particular effort on his own responsibility. If Washington had been commander-in-chief of the Continental army and Schuyler in charge of the northern department when Arnold left Cambridge for Ticonderoga, and if he had had their definite instructions, he might have triumphed and remained there as general and commodore of the lakes. But in the conflict of instructions and of officers of rank equal or nearly equal with his, Arnold was restive and arrogant. He could not turn philosopher and patiently endure small irritations day by day. He was passionate and personal in almost all his judgments. Whoever doubted that Arnold should have his way was a fool and an enemy. Arnold knew he was a better soldier than any other at Ticonderoga or Crown Point. "Colonel Allen is a proper man to head his own wild people," Arnold wrote, "but entirely unacquainted with military service."[14] This was a military expedition, not a raid of freebooters. At the same time, Arnold was a whirlwind hero who could not be bothered with keeping track of small expenses. Spend what had to be spent, and figure the amount up later. Let civilians supply what soldiers needed. Here Arnold was bound to be at odds with civilian auditors. If he was reckless with public money, might he not be keeping some of it for himself? As long as Arnold served in the Continental army quarrels went with him and unsettled accounts trailed after him.

III

Congress, changing its mind about the forts on Champlain, decided not only to hold them but also to send an expedition by way of the lake against Montreal. It was led by Brigadier General Richard Montgomery, formerly a captain in the British army but now ardent for the liberties of America. Another expedition was to go up the Kennebec, through the wilderness, and down the Chaudière to Quebec. Washington gave the command of this to Colonel Arnold, who in September 1775 set out from Cambridge on the fabulous march which brought his little army to the St. Lawrence on November 11. Montgomery, who captured Montreal the next day, joined Arnold in a desperate, unsuccessful assault on Quebec on December 31 in which Arnold was wounded in the left knee and Montgomery was killed.

"I have no thoughts of leaving this proud town," Arnold wrote lying on his back a week later, "till I first enter it in triumph." Five weeks after that he learned of his promotion to the rank of brigadier general, and at once asked Congress to relieve him of his heavy duties in managing the accounts of the expedition.[15] No relief came, and early in April Arnold had to give up the command before Quebec to Brigadier General David Wooster of New Haven, who was Arnold's senior, and take an inferior command at Montreal. The incompetent Wooster was superseded within a month by Major General John Thomas, sent from Cambridge, who died of smallpox on June 2. Before that, the siege of Quebec by the hungry, sick, demoralized Americans had been broken by the arrival in May of strong British reinforcements from England and the headless rout of the rebels. Arnold hoped to have the chief command, but Washington thought Arnold's "little tincture of vanity" and "over-desire of being popular" made him less suitable than Sullivan.[16] Arnold was in charge of the disorderly retreat from Montreal to Champlain, and he was, on June 17, the last American to leave Canadian soil, in sight of the pursuing enemy.[17]

The expedition having failed, the rebels faced a counter-invasion led by Sir Guy Carleton who commanded the forces in Canada. Schuyler, commanding the northern department at Albany, and Gates, who had left Boston for Ticonderoga, put Arnold in charge of the defence on Champlain. Since there were no roads by which an army could march through the heavy forest on either side of the lake, Carleton had to come by water. Drawing on the powerful British squadron on the St. Lawrence, he ascended the Richelieu to the rapids, took a ship and two schooners apart, transported them to St. John's, and made preparations for a formidable advance. Arnold lacked money, materials, skilled workmen (though ship carpenters came from Philadelphia), and trained sailors. But with immense and contagious energy he got together a rough flotilla which engaged the British at Valcour island on October 11. There and in engagements on the two following days he sacrificed his fleet, but he damaged the British. Carleton stopped at Crown Point, decided not to venture against Gates at Ticonderoga, and in November retired to Canada for the winter. Arnold's desperate effort helped give the Americans another year to get ready for the invasion of 1777 which ended in the surrender of Burgoyne—and France's recognition of American independence.

Arnold, who afterwards claimed he had been opposed to the Declaration, only once mentioned it in his surviving letters of that year. When Gates on September 12 directed him to send a copy of the "Act of Independence" whenever he sent a flag to the enemy, Arnold on the 15th replied: "The Act of Independence I will send, agreeable to your directions."[18] The Declaration was first read to the troops at Ticonderoga, "immediately after divine worship," on July 28. Arnold was then at Skenesborough and may have heard nothing till he returned to Ticonderoga the next day. Gates, writing to Congress on the 29th, said his army had received the news of independence with applause but said of Arnold merely that he was "ever active and anxious to serve his country."[19] On October 7 Arnold, writing to Gates from Valcour, showed no decline in his ardour for the patriot cause. The recent evacuation of New York must have been faint-hearted, Arnold declared. "Is it possible my countrymen can be callous to their wrongs or hesitate one moment between slavery and death? What advantage can we derive by blockading the enemy when they are in possession of a part of the country sufficient to support them? It appears to me coercive measures should be adopted." But he did not wish to judge too rashly. "That Being in Whose hands are all human events will doubtless turn the scale in favour of the just and oppressed."[20]

The nearest Arnold came to politics this year was in a letter he wrote to Gates the day before the Valcour fight. "If you have read Price's pamphlet sent you by Mr. Franklin, I will take the loan of it a favour." This was Richard Price's *Observations on Civil Liberty,* an English defence of the Americans and their conduct.

Arnold must have meant to examine its political arguments.[21]

Throughout 1776 Arnold was on good terms with Schuyler and Gates, but he had sharp clashes with three officers of lower rank. Captain Jacobus Wynkoop had in May been ordered by Schuyler, under direction of Congress, to take charge of the lake fleet as temporary commodore. He was at Crown Point, on the schooner *Royal Savage*, when Arnold arrived late at night on August 15 with Gates's orders to take command. Wynkoop insisted that he had not "received any intimation of being superseded"; Arnold that "I acquainted you some time since." Arnold on the afternoon of the 17th heard an enemy party was approaching and ordered two schooners to go down the lake to investigate. Wynkoop, who had not been told of this, saw them making sail and suspiciously feared "that some design had been formed by the captains of the schooners or their crews to go over to the enemy." He halted them by firing a gun, learned they had Arnold's orders, and sent Arnold a note saying: "I know no orders but what shall be given out by me." Arnold, "a little feverish" with malaria and in no mood to argue in the face of possible danger, answered: "You surely must be out of your senses to say no orders shall be obeyed but yours." If Wynkoop did not immediately obey he would be immediately arrested. Arnold, storming, followed his letter on board the *Royal Savage*. Wynkoop, though he ordered the schooners on their errand, still held that only Congress could place another officer over him, and he was "resolved to go under command of no man."

Gates of course supported Arnold and directed him to send the insubordinate Wynkoop under arrest to Ticonderoga. "A little of the dictatorial power was exerted," Gates admitted to Congress, "but perhaps it was never more necessary than on that occasion." When Arnold sent Wynkoop on the 19th to Ticonderoga it was with a generous letter to Gates. "I believe the Commodore was really of opinion that neither of us had the authority to command him. He now seems convinced to the contrary and sorry for his disobedience of orders. If it can be done with propriety, I wish he may be permitted to return home without being cashiered." Gates agreed to give Wynkoop a pass to go at liberty to Albany, but not to return.[22]

Though Arnold was brusque in the Wynkoop matter he was

right and just, and there were no lasting consequences. His clashes with Colonel Moses Hazen and Lieutenant Colonel John Brown were confused and chronic. Hazen, a New Hampshire man living in Canada when the war broke out, seemed to be first a loyalist, then a patriot, and for a time was suspected by both sides. But he joined Montgomery in the attack on Quebec and remained with the Americans. Arnold charged that in the retreat from Canada Hazen was so negligent of stores bought or seized in Montreal that they were plundered by the soldiers and wasted.[23] But when, late in July, Hazen was tried on Arnold's charges, the members of the court martial at Ticonderoga evidently believed that Arnold himself had benefited from the plunder. They refused to hear the testimony of his chief witness, on the ground that he was "interested in the event" of the trial—as Arnold's agent in the transaction.

Arnold in a written protest called the court's action "unprecedented and, I think, unjust." These words were temperate enough, but according to the president of the court "the whole of the General's conduct during the trial was marked with contempt and disrespect." The court, possibly prejudiced and certainly irritated, called the protest "illegal, illiberal, and ungentlemanlike" and informed Arnold that "nothing but an open acknowledgment of your error will be conceived as satisfactory." At the last word Arnold flamed up. They had made, he wrote on August 1, "ungenteel and indecent reflections on a superior officer." Let Congress decide between them as to the justice of their decision. As to their reproach: "This I can assure you, I shall ever, in public or private, be ready to support the character of a man of honour; and as your very nice and delicate honour in your apprehension is injured, you may depend, as soon as this disagreeable service is at an end (which God grant may soon be the case) I will by no means withhold from any gentleman of the court the satisfaction his nice honour may require." At this hint of duels to come the court acquitted Hazen with honour and ordered Arnold to be put under arrest.[24]

Gates, commenting on the trial in his report to Congress, admitted that "the warmth of General Arnold's temper might possibly lead him a little farther than is marked by the precise line of decorum to be observed before and towards a court martial. Seeing and knowing all circumstances, I am convinced if there was a fault on one side there was too much acrimony on the other. Here again I was obliged to act dictatorially and dissolve the court martial. . . . The United States must not be deprived of that excellent officer's services at this important moment." Though he was required to send the proceedings of the court martial to Congress Gates felt sure the members "will view whatever is whispered against General Arnold as the foul stream of that poisonous fountain, detraction."[25] But Arnold on September 7 had heard that "my character is much injured by a report prevailing in Philadelphia of my having sequestered the goods seized in Montreal. . . . I cannot but think it extremely cruel, when I have sacrificed my ease, health, and a great part of my private property in the cause of my country, to be calumniated as a robber and thief; at a time, too, when I have it not in my power to be heard in my own behalf."[26]

John Brown was an early and persevering source of the Philadelphia report. He had studied law in Providence with Arnold's cousin Oliver Arnold (Brown's brother-in-law), served with the Berkshire company at the capture of Ticonderoga and carried the news to Congress, ventured into Canada with Ethan Allen and (after Allen's capture by the British) gone with Montgomery to the siege of Quebec. Distrustful of Arnold from the first, Brown had quarrelled with him when after Montgomery's death Arnold refused to promote Brown (then a major) as Montgomery had promised to do. The reason for this refusal, Arnold explained to Congress in a letter of February 1, was that Montgomery though he had made the promise had decided to withhold promotion when Brown was "publicly impeached for plundering the [British] officers' baggage taken at Sorel, contrary to articles of capitulation and to the great scandal of the American army." Brown, indignantly and persistently denying that he was guilty of this "worst and blackest of crimes," applied in turn to Arnold, Wooster, and Schuyler for a court of inquiry, but in each case was put off. In June he petitioned Congress, which in July commissioned him lieutenant colonel and requested Schuyler to order the court. Schuyler regretfully passed the order on to Gates in August. Brown on September 3 filed a complaint with Gates at Ticonderoga, saying Arnold's accusations were "false, scandalous, and malicious" and demanding that the accuser be brought to trial. Gates thought "a man of honour in an exalted station" would "ever excite envy in the mean and undeserving," and postponed action week after week while Arnold prepared his navy, met the British, and waited for them to withdraw to Canada.[27]

At Valcour Arnold lost, he said, "all my papers" when the *Royal Savage* was burned. The next day he sent what he called "all my public and private papers and accounts, with a considerable sum of hard money" to Schuyler at Saratoga for safe-keeping. After the retreat of Carleton in November Arnold, no longer needed on the lakes, went by way of Saratoga to Albany where on the 27th he was "anxious, after his very long absence, to see his family and settle his public accounts."[28] But the hero of Champlain was still implacably dogged by Brown and Hazen, who attacked again at Albany.

Brown, referred by Gates to the board of war, on December 1 furiously summed up the history of his affair. "I have been led," he wrote to Gates, "an expensive dance from generals to Congress and from Congress to generals." He now brought thirteen charges against Arnold, several of them preposterous, none of them proved though Brown said he was "ready to verify" them all. He repeated last year's story that when Arnold was superseded at Ticonderoga in May 1775 he planned "a treasonable attempt to make his escape . . . to the enemy." Gates sent Brown's charges back to Congress. On December 2 a board of inquiry sat to hear Hazen's special complaint. He produced a receipt on the back of which Arnold in June had charged in writing that Hazen had taken garrison brandy and tobacco for his private use and had disposed of garrison rum to a tavern-keeper. "Colonel Hazen can best tell how much he sold." The board after hearing both Hazen and Arnold were of the opinion that this sentence was "an aspersion of Colonel Hazen's character, and therefore think the complaint just." Hazen had won a second round with Arnold, and Brown though still officially unheard was not yet quieted.[29]

At once after the Hazen inquiry Arnold started south to Washington's army facing Howe in New Jersey, only to be sent off on the 23rd for Providence to aid Sullivan against Clinton, who had just taken Newport. Nathanael Greene, writing to Rhode Island, commended Arnold as "a fine, spirited fellow and an active general."[30] Connecticut praised and honoured him as he rode across his native state to visit his children at New Haven and on to Providence where he arrived on January 12. He had had no time to settle his public accounts, which were in fact never to be settled.

IV

Arnold was at once busy with plans to attack the British at Newport. Needing reinforcements, he went about the middle of February to Boston to try to get four or five battalions from Massachusetts. On his journey he fell in with his old friend John Lamb, whom Montgomery had found "turbulent and troublesome" in Canada but who by his bravery and wounds at Quebec had won Arnold's regard. Lamb, now a colonel, was short of funds for the regiment of artillery he had been commissioned to raise. Arnold open-handedly advanced him £1000, in the form of an order on Hannah Arnold who furnished the money "with alacrity."[31] It was characteristic of Arnold to lend the money in such hard times, and to have it to lend so soon after he declared he had sacrificed a great part of his property in the service of his country.

In Boston, as later in Philadelphia, Arnold seems to have been friendly with loyalists. He was particularly attracted by Elizabeth Deblois whose father had fled to Halifax.[32] Arnold, a downright suitor, sent "the heavenly Miss Deblois" through a friend a "trunk of gowns, etc." which he hoped she would "make no objection to receiving." No matter how downright he was, Arnold can hardly have attempted such a present in his character of merchant; more likely in his character of smuggler or captor of enemy loot. He was a soldier rather than a man of taste. Betsy Deblois seems to have rejected the unimaginative offer.

Having failed to win the help of Massachusetts in the projected offensive, Arnold at Providence on March 10 received a letter from Washington that brought bitter news. Congress, then sitting at Baltimore, after a week of "perplexed, inconclusive, and irksome debate," had promoted five officers, all of them Arnold's juniors in the service and his inferiors in ability, to the rank of major general. This was without consultation with Washington, who was left to read about it in the newspapers. He thought there must be some mistake and wrote to Arnold on March 3 to beg him not to "take any hasty steps in consequence of it" before the error had a chance to be righted. "My endeavours to that end," Washington said, "shall not be wanting." On the 6th, before Arnold had received this letter, Washington wrote privately to Richard Henry Lee to ask whether it was "owing to accident or design" that Congress had slighted the senior brigadier. Washington, who did not want to lose Arnold, took it for granted he would resign. When Washington later heard that because Connecticut had already two major generals Congress had decided against appointing a third from that state, he wrote to Arnold that this seemed "a strange mode of reasoning," but pointed out that it did not necessarily imply "want of merit in you."[33]

Arnold's first reply, on March 11, said he viewed the action of Congress as "a very civil way of requesting my resignation, as unqualified for the office I hold. My commission was conferred unsolicited, received with pleasure only as a means of serving my country. With equal pleasure I resign it when I can no longer serve my country with honour. The person who, void of the nice feelings of honour, will tamely condescend to give up his rights, and hold a commission at the expense of his reputation, I hold as a disgrace to the army and unworthy of the glorious cause in which we are engaged. . . . In justice, therefore, to my own character and for the satisfaction of my friends, I must request a court of inquiry into my conduct. And though I sensibly feel the ingratitude of my countrymen, every personal injury shall be buried in my zeal for the safety and happiness of my country, in whose cause I have repeatedly fought and bled and am ready at all times to resign my life." But he would, he promised Washington, avoid any hasty step "that may tend to injure my country." On the 26th Arnold thought he could soon leave Providence "without any damage to the public interest. When that is the case I will wait on your Excellency, not doubting my request will be granted and that I shall be able to acquit myself of every charge malice or envy can bring against me."[34]

A month later in New Haven he heard that General Tryon had come from New York by Long Island Sound to Connecticut in a powerful raid aimed at the rebel stores at Danbury. Feebly defended, the stores and part of the town were burned. But as in the retreat from Lexington, the British on their way back from Danbury to the Sound were plagued by the rebels. Arnold, hurrying from New Haven, threw up a barricade at Ridgefield where on the 27th he boldly resisted 2000 regulars with 500 half-trained militiamen. Though the British carried the position and got to the shore and away in spite of a damaging pursuit, Arnold was for Americans the hero of the episode. One of his horses was killed, another wounded. A bullet passed through the collar of his coat. He seemed invulnerable and magnificent. Congress could not overlook his exploit, and on May 2 made him a major general.

But just before or just after his heroic exploit he learned that the unrelenting John Brown had published a handbill at Pittsfield on April 12 which renewed the long attack on Arnold and ended with the words: "Money is this man's god, and to get enough of it he would sacrifice his country."[35] On May 12 Arnold was at Washington's Headquarters at Morristown, still "anxious to settle his public accounts, which are of considerable amount," Washington wrote that day to Congress. Washington hoped Congress would appoint a committee to settle them, investigate charges against Arnold, and confer with him on the matter of his rank. For though Arnold was now a major general, he ranked after the five former brigadiers who had been promoted and was "subject to be commanded by those who had been inferior to him."[36] Congress, doing Arnold belated justice, had not quite made up for the slight in February.

On the 20th, then in Philadelphia, he wrote Congress a letter enclosing Brown's handbill. Having made "every sacrifice of fortune, ease, and domestic happiness to serve my country," Arnold said, he had been accused of "crimes which if true ought to subject me to disgrace, infamy, and the just resentment of my countrymen. Conscious of the rectitude of my intentions, however I may have erred in judgment," he asked that "my conduct, and that of my accusers, may be inquired into, and justice done to the innocent and injured."[37]

Congress had to do something. It resolved the same day that Arnold be presented with a horse, "properly caparisoned," as a "token of their approbation of his gallant conduct in the action against the enemy in their late enterprise to Danbury." His letter and "such complaints as have been lodged against General Arnold" were referred to the board of war.[38] Richard Henry Lee, writing to Jefferson on the 20th, said an "audacious attempt" had been made to assassinate Arnold's character. John Adams on the 22nd wrote his wife: "I spent last evening at the war office with General Arnold. He has been basely slandered and libelled."[39] On the 23rd the board reported that they had had a conference with Arnold about the charges in the handbill; "that the general laid before the board a variety of original letters, orders, and other papers which, together with the general's account of his conduct confirmed by the relations of Mr. [Charles] Carroll, one of the late commissioners to Canada, now a member of this board, have given entire satisfaction to this board concerning the general's character and conduct so cruelly and groundlessly aspersed in the publication."[40]

But there were still sceptics about Arnold in Congress. His accounts were not settled, or even put on record. They presumably showed—what they showed three years later—that Congress had advanced him $66,671\frac{12}{90}$ for the Canada expedition, out of which more than $55,000 was not satisfactorily accounted for. Though Arnold may have turned it over, as he claimed, to officers and other persons for public use, there was not sufficient proof of this, and Arnold was still held accountable. However great the confusion of the campaign, this seemed a large discrepancy to be explained as the result of accidents and delays in book-keeping.

Howe was threatening Philadelphia, to keep Washington from moving troops north against Burgoyne. Arnold, appointed by Congress on June 14 to command the militia on the Delaware, acted with his usual spirit and won the enthusiastic admiration of his rank and file. When Howe withdrew the British forces later in the month, Arnold resumed his arguments with Congress. (In July Pierre Du Simitière did the "picture in black lead . . . form of a medal"[41] which is the only likeness of Arnold known to have been made from the life and probably the most lifelike.)

On July 11 he sent in his resignation, not because he loved his country less than before but because he cherished his honour as much as ever. "Honour is a sacrifice no man ought to make; as I received, so I wish to transmit it to posterity."[42] That same day

Le Général ARNOLD

deserté de l'Armeé des États-Unix

le 3 Octobre 1780.

BENEDICT ARNOLD IN 1777

Congress received a letter from Washington asking that Arnold be sent to command the northern militia under Schuyler. "He is active, judicious, and brave, and an officer in whom the militia will repose great confidence." Arnold, to whom Congress forwarded Washington's request and praise, asked that his resignation be suspended, and on the 18th was at Washington's Headquarters near the Hudson. Washington that day wrote to Schuyler that Arnold had generously waived "for the present all dispute about rank" and would not complain if the "good of the service" should require him to yield to St. Clair who had been promoted over Arnold's head.[43]

"No public or private injury or insult," Arnold wrote to Gates on August 5, "shall prevail on me to forsake the cause of my injured and oppressed country until I see peace and liberty restored to her, or nobly die in the attempt."[44] The next day Congress again took up the matter of Arnold's grievance on a motion to send him a new commission as major general, dated February 19, "on account of his extraordinary merit and former rank in the army."[45] After contentious debate the motion was put and lost on the 8th. New Hampshire, Rhode Island, Connecticut, and Georgia voted for it; Massachusetts, New York, New Jersey, Pennsylvania, Delaware, Maryland, North Carolina against it. The delegates of Virginia and South Carolina were absent or silent that day. On the demand of Rhode Island, the six ay's and sixteen no's were recorded. The four states voting for the motion were represented by only a single member each. Though one delegate from New York and one from Pennsylvania favoured the motion, they were outvoted by the other members from those states. All the remaining states voted solidly no. John Adams, who in May had thought Arnold slandered and libelled, in August opposed the restoration of his rank.

The record gives the motion, the action on it, and the names of the individual voters, but does not hint at the course the debate took or the motives behind it. Nor do the surviving private letters of the delegates clarify the incident. James Lovell of Massachusetts wrote on the 8th that this had been "really a question between monarchical and republican principles put at a most critical time." Lovell probably had in mind a conflict between military and civilian prejudices. He felt on the 11th that Arnold had resigned merely because his "self-love was injured in a fanciful right incompatible with the general interest." Like John Adams, wearied with the quarrels of officers "scrambling for rank and pay like apes for nuts," the Massachusetts delegates who headed the opposition had little patience with the fine points of military honour and did not sympathize with men who held that it was more honourable to give up the cause altogether than to tolerate the loss of a grade in rank. Other officers besides Arnold were pestering Congress on matters of rank which they all considered points of honour. But Henry Laurens of South Carolina, a newcomer to Congress who took no part in the debate over Arnold, thought "the reasoning upon this occasion was disgusting. He was refused not because he was deficient in merit or that his demand was not well founded but because he asked for it and that granting it at such instance would be derogatory to the honour of Congress."[46]

In the north Arnold at once found work more suited to his talents than wrangling in Philadelphia. Burgoyne had made his way to the Hudson near Saratoga. Colonel Barry St. Leger, coming by Lakes Ontario and Oneida to the Mohawk, had laid siege to Fort Schuyler and routed one American force sent to relieve it. If St. Leger, with his loyalists and Indians, should capture the fort he might be joined by other loyalists in Tryon county and proceed with heavy reinforcements for Burgoyne. Most of the officers with General Schuyler, facing Burgoyne, thought it unwise to reduce their army by sending another force to Fort Schuyler. Arnold, always ready to take the offensive, offered to lead a volunteer expedition to the rescue. Schuyler appointed him to the command, and he set out on August 15. "Nothing shall be omitted that can be done to raise the siege," he wrote to Gates from the German Flats (Herkimer) on the 21st. "You will hear of my being victorious, or no more."[47]

He issued a proclamation full of the most patriotic hostility to "the —— George of Great Britain" and St. Leger's "banditti of robbers, murderers, and traitors," offering pardon to all frontier loyalists or renegades who within ten days (from August 20) would "come and lay down their arms, sue for protection, and swear allegiance to the United States of America."[48] Though on the 21st his officers thought an attack on the fort too hazardous to be undertaken, Arnold the next day "determined, at all events, to hazard a battle rather than to suffer the garrison to fall a sacrifice."[49] But by a ruse that turned out to be incredibly effective he caused first the besieging Indians, then the loyalists, then the British troops to imagine that Arnold was coming with an immense force. They fled in panic confusion, leaving artillery and stores to be captured by the Americans. Arnold entered the fort on the 24th, and four days later wrote to Gates: "I believe there is nothing to be feared from the enemy in this quarter at present."[50]

It was hard for Arnold to turn back from the relief expedition, where his fierce and original energy could have full outlet, to the northern army, where he was not only subordinate to Gates (who had superseded Schuyler) but also uncertain as to his rank and status. In command of the American left at Freeman's Farm on September 19, Arnold tempestuously attacked the advancing enemy instead of waiting for them to come up to his own lines. Burgoyne believed that only this attack saved the Americans from absolute defeat. Again Arnold was a hero. But Gates, reporting the engagement to Washington, failed to mention either Arnold or the detachment he had led. Arnold had an angry altercation with Gates on the 22nd. Gates pointed out that Arnold had sent in his resignation and had no regular command. Arnold, alert for conspiracy, suspected he had been "traduced by some designing villain." Gates thought that he had been slandered by Arnold, and Arnold that he had been "huffed" and neglected by Gates. Arnold asked for a pass to Philadelphia. Gates gave him an open letter to the president of Congress, which was in effect a pass and more. Arnold was offended. But other officers urged Arnold not to go, and he remained in camp as a disgruntled, indispensable volunteer major general to whom the northern commander paid no attention.[51]

At Bemis Heights on October 7 Arnold once more fought on his own terms. Denied a command, he assumed it, rushing from his tent to the field and everywhere a blazing example and exhortation. Again his horse was killed under him, and again he was wounded: his right thigh broken by a musket bullet. The most conspicuous American officer on the field, and the only one who was badly hurt, Arnold was more than ever a hero. Congress on November 4 officially thanked Gates, Benjamin Lincoln, and Arnold "for their brave and successful efforts in support of the independence of their country"; and on the 29th resolved that Washington should regulate Arnold's seniority. Washington on January 20 sent Arnold a new commission which restored his "violated rank." The delay, Washington explained, had been caused by "the situation of my papers and the want of blank commissions." He hoped Arnold would soon be well enough to rejoin the army and accept a command "which I trust will be agreeable to yourself and of great advantage to the public."[52]

Arnold had been carried in a litter from camp to the military hospital at Albany. So had Lincoln, wounded the day after Bemis Heights. "Last night," one of the surgeons noted on October 12, "I watched with the celebrated General Arnold. . . . He is very peevish and impatient under his misfortunes."[53] Another surgeon on December 24 wrote a letter comparing his two most distinguished American invalids. "General Lincoln is in a fair way of recovery. . . . He is a patient Christian, etc. . . . Not so the gallant General Arnold, for his wound, though less dangerous in the beginning than Lincoln's, is not in so fair a way of healing. He abuses us for a set of ignorant pretenders."[54] It was as impossible for Arnold, with his dynamite vigour, to be long-suffering in a hospital as it is for a healthy child to sit still for more than a few minutes.

During his slow recovery Arnold may have thought of fresh reasons for distrusting Congress and regretting the Declaration of Independence. As he may have talked in Albany with Philip Skene, so may he with wounded British officers like Major Acland in the same hospital with him. But Acland, leaving at the end of December, told Clinton in New York that Schuyler was disposed to peace and reunion but said nothing—so far as is known—about Arnold.

V

Making his convalescent way homewards, Arnold was at Middletown, Connecticut, on March 12 when he wrote to Washington about the new commission. His wounded leg, Arnold said, must for some time longer keep him from going back to camp.[55] While he waited in Middletown his thoughts shifted from war to love, and on April 8 he returned to his courtship of Betsy Deblois in Boston.[56]

"Twenty times have I taken my pen to write to you," he told her, "and as often has my trembling hand refused to obey the dictates of my heart. A heart which has often been calm and serene amidst the clashing of arms and all the din and horrors of war trembles with diffidence and the fear of giving offence when it attempts to address you on a subject so important to its happiness. Long have I struggled to efface your heavenly image from it. Neither time, absence, misfortunes, nor your cruel indifference have been able to efface the deep impression your charms have made. And will you doom a heart so true, so faithful, to languish in despair? Shall I expect no returns to the most sincere, ardent, and disinterested passion? Dear Betsy, suffer that heavenly bosom (which surely cannot know itself the cause of misfortune without a sympathetic pang) to expand with friendship at last and let me know my fate. If a happy one, no man will strive more to deserve it; if on the contrary I am doomed to despair, my latest breath will be to implore the blessing of heaven on the idol and only wish of my soul."

The lady entreated him, as it appears from Arnold's letter of the 26th, "to solicit no further" for her affections. Since she did not positively forbid him to hope, he renewed the siege. "A union of hearts, I acknowledge, is necessary to happiness; but give me leave to observe that true and permanent happiness is seldom the effect of an alliance formed on romantic passion where fancy governs more than judgment. Friendship and esteem, founded on the merit of the object, is the most certain basis to build a lasting happiness upon; and when there is a tender and ardent passion on one side, and friendship and esteem on the other, the heart must be callous to every tender sentiment if the taper of love is not lighted up at the flame." She had inspired in him a "pure and exalted passion . . . which cannot admit of an unworthy thought or action." He had, he said, "enclosed a letter to your Mama for your Papa and have presumed to request his sanction to my addresses. May I hope for your approbation? Let me beg of you to suffer your heart if possible to expand with a sensation more tender than friendship. Consider the consequences before you determine. Consult your own happiness, and if incompatible with mine, forget there is so unhappy a wretch; for let me perish if I would give you one moment's pain to procure the greatest felicity to myself. Whatever my fate may be, my most ardent wish is for your happiness." But Betsy Deblois remained obdurate and Arnold gave up the chase, though he economically preserved the text of his letters to use again in September in another courtship.

On May 1 he reached New Haven, where soldiers and civilians went out to welcome him, and a salute of thirteen guns was fired in his honour.[57] Washington on the 7th wrote affectionately from Valley Forge: "A gentleman in France having very obligingly sent me three sets of epaulettes and sword-knots, two of which professedly to be disposed of to any friends I should choose, I take the liberty of presenting them to you and General Lincoln, as a testimony of my sincere regard and approbation of your conduct. I have been informed . . . of your intention of repairing to camp shortly; but, notwithstanding my wish to see you, I must beg that you will run no hazard by coming out too soon." Washington had heard from a surgeon at Albany that Arnold and Lincoln could not be fit for duty for another month.[58]

But before the end of May Arnold was at Valley Forge. Because the state of his wound would not "permit his services in a more active line," Washington on May 28 assigned Arnold to command in Philadelphia as soon as the British should evacuate the town.[59] On the 30th he took the oath which since February had been required of all officers in the American army. Arnold's oath (still preserved in the National Archives) was administered at Artillery Park at Valley Forge by Brigadier General Henry Knox who had transported the Ticonderoga guns to Boston and whose wife, daughter of a Boston loyalist, had introduced Arnold to Betsy Deblois.[60]

Whatever Arnold may have said after his treason about his stand on independence, and whatever may have been his private reservations in May 1778, he then said that he did "acknowledge The United States of America to be free, independent, and sovereign states and declare that the people thereof owe no allegiance or obedience to George the Third, king of Great Britain; and I renounce, refuse, and abjure any allegiance or obedience to him, and

I do swear (or affirm) that I will to the utmost of my power support, maintain, and defend the said United States against the said King George the Third, his heirs and successors and his and their abettors, assistants, and adherents, and will serve the said United States, in the office"—of major general—"which I now hold with fidelity according to the best of my skill and understanding."

Approach to Treachery

WASHINGTON, assigning Arnold to command in Philadelphia, may have reasoned that this would not only give him a post worthy his rank and merit but would also save him from friction with other officers, somewhat as if he were leading an expedition. He had so pleased the "principal inhabitants" on Lake Champlain by his handling of affairs in the summer of 1775 that they thanked him in a farewell address for "the uncommon vigilance, vigour, and spirit" of his conduct toward the enemy and his "humanity and benevolence" toward friendly civilians.[1] He might prove equally pleasing to the people of Philadelphia.

The Philadelphians were not frontiersmen in daily fear of invading troops or marauding savages. Both a federal and a state capital, Philadelphia after the British left was under the double, jealous rule of Congress and of Pennsylvania. Arnold as commander of the military was bound to be a third in the conflict, and he was neither patient nor diplomatic. "You will take every prudent step in your power," Washington instructed Arnold on June 19, "to preserve tranquillity and order in the city and give security to individuals of every class and description; restraining, as far as possible, till the restoration of civil government, every species of persecution, insult, or abuse, either from the soldiery to the inhabitants or among each other."[2] But the Philadelphia patriots returned after nine months of British occupation to find the town damaged and dirty. If they hated the avowed loyalists who had gone away with Clinton, so did they hate the neutrals who, unprotesting and perhaps prospering while the British were there, now seemed enemies to their country because they had not shared the adversity of its friends. Many of the patriots were angry and vengeful.

Arnold came in from Valley Forge on the 19th. Ccngress had requested Washington to prevent plundering or the "removal, transfer, or sale of any goods, wares, or merchandise in possession of the inhabitants" until a joint committee of Congress and of the supreme executive council of Pennsylvania could "determine whether any or what part thereof may belong to the king of Great Britain or to any of his subjects."[3] Public stores belonging to the enemy would of course be seized. Washington instructed Arnold to "adopt such measures as shall appear to you most effectual, and at the same time least offensive, for answering the views of Congress." Arnold on the first day of his command, with the advice of Joseph Reed who was a delegate from Pennsylvania to Congress, proclaimed military law in the city and suburbs, and ordered that all British or loyalist property be reported to the town major and also all "European, East or West India goods, iron, leather, shoes, wines, and provisions of every kind, beyond the necessary use of a private family . . . in order that the quartermaster, commissary and clothier generals may contract for such goods as are wanted for the use of the army." To prevent removal, transfer, or sale the shops were closed till further notice.[4]

In this Arnold was doing only what Congress and Washington had ordered him to do. It was no fault of his if certain Philadelphians, scrambling over property accumulated under British rule, were furious at his interference with their schemes, or if many Philadelphians were inconvenienced by the closing of the shops for a week. But Arnold was not merely a soldier acting under orders. On the 23rd, four days after he came in and before the shops were opened, he entered into a secret agreement with James Mease, clothier general, and his deputy William West. "Whereas," they recklessly put in writing, "by purchasing goods and necessaries for the use of the public, sundry articles not wanted for that purpose may be obtained, it is agreed by the subscribers that all such goods and merchandise which are or may be bought by the clothier general, or persons appointed by him, shall be sold for the joint equal benefit of the subscribers and be purchased at their risk."[5]

Under this arrangement Mease and his deputy might buy whole stocks if they chose, using public credit instead of their own capital, charge the army with what it could use, sell the remainder at whatever profit to them, account only for the sum originally paid, and divide the stealthy proceeds with Arnold who, while it was officially his duty to denounce such transactions, privately gave this one his interested countenance.

Though the agreement with Mease and West did not come to light till after Arnold's treason, he seems to have been almost at once suspected of corruptly profiting from the disorder in Philadelphia. He confirmed suspicion when, as if he despised it, he soon moved from his temporary headquarters to the John Penn house in Market Street and an establishment quite out of keeping with any income he was known to have. His pay as major general and the expenses allowed him in Philadelphia amounted to $332 a month in Continental currency—then worth about a third of its face value. He owned no real estate except his New Haven house, occupied by his sister, and a small farm in Connecticut. His business, neglected for three years, brought him little revenue. Congress did not vote him any money till October 28, when he was ordered $8000 "on account, he to be accountable."[6] Yet Arnold, with a coach-and-four and liveried servants, kept up a show much like that of General Howe who from the same house had ruled the city as a conqueror. Plain Philadelphians were resentful, and some possibly envious.

The Fourth of July was celebrated for the second time that year, with a "grand festival" at the City Tavern to which all the "principal civil and military officers and strangers in town" were invited.[7] The shops were again open. Congress had returned to Philadelphia from York, the Pennsylvania council from Lancaster. Though military authority gave way to civil government, Arnold was chosen by Congress to be first host to the new French minister, who arrived on the 12th. "On Sunday last," Henry Laurens wrote to South Carolina, "the committee appointed for the purpose received Monsieur Gérard at Chester, and under a respectable cavalcade conducted him to temporary apartments at General Arnold's, where the committee [and] a few other members of Congress including myself dined with him."[8]

Though Arnold later claimed he had always been against the French alliance, he kept silent, so far as any record shows, while Philadelphia exulted. If he talked, it may have been with Silas

Deane. Deane, distrusting France and already in dubious relations with the British king and ministry, came in the same fleet with Gérard. Arnold invited Deane to lodge at headquarters, and letters came to Deane addressed in care of Arnold.[9] Joseph Reed, suspicious of Arnold, advised Deane to lodge elsewhere.[10] But he received "many civilities" from his old friend and in time from his friend's new wife.[11]

During the latter days of June Elias Boudinot thought Arnold seemed ill from overwork, and on July 4 he was suffering from a "violent oppression" in his stomach.[12] His sickness was probably the intolerable, intolerant restlessness of a soldier who could not endure garrison duty, even as commander of a capital. Moreover, Arnold was feverish with schemes for a different career or a larger income.

Three days after Gérard arrived at headquarters he reported to Vergennes that Arnold had the reputation of being as ingenious and active in council *(aussi ingénieux et aussi actif dans le cabinet)* as he was audacious and enterprising in the field.[13] He was in charge, Gérard said, of plans for a new American navy. There is no evidence that these plans then existed anywhere but in Arnold's mind. But on the 19th he asked Washington's advice on a naval matter. Since his wounds would not allow him for some time yet to take a military command he thought of retiring "from public business, unless an offer which my friends have mentioned should be made to me of a command in the navy, to which my being wounded would not be so great an objection as it would remaining in the army. I must beg leave to request your Excellency's sentiments respecting a command in the navy." Washington, who left marine matters to Congress, declined to give advice "on a subject so far out of my line."[14] Nothing came of this scheme, which might have brought Arnold renown, might have brought him prize money. But on September 7 Arnold laid before Congress a "secret paper respecting a secret expedition" which was not entered in its journals. According to Gérard, this was to be an expedition to capture one of the British Windward islands and seize the European goods found there.[15]

On July 15 Arnold sent $500 to Boston for the children of his friend Joseph Warren, killed at Bunker Hill, and promised, if

Congress would not provide for them, to do it himself "in a manner suitable to their birth."[16] Arnold then had money to spare, and expected to have more. Three days after this generous offer he made an agreement with John R. Livingston to buy "a quantity of goods in New York on a prospect that in the course of a few months that city would again fall into the possession of the Americans."[17] During July Arnold made what was probably a similar agreement with Benjamin Seixas a Philadelphia merchant (or with Moses Seixas a Newport merchant) and on the 31st wrote to General Sullivan who was then in command of the forces which hoped to drive the British out of Newport. "Mr. Seixas," Arnold wrote, "has a plan to propose to you which I believe will be agreeable. If so, I have promised him I will be concerned and think it may be of service to the public as well as conducive to our private interest. If you approve the plan, I will take one-third or one-fourth the risk."[18]

Other American generals besides Arnold, paid in falling currency at a time of rising prices, were engaged in speculations, like many civilians whose love of country did not interfere with their love of profits. Though Arnold's agreement with Mease and West was to the certain disadvantage of the public, his designs with Livingston and Seixas need not have been, nor is there any clear evidence that they went beyond proposals. But they are proof of how persistently Arnold was thinking about money. Congress, unaware of his secret ventures, thought he was granting too many passes to persons who wanted to go from Philadelphia to New York, and on August 13 resolved that such passes should in the future be granted only by Congress or Washington and that Arnold should recall any of his which had not yet been used.[19] But Congress probably had in mind only that Arnold was likely to be more obliging to loyalists than the patriots thought desirable.

II

Two of Arnold's ventures left records full enough to be examined. They had to do with the schooner *Charming Nancy* and the sloop *Active*.

On June 4, after Arnold knew he was to command in Philadelphia but while he was still at Valley Forge, a Philadelphia trader, Robert Shewell, came to camp for permission to sail the *Charming Nancy* and her cargo out of the Delaware, still held by the British, to some port held by the Americans. Congress that same day at York resolved that no property should be removed from Philadelphia till its owners were identified. News of the resolve could not have got from York to Valley Forge on the 4th, and Shewell may have been honest in his claim that he and his partners patriotically wished to put their goods into American hands. But it was common knowledge in Philadelphia that the British were nearly ready for the evacuation, and it could hardly have been thought that the available ships would have room for confiscated American property. If Shewell and his partners wanted to save their cargo for the Americans, they had only to remain in Philadelphia till the Americans should come in. By the time they sailed (on a day not stated) they may have had a chance to know that the linens, woollens, glass, loaf sugar, tea, and nails they carried were all subject to control by Congress. But would the army pay as much as private buyers in some other port? Two of Shewell's partners, James Seagrove and William Constable, were New York traders who had come to Philadelphia to pick up profits during the British occupation, and the *Charming Nancy* had been sent there in December by a firm of British outfitters in New York. For Shewell, Seagrove, and Constable business was apparently business.

Arnold seems to have agreed with this equation. He accepted Shewell's claim as to the partners' motive and, without consulting Washington who was then at Valley Forge, gave Shewell a pass— or "protection"—for the schooner, "New England built, about seventy-five tons burthen . . . [of] which schooner William Moore is master," to sail from Philadelphia "into any of the ports of the United States of America" without "any umbrage or molestation" from "officers and soldiers of the Continental army, and other persons." While much effort was later made to find out whether Arnold took a share in the venture before giving the pass, it was never proved. He himself did not deny that he subsequently owned a share in it, or that his share was half the amount realized by the sale of the cargo.[20]

Arnold's pass, given to protect the *Charming Nancy* from capture by Americans, was not entirely effective. She was taken by the New Jersey privateer *Xantippe* and brought into Egg Harbor But a New Jersey judge of admiralty on September 22 "acquitted released, and discharged" her from the capture—which meant that the schooner and her cargo were not the *Xantippe's* prize but still the property of Arnold and his associates.[21] At once they faced another danger. Within a few days a British squadron from New York, with the lively Captain André on board, attacked Egg Harbor, which had become notorious for its privateers. On October 11 Arnold wrote Washington that several American houses and vessels had been burned. Washington philosophically observed that "we must at times submit to such losses, or depend on the exertions of the militia for their prevention."[22] Arnold, who was personally concerned, made a prompt move which furnished the Pennsylvania authorities with a special grievance.

That move was to send a brigade of twelve wagons, called up under a Pennsylvania law for the transportation of public goods, to Egg Harbor "to remove property which was in imminent danger of falling into the hands of the enemy." Arnold did not pretend that the property was public, and he arranged to pay privately for the use of the wagons. Nor does there seem to have been, as the deputy quartermaster general said, "any inconvenience to the service" in letting Arnold have the wagons he needed. Arnold by October had become so unpopular that all his moves were being watched for any fault that might be found with them.

The quarrel over the episode was long and complicated. The gist of it is that the twelve wagons, in charge of Jesse Jordan, left Philadelphia on the 22nd, travelled empty to Egg Harbor, were loaded under the direction of Captain Moore of the *Charming Nancy,* and came back to Philadelphia on the 30th to be unloaded at the house of Stephen Collins. The wagons contained, besides linens, woollens, glass, loaf sugar, tea, and nails, the sails of a schooner, and half a dozen swivel guns. Collins afterwards affirmed that he "sold all these articles upon commission, at the request of Seagrove; that he was spoken to at different times about the goods by Robert Shewell [and] Constable; and that after the sales he paid the money, agreeable to the directions of the three last-mentioned persons, about one-half to General Arnold and the remainder among the same three persons." It was for the present not settled whether the wagoners were to be paid at the fixed public rate or at some private rate to be agreed upon.[23]

Arnold, not foreseeing the trouble to come, seems to have thought his venture satisfactory, for on November 2 he planned to continue dealings with two of his partners in it. "Whereas," they agreed in a document which Arnold's enemies would have been happy to learn about, "it is apprehended that the British troops will soon leave New York, it is mutually agreed by and between the subscribers that Captain James Duncan, who is going into New York, shall there purchase (if he is of opinion the city will soon be evacuated) so many European, India, and other goods as he can procure, for what money, bills, and credit he has in New York, on our joint accounts and risk; which goods are to be held equally between us and for which we do hereby engage our words and honour to pay Captain Duncan, or to his order, for the full amount of our shares, lost or not lost; and we do hereby agree that Captain Duncan, in case he can purchase a quantity of goods in New York on our joint accounts, that he shall be fully entitled to, and come in for, an equal share of any purchase of rice and vessels that we shall purchase in Carolina or Georgia, which shall be made on our joint account and risk; and all such goods purchased by either party shall be on account and risk of all."[24]

So far, the agreement limited itself to lawful trading. But it might extend to forbidden trading within the enemy lines. "And in case Captain Duncan finds the British troops intend remaining in New York and he has the opportunity of conveying any goods out to us, all such goods shall be of the joint account and risk of the subscribers." Arnold signed the agreement first, then Seagrove and Constable, and last Major Matthew Clarkson, Arnold's dashing aide who had just passed his twentieth birthday. An accompanying agreement between Arnold and John R. Livingston said that three copies of the principal agreement were to be sent to New York, presumably for Duncan to show in making his purchases. How or why Duncan, a captain in Hazen's 2nd Canadian regiment, was allowed to go to New York does not appear. But there seem to have been dealings under the agreement. At any rate, when Arnold after the treason asked the British to compensate him for his losses, he

said he had lost "money in hands of Seagrove & Constable, mer
chants, balance of profits arising on £10,000 worth of goods bough
and sold jointly." His share he then put at £1200.[25]

And there was the *Active*, which was to become celebrated ir
American legal history.[26] British-owned, she left Jamaica in Augus
1778 for New York, with four captured Americans forcibly enlistec
in her crew but determined not to end the voyage in a British
prison. Under Gideon Olmsted of Connecticut, unwilling second
mate, the Americans rose on the night of September 6 off Long
Island, confined the other nine officers and men below, and steered
for Egg Harbor. On their way they were picked up and escorted
to Philadelphia by the brig *Convention*, belonging to Pennsylvania
and the privateer *Gérard*. Both of these claimed to have assisted in
the capture of the sloop and to be entitled to share in the prize of
130 hogsheads of rum, with smaller quantities of coffee, cocoa,
beef, limes, and pimento. When the case came before a Pennsylvania judge of admiralty, with a Pennsylvania jury, Olmsted and
his companions were awarded only one-fourth of the prize. Arnold,
admiring their exploit and thinking them ill-treated, took up their
cause with his usual energy. But with his usual concern for money,
he took a half interest in their prospects in return for his influence and the funds he advanced for the cost of an appeal to
Congress.

His agreement with Olmsted was secret but suspected in Philadelphia, and gave rise to one of the earliest nagging paragraphs
against Arnold in the *Pennsylvania Packet*. On November 12 an
anonymous writer, who was actually Timothy Matlack the secretary of the Pennsylvania council, commented on the recent admiralty decision and the proposed appeal. "It is whispered that
some gentlemen of high rank, now in this city, have introduced a
new species of champerty, by interesting themselves in the claim.
. . . If this be so, there is no doubt but that the contract is in itself
void, and the seamen are not bound to fulfil it." Arnold sent an
aide to find out who had written the paragraph, and when he was
refused the name wrote a signed answer in the *Packet* five days
later. His reputation, he said, was not the main issue. "Some of
my countrymen [from Connecticut] and neighbours were here in
distress." He had interested himself in them to keep them from

being cheated. Any public discussion might prejudice their cause.

A committee of Congress on December 15 annulled the Pennsylvania verdict and gave the whole of the prize to Olmsted and the three who had been with him on deck. The marshal of the city and county of Philadelphia, who was Arnold's aide Clarkson, was ordered to sell the *Active* and its cargo, pay the costs and charges ($280), and turn the rest of the sum received over to the appellants. But the Pennsylvania court refused to yield and on January 4, in spite of the efforts of Arnold and the Congressional committee, got possession of the £47,981 2s 5d, Pennsylvania currency, for which the cargo—not yet the sloop—had been sold. The committee hesitated to "enter into any proceedings for contempt lest consequences might ensue at this juncture dangerous to the public peace of the United States."[27] More bluntly, Congress did not care to try its strength with Pennsylvania.

If Olmsted was a victim of this conflict of jurisdictions, so was Arnold. The amount he had failed to get was considerable even in a currency which was depreciating more rapidly each month; and he had no doubt advanced Olmsted and the others money to live on as well as to pay costs of litigation. On January 25, according to Jean Holker the French consul in Philadelphia, Arnold borrowed £12,000 from him and then or later tried in vain to persuade him to buy a share in the speculation.[28] The matter came before Congress repeatedly during 1779, but nothing was done. Pennsylvania on October 21 had paid Olmsted only £12,750 of the £51,000 which Congress now considered due him.[29] Arnold, whose taste was for large risks and quick returns, had involved himself in a case which ran eight years longer than he lived. Though the Supreme Court of the United States finally ordered, in 1809, that Pennsylvania pay Olmsted all that the Continental Congress had awarded him, the nearest Arnold ever came to payment was when he asked the British government, after the war, to compensate him for his loss of "one half of a prize ship and cargo of 130 puncheon of Jamaica spirits, £1893." And this claim he afterward withdrew.[30]

The charge has been made that Arnold was actively engaged in privateering, but in the surviving naval records he appears as owner of only one ship which gave bond for letters of marque.

This was the *General McDougall* of Connecticut, guns 10, crew 30, bond $10,000, registered April 6, 1778, before Arnold took command at Philadelphia. He was one of six owners.[31]

III

Two days after Matlack's hinting paragraph about Arnold and the *Active* the *Packet* gave space to a complaint from A Militia Man. He was willing, he said, to serve his country whenever he was needed. But "to be called upon, out of mere parade, to stand at the door of any man, however great, but at the whim and caprice of any of his suite to be ordered on the most menial services, piques my pride and hurts my feelings most sensibly. . . . I cannot think that the commanding officer views himself as exposed to any real danger in this city. From a public enemy there can be none. From Tories, if such there be amongst us, he has nothing to fear, for they are all remarkably fond of him. The Whigs, to a man, are sensible of his great merit and *former* services and would risk their lives in his defence."

Probably written by Matlack himself, this concerned his son William, a sergeant in the Pennsylvania militia. The younger Matlack, on guard at Arnold's headquarters, had been offended early in October when he was ordered to fetch a barber for Major David Solebury Franks, another of Arnold's aides. William Matlack considered it a servant's duty, not a citizen soldier's, and Timothy Matlack wrote Arnold a letter of protest against such indignities. "No man," Arnold replied on the 6th, "has a higher sense of the rights of a citizen and freeman than myself. They are dear to me, as I have fought and bled for them, and as it is my highest ambition and most ardent wish to resume the character of a free citizen whenever the service of my country will permit. At the same time, I beg leave to observe that whenever necessity obliges the citizen to assume the character of a soldier, the former is entirely lost in the latter, and the respect due to a citizen is by no means to be paid to the soldier, any farther than his rank entitles him to it."

Matlack, insisting that the freemen of the Pennsylvania militia must not be subject to improper orders, declared that if Arnold supported Franks in this case, then "it is my duty as a father to withdraw my son from a service in which commands are to be given him which to obey would lessen him in the esteem of the world; and I shall consider it as a duty which I owe to myself to acquaint my fellow-citizens of my reason for so doing." Arnold closed the correspondence by saying it was "needless to discuss a subject which will perhaps be determined more by the feelings than the reason of men. If the declaration that you will withdraw your son from the service and publish the reasons is intended as a threat, you have mistaken your object. I am not to be intimidated by a newspaper." He admitted that Franks was blameable if he had given the order "in a haughty, imperious, or insolent manner." But "the affair is now out of my hands and lies betwen the sergeant and the major."[32]

The Matlacks may have been as sensitive on a point of honour as they appeared to be; or Timothy Matlack may merely have seized this fresh occasion to add to the odium in which Arnold was increasingly held. But the sting of the *Packet* piece of November 14 was its remark that the Whigs were aware of Arnold's *former* services, the Tories remarkably fond of Arnold now.

No man in Arnold's position, and certainly not Arnold, could have kept a responsible course in Philadelphia in 1778 without being accused of siding with one party or the other. Though the most conspicuous loyalists had left with Clinton at the evacuation, the patriots found other doubtful persons remaining in Philadelphia and tried twenty-three of them on the charge of high treason. Of these only the Quakers Abraham Carlisle and John Roberts were convicted, for having joined the enemy and served against their countrymen. In spite of recommendations of mercy from the grand and petty juries and petitions from influential patriots as well as neutrals, the supreme executive council felt obliged to make an example of the two offenders, who were hanged on November 4. Joseph Reed, in a letter written the next day, had no patience with people who openly held that "treason, disaffection to the interests of America, and even assistance to the British interest" were to be regarded as "error of judgment which candour and liberality will overlook. . . . Will you not think it extraordinary that General Arnold made a public entertainment the night before last, of which not only numerous Tory ladies but the wives and daughters of persons proscribed by the state, and now with the enemy at New York, formed a very considerable number?"[33]

Arnold, who must have known that Carlisle and Roberts were to be hanged the day after his entertainment, must have meant it as a gesture of humane sympathy for the party of the victims. General John Cadwalader, as good a patriot as Reed though not so single-minded, a month later wrote of Arnold that "every man who has a liberal way of thinking highly approves his conduct. He has been civil to every gentleman who has taken the oath, intimate with none," and civil to Whig and Tory ladies without discrimination.[34] But for the most part the liberal patriots and suspected loyalists kept quiet while the zealous enemies of Arnold abused him and his Tories.

On December 1 the *Packet* had an Anecdote for the Military Gentleman. "At a ball last week in this city, not a mile from headquarters, a lady well known in the Tory world, seeing an American officer of great merit come in dressed in scarlet, 'Heyday,' says she to some other officers standing near her, 'I see certain animals will put on the lion's skin.'" Various readers knew that the lady was Rebecca Franks, whose father David Franks had lately been arrested for clandestine correspondence with the British and dismissed from his post as commissary of British prisoners in Philadelphia, and whose cousin was Arnold's aide. The anecdote hardly called for an answer, but Observator took it up and sent a pert rejoinder to the *Packet* of the 3rd. "There are many persons so unhappy in their dispositions that, like the dog in the manger, they can neither enjoy the innocent pleasures of life themselves nor let others, without grumbling and growling, participate in them. Hence it is we frequently observe hints and anecdotes in your paper respecting the commanding officer, headquarters, and Tory ladies. This mode of attacking characters is really admirable, and equally as polite as conveying slander and defamation by significant nods, winks, and shrugs. Poor beings indeed, who plainly indicate to what species of animals they belong, by the baseness of their conduct." Nagging was a game at which two could play.

Whatever favouritism Arnold may have shown toward suspected loyalists, the details are singularly few. The Pennsylvania council, formulating its charges on this point, did not specify. "The discouragement and neglect manifested by General Arnold, during his command, to civil, military, and other characters who have adhered to their country, with an entire different conduct toward those of another character, are too notorious to need proof or illustration." Taking up the point at his court martial, Arnold had nothing definite to disprove and was no more specific than his accusers. "I am not sensible . . . of having neglected any gentlemen, either in the civil or military line, who have adhered to the cause of their country and who have put it into my power to take notice of them. With respect to gentlemen in the civil line and army I can appeal to the candour of Congress and to the army, as scarcely a day passed but many of both were entertained by me. They are the best judges of my company and conduct. With respect to attention to those of an opposite character, I have paid none but such as in my situation was justifiable on the principles of common humanity and politeness. . . . It is enough for me . . . to contend with men in the field. I have not yet learned to carry on a warfare against women or to consider every man as disaffected to our glorious cause who, from an opposition in sentiment to those in power in the state of Pennsylvania, may, by the clamour of party, be styled a Tory."[35]

In the prevailing bitterness and suspicion the zealous patriots were intolerant of opposition or dissent. The British peace offers in June, and the lingering presence of the peace commissioners in New York till November, made many honest Philadelphians wonder if it would not be wiser for America to return to its old place in the Empire on favourable terms than to go on fighting bloodily for independence—and in the end perhaps fail to win it. Independence was an idea, the Empire a reality. Other Philadelphians honestly dreaded the French alliance, out of doubt as to French motives. The United States, even independent of Great Britain, might find themselves disagreeably subordinate to so powerful and so alien an ally as France. At home there were hostile cabals in Congress, and recurring conflicts between the loose federal union and the separate states. The Continental currency fell from a third of its face value in June 1778 to a tenth in February 1779. Business was moving into panic, with the public in a mounting resentment toward the inevitable speculators. The resolute

Philadelphia patriots could not help being aware of a general ir-resolution throughout the city—and the whole country. Men talked longingly of the good old days of peace and prosperity under British rule, and asked if they might not come back again if the stubborn Congress would listen to the British commissioners. This irresolution and this longing were extremely dangerous to the patriot cause. Fear of them made the resolute and zealous patriots fiercely watchful. Anybody might be a secret loyalist, ready at the first chance to go over to the British. And anybody who, like Arnold, was polite to Tories was being impolite, if not treacherous, to Whigs.

Since Arnold, as it turned out, did treacherously turn to the British early in 1779, he must have been inclining toward them during 1778. But his recorded actions prove no more than that he refused to take sides in the violent political controversies of Phila-delphia. And near the end of that year he showed himself so little tender to loyalists on principle as to make an effort to obtain a confiscated loyalist estate as a reward for his patriotic services.

The suggestion seems to have come from Schuyler. "In a former letter," Arnold wrote him on November 30, "you mentioned that the gentlemen of the state of New York were satisfied with my conduct when commanding in the state, and wished to give me some mark of their approbation of my conduct. I have thought of proposing to the state to purchase a tract of forfeited or unlocated lands on the frontiers of the state, and making a settlement when-ever the times will admit." James Duane, member of Congress from New York, had spoken to Arnold of "the grant made to Sir William Johnson called Kingsland"—Kingsborough. This was 66,000 acres ceded by the Mohawk to Johnson, who was dead and whose son was in exile in Canada. "I have some thoughts of Skenesborough"—34,000 acres.[36] After the treason Arnold could claim that he had made a confidant of Skene early in the war, and he could testify in favour of Skene before the commission on loy-alist claims.[37] But in November 1778 Arnold realistically thought of buying Skenesborough, which was forfeit in any case, and taking over Skene's interrupted plans. Either project was congenial to Arnold's temper: to become a great Mohawk or Hudson land-owner, dominating a whole settlement.

"Can you inform me," Arnold wrote again to Schuyler on February 8, "of the sentiments of your assembly with respect to selling or granting the forfeited lands, and the price they would probably expect for a large tract, the purchaser being obliged in three or four years after the war to settle a family on every thousand acres?"[38] By that time Arnold had got the approval of John Jay, newly elected president of Congress, and of the other delegates from New York. Jay, writing to the New York governor, hoped that the legislature in dealing with Arnold would "recollect the services he has rendered to his country and the value of such a citizen to any state that may gain him. . . . I have no doubt but that generosity to General Arnold will be justice to the state."[39] This scheme also came to nothing. Though in February Arnold had set out for Poughkeepsie to confer with Schuyler, he got only to Washington's camp at Middlebrook from which he had to turn back to answer the charges of maladministration brought against him by Pennsylvania.

IV

What Arnold to Schuyler called Pennsylvania's "cruel and villainous proceeding" and the "excessive badness of the roads" forced the postponement of the journey, to what Arnold said was his great mortification and disappointment. But on the 8th he wrote another letter, to Peggy Shippen in Philadelphia, which was less disconsolate. "Six days' absence, without hearing from my dear Peggy, is intolerable. Heavens, what must I have suffered had I continued my journey—the loss of happiness for a few dirty acres. I can almost bless the villainous roads, and still more villainous men, who oblige me to return. I am heartily tired with my journey, and almost so with human nature."[40]

Peggy (Margaret) Shippen, who was to become Arnold's second wife and the most mysterious and controverted element in his treason, was the youngest daughter of Edward Shippen. The Shippens, like other notable families in Philadelphia, were divided during the Revolution. Dr. William Shippen was chief of the medical department of the Continental army. His cousin Judge Edward Shippen, too conservative to be a rebel, was moderate enough to be a neutral. Though for a time during 1777 he was on parole at his country house on the Schuylkill, he was given the liberty of the state in August and lived in Philadelphia unmolested by the British under Howe, as later by the Americans under Arnold. It was less the politics of Edward Shippen than the charm of his daughters which brought many British officers including André to their house in Fourth Street. The Shippen family was the only one that had three daughters—Polly (Mary), Sally (Sarah), and Peggy—invited to be ladies of the tournament at the Mischianza.

They seem to have accepted, but almost certainly did not attend. Their father, according to a Shippen tradition, decided that the "Turkish" costumes designed by André were immodest and forbade the girls to take part in the affair.[41] This tradition has been questioned because it conflicts with the account dated May 23, naming the three, which André sent to London and the *Gentleman's Magazine*.[42] But André himself contradicted this in a second account, dated June 2, which he wrote for Peggy Chew, and in which he left out the Shippen names.[43] The most likely explanation of the change is that the earlier version, written in haste to sail with Howe, contained the names of the ladies as originally invited; while the later, written for Peggy Chew, who would know the facts, corrected the list. And yet another contemporary version, written by an unidentified guest who went with Dr. M. and Mr. F. in Mr. T. F.'s coach, indicates that a Miss Auchmuty, who was probably from New York, took the place of Peggy (or Polly) Shippen, and Rebecca Franks the place of one of the older sisters.[44]

When the Americans came back the Mischianza ladies were for a time under a patriotic ban. On June 22 "an elegant evening entertainment was given at the City Tavern, by the officers of the army and some of the gentlemen of the city, to the young ladies who had manifested their attachment to the cause of virtue and freedom by sacrificing every convenience to the love of their country." A paragrapher in the *Packet* for August 29 complained that leading members of Congress managed balls "graced with Mischianza ladies equally noted for their Tory principles and their late fondness for British debauchees and macaronies."

Patriotic sentiment ran as well against the reopening of the Old Southwark Theatre in September. Some of the American officers,

Miss Margaret Shippen
daughter of Chief Justice Shippen

MARGARET SHIPPEN

DRAWN BY JOHN ANDRÉ

Samuel Adams wrote on October 17, "have condescended to act on the stage; while others, and one of superior rank [probably Arnold], were pleased to countenance them with their presence."[45] Sober Philadelphia disapproved these British frivolities in Americans, who ought to be austere. Congress on the 12th recommended that the states take measures "for the suppressing of theatrical entertainments, horse racing, gaming, and such other diversions as are productive of idleness, dissipation, and a general depravity of principles and manners." Then, when a performance was repeated at the Southwark as if in contempt of the resolution, Congress on the 16th drastically resolved that "any person holding an office under the United States who shall act, promote, encourage, or attend such plays shall be deemed unworthy to hold such office and shall be accordingly dismissed."[46]

Arnold did not share the prejudice against Mischianza ladies or the theatre. He may have met Peggy Shippen soon after he took command, when she was barely past her eighteenth birthday, or may even have been with her at the Old Southwark. According to André's pencil drawing of her, made the past year, she had a spoiled mouth and direct, determined eyes. But the drawing is too conventional to say much except that she was pretty, blonde, and young. The only surviving comment on her as a young girl is that she was devoted to her father and "never fond of gadding."[47] Not a word known to be hers has been preserved from the period before her marriage, nor a hint as to her early impressions of the swarthy general, with his bright black hair and ice-grey eyes, who was twice her age though only thirty-seven.

And there is remarkably little to show what Arnold's feelings were. In his earliest letter, dated September 25, he simply reworked the stilted text of two of his April letters to Betsy Deblois. "Twenty times," he said again, "have I taken up my pen to write to you, and as often has my trembling hand refused to obey the dictates of my heart. . . . My passion," he explained in a sentence he had not used before, "is not founded on personal charms only; that sweetness of disposition and goodness of heart, that sentiment and sensibility which so strongly mark the character of the lovely Miss P. Shippen, renders her amiable beyond expression and will ever retain the heart she has once captivated." He told her, as he

had told Betsy Deblois: "On you alone my happiness depends."
He asked her, as he had asked Betsy: "And will you doom me to
languish in despair? Shall I expect no return to the most sincere,
ardent, and disinterested passion? . . . Dear Peggy"—it had been
"Dear Betsy" in April—"suffer that heavenly bosom (which cannot
know itself the cause of pain without a sympathetic pang) to expand with a sensation more soft, more tender than friendship."
He described for Peggy as for Betsy "the most certain basis to
build a lasting happiness upon; and when there is a tender and
ardent passion on one side"—Arnold's side in either case—"and
friendship and esteem on the other"—Betsy's or Peggy's as the
case might be—"the heart"—here he put in a special parenthesis
"(unlike yours)" for Peggy—"must be callous to every tender sentiment if the taper of love is not lighted up at the flame."

He had written, he told her, to her father for his sanction and
hoped also for her approbation. "Consider before you doom me to
misery, which I have not deserved but by loving you too extravagantly. Consult your own happiness, and if incompatible, forget
there is so unhappy a wretch; for may I perish if I would give you
one moment's inquietude to purchase the greatest possible felicity
to myself. Whatever my fate may be, my most ardent wish is for
your happiness, and my latest breath will be to implore the blessing of heaven on the idol and only wish of my soul."[48]

Writing to her father, Arnold said that his fortune while not
large was "sufficient (not to depend upon my expectations) to
make us both happy. I neither expect nor wish one with Miss
Shippen." Except for his Connecticut house and farm he can have
had actually little but expectations. But he was too proud to be a
fortune-hunter, and too sure of himself to doubt his future. He
did not pretend to be a neutral. "Our difference in political sentiments will, I hope, be no bar to my happiness. I flatter myself the
time is at hand when our unhappy contests will be at an end, and
peace and domestic happiness be restored to every one."[49]

Peggy seems to have refused Arnold at first, and to have been as
cool as Arnold hinted Philadelphia girls generally were. On October 22 Sarah Franklin Bache wrote to her father in Paris about her
daughter Betty, then a year old. "You can't think how fond of
kissing she is, and gives such old-fashioned smacks. General Arnold

says he would give a good deal to have her for a schoolmistress to teach the young ladies how to kiss."[50] In November Mrs. Robert Morris wrote to her husband that "Cupid has given our little general"—Arnold was five feet nine—"a more mortal wound than all the host of Britons could." In December Peggy's sister Elizabeth was married to Major Edward Burd of the Continental army, and Edward Shippen on the 21st wrote his father: "My youngest daughter is much solicited by a certain general on the same subject. Whether this will take place or not depends upon certain circumstances" as to which the letter disappointingly gives no clue.[51]

On the 30th a cousin of Peggy's sister Elizabeth asked her if Peggy was to follow her example. "Every one tells me so with such confidence that I am laughed at for my unbelief. Does she know her own mind yet?" Four days later Edward Burd declared he had never put faith in Peggy's refusal. "A lame leg is at present the only obstacle. But a lady who makes that the only objection, and is firmly persuaded it will be well again, can never retract, however expressly conditioned an engagement may have been made. However, we have every reason to expect it will be well again, though I am not so sanguine as he is with respect to the time. But the leg will be a couple of inches shorter than the other, and disfigured." On January 29 another cousin assumed the matter was not yet settled. "They say she intends to surrender soon. I thought the fort could not hold out long. Well, after all, there is nothing like perseverance and a regular attack." After the marriage this same cousin was pleased that Peggy, for all she had vowed never to marry, had been "Burgoyned" by "her adoring general."[52]

All this seems in the contemporary pattern of coy nymph and pursuing hero. But as it is now known that within a month after the wedding Peggy was a partner in Arnold's plans for treachery, it may be guessed that the two had before it come to some kind of understanding—about which they would naturally have been as silent as they were. It is possible, too, that she affected his decision to give up the project of a manorial settlement on the New York frontier and to fix his residence in Philadelphia. On March 22 he bought the handsome estate on the Schuylkill known as Mount Pleasant and settled it on her for life, the remainder in equal proportions to his sons by his first marriage and any children to be born of the second. On April 8 Arnold and Peggy Shippen were married at Judge Shippen's house. The wounded bridegroom was supported by a soldier during the ceremony and during the reception sat with his leg on a camp-stool.[53] Before the end of the honeymoon Arnold was ready to give up the cause of America.

V

The conflict between Arnold and the Pennsylvania council came to a sudden break late in January. It was less like impartial justice closing inexorably in on a distinguished malefactor than like furious vigilantes pouncing on a hated suspect. The council, unaware of Arnold's principal offenses or unable to prove them, fixed upon his private use of public wagons as an undeniable instance of his misconduct.

On January 21 Matlack, as secretary, wrote to Arnold requesting him "to inform this board whether the property for which the said wagons were ordered was public or private; if the latter, to whom the same belonged; and farther to inform this board by virtue of what resolve of Congress, or other authority, public wagons of this state were sent to another state to do business merely of a private nature." Arnold on the 25th said he thought it extraordinary they should question him when they already knew the essential facts from the quartermaster general's office. As to himself: "I shall only say that I am at all times ready to answer my public conduct to Congress or General Washington, to whom alone I am accountable." Joseph Reed, now president of the council, that same day wrote to Congress complaining of "the indignity offered us upon this occasion." They proposed, Reed said, to call on Congress for justice. "But as we learn that General Arnold is about to depart this city for some time and may thereby elude inquiry into this transaction, we request he may be detained till the whole proceedings can be laid before you in form, and that he forbear exercising any further command in this city until the charges against him are examined."[54]

On Saturday the 30th Jordan, who had been in charge of the wagons sent to Egg Harbor, called on Arnold for his pay, figured at £553 10s. Arnold questioned the amount, believing—later at least—that the council had put Jordan up to asking for more than he should have. The council implied that Arnold expected the public to pay the wagoners for part of the time consumed and for the forage and rations required. Jordan did not get his money on either of two calls on Saturday, and did not go back for it. Arnold claimed this was on the advice of the council, so that there could be another accusation against the victim.[55] Actually, he said, he arranged on Monday or Tuesday to have Jordan paid, and left £500 for that purpose in the hands of Clarkson.[56]

On Wednesday the 3rd Arnold set out for camp on his way to Poughkeepsie. Again there was a cross-fire of recriminations. The council held that Arnold, having learned late on the evening of Tuesday that action was to be taken against him, left for another state in order to be out of reach.[57] Arnold declared that the council purposely waited till after he had gone and then laid their charges against him, to make him look guilty and afraid. It seems clear that he did get away on Wednesday before the council met and passed its resolutions. In a letter which has been overlooked he wrote, on February 19: "I crossed the Delaware at Philadelphia, the 3rd instant in the morning, reached Burlington that night, next day at ten o'clock I crossed the river to Bristol, where the resolutions were delivered to me by an express, sent for that purpose."[58] He might at once have turned back to face his accusers. Instead, he went on to Middlebrook to confer with Washington, who advised him to demand a court martial.

The council, which had sent copies of their resolves to Congress, Washington, and the authorities of every state, on February 9 published them in the newspapers. The public now had a chance to learn that Arnold had been, in the opinion of the council, "oppressive to the faithful subjects of this state, unworthy of his rank and station, highly discouraging to those who have manifested their attachment to the liberties and interests of America, and disrespectful to the supreme executive authority." The council had resolved on the 3rd that it could not, except on "the most urgent and pressing necessity," call forth wagons or militia "or otherwise subject the good people of this state to the power and command of the said General Arnold within the state, should he resume it upon his return." The attorney general of Pennsylvania was to prosecute Arnold for "such illegal and oppressive conduct as is cognizable in the courts of law."

To support these resolves the council listed eight "articles in which they have sufficient ground to esteem General Arnold culpable." These had to do with (1) the pass for the *Charming Nancy;* (2) the closing of the shops "while he privately made considerable purchases for his own benefit, as is alleged and believed"; (3) "imposing menial offices upon the sons of freemen of this state" in the militia; (4) "an illegal and unworthy purchase of the suit, at a low and inadequate price," in connexion with the *Active;* (5) using public wagons for transporting private property; (6) writing a letter to recommend a pass which Arnold had no right to give, and having Clarkson sign the recommendation; (7) indecently and disrespectfully refusing to explain the wagon transaction; and (8) showing favour to Tories. "And if this command has been, as is generally believed, supported at an expense of four or five thousand pounds per annum to the United States, we freely declare we shall very unwillingly pay any share of expenses thus incurred."[59]

To the resolves and charges published on the 9th the council added the information that " a certified copy of the foregoing resolves were delivered to Major General Arnold before he left this state"; and that payment to the wagoners had been ordered "until they can procure farther redress," since Arnold "is departed from this city while the complaint against him was pending." Clarkson with justified spirit protested, in the same issue of the *Packet,* against "condemning an absent man unheard and ordering him to be prosecuted afterwards."

Arnold, who was more guilty than the council could know, denied any guilt with his usual bold vigour. The council had to make the most of what charges it had a chance to prove. Matlack dug up the old charges brought against Arnold by Brown and Hazen, reproducing all of Brown's in the *Packet* for February 27, over the initials T. G. Arnold on March 4 replied: "Envy and malice are indefatigable. Where they have not invention enough to frame new slanders, or the slanders newly framed are found totally inadequate to their purpose, they will call in the feeble aid of old calumnies." He pointed out that Congress had dismissed Brown's charges as cruel and groundless. "Pride and folly," Matlack retorted as T. G. on the 6th, "are perpetually exposing themselves." He admitted that Arnold could hardly have committed so many crimes as Brown alleged. But "when I meet your carriage in the street, and think of the splendour in which you live and revel, of the settlement which it is said you have proposed in a certain case, and of the purchases you have made, and compare these things with the decent frugality necessarily used by other officers in the army, it is impossible to avoid the question: From whence have these riches flowed if you did not plunder Montreal?"

On February 16 every other state represented in Congress voted to postpone Pennsylvania's motion to suspend Arnold from command, and the Pennsylvania charges were referred to a committee which was to confer with the president and council of the state. The committee did not report till March 17, chiefly because Pennsylvania was slow in producing the needed evidence.[60] On the 17th the Congressional committee reported that, in their opinion, only the 1st, 2nd, 3rd, and 5th charges were triable by the court martial which Arnold demanded, and the 1st and 2nd were not proven.[61]

Arnold that same day urged Congress to move as speedily as possible. "As an individual, I trust I shall ever have spirit to be the guardian of my own honour; but as the servant of Congress, when attacked by a public body I consider myself bound to make my appeal to that honourable body in whose service I have the honour to be. And whilst my conduct and the charges against me are under their consideration, I think it my duty to wait the issue without noticing the many abusive misrepresentations and calumnies which are daily circulated by a set of wretches beneath the notice of a gentleman and man of honour. Yet permit me to say that these calumniators, employed and supported by persons in power and reputable stations, whilst my cause remains undetermined before Congress, consider themselves secure and industriously spread their insinuations and false assertions through these United States, to poison the minds of my virtuous countrymen and fellow-citizens and to prejudice them against a man whose life has ever been devoted to their service and who looks on their good opinion and esteem as the greatest reward and honour he can receive. Thus circumstanced, I cannot be charged with undue impatience for soliciting an immediate decision."[62]

Two days later Arnold resigned his command in Philadelphia. On April 3 the Congressional committee had come to an agreement with the Pennsylvania authorities. In the interest of harmony between Congress and Pennsylvania the complaints against Arnold were to be turned over to Washington for trial by court martial, on the 1st, 2nd, 3rd, and 5th charges. In the excitement of debate Thomas Burke of North Carolina said that the Pennsylvania Council had been "waspish, peevish, and childish," and was called to order. But the committee's report was accepted, the resolutions passed.[63] "If Congress," Arnold wrote on the 14th, "have been induced to take this measure for the public good, and to avoid a breach with this state, however hard my case may be and however I am injured as an individual, I will suffer with pleasure until a court martial can have an opportunity of doing me justice by acquitting me of these charges a second time."[64]

Again there were delays and recriminations. Washington on the 20th ordered the inquiry for May 1, then on the 27th had to postpone it to either June 1 or July 1. Arnold charged that Reed was using "every artifice to delay the proceedings of a court martial, as it is his interest that the affair should remain in the dark." Reed charged that Arnold's aides Clarkson and Franks, who had gone to South Carolina, were "designedly absent" so as to avoid having to give testimony which might prove to be damaging to their late chief.[65]

On May 5 Arnold wrote to Washington with peculiar violence. "If your Excellency thinks me criminal, for heaven's sake let me be immediately tried and, if found guilty, executed. I want no favour; I ask only justice. If this is denied me by your Excellency, I have nowhere to seek it but from the candid public, before whom I shall be under the necessity of laying the whole matter. Let me beg of you, Sir, to consider that a set of artful, unprincipled men in office may misrepresent the most innocent actions and, by raising the public clamour against your Excellency, place you in the same situation I am in. Having made every sacrifice of fortune and blood, and become a cripple in the service of my country, I little expected to meet the ungrateful returns I have received from my countrymen; but as Congress have stamped ingratitude as a current coin, I must take it. I wish your Excellency, for your long and eminent services, may not be paid in the same coin. I have nothing left but the little reputation I have gained in the army. Delay in the present case is worse than death."[66]

The letter was hysterical. Nobody had charged Arnold with anything for which he could possibly be executed. Saying that Washington too might be in danger from the misrepresentations of artful, unprincipled men and consequent public clamour, Arnold was unconsciously reassuring himself with the thought that even Washington, given Arnold's grievance, might take Arnold's course. And why was delay worse than death? On May 5 Arnold did not expect to have to wait more than a month or two: a trying delay, but not a mortal one. What lay back of this desperate letter must have been that within a few days of it, before or after, Arnold finally decided to send an emissary to New York and offer his treacherous services to the British.

VI

There is nothing to support the traditional conjectures that Arnold was won over by the persuasions of some British agent, either Beverley Robinson[67] or Christopher Hele.[68] Robinson had tried to win Israel Putnam in October 1777 and in April 1780 was to make advances to Ethan Allen; but he is not known to have had any early communication with Arnold. Lieutenant Hele, in command of the British tender *Hotham,* sailed in October 1778 into the Delaware with the Manifesto and Proclamation of the British commissioners. Arrested and jailed by order of Congress, he was in December released on parole not to leave Philadelphia.[69] He may have talked with Arnold that winter, but it is only a guess that he had any influence.

The British in New York were watching Arnold's quarrels. Clinton on February 16 wrote Germain that Arnold was said to have resigned. On the 17th the *Royal Gazette,* praising Arnold as "more distinguished for valour and perseverance" than any other American commander, said: "General Arnold heretofore has been styled another Hannibal, but losing a leg in the service of Congress, the latter considering him unfit for any further exercise of his military talents, permit him thus to fall into the unmerciful fangs of the executive council of Pennsylvania." This might have seemed a time to appeal to Arnold to change sides. But Clinton after the treason specifically said that Arnold had offered his services "without any overtures from me."[70]

In an angry conference during the Saratoga campaign Arnold declared that "his judgment had never been influenced by any man."[71] And everything in Arnold's career shows how independently—not to say touchily—he made up his mind. Not a hint survives of the disgruntled conversations he may have had with his friend Deane, who also had bitter grievances against Congress. Nor need the later statement of Peggy Arnold, reported at third-hand long after her death, concern Arnold's earliest move. She was said to have said that she had urged Arnold to obtain and then surrender West Point.[72] In May 1779 there was yet no thought of West Point, nor was there to be for another year. If Peggy at the time of her marriage was disgusted with some of the rebel leaders, so was Arnold. And however beguiling she may have been in the warm days of courtship and honeymoon, she could hardly have done more than confirm a powerful will like Arnold's in its own decision. Even if it was actually she who proposed the treachery—and there is no first-hand evidence that she did—the final responsibility must lie with the mature and experienced Arnold for undertaking to carry it out.

In spite of Arnold's later claim that he had been opposed to independence and the French alliance, he seems never to have put a syllable of dissatisfaction on record anywhere before May 1779. Whatever political motives he may then have had, he gave no sign of being actuated by any but personal ones. There was, as always with Arnold, the desire for money. His income had been reduced by his loss of command in Philadelphia, and his expenses increased by his marriage. His share of profits from the *Charming Nancy* had no doubt been spent, and he may or may not have got the money he expected from his trading ventures. The case of the *Active* was still unsettled. Not only had Arnold failed to receive his half, but he is said to have said on April 25 that he must pay £5000 of debts owed by the other claimants, so as to hinder them from selling their shares and revealing their agreement with him.[73] On the 27th his accounts, instead of being settled by Congress, were referred to the treasury board for further examination. Continental currency kept on depreciating, Continental credit growing more shaky. And there were the British in New York with pounds sterling for rebels who would return to their lawful allegiance.

For the rest, there was Arnold's fierce resentment against the civil authorities—in Massachusetts, Congress, Pennsylvania—who had questioned his public accounts and mishandled his promotion and objected to his methods of command. And there were the tricky devices of his enemies, infuriating him with insults while they plotted for a chance to strike. Arnold, who could not believe there could be any guilt in doing what he wanted to do, had none of the weakness of self-doubt. He was right, his enemies were wrong. He had none of the philosophy of Franklin or the magnanimity of Washington, who also had been abused and insulted. Arnold was a man of action only. He must act, or else be sick. To be crippled in the leg was enough to make him desperate. To be hemmed in by pettifogging civilians, expected to account to them for his audacities, checked whenever he turned in any free direction: this was unendurable. Unable to be patient, Arnold had to be violent. In a fury of irritation, he felt he could not wait. Delay was, at that moment, worse for him than death. But it will be seen that, once started on his treacherous career, he developed the cold, sly patience of conspirators.

Hero for Sale

WHATEVER the state—or states—of mind that brought Arnold to the point of treason, his first active steps were simple. "About the month of June 1779," Joseph Stansbury later certified, "General Arnold sent for me and, after some general conversation, opened his political sentiments respecting the war carrying on between Great Britain and America, declaring his abhorrence of a separation of the latter from the former as a measure that would be ruinous to both." Arnold may then, it is true, have expressed such sentiments, but Stansbury did not report them till after the war when Arnold was asking compensation from the British for his losses.[1] "That General Arnold then communicated to me, under a solemn obligation of secrecy, his intention of opening his services to the commander-in-chief of the British forces in any way that would most effectually restore the former government and destroy the then usurped authority of Congress, either by immediately joining the British army or co-operating on some concealed plan with Sir Henry Clinton." Either in error or with some unexplained design both Stansbury and Arnold put the date of this interview in June. It was at least a month earlier.

Stansbury, born in London, had lived in Philadelphia for a dozen years, a mild, pliant man who kept a glass and china shop in Front Street. Though moderately opposed to some of the American measures of the British ministry before 1775, he had been utterly opposed to armed resistance and to the turn toward independence. In October 1776, an informer reported, Stansbury had "sung *God Save the King* in his house, and a number of persons present bore him chorus."[2] Confined for a time to his house for this offence, he had the next year welcomed the coming of the British. With such rewards for his loyalty as being chosen one of the commissioners for selecting and governing the city watch, one of the directors of the Library Company, one of the managers of Howe's lottery for the relief of the poor, Stansbury had enjoyed a minor eminence. He was perhaps best known for his easy verses for various occasions: meetings of the Sons of St. George and of the Church-and-King Club, the arrival of Howe, the recurrent crises of Continental money.

After the British withdrew to New York in June 1778 Stansbury in Philadelphia had adroitly kept to a cautious middle course which included taking the oath of allegiance and abjuration while in his verses privately encouraging the loyalists.

> Think not, though wretched, poor, or naked,
> Your breast alone the load sustains;
> Sympathizing hearts partake it:
> Britain's monarch shares your pains.
> This night of pride and folly over,
> A dawn of hope will soon appear.
> In its light you will discover
> Your triumphant day is near.[3]

Stansbury was conspicuous enough in Philadelphia for Arnold to have met him, and discreet enough for Arnold to trust in his dangerous negotiations. "In order to facilitate the completion of his wishes," Stansbury further certified, "I went secretly to New York with a tender of his services to Sir Henry Clinton."

In New York there was another loyalist poet, the Rev. Jonathan Odell, a graduate of the College of New Jersey (Princeton) and a grandson of its first president. Odell, physician as well as clergyman, had gone to the British early in 1777 from Burlington, where his *Birthday Ode* for that year had been sung the past June by British prisoners of war, to the irritation of the public and the patriot authorities.

> Long as sun and moon endure
> Britain's throne shall stand secure,
> And great George's royal line
> There in splendid honour shine.
> Ever sacred be to mirth
> The day that gave our monarch birth.[4]

In New Jersey Odell had had William Franklin for his patron, and had named his eldest son for the royal governor. In New York Odell, whose New Jersey property was confiscated, lived and supported his wife and three children in Burlington on the six shillings a day which he received as chaplain to the Pennsylvania Loyalists, with a precarious appointment as deputy chaplain to the Royal Fusiliers and irregular gratuities from the commander-in-chief. With the knowledge and probably with the help of Odell, Stansbury had a meeting with André, Clinton's aide, on the morning of Monday, May 10, possibly at Odell's house in Wall Street, more likely at Headquarters at 1 Broadway.

André had probably known Stansbury during the winter the British held Philadelphia. Though he seems to have had no personal acquaintance with Arnold, he had been often at the Shippen house with its amiable daughters. There is only the slightest foundation for the romantic story that André had been in love with Peggy Shippen, or she with him: "Poor André was in love with her," one of her grandsons wrote more than a century later, "but she refused him for Arnold, keeping a lock of André's hair, which we still have."[5] If there had been any correspondence between them through the lines after André left Philadelphia, it apparently took the harmless form of commissions to him to buy her articles of finery in the New York shops. Other pretty smugglers in Philadelphia made the same use of their New York friends if they could, without worrying about the colour of the coat that ran their errands.

The overtures Stansbury brought took André by surprise. He spoke of them that same day, in a note to Clinton, as "such sudden proposals," and of "the kind of confusion" they "created when one must deliberate and determine at once." Stansbury had to hurry back to Philadelphia or run the risk of being missed there, and so suspected if not confined again. While André "mentioned" the matter to Clinton, it was André who gave Stansbury his answer, though not till later in the day, when André had reflected further, did he take time to write out in detail the terms of their agreement.[6]

"On our part," he then wrote, "we met Monk's overtures with full reliance on his honourable intentions and disclose to him, with the strongest assurance of our sincerity, that no thought is entertained of abandoning the point we have in view. That on the contrary, powerful means are expected for accomplishing our end." Arnold, it appears, called himself Monk in these first negotiations, to emphasize the parallel between him and the Scots general who in 1660 had turned against the Parliament and restored the monarchy—and by a grateful monarch had been made captain general, knight, baron, earl, duke, and first lord of the treasury. Naturally Arnold, before changing sides, wished to be assured that the British had no intention of abandoning the war and conceding independence. If he changed sides it was to be to the side he thought would win. ⸺

And what reward might he look for, win or lose? André's statement of their understanding went on: "We likewise assure him that in the very first instance of receiving the tidings or good offices we expect from him, our liberality will be evinced; that in case any partial but important blow should be struck or aimed, upon the strength of just and pointed information and co-operation, rewards equal at least to what such service can be estimated at will be given. But should the abilities and zeal of that able and enterprising gentleman amount to the seizing an obnoxious band of men, to the delivery into our power or enabling us to attack to advantage and by judicious assistance completely to defeat a numerous body, then would the generosity of the nation exceed even his most sanguine hopes; and in the expectation of this he may rely on that honour he now trusts in his present advances." Even in case of failure the British would be generous. "Should his manifest efforts be foiled and after every zealous attempt flight be at length necessary, the cause for which he suffers will hold itself bound to indemnify him for his losses and receive him with the honours his conduct deserves."

Stansbury, Arnold, and Clinton all subsequently agreed that Arnold's original offer had left it to Clinton to decide whether Arnold should at once join the British army or remain where he was, and that Clinton had preferred the second arrangement. But André's written instructions to Stansbury on May 10 contain not a syllable about this offer or this preference. The whole assumption was that Arnold would serve the British while in the confidence of the Americans. "His own judgment," André wrote, "will point out the services required, but for fair satisfaction we give the following hints. Counsels of [Congress]. Contents of dispatches from foreign abettors. Original dispatches and papers which might be seized and sent to us. Channels through which such dispatches pass, hints for securing them. Number and position of troops, whence and what reinforcements are expected and when. Influencing persons of rank with the same favourable disposition in the several commands in different quarters. Concerting the means of a blow of importance. Fomenting any party which when risen to a height might perhaps easily be drawn into a desire of accommodation rather than submit to an odious yoke [the yoke of France]. Magazines—where any new are forming. To interest himself in procuring an exchange of prisoners for the honour of America." This last referred of course to Burgoyne's captured army, still held by Congress on grounds which the British called highly dishonourable.

The correspondence between André and Stansbury was to be in cipher. Each of them would have a copy of a long book: in the first case, a volume of Blackstone's *Commentaries,* though it is not named in André's instructions. Each word in their letters would be represented by three figures: the number of the page on which the word might be found, the number of the line, and the number of the word in the line. Or they might use invisible ink, to be brought out by the application either of heat or of acid. If they did this they were to put a mark on each letter to indicate the kind of ink used. "In writings to be discovered by a process, F is fire, A acid."

These devices were not enough for the ingenious André. Certain topics in their letters might be in a veiled language. "In general information, an old woman's health may be the subject." His plans for a correspondence with Peggy Arnold make it impossible to doubt that she was perfectly aware of the conspiracy from the beginning, and that Stansbury brought word from her as well as from her husband. "The lady might write to me at the same time with one of her intimates, she will guess who I mean, the latter remaining ignorant of interlining and sending the letter. I will myself write to the friend to give occasion for a reply." That is, he would write to Peggy Arnold's friend Peggy Chew, as he shortly did. Peggy Chew, answering in good faith, would turn her letter over to Peggy Arnold to be sent. Peggy Arnold would inter-line the letter with a message in invisible ink. "This will come by a flag of truce, exchanged officer, etc., every messenger remaining ignorant of what they are charged with. The letters may talk of the Mischianza or other nonsense."

André arranged that Stansbury should be taken that night by sloop and whale boat to Prince's bay, recommended to the com-mander of the armed vessel stationed there, and put ashore pre-sumably at South Amboy for his furtive journey across New Jersey and home. "Not finding myself very well," André wrote to Clin-ton a few hours later, "I in consequence of your indulgence on these occasions came into the country," somewhere on York (Man-hattan) Island. The more he thought about the Arnold business the more important it seemed that it should not be left to the hazards of an oral agreement. It was then he set down all he had said to Stansbury and sent it off to Clinton with the request that the commander-in-chief, if he agreed, should seal and transmit it.

The draft which was kept in the Headquarters file is the earliest essential document in the famous conspiracy. It is even more in-teresting than the fair copy which may be supposed to have gone with Stansbury. In his first reference to Monk André started to write "Arnold" then struck it out, realizing that the letter might fall into the hands of the watchful Americans. He referred to defeating "our enemy," and then changed it to "a numerous body." Arnold was after all still in the ranks of that enemy.

II

André's letter to Peggy Chew must have been written soon, though the Headquarters copy is not dated. She had been his lady in the Mischianza and would remember the costumes he had de-signed for the mimic tournament. "I hardly dare write to you," he began, "after having neglected your commissions and not apolo-gized for my transgressions. I would with pleasure have sent you drawings of headdresses had I been as much of a milliner here as I was at Philadelphia in Mischianza times; but from occupation as well as ill health I have been obliged to abandon the pleasing study of what relates to the ladies. I should however be happy to resume it had I the same inducements as when I had the pleasure of frequenting yours and the Shippen family. I know besides that you have everything from Paris, the fountain-head, and therefore have the less regret in neglecting your orders in this particular." In speaking of Paris he was hinting a reproach for the French alliance. "I trust I am yet in the memory of the little society of Third and Fourth Streets and even of the *other Peggy*, now Mrs. Arnold, who will I am sure accept of my best respects and with the rest of the sisterhood of both streets peruse not disdainfully this page meant as an assurance of my unabated esteem for them.'

He sent Peggy Chew news of special British friends in New York, and told her how much he had hated to disagree with Colonel Harrison, Washington's aide, at their recent meeting to discuss the exchange of prisoners. "I intended in case of agreement to have subjoined a clause that all hearts on either side should be restored or others sent in exchange. This would have afforded considerable relief to many swains who still magnetically turn to the banks of the Delaware." He marked his letter A for acid.

This letter, apparently so innocent, actually so well devised for its secret purpose, may or may not have been sent, may or may not have reached Peggy Chew and Peggy Arnold. No answer from either of them survives. André, with his melodramatic turn, could not help embroidering his plot as if for a bad play, but he had no luck in his effort to involve Peggy Chew in a dangerous correspondence of which she knew nothing, or Peggy Arnold in a superfluous subplot.

There were theatrical mishaps enough before a reply could be obtained from Arnold. On the 16th Odell sent an express to Stansbury by a trusted messenger, John Rattoon of South Amboy. That letter seems to have been lost. On the 21st Arnold gave Stansbury an answer which got through the lines and arrived at Odell's house ten days later, enclosed in a letter from Stansbury to Odell. Odell could not wait to carry Arnold's letter to André, for whom it was intended, but made an unlucky effort to read it himself. In a few minutes he had to sit down and write a troubled letter to André.

"I am mortified to death, having just received (what I had been so anxiously expecting) a letter from S——, and, by a private mark agreed on between us, perceiving it contained an invisible page for you. I assayed it by the fire, when, to my inexpressible vexation, I found that the paper, having by some accident got damp in the way, had spread the solution in such a manner as to make the writing all one indistinguishable blot, out of which not the half of any one line can be made legible. I shall use every diligence to forward a letter to him, and to instruct him to guard against the like accident in the future, and hope it will not be long before I shall receive a return." Since Stansbury's letters to Odell came in the same cipher as Stansbury used to André, Odell thought he might be of service. "If you think proper to confide so far in my discretion, I shall make it a rule to assay and carefully transcribe such passages as may come to you for your perusal." André agreed to this, and much of the following correspondence from Arnold is Odell's decipher in Odell's hand.

There were mishaps also at Stansbury's end of the stealthy line. "The confusion of a town meeting," he wrote Odell on May 26, "hath banished me to Moorestown [New Jersey] for preservation." A noisy parade of the militia in Philadelphia on the 24th had been followed the next day by a meeting at which a noisy party had protested against the rising prices caused by the depreciation of the Continental currency. Rich merchants, like Robert Morris with his warehouses full of flour, were particularly blamed for forcing prices up without concern for the public distress. Stansbury, not a rich merchant but uncertain as to his standing with the Whigs, took no chances. "You know the antipathy, or rather fear," he metaphorically explained to Odell in a letter of June 9, "which I have of thunder; and I have sought a temporary shelter here, where the tall trees and high buildings which surround and make my dwelling [in Philadelphia] rather dangerous in stormy weather are not to be met with."

It was probably at Moorestown that he wrote his lively satire *The Town Meeting* (printed in New York in Rivington's *Royal Gazette* for June 26) which certain Philadelphia politicians never forgave. He must have taken a sly pleasure in appearing to be indignant because "*Morris* the wise, *Arnold* the brave" were by the Philadelphia riffraff equally "Confounded with the Tory."[7]

At the distance between them Odell and Stansbury could not help working at cross-purposes. Stansbury in his letter of May 26 said that the cipher of two (missing) letters he had sent was based on Bailey's *Dictionary*, the 25th London edition. Odell on June 9 asked him "to stick to your Oxford Interpreter"—meaning the Blackstone volume. Stansbury, writing in Moorestown that same day, hinted that there were disadvantages in using Blackstone and that he preferred Bailey. He had just received Odell's letter—now lost—of the 3rd which told of the damaged first reply from Arnold. "The original," Stansbury had to report, "is either mislaid or destroyed." He could only hope that some of the other letters he had written would get through the lines.

The conspiring poets sent letter after letter on the perilous way, never sure whether one of them would be received or intercepted. A duplicate of one letter from Odell went "by Mrs. Gordon, who accompanies Mrs. Chamier to Philadelphia." One letter from Stansbury to André was brought by way of Shrewsbury by "Tilton and Hulitt, the two young men for whom I [Odell] have lately requested ensigns' commissions in the militia."[8] Most of the letters were carried by the conspirators' "slender friend" John Rattoon, of "whose fidelity," Odell told André on July 18, "I am more fully assured than I can be of almost any other." Odell might not have been so confident if he had known that on May 22 Washington received a letter "from Mr. Ratton So. Amboy recomd. by Colo. Moylan," with information about the sailing of a British fleet for the Chesapeake, movements of troops on Long Island, and loyalist preparations for raids on the patriots.[9] Or could this have been a conspiratorial device for giving Rattoon a good name with the Americans while he was serving the British? Or was Washington's letter perhaps not from John Rattoon, vestryman of St. Peter's at Amboy, but rather from Robert Rattoon who kept an inn there and was afterwards postmaster?[10]

"As my present situation," Stansbury wrote on June 4, "cuts me off from my favourite sphere of usefulness, I endeavoured, in a circuitous manner, to procure a letter from A. G. [General Arnold] to forward by this favourite conveyance. From some unknown cause I have received none, probably owing to the shortness of the notice." Arnold, whose court martial had been set for May 1, then postponed a month, had gone to Headquarters at Middlebrook for the first session on June 1, only to have it adjourned, on account of the movements of the British on the Hudson. On the 9th Stansbury reported that "Mr. A. G. is at present out of town on private business." But "I have some time since forwarded to Mr. Andrews [André] a plan of trade which will, I hope, be to the satisfaction of the concerned." Odell, who on the 9th had written Stansbury that "Lothario [André] is impatient," on the 13th wrote André there was fresh hope in the news that the "plan of trade" had been sent. It seems to have come soon after, dated May 23, in a cipher based—as if to make things more complicated than they already were—on the 21st edition of Bailey.

III

"Our friend S——," Arnold had had Stansbury write, "acquaints me that the proposals made by him in my name are agreeable to Sir Henry Clinton and that Sir Henry engages to answer my warmest expectations for any services rendered." Arnold's first thought was about his reward for changing sides. "As I esteem the interest of America and Great Britain inseparable S. H. may depend on my exertions and intelligence [information]. It will be impossible to co-operate unless there is a mutual confidence. S. H. shall be convinced on every occasion that his is not misplaced."

Arnold sent an assortment of military and political secrets. "General Washington and the army will move to the North [Hudson] river as soon as forage can be obtained. Congress have given up Charles Town [Charleston, South Carolina] if attempted. They are in want of arms, ammunition, and men to defend it. Three or four thousand militia is the most that can be mustered to fight on any emergency." As to André's suggestion about original dispatches: "Seizing papers is impossible. Their contents can be known from a member of Congress." Just how they could be known, or from what member, Arnold did not say. "Four months since the French minister required Congress to vest their agents with powers to negotiate peace with Britain. The time is elapsed in disputing if they shall demand independency with their original terms or insist on the addition of Newfoundland. No decision, no

measure taken to prevent the depreciation of money, no foreign
loan obtained. France refused to become surety. No encouragement from Spain. The French fleet has conditional orders to return to this continent. They depend on great part of their provisions from hence."

Not all these military secrets were very important, nor all the
political ones too accurate. But Arnold meant to do what he could.
"I will co-operate when an opportunity offers, and as life and
everything is at stake, I shall expect some certainty: my property
here secure and a revenue equivalent to the risk and service done.
I cannot promise success; I will deserve it. Inform me what I may
expect. Could I know S. H.'s intentions he should never be at a
loss for intelligence. I shall expect a particular answer through our
friend Stansbury." Arnold added a postscript: "Madam Arnold
presents her particular compliments."

Even if Arnold's reply had come more promptly André could
not have answered it at once. He had accompanied Clinton on a
sudden successful expedition against the Highland forts up the
Hudson. The British forces moved on May 31, took Stony Point
that day, Verplanck's the next. André, sent under a flag of truce to
receive the surrender of Fort Lafayette at Verplanck's, dramati-
cally granted terms "on the glacis of Fort Fayette." Clinton and
André returned at once to New York. It was this expedition which
forced the second postponement of Arnold's trial: "the exigency
of the public service not permitting it to sit at this time."[11] But
Arnold while at camp had picked up some military information
which he sent André on June 18.

The Headquarters copy of André's first answer to Arnold is
marked "Middle of June." "I have your letter of the 23rd May,"
André wrote. "One in cipher received before was injured by the
damp and not legible. Some messages through S. will have shown
my wish to hear from you, and that in a tone consonant to the
enlarged plan upon which S. H. C. is taught to expect your concurrence." By "enlarged" André probably meant "large." There is
no evidence that there had been any change in the magnitude of
their undertaking. But he was precise enough in his response to
Arnold's wish to be told Clinton's plans for the year's campaign.
"With the same candour which you will experience when engaged

in any operations concerted with him, his Excellency wishes to apprise you that he cannot reveal his intentions as to the present campaign nor can he find the necessity of such a discovery or that a want of a proper degree of confidence is to be inferred from his not making it. He informs you with the strictest truth that the war is to be prosecuted with vigour, and that no thought is entertained of giving up the dependency of America, much less of hearkening to such a claim as you have been told the Congress affect to debate upon": that is, independence for Newfoundland.

Clinton could not, André was politely saying, be expected to treat with Arnold altogether as an equal. He was only one of the American generals, and he was not in command anywhere. A British soldier who had escaped from Philadelphia told André, who entered it in his notebook of intelligence on the 24th, that Arnold was "in no repute."

André in his answer to Arnold went on with a delicate reminder from Clinton. "He begs you to observe that you proposed your assistance for the delivery of your country. You must know where the present power is vulnerable, and the conspicuous commands with which you might be vested may enable us at one shining stroke, from which both riches and honour would be derived, to accelerate the ruin to which the usurped authority is verging and to put a speedy end to the miseries of our fellow-creatures." It was sufficient for Arnold to know that Clinton's army was "now centrically stationed fifty miles up the North river" since his recent occupation of the Highland forts. "A few hours can embark him for any part of the coast, and an irruption into the country in any direction is equally at his choice. He forbids any but a circuitous communication between the southern and eastern provinces. In this situation, whatever may be his designs, he can concur with you in almost any plan you can advise and in which you will cordially co-operate."

Clinton had a specific suggestion for Arnold. "Join the army, accept a command, be surprised, be cut off: these things may happen in the course of manœuvre, nor you be censured or suspected. A complete service of this nature involving a corps of five or six thousand men would be rewarded with twice as many thousand guineas."

Here was the first mention of an actual amount that might be paid Arnold for his double-dealing. "The method," André explained, "would be arranged by my meeting you as flag of truce or otherwise as soon as you come near us. It is service of this nature, or intelligence having evidently led to such strokes, which S. H. C. looks for. It is such as these he pledges himself shall be rewarded beyond your warmest expectations. The colour of the times favours them, and your abilities and firmness justify his hopes of success. In the meantime your influence might be generously, as well as profitably, employed in procuring the exchange of General Burgoyne's army. It could be urged by none with more propriety," since Arnold had been among the victors at Saratoga, "nor would you be sorry to see this act of justice superadded to the shining revolution you may perhaps be instrumental in effecting." (Here André proposed what was to be their fatal interview.)

Whatever the uncertainty as to the date of this letter, there is none as to the circumstances of its reception. Stansbury narrated them on July 11 in a letter to Odell which Odell quoted in part in a letter to André a week later.

"It was on the evening of the 7th Mr. Anderson's [André's] favour came to hand, which I immediately delivered to Mrs. Moore." The change from "Mr. A. G." to "Mr. Moore" for Arnold was presumably made out of caution, and the name Moore may have been chosen because Stansbury had been at Moorestown. "A multiplicity of business prevented Mr. M—— giving it the requisite attention. I waited on him yesterday morning, found he had made some progress in the account and promised me cash in the evening, and to send me a sketch that I might draw out a fair account and send Mr. Creek home." The terms "account" and "cash" meant nothing except that Stansbury was aiming to disguise his language so it would seem, if it fell into the wrong hands, to be about some simple business transaction. "Instead thereof I received a note from him, that he had carefully examined the letter [from André] and found, by the laconic style and little attention paid to his request, that the gentleman appeared very indifferent respecting the matter. He therefore omitted sending me the memorandum he intended in the morning, and wished to see me. We had a long conversation, the result whereof forms the enclosed letter to Mr. Anderson on the 23rd principle"—based as to its cipher on the 23rd edition of Bailey.

Moreover, Arnold had been suspicious. Since André's letter had come in Odell's handwriting, Odell might know the identity of Monk, A. G., Moore—as Odell unquestionably did. Stansbury had insisted that "Mr. Osborne [Odell] only knew that a Mr. Moore was concerned in the business." The poet had had no scruple about hoodwinking the conspirator. Nor did Odell, quoting this part of Stansbury's letter to André, object to further deception. "I mention this that, if you should think proper, without seeming to know he had entertained such a suspicion (which I presume respected not you but S——), you might somehow express yourself, whenever you next write, in such a manner as to reassure him on this head."

Stansbury's letter to Odell had a paragraph concerned with Peggy Arnold. "Mrs. Moore requests the enclosed list of articles for her own use may be procured for her and the account of them and the former sent, and she will pay for the whole with thanks." The list ran: 18 yards wide or 22 yards narrow pale pink mantua (silk or other rich material for a loose cape such as women then wore); 1 piece broad pale pink ribbon; 6 yards satinet for shoes; 1 piece diaper for napkins (heavy silk or linen cloth for table napkins); 1 pair neat spurs; 1 piece clouting diaper (for towels or baby's napkins, though she had no baby).

Efforts have been made, with agile ingenuity, to prove that this matter-of-fact list conveyed some secret message to André. It can hardly have signified more than that she thought herself on the same friendly terms with André as ever, even though her husband may have been disappointed in the negotiations; and possibly that André was not to think of the negotiations as ended yet. André seems to have neglected the list and Odell to have done nothing about it till December 21, when he noted in a postscript to André: "A parcel, long since requested by S—— to be sent for Mrs. Moore, is now made up, and I hope soon to be able to send it. Shall I charge it to S—— or is it, as one before, to be accounted between yourself and your humble servant?"

IV

The important communication of July 11 was not from her but from Arnold, referred to as Gustavus, through Stansbury, who now called himself Jonathan Stevens, to André. "I delivered Gustavus your letter. It is not equal to his expectations. He expects to have your promise that he shall be indemnified for any loss he may sustain in case of detection, and, whether this contest is finished by sword or treaty, that £10,000 shall be engaged to him for his services, which shall be faithfully devoted to your interest." Here was Arnold's first statement of his price, at a figure to which he was reiteratively faithful in all his later bargaining.

As if to soften his curt answer, or to show how valuable his services might be, Arnold went on, though curtly, with his supply of information. Washington had 10,000 effectives with him, and might be joined by from 4000 to 8000 militia. "Plenty of everything at camp—supplied from everywhere." General Sullivan, leading the expedition against the Iroquois who with the loyalists had devastated the frontier for two terrible summers, "commands 5000 regulars—are now sixty miles above Wyoming" on the Susquehanna. "Detroit the object—usual route. Six or eight field-pieces—plenty of provisions carried on 1500 pack horses. Whether likely to succeed you must be the best judge." Gates was at Providence, Heath at Boston. Benjamin Lincoln, commanding in the southern department, had 3000 regulars and 500 militia. "Not likely to collect any army of consequence—the militia do not turn out with alacrity. . . . The forts in our rivers are in better state than ever before. No heavy cannon, garrison small, no stores, being supplied from this town occasionally. D'Estaing coming here this summer depends on the British admiral. We know nothing about it."

This letter, brought by Rattoon, who was "detained by some embarrassments in his way," reached Odell on Sunday evening July 18. Odell at once wrote at length to André. Stansbury's packet had contained, besides letters to André and Odell, one "for a Major Giles at Flatbush" which Odell thought was "really intended for the person to whom it is addressed." Aquila Giles had been captured at Brandywine and sent prisoner to Long Island, where he married a loyalist girl and helped Peggy Arnold with her shopping through the lines. From what Stansbury had told him Odell was aware that "my friend's friend has misunderstood your [André's] letter and disappointed, I apprehend, your expectations. Yet if I might take the liberty to suggest my own opinion, I could wish you to write once more at least, as it cannot do any harm and may possibly be still worth while." Odell at that point, and perhaps also André, was afraid that the negotiations with Arnold had fallen through. "But I am in much greater pain from an apprehension that the late unfortunate event"—the recapture by Wayne of Stony Point two days before—"may be so consequential as to render it difficult for you to find time at present for attending to a seemingly fruitless correspondence.

"I must, however, beg a line from you as soon as possible, as our Mercury [Rattoon] is already suspected of having been here and therefore wishes to return without delay, lest, if long absent, the danger from such suspicion should be the greater. If you have not time to write, would you approve of my mentioning your being at present out of town as a reason, and at the same time renew my assurances to my friend that his employer [Arnold] may most surely rely upon your being absolutely in earnest, on your part, to conduct the business proposed in a manner that cannot fail, but through his own groundless hesitation, to surpass his most sanguine expectations?"

Three days later Odell again wrote to André. He was sending his copy of the 23rd edition of Bailey, which Stansbury had used in his latest letters, but wanted the book back with André's answer, "in order that I may execute the commission properly respecting the queries I am to propose. I am glad to find you are still patient enough to continue the correspondence. Something surely may be expected from it, and I am, I confess, still in hopes of something 'on a large scale.' Otherwise the conduct already shown is utterly unaccountable to me." If André should write to Stansbury's partner [Arnold] directly, he must use the 25th edition of Bailey which he had formerly taken with him from Odell's house. The 23rd, now being sent, had cost 60 Continental dollars in Philadelphia, and Rattoon had brought it from Stansbury. "Mercury waits till I hear again from you."

"I am sorry," André's answer began, written directly to Arnold and in the Headquarters copy marked "End of July," "any hesitation should still remain, as I think we have said all that the prudence with which our liberality must be tempered will admit. I can only add that, as such sums as are held forth must be in some degree accounted for, real advantage must appear to have arisen from the expenditure, or a generous effort must have been made." In directer words, Clinton might be liberal but he must be prudent. He could not pay out £10,000 without question from the British government, and could not justify any such payment except for notable, unmistakable services. He would not fix an amount for indemnification in advance, certainly not on Arnold's unsupported estimate of the value of the property he stood to lose.

"We are thankful for the information transmitted, and hope you will continue to give it as frequently as possible. Permit me to prescribe a little exertion." So far Arnold had told them only facts he was easily in possession of. "It is the procuring an accurate plan of West Point, New Windsor [Washington's Headquarters near Newburgh], Constitution [the fort opposite West Point], etc." This was the earliest reference between them to West Point, but without any thought that it was to become the most weighty matter in their negotiations. "An account of what vessels, gunboats, or galleys are in the North river or may be shortly built there, and the weight of metal they carry. The army as brigaded with the commanding officers in the form commonly called the order of battle. Sketches or descriptions of harbours to the eastward which might be attacked, and where stores and shipping might be destroyed.

"The only method of completing conviction, on both sides, of the generous intentions of each and making arrangements for important operations is by a meeting. Would you assume a command"—again André reminded Arnold that he was not in the field, where he could be really useful to the British—"and enable me to see you, I am convinced a conversation of a few minutes would satisfy you entirely and I trust would give us equal cause to be pleased. In any concerted plan which may not be carried into execution before that time, General Phillips's coming here on parole would be an exceeding good opportunity for further explanations." Phillips was in Virginia, still unexchanged. "He is S. H. C.'s firm friend and a man of strict honour. But neither to him nor any person can we give the smallest hint without your permission, which we do not mean to ask unless you are perfectly willing to grant it. But above all, Sir, let us not lose time or contract our views, which on our part have become sanguine from the extensive strain of your overtures, and which we cannot think you would on your side confine to general intelligence whilst so much greater things may be done and advantages in proportion as much greater can be reaped."

Arnold replied through Stansbury in a letter dated "Saturday 3 A.M.," probably by the middle of August. "I have had an interview with ——," Stansbury wrote, "who showed me your letter and remarked that it contained no reply to the terms mentioned in my last"—to the request for a promise of £10,000. "Though he could not doubt your honour yet there was no assurance given that his property in this country should be indemnified from any loss that might attend unfortunate discovery. However sincerely he wished to serve his country in accelerating the settlement of this unhappy contest, yet he should hold himself unjust to his family to hazard his all on the occasion and part with a certainty (potentially at least) for an uncertainty. He hopes to join the army in about three weeks, when he will if possible contrive an interview. He will make a point of seeing General Phillips if he comes here, and may perhaps open himself to that general. At [the] same time, he depends on your honour that nothing ever transpires to his disadvantage. I wished him to put pen to paper, but he said he had told me his sentiments and confided in me to represent them, which I have done with fidelity."

If André could hint, so could Arnold. "In the course of the conversation he asked me if I knew that Sir Henry was going home and Lord Cornwallis was to have the command." Clinton on the 20th of that month did desire, he wrote Germain, to give up his command to Cornwallis. As to André's latest queries Arnold "said he had nothing to communicate at present that could be of service. He had not the plan of West Point—being only in General Washington's hands and the engineer's who made the draft. It had many new works, and he could when there make a drawing of it easily. The number of men and the commanding officers were shifting daily, the commanding officer of a wing today being ordered perhaps to some post to-morrow. The harbours, etc., to the eastward he thought you must be well acquainted with, and also knew where the vessels, stores, etc., lay, as Boston, Newburyport, Salem, etc." Gérard, minister from France, was still "detained by Congress, not having come to any definitive terms to offer Great Britain." Congress defined those terms on the 14th, though Arnold may not have known it at once.

V

With this reply the first chapter of the negotiations came to a standstill. Arnold had named his price, and Clinton had refused to meet it. André did not for the present write to him again, but instead wrote on the 16th to Peggy Arnold. "Major Giles," he told her, "is so good as to take charge of this letter, which is meant to solicit your remembrance, and to assure you that my respect for you and the fair circle in which I had the honour of becoming acquainted with you remains unimpaired by distance or political broils. It would make me very happy to become useful to you here. You know the Mischianza made me a complete milliner. Should you not have received supplies for your fullest equipment for that department, I shall be glad to enter into the whole detail of cap-wire, needles, gauze, etc., and, to the best of my ability, render you in these trifles services from which I hope you would infer a zeal to be further employed."

Peggy Arnold may have reflected that André had not yet taken the trouble to execute her month-old commission, but she could not miss his "zeal to be further employed," or misunderstand what he meant. Possibly she agreed with her husband as to his value to the British. At any rate, she did not answer André till October 13, and then in as prim a note as was ever written by a conspirator. "Mrs. Arnold presents her best respects to Captain André, is much obliged to him for his very polite and friendly offer of being serviceable to her. Major Giles was so obliging as to promise to procure what trifles Mrs. Arnold wanted in the millinery way, or she would with pleasure have accepted of it. Mrs. Arnold begs leave

to assure Captain André that her friendship and esteem for him is
not impaired by time or accident. The ladies to whom Captain
André wished to be remembered are well and present their compliments to him."

The feelings of the disappointed poets may be guessed from a
letter Odell, signing himself James Osborne, wrote in reply to two
lost letters from Stansbury dated September 13 and 26. "Your notions concerning the merit and the views of your friend the Overseer [Arnold] seem to be the same with mine, and I believe we are
not alone in our ideas on this head, for I am desired by our common friend pd 53 [André?] to address myself on this occasion
directly to you"—rather than to the unresponsive Arnold—"and
to request authentic information concerning any points that you
may suppose important at this time." He asked, he explained in
his commercial jargon, only for such articles "as are now most in
demand, and if they are genuine they will fetch a very good price;
but unless they are of the best quality they will not be so readily
saleable, and by no means turn to so good account." Odell had not
lost all hope. In his poem *The Congratulation* (printed in the
Royal Gazette for November 6 and again as from popular demand
on the 24th) he insisted there were secret forces that would overthrow the tyrant Congress in the end:

> Seen or unseen, on earth, above, below,
> All things conspire to give the final blow.
> Heaven has ten thousand thunderbolts to dart;
> From hell ten thousand living flames will start;
> Myriads of swords are ready for the field;
> Myriads of lurking daggers are concealed;
> In injured bosoms dark revenge is nursed.
> Yet but a moment and the storm shall burst.[12]

"In injured bosoms dark revenge is nursed." A letter which
Stansbury by a slip dated November (for December) 3 brought
news from Arnold that the American army was going into winter
quarters. There was a shortage of flour in camp and in Philadelphia, though plenty in Maryland. "M—— [Arnold] proposes landing troops in Maryland to cut off these supplies." The American
prospects in the southern department were not encouraging. "Tell

me if you wish to have a useful hand in their army, and to pay what you find his services merit." In the middle states "Washington had about 9 or 10,000 before Sullivan joined him with 3000, and Gates is going to join him with 1500, making together 14,000. All these, except 2000, are veterans enlisted during the war. Blankets are scarce with them: one to four men." Bad news had leaked out of New York. "Some insect of your place has written the president of Congress that the October packet was arrived, the contents not transpired, but that your officers looked very blue." Philip Schuyler had proposed that Congress move from Philadelphia, "because they could do no business but it was instantly communicated to you. The questions to be put are: shall they move to the eastward or southward? If the latter, Baltimore and Bladensburg are mentioned; if the former, Hartford in Connecticut." It was no secret to Congress that the British were getting ready to embark in force from New York, and it was supposed they were "destined for the southward as soon as the French leave the coast." Congress was scheming to get money from Holland. "If the bait takes, they will continue fishing. If not, they must soon leave off." Arnold believed the Comte d'Estaing with the French fleet "has not left us yet, but none of us know where he is, and some of us think he has too much understanding to tell his intentions even to Congress itself." Though Arnold still held out for his own price for his total services, here was some of the small change of treason.

In a letter to André on the 18th Odell, who at William Franklin's suggestion and with Clinton's approval had been writing for a year for the newspapers in support of the British cause, declared that: "However ineffectual my political publications may be, I cannot but hope that, with some assistance, I may yet make my private correspondence essentially useful." Something yet might come through Stansbury from Arnold.

Subplots

S TANSBURY, bringing overtures from Arnold, brought a separate offer from another conspirator, hitherto undetected and unsuspected, who at the time knew nothing of the larger conspiracy, though a year later he was to replace Stansbury as Arnold's agent and handle the first money paid Arnold for his treason.

The minor conspirator appears without a name in André's instructions to Stansbury about Arnold on May 10. "The other channel you mentioned to me this morning, through which a communication was formerly held, must be kept unacquainted with this, and with regard to it the same may be said as with regard to Monk: that liberal acknowledgments will infallibly attend conspicuous services." The missing name was supplied by Stansbury on July 12 in the second part of the letter of the day before about the £10,000 Arnold demanded. "I have since conversed with Mr. Samuel Wallis, who with his [unidentified] friend was extremely useful to General Howe, as mentioned to you at our last interview."[1]

Wallis, born in Maryland but long established as shipper and speculator in Philadelphia, had after the treaty of Fort Stanwix bought a tract of land and built a stone house at Muncy in Northumberland county on the West Branch of the Susquehanna. Though he seems for some years to have lived in Muncy only during the summer, and was a Quaker, he was in February 1776 elected a captain in the Northumberland militia. Beyond Muncy, which was in effect a northwest bastion of Pennsylvania facing the Indian country, white settlers had taken up lands on the West Branch, some of them in lawless trespass on the Indians in spite of sharp resistance. In the summer of 1778, just before the Wyoming raid, an Indian war party fell upon the West Branch settlers and drove them all back to Wallis's house, and on to the shelter of Fort Augusta at Sunbury, in what the district still remembers as the Big Runaway.[2]

Wallis, who had been in Philadelphia during the British occupation and had then, presumably, been of some unrecorded use to Howe, was back at Muncy in July, disgusted with the failure of Pennsylvania to send regular troops to the border. "Such confusion has already happened by trusting to the militia here," he wrote to Matlack on July 24, "that I will not stay a single moment longer than I can help after being assured that we are to be protected by them only. . . . Unless some speedy interposition in our behalf, I do again with great confidence assure you that we shall be no longer a people in this county."[3] In August a detachment of the 6th Pennsylvania established a fort near Wallis's house, and encouraged some of the settlers to return to their farms. In November Wallis was once more in Philadelphia.

On the 3rd he went before a justice of the peace and testified in favour of Roberts who with Carlisle was to be hanged the following day. "Some time in April last, while the enemy were in possession," Wallis affirmed, he had "happened to overhear a conversation pass between Joseph Galloway, late of this city, Esquire, and Colonel Balfour of the British army," one of Howe's aides. Galloway had recommended Roberts as a "proper person" to guide a British force sent against some Americans across the Schuylkill. "On which Balfour shrugged up his shoulders and said he believed John Roberts was a good kind of man, but that he (Balfour) thought he was not to be depended on." Wallis had understood from this that Roberts was "a person in whom the enemy had no confidence."[4] Other patriots besides Wallis tried to save Roberts, and apparently no one guessed that Wallis—possibly through Galloway—had served Howe in secret as Roberts had in public.

Still keeping his secret, Wallis sent his offer by Stansbury to Clinton in May. By July Wallis had special information in return for the assurance that liberal acknowledgments would attend conspicuous services. "If a perfect knowledge of everything relating to Sullivan's army is an object with the General [Clinton]," Stansbury wrote in his letter of the 12th, Wallis would "engage to furnish exact accounts thereof every week or fortnight, and that his friend shall go with them as a volunteer and furnish him with intelligence to hand through me. All they ask is that their expenses should be paid and that in the end if they are thought to have deserved anything that they may be considered. It being agreeable to your system to reward in proportion to services done, I have encouraged the matter, that there may be no time lost."

Sullivan was then organizing his expedition against the Six Nations, to destroy their towns and crops and consequently their power to threaten the frontier. Like William Rankin in York county, Wallis sided with the Indians and loyalists against his own neighbours. "Mr. Wallis," Stansbury went on, "is a gentleman of large estate in this province and better acquainted with the Indian country than almost any other person. As such he was applied to by the [Pennsylvania] council to furnish a drawing of the country and to assist them in their plan of the Indian expedition. To have refused would have exposed him to sufferings. His drawing was laid by Reed before Washington and the expedition formed on it. He leads them by it to 100 miles southwest of Tioga. A corrected copy of this drawing will be ready by return of your next. As it will be large it will require some address to get it through."

Here was one of the most extraordinary schemes ever contrived by a loyalist. Wallis would furnish Sullivan with a false map to mislead him, and Clinton with a true map to give the British an advantage. But no such drawing as Wallis said he furnished has been found, nor any corrected copy in the British files. Certainly the expedition was not formed on Wallis's treacherous design. While Washington had in February applied to Reed for maps of the Indian country, he had also consulted numerous experts and laid his plans with great care.[5] Sullivan's comment, in his official report, that "the maps of the country are so exceeding erroneous that they serve not to enlighten but to perplex,"[6] was true of all of them. Wallis not only said he would do more than he could but also said he had done more than he had. If his unidentified friend went with the expedition, he at least made no reports that have been found.

André, signing himself Joseph Andrews, replied to Stansbury about Wallis late in July in a note of which Headquarters kept what seems to be an abridged copy. "Obliged to him for his exactness and assiduity. Intelligence concerning Sullivan will be acceptable and the drawing we are anxious to receive. Expenses of a limited nature shall be paid and, as you judge, services considered hereafter in proportion to their importance. This kind of information, however, has but a very indirect influence here and does not enable us to distress or counteract. Immediate information of the movements of the army opposed to us is the main point. Our compliments and thanks to Mr. W."

Though Wallis's information was not very valuable, his house might be, as a safe and secret rendezvous on the frontier. In an undated letter to an unidentified loyalist André wrote after hearing from Wallis: "We have received favourable impressions of your sentiments and are acquainted with your influence and abilities. You may render essential services and these would be amply rewarded. The word is ———. When that is sent to the house of Wallis at [Muncy] then you must communicate with Colonel Brant or whoever commands. Give him information and when he meditates a blow second him by a sudden meeting of loyalists at a particular place which you may concert, to join and strike with him, or by intercepting convoys, burning magazines, spiking cannon, breaking down bridges, or otherwise as you shall see expedient. Send us in answer the state of the back country as to defence, your ideas as to the most proper points to be attacked and posts to be maintained. And think of some handsome scheme for an important service to government. We shall not be idle on this side." Wallis's scheme of the false map was hardly more extraordinary than his readiness to let his house be used as the centre of frontier intrigue; the Quaker conspiring with the Mohawk.

II

The frontier conspirators Wallis of Northumberland and Rankin of York possibly did not know about each other's plans during 1779. On November 27 Christopher Sower, Rankin's agent, warned André against Wallis's agent Stansbury, who Sower had heard "insinuates to be employed on secret services for government." André, directing the plots, carefully kept the plotters separate.

On June 20 Alexander MacDonald and three followers came to New York with the watchword that had been sent to Rankin in March. MacDonald claimed to have raised 600 men in York county independent of Rankin's. But because MacDonald was a deserter from the British army who had escaped to the frontier, he was suspected of inventing a story to save his skin, and was arrested. André wrote to Rankin: "We are sorry you have extended your confidence so much, fearing you may be drawn into difficulties by your zeal unless tempered with much prudence. We send you a new word which you will please not to divulge, but only make use of it according to our first intentions for a check on any false messenger. You shall be called upon when your services in a body can be useful to his Majesty. In the meantime, certain services which the messenger [Fürstner] will explain can be rendered."[7] These immediate services, according to Sower, were that Rankin should "destroy the [Carlisle] magazine clandestinely and order the perpetrators to retreat to this place [New York] where they should be handsomely rewarded."[8]

Fürstner went again to York and was back in August. MacDonald had told the truth, Rankin said, "having actually raised 623 men who might have been collected in one night's time for action. These men have now put themselves under the command of Colonel Rankin and renounce all further connexion with MacDonald, since they have learned that he is a deserter. . . . That one Scherrop, a man of good repute living near Hanover alias McAllister's Town, had also founded a body of 600, mostly Romans [Catholics], who had now put themselves under Colonel Rankin." Two of MacDonald's followers had been captured on their way back from New York, and Rankin thought they might confess for fear of being treated as spies. "In which case it was resolved by Colonel Rankin and his party, now amounting to 1800 men, to take up arms, act openly against the rebels, and, if in danger of being overpowered, retire to the mountains and there defend themselves. But they hope upon their first appearance in arms to be joined by many loyalists from all quarters who as yet know nothing of their design. And at the same time they rely upon his Excellency the commander-in-chief to afford them some relief and assistance if in his power.

"In answer to Captain André's proposal for destroying the magazines at Carlisle in a private manner, they reply that they have appointed proper persons who will enlist in the rebel artillery at that place and execute the business if his Excellency still inclines to have it done secretly. But prior to this, they beg leave to observe that the loyalists know of no other method for procuring a sufficient quantity of arms and ammunition than by seizing instead of destroying the said magazines. Nevertheless, upon the receipt of orders the matter shall be instantly set about, trusting that his Excellency's wisdom will supply them in some other manner."[9]

Clinton's reply, sent at once by André through Fürstner, was not too encouraging: "That the General applauded their zeal and loyalty and was sorry to find them involved in difficulties at this time, in particular as he could not have a share in their danger; that the report of the French fleet being on the coast had made some other measures necessary which were not foreseen, but [he] expected they would soon return to the West Indies and pursue their object there; that he would advise them to remain quiet, and if the rebels should confine any of the leading men he wished to be informed of it, that he might by some means or other procure their releasement."[10]

On October 5 another messenger came from Rankin. The messenger had on his way fallen into the hands of the rebels, destroyed the letter he carried, escaped after three weeks, and got to New York. But he had read the letter and could give Sower its purport. "Some of MacDonald's party had inadvertently betrayed the secret and thereby alarmed the rebels," who had confined supposed loyalists in the York jail. Rankin was "universally suspected as the author of this combination" and "great threats are thrown out against him. That his party is exceedingly numerous and determined to rescue their friends whose lives are in danger, and to support his Majesty's cause. That he relies on his Excellency's humanity and hopes he will not let so many loyalists fall a sacrifice to rebellion. That he would humbly represent, if a body of troops with vessels were sent to Baltimore or the lower counties on Delaware, they could at all events secure a retreat but should most probably bring Pennsylvania to a sense of its duty. That if they could get no assistance his men were determined to make the rebels purchase their lives dearly, being resolved to go to the extremes of fire and sword. That he prays for his Excellency's advice and an answer to his representation by Andrew Fürstner without delay. That he will undertake to do the fighting part, praying only for a small detachment of ships and troops upon the coast to give countenance to the matter."

André's answer on November 9 once more asked the conspirators to be patient. "We are happy to find our friends continue so zealous and hope they will soon experience that our attention to them is not relaxed. We recommend prudence, but at the same time every preparatory measure to act when called upon."

Rankin's party no doubt expected more from Clinton than he could do, and he more from it than it would undertake without full support or authorization from him. But the scheme, according to the messengers who kept coming in all winter, grew formidably. On May 1, 1780 Sower sent an enthusiastic report to Clinton, then in South Carolina. Rankin now had 6000 men, Sower said, "spread all over the country" into Lancaster and across the Pennsylvania boundary into Maryland, where "great numbers" were ready to take an active part. "Many of those who heretofore professed to be conscientiously scrupulous of bearing arms [Quakers and German quietists] do now promise to exert themselves in seizing and securing the ringleading rebels." Thomas McKean, chief justice of Pennsylvania, "had been informed of their association and went to Lancaster and York counties to make further discoveries," but "returned without making any." Clinton's messages had satisfied Rankin's people for a time, but they had become impatient, "and often it is with the utmost difficulty he can restrain them from acts of violence. He dreads much that some warm indiscreet person will take the lead out of his hands and endanger the whole. That a certain Dr. McCartney and some others had already begun to burn the houses, mills, and barns of the rebels in Cumberland county and that the [Pennsylvania] council by public proclamation has offered a reward of $1000 for each of them." The border loyalists kept expecting relief by way of the Chesapeake and could not understand why Clinton was so slow in coming to support them.

"Very many were dubious whether their situation, loyalty, and numbers were properly represented, since they have not been relieved before now, and therefore wished me [Sower] to request Governor Franklin to interest himself with his Excellency." Sower had applied to William Franklin and introduced the messengers to him. "The governor offers, if his Excellency will give him the New Jersey Provincial brigade and such other Provincial corps as will turn out voluntarily, and permit [him] to raise as many more refugees as may be in his power; and at the same time that a diversion be made in his favour so as to keep off Mr. Washington's army; he will undertake to penetrate into the loyal county of Sussex in New Jersey, reinforce himself, and form a junction with those people on the frontiers of Pennsylvania."

But Clinton did not yet think it advisable or practicable either to send a relief expedition to the Chesapeake or to commission loyalists from New York and New Jersey to undertake to fight their way overland to the back counties. Though he had come to think Rankin's party important, Clinton let matters drag another year, and the loyalists had not the enterprise to rise on their own account, as the rebels had done five years before.

III

There was the mystifying episode of Edward Fox, whose dubious transactions left a record in the British Headquarters papers. Fox had had a minor post under the last royal governor of Maryland, Robert Eden, and had continued as clerk to the state board of accounts. On May 8, 1778 he was paid £423 12s 6d for whisky he had furnished the state, presumably an army contract.[11] By the 18th he was in Philadelphia, where on that day he became a clerk in the Continental treasury. In August he was chosen one of thirty men authorized to sign Continental currency, and in October was nominated by John Penn for the office of commissioner to one of the chambers of accounts under the treasury board. Though he was not elected, he retained his clerkship.[12]

In some unexplained fashion Fox was taken prisoner by the British about the end of August 1779 and carried to Long Island, from which by the connivance of his captors he made his way to

New York. There on September 11 he wrote a letter to Dr. Henry Stevenson, a Maryland refugee who the year before had urged Howe to take Baltimore as the best means of obtaining provisions and getting at the rebel magazines at Carlisle.[13] Fox had talked with André, he told Stevenson, about a plan to transfer some unidentified person from Boston to Philadelphia to pick up official secrets. Though André had not been encouraging, Fox was still hopeful. He had bigger game in mind than his Boston spy: a friend in Annapolis whom Fox in his letter to Stevenson called merely C. "Would it not be doing great things to bring him over in the course of two or three months? Surely it would. Who persuaded the people of Maryland to accede to independence? C. Who could persuade them to give it up? C. Who can persuade them to anything? C."

Stevenson must have spoken or written to André, for on the 15th André wrote Stevenson that Clinton knew all about Fox's proposals but was not certain that Fox could or would carry them out. André had plans of his own. "Mr. Fox may quit this place and endeavour to convince us of his good intentions by speedily giving tokens of it and claiming the promise we hereby make him of most largely requiting him. A man shall moreover be sent to Philadelphia or wherever he [Fox] pleases to receive his dispatches. Or Mr. [Fox] may be detained here in the following manner. His coming to New York [from Long Island] is clandestine. He may be confined for a day as a suspected person and admitted to bail so as to preclude his exchange. He shall be handsomely maintained here by a private salary. He shall solicit the correspondence of C—— by means we will procure him; and if he deems any other persons willing and capable of serving us (such as old friends of Governor Eden) we may write to them. Such correspondence being settled to our satisfaction, his reward will flow in to him."

A letter from Fox to Stevenson on the 16th indicates that Fox had seen André's letter. Fox said that he did not want any reward in advance but that he would need small sums in gold. "Some person must be placed in the secretary's [Charles Thomson's] offices" in Philadelphia. It would require, Fox thought, two or three letters between him and C. before "I could speak so plain as to put it out of his power to mistake my drift." Going back to Philadelphia as an exchanged prisoner seemed to Fox better for his purposes than staying in New York.

Some time after the 18th André wrote out a statement of the Fox affair as it then stood. James Rivington the printer, André said, had told Stevenson about "a young man who had been employed in a public office under Governor Eden and since in the treasury of Congress. He had been carried prisoner into Jamaica and had from thence found his way here and was soliciting his exchange. He is in partnership with C——, a member of Congress, and on the information derived from their stations they speculate. He has received from us on the 17th September 30 guineas, is gone, and is to send us intelligence." When he should send Stevenson the watchword—*The compliments of Clapham*—a messenger was to go at once from New York to Philadelphia, where he would communicate with Fox by one of André's melodramatic devices. "The messenger is to make a cross in chalk on the pit door of the playhouse at night, and on the next day is to find an hour and address marked over it when to call for a parcel."

There can be no reasonable doubt that Fox's friend C. in Annapolis was Samuel Chase, signer of the Declaration, member of Congress 1774–78, but just now under a cloud because of his practices as speculator. Alexander Hamilton in the *New York Journal* at Poughkeepsie had bitterly attacked Chase on October 26 and November 1, 1778. "You have shown that America," Hamilton wrote, "can already boast at least one public character as abandoned as any the history of past or present times can produce. . . . It is your lot to have the peculiar privilege of being universally despised. . . . When you resolved to avail yourself of the extraordinary demand for the article of flour which the wants of the French fleet must produce, and which your official situation early impressed on your attention, to form connexions for monopolizing that article and raising the price upon the public more than 100 per cent; when by your intrigues and studied delays you protracted the determination of the C——tt—e of C——ss on the proposals made by Mr. W——sw—th [Jeremiah Wadsworth], C—ss—y G—n—l, for procuring the necessary supplies for the public use, to give your agents time to complete their purchases; I say, when you were doing all this, and engaging in a traffic infamous in itself, repugnant to your station, and ruinous to your country, did you pause and allow yourself a moment's reflection on the consequences?"[14] Chase had failed of re-election to Congress in November 1778, though Fox seems to have told André—or let him think—that Chase was a member. If Fox was, as he said, Chase's partner in speculation, Chase still had a private source of information from Philadelphia which he could make use of in his trading. "On the information derived from their stations they speculate," as André put it.

There is no evidence that Chase ever thought of treachery as a form of speculation, or that letters were sent to him as André said they might be. Fox may only have guessed that Chase was purchasable, or may only have hinted at it as a ruse for getting himself released. But Fox did hint at this and other treacheries, and did obtain his liberty and his guineas. Treachery was a commodity which could be offered in large or small amounts at Headquarters and paid for according to what it promised or performed.

On the 20th Fox on his way home arrived at the American outpost at Elizabeth and promptly reported that the British were sending an expedition by sea to the south, "their destination said to be Virginia." Washington had already for ten days been getting word to the same effect from his New York and Long Island informers, and mentioned Fox among them in a letter to Congress on the 25th.[15] The day before that Fox, once more in Philadelphia, had himself written Congress a letter, which was copied and sent to the governors of Maryland and of "other states to the southward."[16] Fox's reason for thinking Virginia the destination was that he had during his "stay in York discovered that several of the Virginia refugees are making preparations to go with this embarkation, not only with stores but some with their families."[17] A few days later he laid before Henry Laurens a plan for "effectually preventing the future circulation of counterfeit bills" which Fox said had been formed at considerable risk during his three weeks' captivity. Congress appointed a committee to investigate the plan, but nothing was done. On December 2 Fox wrote to Congress asking to be absolved from his promise to "be a principal actor in bringing the business into such a train as to answer the purpose."[18]

If this plan remains a mystery, so do the motives behind Fox's dealings with André. Was Fox a spy for the Americans, or for the British, or for both? Or was he an opportunist double-dealer who could take money from the British for services he may or may not have meant to render, and yet as soon as he had a chance could hurry to Congress with news which was of the greatest importance to the rebel government? He continued throughout the Revolution to be a treasury clerk and later one of the treasury commissioners.

IV

There is an undated paper in André's handwriting in the British Headquarters files that runs through what André thought were some of the prospects for American treachery in the summer of 1779.[19] It began as the draft of a letter to Arnold, written probably about the middle of June.

"The most essential services for wresting this country from ruin and oppression," André wrote, "would be in revealing the counsels of its rulers so as to counteract them and in affording an opportunity to defeat the army. . . . The operation of the former of these services is slow but has its importance and must be attended to. . . . But the most brilliant and effectual blow finally to complete the overthrow of the present abominable power would be the destruction of the army. This may be effected by a grand stroke or by successive partial but severe blows. Here follow hints for both.

"I should style a partial blow the taking possession of a considerable seaport and defeating the troops assigned to the defence of the province so as to be able to make a progress through it, drive away or disarm the disaffected, and by curbing the trade and displaying at the same time our prowess and lenity give a spring to the just indignation of the suffering people and induce them to return to their allegiance. Could you obtain the command in Carolina? The rest you must understand."

André was clearly hinting at the expedition against Charleston which Clinton had already planned for the end of the year,[20] and hoping that Arnold might command the southern army and treacherously lose it to the enemy. Arnold on May 23 had asked to be told Clinton's intentions. André in this draft gave a tentative answer. But Clinton, it appears, disapproved the answer as André had first drafted it. In the letter actually sent about the middle of June[21] Clinton said he could not reveal his intentions but advised Arnold in more general terms to "join the army, accept a command, be cut off," for a reward of two guineas a head for soldiers surrendered up to the number of 5000 or 6000. Clinton's revision made the answer more prudent for him and yet more tempting to Arnold.

Of other partial blows which might be struck André in his unsent letter listed these: "A surprise of a considerable body of men, or the means pointed out of ambuscading them, crossing upon their march, etc. Such a body might be collected and put in motion in consequence of operations on our part, and the most effectual ones for that purpose you might suggest, such as our threatening a magazine, a fort in the Sound, etc." Or: "The intercepting a convoyed fleet to or from France or the West Indies might be effected by means of proper intelligence." Or: "Magazines might be burnt and on certain occasions all the guns of a fort or field artillery spiked.

"As to a general project against the whole army, could anything take place on the west side of the North river? We should be glad of your sentiments on that head.

"Here are our ideas for movements to the eastward. A considerable corps shall march into New England. The consequences will be that Washington will cross the North river and hasten to the points attacked. He would possibly be preceded by a corps similar to that in Jersey under General Lee which would have orders to harass, attack, awe the country, etc." Since General Charles Lee no longer had a command in New Jersey—or anywhere else— André must have referred to Major Henry (Light Horse Harry) Lee and Lee's Legion. "Could you command that corps it might be concerted where and when it should be surprised, defeated, or obliged to capitulate. Complete information might be received concerning the main body, its baggage, its means of supply, etc. Convoys might be intercepted, magazines burnt, boats in the North river seized, and the passage back prevented by a reembarkation of the [British] corps to the eastward or by the co-operation of troops from New York. A chain of connivance must be very artfully laid to multiply difficulties and baffle resources. Under the circumstances Washington might be attacked or be left to disperse from want of supplies. At such an hour, when the most boisterous spirits were with the army and every one intent on its fate, the seizing the Congress would decide the business. You must observe that our navy would not be idle during this time and that a small corps attending a few ships of war might either be assisting in bringing off the Congress or in increasing the general confusion by descents on the coast."

This letter, never sent, belongs less with Arnold's conspiracy than with André's projects. André did not destroy the unused draft but added to the same manuscript a series of Observations which may be of various dates. Some of the projects and conjectures are revealing, some startling, some incomprehensible.

"Mifflin would be the man to remain at Philadelphia to seize the Congress. Is he enterprising?" Major General Thomas Mifflin had been a negligent quartermaster and Congress had accepted his resignation from the army the past February. But nothing in his record indicates that he ever thought of treachery.

"If added to this Fort Pitt were taken by expedition from Detroit, in which Th—— and Mons. [name illegible] and Rankin might assist and an effort defeated which is projecting against Detroit, there could remain no resource." By the effort against Detroit André meant Sullivan's march against the Six Nations, which the British expected to go farther than it did. It is possible that Th—— may have been Thayendanegea (Brant), with whom Rankin had offered to co-operate on the Pennsylvania frontier, though André nowhere else uses the Mohawk name. The illegible name eludes conjecture.

"L. might help us as to the boats and convoys across the North river. We may call upon the two quartermasters from whom we hear by General Tryon's scouts from [Andreas] Emmerich's corps" of partisan chasseurs. These two quartermasters are unidentified. But a letter André wrote to L. on July 31 adds a few details about him.

"We should be very happy to see the zeal you formerly showed in our cause renewed and to open our communications afresh. Sir Henry Clinton will show himself as sensible of the value of your services as you can desire and will treat the business with the utmost discretion and attention to your safety. The points on which we wish information are" detailed military matters: "in short, things which your own judgment will suggest as enabling us to counteract the enemy's views and to take advantage of opportunities to distress them. S. H. C. and Lord Cornwallis express the greatest confidence in you and have been desirous to avail themselves of the bearer being here to renew the correspondence, especially as the method by flag to Elizabethtown which I had in view is so precarious." Clinton did not make such outspoken promises to ordinary informers, and he and Cornwallis would hardly have joined in a message to anybody not a man of weight. The letter was "sent by P. who received five guineas" and who was probably John Potts, skilful in forwarding letters to Philadelphia. No answering communications from the unidentified L. have been found in the Headquarters papers.

"Schuyler," André went on in his Observations, "should be encouraged, as the people near Albany begin to show signs of impatience under the present rulers and as the Indians are threatening in that quarter. Could he negotiate the purchase of [Forts] Montgomery and Clinton, spike their guns at a certain time?" Clinton had recently taken Stony Point and Verplanck's and might advance higher with the help of treachery from Schuyler who, the British kept thinking, could be won over by proper arguments. Few things were less likely than that Schuyler would make such a traitorous deal as this. André's scheming was directed rather by his active hopes than by any accurate knowledge of the characters of the patriots he thought of as possible renegades.

"Rankin should have a cipher —— and a word, Houseker a word, and they should point out a house on the frontier by which Brant might by sending the parole have communication and arrange his operations." At the time André wrote this he had not yet hit on Wallis's house as the rendezvous, as he did later. Houseker (if the name is not Honseker in the manuscript) may be Colonel Nicholas Haussegger who had been captured by the British in January 1777, sent on parole to his home in Lancaster county, suspected and watched by Washington's orders, and ordered by the British to return to captivity in January 1779.[22] As Haussegger later joined the British, he may already have offered them his services as a secret assistant to Rankin. But his mysterious career has left so few records that it seems impossible to do more than make guesses about him.

"White might carry this information to Brant. Neither would know the other to be concerned." The White referred to was probably Abraham White, sheriff of Tryon county, who had adhered to the Johnson dynasty on the New York frontier. "If a proper plan of this nature could be concerted, General Haldimand," governor of Canada, "should have it explained to him that White might be encouraged.

"Might it not be advisable to exchange the Frenchman who has 200 per annum from government and was taken at Fort Chartres, and send him to Canada if the posts on the Mississippi are to be repossessed? He was probably a man of some influence with the Indians." This was Philippe François Rastel, Sieur de Rocheblave, who had been captured by George Rogers Clark at Fort Gage (not Chartres) in Kaskaskia on the Mississippi on July 4, 1778 and sent to prison in Virginia.[23] He was paroled and returned to New York the month after André's memorandum.

André's Observations end with a set of miscellaneous queries. "Is it impossible to do anything with [General] Maxwell?" It would almost certainly have been impossible. "Mr. Elliot." Who this was does not appear. There were two Elliots who were conspicuous loyalists but no patriot of that name likely to be useful to the British. André may have meant that Maxwell might be approached through Andrew Elliot, the loyalist refugee in New York. "Has Sinclair [General St. Clair] been thought of lately?" It is not known that he had ever been thought of at Headquarters, which knew how absurd the story was of his selling Ticonderoga for silver bullets fired by the British into the fort. "Hazen may be had." This was Arnold's enemy Colonel Hazen. "He is artful and enterprising. He will be a good creature of [Arnold] whom he knows and to whom he has betrayed us in Canada." André apparently knew that Hazen had first seemed to side with the British in Canada, then joined the Americans; but he could not have known how much Hazen hated Arnold. "May [Arnold] be promised Provincial major general's rank? He asks his own rank in the British army." None of Arnold's surviving letters mentions the rank he expected if he changed sides. Perhaps it had been reported by Stansbury.

From May 26 to August 10 André made many entries in a manuscript book of intelligence he kept, much of it information from American deserters or British prisoners who had escaped or been exchanged. Deserters regularly got a guinea each for coming in, and British soldiers a guinea for each American prisoner taken.[24] On October 23 André was rewarded for his activity by being appointed deputy adjutant general with the rank of major until the king's pleasure could be known.

Such an appointment in the British army in 1779 was not merely a promotion but also a business transaction. Lord Rawdon, who had been adjutant general, resigned his post on September 3, telling Clinton he had "no longer the honour of being upon those terms of mutual confidence with your Excellency which alone could prevail on me to continue in a station whose duties are most irksome to me." Lieutenant Colonel Stephen Kemble, deputy adjutant general, found Clinton evasive when asked about the succession. On the 16th Kemble resigned by arrangement with André.[25] Though Kemble was to give up his post and André succeeding to it would become a major, he was to turn over to Kemble the extra pay of £300 a year and if he quit the post was to pay Kemble another £200. By this arrangement André had an advance in rank and Clinton a favourite at his right hand, instead of Rawdon or Kemble whom Clinton did not like. Since no adjutant general was appointed, André though he had been only a captain and was only twenty-eight took charge of all the duties of the office.

V

Clinton in his efforts to win Americans over to the British cause was supported by advice from London. A letter of May 27 from Eden said: "Our spirits in general with regard to your prospects are not very high; therefore if by any fortunate or able stroke you can get us out of our scrape you will be worshipped by a very grateful country." Eden was not thinking of military strokes alone. "If it comes to a crisis among the leaders, you should not hesitate at any expense, promises, threats, management, etc. etc. etc., that may tend to carry the point or disarm the rebellion before the mischief makers [opposition] on this side of the water can interfere." Clinton, Eden held, might safely influence, divide, or bribe as much as he could.

Germain on September 27 echoed and confirmed Eden, though in a letter which did not reach Clinton till the following May in Charleston. "I have heard with great pleasure from Captain Dixon that the dissensions and jealousies among the members of the Congress continue to increase, and that the people's repugnancy to serve in their army becomes every day greater. It will not, I am persuaded, escape your sagacity that the gaining over some of the most respectable members of that body, or officers of influence and reputation among their troops, would, next to the destruction of Washington's army, be the speediest means of subduing the rebellion and restoring the tranquillity of America. Your commission authorizes you to avail yourself of such opportunities; and there can be no doubt that the expense will be cheerfully submitted to." And there could be no doubt that this letter authorized Clinton to use any means he chose with respect to Arnold or any other influential American.

Eden, returned from America, pulled wires at home. All the men he proposed[26] for members of a council to assist Clinton were appointed by the king on July 22: Eden's wife's uncle Andrew Elliot, Elliot's neighbour William Smith the royal chief justice of New York, Frederick Smyth the royal chief justice of New Jersey, and John Tabor Kempe the royal attorney general of New York. To these the king added Cornwallis, James Roberton the newly appointed royal governor of New York, and the royal governors Martin of North Carolina and Franklin of New Jersey. It does not appear that Clinton took much advice from his council, though one of his enemies accused him of being excessively influenced by William Smith.[27] New York was an occupied city under military government.

Of the Americans on the council William Franklin made himself the most conspicuous. He thought Clinton sluggish and unintelligible; Clinton thought him "sanguinary and mercenary."[28] Franklin's aims were chiefly concerned with what the loyalists might do if allowed a chance, unhampered by British caution. On May 29, following his January plan for an armed association of loyalists, he proposed that "some of the principal gentlemen among the loyal refugees" then in New York be "united and employed as a kind of board for the purpose of procuring, digesting, and communicating intelligence of the designs and motions of the enemy from time to time." He set his own name at the head of the list, with Daniel Coxe of New Jersey next, and then—written in as though an afterthought—"Rev. Mr. Odell." It is difficult not to suspect that Franklin, Odell's patron, had got wind through Odell of the Arnold overtures from Philadelphia.

Franklin's other nominees for his board were John Potts and Samuel Shoemaker of Pennsylvania (both of whom like Coxe had served as magistrates under Howe in Philadelphia); Anthony Stewart and Robert Alexander of Maryland; Captain James Parker of Virginia; Abraham C. Cuyler of Albany and Peter Dubois of Ulster county, New York; and Metcalf Bowler, Clinton's Rhode Island spy, who Franklin thought lived in Massachusetts. They were to have power to call and examine persons who came to New York, to inspect intercepted letters, and to give rewards for intelligence received. "The board shall endeavour to settle a regular correspondence not only with their friends and connexions in the different colonies but also with some persons of note in the Congress, armies, councils, and assemblies of the rebels." They were to be provided with various facilities by the commander-in-chief and would leave it to him "to make them such allowance or consideration for their services as he may hereafter think they merit."

Clinton seems to have given no encouragement to the scheme, which would have set up a loyalist office supplementing—or competing with—the adjutant general's. But the proposed members of the board were unofficially active. A letter from Coxe to André on June 5 indicates that Coxe had some share in the Arnold matter. "The impatiently expected letter is not yet arrived, nor can I divine the reason, unless from the great pains taken at present [by the Americans] to stop all communications. . . . The one I forwarded, and to which I expected an answer, I have an intimation has got to hand, but so much a blot (an experiment) as not scarcely to be understood." This was five days after Odell received the first letter from Stansbury and, trying to bring out the invisible page by heating it, found it "all one indistinguishable blot." Franklin on the 11th asked André if a certain American prisoner of war on Long Island might be released on parole. "He is a secret friend of government, as I am well assured," Franklin said, "and I expect to derive some advantages to the king's service from his return." Potts forwarded letters, like the one to L. of July 31. Odell was busy with his Stansbury correspondence.

Dubois furnished minor items which André entered in his intelligence book on August 10. One of Dubois's correspondents, and possibly Dubois himself, reported sometimes in French. André made, in his own French, an undated memorandum about "a person in question" who was to stay where he was rather than "come to us. It would be still better if he were in the service [the American army] and could be nearer . . . for instance, coming to Morristown from which we could get news from him more frequently." An unidentified mysterious "Madame de Rambouillet" had been paid £100 for unspecified services, and Dubois would have had the watches if there had been any safe way of getting them to him.[29]

At the same time, plans went on for what came to be called the Associated Loyalists with William Franklin at the head. The first meeting of the loyalists in London was held on May 29, with Sir William Pepperell as chairman and Galloway on the committee appointed to draw up an address to the king.[30] Tryon in New York, supporting the plan as outlined by Franklin, on June 30 hoped in a letter to Clinton that the British government would see fit to embody loyalists "who for various reasons will not enlist themselves soldiers, and many of whom are nevertheless willing to take up arms and contribute their aid for the suppression of the rebellion." They should, Tryon thought, "be entitled to the plunder they take, which is to be only from rebels, and not from loyalists that live among them." Clinton might advance Franklin money and credit to the amount of £20,000, or even £30,000, as capital for the undertaking. Franklin, writing to Clinton on November 10, agreed with Tryon that the loyalists should be separately embodied, not attached to regular military posts "under the directions and restraints of the commanding officers." Though Franklin did not say so, it is clear enough that he and the other loyalists had revenge and plunder in mind as well as armed efforts against the rebels.

VI

The Headquarters files during 1779, as during 1778, contain the documents of many tantalizing minor episodes of secret activity. On February 27 H. E. wrote from Bedford (presumably in Westchester) that he thought the offers of the Carlisle commission should have been accepted and that he hated the French alliance. He was leaving in a few days for Philadelphia, where he hoped he might learn something valuable from his intimate friend John Jay, president of Congress. "I am settling my public accounts, which causes my journey to Philadelphia." He meant to put his Continental money into New Jersey land as an investment.

On April 2 another letter, marked "From G. T. [General Tryon's?] friend," said that H. E. had returned the day before. "I have fixed matters upon a tolerable good plan to obtain further information which I shall convey to you from time to time. But it will be difficult getting through the lines." He had learned of the Iroquois expedition but did not know that Sullivan was to command it. H. E. had "drinked freely" with an officer of the Maryland line. "As we were both in the service he thought it no harm to tell me, but he enjoined it upon me as a secret." Congress had prospects from Europe. "If I could see you I could give you particulars as I received it from Mr. Jay," who of course did not suspect H. E. of treachery. He might come in under a flag to inquire about Peter Van Tassel, "who has been long confined with you. Application has been made to me by his friends to get him exchanged, which is a good excuse." Several leading men in the neighbourhood, H. E. said, were "almost ripe to join you" if he could show them instructions in writing to assure them "they may act safe." H. E. was Captain Elijah Hunter, formerly of The 2nd New York, and was actually one of Washington's secret agents.

On June 27 Washington wrote to Colonel Benjamin Tallmadge, of the American secret service, about the American spy who had replaced the invaluable Abraham Woodhull (known as Culper Senior) in Manhattan. Washington did not know the name of Culper Junior (actually Robert Townsend) or desire to know it, but he wished that the new spy would "endeavour to hit upon some certain mode of conveying his information quickly." There was "a man on York island, living on or near the North river, of the name of George Higday, who I am told hath given signal proofs of his attachment to us, and at the same time stands well with the enemy." Perhaps Higday might get messages across the river and to American Headquarters. "He is enterprising and connected with people in Bergen county who will assist in forming a chain to me, in any manner they shall agree on." This letter was taken by the British at an American advanced post. Washington at once saw that Higday was in danger and on July 5 asked that he be warned if possible.[31]

Higday, arrested in New York, on the 13th wrote a penitent, frightened, illiterate letter from prison to Clinton. About three or four weeks before, Higday admitted, he had taken three rebel officers across the Hudson to New Jersey. "On going over thire Decourse wass what a fine thing it might be for me to fech Information over for Washenton that he would make me rich in so doing A Cordingly i being left by God and his Devine purtecktion to my Self," apparently but illegibly yielded to temptation. He went with the officers to Washington, "and ofered the Above purposals but he wass afreaid to venter but said he would consither on it And did not countence me much & had sum Congress munney & thought to by A Cow on time with it—the Monney wass So bad I could not by one So I returned home for which Reson I supose he hath sent this Letter that now is taken. . . . Now I did not think Even they would write to me for Washington Said my name was in the black book for being A friend to Government and would not trust me." Higday promised that if any letters should come to him from the rebels he would turn them over to Clinton.

There is no record of what was done with Higday, but he would obviously not offend again, and Clinton was always disposed to be lenient. "From good policy and perhaps a little more feeling than is usual for those in my situation," Clinton wrote after André's arrest, "I have never executed a spy." As he went on to explain it, "I have made good use of them by employing them double."[32]

Earlier than has hitherto been realized Clinton made—or thought he had made—overtures to Ethan Allen, who on July 3 had appeared before Congress soliciting a union of Vermont "with the other free and independent states of America." Congress hesitated to acknowledge the independence of a district claimed by existing states and put off the decision. This seemed "the moment for tempting E. A.," Clinton wrote confidentially on August 21–22 to Eden, who was not yet to speak of it to the ministry. Clinton said he had instructed Allen—apparently by messenger—to retire with his militia to Canada and operate with Haldimand. If he preferred to join Clinton, "I would meet him from King's Ferry, either on the east or the west side of the river as Washington's situation should decide. . . . Since the above I have not heard from him."

Congress on September 24 put off further consideration of the dispute till February, and Clinton on October 10, he wrote Eden, had received an answer from the Green Mountain chief. "The messenger whom I told you in a former letter I had dispatched to Ethan Allen is returned and informs me that he met him and Colonel [Seth] Warner on the 10th of August at a place called Williamstown to the northward of Albany. That the former entrusted him with a letter for me, but being in danger of falling into the hands of the enemy he was obliged to destroy it." According to the messenger, Allen had about 1500 men, "properly armed and equipped, and is daily joined by people from different parts of the country." This must have sounded to Clinton like the news from Rankin on the Pennsylvania border. Allen "declares himself well affected to his Majesty and assigns as a reason for not proceeding with his troops" that the rumours of French and Spanish assistance had "created a temporary division" of opinion in Vermont.

Warner, like Rankin's colleagues in Pennsylvania, could "raise about 700 men and declares himself ready to join any body of men in opposition to the Congress, but particularly Colonel Allen." Still according to the messenger, Colonel Israel Williams of Hatfield, Massachusetts, an avowed loyalist, "approves of Colonel Allen's plan of advancing with his men and thinks he will meet with little opposition. He says he assured him that he had a correspondence with General Schuyler and that the general was at bottom a friend to government." Again Schuyler, whom the British still hoped to hear from! "The messenger further says that Allen had written to General Haldimand but received no answer. In short, we are as sure of Allen's joining us as is possible without we had seen him ourselves, but I cannot consent to its being made known to government in form, as there is no being sure of a person of Allen's character; nor can we expect him to show himself without we are in a situation to give him support."[33]

No plan for a loyalist uprising had more promise than this seemed to have. Allen's militia were in the open, not hidden like Rankin's followers, and Haldimand might help them from Canada. The British ministry, unlike Congress, thought the separation of Vermont might be advantageous and saw no objection, Germain had written to Haldimand on March 3, to giving the Vermonters "reason to expect that the king will erect their country into a separate province."[34] To be a separate province under the Crown might seem more desirable to Vermont than to be a state unrecognized by Congress and litigated over by New Hampshire and New York. And now Ethan Allen, brigadier general of militia in Vermont and the most powerful Vermonter, was reported to be ready to turn to the British.

But again Clinton was disappointed. On December 11 he had to write to Eden that "the information I gave you respecting Ethan Allen was premature. The messenger has proved a rogue and confesses that not being able to get to him he returned and invented the story. I have however sent other messengers to him, and as 'tis his interest I am persuaded he will join us."[35] When Clinton sailed for Charleston on the 26th he left the Allen negotiations to Beverley Robinson, who did not get a messenger to Allen till the following July.

Double-Dealer on Trial

THOUGH Arnold was secretly bargaining with the British over his price for treachery he was still determined to prove to the Americans that he had done nothing wrong as commander in Philadelphia. After his hysterical letter of May 5, 1779 protesting against delay of his trial as worse than death, he wrote again to Washington on the 14th, when Stansbury had had four days in which to get back from New York with the first encouraging answer from Clinton. Arnold now particularly desired, he said, to rejoin the army and "to render my country every service in my power at this critical time; for, though I have been ungratefully treated, I do not consider it as from my countrymen in general but from a set of men who, void of principle, are governed entirely by private interest. The interest I have in the welfare and happiness of my country, which I have ever evinced when in my power, will I hope always overcome my personal resentment for any injury I can possibly receive from individuals."[1]

Washington, who was sorry that the trial had to be held at camp instead of in Philadelphia, as Arnold wished, and that it could not take place at once, chose Major General Robert Howe of North Carolina to be president of the court martial "for particular reasons." These had, it may be guessed, something to do with Howe's experience as commander of Charleston and Savannah, where he had during the past fall and winter been involved in such conflicts that he had been ordered north in April. He would be acquainted with troubles like Arnold's and he would hardly be prejudiced against a soldier complained of by civilians. "I shall endeavour," Washington wrote Reed on the 20th, "to have the affair conducted in its future progress with unexceptionable propriety."[2]

Arnold made this propriety somewhat difficult by assuming that he had the full—if not violent—support of everybody at camp. "I am treated with the greatest politeness by General Washington and the officers of the army, who bitterly execrate Mr. Reed and the council for their villainous attempt to injure me," he wrote to Peggy. This Washington afterwards declared, when the letter came to light, was "an absolute falsehood" so far as it applied to the commander-in-chief. "It was at no time my inclination, much less my intention, to become a party in his cause; and I certainly could not be so lost to my own character as to become a partisan at the moment I was called upon, officially, to bring him to trial. . . . True it is, he self-invited some civilities I never meant to show him (or any officer in arrest); and he received rebuke before I could convince him of the impropriety of his entering upon a justification of his conduct in my presence, and for bestowing such illiberal abuses as he seemed disposed to do upon those whom he denominated his persecutors."[3] Washington did not like Arnold's claiming to be always a hero beset by villainous enemies.

At eleven o'clock on the morning of June 1 the court met at Howe's quarters at Middlebrook. Besides Howe, the only major general, there were four brigadiers—William Smallwood of Maryland, Henry Knox of Massachusetts, William Woodford of Virginia, and William Irvine of Pennsylvania—six colonels, and three lieutenant colonels: by mistake a total of fourteen instead of the thirteen required. Arnold peremptorily challenged General Irvine, Colonel Richard Butler, and Lieutenant Colonel Josiah Harmar, all of whom were Pennsylvanians. Though the articles of war were "entirely silent on the right of the prisoner to challenge the members of a court either peremptorily or otherwise," the challenge was allowed, and the court adjourned to the next day. But that evening the members, at a hurried conference with Washington who had just heard of Clinton's expedition up the Hudson, voted to postpone the trial. Washington wrote Matlack that in the emergency all the general and field officers were needed for active service. He added a postscript: "As the movements of the enemy may possibly admit of the court martial's sitting in the course of two or three or a few days, I am just informed that General Arnold intends to go to Morristown and to wait events."[4]

Arnold, who before he left Philadelphia for Middlebrook had sent a reply to André, was not at home in Philadelphia till after the 9th, the day on which Stansbury at Moorestown learned that the reply had been illegible in New York. By the time a duplicate could be sent and an answer received, it was July 7. On the 11th Arnold, dissatisfied with Clinton's promises, sent word that his price was £10,000 indemnity, "whether this contest is finished by sword or treaty." Two days later Arnold wrote to Washington asking about the trial and hoping that it might, because of "the cruel situation I am in," be held as soon as possible. "My wounds are so far recovered that I can walk with ease and I expect soon to be able to ride on horseback. If there is no probability of the court's meeting soon I must request the favour to know it, in which case I shall beg of Congress a few months' absence on my private affairs."[5] But Washington could not spare the necessary officers till December, when the court finally convened on the 23rd at Norris's tavern in Morristown, after Arnold had sent the British his last stealthy information of the year and put off treason for the winter.

There had been several changes in the court. Howe still presided, but of the brigadiers nominated in June only Knox remained, to sit with William Maxwell of New Jersey and Mordecai Gist of Maryland; and only two of the colonels. John Laurance, judge advocate general of the Continental army, managed the prosecution, and Arnold his own alert and lawyer-like defence. The witnesses heard during the trial were Timothy Matlack and his son William, Arnold's aide David S. Franks, Washington's aide Alexander Hamilton, John Hall who was clerk to John Mitchell, John Mitchell the deputy quartermaster general, and a Mr. Nicholson whose testimony was struck from the record as irrelevant. The court sat December 23–24, met on the 27th only to adjourn to the 28th, sat daily through the 30th, and adjourned for want of evidence till called together by Washington's order on January 19. Mitchell, for whom the court had been waiting but whom the Board of War could not earlier release from his duties elsewhere, testified on the 20th. On the 21st Arnold summed up his defence.[6]

The judge advocate had confined himself, according to the resolution of Congress, to the 1st, 2nd, 3rd, and 5th charges brought by Pennsylvania. Arnold went through all eight with the vigour of affronted innocence. "When the present necessary war against Great Britain commenced I was in easy circumstances and enjoyed a fair prospect of improving them. I was happy in domestic connexions and blessed with a rising family who claimed my care and attention. The liberties of my country were in danger. The voice of my country called upon all her faithful sons to join in her defence. With cheerfulness I obeyed the call. I sacrificed domestic ease and happiness to the service of my country, and in her service have I sacrificed a great part of a handsome fortune. I was one of the first that appeared in the field; and from that time to the present hour have not abandoned her service"—except that eight months before he had offered his treacherous services to the enemy.

"When one is charged with practices which his soul abhors and which conscious innocence tells him he has never committed, an honest indignation will draw from him expressions in his own favour which on other occasions might be ascribed to an ostentatious turn of mind." With proper pride the accused man read letters from Washington and resolutions of Congress recognizing and commending Arnold's unquestionable merits. Was it probable, he asked, that having won such honours he could "sink into a course of conduct equally unworthy of the patriot and soldier?" Yet the Pennsylvania council had gone to every length in slandering and abusing him. "Such a vile prostitution of power, and such instances of glaring tyranny and injustice, I believe are unprecedented in the annals of any free people."

As to the pass given to the *Charming Nancy* and her cargo Arnold said that the owners' design "of saving them for the use of the citizens of the United States" had seemed to him highly laudable and he had felt obliged to further it. No mention, naturally, of the fact that he had been, at least afterwards, half-owner. He ridiculed the notion that Pennsylvania should think itself concerned in the matter, or should worry because Washington was not consulted. Perhaps, he hinted in Virgil's Latin, Washington did not need such help or such defenders (*Non tali auxilio eget, nec defensoribus istis*). "The General is invested with power, and he possesses spirit to check and to punish every instance of disrespect shown to his authority; but he will not prostitute his power by exerting it upon a trifling occasion; far less will he pervert it when no occasion is given at all."

On the charge that he had closed the Philadelphia shops to keep even officers of the army from purchasing goods while he "privately made considerable purchases for his own benefit, as is alleged and believed," Arnold was especially vehement. In closing the shops he had only been carrying out the orders of Congress, with the approval of Joseph Reed who now complained of the action. If it were true, Arnold declared, that he had made private purchases in violation of his own order, then "I stand confessed, in the presence of this honourable court, the vilest of men; I stand stigmatized with indelible disgrace, the disgrace of having abused an appointment of high trust and importance to accomplish the meanest and most unworthy purposes. The blood I have spent in defence of my country will be insufficient to obliterate the stain. . . . Where is the evidence of this accusation? I call upon my accusers to produce it; I call upon them to produce it, under the pain of being held forth to the world and to posterity, upon the proceedings of this court, as public defamers and murderers of reputation." He knew they could not produce the written agreement he had made with Mease and West, while the shops were closed, to buy goods "for the joint equal benefit of the subscribers." So, before this honourable court, "on the honour of a gentleman and soldier, I declare to gentlemen and soldiers that the charge is false."

To the charge that he had imposed menial duties on the sons of Pennsylvania freemen Arnold returned the countercharge that this was mere clamour raised to alienate the militia from him. "My ambition is to deserve the good opinion of the militia of these states, not only because I respect their character and their exertions but because their confidence in me may (as I flatter myself it has hitherto been) prove beneficial to the general cause of America. But having no local politics to bias my voice or my conduct, I leave it to others to wriggle themselves into a temporary popularity by assassinating the reputation of innocent persons and endeavouring to render odious a principle the maintenance of which is essential to the good discipline of the militia and consequently to the safety of these states." He thought Pennsylvania was ungrateful and ungracious in abusing a soldier who had, instead of resigning when junior brigadiers were promoted over him, suppressed his wounded feelings and in June 1777 taken command of the Pennsylvania militia facing Howe on the Delaware. "How far the good countenance of the militia under my command operated in deterring General Howe from marching to the city of Philadelphia I will not pretend to say. Certain it is, he altered his route."

In connexion with this 3rd charge Arnold made his one recorded statement before the treason on the subject of independence, which he later told the British he had always been opposed to. "I flatter myself the time is not far off when, by the glorious establishment of our independence, I shall again return into the mass of citizens. 'Tis a period I look forward to with anxiety. I shall then cheerfully submit, as a citizen, to be governed by the same principle of subordination which has been tortured"—in Pennsylvania's charge—"into a wanton exertion of arbitrary power."

With regard to the *Active* Arnold pointed out that this was a matter for the civil courts and that the indictment against him for unlawfully maintaining the suit had been dismissed by the grand jury the past April for want of evidence to support it. He had helped Olmsted and the others out of sympathy: not a word about the half-interest he owned in their prospects, nor about the witnesses he had brought before the grand jury to swear that he had no interest in the case.[7] The Pennsylvania council, according to him, had been actuated by interest and vengeance. Arnold praised the jurors who had been "impregnable to all the arts made use of to poison the fountain of justice. And here I cannot but congratulate my countrymen upon the glorious effects of the exertions we have made to establish the liberties of ourselves and posterity upon the firm basis of equal laws. Had it not been for the grand bulwark against the tyranny of rulers, the trial by peers, it is easy to foresee, from the spirit of those who have been my accusers, what must have been my fate." Sooner or later posterity would "feel the blessed effects of my efforts, in conjunction with you [the court martial] and others, in rescuing them from a tyranny of the most cruel and debasing nature."

Though Arnold did not deny that public wagons had been sent for private property in which he was interested, he did deny that the wagons were then needed by the public or that he had ever meant to avoid paying privately for them. The Pennsylvania council, Arnold claimed, had persuaded the wagonmaster not to call for his pay but to raise his charges to double the first amount and then to sue. "There is now an action against me, depending in one of the courts of Pennsylvania, for upwards of £1100 for the hire of those wagons. Is it not very extraordinary that I should be accused and tried before this honourable court for employing public wagons, and at the same time and by the same persons be prosecuted in a civil court of Pennsylvania for employing the same wagons as private property?"

Congress had dismissed the 6th charge, and the judge advocate had not brought it before the court, but Arnold preferred to justify his conduct on this point too. "To attempt a serious refutation would be as ridiculous as the charge itself." What had happened, he said, was that (in October 1778) he had written a letter, signed by Clarkson, to Maxwell in command at Elizabeth, recommending that Maxwell give a pass which Arnold was not authorized to give. Arnold had kept no copy but thought he could remember his letter. "The bearer," he quoted from memory, "Miss Levy, is a young woman of good character who has an aged parent that is blind, depending on her for support. She has money due to her from people in New York and wishes for a permission to go there for the purpose of collecting it, for the relief and support of her mother, who will be greatly distressed without it. I believe she will not make an ill use of a pass if granted to her."

But Arnold's explanation before the court martial did not agree with the account he had furnished in writing to Matlack in March 1779.[8] Matlack had informed him that the council knew of a Mr. Templeton in New York "to whom Miss Levy was to apply by your direction. I give you this notice, to afford you an opportunity of showing any reasons you may be possessed of why his name ought to be concealed" in the charges, "conceiving it possible that you may have such reasons." The council would not make the name public if discretion was advisable. Arnold on the 5th urged discretion. "My request to Miss Levy to apply to Mr.

Templeton was for purposes of importance to the United States. I therefore, for his sake, wish his name may not be mentioned publicly, as it will doubtless operate to his prejudice and [endanger his] personal safety in New York." Nothing is known of any relations between Arnold and Templeton, who was possibly Oliver Templeton an auctioneer. Arnold was at least as likely to have been engaged in forbidden trading with Templeton as to have employed him on any secret service. There seems to be nothing notable in the episode except that Arnold kept from the court martial something he had told Matlack; and this may really have been for Templeton's sake.

The Pennsylvania council had charged Arnold with making an "indecent and disrespectful refusal of any satisfaction whatsoever" when he was asked for a statement about the wagons. Arnold claimed they had first insulted him by asking him to account for his conduct. "I beg leave to observe that no one has a greater respect than myself for the civil authority, and no one is more convinced of the necessity of supporting it. But when public bodies of men show themselves actuated by the passions of anger, or envy, and apply their effects to sap the character of an individual and to render his situation miserable, they must not think it extraordinary if they are not treated with the deference which they may think their due. It is the dignity with which an office is executed, much more than the name, that can ever secure respect and obedience from a free people; and true dignity consists in exercising power with wisdom, justice, and moderation."

For the answer to the final charge, that of favouring Tories in Philadelphia, Arnold saved his bitterest rejoinder, aiming at Reed and charging him with a former inclination to such treachery as Arnold had recently committed himself to—if he could get his price. "Conscious of my own innocence," Arnold told the court, "and the unworthy methods taken to injure me, I can with boldness say to my persecutors in general, and to the chief of them in particular, that in the hour of danger, when the affairs of America wore a gloomy aspect, when our illustrious General was retreating through New Jersey with a handful of men [in November–December 1776], I did not propose to my associates basely to quit the General and sacrifice the cause of my country to my personal safety, by going over to the enemy and making my peace. I can say I never basked in the sunshine of my General's favour, and courted him to his face, when I was at the same time treating him with the greatest disrespect and vilifying his character when absent. This is more than a ruling member of the council of the state of Pennsylvania can say, as is alleged and believed." Reed seems never to have done more than temporarily lose confidence in Washington as commander and he had not deserted the patriots. But Arnold seized an opportunity to turn the tables on his antagonist with what was, in their relative circumstances, an insolence as bold as Arnold's attack on the attacking Burgoyne at Saratoga.

"If in the course of my defence," Arnold concluded, "I have taken up the time of the court longer than they expected, they will, I trust, impute it to the nature of the accusations against me; many of which, though not immediately before you as charges, were alleged as facts and were of such a complexion as to render it necessary to make some observations upon them; because they were evidently calculated to raise a prejudice against me, not only among the people at large but in the minds of those who were to be my judges. I have looked forward with pleasing anxiety to the present day when, by the judgment of my fellow-soldiers, I shall (I doubt not) stand honourably acquitted of all the charges brought against me and again share with them the glories and danger of this just war."

The court met on the 22nd for the judge advocate's summation, and adjourned to the 26th. On that day the verdict was agreed upon. The officers were "clearly of opinion he had no right to give" the permit to the *Charming Nancy,* "circumstanced as he was." They thought him justified in closing the shops and found the charge that he had made private purchases "entirely unsupported, and they do fully acquit General Arnold of it." They acquitted him without comment on the charge of treating militiamen as menials. "Respecting the fourth charge, it appears to the court that General Arnold made application to the deputy quartermaster general to supply him with wagons to remove property then in imminent danger from the enemy; that wagons were supplied him by the deputy quartermaster general on this application which had been drawn from the state of Pennsylvania for the public service; and it also appears that General Arnold intended this application as a private request and that he had no design of employing the wagons otherwise than at his private expense, nor of defrauding the public, nor injuring or impeding the public service; but considering the delicacy attending the high station in which the general acted, and that requests from him might operate as commands, they are of opinion the request was imprudent and improper and that, therefore, it ought not to have been made. The court, in consequence of their determinations respecting the first and last charge exhibited against Major General Arnold, do sentence him to receive a reprimand from his Excellency the commander-in-chief."

As Washington was at Morristown during the whole of Arnold's trial there was no occasion for letters between them that might show how Arnold resented or Washington regretted the court's verdict. On the 30th Washington sent the proceedings to Congress, which on February 12 confirmed the sentence with only three dissenting votes out of twenty-six: Robert R. Livingston of New York, Thomas Burke of North Carolina, John Mathews of South Carolina.[9] The notice of confirmation was not sent to Washington for a month, and it was not till April 6, after the proceedings had been published by Congress in a small edition of fifty copies, that he delivered the reprimand—which was never actually spoken to Arnold—by including it in the day's general orders.

An orotund and mellifluous version of the reprimand, invented by Barbé-Marbois,[10] has been repeated over and over by Arnold's biographers'. Washington's own words were considerate but brief and downright. "The Commander-in-chief would have been much happier in an occasion of bestowing commendations on an officer who has rendered such distinguished services to his country as Major General Arnold; but in the present case a sense of duty and a regard to candour oblige him to declare that he considers his conduct in the instance of the permit as peculiarly reprehensible, both in a civil and military view, and in the affair of the wagons as imprudent and improper."[11]

Washington meant what he said. Arnold on March 22 wrote to Deane: "I believe you will be equally surprised with me when you find the court martial have fully acquitted me of the charge of employing public wagons, of defrauding the public, or of injuring or impeding the public service, and in the next sentence say 'as requests from him might operate as commands,' I ought to receive a reprimand. For what? Not for doing wrong, but because I might have done wrong; or rather, because there was a possibility that evil might have followed the good I did." Arnold had missed the whole point of the court's opinion, with its emphasis on the lack of delicacy in his conduct. As it was hard for him to think it could be wrong for him to do what he wanted, so was it hard to think that any way he chose to do it in was a wrong way. As if with the clearest conscience, he sent Deane a copy of the proceedings "which I must beg the favour of you to have translated into French and published when you arrive in France, and dispersed wherever you think necessary; the expense of which I will repay you with thanks."[12]

II

Waiting for both a vindication by the Americans and a better offer from the British, Arnold was at the same time waiting for the settlement of his public accounts with Congress. The treasury board to whom they were referred in April 1779 reported after months of difficulty and delay to Congress on September 29, and two days later the report was turned over to a committee with the friendly Henry Laurens as chairman. There it rested till February 14, when the committee reported that the matter was too intricate for them and asked that it be sent back to the treasury for adjustment.[13] Arnold on the 18th in a petition to Congress declared that the treasury commissioners had been governed by "private resentment or undue influence," and that some of them, with whom he had had "several disputes, are now become parties in the matter and by no means disinterested and proper persons to judge of his accounts and claims."[14]

Almost nothing is known of Arnold's life during these impatient, angry months. He lived on a good scale in Philadelphia, to which his sister Hannah and his three sons by his first wife had come from New Haven. Hannah Arnold was a devoted sister, but—at least later—seems to have been jealous of Arnold's wife, who may have resented the presence of an older woman in the household. To these discomforts was added a suspicious and hostile popular attitude toward Arnold. Early in October a riotous mob, made up partly of militiamen, attacked James Wilson's house where a group of notables including Robert Morris, all accused of profiteering, had taken refuge. Arnold came to quiet the rioters but was driven away, according to a contemporary letter, "pursued by two men. But he happened to have his pistols and prevented them from hurting him by threatening to fire at them."[15]

On the 6th Arnold wrote to Congress asking for a Continental guard of twenty men and a good officer to protect him. "A mob of lawless ruffians have attacked me in the street and threaten my life, now I am in my own house, for defending myself when attacked." There was, he said, "no protection to be expected from the authority of this state for an honest man. . . . This request I presume will not be denied to a man who has so often fought and bled in the defence of the liberties of his country."[16] Congress assured him it had full confidence in Pennsylvania's "disposition to protect every honest citizen . . . and highly disapprove the insinuations of every individual to the contrary."[17]

Arnold, who would never admit that anybody was more honest and patriotic than he, had now another grievance against Congress. The verdict of his court martial in January 1780 and the action on his accounts in February multiplied his resentments. Moreover, he must have been, like other officers and officials paid in a Continental currency which had become almost worthless, seriously in need of money. This, more perhaps than his restless need to have something to do, led him in March to think again of a naval command and possible prizes. To Deane, on the 22nd, Arnold wrote that he himself had proposed the matter to the admiralty board; and if it should not be carried out, that he thought of going to Boston "with the intention to take the command of a private ship." But to Washington, on the 10th and also ten days later, Arnold implied that the admiralty board had made its plans first and then called him.[18]

"I am requested by the board of admiralty to inform your Excellency that they have in contemplation an expedition with several of their frigates, which will require three or four hundred land forces to act in conjunction and who may act as marines when on board, which will obviate the great difficulty of procuring men for the ships. They wish to be informed if the men can be spared from the army. They will be wanted to embark (probably at New London) by the middle of April, for an expedition of about two months. If seamen can be drafted, they will be much preferable to other troops. From the injury I have received in my leg, and the great stiffness in my ankle, my surgeons are of opinion it will not be prudent for me to take a command in the army for some time to come."

Washington, having received Arnold's first letter, wrote directly to the admiralty board saying he thought the needed men could not be spared from the army "consistently with prudence or policy," and that without orders from Congress he could not take it upon himself either to send them or to express an opinion about Arnold as commander.[19] Arnold in his second letter said that if the expedition could not be undertaken, "I must request of your Excellency a leave of absence for the ensuing summer, or until my wounds are so well as to admit my riding and walking with some degree of ease and, of course, being able to take the command of a division in the army." He told Washington that Peggy's first child, Edward Shippen, had been born on the 19th.

Washington, sending his affectionate congratulations on the 28th, explained that he had written to the admiralty board because the decision rested with them and Congress. As to a leave of absence, "you have my permission (though it was my wish and expectation to see you in the field); but, provided your views extend to a voyage, leave for this purpose must be obtained from the Congress, as I have in no instance whatever ventured to grant a furlough to any place not within the United States."[20] Arnold had not said and Washington did not ask where the expedition was to be bound. As reasonable a guess as any other is that Arnold was still remembering his proposal of July–September 1778 to raid a West India island and plunder it. If he could get no official backing, then, as he told Deane, he might go to sea as a privateer. But the admiralty board on the 23rd wrote Washington that the naval project had been abandoned.[21]

Another scheme which Arnold is said to have tried rests, without first-hand documents, on a few sentences in the *Pennsylvania Packet* immediately after the treason and on an episode told a generation later by Barbé-Marbois. Among the papers seized at Arnold's house in Philadelphia, as soon as news came that he had escaped to the enemy, were found "private correspondence of himself and family" containing "the most sarcastic and contemptuous expressions of [about] the French nation and of an eminent personage of that country, whose hospitality and politeness they were at that time frequently experiencing."[22] As Barbé-Marbois put it, the investigators found "in the apartment of Mrs. Arnold some letters in which the character of the Chevalier de La Luzerne [the French minister who had succeeded Gérard] was roughly handled. They were brought to this minister. He consigned them to the flames, without having read them."[23]

On such a point Barbé-Marbois, the active young secretary of the French legation at Philadelphia, was closer to his materials than anywhere else in his often romantic and misleading narrative. According to him, Arnold after the court martial applied to La Luzerne for a loan. Unless he could pay off his debts, Arnold declared, he must leave the American army for civil life to restore his broken fortunes. Surely it was to the interest of France to keep such a soldier as he was in the service of her ally, and grateful to France. La Luzerne is said to have refused the loan, in lofty words obviously made up by Barbé-Marbois, on the ground that it would degrade the minister to behave as though the alliance needed secret means to maintain it, and the soldier to take money from one country to fight for another. Arnold, still according to Barbé-Marbois, was unconvinced and resentful. And it is true that the hearsay details of this episode, for whatever they may be worth, give the earliest hints of that dislike and distrust of France which Arnold later gave as one of his chief reasons for joining the British.

As there was to be no prize money and no French loan, neither was there to be an immediate settlement of Arnold's accounts. On April 27, a year to a day after this tangled business was referred to the treasury board, the board reported at some length to Congress.[24] Confusing then, the accounts are no less confusing now. Of the $70,004\frac{42}{90}$ charged against him, $3333\frac{30}{90}$ (£1000), Arnold claimed, had been turned over to a commissary of provisions in Canada who denied having received the amount or having given a voucher for it. Arnold insisted that this voucher had been among the papers he left in the treasury office, but that it had been mislaid or pilfered. There was a further total of $51,993\frac{68}{90}$ set down as "payments and advances made by the general to sundry persons who, if he is to be credited with them, must be charged and accountable to the United States." Yet while the board held that the smaller sum must be charged against Arnold till he could produce sufficient vouchers, the larger was to be credited to him, subject only to revision by the commissioners of accounts at Albany. That is, Arnold's public accounts would be settled though about five-sixths of the money advanced him on the Canada expedition was still not strictly accounted for.

Arnold on May 12 wrote Congress a long letter appealing from the treasury board's recommendation and sending numerous documents (hitherto little studied by his biographers) to support his claim.[25] As to the missing voucher Arnold was convinced, he said, that there had been carelessness if not fraud in the treasury office. He declared that Elbridge Gerry of Massachusetts, formerly a member of the board, had privately used his influence with the treasury accountants to prevent a settlement satisfactory to Arnold. (This Gerry indignantly and convincingly denied.) The board had passed over in silence, Arnold complained, his charge of £1000 to pay him for acting as commissary and quartermaster in Canada and handling more than £25,000. He had charged only about 4 per cent, "which is less than has been paid to others, and less than any person could have been hired to receive and pay so much money in our situation, taking the risk and expense upon himself." He objected that too much of the money still due him, according to the treasury accountants, was to be paid in paper money and not enough in specie. "Upon the whole, I beg leave to observe that I think there is justly due me from the public upwards of £2500 lawful money and that upwards of £2000 of this sum ought to be paid to me in specie or paper equivalent." A dollar in specie was then worth about fifty in Continental currency.

The disagreement between Arnold and the treasury board was chiefly over the £1000 commission for special services in Canada which he demanded and which the board disallowed; and the £1000 involved in the missing voucher, which the board said Arnold might claim whenever he could furnish proof that the commissary had received the amount and was himself accountable. In the state of Arnold's affairs £2000 was so important that he fought hard for it, furious at the officials who seem honestly to have thought it was not due him. He would not see that in the interests of the public they had every right to question his lax accounting.

How difficult their problem was appears in the smaller but bitterly controverted affair of his brigantine *Peggy* and its cargo, taken by the American army in Canada according to certificates which Arnold sent to Congress. The *Peggy,* commanded by John Gordon and "partly loaded for the sea," was in January 1776 "lying at the island Orleans before Quebec when Captain Gordon was seized with the smallpox and died," according to Freegift Arnold, mate. "Previous to which Captain Gordon had passed a bill of sale of said brigantine and cargo to Simon Frazer of Quebec to prevent her being seized" by the British. "Said Frazer had (by his interest) obtained liberty of the governor for said brigantine to winter at Orleans." The cargo in January consisted of 25 horses on shore, "cost on average in and about Quebec £10 lawful money" each; 500 bushels of oats, valued at £37 10s; 40 water hogsheads, £24; 40 bundles of hay, £30; 30 barrels of fish, £45; 10 barrels of provisions, £25: a total of £411 10s. The value of the brigantine Arnold put at £800.

Before Arnold left for Montreal in April he planned to send two fire-ships, "one at Orleans," into the harbour at Quebec in an attempt to burn the British vessels there.[26] Later in the month, according to the mate, the provisions and fish on board the *Peggy* were "landed for the use of the army, the oats was put on board another vessel lying at Orleans," and the hay and hogsheads left on the brigantine as extra fuel. The attempt to fire the "English frigates and transports" on May 3 failed but the *Peggy* was consumed. Arnold charged the entire value of brigantine and cargo to the army.

There was no question that the *Peggy* had been burned, and the treasury board did not ask for proof that the bill of sale to Simon Frazer, a Quebec merchant, had been a mere subterfuge, with no money actually paid to Arnold. But the evidence that the cargo had been put to public use was insubstantial. Wooster, in a certificate written in New Haven (at Arnold's request) a year after the event, said that the *Peggy,* "the property (as I was informed) of General Arnold," was burned "with part of her cargo, such as hay, hogsheads, etc.; some part of her cargo, being provisions, was received by the commissary of provisions for the use of the army." Whether the army had used all the provisions or part of them, or any of the horses, Wooster did not say, and Wooster was now dead. The statements as to the horses had not been made till August 1779, in Philadelphia. Then all John Taylor, who had been in the commissary department in Canada, could say was that the *Peggy's* horses were, "I have been often told, 25 or 28 in number. In December the captain of said vessel brought three of said horses to headquarters before Quebec, where he died of the smallpox, and the horses were kept there and made use of in the public service. I have also good reason to believe that the above-mentioned cargo of horses were taken into public service and not returned." The treasury board, which existed rather to safeguard the public funds than to satisfy Arnold, held that he should not be credited with 25 of the horses till he could produce better proof than this that the army had used them all.

On May 16 Arnold's appeal from the treasury board was referred to another committee of Congress in what Arnold must have thought another intolerable postponement. For the present he could do nothing about his accounts with Congress. And he had hit upon a scheme which might this year bring the British to meet his terms.

III

Although on March 20 Arnold had asked for leave, by the end of April he was inclined to continue in the service. He made a confidant of Schuyler, who had come early in March as a delegate to Congress, and who on April 13 was elected chairman of a committee to go to Headquarters at Morristown to confer with Washington on the organization of the staff departments and co-operation with the French. Schuyler arrived at Morristown on the

28th and on May 11, after a conversation about Arnold with Washington, wrote Arnold a letter which seems to have been much delayed and probably lost.

On May 25 Arnold wrote to Schuyler: "I have not had the pleasure of receiving a line from you since you arrived at camp, and know not who is to have the command at the North river." This is the earliest hint of Arnold's scheme to get himself appointed to command on the Hudson, at West Point. He hinted discreetly, as if not expecting too much. "If General Heath joins the army, as I am informed he intends, that post will of course, I suppose, fall under his command, unless some other arrangement is more agreeable to him." Heath, who had commanded the Highlands posts including West Point for nearly a year, was now on furlough, and Robert Howe was in charge.

"When I requested leave of absence of his Excellency General Washington for the summer," Arnold explained, "it was under the idea that it would be a very inactive campaign, and that my services would be of little consequence, as my wounds made it very painful for me to walk or ride. The prospect now seems to be altered, and there is a probability of an active campaign; in which, though attended with pain and difficulty, I wish to render my country every service in my power, and with the advice of my friends am determined to join the army; of which I beg you will do me the favour to acquaint his Excellency General Washington, that I may be included in any arrangement that may be made. A violent cold which has confined me for some days will prevent my setting out for camp for some days longer."[27]

Arnold here gave his reasons for changing his plans with an explicit formality that meant he expected Schuyler to show the letter to Washington. Schuyler, who with his wife and daughter had been on the friendliest terms with the Arnolds in Philadelphia, wrote less formally on June 2. In the missing letter of May 11, he now said, "I advised you that I had conversed with the General on the subject which passed between us before I left Philadelphia; that he appeared undecided on the occasion, I believe because no arrangement was made, for he expressed himself with regard to you in terms such as the friends who love you could wish. When I received yours of the 25th May, I read it to him; he was much engaged; next day he requested to know the contents again. I put it into his hands. He expressed a desire to do whatever was agreeable to you, dwelt on your abilities, your merits, your sufferings, and on the well-earned claims you have on your country, and intimated that as soon as his arrangements for the campaign should take place that he would properly consider you. I believe you will have an alternative proposed, either to take charge of an important post, with an honourable command, or your station in the field. Your reputation, my dear sir, so established, your honourable scars, put it decidedly in your power to take either. A state [New York] which has full confidence in you will wish to see its banner entrusted to you. If the command at West Point is offered, it will be honourable; if a division in the field, you must judge whether you can support the fatigues, circumstanced as you are."[28]

Whatever Arnold may have said in Philadelphia, he had in his letter mentioned only the Highlands and West Point command and had twice referred to the pain it would cost him to take the field. He was asking for West Point as plainly as was prudent. Washington, it seems clear from Schuyler's letter, desired to put Arnold to some more active use. Schuyler, innocent intermediary, thought Arnold might be offered his choice. Schuyler could not know, and would never have suspected, that Arnold while offering his services to Washington was at the same time offering them again to the British.

Better Bargains

WHEN Arnold reopened his negotiations with the British, apparently in May, there was no André in New York to take up the records begun the year before. André had gone on the southern expedition against Charleston, which Clinton after siege and assault had captured on May 12 with Lincoln's entire army defending it. Lieutenant General Wilhelm von Knyphausen commanded in New York during Clinton's absence, and Captain George Beckwith, his aide, set down neither the date of Arnold's new offers nor the name of the emissary. But on the whole the transaction is clear from the overlapping documents which Beckwith saved for Clinton's and André's return.

What Beckwith called "Mr. Moore's offers" seems to have been written out after a conference with Stansbury. "That he [Arnold] will undertake the part in question [an American command with treacherous intentions], confiding in the former assurances made by his Excellency the commander-in-chief; provided he now obtains from Sir Henry Clinton or General Knyphausen the security as expressed in the enclosed note written by his friend." The note is missing, but the stipulations appear later. "This [security] Mr. Moore destines for his family, or any proportion of it which he may not be able to dispose of": that is, any part of the security, or indemnification, which Arnold might have to leave for the present in the hands of the British. "He asks for a small sum of ready money to employ in a particular channel. He is now at Philadelphia; goes in a few days to Connecticut on his private affairs; after which, he returns to camp and remains there in a military capacity." It will be remembered that Arnold on May 25 said he had been delayed for some days by a cold but expected to leave soon; he may have been waiting for Stansbury's return from

New York. "He particularly desires to have a conference with an officer of confidence. He will take a decisive part in case of an emergency or that a capital stroke can be struck. He requests that a particular signature may be sent to him; that he may be furnished with a token to prevent fraud; and that a regular mode of communication may be fallen upon. Were it not for his family, he declares he would join the army without making any terms."

"General Knyphausen's answer to Mr. Moore's proposals," of which Stansbury must have carried the substance if not a copy back to Arnold, was friendly but discreet. "The affair in agitation is of so important a nature that General Knyphausen does not think himself authorized to give an answer to it in its full extent; and the more so as the matter is already known to the commander-in-chief. The general will therefore take the first opportunity of communicating the transaction to Sir Henry Clinton; and in the meantime will feel happy in cultivating the connexion and in giving Mr. Moore every testimony of his regard, from the persuasion which the general entertains of his rectitude and sincerity. Any trifling expenditures which may be made in the channel of communication, previous to a full answer from Sir Henry Clinton, will be readily reimbursed. An officer will give Mr. Moore the meeting which he solicits, whenever the practicability of it can be pointed out. In the meantime, two rings are procured which are exactly alike and one of them is sent to him by his friend, with whom a mode of correspondence by cipher is likewise settled." Another draft of the same answer has a different ending which indicates that the cipher was to be based on "two pocket dictionaries."

The third document is a "Memorandum" drawn up as a digest of the affair for Clinton. "A Mr. Moore had made proposals to [Clinton] previous to his departure from hence, relative to himself. The proposals were declined at first from particular circumstances; but offers were then made which Mr. Moore has now accepted of, provided that assurances are given to him of certain indemnifications for himself and family in cases of emergency." The only apparent change in Arnold is that he now said he was ready to take a treacherous command in the American army and he talked about his family; he had not reduced his price. "The indemnifications required are as follows: the loss of his private fortune, £5000 sterling; the debt due to him by the community, £5000 sterling, to be made good, or whatever part is lost; and to have a new-raised battalion here upon the common footing; to be supplied with money from time to time as circumstances may require. Mr. Moore is now at Philadelphia and waits there for a few days; he intends going to Connecticut and to return in three or four weeks to camp, where he is to remain in a military line. He wishes to have a conference with a military officer. He offers to take a decisive part in case of an emergency, or in view of attack on Boston or Philadelphia or any other place. He declared were it not for his family he would without ceremony have thrown himself into the protection of the king's army.

"This to go no further here. It may be communicated to S. H. C. with the particulars of the indemnification required, in addition to promises made him formerly, on which he relies.

"To fix upon a particular token, place of meeting, cipher, and channel of communication." Clinton, after he had returned and read the digest, added in his handwriting the words: "permission for a few articles" which were supposedly to be sent to Arnold or his wife, or to Stansbury.

In the negotiations of 1779 Arnold had never committed himself to specific services but had only asked to be promised £10,000 for what he might do, whatever came of it; and Clinton had made no specific offer except of payment (according to number) for soldiers, commanded by Arnold, whom he might arrange to lose to the British. If in 1780 Arnold was willing to accept that offer, it was because he had thought of a command he might take and a valuable post he might surrender. So while he was carefully planning to get West Point from Washington, he was no less carefully preparing to give it up to Clinton.

Though neither of these matters could yet be settled, Arnold could at once send the British some American secrets. The first of these had to do with Lafayette, who had returned from France with news of another French loan and of ships and soldiers on the way. Conferring at Morristown, he and Washington planned to issue a proclamation to the Canadians, announcing a combined French-American attack on British Canada and urging the French in

Canada to join with the French from overseas in the cause of the United States. This was intended only to deceive Clinton in New York, against which the combined attack was actually to be made. Washington on June 4 sent Arnold "the draft of a proclamation addressed to the inhabitants of Canada. You will be pleased to put this into the hands of a printer whose secrecy and discretion may be depended on and desire him to strike off a proof sheet with the utmost dispatch, which you will send to me for correction. We shall want at least 500 copies. The importance of this business will sufficiently impress you with the necessity of transacting it with every possible degree of caution. The printer is to be particularly charged not on any account to reserve a copy himself or to suffer one to get abroad."[1]

Sent on the 4th, this reached Arnold at Philadelphia the next day. "Immediately on receipt of it," he reported on the 7th, "I applied to several printers, but could not find one who had any person in their employ who understood French, that could be confided in. I was therefore obliged to have a proof sheet struck off by a person who did not understand French and who was greatly at a loss with respect to many of the letters. The first proof sheet was so very erroneous I was obliged to send it back cancelled, and have this minute received the second which is enclosed. Tomorrow or next day I expect to set out for Headquarters. I have therefore sealed up the original draft with a proof sheet similar to the one I enclosed, which I have left with Mrs. Arnold to be delivered to your Excellency's order. The printer employed is Mr. Claypole in Second Street, who will print any number of copies you will please to direct, and carefully seal and deliver them to any person your Excellency will name to send them to Headquarters. I make no doubt he will observe the greatest caution and secrecy."[2]

But Arnold himself was so far from observing caution and secrecy that he wrote that same day to Beckwith at British Headquarters. "I have received from the commander-in-chief," the first paragraph of the letter read, "a proclamation in order to have a number of copies printed, the purport of which will be transmitted to you by Joseph Stansbury to whom I have communicated it." Arnold did not know that the proclamation was a ruse and was intended for the British later. He thought that in betraying a confidence of Washington he was acting in good faith to Clinton. He had made his choice between the two.

Arnold went on: "The minister of France this day assured me that the French troops destined for Canada amount to 8000. The 8th instant I propose going to camp; will be at Morristown the 12th, King's Ferry the 16th, New Haven the 20th, and return to camp on the 4th of July." He was precise about his itinerary in order to give some British agent a chance to confer with him. "If I meet a person in my mensuration [of something like my rank] who has the token agreed on, you may expect every intelligence in my power which will probably be of consequence. When fully authorized by Sir Henry Clinton to treat I wish to have a conference with one of your officers in whom we can place a mutual confidence. The American army intended to co-operate with the French will probably go up Connecticut river to Number Four [Charlestown, Vermont] and cross the country to St. John's."

Stansbury the same day put the proclamation into cipher and sent it off addressed to "G. B. Ring, executor to the late John Anderson, Esq., in care of James Osborne." This was of course George Beckwith, who had kept one of the rings agreed on as a token to prove the message was authentic, who had temporarily taken the place of John Anderson (André), and who was to be reached through James Osborne (Odell). So far as Stansbury knew, André might be back in New York by the time the proclamation got there. The renewed conspiracy would then be in the hands of last year's conspirators. The proclamation, Stansbury said, "must be a profound secret."

II

Arnold may not have set out till the 9th, or after, for he carried a letter of that date to Schuyler from Robert R. Livingston,[3] who had voted in Congress against confirming the verdict of Arnold's court martial and who was a friend of both Arnold and his wife. Livingston, whom there is not the slightest reason to suspect of any treachery, knew of Arnold's desire to command at West Point, and approved it. Like Schuyler, he hoped to see Arnold at a post which New York very much wanted to have securely held. On the 22nd

Livingston wrote to Washington about the West Point command. Instead of to Robert Howe, might it not be "confided to General Arnold, whose courage is undoubted, who is the favourite of our militia, and who will agree perfectly with our governor?"[4] Arnold had been a hero to New York ever since Saratoga.

The journey to Connecticut in June has been hitherto a mystery almost without a record. Part of it may now be closely followed in Arnold's own words sent secretly to the British.

As he promised them, he was at Morristown on the 12th, and he that day wrote two letters. "Six French ships of the line," he reported in the first, "several frigates, and a number of transports with 6000 troops are expected at Rhode Island in two or three weeks to act under General Washington." This was true, and was to be of the greatest interest to Clinton. "It is probable three or four thousand rebels will be embarked with them and proceed up the St. Lawrence to Quebec, while the Marquis Fayette with two or three thousand will go from Connecticut river to St. John's and Montreal." This was what Washington hoped the British would think and what many Americans, not in his confidence, did think. "Governor Trumbull is laying up flour and pork at Connecticut river for the French. The drafts when completed will make General Washington 20,000, but some states are so dilatory he does not expect strong reinforcements before August." Washington on the 6th had told his council of war that he might have 24,000 by the 20th, but on the 12th he had heard that some of the states planned to send fewer soldiers than Congress had requested.[5]

At ten o'clock at night Arnold wrote a second letter, possibly after he had talked with Washington. "Mr. Moore expects to have the command of West Point offered him on his return. Troops and provisions wanting there. Only 1500 [men]. Little flour, and none to be had but from Pennsylvania, whence they have required 10,000 barrels. Mr. Moore thinks it would be a good stroke to get between General Washington and West Point."

What Arnold told the British he expected was not what Washington understood. According to his later recollections, he had discussed the West Point command with Schuyler without anything like a promise, and had said "it was my intention to draw my whole force into the field when we were in circumstances to commence our operations against New York, leaving even West Point to the care of invalids and a small garrison of militia"; but that if Arnold were unfit for active duty "I should readily indulge him" in his preference. "This, to the best of my knowledge and recollection, is every syllable that ever passed between me and General Schuyler respecting Arnold or any of his concerns."[6] And when Arnold himself at Morristown "intimated a desire to have the command at West Point, I told him I did not think that would suit him, as I should have none in his garrison but invalids because it would be entirely covered by the main army." But Arnold had set his mind on commanding West Point and surrendering it to the British. He might drive a better and quicker bargain if he mentioned his prospect as a fact.

As the extracts from these two letters preserved in the Clinton papers are dated the 15th, Arnold must have found some way of sending them direct from Morristown. He continued on his journey by King's Ferry and wrote again from Fishkill on the 16th.

"I called on General Howe at West Point, which I never saw before," Arnold said; "was greatly disappointed both in the works and garrison. There is only 1500 soldiers, which will not half man the works. But General [James] Clinton's brigade of 1200 men are ordered to join the garrison and are on their march from Albany. It is hoped they will arrive before the English can make an attack which it is thought they have in contemplation." Washington had not yet disposed his army below the Highlands for the attack on New York, and a sudden land and river thrust at West Point would find it unable to defend itself.

"This place has been greatly neglected. General Howe tells me there is not ten days' provision for the garrison. A quantity is on the way and soon expected; but if the English were to cut off the communication with Pennsylvania they would be distressed for flour, which is not to be procured in this part of the country. It is surprising a post of so much importance should be so totally neglected. The works appear to me, though well executed, most wretchedly planned to answer the purpose designed: viz., to maintain the post and stop the passage of the river. The Point is on a low piece of ground comparatively to the chain of hills which lie back of it. The highest, called Rocky Hill, which commands all the other works is about half a mile from Fort Putnam, which is strong. On Rocky Hill there is a small redoubt to hold 200 men and two six-pounders pointed on the other works. The wall six foot thick and defenceless on the back; and I am told the English may land three miles below and have a good road to bring up heavy cannon to Rocky Hill. This redoubt is wretchedly executed, only seven or ten feet high and might be taken by assault by a handful of men. I am convinced the boom or chain thrown across the river to stop the shipping cannot be depended on. A single ship, large and heavy-loaded with a strong wind and tide, would break the chain.

"The committee of Congress have made requisition to the different states which, if complied with, will enable us [the Americans] to act offensively this summer and to some purpose."

Arnold went into treason as into a business, surveying the ground and estimating the possible profits. Robert Howe afterwards remembered that Arnold "spoke so particularly of the Rocky Hill work and with what ease it could be taken as struck me oddly even then, though I had not the least suspicion of him."[7] If Arnold was pleased to find what he thought a vulnerable point in the fortress, so was he to be able to report it to Clinton, who would be encouraged to the attack he had in mind.

From Fishkill Arnold travelled to Hartford where the Connecticut assembly was in session. The assembly the past October had voted allowances to the officers and men of the Connecticut line in the Continental army which would make up what they had lost by the depreciation of the currency. The present session voted to admit Arnold to the same "benefits and advantages." His pay was to be balanced to January 1, 1780, by a committee appointed to examine the officers' accounts, and he was to receive the amount due him in four instalments beginning June 1782 and thereafter paid annually in that same month. What he would now actually receive would be notes on the state treasury.[8] These notes he apparently expected to discount for cash which he presumably hoped he might have with him at West Point when he surrendered it.

But on his hurried visit to Hartford he had no time to get his accounts examined and the sum due him settled upon. (He later, asking the British for compensation, put the amount at £1125.)[9] The best he could do was to leave the matter in the hands of his friend Titus Hosmer of Middletown, who was then at Hartford in the assembly. With Hosmer, too, Arnold left another claim, in connexion with the *Active* case which was still undecided in Philadelphia. Perhaps the Connecticut legislature might "think it their duty to obtain justice to a subject of the state and defend its rights and dignity so grossly violated." Arnold gave Hosmer a fee of $1000 to handle the matter so that, possibly, Connecticut could urge Pennsylvania to make a settlement satisfactory to the Connecticut captors of the sloop—and to Arnold.[10]

On the 23rd Arnold was at Middletown, where he that day got an order for £12 10s from David Hopkins, who had gone as volunteer on the march to Quebec. (The order was on David Lenox of Philadelphia, who later said he did not owe Hopkins a shilling.)[11] In New Haven on the 25th Arnold was making efforts to sell his house there to Enoch Brown of Boston.[12]

There had been several offers, Arnold wrote Brown, and the price was low at £1000. "Nothing could have induced me to take double the sum, did not my connexions induce me to leave this place." The house was large and elegant, "about one-half completed within and materials (of the best kind) sufficient to complete it." Besides the house there were neat stables for ten or twelve horses and a coach house for two carriages, on a lot of two acres. A hundred fruit trees—pears, peaches, apples, plums, cherries, nectarines, apricots, etc.—had been planted seven years before. The whole had cost £1800. Arnold wanted cash for the property, "or good sterling bills on France, Holland, or England, or paper currency equivalent, the one-half in hand and the other payable in six or twelve months." Since Brown was a stranger, the house would have to remain as collateral till the whole was paid. Arnold would much prefer the whole at once, "as I have an opportunity of making a purchase that is convenient to me." The current rate of exchange of paper for specie at Philadelphia was 60 for 1. If Brown would take the house and pay for it within a month, Arnold would accept paper at the Philadelphia rate. Or Arnold would take £1200 and insure the house against damage or destruction by the enemy while the war lasted. But Arnold did not complete the sale,[13] and after the treason he asked the British £1800 for the loss of the New Haven house.[14]

His stay in Connecticut was shorter than has been supposed, for he was back in Philadelphia early in July. On the 8th he wrote to Hosmer, now at Middletown, about the pay due Arnold as a Connecticut officer. "I must beg the favour of a line of advice (on the settlement and receipt of the treasury notes) of their value in specie and paper, and I wish to realize a part of them in this or the state of New York. I expect in a few days to set out for the army and have my choice of a command in the main army or West Point. I believe I shall accept the latter."[15]

Though Arnold seemed sure of the command which would enable him to co-operate with the British, he was disappointed on his return to Philadelphia to find no answer to his letter of June 7 asking for a conference. Stansbury, for some reason using the name Thomas Carleton, on July 7 wrote to Odell: "My partner is come to town and has set those matters right that were not clearly entered in my last account current and which you will perceive make a great difference in the general balance." This was, probably, a discreet commercial way of saying that Arnold had learned of Washington's intention to move against New York rather than Canada. "He thinks it strange that no steps are taken on your part to come to a settlement which rightly considered is of consequence to you both. He intended to have wrote you on that head this day, but though I left a person waiting all day in town on that account, business would not permit him an hour's leisure." Then Stansbury (Carleton) added: "I got a verbal message about *minuit* and I shall forward it to you. My best respects wait on Mr. Anderson and M. de l'Anneau"—Ring, or Beckwith.

If the surviving communciation from Moore of the same date is based upon this verbal message, Arnold must have seen Stansbury at midnight and told him what was to be sent in cipher to New York. "Mr. Moore requests a very explicit answer to his letter of June 7th, and that some method may be fallen on to obtain an interview with Major General Phillips or some other proper officer, as nothing further can be done without it." To correct the earlier mistaken information Moore had now to say: "On the arrival of the French troops New York is the object, if an army can be raised which is thought equal to the attempt. The Canada expedition is a secondary object in case the other fails. General

Washington will throw a detachment over the North river [from New Jersey] when the French fleet arrives at Newport, but not before." Arnold gave some fresh information about the Highland forts which he had got on his way back from New Haven; and he had talked with Howe at West Point.[16] "Two or three persons in whom you confide as spies on General Howe are in his pay and often give him important intelligence." The spies of either side were throughout the war frequently spies of both.

"He [Moore-Arnold] thinks General Phillips might come out to negotiate on an exchange of prisoners, or his own for Lincoln" who had been captured at Charleston. "He begs you would write to him only by such channels as may be fully depended on. He is to take the command of West Point immediately on the fleet's arrival, or at any rate in the course of this month." Arnold had stopped saying he expected the West Point command. "He has a drawing of the works on both sides of the river done by a French engineer, and thinks he could settle matters with a proper officer that you might take it [West Point] without loss, and also [besides settling matters] lay down a plan of communication whereby you should be informed of everything projected at [American] Headquarters."

III

There were reasons for the delay of the British answer to Arnold's letter of June 7. Clinton, returning in triumph from his capture of Charleston which he hoped and believed would end the rebellion in the Carolinas, did not arrive off Sandy Hook till the 17th. He found that Knyphausen had crossed with 5000 men into New Jersey on a report that the American army was mutinous and might be won over. If the Americans were mutinous it was because they were hungry, not because they were disaffected. The Continentals fought with rebel stubbornness, and the militia rose like angry magic. Knyphausen could make no headway, and waited for Clinton. Together they concerted a feint on Springfield and a more important attack on Morristown on the 23rd. Though Springfield was burned, the British were checked and retired that night to Staten Island. The New York loyalists were bitter with complaints of what seemed to them Clinton's incomprehensible lack of enterprise.[17]

There can be little doubt that the British withdrawal from New Jersey owed something to the reports from Arnold which Clinton found waiting for him. On the 20th Beckwith, then with the Hessian command at Elizabeth, wrote André that "our friend [Arnold] is certainly travelling to Connecticut." André had already taken precautions to have Arnold investigated. Joseph Chew, a New London loyalist (then in New York) who was often useful to André, wrote him the same day: "I received your note at half after two yesterday and before five put two persons out in order to obtain an account of Mr. Arnold's movements and what other intelligence they can get from that part of the country." But though it was prudent to set spies to watch him, Clinton was convinced by Arnold's news of the 12th from American Headquarters that the French would shortly be at Newport. As Clinton wrote to Eden: "Immediately on my arrival from the southward I received, from such authority as I should have risked an action upon, intelligence that the French fleet and 6000 troops were expected at Rhode Island."[18] If he risked too many men against Washington, in what Clinton knew might be a difficult campaign, this would leave New York open to possible attack by the French. And Clinton's strategy was first of all to hold New York, with such punishing raids elsewhere as he might be able to carry out. Arnold, betraying Washington's secret to the British, unintentionally helped save Washington from further British operations in New Jersey.

On the 22nd Clinton asked Admiral Marriot Arbuthnot, in command of the fleet, to have transports for 6000 men ready "at a moment's notice, as the movements of the army at this time might be important." Part of Clinton's force moved up the Hudson to Phillipsburgh, for fear Washington should try to cross the river, and the transports returned to Manhattan to carry another part, if necessary, to Rhode Island. The French did not arrive at Newport till July 12, nor word of it reach New York till the 18th; and Washington did not cross till the 31st. But Clinton was so much occupied at the end of June and the beginning of July that he apparently made no effort to communicate with Arnold on his way to and from Connecticut.

Arnold, impatient in Philadelphia, waited only four days after his message of the 7th by Stansbury before writing again. "A mutual confidence between us is wanting," he said. "The persons we have employed have deceived us, or we have been unfortunate in our negotiations. . . . If the first, here our correspondence ought to end. If the second, an opportunity offers of redressing any abuse." Suspicious of Stansbury and Odell, Arnold had trusted his secret to another intermediary, then unnamed but actually Samuel Wallis. Though André, dealing with both Wallis and Arnold, had tried to keep them each in ignorance of the other, they had somehow come to an understanding.

Arnold had, he said, through Stansbury reported matters of great importance. "The bearer [Wallis], in whom a confidence may be placed, is charged with others and is instructed—preliminaries being first settled—to fix on a plan of safe conveyance and operation." The preliminaries which must be settled before the business could go on were the rewards Arnold demanded. Though he wrote in a commercial language which might deceive interceptors or accidental readers, his meaning would be clear enough to Clinton and André. "My stock in trade (which I have before mentioned) is £10,000 sterling, with near an equal sum of outstanding debts. An equal sum I expect will be put into stock and the profits arising be equally divided." Still faithful to his first price for indemnification, win or lose, Arnold insisted that the amount be guaranteed him (put into stock) and additional payments (profits) be left to depend on services rendered. "I have advanced several sums already, and risked still greater, without any profit." These were payments and promises to his messengers, and possibly also to the intermediaries. "It is now become necessary for me to know the risk I run in case of a loss. I expect you will pay into the hands of the bearer 1000 guineas to be invested in goods suitable for our market; on receipt of which I will transmit to you their full value in good French bills drawn on sight or at a short time": less cryptically, information which Arnold counted on getting from the French minister or generals. "For other advances you shall have good sterling bills well endorsed": presumably, American military information which would be as good as gold.

"I wish for a personal conference with Captain P—— [perhaps a slip for B—— for Beckwith] or some one of the co-partnership, without which it appears difficult to make a proper arrangement. This I apprehend may very easily be brought about. If you have any regard for your own interest or my safety, by no means trust to any conveyance that is not known and approved, or proved. You may be deceived with false friends. Mention no names. Write me in cipher and through some medium. A clear, explicit, and confidential avenue in cipher will enable us to co-operate to mutual advantage, or end this correspondence to the mutual safety of all concerned; as I make no doubt the strictest honour will be observed."

The next day, the 12th, Arnold wrote still another letter to go with this one. Saying "I expect soon to command at West Point" he did not mean to imply that there was any question whether he would have the command, only how soon. Once there, he could arrange the conference he desired. "An officer [British] might be [voluntarily] taken prisoner near that post and permitted to return on parole, or some officer on parole sent out to effect an exchange. . . . I have accepted the command at West Point"—which had not yet been offered him—"as a post in which I can render the most essential services and which will be in my disposal. The mass of the people are heartily tired of the war and wish to be on their former footing. They are promised great events from this year's exertion. If disappointed, you have only to persevere and the contest will soon be at an end. The present struggles are like the pangs of a dying man, violent but of a short duration.

"As life and fortune are risked by serving his Majesty, it is necessary that the latter shall be secured as well as the emoluments I give up; and a compensation for services agreed on; and a sum advanced for that purpose which I have mentioned in a letter which accompanies this, which Sir Henry will not, I believe, think unreasonable." Arnold added a postscript: "I have great confidence in the bearer, but beg Sir Henry will threaten him with his resentment in case he abuses the confidence placed in him, which will bring certain ruin on me. The bearer will bring me 200 guineas and pay the remainder to Captain André who is requested to receive the deposit for Mr. Moore."

The next day Arnold got his first answer from Clinton, undated, unsigned, bland, and vague. As Clinton had not yet seen Arnold's July letters naming the reward expected, this reply acknowledged only the June letters sending secrets, telling of the West Point plan, and asking for a meeting. "His Excellency Sir Henry Clinton is much obliged to you for the useful intelligence you have transmitted him. It corresponds with other information and gives him full conviction of your desire to assist him. He had hoped to communicate with you in a very satisfactory manner but is disappointed. His Excellency hopes you still keep in view the project of essentially co-operating with him. He thinks the having the command of West Point would afford the best opportunities for it, and would willingly know from you some scheme for effecting a service of importance there. The General could point out such plausible measures as would ward off all blame or suspicion and be very eligible at the juncture of an attack upon Canada. An interview between you and a person he [will send is] absolutely necessary. Your visiting Elizabethtown [the American advanced post in New Jersey] or some place near us, which a flag of truce could reach and where you might be supposed to be detained by sickness, is the expedient which strikes Sir Henry Clinton as a practicable one. The General trusts that in the same confidence in which you communicate with him you will rely on his promise that upon effectual co-operation you shall experience the full measure of the national obligation; and his Excellency will in the meantime give you in such manner as you may require it an ample stipend."

To Arnold, hot with anxiety, this was cold and unsatisfying. In a reply of the 15th he made his terms unmistakable. "Two days since I received a letter without date or signature, informing me that Sir Henry ——— was obliged to me for the intelligence communicated and that he placed a full confidence in the sincerity of my intentions, etc., etc. On the 13th instant I addressed a letter to you expressing my sentiments and expectations." There is no surviving letter of the 13th, and Arnold may here have meant his letter of the 12th, to judge by his account of the contents. He had asked, and now repeated, that "the following preliminaries be settled previous to co-operation: that Sir Henry secure to me my

Arnold's code letter of July 15, 1780
offering to sell West Point to the British for £20,000

Inclosed in a cover addressed to Mr. Anderson.

Two days since I received a letter without date or Signature, informing me that S. Henry — was obliged to me for the intelligence communicated, and that he placed a full confidence in the Sincerity of my intentions, &c. &c. — On the 13th Instant I addressed a letter to you expressing my Sentiments and expectations, viz. that the following Preliminaries be settled previous to cooperating— first, that S. Henry secure to me my property, valued at ten thousand pounds Sterling, to be paid to me or my Heirs in case of Loss; and, as soon as that shall happen, — hundred pounds per annum to be secured to me for life, in lieu of the pay and emoluments I give up, for my Services as they shall deserve — If I point out a plan of cooperation by which S.H. shall possess himself of West Point, the Garrison, &c. &c. &c. twenty thousand pounds Sterling I think will be a cheap purchase for an object of so much importance. At the same time I request a thousand pounds to be paid my Agent — I expect a full and explicit answer — The 20th I set off for West Point. A personal interview with an officer that you can confide in is absolutely necessary to plan matters. In the mean time I shall communicate to our Mutual Friend S— y all the intelligence in my power, until I have the pleasure of your answer.

July 15th

Moore

To the line of my letter of the 13th
I did not add Seven.

N.B. the postscript only relates to the manner of composing the Cypher in the letter referred to —

Arnold's letter of July 15, 1780
as decoded by Odell

property, valued at £10,000 sterling, to be paid to me or my heirs in case of loss; and, as soon as that shall happen, —— hundred pounds per annum to be secured to me for life, in lieu of the pay and emoluments I give up, for my services as they shall deserve. If I point out a plan of co-operation by which Sir Henry shall possess himself of West Point, the garrison, etc., etc., etc., £20,000 sterling I think will be a cheap purchase for an object of so much importance. At the same time, I request £1000 to be paid my agent [Wallis]. I expect a full and explicit answer. The 20th I set off for West Point. A personal interview with an officer that you can confide in is absolutely necessary to plan matters. In the meantime I shall communicate to our mutual friend Stansbury all the intelligence in my power, until I have the pleasure of your answer."

Arnold's positive statements that he had accepted the West Point command and would leave Philadelphia in five days were founded, it may be fairly guessed, on more than his ardent wishes. Washington on June 29 had written to Livingston in answer to his recommendation of Arnold instead of Howe for West Point. "When a general arrangement is gone into and a disposition made for the campaign," Washington said, "I can with propriety, and certainly shall, bring General Howe into the line of the army and place the gentleman you have named at that post if the operations of the campaign are such as to render it expedient to leave an officer of his rank in that command."[19] Livingston, pleased himself, could hardly have failed to tell his interested friend Arnold of Washington's conditional agreement, and the sanguine Arnold took it as a promise.

Two days after Arnold on the 15th wrote the British what his price for the surrender of West Point would be, he wrote Congress a letter asking for money from the Americans. "I am under the necessity of informing Congress that there is due to me upwards of four years' pay; and to request that honourable body that they will give orders that I may receive four months' pay in specie or paper equivalent, to enable me to purchase horses, camp equipage, etc., that I may be enabled to take the field, which I am called upon by his Excellency General Washington to do immediately."[20] Though he had West Point firmly in mind, he said nothing about this to Congress, which might make him a larger advance if he asked for money to buy field equipment. He might as well be supported by Congress while he bargained with Clinton. The treasury board did not admit that so much back pay was due him; his pay was involved in his total account. But on the 21st Congress ordered that $25,000 be "advanced to General Arnold on account of his pay; and for which he is to be accountable."[21] At the rate of 50 to 1 this was roughly the four months' pay Arnold requested, without the additional allowance provided for a major general in a separate command. Congress assumed that Arnold would be in the field with the main army, as he had himself implied.

It is unlikely that Arnold set out from Philadelphia till the 21st or after, or without the money ordered him by Congress. But between the 21st and the 30th, when he was or had been at Headquarters near the Hudson, there seems to be no record of his movements or activities. By the roads he probably took he had to ride about 125 miles; and if his leg was as painful as he claimed, he probably took five or six days. He left his treacherous correspondence in the hands of Stansbury, Wallis, and Peggy Arnold, for what turned out to be a month of confused delay.

IV

It was easier to write secret letters in Philadelphia or New York than to get them safely and promptly through the lines, or in the order in which they were written. The message from Moore (Arnold) written by Carleton (Stansbury) on July 7 was answered by André on the 23rd. Since Arnold's statement of his terms had not yet been received, the answer (undated and cautious) said nothing of any reward except "the supplies mentioned both for Mr. Moore and yourself." Ostensibly the letter was to Stansbury, addressed as Stevens or Carleton. Intercepted, it would not point to Arnold. But Arnold could not miss knowing that it was to him through André from Clinton. "You must not wonder if we take a view of our new arrived foe and, if prudence justifies it, make some attempt on him." Clinton was then busy with plans for an expedition by the Sound against the French in Newport. "Our main purpose is, however, the manner which your co-operation is to render successful. Stony Point will be taken possession of, and from thence I shall find some pretence which you will understand for a meeting; not with the person at first wished for, as you will have learnt the objection of it, but with one you know and will confide in." Phillips was in process of being exchanged for Lincoln, and consequently not available for an interview with Arnold.

Arnold, distrusting Stansbury, had sent his letters of the 11th and 12th by Wallis, then given the letter of the 15th to Stansbury to send. Stansbury's messenger, the expert Andrew Fürstner, reached New York on the 23rd, after that day's answer had already gone. The next day an answer was drafted which at last met Arnold's terms with Clinton's final offer.

"Your letter of the 15th is arrived; that of the 13th [12th] is not yet come to hand. Though West Point derives its importance from the nature of the operations of our enemy, yet should we through your means possess ourselves of 3000 men and its artillery and stores with the magazine of provisions for the army which may probably be there, the sum even of £20,000 should be paid you. You must not suppose that in case of detection or failure that, your efforts being known, you would be left a victim; but services done are the terms on which we promise rewards. In these you see we are profuse; we conceive them proportioned to the risk. As to an absolute promise of indemnification to the amount of £10,000 and annuity of 500 whether services are performed or not, it can never be made. Your intelligence we prize and will freely recompense it. £200 shall be lodged in your agent's hands as you desire, and 300 more are at your disposal." Arnold had asked for £200 to be paid to Wallis and 800 left with André. Clinton cut the balance down, and refused once for all to guarantee Arnold against losses unless he performed services to match.

Odell that same day, writing to Stansbury, seemed to soften the answer a little. "I have this morning had the honour of a conversation with the commander-in-chief on the subject. In addition to what is stated in the enclosed for Mr. Moore, his Excellency authorizes me to repeat in the strongest terms the assurances so often given to your partner: that if he is in earnest and will to the extent of his ability co-operate with us, he shall not in any possible event

have cause to complain, and essential services shall be even profusely rewarded far beyond the stipulated indemnification, etc.
But indemnification as a preliminary is what Sir Henry thinks
highly unreasonable. However, he has not the smallest doubt but
that everything may be settled to mutual satisfaction when the
projected interview takes place at West Point; from whence it is
expected Mr. Moore will take occasion (upon entering on his command there) to correspond with Sir Henry by flag of truce. Mr.
Anderson is willing himself to effect the meeting either in the way
proposed or in whatever manner may at the time appear most
eligible."

Stansbury had proposed, possibly in a missing letter of the 18th,
a speculation of his own which Odell said Clinton approved. This
was a scheme to ship lumber through the lines to the British garrison. Vessels were to be—and were—cleared from Philadelphia
with papers for Boston, but deliberately exposed to capture by the
British. Brought into New York, their cargoes of lumber were
taken to the king's yard and paid for through agents conniving
with the shippers in Philadelphia and New Jersey. The captains
and crews were quickly exchanged and allowed to go back for another forbidden voyage. One of the captains had been five times to
New York on this arrangement before November, when the scheme
was discovered by the Pennsylvania council. Stansbury, having
brought Clinton's permission and protection to the venture, shared
in the profits.[22]

When Wallis arrived in New York on the 28th, with Arnold's
letters of the 11th and 12th, Clinton and André were off on the
expedition against Newport which got no further than Huntington, Long Island. In André's absence the Arnold correspondence
was left in charge of Beckwith. But as Beckwith was then stationed with Knyphausen at Morris House (Jumel Mansion) in
upper Manhattan, Wallis had to apply to Odell in Wall Street and
consequently to reveal to him the suspicions Arnold entertained.

Wallis, Odell wrote to André on the 29th, had been sent "chiefly
with a view of ascertaining whether Mr. Stevens or your humble
servant had faithfully conducted the correspondence, and as an
agent to receive the first fruits. Mr. Moore will be convinced that
his jealousy [suspicion] of 'the persons employed' was utterly

groundless; and when Mr. Wallis returns, which he says he must of necessity do without delay, Mr. Moore will probably leave 'harping on my daughter' and think the terms contained in your last letter every way equal to what he can in reason expect." Odell wished "a new harvest of glory to our noble chief and his gallant train of myrmidons."

Odell sent word to Beckwith, who, as he wrote André the next day, rode down to Headquarters and talked with Wallis. "In consequence of a letter which Mr. Odell produced to me of yours, and Mr. Moore's application, I paid the 200 guineas and took his receipt, which I hope the commander-in-chief will approve of. I could not take it upon me to fix a direct mode of communication by the Hudson." That would have to wait for André's return. "I have fixed on a mode of corresponding with the gentleman . . . but the manner is tedious although certain, being by Philadelphia." Beckwith "also wrote three or four words to Mr. Moore, relative to the sum paid Wallis on his account."

(The 200 guineas which Odell called Arnold's first fruits had an involved history. André entered the payment in his account of expenses on September 13: "Captain Beckwith for W. for Moore 210" pounds (200 guineas). But Wallis, the agent who was to expedite communication, apparently did not carry the money with him to Philadelphia, or if he did, did not turn it over to Peggy Arnold. Instead, he gave it—then or later—to Daniel Coxe, who after the treason had been discovered and Peggy had taken refuge in New York, paid it to her and got her receipt on January 6, 1781: "Received of Daniel Coxe for, and on account, and in full of all accounts of Mr. Samuel Wallace of Pennsylvania, the sum of two hundred guineas, ordered to be paid by Mr. Wallace to General Arnold.")[23]

The manner of communication by way of Philadelphia was as tedious as Beckwith foresaw it would be. John Rattoon, with the replies of the 24th, and Wallis, with Beckwith's note to Arnold of the 30th, did not reach Stansbury till August 8; and Stansbury's acknowledgment of the 14th did not come, by Rattoon, till the 23rd. "Mr. Moore commands at West Point," Stansbury wrote on the 14th, "but things are so poorly arranged that your last important dispatches are yet in *her* [Peggy Arnold's] hands, no unquestionable carrier being yet to be met with. When you have opened your communications on the spot these delays will be avoided."

Three weeks after Clinton agreed to pay £20,000 for the surrender of West Point Arnold still did not know that his terms—except for the indemnification—had been accepted; and Clinton had heard nothing from Arnold since he left Philadelphia to rejoin the army. But Peggy had received letters from Arnold and she allowed Stansbury to forward extracts on the 14th to Odell, who received them on the 23rd and the next day gave or sent them to André. As Odell explained, the extracts were "from letters written to Mrs. Moore, but with a view of communicating information to you." Using this device, Arnold could assume that his letters would get safely to Philadelphia, and even if intercepted would seem to be only innocent confidences to his wife.

"General Washington had just arrived at Kakiat [near New City, New York]," Arnold wrote on July 30, "when he received intelligence that Sir Henry Clinton had gone up the Sound with a considerable force. He went immediately to King's Ferry and from thence proposed to go to West Point to put the troops there in motion to join this army, who cross the Ferry tomorrow morning. When the whole form a junction I believe we shall have near 10,000 men together, who will probably move towards New York in order to draw the attention of S. H. C. from Rhode Island. I wish our force and the provision made for it would enable us to attack New York in his absence and end the dispute. But I am sorry to say that I believe it will be unequal to the undertaking, and am very apprehensive for the French fleet and army who are in a critical situation." This might be bad news for the Americans, but it would be good news for the British. "However, another division of 2500 men and several ships of the line were to sail from Brest as soon as transports could be procured. . . . If this division should arrive soon they will probably make the French fleet nearly equal, perhaps superior, to the British, and there is some expectation of a reinforcement from the West Indies. So that upon the whole our affairs, which do not wear a pleasing aspect at present, may soon be greatly changed."

In another extract, undated, Arnold wrote: "In consequence of S. H. C.'s return our army is ordered to recross the North river at

King's Ferry and will march to Dobbs Ferry"—that is, to the Dobbs Ferry landing on the west side of the Hudson—"where the General intends to establish a post and build works which will confine the British within narrower bounds and shorten our communication with New England. The preparations against New York are at present laid aside, as there appears no prospect of our collecting a force sufficient this summer, and we are in want of almost every requisite for the purpose." Arnold probably wrote this undated note on August 3, when general orders announced that the army would "recross the river tomorrow" and Washington wrote to Congress to say that he had given up his plan to march on New York and would, having recrossed the Hudson, "proceed with our whole force to Dobbs Ferry."[24] Arnold, who the same day received his instructions for the command at West Point, wrote from his new headquarters on the 5th that all the Continental troops at the post had left for the main army. "At present there are no troops there but about 1500 of the militia of Massachusetts Bay, who are destitute of almost every necessary. They are in want of tents, provisions, and almost everything."

Marking time, Arnold sent his odds and ends of information. He sent more in a letter dated the 25th, though apparently written earlier. There was a report, he said, that Clinton had "embarked a considerable force. It is imagined he has some enterprise in contemplation. If he should draw off a great part of his force, General Washington has a fine army of 12,000 men ready to make an attack on New York. One circumstance is indeed rather against us, owing to the derangement of the commissary department." Nathanael Greene had that month angrily resigned as quartermaster general. The army, Arnold went on, had "been three days without a mouthful of meat, and the post [West Point] is very little better. The commissaries drive the cattle provided for us to the French, who give them a better price, which will probably create a jealousy *entre eux*. Our army cannot keep the field late, unless better supplied."

What makes it appear that Arnold had written this letter before the 25th is that he did not refer in it to Clinton's final offer of July 24 which got to Arnold on August 24. Treason had stood still exactly a month.

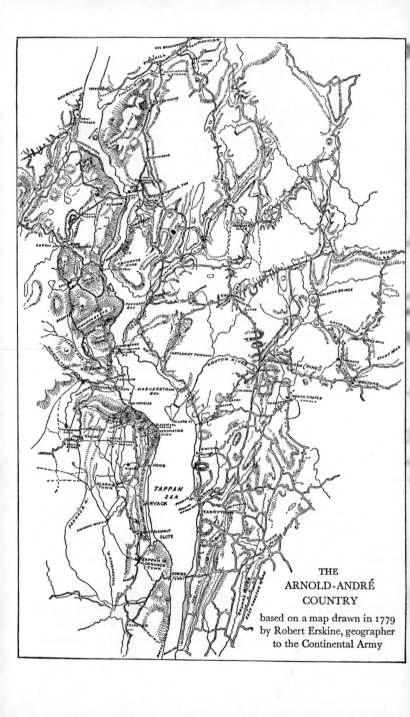

THE
ARNOLD-ANDRÉ
COUNTRY

based on a map drawn in 1779
by Robert Erskine, geographer
to the Continental Army

Traitor in Suspense

THOUGH Arnold was at Headquarters at Kakiat by July 30 and hurried off a note to tell the British that the Americans would cross the Hudson the next day, he did not then see Washington. But on the 31st, "while the army was crossing at King's Ferry," as Washington remembered, "I was going to see the last detachment over, and met Arnold, who asked me if I had thought of anything for him. I told him that he was to have the command of the light troops, which was a post of honour, and which his rank entitled him to. Upon this information his countenance changed and he appeared to be quite fallen; and instead of thanking me, or expressing any pleasure at the appointment, never opened his mouth."[1]

The general orders for the next day had perhaps already been drafted, for on the 1st they announced that Arnold would command the left wing. But on the 3rd, after he had once more pleaded his three-year-old wound as his excuse, the assignment was changed and he was instructed to "proceed to West Point and take the command of that post and its dependencies." These included the forts at Stony Point and Verplanck's below West Point, on each side of the Hudson, and the posts east of the river from Fishkill to King's Ferry as well as the corps of infantry and cavalry "advanced towards the enemy's lines" as far south as North Castle (near Armonk).[2] Since the main army was preparing to return to New Jersey, this would leave Arnold in charge not only of the river forts but also of the disputed district north of New York through which Clinton would have to send any land troops marching to assist an expedition by water.

In the manœuvres of Washington and Clinton during the last days of July and the first of August Arnold had a secret share.

When Clinton on the 26th took his transports through Hell Gate on their way, he hoped, to attack the French at Newport, he already believed that Arnold might soon command West Point and conspire to surrender it. Believing this, Clinton could risk a movement against the French with part of his forces, leaving the rest to hold New York till his return. But he had such grudging and delaying support from Arbuthnot and the fleet, Clinton claimed, that he brought the transports to at Huntington, decided he could not afford to be held up so long as it seemed he would be, and was back at threatened New York on the 31st. Washington, who that day got his army across the Hudson, crossed expecting to move south and attack New York in Clinton's absence. On hearing of Clinton's return Washington changed his plans, left Arnold in the Highlands, and moved the main army to Tappan in New Jersey. An attack on New York might still be possible. In the meantime the army at Tappan would be between West Point and Clinton if he attacked first, as Washington thought not too unlikely. Clinton put off his attack. The prospects of success would be much brighter once Arnold had established himself and completed his plans for treachery.

On the 3rd, the day Arnold received his instructions for West Point, he wrote from Fishkill to Mercy Scollay in Boston about the Warren children in whom he had for more than two years kept up his interest. Congress had in July voted to allow, through the Massachusetts authorities, a major general's half pay for the maintenance of Warren's second son and two daughters (the elder son being already provided for), to commence with Warren's death and to continue till the youngest of them should be of age. Arnold, claiming more credit for Congress's action than he probably deserved,[3] regretted that he had not himself been able to do what he would have liked, while the children were being cared for by Mercy Scollay and her father. "The public are indebted to me for a considerable sum which I advanced for them in Canada, and for four years pay which I cannot obtain. I must request you will present the account of expenses incurred to the president and council of Massachusetts Bay without any mention of my name, and request payment, which I make not the least doubt they will not only comply with but reimburse the sum advanced. . . . If the state refuses to pay the account I shall esteem myself obliged to. . . . Your observations on the charitable disposition of people of opulence is very just. Charity, urbanity, and the social virtues seem swallowed up in the tumult and confusion of the times, and self wholly engrosses the nabobs of the present day."[4] Characteristically, Arnold was offering to be generous again and also hinting that he, "without any mention of my name," might be reimbursed for what he had already given. As on his trip to Connecticut in June, he was busy with schemes for realizing his American assets before he went over to the British.

Possibly on the 4th, certainly by the 5th, Arnold was at Robinson's House opposite West Point. "I have not been on the Point since I came here," he wrote on the 5th to Robert Howe.[5] "I shall carefully inspect both sides of the river and take quarters where I think myself free from danger and in a condition to render the greatest service. At present I apprehend no danger in these quarters, which are the most convenient for an invalid." He stayed on at this manor house of Beverley Robinson, used by the Americans as headquarters, and occupied immediately before Arnold by Howe. One of the surgeons who had been there in 1778 thought that Robinson in the choice of his country seat must have been "guided altogether by a taste for romantic singularity and novelty. It is surrounded on two sides by hideous mountains and dreary forests, not a house in view, and but one within a mile."[6] Arnold seems to have been neither repelled nor attracted by the wild scenery or the isolation of the house. It was safer than a house on the Point might be—for him and for his wife and youngest child who were soon, Arnold planned, to join him. They would be out of range of British guns attacking the fortress. And the Highlands command might still be exercised from the east side of the Hudson, as it had been for the past three years.

Major Franks, who had been aide to Arnold in Philadelphia, was now with him again; and on the 5th Arnold wrote to Lieutenant Colonel Richard Varick at Hackensack. "I am in want of a secretary, having within a few days been appointed to this command. General Schuyler"—then at Washington's Headquarters—"informed me yesterday that he believed it would be agreeable to you, as the duty would engross only a part of your time and leave a

considerable time for you to prosecute your studies, if you choose.
. . . As this has the appearance of a quiet post, I expect Mrs.
Arnold will soon be with me."[7] Varick had been military secretary
to Schuyler in the northern army, and a friend to Arnold during
the Saratoga campaign. Out of active service since the past January,
Varick had resumed his interrupted legal studies at his father's
house but had found himself so often called on for militia duty
that he was glad to return to the army as Arnold's writing aide. In
accepting the offer on the 7th Varick spoke of his pleasure at the
chance to serve "under an officer than whom none in the army
claims greater respect from, and will be more agreeable to, me than
yourself. . . . The presence of Mrs. Arnold will certainly make
our situation in the barren Highlands vastly more agreeable, and
I am persuaded will more than compensate for every deficiency of
nature." But Varick needed a week to get proper clothes for his
new appointment, and could not reach Robinson's House till
the 13th.

In the selection of his aides Arnold did not look for disaffected
men whom he might take into his confidence. Any confidant would
add to the peril of the undertaking. Franks had broken with his
loyalist father in Montreal while the Americans were there in
1776 and had been with Arnold most of the time since. Arnold
was used to Franks as aide, and could feel sure that Varick, as
Schuyler said, would be a capable secretary. Nor can there be
much doubt that Arnold chose aides—both in their twenties—
who would be congenial not only to him but also to his wife,
transported from elegant Philadelphia to what she might think a
lonely wilderness.

Arnold's solicitude for Peggy appears in many of his letters:
references to her coming, efforts to get beds, dishes, and other
household equipment suitable for her. And there is a revealing
passage in a letter to Howe on September 12. Howe, a bachelor of
nearly fifty with a reputation for gallantry, had congratulated
Arnold on his good fortune in being so happily married. "I thank
you, my dear Sir," Arnold replied, "for your friendly wishes to me
and Mrs. Arnold . . . and for the favourable opinion you are
pleased to entertain of the state of our connubial connexion. Be
assured, Sir, no sensations can have a comparison with those arising

from the reciprocity of concern and mutual felicity existing between a lady of sensibility and a fond husband. I myself had enjoyed a tolerable share of the dissipated joys of life, as well as the scenes of sensual gratification incident to a man of nervous constitution; but, when set in competition with those I have since felt and still enjoy, I consider the time of celibacy in some measure misspent."[8] In these stiff sentences, with these heavy words, Arnold was unmistakably implying that he had found in Peggy a wife that any husband, a mistress that any lover, might covet. The Shippens all thought of her as demure and shy. Arnold knew better.

II

It will be remembered that Arnold, at Robinson's House by the 5th, did not know till the 24th that his price of £20,000 for the surrender of West Point to the British had been agreed to; and it is conceivable that he might never have consented to the bargain on less satisfactory terms. But whether or not he was fully bent on treason during August, he was bound to act with at least the appearance of his customary vigour, so as not to be suspected. Washington furnished definite instructions for the West Point command, and he was attentive to all that went on in Arnold's department. Arnold could treacherously weaken the post only by stealth, in spite of Washington's supervision and in the face of objections sure to come from Colonel John Lamb, commandant of artillery at West Point; Lieutenant Colonel Udny Hay, in command of the troops at Fishkill; Colonel James Livingston, commanding the works at Verplanck's and Stony Point; and Colonel Elisha Sheldon, in charge of the forces watching the enemy's lines. Whatever Arnold might do for the sake of the British had to seem to be for the sake of the Americans.

For instance, there was his asking Lafayette at Headquarters for the names of his spies in New York. Though Arnold may have meant to put an end to that information, he could claim that he wished to facilitate it, now he was in the Highlands command. Lafayette refused to tell the names, because he had promised not to, but he did not then think of Arnold as more than zealous in the matter.[9] Nor did Howe, turning West Point over to Arnold, consider it strange when Arnold said in his letter of August 5: "As the safety of this post and garrison in a great measure depends on having good intelligence of the movements and designs of the enemy, and as you have been fortunate in the agents you have employed for that purpose, I must request (with their permission) to be informed who they are, as I wish to employ them for the same purpose. I will engage upon honour to make no discovery of them to any person breathing."[10]

Howe naturally did not know that Arnold, after his visit to West Point in June, had written Clinton that some of his spies on Howe were in Howe's pay also. On the 14th Howe replied much as Lafayette had done. The agents were not willing to have their names divulged to anybody. The two most intelligent of them "are persons of character and property who cannot without utter ruin get out of the enemy's power and yet, devoted to America, have agreed to serve in a way they do not like but which is the only way they can at present serve her in." Another agent, on Long Island, would continue to report under the name of John Williams, if Arnold would make no attempt to find out his real name.[11] Arnold on the 16th hoped the secret agents would in time give him their confidence. "You have my honour," he assured Howe, "that I will not be solicitous about the real name of Mr. Williams, and you may pledge my faith to him that if accident should disclose to me his real name I will not discover it. I will take proper precautions that no gentlemen of my family open any letters addressed to me as *Private*."[12] But Howe's spies seem never to have served Arnold. Perhaps they were wary because they did not know him as they knew Howe. Perhaps they distrusted Arnold. One of them insisted that "a general officer high up was in compact with the enemy."[13] Though no suspicion yet pointed particularly at Arnold, spies must be careful.

Arnold, being a double-dealer, had a double use for secret agents. He might get information from them which he honestly needed as commander, or which as treacherous informer he might forward to New York. Most of all, he desired a channel of communication with Clinton by way of the Hudson instead of the long way round through Philadelphia. He may have wished that he could get hold of some spy who had served both Clinton and Howe and who would become Arnold's messenger.

In the hunt for secret agents Arnold formed what was to be his fateful connexion with Joshua Hett Smith. Smith lived near Haverstraw on the west bank of the Hudson, not far below King's Ferry, in a country house belonging to his refugee brother William Smith, the royal chief justice of New York. Joshua Smith had been an active Whig in the early years of the Revolution, member of the New York provincial congress, and energetic in the patriot militia of his neighbourhood. Married to a South Carolina woman, he had in 1778 made the acquaintance in Charleston of Robert Howe, and after his return to Haverstraw and Howe's appointment to West Point had zealously concerned himself with obtaining and transmitting the reports of Howe's secret agents.[14] Howe seems to have recommended Smith to Arnold, who had met him in Philadelphia two years before. Arnold may have stopped at Smith's house on the ride to King's Ferry at the end of July, and he then or soon afterwards asked Smith about the sources of Howe's information. Smith, in a letter to Arnold of August 13, preferred not to be too explicit on paper but promised to come to Robinson's House and furnish the secret details. He hospitably offered to entertain Peggy Arnold if she should pay her husband a visit. She might "make my house a stage until your barge can meet her at the ferry." Smith wished Arnold might grant passes to two loyalist women and their children, so they could go to New York and join their husbands. This, Smith said, would be humane to the women and children, and burdensome to the British who would have to feed and house them.[15]

Nothing in the letter indicated any disaffection on Smith's part, nor in Arnold's answer of the 16th, thanking Smith for his "civilities tendered to Mrs. Arnold," and saying the passes were enclosed. They were actually not sent. Varick, who had arrived at Robinson's and taken up his duties, was suspicious of Smith, chiefly on account of his brother. There was always danger that women sent into New York with a flag might carry messages—and Arnold did later smuggle his first message from West Point to André by such means. On Varick's insistence, Arnold held up the passes and wrote on the 17th to Governor George Clinton of New York asking for instructions in regard to flags of truce. Clinton on the 22nd replied that passes of the kind were to be granted to inhabitants of the state only with the permission of the civil government.[16] Arnold accepted the ruling, but defended Smith's character till Varick was irritated.

Then there was the affair of the woodcutters. On August 12 Arnold wrote to Washington: "Colonel Hay has requested 200 men to cut wood and make brick for the use of the garrison next winter. He informs me that the wood must be transported a considerable distance by water; that the vessels employed are so badly found with cables, anchors, and sails that they cannot ply after the middle of October. I find on inquiry that the wood is destroyed in the vicinity of the garrison, and unless a stock is laid in this fall they will be put to the greatest difficulty for fuel next winter. Colonel Hay is of opinion that with 200 men he can furnish a sufficient quantity for the garrison. I wish your Excellency's directions in this matter."[17] Washington the next day thought providing wood in season so essential that Arnold should allow Hay the men he required.[18]

Here again Arnold appeared to be merely prompt and forehanded. But a letter from Hay to Arnold on the 15th, three days after the letter to Washington, proposed the woodcutting scheme as if Hay had not yet heard of it. "I beg leave to mention the necessity of adopting some certain plan by which a quantity of wood may immediately be cut for, and be conveyed to, the garrison at West Point. When you view the distance from which that article must be brought by land if not laid in before the river shuts, you will be fully convinced of the necessity of procuring an immediate and, as far as possible, a full supply. I would likewise observe that there are but very few vessels in this river that have either sails or cables fit for the fall; of consequence the conveyance of wood as well as forage and provisions must become very precarious."[19]

It is of course possible that Hay had already spoken to Arnold, and wrote his letter only for the headquarters record. But Arnold wrote the next day: "I have ordered 200 good axemen to be drafted tomorrow morning and put under your direction to procure wood, etc., for the garrison."[20] This was the number Arnold had told Washington that Hay required, though Hay in his letter had not specified it or any other. It looks as if Arnold had originated the idea and set the figure himself, while letting both Washington and Hay think that Hay was responsible. Was Arnold acting as a commander genuinely interested in the winter's fuel, or was he acting as a traitor set on weakening the post he intended to surrender? Colonel Lamb at West Point sharply protested on the 18th. He had already sent 200 militiamen to Hay at Fishkill for a guard. "What occasion there is for such a guard at that place I cannot possibly conceive. Half the number will be sufficient." And now he must send an equal number to cut wood. "If such drafts as are called for are made from the garrison we shall neither be able to finish the works that are incomplete nor in a situation to defend those that are finished."[21] But the woodcutters soon went off up the river to Staatsburg. As Arnold must have calculated, they would provide fuel for West Point if it was still to be an American fort that winter; and they would not be on hand to help defend it if it was to be taken by the British that summer.

Arnold has been accused of taking up, or partially dismantling, the chain which had been laid across the Hudson at West Point to prevent the passage of enemy ships. There is no evidence that he did. Major Villefranche, the French engineer sent by Washington to superintend the reconstruction of the works, reported on the 19th that he had examined the chain and thought new logs should be installed as soon as possible under the chain.[22] Arnold on the 22nd applied to Governor Clinton for teams to be used in drawing the chain out for repairs (teams which Clinton could not provide),[23] and complained the next day to Timothy Pickering, quartermaster general of the the Continental army: "I am informed . . . that the middle part of the chain . . . is sinking and in a dangerous situation, on account of the logs, which it has hitherto floated on, being water-soaken; that unless this be speedily remedied it will be out of our power to raise it but with great expense of time and trouble; that new timber cannot be hauled for want of teams, of which we have not half sufficient for the daily necessities of the garrison."[24] Instead of taking up the chain, Arnold did nothing. He had in June reported to Clinton that it could be broken by a single heavily loaded ship. There was enough treachery in neglecting the chain altogether.

III

In the midst of the heavy routine duties of his command Arnold found time to carry on a persistent if disappointing correspondence about his private affairs. Titus Hosmer, on whom Arnold had depended to represent him in Hartford, died suddenly August 4, and Caleb Bull took his place. Arnold on the 15th asked whether Bull had yet received the notes on the Connecticut treasury, for Arnold's back pay, and what they were worth. If they could be sold, he wished "to convert them into specie or sterling bills that I may have an opportunity of improving the money in a purchase."[25] Three days later Arnold sent Bull an order on the state treasury for the notes, and requested him to put the *Active* claim in charge of some other lawyer or lawyers, "with a suitable fee and a promise, in case their exertions shall prove successful in obtaining speedy justice to the captors of the *Active*, of $1000 specie which I will pay to him or them who will undertake and prosecute the affair to issue. . . . Of this offer you will please to make no mention to any other person." Bull on the 26th replied that he had found a lawyer who thought he could manage the claim, but that the treasury notes could not be obtained "till three of the committee are together to adjust your accounts, which I shall get done as soon as possible."[26] This was two days after Arnold had learned that he might have his price for the surrender of West Point. He seems to have given up his expectations of money from Connecticut, and to have dropped the futile correspondence with Bull.

Nor was Arnold more successful in his efforts to raise money in New London or New Haven. On the 10th he wrote to Nathaniel Shaw, Continental prize agent for Connecticut, who was then in New London. Joseph Packwood, according to Arnold, had returned from a profitable voyage to the West Indies in the sloop *John* more than a year ago and had never accounted to the owners, of whom Arnold was one. Shaw might settle the business.[27] Apparently no answer ever came from Shaw to Arnold. On the 22nd Jacob Thompson of New Haven reported that Arnold's accounts were not yet settled there. His china had been sold, but the enemy had taken the money from Mr. Shipman, Mr. Shipman said. The house had not been sold, but Captain Sloan had come back from a prosperous voyage, moved in, and repaired the roof. "He will take every meathard [method] to secure the house from further damegg he intends to purchase it if he goes safe the next voyg."[28] On the 28th Arnold wrote to Thompson in detail, and again on the 31st; and on the 31st he dispatched Jesse Penfield with several letters to Thompson and others in New Haven. In particular, he wanted a feather bed belonging to his sister Hannah, which was to be brought from Cheshire to Fishkill with every care to keep it from getting dirty or wet on the road.[29] The bed may have reached Arnold just before he fled West Point,[30] but not, it appears, any of the money he thought due him in New Haven.

Like most Continental officers without sound private incomes Arnold was in serious need. On August 3 the general officers had presented a memorial to Congress, asking for increase of pay. Congress, itself desperate, in its resolution of the 12th observed: "that patience and self-denial, fortitude and perseverance, and the cheerful sacrifice of time, health, and fortune are necessary virtues which both the citizen and soldier are called to exercise while struggling for the liberties of their country; and that moderation, frugality, and temperance must be among the chief supports, as well as the brightest ornaments, of that kind of civil government which is wisely instituted by the several states in this union."[31] Nor were the various adjustments of compensation in the resolutions of the 12th and the 24th[32] much more satisfying to the officers than these moral remarks.

Arnold was infuriated. The promise that he, as major general, would after the war get seven years' half-pay and 1100 acres of land meant nothing to him now. Writing on the 27th to Parsons, in command of the Connecticut forces, Arnold sent a copy of the resolutions which he bitterly said were "founded on principles of genuine Congressional virtue, magnanimity, benevolence, patriotism, and justice. I hope they meet with a proper reception by all who are interested in them. The insult added to injury is too pointed to pass unnoticed."[33] Both to Nathanael Greene on the 23rd and to Parsons on September 8 Arnold proposed that a committee of 1000 or 1500 men from all ranks of the army be sent to Congress "to present a spirited but decent memorial setting forth their claims and requesting immediate justice as far as the public are able. This measure I think would be attended with happy consequences to the country; for if justice is not done to the army their necessities will occasion them to disband, and the country will of course be left to the ravages of the enemy."[34] Arnold was, when he made this proposal to Parsons, already in communication with André on the subject of a meeting to arrange for the surrender of West Point; in the meantime, it might be worth while to encourage a sense of grievances in Parsons, who had just been ordered to take command of all Arnold's troops advanced towards the British lines.

Possibly with a sense of his own grievances, Arnold at headquarters had no scruple about trading in public stores for his own benefit. Catherine Martin, wife of a sergeant major in the 3rd Pennsylvania and housekeeper for Arnold, noticed that he secretively kept his stores "in his own private room, and afterwards in a room appointed for the purpose, to which no person had access except himself," his servant, and the housekeeper.[35] Arnold seems to have drawn the salt meat and rum allowed him and his household from the commissary in bulk, stored them, and then as he chose exchanged them for fresh meat or vegetables from farmers— as he allowed other officers of the garrison to do, over the protest of the field officers who found they could not buy country produce for money.[36] Besides this, Arnold's aides found that he sold wine, pork, and salt for cash, which he pocketed. As the memorandum book in which he noted down such sales is missing, there is no certainty how much he disposed of. Varick managed to prevent one sale of rum—to a Tory skipper—and thought he had prevented another of three barrels of pork. But Arnold, giving his orders about the pork "in so singularly low a tone of voice as not to be audible where Colonel Varick sat writing in the same room," got the barrels taken out of the cellar and moved down to the landing without the knowledge of his punctilious aide.[37] Arnold's defence of his conduct was simple: he claimed he had back rations coming to him as part of his unsettled accounts and would hereafter draw all his rations and sell what he did not need.[38]

Faithful as Franks had long been to Arnold, and much as Varick admired his chief, Arnold's official family was not harmonious.

When Varick arrived on the 13th he found Franks dissatisfied. Arnold for some months had been short and fault-finding. The money Franks had brought from Canada had depreciated in value, and he felt he must soon discover a way of earning more for the support of his sister. He thought of going to Spain, where his friend Brockholst Livingston was now private secretary to John Jay, minister at that court. Three years with Arnold was enough. But Franks was in no great hurry, and he willingly set off for Philadelphia on the 23rd to escort Peggy Arnold and her child back to West Point.

Varick had come to his post in the belief that his work as secretary would not occupy all his time but would give him leisure for his studies. In this he was disappointed. Because of his "constant confinement to the writing table," he refused to have anything to do with Arnold's household or stores or in any way to act "as caterer or steward." Arnold had brought so many stores to Robinson's House, Franks said a day or two after Varick's arrival, that if the enemy should make a surprise attack "either our baggage or our stores must be lost. I [Varick] replied that the stores should go to the devil before I should lose my baggage, and that with Arnold's conduct in that respect I had no concern." But Varick was too honest not to object to Arnold's peculations, as he was too patriotic not to object to Arnold's friendship with Joshua Hett Smith.[39] Yet while Varick thought Arnold was sly and avaricious, he did not at all suspect him of treachery.

I V

A man as arrogant as Arnold must have hated the indignity of being watched and checked by his aides, though he may have been too much absorbed in his conspiracy to fret over minor inconveniences. A month after he left Philadelphia he had still not heard from Clinton. Arnold waited in anxious tension. His terms might be rejected. Even if they were accepted, the answer had to come by a dangerous road, with many chances of detection which would mean ruin and probably death. How the answer came is not certain. A guess is that it was brought by an innocent messenger, Jonathan Copp, who on the 21st wrote from Fishkill that he had last Thursday seen Mrs. Arnold "perfectly well" and that he had with him a parcel and letters from her which would be forwarded.[40] If these included the letters from British Headquarters, they did not reach Arnold for three days more; and it was six days after that before he found an opportunity and a messenger for his reply.

Just why William Heron of Redding, Connecticut, decided to go on a treacherous errand to New York at the end of August remains a mystery. He had hitherto been publicly an active patriot, member of the assembly, and trusted friend of General Parsons. Parsons, understanding that Heron's errand was to collect a debt, sent him to Arnold for the necessary pass. "Mr. Heron is a neighbour of mine, for whose integrity and firm attachment to the cause of the country I will hold myself answerable. . . . I am certain he will conduct with strict honour any matter he undertakes."[41]

As Heron later told his story to the Americans, he applied to Arnold for the pass on the 29th and was told to come back the next morning at eight. "I waited on him according to his directions. He intimated (by Colonel Varick) that I must wait two hours before he could dismiss me. I stayed (I believe) a longer time than that. I sat in the room with Colonel Varick, when the general came in and desired the colonel to write a permit (or a flag) for me, which he did, and the general signed it. The general then retired to his room and immediately sent word to me that he wanted to speak to me. I waited on him, and as soon as I entered the room (he being alone) he asked me if I thought the person with whom I expected to transact my business at the enemy's lines would transmit that letter (meaning a letter he held out to me) to the person to whom it was directed. I answered in the affirmative. He said if I could rely on him he should be obliged to me if I could give him (meaning the person I was to meet) a particular charge with regard to the delivery of the letter. As soon as I received the letter and viewed the superscription, which was written in a feigned hand, I must confess that I felt a jealousy or a suspicion that I never before experienced concerning any person of his rank."[42]

Arnold said that the letter, originally sealed with a wafer, had been opened for examination and sealed again with wax. But

when Heron scrutinized it he found the wafer "entirely whole."
This must, he reflected, be a letter which Arnold himself was sending secretly to New York, taking special pains that Varick should
not know about it. Might not Arnold have written it while Heron
waited, seizing this occasion to get some forbidden message safely
carried? "Considering the impression the foregoing circumstances
made on my mind, it will not be thought strange if I deemed it my
duty to deliver the letter in question to General Parsons, instead
of carrying it where it was directed, which I accordingly did on
my return from the lines."

What is to be thought stranger is that Heron did not transmit
the letter addressed to "Mr. John Anderson, merchant, to the care
of James Osborne to be left at the Rev. Mr. Odell's, New York."
For Heron in New York made terms with the British and became
their spy for the duration of the war. On September 4 he talked
for three hours with Chief Justice William Smith, brother of
Arnold's friend at Haverstraw, said he had dined with Arnold at
Robinson's House, and reported a general discontent among the
Highlands officers, as well as wide-spread despair among the people
everywhere. "Undoubtedly the majority of the Continent have
long been for a reunion with Great Britain." Smith, hearing the
kind of talk loyalists liked and almost always heard, took down a
long record of Heron's conversation[43] and noted in his own manuscript memoirs: "It is very material. I gave him some information
of which he will make good use."[44] But Heron with unexplained
caution took Arnold's letter back to Redding and gave it to Parsons on the 10th. Parsons, reading it, did what Arnold hoped any
chance reader would do: supposed it "to refer merely to commerce" and did not turn it over to Washington till after Arnold's
treason had come to light.

The intercepted letter played no part in the conspiracy, but it
is a part of Arnold's story. It was written as from Gustavus about
Moore (Arnold). "On the 24th instant," he wrote, "I received a
note from you without date, in answer to mine of the 7th July;
also a letter from your house [British Headquarters] of 24th July
in answer to mine of the 15th, with a note from Beckwith of the
30th July; with an extract of a letter from Mr. James Osborne of

the 24th." Peggy or Stansbury had presumably thought only part of Odell's letter worth forwarding. "I have paid particular attention to the contents of the several letters. Had they arrived earlier, you should have had my answer sooner. A variety of circumstances has prevented my writing you before. I expect to do it very fully in a few days, and to procure you an interview with Mr. Moore, when you will be able to settle your commercial plan, I hope, agreeable to all parties. Mr. Moore assures me that he is still of opinion that his first proposal"—for £10,000 indemnification win or lose—"is by no means unreasonable, and makes no doubt, when he has a conference with you, that you will close with it." Arnold seemed incapable of realizing that he could not, somehow or other, have the price he had set his mind on. "He expects when you meet that you will be fully authorized from your house; that the risks and profits of the co-partnership may be fully and clearly understood.

"A speculation might at this time be easily made to some advantage with ready money [British forces], but there is not the quantity of goods [men and stores] at market [West Point] which your partner seems to suppose, and the number of speculators [American forces] below I think will be against your making an immediate purchase [attack]." Clinton had spoken of 3000 men to be surrendered at West Point for £20,000, and Arnold had nothing like that number in the garrison. From then on he was less concerned with scattering his men than with concentrating them at West Point. He wanted his full price for the surrender, though the capture might be harder and bloodier. He may even have counselled delay with a thought to his own surer profit. "I apprehend goods will be in greater plenty and much cheaper in the course of the season; both dry and wet [provisions and rum?] are much wanted and in demand at this juncture. Some quantities are expected in this part of the country soon.

"Mr. Moore flatters himself that in the course of ten days he will have the pleasure of seeing you. He requests me to advise you that he has ordered a draft on you in favour of our mutual friend Stansbury for £300, which you will charge on account of the tobacco [the balance kept for Arnold in New York]."[45]

As Heron guessed, he had probably been kept waiting while Arnold wrote this letter. For it was only an acknowledgment of the offers received, and an acceptance of them. Arnold had not yet had time, and could not that Wednesday morning take time, to arrange in clear detail the indispensable interview with André.

Plans for a Meeting

ARNOLD had not only to get word to André of the place of meeting but also to arrange matters so that André could come to it without being detected. There was no public business to bring the Highlands commander and the British adjutant general together, and if there were, there would hardly be a chance for them to have a long private conversation. Arnold might be safe from the British if he went near the British lines, but not from the Americans who would be sure to know so conspicuous a figure had gone. André, comparatively a stranger, might be safe among them if he came unidentified on an errand approved by Arnold. So, apparently, Arnold reasoned, not thinking—or too much caring—that on those conditions André would be counted a spy and liable to death if found out. Still, he could hardly be convicted without the discovery of Arnold's share in the plot and his equal guilt. They were both in danger. André was as eager to buy West Point as Arnold was to sell it. Success in the transaction would make their fortunes forever.

The most innocent-looking device would be to have André appear in the role of a secret agent such as Arnold had been trying to engage in his service since he took command. A good deal of mystery would be tolerated in them, even expected. Arnold's first mysterious moves roused no suspicion. Colonel Sheldon at the advanced post at Lower (South) Salem had for some time been using a double spy (Elijah Hunter) who was loyal to the Americans but trusted by the British. Arnold, who heard Hunter had gone into New York, wrote on September 1 to Sheldon: "I wish to be informed if the person you mentioned is returned from his excursion. On considering the matter," evidently discussed before, "I am convinced that material intelligence might be procured through the channel I mention": that is, André.[1] André could seem to be Arnold's agent as Hunter was Sheldon's. And Arnold may have thought that he could contrive André's first—and only—visit through Hunter.

But Hunter was delayed. Arnold on the 3rd found another opportunity to send a letter to André, by a woman who came with a pass from Governor Clinton on her way to the British. This time Arnold was not so secretive with Varick, but—without letting him read the letter—boldly told him it was written "in a mercantile style to a person in New York whose fictitious name was John Anderson, to establish a line of intelligence of the enemy's movements." Varick thought "the correspondence was proper, in discharge of his duty, and commendable if he could procure intelligence. . . . I never was solicitous to know the real characters or names of his emissaries, further than he chose to communicate them to me, as I thought it none of my business and improper to be known by any person."[2] Varick himself wrote an order to West Point for an artillery officer to serve as escort. Lieutenant Barber's instructions the next day were in Arnold's handwriting. "You are to proceed in a barge with a flag, one sergeant, and seven privates to Fort Washington or other British post on the river, taking with you Mary McCarthy and her two children, late of Quebec, who have my permission to enter the British lines, where you are to leave them and return without delay."[3] Mrs. McCarthy may or may not have had an inkling of the nature or purposes of the letter she carried.

No one knows exactly what it said: it is not in the British Headquarters files. But, as Arnold afterwards took occasion to explain to Sheldon, it asked the supposed secret agent to meet Arnold at Sheldon's quarters, and told him that Sheldon already knew he might write or come and would "send any letter to me, or inform me of his arrival."[4]

Arnold had yet another scheme, involving Peggy. She had sent her husband a letter to Major Giles who the year before helped her smuggle finery through the lines from New York to Philadelphia. This letter Arnold sent to Sheldon, who on the 6th wrote: "I have forwarded Mrs. Arnold's letter for Major Giles to Colonel DeLancey and wrote him on the subject." The younger Oliver

DeLancey was a loyalist close to Clinton who was to succeed André as adjutant general. "In answer he writes me that if any articles are sent to him for Mrs. Arnold he will take particular care of them and inform me immediately." But, Sheldon pointed out, Parsons was to take command on the lines tomorrow and might object to such official connivance.[5] Arnold the next day replied that he was on the "most friendly footing" with Parsons and expected no difficulty about the "articles for the lady."[6]

The day after that he explained the circumstances in a letter to Parsons. "A lady of my acquaintance had some trifling articles purchased for her in New York by Colonel Webb and Major Giles about eighteen months past, which they could not bring out. They have lain there ever since with Major Giles. By her desire I have some little time since requested Colonel Sheldon to endeavour to get them out by one of his flags, which he promised to do, and gives me encouragement of their being sent out. They will be in a box or small trunk. If they come out when you are on the lines I beg the favour of you to take care of them and send them to me. I am told there is a general order prohibiting any goods being purchased and brought out of New York, but as the goods were bought many months before the order was issued, I do not conceive they come under the intentions or spirit of it. However, I would not wish my name to be mentioned in the matter, as it may give occasion for scandal."[7]

Arnold, so plausible about this technical infringement, was almost certainly referring to the purchases made for Peggy by André or Odell, and never sent her. If DeLancey permitted them to come, André would know about it; and André might send with the stealthy goods a still more stealthy communication.

II

It seems significant that not one of Peggy's letters to Arnold during their separation has survived, and only one of his to her, besides those meant for Clinton. The married conspirators were either careful not to keep each other's letters or else able to destroy them immediately after they saw the plot must soon be exposed.

What went on between them has to be conjectured from a few hints and hearsay incidents.

According to Robert Morris, Peggy dined at his house not long after Arnold left Philadelphia. That evening "a friend of the family came in and congratulated Mrs. Arnold on a report that her husband was appointed to a different but more honourable command" than West Point. The friend had possibly heard of the general orders of August 1 assigning Arnold to the left wing, but not yet of Arnold's changed appointment to the fortress on the 3rd. "The information affected her so much as to produce hysteric fits. Efforts were made to convince her that the general had been selected for a preferable station. These explanations, however, to the astonishment of all present produced no effect."[8] It must have seemed to her that those promising dark plans had failed. Arnold would have no chance at the surrender she had set her heart on. She was only twenty and in dire suspense. As was to appear later, she had the habit of hysteria—perhaps voluntary—at times of sudden stress.

She had, too, a sharp pen. In one of her letters, found and read after the treason but now missing, she told Arnold of a concert at the French minister's, with malicious comments on La Luzerne and various ladies present.[9] She need have been no more malicious than any lively girl at the expense of an official she did not like and of too-familiar acquaintances who bored her. There was something more nearly conspiratorial in a missing letter from Arnold in August, telling her to draw all she could from the commissary and sell or store it.[10] If she did this, she agreed with her husband that they should collect their property before deserting their country. And in writing a letter to Giles in New York, whether she thought of it herself or took the hint from Arnold, she was a partner in the conspiracy.

Hannah Arnold, in Philadelphia with her brother's young wife, wrote in spinster acid to her brother on September 4.[11] She herself knew, she told him, nothing of fashions or gossip: "ill nature I leave to you, as you have discovered yourself to be a perfect master of it; witness yours of August 18"—which is missing. "As you have neither purling streams nor sighing swains at West Point, 'tis no place for me; nor do I think Mrs. Arnold will be long pleased with it, though I expect it may be rendered dear to her for a few hours by the presence of a certain chancellor; who, by the by, is a dangerous companion for a particular lady in the absence of her husband." The only chancellor in their circle was Robert R. Livingston, friend of the Arnolds but accused only by Hannah, so far as is known, of special attentions to Peggy. Hannah, from Norwich and New Haven, disapproved of the fashionable manners of Philadelphia. "I could say more"—about Livingston—"than prudence will permit. I could tell you of frequent private assignations and of numberless *billets doux,* if I had an inclination to make mischief. But as I am of a very peaceable temper I'll not mention a syllable of the matter." And there was another scandal to hint at. "Your neighbour Mrs. Meade is or pretends to be very unwell. He [her husband] sees how matters are going and will make sickness a pretence for discontinuing his visits." (George Meade on August 24 had written to Arnold: "I have been very unwell since you left us, which has prevented my showing Mrs. Arnold those attentions I would wish to have done.")[12]

Any popular young woman married to a much older man is sure to incur gossip of this sort. There is nothing but random tattle to support the gossip about Margaret Arnold. A woman in Philadelphia the following February, after Peggy had gone to New York, said all that can be said with any assurance on the subject. "They tell strange stories of her here, and strive to blacken her character in a way which her uncommon affection for the general renders very improbable."[13]

Though Arnold from the first expected that Peggy would join him at West Point before the surrender, he spoke of her coming as a visit. His two elder sons were at the Needwood Academy of the Rev. Bartholomew Booth in Maryland; his younger son by his first wife would remain in Philadelphia with Hannah Arnold. If Arnold was worried about the three boys, he doubtless reflected that they were too young to be blamed or punished for his change of sides, no matter how it came out. His principal concern was for his wife. Even his sister admitted that in Peggy's "life and happiness his consists."[14] Franks, writing on the 28th from Philadelphia that he and the party would set out in a few days, hoped "soon to put safe into your hands the greatest treasure you have."[15]

Arnold's feeling for his wife and baby appears in the solicitous directions he sent her for the journey.[16] "You must by all means get out of the carriage crossing all ferries and going over large bridges, to prevent accidents." He marked off the best route for her, day by day. "(1) Your first night's stage will be at Bristol, Mr. Coxe's, 20 miles. (2) The second at Trenton, Banager's, unless you [go] to G. Dickinson's or Colonel Cadwalader's, 10. (3) The third night to Brunswick, Wm. Marriner's, a good house, 28. If the weather is warm, and this stage too long, you can lodge at Princeton, 12 miles from Trenton. (4) The fourth night at Newark, 26. If this stage is too long you can stop 6 miles short, at Elizabethtown; or if any danger is apprehended from the enemy, you will be very safe by riding a few miles out of the common road. (5) The fifth night at Paramus, 12. (6) The sixth night, Judge Coe's [at Kakiat], 14 miles; and, if not fatigued, to Joshua Smith, Esq., 6 miles further and only 3 from King's Ferry, where you will be hospitably received and well accommodated.

"You will get tolerable beds at Coe's, and from thence, or Smith's, can reach West Point next day with ease, as you will go from King's Ferry by water, so that in seven days, if the weather is cool, you will perform the journey with ease. You must not forget to bring your own sheets to sleep in on the road, and a feather bed to put in the light wagon which will make an easy seat; and you will find it cooler and pleasanter to ride in in smooth roads than in a close carriage; and it will ease your carriage horses. At Paramus you will be very politely received by Mrs. Watkins and Mrs. Prevost, very genteel people." This was the loyalist widow Theodosia Prevost with whom Peggy stopped on her tormented journey back to Philadelphia at the end of September. "Let me beg of you not to make your stages so long as to fatigue you or the dear boy, [even] if you should be much longer in coming."

On September 5 the impatient husband sent one of Sheldon's dragoons off to meet the little caravan, with a letter for Peggy.[17] "You will go to Paramus," the dragoon's orders read, "unless you should meet her on the road. At Paramus inquire at Mrs. Watkins's for Mrs. Arnold. If you hear nothing of her, proceed on to Newark,

Elizabethtown, and on to Brunswick. If you do not meet her, make particular inquiry of any express [rider] or gentleman you may meet from Philadelphia if they have seen her on the road." On Friday the 8th Arnold went with his barge down to King's Ferry, saying he expected to meet his wife and probably having no other purpose. But, as it turned out, she had not left Philadelphia till the 6th and so did not arrive as Arnold hoped. He spent the night at Smith's house and came back the next evening with two officers from South Carolina and Sir James Jay as guests.

III

He found at his headquarters a very troubling communication of that day from Sheldon.[18] "Enclosed I send you a letter," Sheldon said, "which I received last evening from New York, signed John Anderson, who mentions his name being made known to me. If this is the person you mentioned in your favour of yesterday, he must have had your information by letter, as I never heard his name mentioned before I received the letter." Reading the letter Sheldon enclosed, Arnold saw at once that his message by Mrs. McCarthy had got to André and that André had promptly written to Sheldon on the 7th. But, Arnold saw also, André proposed another place of meeting and referred to a British officer who might be sent instead of the expected agent. Arnold had prepared Sheldon for a private emissary; André assumed that an officer would do as well. Sheldon might suspect that Anderson had official backing and therefore needed watching. Nor did Arnold quite understand why his plans for the interview had not been satisfactory.

What had happened in New York was reasonable and fairly simple. Sir Henry Clinton, aware how risky it would be to let André go disguised to the American lines out of reach of British protection, insisted that the meeting be held somewhere in the neutral ground between the armies, and on the Hudson not too far from British armed vessels. André accordingly wrote, as John Anderson, to Sheldon on the 7th and sent the letter by a flag to the lines.[19] "I am told my name is made known to you, and that I may hope your indulgence in permitting me to meet a friend near your outpost. I will endeavour to obtain permission to go out with a flag, which will be sent to Dobbs Ferry on Monday next, the 11th, at twelve o'clock, when I shall be happy to meet Mr. G——. Should I not be allowed to go, the officer who is to command the escort, between whom and myself no distinction need be made, can speak on the affair. . . . I trust I shall not be detained; but, should any old grudge be a cause for it, I should rather risk that [letting an officer undertake the mission] than neglect the business in question, or assume a mysterious character to carry on an inno- cent affair and, as friends have advised, get to your lines by stealth."

Replying to Arnold through Sheldon, André had to be guarded. He must appear to be John Anderson, a secret agent meeting a friend on private business. He was careful not to identify the friend, in writing, as Arnold, but to call him only Mr. G——. Because of Sheldon André did not dare say that Clinton had for- bidden him to "assume a mysterious character . . . as friends [Arnold] have advised." Sheldon had no idea that any British offi- cer was concerned. To prevent Sheldon's surprise, or suspicion, if André should have to come as an officer, André pretended that he, as Anderson, might not be allowed to leave New York. Arnold of course would realize that the officer, "between whom and myself no distinction need be made," was both André and Anderson in one.

But Arnold realized that this ingenious deception might leave Sheldon still wondering how an American spy could arrange through a British officer to send intelligence to the Highlands command; and then wondering whether Arnold also must not be watched. After a night with his friends Arnold wrote on Sunday to Sheldon, with explanations.[20] "You judge right. I wrote to Mr. Anderson on the 3rd instant, requesting him to meet me at your quarters. . . . I did not mention his name in my letter to you, because I thought it unnecessary. I was obliged to write with great caution to him. My letter was signed Gustavus, to prevent any discovery in case it fell into the hands of the enemy." Anderson's saying he might be represented by an officer mystified Arnold, he said. Possibly his letter to Anderson had been intercepted, and the reply coming as Anderson's was false. Nevertheless Arnold would go to Dobbs Ferry on Monday and meet the flag, whoever came with it. If Anderson should find some other means of coming to Sheldon's post, Arnold wished Sheldon would "send an express to let me know, and send two or three horsemen to conduct him on his way to meet me, as it is difficult for me to ride so far. If your health will permit, I wish you to come with him. I have promised him your protection, and that he shall return in safety." Parsons, too, was to be told of the matter. And Arnold particularly inquired how Anderson's letter had come to Sheldon.

Arnold's guess that his letter to Anderson had been intercepted may not have been altogether a pretence aimed at hoodwinking Sheldon. For that same Sunday the 10th Arnold wrote, again as Gustavus, to André, still as Anderson.[21]

"I have received a letter of the 7th instant with your signature addressed to Colonel Sheldon in which is the following paragraph." Arnold quoted the passage appointing Dobbs Ferry for the interview and saying an officer might represent André there. "From the tenor of your letter and of this paragraph in particular, I suspect my letter to you of the 7th [3rd] instant has been intercepted, and the answer dictated by the enemy [British] in hopes of drawing you into a snare, for I cannot suppose you would be so imprudent as to trust a British officer commanding a flag with our private concerns, although of a commercial nature." Arnold here carefully maintained the fictions of Gustavus and Anderson: this letter might be intercepted. "You must be sensible my situation will not permit my meeting or having any private intercourse with such an officer." Here Gustavus was writing as from Arnold to André. "You must therefore be convinced that it will be necessary for you to come, or send some person you can confide in, to Colonel Sheldon's quarters, to whom I have wrote requesting him to send a pilot [guide] with you to meet me, which he has promised to do, and will perhaps come himself. By no means hint to him or any other person your intention in coming out, as it may prevent our speculation, which can be of no consequence to any one but ourselves.

"If I have been mistaken and the letter directed to Colonel Sheldon was wrote by you, I do by all means advise you to follow the plan you [I] propose of getting to our lines by stealth. If you can do it without danger on your side, I will engage you shall be perfectly safe here."

With his usual obstinacy Arnold still preferred his plan for a meeting with André, disguised, inside the American lines; and if he did not actually think the proposed meeting at Dobbs Ferry a trap, at least he knew it was a hazard, for he could not hope to go at noon on Monday without the Americans' (at least his eight bargemen's) knowing that he had conferred with a British officer. Arnold had no pretext for such a conference and was not aware that André had. But Arnold went down the river in his barge, with his guests, to Smith's house on Sunday evening, spent the night, and the next day proceeded to Dobbs Ferry, to meet André if André came.

André's pretext for the interview had been worked out in collaboration with Clinton and Beverley Robinson. Three years before, Clinton remembered or Robinson reminded him, Robinson had gone up the Hudson to his house, then Putnam's headquarters, ostensibly to arrange about household goods left there, surreptitiously to try to win Putnam over. Now Robinson might go again, making his property his excuse for the flag, and André, accompanying him, might secretly complete his arrangements with Arnold. A note from Clinton to André on Monday morning throws light on their plans. "Colonel Robinson will probably go with the flag himself. As you are with him at the forepost [Kingsbridge] you may as well be of the party. You will find me on your return at General Knyphausen's" headquarters in Morris House in upper Manhattan. The meeting seemed so important to Clinton that he would travel the length of the island to hear André report as soon as he got back.

The British armed sloop *Vulture,* Captain Andrew Sutherland, was regularly stationed at Spuyten Duyvil off Kingsbridge, and sent occasional gunboats up the Hudson on scouting duty. One of these may have taken Robinson and André to Dobbs Ferry on the morning of the 11th and landed them on the east side where they would expect to meet Arnold; or they may have gone from Kingsbridge on horseback. But there were several gunboats on the river, and one or more of them, sighting Arnold's barge as it came down, fired upon it. Arnold got away to the west side and stayed at the blockhouse there till sunset. The British party seem to have been unable to inform their boats that an American officer was coming to meet the flag, and possibly did not identify the barge. Arnold might have identified himself by hoisting a flag of his own. But his taste was for some less noticeable meeting, and he did not let the British know that he was in the barge, or in the neighbourhood. He and André waited, presumably with the river between them, each expecting the other to hunt him up. Their excessive caution cost them their safest opportunity for a meeting.

Arnold, who circumspectly wrote from Dobbs Ferry to Washington to say he was there "in order to establish signals in case the enemy came up the river,"[22] might have met the flag, had his secret interview with André, and reported only the conference with Robinson. While such a conference, between a general and a colonel, was irregular, Arnold could have explained that he had waived his rank because Robinson had formerly owned the confiscated house which Arnold now occupied. Washington would probably have thought the meeting informal, not culpable. No matter what he thought, the treacherous plans would have been laid and the attack and surrender might have been concerted. But Arnold did not know that Robinson was with André, or even certainly that André was at Dobbs Ferry with a flag. They came for a meeting and did not meet. Disappointed, Arnold returned that night to Robinson's House, André and Robinson to New York.

IV

On Tuesday the 12th Arnold wrote with singular insolence to Greene about the recent defeat of Gates at Camden in South Carolina. "It is an unfortunate piece of business to that hero and may possibly blot his escutcheon with indelible infamy. It may not be right to censure characters at a distance, but I cannot avoid remarking that his conduct on this occasion has in no wise disappointed my expectations or predictions on frequent occasions." The censor went on. "It is a matter much to be lamented that our army is permitted to starve in a land of plenty. There is a fault somewhere. It ought to be traced up to its authors, and if it was ['designed' struck out and illegible word substituted] ought to be capitally punished. This is in my opinion the only measure left to procure a regular supply to the army in future."[23] Hang the dishonest rascals.

That same day Arnold wrote to Washington, who had candidly laid the military situation before a council of war on the 6th, asking all the general officers for their opinions as to what should be done. "I will endeavour, agreeably to your Excellency's request," Arnold said, "to transmit my opinion on the matters submitted, by the time required. I sincerely wish the situation of our affairs would admit my giving it with more decision than I am able to do at present." Washington had ordered that the eight soldiers formerly employed by Howe as bargemen at West Point be sent to join their regiment. Arnold replied that "they are now employed as my bargemen" and that he would take the liberty of detaining them until further orders.[24] He needed a barge if anybody did.

Though the routine of his command went on much as usual, Arnold was chiefly occupied with his plot. On Wednesday he heard from Colonel Livingston at Verplanck's Point that Beverley Robinson had come to Tarrytown "in a barge under pretence of a flag, but I think it more probable to reconnoitre the country" in advance of a foraging raid from New York. If Arnold thought it advisable, Livingston would send a force "to give them a check." Arnold, answering the same day, thought "we ought to be exceedingly cautious how we venture small parties as low down as Tarrytown. I am well informed that the enemy generally come out in force." A small American party too far from its base would be in danger. Better not move to meet the British "unless they approach much nearer to you than Tarrytown."[25] This may have been meant as sensible military advice, which it was, or it may have been a scheme for leaving the lower river as free as possible for whatever course André might take.

André might still come to Sheldon's quarters. But Sheldon had been temporarily deprived of his command, and Arnold on Wednesday wrote to Major Tallmadge at North Castle, nearer than Lower Salem to the British lines. "If Mr. John Anderson, a person I expect from New York, should come to your quarters, I have to request that you will give him an escort of two horsemen, to bring him on his way to this place, and send an express to me, that I may meet him. If your business will permit, I wish you to come with him."[26] Since Arnold was asking Tallmadge, as he had earlier asked Sheldon, to receive the secret agent, it was prudent to seem open with them. But to Tallmadge as to Sheldon Arnold said he would come part of the way to meet Anderson. Possibly it would be better not to confer with him at Robinson's House, with the watchful Varick near at hand.

That Wednesday Arnold was getting together some documents for the treason. He had Major Sebastian Bauman's return of the ordnance at all the forts and batteries at West Point and its dependencies; Bauman's orders for the disposition of the garrison corps "in case of an alarm"; and Villefranche's estimate of the number of men necessary to man the works at West Point: 2438. Arnold himself wrote out on the 13th his own estimate of the men under his command, at West Point, Fishkill, at Verplanck's and Stony Points, and on the lines. He made the total 3086, nearly a hundred more than Clinton had stipulated if the price was to be £20,000. Possibly the same day Arnold set down his Remarks on the Works at West Point, a detailed account of the defects of the forts and redoubts; and copied the statement Washington had made to his council of war on the 6th. These papers, which Arnold intended to give to André when they met, would furnish the British everything they most wanted to know about the stronghold they intended to attack.[27]

The next day, Thursday the 14th, Arnold wrote a letter to Washington "in answer to your Excellency's questions proposed to the council of general officers." There was irony in his saying that "from the fluctuating situation of our affairs, which may be totally changed in a short time by a variety of circumstances which may happen, it appears extremely difficult for me to determine with any degree of precision the line of conduct proper to be observed." But he agreed with Washington that much depended on the arrival of the second division of the French fleet. If that should come soon, and "give us a decided superiority over the enemy, as well by land as sea, I am of opinion that every necessary preparation and disposition should be made to attack New York." If reinforcements should not come within a month, then he thought no offensive could "with prudence be undertaken this fall." The British were likely to send forces to the Carolinas or Virginia. If that happened, the Pennsylvania line, Arnold suggested, "should march to the relief of the southern states." Above all, steps ought to be taken at once to raise an army of men "engaged during the war" instead of the short terms for which so many of them were enlisted.[28]

For some reason Arnold did not send this letter off that day, but he himself went in his barge down to Smith's house at Haverstraw, to meet his wife, spend the night, and design with Smith— and probably with Peggy too—another meeting with André. On the 15th Arnold in a letter to André offered two plans: the original and a new alternative. "If you think proper to pursue your [really Arnold's] former plan, you will be perfectly safe in coming" to the American lines. Arnold explained that Lieutenant Colonel John Jameson had succeeded Sheldon in command at Lower Salem. But either Jameson or Tallmadge at North Castle would provide André with protection and an escort. He was, of course, not to mention his actual purpose to them. "I have no confidants; I find I have made one too many already [Wallis or Stansbury or Peggy?] which has prevented several profitable speculations. . . .

"If you have any objections to this plan, I will send a person in whom you may confide, by water, to meet you at Dobbs Ferry on Wednesday the 20th instant between eleven and twelve o'clock at night, who will conduct you to a place of safety where I will meet you." This person was Smith of Haverstraw, who had consented to bring André to the meeting on the supposition that he was to become Arnold's secret agent. "It will be necessary," Arnold told André, "for you to be disguised, and if the enemy's boats are there it will favour my plan, as the person is not suspected by them." This seems to imply that the British on the river considered Smith a loyalist, though other evidence on the point is lacking. "If I do not hear from you before, you may depend upon the person being punctual at the place before mentioned.

"My partner of whom I hinted in a former letter [Washington] has £10,000 cash in hand ready for a speculation [10,000 men ready for action] if any should offer which appears profitable. I

have about £1000 on hand [1000 men at West Point] and can collect £1500 more in two or three days. Add to this, I have some
credit. From these hints you can judge of the purchase [capture]
that can be made. I cannot be more explicit at present. Meet me
if possible. You may rest assured that if there is no danger in passing your lines, you will be perfectly safe where I propose the
meeting; of which you shall be informed on Wednesday evening
if you think it proper to be at Dobbs Ferry."[29]

This letter Arnold "found means to send by a very honest fellow who went to Kingsbridge on the 16th." And possibly that
honest fellow carried also another note which was of a special and
peculiar treachery. It concerned Washington, who had been Arnold's steadfast friend and of whom Peggy, who had met Washington when she was fourteen, later said that "nobody in America
could revere his character more than I did."[30]

Arnold on his return to Robinson's House in the afternoon or
evening of Friday had found a letter from the commander-in-
chief with a confidential postscript.[31] "I shall be at Peekskill on
Sunday evening, on my way to Hartford to meet the French Admiral [Ternay] and General [Rochambeau]. You will be pleased to
send down a guard of a captain and 50 at that time, and direct the
quartermaster to have a night's forage for about 40 horses. You
will keep this to yourself, as I want to make my journey a secret."
If it was important not to let the British learn that the American
and French commands were meeting to decide on a common effort,
it was even more important not to let the British armed vessels on
the river realize that Washington would cross at a particular place
on a particular day and might be taken by a sudden overpowering
raid by water. But Arnold the very day he heard of Washington's
secret journey put the secret into cipher for André and Clinton.
Both the cipher and the decipher (in Odell's hand) are still among
the Clinton papers.[32]

"General Washington will be at King's Ferry Sunday evening
next on his way to Hartford, where he is to meet the French Admiral and General. And will lodge at Peekskill."

Having dispatched this sinister note, Arnold on Saturday wrote
another to Washington to say that the guard and forage would be
furnished.[33] "My answers to the questions proposed by your Ex-

General Washington will be at King's Ferry Sunday evening next on his way to Hartford, where he is to meet the French Admiral and General. And will lodge at Peak's Kill.

Arnold's code note of September 15, 1780
informing the British when Washington
would cross the Hudson and might be captured,
with Odell's decoding of the note

cellency to the council of war I will do myself the honour to deliver in person." It is just possible that Arnold, in the hurry of getting off down the river on Thursday to meet his wife, had neglected the letter of that date to Washington. Now he had an excuse for his tardiness and could take his answers to King's Ferry and Peekskill on Sunday when he went to pay his official respects to the commander whom he had privately done his best to betray.

This was an uncomfortable week-end at Robinson's House, with the conspiracy stirring beneath the surface. Varick at once told Franks, who returned with Peggy, that during his absence Arnold had sent a letter to John Anderson in New York and had heard from him through Sheldon. Franks thought he remembered "that Arnold had corresponded with Anderson or some such name before from Philadelphia, and had got intelligence of consequence from him."[34] Both the aides seem to have felt no suspicion or anxiety, though Varick was afraid the letter to Anderson might have been intercepted. The arrival on Saturday of Smith with his wife and nephew to stay two days was disturbing. It was reasonable enough that Smith, who had shown the Arnolds his hospitality, should now be offered theirs. Smith's wife had found the Highlands wilderness lonely after Charleston, as Peggy Arnold might find it after Philadelphia. The two ladies could console each other in this rough if picturesque exile. But Varick distrusted Smith, though not yet as much as a few days later, and communicated his distrust to other officers on Arnold's staff.

On Sunday the 17th Arnold invited some of the West Point officers to an early dinner, along with his aides and the members and guests of the household. While they were at table two letters, forwarded by Colonel Livingston, arrived from Beverley Robinson on board the *Vulture,* which the day before had come up from Spuyten Duyvil and anchored at Teller's Point at the lower end of Haverstraw bay. One of the letters was addressed to Israel Putnam, who Robinson knew had recently made a visit to Arnold's headquarters. Robinson's pretence was that he had come up with Clinton's permission to ask for an interview with Putnam. If Putnam had left, Robinson said in an accompanying letter to Arnold, "I am persuaded (from the humane and generous character you bear) that, could I be so happy as to see you, you would readily grant me the same request I should make to him. But for prudential reasons I dare not explain the matter further, until I have some assurances that it shall be secret if not granted."[35] There were grounds for secrecy, even if Robinson meant only to ask for the restoration of his property, which had been confiscated by the state of New York and which Arnold had no right to give up. But Robinson was hinting at a very different matter when he explained why he had sent these letters through the officer commanding at Verplanck's instead of "by my servant, James Osborne." Arnold would recognize this name. He might not know that James Osborne was Jonathan Odell (who was not on the *Vulture*), but he would know that this was Stansbury's correspondent in New York and that Robinson was acting in behalf of André.

With no sign of the excitement he must have felt, Arnold opened the letter addressed to him, "just looked at it, and put it up in his pocket"; and did not hesitate to tell his companions whom the letters were from. To Colonel Lamb, the West Point commandant, Arnold said that Robinson desired an interview. Lamb's advice was against granting so extraordinary a request. If Robinson had anything to communicate that was "of importance to this country, he might do it by letter." If his communication was about his private affairs, "his business would be with the governor of the state, not with the general commanding in the department. . . . I could not suppose what would be the motive, and told him [Arnold] the proposal was of such a nature that it would induce suspicion of an improper correspondence between him and Beverley Robinson." Lamb strongly urged that Arnold, who was to see Washington that evening, submit the letters to him and let him decide what should be done.[36] Arnold remarked, with apparent indifference, that whatever proposal Robinson had in mind he had first to make it "through some channel" or other; "and here the conversation ended."[37] Smith, who had before this heard only of Anderson, still did not suspect Arnold of treachery and accepted his assurance that Robinson, coming with Clinton's leave, would bring intelligence somehow beneficial to the Americans.

That afternoon or evening Arnold went with Franks to Peekskill to greet Washington on his journey.[38] Though they did not take the barge down the river, they may have ridden by land as far as King's Ferry, met him there, and accompanied his party to its next stop. But there is nothing to support the melodramatic story told by Barbé-Marbois that Washington, crossing the Hudson in Arnold's barge, studied the *Vulture* through a glass with such attention that Arnold, guiltily aware that Beverley Robinson was on board the ship, boldly brought up the matter of Robinson's communication; or that Lafayette alarmed Arnold by a pleasantry about the ease of intercourse with the enemy up and down the river.[39] If Arnold was at the ferry, and did hope—or fear—that the British, acting on his information, might take advantage of the high wind blowing from the south and try to capture Washington at the ferry, there can have been small chance of it. For it is not likely that Arnold's information had reached the *Vulture* or that if it had Clinton would have made any such attempt while the West Point conspiracy was still unsettled. Arnold probably asked Washington's advice about Robinson at Peekskill, and there agreed to have no further dealings with him.

In spite of this agreement Arnold, back at his headquarters on Monday, promptly wrote to the loyalist on the *Vulture*. Varick disapproved of the letter, saying it "bore the complexion of one from a friend rather than one from an enemy" and insisting that Arnold alter it.[40] In the revised version Arnold said he had consulted with Washington and that Robinson's application must be made to the civil authorities. "If you have any other proposals to make, and of a public nature of which I can officially take notice, you may depend on it that the greatest secrecy shall be observed, if required, as no person except his Excellency General Washington shall be made acquainted with them. The bearer, Captain Archibald, will take particular care of your letters and deliver them to me with his own hand."[41] The reference to Washington was for the sake of Varick. Robinson would understand that his reply was to come by Archibald straight to Arnold.

But Varick did not see the private letter to Robinson sent with the official one.[42] Arnold could not, he said, safely or properly confer with Robinson in public. "I shall send a person to Dobbs Ferry, or on board the *Vulture,* Wednesday night the 20th instant, and furnish him with a boat and flag of truce. You may depend on his secrecy and honour, and that your business of whatever nature shall be kept a profound secret. . . . To avoid censure, this matter must be conducted with the greatest secrecy. I think it will be advisable for the *Vulture* to remain where she is until the time mentioned"—not drop down to Dobbs Ferry as if this letter had given some kind of signal. "I have enclosed a letter for a gentleman in New York [André] from one in the country [Gustavus] on private business, which I beg the favour of you to forward, and make no doubt he will be permitted to come at the time mentioned." Arnold added a postscript: "I expect his Excellency General Washington to lodge here on Saturday night next, and will lay before him any matters you may wish to communicate." This would let Clinton know how long Washington was to be away, if it had been planned to attack West Point in his absence.

Sending this private letter without Varick's knowledge, Arnold practised another device which is now for the first time made known. He enclosed both the letter to Robinson and the letter to André in a sealed cover addressed to William Smith in New York with a note telling Robinson he might open the cover.[43] Why did Arnold risk involving William Smith, who knew nothing of the conspiracy? It may have been because Arnold had understood from Heron that he was to communicate with Smith; perhaps Arnold, who could not know what Heron had done with the letter of August 30, thought that he may have turned it over to Smith for André and that Smith might transmit this one also. Or it may be that Arnold used William Smith's name as a subtle way of hinting that Joshua Smith would come to the *Vulture* for André. Robinson, on first seeing the cover addressed to one Smith, might not take the hint; but when another Smith came on Wednesday night, Robinson and André might remember the name and for that reason put more confidence in Joshua Smith than they would otherwise have done.

The letter enclosed to André was a copy of what Arnold had written on the 10th, asking him to come to the American outpost, and on the 15th, telling him that he would be met at Dobbs Ferry on the 20th. Since this copy came by a flag of truce from Arnold it would prove that the earlier letters had been genuine. The present plan would supersede the earlier, with the changed arrangement that Arnold's messenger would go at night and might go to the *Vulture*.[44]

There was tension in the household on Monday. Franks came back from Peekskill full of resentment. He had set out in the hope that through Hamilton he might obtain a transfer to the staff of Rochambeau or some other French general in Rhode Island. Nothing apparently had come of that, and Franks had had such "repeated insults and ill treatment" from Arnold that he was "resolved not to remain with him on any terms whatever." Varick, to whom Franks confided this, had to report an altercation with Smith on Sunday evening after Arnold and Franks had left. Smith had said that "America might have made an honourable peace with Great Britain when the commissioners came out in 1778." To this Varick, devoted to independence, objected. They had a sharp dispute, in the course of which Varick did his best to insult Smith, who would not be insulted. Peggy Arnold, who was present, told Franks the next day that Varick seemed to be a very "warm and staunch Whig."[45] Franks and Varick had already noticed that she had spells of nervous excitement "during which she would give utterance to anything and everything on her mind . . . so much so as to cause us to be scrupulous of what we told her or said within her hearing."[46] But neither her hysteria nor Arnold's rudeness was ascribed, by the critical aides, to its true and sufficient cause.

By the time Arnold got back from Peekskill on Monday the 18th Smith had probably left for Fishkill with his wife and nephew. This was, without much question, part of the Arnold-Smith plan laid the week before. Smith would get his entire family out of his house for the sake of privacy when André should come there from Dobbs Ferry. The week-end with Arnold, while natural in itself, was also incidental to the secret. Now that Arnold had made arrangements to send Smith to Dobbs Ferry at night on the 20th, and possibly to the *Vulture*, it was necessary to inform Smith of the change. Smith, returning from Fishkill by way of Robinson's House on the 19th or 20th, seems to have consented. Arnold wrote him a pass, dated the 20th: "Permission is given to Joshua Smith, Esquire, a gentleman Mr. John Anderson who is with him, and his two servants to pass and repass the guards near

King's Ferry at all times."[47] With this, and an order from Arnold
to the quartermaster at King's Ferry to furnish Smith with a light
boat, Smith called on Livingston at Verplanck's on the east side of
the ferry. "Mr. Smith then informed me," Livingston later testified, "that he was upon a plan, in conjunction with General Arnold, to gain intelligence of the utmost importance, and that he
expected to meet a gentleman for that purpose near Dobbs Ferry,
but did not mention the time when he expected to meet him."[48]
On the afternoon of Wednesday the 20th neither Arnold nor
Smith can have supposed there would be any hitch in that night's
meeting.

V

Meanwhile André, disappointed at Dobbs Ferry on the 11th, had
been waiting in New York for an explanation and another opportunity. On the 12th he wrote a discreet note to Lieutenant Colonel John Graves Simcoe, commanding the Queen's Rangers on
Long Island and eager to make energetic use of them. There was
talk of an expedition to Maryland and Virginia, and Clinton had
invited the refugees from those provinces to assist him. Troops
were being transferred from Long Island to Manhattan and transports made ready. Simcoe, who preferred to fight the rebels near
at hand, was afraid he might be sent off to the South. André could
not tell him that Clinton was partly feigning the Chesapeake foray
as an excuse for preparing a dash up the Hudson. But neither
could André let his friend Simcoe worry. "Rely upon it," André
wrote, "your alarms are vain. Colonel Watson or you, one or other,
will not embark. I should have been happy to have seen you and
hinted that apparent arrangements are not always real ones, but I
beg you to seek no explanations. I should not say what I do, but I
cannot without concern see you in any uneasiness I can remove."[49]

On the 13th André reimbursed Captain Beckwith for the 200
guineas he had given Wallis for Arnold six weeks before, and paid
Odell £42 presumably for expenses of the Stansbury correspondence.[50] It must have seemed to André that the negotiations which
had dragged on for sixteen months looked now to their triumphant end. He had been recommended on August 31, in a letter

JOHN ANDRÉ

AN UNPUBLISHED PORTRAIT BY SIR JOSHUA REYNOLDS

from Clinton to Germain, to the full rank of adjutant general. André may already have been promised that he might lead a select corps in the assault on Fort Putnam, the citadel at West Point, with a chance at the spectacular glory of taking it. This might make him a colonel, or even a brigadier, and assure his future in his profession.[51] Possibly this week he was composing the third part of his burlesque epic-ballad *The Cow-Chase,* of which two parts had been printed in Rivington's *Royal Gazette* and one, left behind with the printer, was to appear on the day André himself was taken at Tarrytown. The ballad commemorated the spirited action of some loyalists at Bull's Ferry, New Jersey, who had been attacked by a much larger number of patriots under General Wayne and had driven them off. What more could be expected, André laughed in his brisk verses, from a rebel general who was a tanner, at the head of those "dung-born tribes" the rebels?[52]

He ought to hear from Arnold any day now. Arnold's letter of the 10th had perhaps reached André, but it still asked for the meeting inside the American lines which Clinton would not permit. By Saturday the 16th Clinton and André had arranged to send Beverley Robinson up on the *Vulture,* to appoint a safer meeting. No answer came from Robinson till Tuesday. But at eight o'clock on the evening of Monday the 18th Beckwith at Knyphausen's headquarters at Morris House wrote to André about a packet of letters that had just come in by a flag of truce "from the general officer commanding upon the North river [Arnold]." The packet was "sealed, and addressed upon the outer cover to Mr. Loring, commissary general of prisoners. General Knyphausen having thought proper to desire me to open the packet, I found it enclosed in a second cover addressed to Colonel Cuyler; upon opening which, there are several letters which, with the covers, are forwarded to Headquarters without being examined; and amongst the rest, one from Mr. Moore which I enclose and forward by express." Beckwith guessed that this letter from Moore [Arnold] was the important one of the lot.[53]

Knyphausen would, Beckwith wrote, "grant to the countryman" who had brought the packet "a certificate of his having fulfilled his orders, which certificate I signed, and it will be delivered to him when he is dismissed to-morrow, possibly some of the letters requiring answers, or if you have any commands for him." Possibly this was the person who had come to the lines at Kingsbridge "a few days ago." It is a fair guess that the countryman was the honest fellow whom Arnold on Saturday had sent to Kingsbridge with the letter of the 15th asking André to come to Dobbs Ferry on the 20th; and consequently that on Monday evening Clinton heard direct from Arnold what he heard from Arnold through Robinson on Tuesday when Robinson sent down Arnold's letters of the 18th.

Clinton, who was to spend so much ink and paper in explaining what he had intended to do, was never entirely clear about it. But it appears that so long as he expected Washington, co-operating with the French, to attack New York, Clinton had in mind to wait till the combined forces had advanced on the town and then to strike up the Hudson, possess West Point and its garrison and stores, dominate the river, and force Washington to retire.[54] This Clinton seems to have believed would be as mortal to the rebellion in the north as he believed his capture of Charleston had been in the southern provinces. Cornwallis, following up that capture, had dispersed the remaining southern army at Camden. Clinton himself might follow up a victory at West Point by the destruction of Washington's army. The arrival of Admiral Sir George Rodney from the West Indies on the 14th, with a fleet which gave the British a decided naval superiority over the French, rightly convinced Clinton that the attack on New York would not be undertaken. He need wait no longer. He confided the Arnold plot to Rodney (possibly the first person in New York who knew definitely about it outside of Clinton, Odell, André, Knyphausen, and Beckwith). On Tuesday the 19th the plans were carried as far as they could be before the final settlement of details with Arnold. Troops and transports were ordered to be ready for a swift movement up the river as soon as the last word should come.

That could not come till André had conferred with Arnold. Clinton later said, again and again, that he sent André because Arnold insisted on it. But André, at Clinton's direction, had been the first to propose such a meeting, as far back as June 1779. "The method [of surrendering American soldiers at two guineas a head] would be arranged by my meeting you as flag of truce or otherwise as soon as you come near us." Other emissaries had been mentioned, but not since the past July 24, when Odell was authorized by Clinton to tell Arnold that "Mr. Anderson is willing himself to effect the meeting" in regard to the surrender of West Point. Clinton had expected to send André, and André to go.

Nor can Clinton have had much reason to feel uncertain, as he later claimed he had, whether his long correspondence had actually been with Arnold or with some incredible plotter playing a sly game with the British command. But Clinton was suspicious and cautious and knew that André's mission would be hard to distinguish from a spy's errand. André was not, Clinton stipulated, to disguise himself or go within the American lines. These two stipulations André understood. He may not have understood what Clinton later said was the third stipulation: not to take any papers. Neither at his trial nor in his letter to Clinton after the trial did André mention any injunction against carrying papers back with him. And there seems to be no record that Clinton ever spoke of it till after he had heard from Arnold of André's capture with the damaging papers in his possession.

A romantic story tells that on the night before André left New York Clinton and his staff dined with Colonel Williams of the 80th regiment at Kip's Bay, and that André sang, to officers all supposed to know what he was to do, the famous song *How Stands the Glass Around?* which James Wolfe is said to have sung the night before the battle of Quebec at which he fell.[55] There was no Colonel Williams of the 80th, which was then commanded by Sir William Erskine; and there is little likelihood that so close a secret was revealed at any convivial table at a time when every care was being taken to avoid premature disclosure of the crucial plot.

On Wednesday the 20th, the day set for the meeting, André went to Dobbs Ferry with letters—to Robinson and Sutherland—from Clinton ordering the *Vulture* to drop down the river to that place, to which André had said that he would come and Arnold that he would send a boat. Instead of sending the letters by sloop from the Ferry André chose to go up in the sloop himself, and got on board the *Vulture* about seven o'clock. It was true that Arnold had spoken of sending to the Ferry, but he had also spoken of sending to the ship. Robinson, answering Arnold, had said he would wait on board till Anderson came. André, Robinson, and Sutherland decided it was natural to expect the boat at the *Vulture*. If it came from West Point, it would have to pass the ship on the way to Dobbs Ferry, which was a dozen or so miles further. And, though André wrote nothing of this to Clinton, the conspirators on the *Vulture*—as will appear—had taken Arnold's hint that a man named Smith was concerned, and already expected Joshua Smith who they knew lived not far from where the *Vulture* lay. Whatever their arguments, they disregarded Clinton's orders to drop down and instead waited where they were.

ༀ༅ༀ༅ༀ༅ༀ༅ༀ༅ༀ༅ༀ༅ༀ༅ༀ༅ༀ༅ༀ༅ༀ༅ༀ༅ༀ༅ༀ༅ༀ༅ༀ༅ༀ༅ༀ

Five Days

JOSHUA SMITH in the late afternoon of that Wednesday had an order for a boat, but he had not yet obtained one or engaged the necessary oarsmen. He applied to his tenant Samuel Cahoon (Colquhoun), who at Smith's trial told all that is known of the episode.

"Mr. Smith had been up at Fishkill, as he told me, and came down in the evening and told me he wanted to speak a word with me, and I went with him up in his room, and he asked me to go that night a piece, he said, down the river. I told him I had no mind to go, and did not want to go; he did not urge me hard to go. Then he said he must send me up express to General Arnold, and we should go over to the other house; but, upon my telling him I had no mind to go [to Arnold], he seemed to urge my going, and said it was great business. I thought it was best to go, and agreed to go. We went over to his brother's [Thomas Smith's], where I consented to go to General Arnold's, and was furnished by Mr. Smith with a horse, and a paper to Major Kierce, and went off." Kierce (or Kiers) was the quartermaster at King's Ferry who was to furnish the boat. "I went as fast as I could, and got to General Arnold's just after sunrise. The general was not up, and I delivered the letter from Mr. Smith to General Arnold, to a gentleman there; and I was informed by the gentleman there was no occasion for an answer; and I was told by him I might go on as quick as I could."[1]

André, waiting all night on the *Vulture* for the boat that did not come, had again been disappointed. But instead of returning to New York he simulated such a bad cold that Robinson and Sutherland urged him to wait another day. Outwardly yielding to their insistence, he wrote privately to Clinton on Thursday morning:

"This is the second excursion I have made without an ostensible reason, and Colonel Robinson both times of the party. A third would infallibly fix suspicions." Robinson was known to have business with Arnold. André must have some casual excuse or else be thought to have important business too: important enough to bring the British adjutant general to confer with the American commander on the Hudson. If the suspicion got started, it might travel far. "I have therefore thought it best to remain here on pretence of sickness . . . and try further expedients." The day before some American irregulars at Teller's Point had fired on a *Vulture* boat carrying a flag. "Captain Sutherland," André told Clinton, "with great propriety means to send a flag to complain of this to General Arnold." If this was with propriety, it was also with craft. For the protest sent, while signed by Sutherland, was in André's handwriting and countersigned John Anderson, Secretary, to let Arnold know that André was on board.[2]

To make this more convincing still, Robinson wrote a hitherto unknown letter to Arnold which would show that his hint about Smith had been understood.[3] "I have been greatly disappointed in not seeing Mr. Smith at the time appointed, being very anxious to conclude our business, which is very necessary should be done without delay; and I can now make a final settlement with him, as my partner [André] upon the receipt of the letter I forwarded to him yesterday immediately set off from New York and arrived here last night. If Mr. Smith will come here we will attend him to any convenient and safe place."

André's identifying letter, and presumably Robinson's, reached Arnold at Verplanck's Point to which he had come down in his barge after learning at sunrise that Smith had not gone to the *Vulture* the night before. Arnold's plans had been less deranged than André's. For it seems evident that Arnold had expected André to be taken to Smith's house for a conference on Thursday the 21st, when Arnold intended to visit Verplanck's on military affairs.[4] He would sleep discreetly in his own bed while André at enormous risk left the *Vulture* to go within the American lines.

At Verplanck's on Thursday Arnold spent half an hour with Colonel Livingston and mentioned the Sutherland letter about "our people firing upon a party of theirs." He seemed to Livingston "a good deal reserved." On one side of the Ferry or the other, Arnold talked with Major Kierce about the boat that had been ordered. Because there was none available at Verplanck's or Stony Point Arnold sent his barge up the river to borrow a boat and tow it down. Though Arnold could not wait, he asked Kierce, when the boat should come, to send it into Haverstraw creek, near Smith's house, and "let him or Mr. Smith know by express, by land. . . . General Arnold informed me . . . that Mr. Smith had furnished General Howe with very good intelligence; and that he, Mr. Smith, was going down the river to procure intelligence for him; and desired me not to delay the boat a minute, but as soon as it arrived to send it into the creek."⁵ From Stony Point Arnold went on horseback to Smith's, where before he had heard about the delivery of the boat he was looking for men to row it.

"Near sundown," according to Samuel Cahoon again, "Mr. Smith spoke to me as I was going for the cows, and told me to come up, as the general wished to speak to me. I went up with Mr. Smith in the room where General Arnold was, who asked me to go with him a piece that night. I said I could not go, being up the night before, and told him I was afraid to go; but General Arnold urged me to go, and told me if I was a friend to my country I should do my best; and at last I asked the general where he wanted me to go, and the general and Mr. Smith said on board of the ship in the river, and that there was a man there the general wanted to see very much." There was now no question, as there may have been on Wednesday afternoon, of going to Dobbs Ferry. Arnold knew that André was on the *Vulture*. "Upon my saying what was the reason he could not stay till the morning, General Arnold said it must be done that night; and upon my saying I could not go alone, Mr. Smith desired me to go and fetch my brother. I went, and my wife being dissatisfied with my going, I went back to General Arnold, and told him that I did not want to go, and told him there were [American] guard boats out; he said there was no danger of them, and said if I did not go he would look upon me as a disaffected man. I then went and fetched my brother; and when we came back we stood out a great while before we consented to go."⁶

Joseph Cahoon, also Smith's tenant, sitting with Smith on a

bench outside the door, told him: "I was sorry I was wanted for that purpose, and said upon any other thing I was willing to serve him or the general. Mr. Smith asked me why, and said there was no hurt in going, as it was general business." The guard boats need not trouble them. "He had a pass from the general to go, and the countersign; and he said the countersign was *Congress.* . . . I asked him why the flag was not sent down in the daytime, as it ought to be done. He said because it was to be kept private from the inhabitants and common men. . . . I then told him I did not choose to go. He said there was no hurt in going, at all; and said if anything should come against me, he would defend me and clear me from all. I told him he could not clear me if there was any bad in it; and Mr. Smith afterwards got up and went into the house to General Arnold.

"General Arnold came out soon after Mr. Smith went in, and said, upon his coming out, I need not be afraid to go with Mr. Smith, and said it must be done for the good of the country; and said it was not done in private, for the officers at the Ferry knew it, the captain of the water guard also. . . . I thought at first it was not good, but thought otherwise upon the general's mentioning that it was known." Smith, told that Joseph Cahoon had changed his mind, asked him to ride to the landing to see if the boat had come. "I said no, he ought to send his Negro. He ordered the Negro to get the horse, and the Negro went off. While the Negro was gone, myself and my brother concluded not to go, but both were afraid to tell the general of it." The Negro met an express from Kierce with a letter saying the boat was in the creek.

Joseph Cahoon, without knowing what the letter said, got up courage to go into the house and tell Arnold the brothers "had no mind to go; and as I was going up I met Mr. Smith in the entry, and he told me the general wanted to speak with me; and he passed out to the stoop, and I went into the room to the general, who was sitting by a table, with paper; and [upon] his speaking to me, I acquainted him I had no mind to go, as it was late; and said I would rather go in the morning. General Arnold said he must go to headquarters by ten o'clock in the morning; and if I did not assist when I was required for the good of my country and Congress he would put me under guard immediately.

"Upon which Mr. Smith came in, and I went out; and just after that Mr. Smith came out to the stoop, asked my brother and myself if we would have a dram, and gave us each one; and afterwards the general came out, and Mr. Smith and myself and brother were there together. The general and Mr. Smith talked together, but what they said I do not know . . . as they talked low . . . maybe two minutes, maybe more or less."[7]

Some time during the long discussion Arnold offered each of the Cahoons fifty pounds of flour (which they never got), but his promises probably affected them less than his threats. Toward midnight they finally consented, left Arnold at the house and went with Smith to the landing in the creek, muffled their oars in sheepskins as Arnold had ordered, and rowed about six miles down and across the stretch of the Hudson known as Haverstraw bay to the *Vulture*. "We were hailed by the vessel," as Samuel Cahoon told the story, "and Mr. Smith answered 'Friends,' and said we were from King's Ferry and bound to Dobbs Ferry; and we were ordered alongside immediately." Smith went on board and the Cahoons stayed in the boat.

II

The accounts of what happened on the *Vulture* are conflicting. Smith told one set of stories at his trial, when he was trying to prove to the Americans how good a patriot he was, and another in his *Authentic Narrative* twenty-eight years later, when he was trying to prove to the British how good a loyalist he had been. Robinson and Sutherland, after André's capture and sentence, anxiously insisted, for André's sake, that Smith had brought Arnold's request, virtually an order, to André to come on shore under the assumed name John Anderson. None of these accounts seems as trustworthy as the letter, now first made known, which Robinson wrote to Clinton on the 24th before the officers on the *Vulture* knew for certain that André had been captured.[8]

The only apparent error in Robinson's letter is his statement that his note to Arnold, saying Smith was expected, "and Captain Sutherland's flag"—note of protest—"met Arnold at or near Smith's house about twelve o'clock that night (Thursday)." Arnold must have received the protest earlier in the day, for he spoke of it to Livingston at King's Ferry. Smith, Robinson's only possible informant, may have misled him or been misunderstood by him. But Robinson knew at first-hand about the visit to the *Vulture*.

"Mr. Smith came on board with two men and brought me the following letter from Arnold open. 'This will be delivered to you by Mr. Smith, who will conduct you to a place of safety. Neither Mr. Smith nor any other person shall be made acquainted with your proposals. If they (which I doubt not) are of such a nature that I can officially take notice of them, I shall do it with pleasure. If not you shall be permitted to return immediately. I take it for granted Colonel Robinson will not propose anything that is not for the interest of the United States as well as himself.' " This open note was intended by Arnold to deceive Smith, if he read it, or any officer of the water guard who might challenge Smith's right to be on the river at night.

"Mr. Smith had a paper from Arnold in the nature of a flag for himself, one man, and two servants to go down by water to Dobbs Ferry, for the purpose of forwarding some letters to New York on private business." ("Permission is granted to Joshua Smith, Esq., to go to Dobbs Ferry with three men and a boy [Smith's Negro] to carry some letters of a private nature for gentlemen in New York, and to return immediately. . . . He has permission to go at such hours and times as the tide and his business suits." As Arnold later[9] explained: "This was done as a blind to the spy [guard] boats.") In addition, Robinson continued, Smith "had a second paper as a pass to bring with him two servants and a gentleman Mr. John Anderson." (This was the pass, already quoted, which Arnold had given Smith on the 20th.) "He had a third small scrap of paper on which was wrote nothing more than 'Gustavus to John Anderson.' " (This was to convince André that Gustavus and Arnold were the same person.)

"Upon considering all these matters Major André thought it was best for him to go alone, as both our names was not mentioned in any one of the papers, and it appeared to him (as indeed it did to me) that Arnold wished to see him." It seems clear that Robinson did not know quite why or how much Arnold wished this. "I therefore submitted to be left behind, and Major André went off between twelve and one o'clock Thursday night. Smith told me Arnold would be about one o'clock at a place called the Old Trough or Road, a little above De Noyelles's with a spare horse to carry him [André] to his [Smith's] house."

The subsequent British claim that André's going on shore, and going under a fictitious name, had been demanded by Arnold disregarded the facts that André had called himself John Anderson from the beginning of the negotiations and had long planned to meet Arnold at some place designated by him. Nobody had ever proposed that Arnold come on board the *Vulture*. Robinson in his note to Arnold on Thursday morning had specifically said that if Smith would come "here, we [André and Robinson] will attend him to any convenient and safe place." Robinson "submitted to be left behind" because André thought it best. Smith had brought a note from Arnold addressed to Robinson authorizing him to come on shore and return, and a pass mentioning John Anderson; but there was no single paper naming both of them, and no formal pass naming Robinson at all. Some guard boat might notice the irregularity and ask difficult questions. André went on shore because "Arnold wished to see him"—as he wished to see Arnold. A British officer on a British armed ship was in no way subject to the commands of an American, however high his rank. André went voluntarily to the meeting, and—on the evidence of Robinson's letter of the 24th and of André's own statement at his trial—expected Smith, if after the meeting it was "too late to bring me back, to lodge me until the next night in a place of safety."[10]

When the boat was "on the point of setting off," Captain Sutherland later said, "Colonel Robinson observed that as they had but two men in a large boat they would find some difficulty in getting on shore, and proposed that one of ours should tow them some part of the way; to which he [Smith] objected, as it might, in case of falling in with any of their guard boats, be deemed an infringement of the flag."[11] Smith, who almost certainly did not know what André's real errand was, thought they were in effect under a flag of truce, though no actual flag seems to have been carried; and Robinson and Sutherland, whatever they conjectured André's purpose to be, let him go on the strength of Arnold's pass without insisting he come back that night and without themselves providing for it. Only André, aware of his design and consequently of his danger, then realized—and later admitted when his life was at stake—that "it was impossible for him to suppose he came on shore under the sanction of a flag": coming stealthily at night, under a false name, to make final arrangements with a traitor. "I was," he wrote to Washington, "in my regimentals and had fairly risked my person."[12]

Wearing a blue caped cloak or surtout over his scarlet coat, André sat in the stern talking little with Smith who steered the boat while the Cahoons rowed it across the Hudson—at that point two miles wide—to a landing place at the foot of Long Clove Mountain, about two miles below Haverstraw, somewhat below where Arnold had said he would wait with a spare horse. Possibly seeing the boat from the road and riding down to meet it, he was close at hand "when we came on shore," according to Samuel Cahoon. "I heard the noise of a man at a bank above, and Mr. Smith went up and returned immediately; and the person we brought on shore went up, and Mr. Smith stayed with us."

Nothing is positively known about the topics and decisions of the interview. André did not live to report it to Clinton, and Arnold put on record—in a letter to Clinton of October 18—only what he said André had said about money.[13] "In the conference which I had with Major André he was so fully convinced of the reasonableness of my proposal of being allowed £10,000 sterling for my services, risk, and the loss which I should sustain in case a discovery of my plan should oblige me to take refuge in New York before it could be fully carried into execution, that he assured me, though he was commissioned to promise me only £6000 sterling, he would use his influence and recommend it to your Excellency to allow the sum I proposed; and from his state of the matter he informed me he had no doubt your Excellency would accede to the proposal." Up to the very end of the conspiracy, and afterwards, Arnold was faithful to his earliest price for treason; and it was not improbably the first point taken up at the meeting. Once that was settled, they could work out as far as possible the details of the attack and surrender.

Though André had never been at West Point, Clinton had known the country since his temporary capture of the Highlands forts in October 1777, and he had had recent information from spies as well as from Arnold himself. Arnold could now tell André, who was to lead the assault on Fort Putnam, that the fort was "wanting great repairs, the wall on the east side broke down and rebuilding from the foundation; at the west and south side have been a *chevaux-de-frise;* on the west side broke in many places, the east side open; two bomb-proofs and provision magazine in the fort, and slight wooden barrack." (Arnold had written this out in his Remarks on Works at West Point, but he could hardly have shown it to André where they met "hid among firs" on a moonless night.) The detachments at Fishkill and King's Ferry, Arnold could tell André, were under orders to move to West Point at the first alarm: more rebels to defend it, but more to be captured. André could tell Arnold what vessels, of what draught, and with what number of men on board would come up, and consult with him about the safest point of debarkation and the most likely approaches. They may have agreed upon a day when the surprise should be undertaken. But on Friday morning they cannot have hoped that this might be done before Sunday, when Washington would return from Hartford.

The interview seems to have lasted till perhaps four o'clock. According to Smith, he then "deemed it expedient to inform them of the approaching dawn of day" and Arnold came down from the bank and tried hard, though unsuccessfully, to persuade the tired and sleepy farmers to row André back to the *Vulture*.[14] But the Cahoons swore they did not see Arnold at the landing or know for sure that he was the man their passenger conferred with. It was Smith, according to Samuel Cahoon, who "asked my brother and myself if we would go on board the vessel again that night. I told him I was fatigued, being up the night before, and could not go. . . . Mr. Smith said if we could not go we must do as we thought best, and would leave it to us; but made us no offer to return on board the vessel that night."[15] Unaware of André's danger, and assuming that Arnold had the affair in charge, Smith without special concern left them to ride to his house while he went with the Cahoons in the boat to Haverstraw creek, where they arrived about daybreak. (The sun rose that day at 5:59.)

In André's terse statements to Washington and to the court

martial: "I was told that the approach of day would prevent my return and that I must be concealed until the next night."[16] André was of course prepared for this, though he would have preferred to go back at once. "I got on horseback with him [Arnold] to proceed to —— house, and in the way passed a guard I did not expect to see, having Sir Henry Clinton's directions not to go within an enemy's post."[17] Passing the guard, André assured Washington, was "against my stipulation, my intention, and without my knowledge beforehand." But it was too late to refuse, and André, with whatever anxiety he may have felt, considered himself under Arnold's orders. They were at Smith's when Smith with the Cahoons came up from the creek just after daylight. There was apparently no talk of sending André back to the *Vulture* now. He had come in the dark and was to go in the dark, whether one night or the next.

III

And it was not at all certain that he could go to the *Vulture* at any time. For, without orders from Arnold, Colonel Livingston had chosen that Friday morning, at daylight, to open fire on the ship with a four-pounder and a howitzer which had been brought to Teller's Point while Arnold was with André. According to Robinson, the "very hot fire . . . continued two hours, and would have been longer but luckily their magazine blew up. It was near high water, and the tide very slack and no wind, so that it was impossible, though every exertion was made, to get the ship out of their reach sooner. Six shot hulled us, one between wind and water; many others struck the sails and rigging, and boats on deck. Two shells hit us, one full on the quarterdeck, another near the main shrouds. Captain Sutherland is the only person hurt, and he very slightly on the nose by a splinter."[18] Arnold, who according to Smith saw the fight from a window at Smith's house and saw the *Vulture* leave her position about eight or nine,[19] must then have decided that some alternative route would have to be devised for André's return. Even if the *Vulture* should come up again, she would be under scrutiny by the Americans. It might be safer for André to travel by land, in disguise.

Arnold's earliest plan had been for André to come disguised within the American lines, and Arnold was still willing to take that risk. André, who had objected to this before, objected still. When, he said at his trial, mention was made "of my crossing the river and going by another route," he protested vigorously, "and thought it was settled that in the way I came I was also to return." He was possibly of the same opinion when he obeyed orders to carry to Clinton the papers Arnold had brought from Robinson's to Smith's. Arnold "himself made me put the papers I bore between my stockings and my feet. Whilst he did it, he expressed a wish, in case of any accident befalling me, that they should be destroyed, which I said of course would be the case, as when I went into the boat I should have them tied about with a string and a stone."[20] As to the disguise, though Arnold later said he had ordered it, André never claimed that, but seemed to imply he took the step on Smith's "refusal to reconduct me back the next night as I had been brought. Thus become prisoner, I had to concert my escape."[21]

Conflicting as the stories are, the believable parts of them may be fitted into a reconstruction which not too incredibly explains the actions and motives of the three conspirators on Friday the 22nd. Up to the time of the unforeseen cannonading all three expected that André would be rowed to the *Vulture* the coming night. After that André still thought it possible, as well as desirable, but Arnold was not sure. He felt obliged to hurry to headquarters. It was necessary before he left to make at least two plans, either of which might be carried out at discretion without further orders from him. What these were is plain from the passes he furnished, all dated that day at Robinson's house though written at Smith's.[22]

"Joshua Smith has permission to pass with a boat and three hands and a flag to Dobbs Ferry, on public business, and to return immediately." With this Smith might go down to the *Vulture*, no matter where it lay. "Joshua Smith has permission to pass the guards to the White Plains, and to return; he being on public business by my direction." With this Smith might escort André by land, crossing the Hudson at King's Ferry and travelling east of the river so as not to encounter the posts of the American main army. "Permit Mr. John Anderson to pass the guards to the White

Plains, or below, if he chooses; he being on public business by my direction." This would enable André, when Smith turned back, to go on to the British lines and safety.

Knowing André's objections to the land route and the indispensable disguise, Arnold did not absolutely order this: thinking the boat to the *Vulture* still a possibility, or intending to delude André for the present, or merely wishing to avoid an argument. With the same motives he instructed André to destroy the papers if necessary, and assented to André's plan to throw them into the water as if the river route were the only one in prospect. When Arnold after breakfast went off about nine or ten o'clock, André, with the original plan uppermost in his mind, did not understand how far Arnold had gone with his alternative.

Perhaps Smith too did not understand this till he accompanied Arnold to Stony Point where the barge waited for him. Then, if Arnold had not already given Smith his instructions behind André's back, there was an opportunity to do it. According to Smith, Arnold told him that André was a merchant who from false pride had borrowed a British uniform coat, and must not be allowed to continue a disguise in which he could not count on getting through the American lines, whatever pass he might carry.[23] Arnold may have left it to Smith's choice whether he should go by river or by land, and may have agreed that in the boat no disguise would be necessary. Since André if he went by land must be mounted, Arnold provided a horse—possibly the one André had ridden from the Long Clove the night before.

When Arnold set out in his barge for Robinson's House, about fifteen miles up the Hudson from Stony Point, he could think he had taken every essential precaution. His own interests were completely involved with André's. The capture of the intermediary would mean the detection of the principal. It is absurd to suppose that Arnold, in the circumstances, meant to deal treacherously with André, or even negligently. That would have been neglect of Arnold, who always looked out for himself. Nor was the water route to the *Vulture* clearly safer than the land route to White Plains. There were sure to be American guard boats on the Hudson watching the ship the first night after Friday morning's bombardment, and unlikely to pass a boat in which they might find a British officer in uniform. Because André, as it turned out, was actually captured going by land, it has been taken for granted that his route was foolishly chosen. But on all the grounds Arnold could calculate in advance, one route was as safe as the other.

André, when Smith came back from Stony Point, believed he was to be rowed to the *Vulture* Friday night. Some time during the day Smith, either obeying Arnold or suiting himself, refused to undertake this. Long afterwards Smith falsely said that Arnold appeared toward evening, found Smith suffering from a fit of the ague which he insisted must prevent his going on the river, and finally ordered him to take André by land.[24] Arnold unquestionably did not return to Smith's house that evening—as a good part of the afternoon was then called—but Smith may have waited till afternoon or evening to make up his mind and break the unwelcome news to André, who had spent the day in a room on the second floor.

Smith, if he had known who André was and how dangerous it must be for him to put on a disguise, could hardly have failed to make every effort to take him undisguised to the *Vulture*, though that route too was risky. Not knowing these things, Smith did not pay much attention to André's protests. André was only a merchant pretending to be an officer. Even if he were stopped in another borrowed coat at an American post he had nothing to fear but a short delay till Arnold could vouch for him. But Arnold, Smith understood, wished to keep Anderson's coming and going a secret from the public, and Smith sympathized with the prudent wish. Moreover, Smith thought of his own convenience. For him, the trip to the *Vulture* would be so much hard work and wasted time. But as he had to make a trip to bring his family back to Haverstraw, he might kill two birds with one stone—ominous image—by starting off as André's escort and when they parted continuing to Fishkill where the family was.

When Smith, to André's "great mortification, persisted in his determination of carrying me by the other route," and André saw himself as a prisoner who must "concert my escape," he discarded his scarlet coat for a purple or claret-coloured one of Smith's, with gold-laced buttons and button-holes. His nankeen waistcoat and breeches would not identify him as an officer, nor his whitetop riding boots. He wore also the blue cloak in which he had come ashore and a round civilian hat, not cocked. Restless but reserved, he got on his horse "at the decline of the sun" and rode with Smith and his Negro two and three-quarters miles down to the Stony Point landing of King's Ferry. All those who saw him there remembered him as very silent, Smith as jovial and talkative. He stopped for a drink with some officers at Stony Point, urged the ferrymen to row faster, called on Colonel Livingston at Verplanck's.

"I asked him where he was going," Livingston later testified. "He said up towards General Arnold's, or that route; and I gave him one letter to be delivered to General Arnold and another to General Clinton. . . . I then urged him to stay awhile and take supper or a drink of grog. He then informed me that there was a gentleman waiting for him who had just rode on, and was in a hurry to get off, and informed me that his business was very urgent, and I did not insist on his staying any longer. He then rode off and I did not see the person who was with him, it being dark and he having rode forward."[25]

André's intention was to ride all the way to White Plains that night. But near Crompond, about eight miles from Verplanck's, the travellers were stopped by a party of New York militia before nine o'clock. The militia captain insisted on asking questions. When Smith said they planned to put up at Major Strang's, the captain said Strang was not at home. When Smith then spoke of going on to his old friend Colonel Drake's, the captain said Drake had moved away. The captain asked for Smith's pass. It was from Arnold, and in order, but it named Smith as Joshua, whereas the captain had always heard him referred to as Jo and thought his name was Joseph. "I desired him to let me know something of his business," the captain testified later. "He made answer that he had no objection to my knowing it. He told me that he was a brother of William Smith, in New York, though very different in principle, and that he was employed by General Arnold to go with that gentleman—meaning the person who was with him—to get intelligence from the enemy; that they expected to meet a gentleman at or near the White Plains, for the same purpose. If I recollect right, I think Mr. Smith told me he was not so positive as that he should go himself as far as the White Plains or not."[26]

The captain—solicitous or suspicious—advised them to spend the night at a small farmhouse close by and finish their journey next day. "The reasons I gave Mr. Smith were that the riding in the night would be dangerous when they got below Croton river, from the Cowboys"—loyalist partisans. André naturally had no fear of loyalists, but he dared not reveal this to Smith, much less to the militia. He consented to the interruption of his journey, and he and Smith, according to Smith, slept in the same bed, André very restlessly.[27]

Arnold too had an uncomfortable evening. When he got back to headquarters he found both Varick and Franks displeased because he had paid Smith another visit. Though they did not yet think of treachery, they had reflected in Arnold's absence that he was "an avaricious man" and "imagined he had some commercial plan in agitation with some people in New York [represented by Anderson] under the sanction of his own command and through the rascal Smith." The two aides, unwilling to serve a smuggling chief, "agreed on honour to leave him if our doubts were confirmed." They "begged Mrs. Arnold to use her influence with Arnold to prevent" this dubious intimacy. Peggy, who said she had an "unfavourable opinion of Smith, both as a gentleman and as a man of sincerity," informed Franks "afterwards that Arnold had made her fair promises not to countenance Smith at all."[28] But the conflict did not come to a head on Friday, and Arnold can have thought of it as only a minor annoyance compared with his deep anxiety over André's return to Clinton and the consummation of the plot.

IV

On Saturday the 23rd the plot emerged from secrecy into history, the light falling first on André and thereafter recording almost every hour he had to live. He and Smith got up before sunrise and rode together by way of Crompond Corner about seven miles to another farmhouse near Cat Hill where they had breakfast. There, or at Pine's bridge over the Croton river a little further on, Smith turned back, leaving André to ride alone fifteen miles to White Plains by roads unfamiliar to him.[29] Smith was afraid of loyalist marauders who might stop him south of the

Croton, and André was not. Neither of them supposed André would meet armed Americans beyond Pine's bridge, the ordinary limit of the American patrols, and if he should he could produce Arnold's pass for John Anderson.

Riding down Hardscrabble road past Chappaqua and Pleasantville, André heard from a boy at a well that there were rebel scouts on the road to White Plains, and took the Tarrytown road instead. But in that Neutral Ground between the armies, where the more or less loyalist Cowboys and the more or less patriot Skinners kept up a savage warfare of raid and retaliation and plunder—and collusion—no stranger was safe. A party of loyalists had been out the day before, and the Westchester patriots today were vengeful. Three of them—John Paulding, Isaac Van Wart, and David Williams—were lying in wait at a bridge just above Tarrytown. They were, as Congress later called them, "volunteer militiamen"[30] who were operating under a recent New York act which permitted them to claim as prize any property they might find on a captured enemy. They stopped André, who was unarmed, about nine or ten o'clock.[31]

The legend of André's capture is classic, but the facts are obscure. Paulding and Williams at Smith's trial—Van Wart did not testify—told stories so minutely alike that they must have been agreed on and rehearsed for patriotic effect.[32] André told his story in few words: "I was taken by three volunteers who, not satisfied with my pass, rifled me and, finding papers, made me a prisoner."[33] Not much more than this is certain. But it seems fairly clear that André at first mistook his captors for loyalists such as he expected to find in this neighbourhood, told them he was of their party, and did not produce Arnold's pass till he found—too late—that they belonged to the other. Searching him, quite possibly for loot, they came upon the papers in his stockings. He offered, or they demanded, ransom for his release. He had little money with him and they either did not trust his promise to send a sufficient sum out to them or else were unwilling, on account of the papers, to accept a bribe to let him go. They took him cross-country to the American post at North Castle, where Jameson was in command. (The captors, with four other companions in their day's venture, were subsequently allowed André's watch, horse, saddle, and bridle as their prize.)

The officers at the advanced posts had been ordered by Arnold to look out for John Anderson if he came there from New York, and to send him up to headquarters. Jameson, when a stranger was brought in with Arnold's pass for John Anderson, naturally supposed this was the same man. But he had come from the wrong direction and carried papers which, Jameson wrote to Arnold, were "of a very dangerous tendency."[34] While Jameson, obeying orders, sent André (so far known only as Anderson) off to Arnold, he at the same time dispatched a messenger with the captured papers to Washington, who was known to be on his way back from Hartford, and supposed to be between Danbury and Peekskill. It does not appear that Jameson suspected Arnold of treason, and may have thought only that Anderson had stolen the papers. In any case, any lieutenant colonel might well have hesitated to make so grave a charge against his commanding general without first consulting the commander-in-chief.

Later in the day Major Tallmadge returned from scouting duty to North Castle. Active in the American secret service, he was more used to spies than Jameson and possibly more suspicious. (There is little to support the ingenious story that Tallmadge had heard from a spy in New York about the Arnold-André plot.[35]) Tallmadge, learning about the prisoner, at once concluded that since Arnold had arranged to meet Anderson, and Anderson was carrying military secrets back to New York, Arnold must be engaged in some traitorous conspiracy. Long afterwards Tallmadge hinted that he had proposed to go to headquarters, at his own risk, and seize Arnold.[36] But at the time he was able to do no more than persuade Jameson to send after André and order him brought back and held. According to Tallmadge, thirty-three years later, he urged Jameson not to inform Arnold of the capture, as Jameson persisted in doing. According to Jameson, in a letter to Washington four days after the event, Jameson "mentioned my intention to Major Tallmadge and some others of the field officers, all of whom were clearly of opinion that it would be right, until I could hear from your Excellency," to write about Anderson's capture to Arnold. "I did not think of a British ship being up the river, and expected that, if he was the man he has since turned out to be, he would come down to the [British] troops in this quarter, in which case I should have secured him."[37]

André with his guards was overtaken near Peekskill, returned to North Castle, and transferred early on Sunday morning to Lower Salem. So long as he expected to be carried to Arnold he kept silent as to his real name. But when he learned that the incriminating papers had been sent to Washington, who instead of Arnold would have charge of the affair, André on Sunday wrote Washington a letter telling him that "the person in your possession is Major John André, adjutant general of the British army." He had come to ground between the lines, he admitted, to "meet a person who was to give me intelligence" but whom André carefully did not name. He had been "betrayed . . . into the vile condition of an enemy in disguise within your posts." He asked that he be "branded with nothing dishonourable, as no motive could be mine but the service of my king, and as I was involuntarily an impostor."[38]

The lieutenant who had set out with André and then brought him back, left some time on Sunday with Jameson's letter to Arnold. A captain, with the papers which had come back from Danbury, and with André's letter also, hurried off later on Sunday to deliver them to Washington at Arnold's headquarters. It was a kind of race to decide whether Washington or Arnold would first learn that treason had been discovered.

The events which on Saturday began to forecast tragedy for André cost Arnold that day only a shabby squabble with his aides. Smith arrived in time for dinner, with the news, for Arnold, that John Anderson had got quietly past the American outposts. But Varick and Franks, convinced that Smith was Arnold's partner in some trading scheme, resented Smith's presence at headquarters.

"When we were at dinner on Saturday, the 23rd September," Colonel Lamb later testified, "there happened to be a scarcity of butter at the table. On Mrs. Arnold's calling for more butter she was informed by the servant that there was no more. Arnold immediately said: 'Bless me, I had forgot the olive oil I bought in Philadelphia. It will do very well with salt fish,' which was one of the dishes. The oil was produced, and, on Arnold's saying it cost eighty dollars [in Continental money], Smith replied 'Eighty pence' [meaning] that a dollar was really no more than a penny; upon which you [Varick] said with some warmth either 'You are mistaken' or 'That is not true, Mr. Smith.' I do not particularly recollect which. This you said in such a tone of voice as convinced me you was determined to affront him."[39]

"A very high dispute took place," according to Varick's continuation of the story,[40] "in which you [Franks] became a volunteer with me. Arnold opposed you and often addressed to you, with warmth, answers to my observations, and I replied to his answers, addressing myself to Smith. You, as well as myself, were cavalier with Smith till Mrs. Arnold (who also thought ill of Smith), observing her husband in a passion, begged us to drop the matter. I soon quitted the table and went into my room, which was then the office.

"After dinner, Smith went off and Arnold came into the office and took you [Franks] to task in very illiberal language for affronting Smith. He lashed me over your back, without addressing himself to me. He declared that if he asked the devil to dine with him, the gentlemen of his family should be civil to him. You told him if Smith had not been at his [Arnold's] table you would have sent the bottle at his head, and would thereafter treat him as a rascal. I then found it necessary to do you, as well as myself, justice by taking on myself the blame of affronting Smith. You thereupon declared to Arnold that you had of late observed that he viewed every part of your conduct with an eye of prejudice, and begged him to discharge you from his family. You went out of the room in a passion and to Newburgh on business, from which you did not return till the 24th. The dispute between me and Arnold continued very high. I cursed Smith as a damned rascal, a scoundrel, and a spy, and said that my reason for affronting him was that I thought him so. I also told Arnold that my advice to him [against Smith] had proceeded from a regard to his [Arnold's] reputation, which he repeatedly and confidentially told me he wished should stand well in this state, and which I had very often told him would suffer by an improper intimacy with Smith.

"I further told him that Smith's insolence to you and his ungentlemanlike conduct to Mrs. Arnold in speaking impertinently to you before her in a language [French?] she did not understand, justified your treating Smith in the manner you did, and worse, and also merited his [Arnold's] resentment instead of countenance. Arnold then told me that he was always willing to be advised by the gentlemen of his family but, by God, would not be dictated to by them; that he thought that he possessed as much prudence as the gentlemen of his family. Some other words ensued, till I had occasion to leave him to dispatch an express, and when I returned he had left the office."

That evening Varick received a letter from a member of Governor Clinton's staff indicating that the governor did not altogether trust Smith—though giving little reason for this except "the conduct of his connexions and his own loose character." Varick showed the letter to Arnold "and then told him that I considered his past conduct and language to me unwarrantable, and that I thought he did not place that confidence in my repeated friendly assurances and advice which I had a right to expect and which was necessary to put in a person acting in my capacity, and that I could not longer act with propriety. He gave me assurance of his full confidence in me, of a conviction of the rectitude of my conduct, of Smith's being a rascal, and of his error in treating me with such cavalier language; and that he would never go to Smith's house again or be seen with him but in company."[41] Arnold, believing he was now done with Smith's help, could promise this with the private reflection that he was being even more truthful than Varick realized.

V

The messengers sent on Sunday with warnings to Arnold and to Washington, either starting late or halting on the way, did not reach Robinson's till Monday. Washington unexpectedly lodged Sunday night at Fishkill, where Smith had supper at the house where Washington was stopping. They, like Arnold, did not learn that day of André's capture.

Nor did Beverley Robinson and Sutherland, growing more and more uneasy on the *Vulture*. Since they had not thought of André's return Thursday night as a certainty, they did not report to Clinton on Friday. And even on Saturday, after a second night of waiting, they still hoped and did not report. But on Sunday the 24th Robinson, at last informing Clinton of the whole affair, had to write: "It is with the greatest concern that I must now acquaint your Excellency that we have not heard the least account of him since he left the ship. . . . I hope to have your Excellency's further instructions what to do. I shall do everything in my power to come at some knowledge of Major André." If, as is possible, this letter got to Clinton the same day, he as well as André had good reason to know the scheme had failed.

For Arnold, discovery and catastrophe came on Monday. Before breakfast he went into the office, which was also Varick's bedroom, and asked Varick if he had answered some letters that had come from Jameson and Tallmadge. Varick, who had been ill for two or three days, said he had not and was today not able to. Arnold took the Tallmadge letter with him and said he would answer it himself. It was presumably the letter of the 21st telling Arnold that if John Anderson came to North Castle Tallmadge would take care of him: as Tallmadge, in a manner then so unintended, had since done! Varick never saw Arnold again, "but betook myself to my bed."[42]

Washington was expected to breakfast with Arnold. But about nine o'clock Alexander Hamilton and another aide arrived with word that the commander-in-chief would be late and that the meal should go on without him and the other members of his staff, including Lafayette and Knox. While the party, apparently, was at table—though Arnold at the moment may have been out of the room[43] on some official business—the earlier letters from Jameson were handed to Arnold, with the thunderous news that John Anderson had been taken and the papers found.

Arnold, telling the messenger to say nothing about the capture but otherwise showing no sign that tragedy had struck him, "soon after he received the letters . . . went upstairs to his lady," according to Franks. There was barely time to tell her of the downfall of their plot, and none to comfort or quiet her in her panic. "In about two minutes his Excellency General Washington's servant came to the door and informed me that his Excellency was nigh at hand. I went immediately upstairs and informed Arnold of it. He came down in great confusion and, ordering a horse to be saddled, mounted him and told me to inform his Excellency that he was gone over to West Point and would return in about an hour."[44] Nobody thought this particularly strange. And nobody at Robinson's, besides Peggy, knew that Arnold was hurrying down a short cut to his barge at the landing, on his desperate way to refuge on the *Vulture*.

Washington arrived, breakfasted, and instead of waiting for Arnold left for West Point expecting to see him there. Varick, who had got dressed long enough to pay his respects, had to go back to bed. "A considerable time thereafter [probably two or later]," Franks came to Varick's window from outside the house, hastily shoved up the window, and told the sick man there was "a report that one Anderson was taken as a spy on the lines and that a militia officer had brought letters to Arnold and that he had been enjoined secrecy by Arnold." Franks had not seen the letters, but these circumstances made him suddenly wonder if Arnold were not involved with Anderson in treachery rather than in peculation. Varick for a moment was disposed to agree with Franks; "but instantly reflecting that I was injuring a gentleman and a friend of high reputation in a tender point," he said it was "uncharitable and unwarranted even to suppose it." Franks on second thought "coincided in opinion with me, and I lay down secure in the high idea I entertained of Arnold's integrity and patriotism." Even when, in the course of the day, he was told that Arnold's barge had gone down the river, not to West Point, that added "circumstance made no impression on me."[45]

Whatever state Peggy Arnold may have been in when her husband left her, she controlled herself while Washington was in the house. He did not see her or have reason to wonder that she should be upset because her husband had gone, as Washington had been told, no farther than to West Point. Possibly in this interval she destroyed the letters between her and Arnold, if they had been saved. She could not get at the damaging files in the office, because Varick was there in bed. But it was on Varick that she released her hysterics, once Washington had gone.

"About an hour thereafter," as Varick wrote his sister,[46] "Mrs.

Arnold (good woman) inquired how I was from the housekeeper and bid her go and see." Peggy had the day before spent an hour with Varick "while I lay in a high fever, made tea for me, and paid me the utmost attention in my illness." Now, the moment the housekeeper turned her back, Peggy was suddenly "mad to see him, with her hair dishevelled and flowing about her neck. Her morning-gown with few other clothes remained on her—too few to be seen even by gentlemen of the family, much less by many strangers." Varick in his room "heard a shriek, ran upstairs, and there met the miserable lady, raving distracted. She seized me by the hand with this—to me—distressing address and a wild look: 'Colonel Varick, have you ordered my child to be killed?' Judge you of my feelings at such a question from this most amiable and distressed of her sex, whom I most valued. She fell on her knees at my feet with prayers and entreaties to spare her innocent babe. A scene too shocking for my feelings, in a state of body and nerves so weakened by indisposition and a burning fever. I attempted to raise her up, but in vain. Major Franks and Dr. Eustis," the surgeon stationed at Arnold's headquarters, "soon arrived, and we carried her to her bed, raving mad."

Varick is said to have believed, later, that she had been acting.[47] But at the time he was twenty-seven, unmarried, and devoted to the unhappy girl. He could see "no cause for all this" and took it for frantic grief. "When she seemed a little composed she burst again into pitiable tears and exclaimed to me, alone on her bed with her, that she had not a friend left here. I told her she had Franks and me, and General Arnold would soon be home from West Point with General Washington. She exclaimed: 'No, General Arnold will never return; he is gone, he is gone forever; there, there, there, the spirits have carried [him] up there, they have put hot irons in his head'—pointing that he was gone up to the ceiling. This alarmed me much. I felt apprehensive of something more than ordinary having occasioned her hysterics and utter frenzy." As soon as she learned that Washington had come back from West Point without Arnold she insisted that "there was a hot iron on her head and no one but General Washington could take it off, and wanted to see the general."

Dr. Eustis left the room with Varick and Franks and told them that Arnold must be sent for "or the woman would die." The aides, hearing her say so often that her husband was gone forever, had come to suspect that he had gone to the enemy.[48] They took the doctor into their confidence, though they were still not willing to hint such a thing to Washington—who already knew it was true. On his return from West Point he had read the papers which in his absence had come to Robinson's by the second messenger, and had sent Hamilton on horseback to stop Arnold, if it could be done, at Verplanck's. Varick and Franks were keeping their suspicion from Washington for fear it might be unfounded. He was keeping the fact of the discovery from them, because they as late associates of Arnold must for the present be watched, but not warned. They made the first move, after they had decided that "the most eligible mode of conveying our anxious fears and suspicions of Arnold's business was by letting him see her unhappy situation."[49] Varick "waited on his Excellency, informed him of all matters, and Mrs. Arnold's request. I attended him to her bedside and told her there was General Washington. She said no, it was not. The General assured her he was, but she exclaimed: 'No, that is not General Washington; that is the man who was a-going to assist Colonel Varick in killing my child.' She repeated the same sad story about General Arnold. Poor, unhappy, frantic, and miserable lady."

Hamilton returned with a letter which Arnold, safe on the *Vulture*, had sent under a British flag to Verplanck's for Washington.[50] "The heart which is conscious of its own rectitude," he said, "cannot attempt to palliate a step which the world may censure as wrong. I have ever acted from a principle of love to my country, since the commencement of the present unhappy contest between Great Britain and the colonies. The same principle of love to my country actuates my present conduct, however it may appear inconsistent to the world, who very seldom judge right of any man's actions." Arnold had already begun his long apologia.

But for the present he asked no favour for himself. "I have too often experienced the ingratitude of my country to attempt it. But, from the known humanity of your Excellency, I am induced to ask your protection for Mrs. Arnold from every insult and injury that a mistaken vengeance of my country may expose her to. It ought to fall only on me; she is as good and innocent as an angel, and is incapable of doing wrong. I beg she may be permitted to return to her friends in Philadelphia, or come to me, as she may choose. . . . I have to request that the enclosed letter may be delivered to Mrs. Arnold, and she be permitted to write to me." He added a postscript to assure Washington that Varick and Franks, "as well as Joshua Smith, Esq. (who I know is suspected) are totally ignorant of any transactions of mine that they had reason to believe were injurious to the public." So far as Peggy was concerned, Arnold's letter confirmed her hysterics, and Washington was satisfied that she was innocent.

Hamilton, who was twenty-three, was more than satisfied. Though he brought her word that her husband had escaped, and a letter which she was permitted to keep though all Arnold's other papers were seized, she could not afford to become calm at once; and Hamilton saw her still "frantic with distress. . . . It was the most affecting scene I was ever witness to," he wrote to his fiancée, who was Schuyler's daughter.[51] "One moment she raved, another she melted into tears. Sometimes she pressed her infant to her bosom and lamented its fate, occasioned by the imprudence of its father, in a manner that would have pierced insensibility itself. All the sweetness of beauty, all the loveliness of innocence, all the tenderness of a wife, and all the fondness of a mother showed themselves in her appearance and conduct. We have every reason to believe that she was entirely unacquainted with the plan, and that the first knowledge of it was when Arnold went to tell her he must banish himself from his country and from her forever."

Their reasons for believing this were that a traitor had said so and a pretty and clever woman had said so too. Washington had known her since she was a young girl, and probably found it hard not to think of her as still that. He and his staff had had no experience with women as conspirators, in a conflict in which women had almost never taken any active part. And of course whatever part of her behaviour was frustration was lost in her total fear and anxiety, and her knowledge that her great hopes had come to utter ruin. If she had been half-hysterical when, at Robert Morris's house six weeks before, she had heard that Arnold was not to command at West Point, she could be hysterical now. Hysteria, or something like it, was self-preservation.

The next day, according to Varick, "she recovered a little and remembered nothing of what happened on the 25th." As Hamilton put it: "This morning she is more composed. I paid her a visit, and endeavoured to soothe her by every method in my power, though you may imagine she is not easily to be consoled. Added to her other distresses, she is very apprehensive the resentment of the country will fall on her (who is only unfortunate) for the guilt of her husband. I have tried to persuade her that her fears were ill-founded, but she will not be convinced. She received us [including Washington and Lafayette, presumably] in bed, with every circumstance that would interest our sympathy; and her sufferings were so eloquent that I wished myself her brother, to have a right to become her defender." (Did Betty Schuyler guess that Peggy had perhaps artfully chosen her bed for a stage on which to be interesting to the sympathetic officers?) The day after that Peggy, having triumphed over all suspicion at Robinson's, departed with Franks as escort for Philadelphia.

Now comes the story, so often doubted and discredited, of her confidences to Theodosia Prevost at Paramus on the way home. "As soon as they were left alone, Mrs. Arnold became tranquillized and assured Mrs. Prevost that she was heartily tired of the theatricals she was exhibiting." She said "that she had corresponded with the British commander, and that she was disgusted with the American cause and those who had the management of public affairs, and that through unceasing perseverance she had ultimately brought the general into an arrangement to surrender West Point."[52]

The story is only hearsay, first recorded after both the Arnolds were dead, and Theodosia Prevost who is said to have confided it to her second husband Aaron Burr, and Burr himself who left it for his biographer to publish. The Shippen family, when the story appeared, produced another. Burr they said was at Paramus when Peggy arrived there, was her escort the next day (Franks was actually her escort), made advances to her which she repulsed, and invented the scandal out of spite.[53] The notorious Burr has been doubted and abused by chivalrous defenders of Peggy Arnold who believed her husband and her, and had no evidence of her complicity. Now that unmistakable evidence has come to light, there is reason enough to suppose that she may have felt such relief at Paramus as to tell Theodosia Prevost what she told Burr and what he—who also had known Peggy from childhood, and better than Washington—kept secret till it could do no harm to living persons.

VI

The question of Peggy's innocence was a much smaller matter in the afternoon of Monday the 25th than the certainty of Arnold's guilt. Washington, when he had read the damning papers and André's letter and had sent Hamilton to Verplanck's, seems to have waited for Hamilton's return before taking any positive steps. Only his confidential aides knew what had been discovered, though Varick and Franks were more and more suspicious. Dinner was at four. Washington, Lafayette, Knox, the French engineers Gouvion and Villefranche, Lamb from West Point, and the aides dined at Robinson's quietly, as Varick wrote a few days later.[54]

"I had a high fever, but officiated at the head of the table. Franks attended also when Mrs. Arnold's affairs would permit. Dull appetites surrounded a plentiful table. His Excellency behaved with his usual affability and politeness to me. . . . After dinner some time"—perhaps after Hamilton brought word that Arnold had got to the *Vulture*—"his Excellency called to me to take my hat and walk out with him, which I did. He thus declared he had the most indubitable proofs of Arnold's treachery and perfidy. I told him I was sorry for it, and he said he had not the least cause of suspicion of Major Franks or myself, but that his duty as an officer made it necessary to inform me that I must consider myself a prisoner, in which I, as politely as I could, acquiesced. It was what I expected. I then told him the little all I knew."

Varick and Franks could and did tell about Arnold's dealings with John Anderson for the past three weeks, and about Joshua Smith's connivance. Washington at seven sent out the first orders called for by the emergency.[55] Jameson was to bring André at once to Robinson's, with an escort strong enough to keep him from escaping or being recaptured by the enemy. "He had better be conducted to this place by some upper road rather than by the route through Crompond. I would not wish Mr. André to be treated with insult, but he does not appear to stand upon the footing of a common prisoner of war and therefore he is not entitled to the usual indulgencies they receive, and is to be most closely and narrowly watched. . . . André must not escape." These orders reached Jameson about midnight, and André, in the charge of Tallmadge, three other officers, and a hundred dragoons, rode the rest of the night through the rain and were at Robinson's at dawn. Gouvion was sent to Fishkill to take Smith, who was found in bed at his brother-in-law's house and harshly hurried on foot to Robinson's by seven or eight.

Though Arnold had had no confederates in his department, and Washington had no particular reason to suspect anybody, he sent Colonel Lamb early Monday evening to take charge of Verplanck's and Stony Points and summoned Colonel Livingston to headquarters. There might—so far as Washington could know—even now be British vessels in the Hudson moving up to an attack, and the King's Ferry posts must be held by an officer with whom Washington could be sure there had been no tampering. Livingston came and Washington was convinced of his fidelity. West Point was put in a state of defence, reinforcements were ordered, and the militiamen whom Arnold had sent to cut wood called back again.

While Hamilton was at Verplanck's he had sent a note to Nathanael Greene, commanding the main army in Washington's absence, about Arnold's flight and André's capture. At half past seven Washington wrote to Greene: "I request that you will put the division on the left in motion as soon as possible, with orders to proceed to King's Ferry, where (or before) they will be met by further orders." At eleven at Tappan two Pennsylvania brigades were ordered to march immediately and the rest of the army put in readiness. One of the young officers long afterwards still vividly remembered "the dark moment . . . in which the defection of Arnold was announced in whispers. It was midnight, horses were saddling, officers going from tent to tent ordering their men, in suppressed voices, to turn out and parade. No drum beat; the troops formed in silence and darkness. I may well say in consternation, for who in such an hour, and called together in such a manner, and in total ignorance of the cause, but must have felt and feared the near approach of some tremendous shock."[56]

Possibly that night, or early the next morning, a letter came from Beverley Robinson on the *Vulture*.[57] He had "this moment" learned, he said, that André had been taken. Robinson felt he must inform Washington of the truth of André's case. "He went up with a flag at the request of General Arnold, on public business with him, and had his permit to return by land to New York." The public business was Arnold's stealthy design to betray his trust and Clinton's no less stealthy mission to complete and promise to reward the treason. "Under these circumstances Major André cannot be detained by you, without the greatest violation of flags, and contrary to the custom and usage of all nations; and, as I imagine you will see this matter in the same point of view as I do, I must desire you will order him to be set at liberty and allowed to return immediately. Every step Major André took was by the advice and direction of General Arnold, even that of taking a feigned name, and of course he is not liable to censure for it." The feigned name had been chosen by André himself sixteen months before, and he had voluntarily left the *Vulture* under it. The British had begun their defence and justification of André.

Arnold, running to the *Vulture* with empty hands, insisted that the bargemen who had saved his life be carried as prisoners to New York (where Clinton at once released them on parole).[58] This was petty meanness in a man who had aimed to be such a traitor that he would be a hero, another Monk restoring another king. Arnold may furiously have reflected, on the Hudson, that if West Point had been taken, and the American cause lost, then Washington might in time be thought of as a beaten rebel and Arnold as the saviour of his country and the united Empire. Successful treason is not treason, but virtue and triumph. Probably Arnold had never come so close to it as he thought; and probably even the loss of West Point would not have beaten Washington, that magnificent commander who could still count on a devotion from his army and people that Arnold never understood. But Arnold could perceive, in gnawing bitterness, that his great plans had been defeated by little accidents: that unexpected firing on the *Vulture*, those unlooked-for volunteers beyond the American outposts. No single conspirator can call all the turns of chance. One unanticipated slip, and any conspiracy may fall to the ground, as Arnold's had.

Two Fates

THE light of history has fallen on André's final days from every direction. Historians and ballad-makers agree that he was the victim in the tragedy, while the villain Arnold went unpunished. The Americans who were set to be André's guards during his captivity became his friends. Tallmadge, then twenty-six, who first knew that Anderson was André and who was with him almost constantly thereafter, "walked with him to the place of execution and parted with him under the gallows, entirely overwhelmed with grief that so gallant an officer and so accomplished a gentleman should come to such an ignominious end."[1] Hamilton wrote, a few days later, that "among the extraordinary circumstances that attended him, in the midst of his enemies, he died universally esteemed and universally regretted."[2]

From Robinson's House André, who never saw Washington there or later, was taken across the Hudson to West Point, on the 28th in a barge down the river to Stony Point, and under a strong escort of dragoons to Mabie's tavern, André's last prison, at Tappan. Joshua Smith made the same journey, but the two were not permitted to speak together. Washington, who returned to Tappan that day, the next day summoned a board of general officers. They were to examine André carefully and "as speedily as possible to report a precise state of his case, together with your opinion of the light in which he ought to be considered and the punishment that ought to be inflicted."[3]

On Friday the 29th the board met in the Dutch church at Tappan, with Nathanael Greene as president. The other major generals were Lord Stirling (William Alexander, who claimed the title), Lafayette, Baron de Steuben (Frederick William Augustus von Steuben), St. Clair, and Robert Howe. The brigadiers were James Clinton, John Glover, Edward Hand, John Stark, Parsons, Knox, John Paterson, and Jedidiah Huntington. If the questions and answers were taken down, they were not preserved. The only record of the trial is the abstract made by John Laurance, advocate general.[4]

"Major André, adjutant general to the British army, was brought before the board." Washington's letter authorizing the inquiry was read. "The names of the officers composing the board were read to Major André; and on his being asked whether he confessed the matters contained in the letter from his Excellency General Washington to the board, or denied them, he said, in addition to his letter to General Washington dated Salem the 24th September, 1780 which was read to the board and acknowledged by Major André to have been written by him (which letter is annexed): that he came on shore from the *Vulture* sloop-of-war in the night of the 21st of September instant, somewhere under the Haverstraw mountain; that the boat he came on shore in carried no flag, and that he had on a surtout coat over his regimentals, and that he wore his surtout coat when he was taken; that he met General Arnold on the shore and had an interview with him there. He also said that when he left the *Vulture* sloop-of-war it was understood he was to return that night, but it was then doubted, and if he could not return he was promised to be concealed on shore in a place of safety until the next night, when he was to return in the same manner he came on shore; and when the next day came he was solicitous to get back, and made inquiries in the course of the day how he should return, when he was informed he could not return that way and he must take the route he did afterward. He also said that the first notice he had of his being within any of our posts was being challenged by the sentry, which was the first night he was on shore. He also said that the evening of the 22nd of September instant he passed King's Ferry between our posts of Stony and Verplanck's Points, in the dress he is at present in, and which he said is not his regimentals, and which dress he procured after he landed from the *Vulture* and when he was within our posts; and that he was proceeding to New York, but was taken on his way at Tarrytown, as he has mentioned in his letter, on

Saturday the 23rd of September instant about nine o'clock in the morning." Though André had in advance drawn up a written Statement to supplement his letter to Washington, he was allowed to make any oral changes or corrections he chose.

Shown the papers given him by Arnold, André "confessed to the board that they were found on him when he was taken, and said they were concealed in his boot, except the pass." He was shown his letter, as from John Anderson to Sheldon, of the 7th saying he would meet Gustavus at Dobbs Ferry: "which he acknowledged to have been written by him. . . . Major André observed that this letter could be of no force in the case in question, as it was written in New York when he was under the orders of General Clinton, but that it tended to prove that it was not his intention to come within our lines.

"The board having interrogated Major André about his conception of his coming on shore under the sanction of a flag, he said that it was impossible for him to suppose he came on shore under that sanction, and added that if he came on shore under that sanction he certainly might have returned under it.

"Major André having acknowledged the preceding facts, and being asked whether he had anything to say respecting them, answered he left them to operate with the board. The examination of Major André being concluded, he was remanded into custody."

After he withdrew the board heard letters from Beverley Robinson, Arnold, and Clinton, all insisting that André had come under a flag and had acted under Arnold's orders while within the American lines, and could therefore not be considered a spy subject to the usual penalty. These insistences did not, for the board, have as much weight as André's frank admissions. The essential facts seemed to the board to be: (1) that André had come on shore "in a private and secret manner"; (2) that "he changed his dress within our lines and under a feigned name and in a disguised habit" passed the works at King's Ferry to the point where he was captured, "being then on his way to New York" and having in his possession "several papers which contained intelligence for the enemy."

There was no question about the disguise and the papers. On

the subject of the flag, the issue of veracity was between André and Arnold. The board, after a deliberation of which no accurate details are known, came to a verdict which every officer signed: "that Major André, adjutant general to the British army, ought to be considered as a spy from the enemy; and that, agreeable to the law and usage of nations, it is their opinion he ought to suffer death." Washington in general orders the next day approved the sentence and ordered the execution for five o'clock the following afternoon.

It must be borne in mind that André's admissions before the board were, as he said, "in addition" to what he had written in his letter to Washington on the 24th. Then André declared that he had been conducted inside the American lines against his stipulation and had put on a disguise in an attempt to escape from what amounted to imprisonment. Even after he heard the verdict of the board he was still aware that there were certain special circumstances in his case, and still hoped that they might be taken into account.

He had come out, not as an ordinary spy, but as a kind of intermediary between Clinton and Arnold. Clinton had, according to the practices of war and under instructions from his government, as much right to try to win Arnold over as to try to defeat him in the field. André, who would have thought it dishonourable to act as an ordinary spy sent on a furtive, paid mission at his own peril, felt no more dishonoured at being ordered to meet Arnold secretly than he would at being commanded to lead an assault against him. To keep the risk down to the minimum, Clinton did order André to wear his uniform and to stay in neutral ground. But Clinton must have known that André could not go on shore under his own name, since Arnold would not dare to mention it in any pass he could send; and ought to have known that a flag of truce misused by Arnold with treacherous intentions would not protect André if he were discovered by the Americans.

When André left the *Vulture* he doubted that he would be able to come back the same night, and he fully intended, if he could not, to spend the next day at Smith's house. If he did not know that the house was beyond an American outpost, he could at least have inquired. It was either carelessness or daring that let him get as far as the post at Haverstraw without realizing beforehand that the place of safety he was bound for was within the lines—and so could not be a place of safety for him. Though he followed Arnold's directions, because Arnold commanded the district, André never supposed that the dishonest flag gave a sanction to the enterprise, and that he could return under it in any way that was convenient.

Nothing in André's letter to Washington or his statements to the board of general officers said unmistakably that Arnold had ordered André to return by land or in disguise. On the contrary, André said that when "in the morning Arnold quitted me," it was, André thought, "settled that in the way I came I was also to return." This need not call for any change of dress. It was, André said, "Mr. ——— [Smith, not Arnold], who persisted in his determination of carrying me by the other route," by King's Ferry and White Plains. "Thus become prisoner I had to concert my escape," disguised on horseback. André could not compel Smith to row him to the *Vulture*, or to go for further orders from Arnold while André waited hidden where he was. Nor could he reveal his name and rank to Smith, as a means of impressing him with the gravity of the case. Smith might turn frightened patriot and give him up. André was on a secret mission and must pay the price of secrecy. He might have made sure of his life by going, in his uniform, to Stony Point and giving himself up as a prisoner of war. But he could hardly have explained how he came there without involving Smith and Arnold, and at best he could not be exchanged in time to serve in the Arnold negotiations. If he was to obey Clinton's general orders, it was necessary to disregard his particular instructions. Being obedient to Clinton, and ambitious for himself, André took a long chance—and lost.

Gallantly as he faced the consequences, he still would not think of himself as an ordinary spy, though a chain of accidents had made him act and look like one. He was an officer and a gentleman, assigned to a hard duty in behalf of his king and country. If he had failed, he wanted to think he had failed like a soldier, and was entitled to be dealt with as a soldier fallen into the enemy's hands. The Americans might judge him rather by his intentions than by his outward actions.

II

This, the British command went on insisting, was what the Americans ought in honour and decency to do. New light falls on André's case from the direction of New York, where every effort was passionately made to justify him. The journal of Chief Justice William Smith, unpublished and hitherto overlooked in this connexion, furnishes the record.[5]

"The *Vulture* armed ship," he wrote on Tuesday the 26th, "has been ten days up the river with Major André and Colonel Robinson"—in order, the public supposed—"to watch the crossing of the rebel army while Washington was gone to Hartford. The secret is now out, for yesterday General Arnold came to the ship with a whaleboat, and this day to town. The people exult much, but it is not known yet that André was catched with his papers, which forced Arnold to come off before the design was accomplished of delivering up the Highland forts to the British. Some great error has been committed either by André or by Sir H. Clinton, who perhaps has been too slow in collecting his troops to ascend the river. The army is still on Long Island except the light infantry of whom some are drawn to Kingsbridge within a day or two. This defection must have good effects. . . .

"I recollect that Sir H. C. in our conversation of the 7th July said the rebellion would end suddenly in a crash. I told him my opinion was that it would die of a consumption. If he was in treaty with Arnold at that time, he had authority for what he said. . . . I fancy that Sir H. Clinton has intrigued with Arnold for some time, and that his reliance upon its success is the cause of his neglecting Rhode Island."

Apparently Clinton did not call upon his council that day, but asked Arnold to write him a letter which could be sent to Washington to clear André of blame. "I apprehend," Arnold said, "that a few hours must return Major André to your Excellency's orders, as that officer is assuredly under the protection of a flag of truce sent by me to him for the purpose of a conversation which I requested to hold with him relating to myself and which I wished to communicate through that officer to your Excellency."[6]

Arnold had had, he claimed, an "undoubted right to send my flag of truce for Major André. . . . Having held my conversation with him, I delivered him confidential papers in my own handwriting to deliver to your Excellency." Here Arnold, perhaps in part at Clinton's bidding, assumed that the nature of the conference had nothing to do with the validity of the flag, and that André was to be regarded as a messenger under orders. Arnold continued: "Thinking it much properer he should return by land, I directed him to make use of the feigned name of John Anderson, under which he had by my directions come on shore; and gave him my passports to pass my lines to the White Plains on his way to New York." This gave—and was intended to give—the false impression that Arnold was responsible for the choice of a return route, whereas in fact he seems to have left it to Smith's discretion; and that the assumed name was altogether Arnold's scheme, not something expected by André and tacitly concurred in by Clinton who had not forbidden it. It will be noted that Arnold in this letter made no reference to any disguise. On the 26th he knew nothing of the capture except what was in the letters from Jameson which Arnold had brought with him to the *Vulture* and which did not mention Anderson's dress. As they would almost certainly have spoken of his wearing a uniform coat, Arnold could guess that André had worn a civilian's. But it would be imprudent to bring the matter up when aiming to prove that André was not a spy.

Clinton the same day sent Arnold's letter off to Washington, with a brief note informing him that "I permitted Major André to go to Major General Arnold at the particular request of that general officer."[7] Not a word of the weeks during which Clinton had himself particularly requested, through André, that the meeting be held.

No reply came from Washington on Wednesday or Thursday, and André was so closely guarded that the British did not know where he was. Clinton, in mounting anxiety, sent for the chief justice on Thursday, talked with him for an hour, "and concluded," Smith wrote in his journal, "with thanking me for the consolation I had given him in the opinion that he was no spy, which he said agreed with all the others who had been consulted.

"He told me he had corresponded for a considerable time with Arnold; that he gave him the intelligence the French fleet was coming to Rhode Island": intelligence which, Clinton explained, might have been of the greatest benefit to the British but for Admiral Arbuthnot's doubts and delays. Clinton "lamented the last disappointment—blamed Arnold for not sending André back by water. Their interview was at Stony Point, and André seized on this side Croton by three militiamen and carried to the light horse. That he [Clinton] had everything ready for seizing the Highlands and putting an end, he owned, to the war, for he had boats of all draughts for proceeding to Albany. That the interview with Arnold was absolutely necessary to ascertain whether he had really been corresponding with Arnold. Arnold was desirous to favour the capture, but he had insisted upon his being an agent in it, and he [Clinton] was to have paid a great price for the acquisition. He regretted this disappointment as the loss [of] his hope of an instantaneous termination of the war; said he should have had both Washington and Rochambeau prisoners, for they were both there now.

"He should have seized the forts with 5000 and had 5000 more ready, for he thought the [loyalist] militia sufficient to take care of this place. I guess there was design in this enumeration": that is, Smith did not credit Clinton's figures.

"He said he had revealed his secret only to Sir George Rodney. . . . He hinted of his masking the enterprise up the river by giving out a design on the Chesapeake. That he should go there yet. Washington had not sent a man to the southward since Gates's affair. He could not. . . . He did not know whether Washington knew of his design upon the Chesapeake or not.

"I said little, for he spoke much, except what related to André. I enlarged upon the idea he now had of the importance of the Hudson and the acquisition of it as the end of the war. . . . I almost suspect that he still has designs upon the Hudson. There are other generals like-minded with Arnold. On my assenting to it as probable, he questioned me as to the person. I mentioned

Bob Howe. He would not countenance nor gainsay my suspicions, but asserted that he knew of others." If Clinton did have others in mind, the surviving Headquarters papers do not show who they were.

III

Again on Friday the 29th there was no news of André. Late Saturday afternoon Captain Aaron Ogden of the 1st New Jersey came to the British outpost at Paulus Hook (Jersey City) with a reply from Washington to Clinton, enclosing letters from André to Clinton and from Peggy to Arnold. Peggy's, presumably telling her husband that ‚Washington had been kind to her and would let her go to Philadelphia, is missing.[8] Washington's, dated the 30th, informed Clinton of the findings of the board and of the verdict, and clearly summed up the American position with regard to André's status.[9]

"From these proceedings it is evident Major André was employed in the execution of measures very foreign to the objects of flags of truce and such as they were never meant to authorize or countenance in the most distant degree; and this gentleman confessed with the greatest candour in the course of his examination 'that it was impossible for him to suppose he came on shore under the sanction of a flag.' "

André's letter, graceful and dignified, had been written on the 29th in the shadow of "the rigorous determination that is impending." His first concern was to "remove from your [Clinton's] breast any suspicion that I could imagine I was bound by your Excellency's orders to expose myself to what has happened. The events of coming within an enemy's posts and of changing my dress, which led me to my present situation, were contrary to my own intentions as they were to your orders. And the circuitous route which I took to return was imposed (perhaps unavoidably) without alternative upon me." As he would not blame Clinton for sending him on a dangerous errand, neither would he blame Arnold too much for failing to safeguard the return. "I am perfectly tranquil in mind and prepared for any fate to which an honest zeal for my King's service may have devoted me."

André remembered his obligations to Clinton. "With all the warmth of my heart I give you thanks for your Excellency's profuse kindness to me. And I send you the most earnest wishes for your welfare which a faithful, affectionate, and respectful attendant can frame." He asked nothing more except consideration for his mother and three sisters, "to whom the value of my commission would be an object." (A commission was normally for the life of the holder, but in this abnormal case an exception might be made, André hoped.) He closed with reassurances as to his treatment in captivity. "I receive the greatest attention from his Excellency General Washington, and from every person under whose charge I happen to be placed."[10]

These letters were hurried across the Hudson to Clinton, who promptly summoned his council to Headquarters. When William Smith arrived he found several general officers and councillors ahead of him. There was Clinton's close friend William Phillips, captured at Saratoga but recently exchanged, whom Clinton had first proposed to send to Arnold for a conference. There was Lieutenant General James Robertson, royal governor of New York, who had perhaps as much influence with Clinton as any of his officers. Lieutenant Governor Andrew Elliot and Attorney General John Tabor Kempe of New York were present, and Governor William Franklin and Chief Justice Frederick Smyth of New Jersey.

"Sir Henry came in about nine o'clock and introduced his question relating to Major André and caused the letters upon that subject to be read: *viz* that from Arnold to himself, another from himself to Washington enclosing Arnold's of the 26th instant, Washington's of the 30th (that day), with one from André taking leave. At the reading of which last he was very much affected.

"A good many questions were asked, and some by Franklin and Kempe which, as supposing doubts whether André ought not to be considered as a spy, distressed him more; and he called out to me for my opinion. I declared it and opened the reasons, and the whole company concurred except Franklin and Kempe, who promised to change their votes." Even in Clinton's inmost circle there were some who agreed with Washington about André. It is clear that they yielded not only to the outnumbering majority but also to Clinton's agonized desire.

"After various suggestions respecting a letter to be sent in answer to Washington's, Sir Henry retired and after some time came in with a draft which his secretary Captain Smith read. It was in general approved except as to a compliment on Washington's humanity. General Robertson made a proposition for a shorter and more peremptory letter, and with the General's leave went out to frame it; and it was approved. It intimated that Washington and his board of general officers were misinformed; that Lieutenant General Robertson was sent with two other gentlemen to state the facts as they truly were and to declare the General's sentiments and resolutions."

Clinton, according to William Smith, had said in his unused draft: "that he wished them to consult the French and Hessian generals; that he expected André though no spy, in return for his exchanging one Robinson, commandant of one of their regiments, who was certainly a spy; that he had many others in his power and would avenge." It must have seemed to Robertson and the others that this was hardly the time to mention bargains or threats to Washington, and Clinton's original answer was diplomatically overruled and simplified.

The revised draft "being approved, Chief Justice Smyth whispered to me," William Smith wrote, "that I ought to accompany General Robertson, who was to go out in the morning to Dobbs Ferry; and the letter [was to go] this night by Washington's flag from Paulus Hook by land. Soon after, General Robertson wished me to be one of the persons who was to assist him; and upon my approaching the General [Clinton] he asked it. I replied that I had no other objection than, as the question and business was important, it seemed fit to employ persons of the highest rank in it. He replied that he could nominate none of more unexceptionable character. I thanked him and declared my readiness to obey his commands.

"The secretary was now gone to copy the letter, and we had orders to direct a postscript that the two assistants were Mr.

Elliot and myself. The company broke up, and we agreed to breakfast with the governor [Robertson] and go off in the *Greyhound* in the morning by seven or eight o'clock."

The council was probably not told, and Clinton may not yet have known, that Captain Ogden was the bearer also of an informal inquiry about a possible exchange of André for Arnold.[11]

A good many Americans, no matter how confident they were that André had been a spy and his sentence was just, could not without further effort bear to see an unfortunate victim die and a deliberate villain go free. "It was by some suspected," Hamilton wrote to John Laurens, "Arnold had taken his measures in such a manner that, if the interview had been discovered in the act, it might have been in his power to sacrifice André to his own security. This surmise of double treachery made them imagine Clinton might be induced to give up Arnold for André, and a gentleman took occasion to suggest this expedient to the latter as a thing that might be proposed by him. He declined it." Hamilton himself refused to make the suggestion to André. "As a man of honour he could but reject it, and I would not for the world have proposed to him a thing which must have placed me in the unamiable light of supposing him capable of meanness, or of not feeling myself the impropriety of the measure."[12]

But Hamilton, it seems fairly certain, wrote a secret letter to Clinton on the 30th, the day Ogden came to Paulus Hook. Though the letter is in a disguised hand, and signed apparently A. B., it uses the same argument in almost the same language as Hamilton's letter to Laurens. "It has so happened in the course of events that Major André, adjutant general to your army, has fallen into our hands. He was captured in such a way as will according to the laws of war justly affect his life. Though an enemy his virtues and his accomplishments are admired. Perhaps he might be released for General Arnold, delivered up without restriction or condition, which is the prevailing wish. Major André's character and situation seem to demand this of your justice and friendship. Arnold appears to have been the guilty author of the mischief; and ought more properly to be the victim, as there is great reason to believe he meditated a double treachery, and had arranged the interview in such a manner that if discovered in the

Sir,

It has so happened ~that~ in the course of events, that Major André Adjutant General of your army has fallen into our hands. He was captured in such a way as will according to the laws of war justly affect his life. Though an enemy his virtues and his accomplishments are admired. Perhaps he might be released for General Arnold, delivered up without restriction or condition, which is the prevailing wish. Major André's character and situation seem to demand this of your justice and friendship. Arnold appears to have been the guilty author of the mischief; and ought more properly to be the victim, as there is great reason to believe he meditated a double treachery, and had arranged the interview in such manner, that if discovered in the first instance he might have it in his power to sacrifice Major André to his own safety.

I have the honor to be &c
— +B

Sept. 30. 40

No time is to be lost

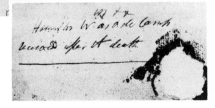

Alexander Hamilton's letter in a disguised hand proposing the exchange of Arnold for André, with endorsement by Clinton

first instance, he might have it in his power to sacrifice Major
André to his own safety." There was an urgent postscript: "No
time is to be lost."

The original letter, still surviving in the British Headquarters
papers, is endorsed by Clinton: "Hamilton W aid de camp received after A death."[13] Simcoe, André's friend, knew of it:
"Amongst some letters which passed on this unfortunate event,
a paper was slid in without signature, but in the handwriting of
Hamilton, Washington's secretary, saying that the only way to
save André was to give up Arnold."[14] If Clinton was right about
the time the letter was received, then it was not slid in among
the papers Ogden brought on the day the letter was written. But
a letter hinting at an exchange was sent to Clinton and did sooner
or later reach him.

There was of course not the remotest possibility that Clinton
would consent to an exchange which would be a sentence of death
to Arnold. From the British point of view Arnold's desertion was
not a crime but a merit. His crime had been his service with the
rebels. In leaving them he was returning to his lawful duty.
Clinton, who had promised to reward and protect Arnold, could
now not send him to the gallows instead, whatever mischance
André had fallen into. Washington must have been aware of all
this. But he deeply sympathized with André, and was willing to
let Clinton save his life if he chose to do it at the expense of
Arnold's. There is nothing to indicate whether Washington
approved of Hamilton's letter, or even knew of it.

The instructions to Ogden,[15] given him in general by Washington and in particular by Lafayette, were that he should take care
to reach Paulus Hook with the flag and letters so late on Saturday
afternoon that he would have to stay the night at the British post
while waiting for an answer. He was then, in conversation with
some British officer, to give it as his opinion that if Arnold were
sent back André might be spared. Ogden did this, talking with
the post commandant, and was asked if he had authority for his
opinion. He said he had not, but he was prepared to say that if
Clinton proposed the exchange Washington might agree to it.
The commandant at once left the post, crossed the river, reported
to Clinton, and came back to tell Ogden that Clinton could not

even consider such a thing. The next morning Ogden set out for Tappan with Clinton's reply to Washington saying that Robertson and the others would go to Dobbs Ferry that day to present "a true state of the facts" in André's case. The day's evening orders postponed the execution to Monday "at twelve o'clock precisely."

IV

William Smith's journal adds some new details to the story—often told—of the Robertson mission. "We met, now Sunday 1 October, and Arnold had prepared a letter to Washington taking all the blame upon himself respecting André and threatening retaliation if the rights of the flag were violated; which we were to withhold or deliver as we saw fit." It is very unlikely that this was without Clinton's knowledge and instructions. He would not make threats himself, in writing, but might allow Arnold to do it.

"At three P.M. we moored off Corbet's point and the general sent Murray, his aide-de-camp, on shore to know whether there was any message from Washington, whose army was four miles behind at Tappan. The officer informed him that Washington's messenger had not returned above two hours from Paulus Hook, but that General Greene was coming and wished to receive General Robertson alone; so that only he and his aide-de-camp went on shore. A long conference ensued apart, while Murray walked elsewhere with Hamilton, Washington's aide-de-camp, and two other rebel officers." (Hamilton may have taken this opportunity to transmit his mysterious letter to Clinton, if it had not gone by Ogden.)

Smith's account of the interview can have come only from Robertson, and differs little from the account Robertson wrote that evening to Clinton.[16] "Greene said," according to Smith, "Mr. Washington considered the right of inquiry and decision as theirs, and that he only met General Robertson as a gentleman. General Robertson supposed they wished to know the truth and that it was immaterial, if carried to Washington, in which light he was considered."

Robertson offered to produce Beverley Robinson and the officers of the *Vulture* to prove that André had gone under Arnold's flag.

"He showed Greene also Arnold's letter to Washington." In this Arnold once more insisted that he was responsible for André's use of an assumed name. Without mentioning the papers again, Arnold now spoke of the disguise, about which he had definitely learned since his former letter. André "with much reluctance and at my particular and pressing instance" had changed his coat, Arnold said: probably lying, certainly contradicting André. "Greene," according to Smith, "produced a letter from André to Washington in which he faults [takes the blame for] his own disguises in the transaction with Arnold, and confesses he had no flag." This sounds less like André's letter to Washington, which Robertson understood it to be, than like André's written statement submitted to the board of officers.

"General Robertson observed properly that André's wrong idea of his securities *jure belli* was of no avail. Greene said Arnold was a rascal and André a man of honour whom he believed; and they would consent to no conference for additional evidence. Greene hinted that André might be safe if Arnold was given up, and talked of satisfying the army. Robertson answered with a look. They parted with Greene's promise to inform Washington of what had passed."

The *Greyhound* lay over night at Dobbs Ferry, while Robertson waited for an answer from Washington. The next forenoon a note came from Greene saying he had communicated to Washington "the substance of our conversation in all the particulars, so far as my memory served me. It made no alteration in his opinion and determination."[17] Robertson seized on the words "so far as my memory served me" as a pretext for writing at length to Washington about the interview.[18] In an affair of such moment the unaided memory was not enough. The written version sent by Robertson was delicately put, barely hinting that Clinton had many persons in his power on whom he might retaliate. But Robertson enclosed the letter from Arnold, with its violent conclusion.[19]

"If after this just and candid representation of Major André's case the board of general officers adhere to their former opinion, I shall suppose it dictated by passion and resentment. And if that gentleman should suffer the severity of their sentence, I shall think myself bound by every tie of duty and honour to retaliate on such unhappy persons of your army as may fall within my power—that the respect due to flags and the law of nations may be better understood and observed.

"I have further to observe that forty of the principal inhabitants of South Carolina have justly forfeited their lives, which have hitherto been spared by the clemency of his Excellency Sir Henry Clinton." These were Americans who, after the capture of Charleston, had accepted British protection and been released on parole, but who had secretly corresponded or conspired with the patriot forces in the state. Arnold declared—either with Clinton's permission or else with amazing effrontery—that Clinton could not "in justice extend his mercy to them any longer, if Major André suffers; which in all probability will open a scene of blood at which humanity will revolt.

"Suffer me to entreat your Excellency, for your own and the honour of humanity, and the love you have of justice, that you suffer not an unjust sentence to touch the life of Major André. But if this warning should be disregarded, and he should suffer, I call heaven and earth to witness that your Excellency will be justly answerable for the torrent of blood that may be spilt in consequence."

Arnold's officious threats could have had no effect on Washington even if they had reached him earlier. As it was, they probably did not get to Tappan till after André's death. "It was twelve o'clock," according to Smith, "when Murray had delivered his letter on shore, and as soon as he returned we weighed anchor and came away." And twelve o'clock was the hour set for the execution.

André's servant had been permitted to come out, perhaps with Ogden, bringing clean clothing, and André on his last day—at least—wore British full dress instead of the borrowed coat he had worn from the time of his capture through his trial. On Sunday he asked, in a note to Washington, that he might be shot like a soldier not hanged like a felon. "The practice and usage of war, circumstanced as he was, were against the indulgence," Washington explained to Congress.[20] Either André was a spy, as the board had decided, and should die a spy's death, or else he was a prisoner of war, and should not be killed at all. Any mitigation of his sentence would imply a doubt that he had been justly condemned. Washington did not answer the note, thinking it more considerate to spare André the unhappy knowledge as long as possible, and he left his prison still believing he might be shot. He learned the truth only when he came in sight of the high gibbet on a hill in a field just outside the village of Tappan but within the limits of the American camp. With affecting courage, before a multitude of soldiers and spectators, he climbed upon the gruesome coffin in the baggage wagon that was to serve as a drop, and himself adjusted the rope round his neck and his own handkerchief over his eyes. All the witnesses agree that when the wagon was driven suddenly from under him he seemed to die during the first great swing of the rope. He was buried on the spot where he had died.[21]

V

Washington could not agree with one of his aides that Arnold must, after the catastrophe, be "undergoing the torments of a mental hell. He wants feeling! From some traits of his character which have lately come to my knowledge, he seems to have been hackneyed in villainy, and so lost to all sense of honour and shame that while his faculties will enable him to continue his sordid pursuits there will be no time for remorse."[22] And it is true that only thirteen days after Clinton had heard of André's death, and was still overcome with grief and regret, Arnold could write a letter asking if he might not yet have the £10,000 he had long haggled for rather than the £6000 he had been promised by André at their interview.[23] Without any reference whatever to André's tragedy, Arnold declared: "I have every reason to believe the step which I have taken will in the consequences have the most happy effect, and will tend to promote his Majesty's service more effectually than an expenditure of a like sum could possibly have done in any other way. I am induced with the greater cheerfulness to submit the matter to your Excellency, in full confidence of your generous intentions, and that you will not think my claim unreasonable when you consider the sacrifices I have made, and that the sum is a trifling object to the public though of consequence to me, who have a large family that look up to me for support and protection."

Even Arnold never wrote a more heartless letter. André was dead, Arnold was alive. Clinton might be willing to pay the living man what he said the dead man had thought the job was worth. Nothing further could be done about André. Arnold had supported Clinton in the case he had tried to make out for his adjutant general: in the preposterous contention that the commander at West Point had authority to protect an enemy agent coming, in full knowledge of his errand, to arrange for the betrayal of the stronghold; in the misleading or false statements Arnold furnished about André's assumed name and disguise and choice of a return route. And Arnold had, as might have been expected, fully agreed with Clinton that Washington and his officers, calling André the spy he undoubtedly was, were actuated only by passion and resentment. Whoever questioned Arnold's right to do what he wanted must have evil motives.

Before the news of André's death came to New York Arnold was already busy with plans for justifying his conversion and serving his new cause. On October 4 Andrew Elliot noted that "the printers have been prevented saying anything till Arnold wrote his own sentiments."[24] In writing his own sentiments Arnold had the help of William Smith. The soldier needed the lawyer.

"A letter this morning from General Arnold," Smith entered in his journal for the 3rd, "requesting a draft of an address from him to the public. I had doubts of complying, and only promised by a note to assist on his draft. . . . General Arnold calls in the evening with his notes for an address. He begs draft of a letter to Lord George Germain and the correction of his intelligence to the minister of the interior state of the country which he will send tomorrow." The next day: "I send General Arnold draft of address to the public and draft letter to Lord George, and promised to return his notes of intelligence tomorrow." On Thursday the 5th: "He calls, alters the first, and shows new draft of the last; copies the former and throws draft into the fire with his notes of it. Begins to copy my alterations or additions to the intelligence. News by Mr. White that André was executed on last Monday;

eported that his servant Peter is come in. He [Arnold] is vastly disconcerted and retires on the chariot's coming for him from General Robertson."

From these journal entries it seems clear that Arnold's address *To the Inhabitants of America* was based on his notes but drafted by Smith with some further alterations by Arnold. Dated the 7th, it was published as a broadside and printed in the *Royal Gazette* of the 11th.[25] "Arnold's justificatory address comes out," Smith wrote on the 9th. "It does not please the refugees, who think their own merits slighted. He is announced today a brigadier general and receives congratulations at the parade."

If Arnold in his argument suddenly took the orthodox loyalist positions, it need not mean, as he insisted, that he had privately held them before the treason; but may mean partly—or largely—that he took them over from a skilful advocate who had been maintaining them for at least two years. Arnold had never before expressed any special dislike of Congress except for its treatment of him. Now he talked about "the tyranny of the usurpers in the revolted provinces," and about "that class of men who are criminally protracting the war from sinister views at the expense of the public interest." Smith and all orthodox loyalists used such words every day.

"When I quitted domestic happiness for the perils of the field," Arnold said sounding more like Arnold, "I conceived the rights of my country in danger, and that duty and honour called me to her defence. A redress of grievances was my only object and aim; however, I acquiesced in a step which I thought precipitate—the Declaration of Independence." But at his court martial three and a half years after the Declaration he had told his judges how eagerly he looked forward to "the glorious establishment of our independence." He had, he said in his address, considered the war "a defensive one until the French joined in the combination" and the British sent new terms for peace and union. Then, Arnold went on in words that sound more like Smith's than his own: "I lamented . . . the impolicy, tyranny, and injustice which, with a sovereign contempt of the people of America, studiously neglected to take their collective sentiments of the British proposals of peace and to negotiate, under a suspension of arms, for an adjustment of differences, as a dangerous sacrifice of the great interest of this country to the partial views of a proud, ancient, and crafty foe. I had my suspicions of some imperfections in our councils, on proposals prior to the Parliamentary commission of 1778; but having then less to do in the cabinet than the field . . . I continued to be guided in the negligent confidence of a soldier. But the whole world saw, and all America confessed, the overtures of the second commission exceeded our wishes and expectations. If there was any suspicion of the national [British] liberality, it arose from its excess." Only loyalists believed that all America was satisfied with the peace offers of 1778: especially loyalists, like Smith, shut up in New York and unfamiliar with patriot opinion.

To the "insidious offers of France," Arnold said (though he had never put it on record at the time), "I preferred those from Great Britain, thinking it infinitely wiser and safer to cast my confidence upon her justice and generosity than to trust a monarchy too feeble to establish your independency, so perilous to her distant dominions, the enemy of the Protestant faith, and fraudulently avowing an affection for the liberties of mankind while she holds her native sons in vassalage and chains." To make his preference effective he had hit on a scheme which he meant altogether for the good of his countrymen. "I affect no disguise, and therefore frankly declare that, in these principles, I had determined to retain my arms and command for an opportunity to surrender them to Great Britain and in concerting the measures for a purpose, in my opinion, as grateful as it would have been beneficial to my country. I was only solicitous to accomplish an event of decisive importance and to prevent, as much as possible in the execution of it, the effusion of blood." No mention here of his first demanding £20,000 for the surrender of West Point and of his taking no final steps till his price had been accepted.

He could now, having been made a British general, "with the highest satisfaction . . . bear testimony to my old fellow-soldiers and citizens that I find solid ground to rely upon the clemency of our sovereign and abundant conviction that it is the generous intention of Great Britain not only to have the rights and privileges of the colonies unimpaired, together with perpetual exemption from taxation, but to superadd such further benefits as may consist with the common prosperity of the Empire. In short, I fought for much less than the parent country is as willing to grant her colonies as they can be to receive or enjoy."

Some loyalists might think he had "continued in the struggle of those unhappy days too long." He could say to them only that he "did not see with their eyes" or perhaps have "so favourable a situation to look from." Some patriots might think he had given up their cause too soon. As to the candid among them, "some of whom I believe serve blindly but honestly in the ranks I left, I pray God to give them all the lights requisite to their own safety before it is too late." As to "that kind of censurers whose enmity to me originates in their hatred to the principles by which I am now led to devote my life to the reunion of the British Empire, as the best and only means to dry up the streams of misery that have deluged this country, they may be assured that, conscious of the rectitude of my intentions, I shall treat their malice and cal- umnies with contempt and neglect." These last defiant words were pure Arnold.

What Smith called Arnold's "intelligence to the minister of the interior state of the country" and altered at Arnold's request be- came The Present State of the American Rebel Army, Navy, and Finances, which Arnold dated the 7th but did not send to Ger- main till the 28th with the letter which Smith had drafted first.[26] In the Present State Arnold reported to Germain what Washing- ton on September 6 had told his council of war about the size of the American armies. To this Arnold added that: "Many of the best officers of the army have resigned, and others are daily follow- ing their example, through disgust. necessity, and a conviction that the provinces will not be able to establish their independ- ence." There was much jealousy, Arnold said, between Congress and the army. The American navy was only three frigates and a few small vessels that were generally in port for want of hands to man them. "The treasury is entirely empty and the finances are at the lowest ebb." Congress had no credit, and the different prov- inces very little more. Much of this was true, and all of it would seem true to Germain, who was used to hearing it from loyalists.

In the accompanying letter to Germain which Arnold began

at the same time with the Present State but for some reason held back for three weeks, there was detailed advice as to specific moves that might be made. "A title offered to General Washington," Arnold fantastically thought, "might not prove unacceptable, and [might] answer a good purpose." The other officers and the soldiers had many of them not been paid for months. Let Great Britain promise to pay all arrears to those who would join the king's army, with promises of 7½ years half pay after the war and of land ranging from 200 acres each for private soldiers up to 5000—or even 10,000—acres for major generals. This would cost the British government less than a few months of waging war. Or an immediate cash reward of 15 or 20 guineas might be offered to every private or non-commissioned officer who would come over, half down and half at the end of the war. This would cost less than procuring soldiers in Great Britain and transporting them.

If Arnold should be authorized to announce this, he was sure he could recruit 2–3000 men in a short time. Perhaps some people might think these schemes "derogatory to the honour and dignity of Great Britain." Arnold thought "the true honour and dignity of the nation consists in promoting peace and union. . . . Forms and etiquette ought to be dispensed with when the nation is in imminent danger." Having been bribed himself, he had no objection to bribing others, and seemed confident that it could be done on a large scale if the bribes were large enough. The whole of Vermont might be won to the British cause by an offer to recognize the territory as a separate province. This was a favourite design of Arnold's collaborator Chief Justice Smith, who claimed land (said to have been nearly 100,000 acres) in Vermont under a New York grant supported by the Crown, and who would lose it if Vermont remained a rebel state.[27]

But of course, Arnold insisted, a powerful British army would have more effect than anything else. In that he hoped he might have the rank of major general. "I beg leave to observe to your lordship that the sacrifices of fortune which I have made are great, and that it is my most ardent wish to have a command in which I can by my conduct testify to his Majesty my sincere attachment to his person and interests and atone for any errors that I may have been guilty of heretofore." Once he had asked for a higher rank than Clinton had given him, Arnold could go on with his military recommendations.

The Provincials enlisted in America, he said, should not be restricted to garrison duty but should be actively employed as light troops. Two or three divisions of 3–4000 men each could in one campaign force the rebel army to disband. "Believe me, my lord, this is not a visionary scheme, but what I know to be practicable." There were two ways to win success. One was to muster the entire British army and overcome Washington, no matter how far he might retreat. "The posts in the Highlands on the North river in my opinion ought to be the first object of the army in the spring." Or the British might go south with all their army except the garrison regiments left to hold New York. Arnold advised against marching up from South Carolina to Virginia (as Cornwallis did the next year, to the end at Yorktown). It would be better instead to take possession of Baltimore and the Chesapeake region. "A formidable force there would immediately awe Maryland and Virginia into obedience, and soon establish a civil government in those provinces, collect the resources of the country both men and provisions, and might proceed to Pennsylvania, New Jersey, and New York, with a force that might bid defiance to all oppositions." Various loyalists had urged this move on Clinton, who chose two months later to send Arnold to Virginia.

Before sending off the letter to Germain, Arnold had already begun—again with William Smith's help—his efforts to seduce the American army. On October 23 the *Royal Gazette* announced: "His Excellency the Commander-in-chief has been pleased to appoint Benedict Arnold, Esq., colonel of a regiment, with the rank of brigadier general." On the 25th the *Royal Gazette* printed Arnold's *Proclamation to the Officers and Soldiers of the Continental Army* (a broadside dated the 20th) and continued to reprint it in every issue twice a week through December 6.[28] The colonel of a regiment, as the British army was then organized, was in a sense a contractor, and Arnold's proclamation was in a sense an advertisement of an enterprise which might bring him profit as well as renown.

Arnold aimed his proclamation, he said, at officers and soldiers "who have the real interest of their country at heart and who are determined to be no longer the tools and dupes of Congress or of France." He believed that his present principles "animated the greatest part of this continent" and therefore rejoiced at "the opportunity I have of inviting you to join his Majesty's arms.

"His Excellency Sir Henry Clinton has authorized me to raise a corps of cavalry and infantry, who are to be clothed, subsisted, and paid as the other corps are in the British service; and those who bring in horses, arms, or accoutrements are to be paid their value or have liberty to sell them." This would of course apply not only to the private property of deserters but also to any property of the American army which they might bring away with them. "To every non-commissioned officer and private a bounty of three guineas will be given; and, as the commander-in-chief is pleased to allow me to nominate the officers, I shall with infinite satisfaction embrace this opportunity of advancing men whose valour I have witnessed and whose principles are favourable to an union with Britain and true American liberty. The rank they obtain in the king's service will bear a proportion to their former rank and the number of men they bring with them." Lieutenant colonels, of cavalry or infantry, would be expected to bring 75 men; majors, 50; captains, 30; lieutenants, 15; cornets of horse or ensigns of infantry, 12; sergeants, 6.

"N. B. Each field officer will have a company. Great as this encouragement must appear to such as have suffered every distress of want, pain, hunger, and nakedness from the neglect, contempt, and corruption of Congress, they are nothing to the motives which I expect will influence the brave and generous minds I hope to have the honour to command; and I wish to have a chosen band of Americans to the attainment of peace, liberty, and safety (that first object in taking the field) and with them share in the glory of rescuing our native country from the grasping hand of France as well as from the ambitious and interested views of a desperate party among ourselves who, in listening to French overtures and rejecting those from Britain, have brought the colonies to the very brink of destruction."

Arnold repeated the familiar loyalist arguments, with special emphasis on the horrors of a French alliance. "What is America but a land of widows, beggars, and orphans? And should the parent nation cease her exertion to deliver you [from Congress] what security remains to you for the enjoyment of the consolations of that religion for which your fathers braved the ocean, the heathen, and the wilderness? Do you know that the eye which guides this pen lately saw your mean and profligate Congress at mass for the soul of a Roman Catholic in purgatory and participating in the rites of a church against whose anti-Christian corruptions your pious ancestors would have witnessed with their blood?" Arnold was referring to the past May when Congress attended the funeral of the Spanish agent in Philadelphia, Don Juan de Mirailles.[29] There is no record that Arnold, attending the service, made any difficulty then; but now he might speak of it as a warning to Protestants. Smith, on October 28, noted in his journal that Congress had appointed December 7 as a day of general thanksgiving "for deliverance from Arnold's plot, etc., and for continuing the enjoyment of the gospel of peace! How opportune Arnold's proclamation of 20th instant asserting that the Congress assisted a mass in praying for the soul of Don Juan from purgatory!" Smith was an ardent Presbyterian.

The Continental soldiers, Arnold declared, must be certain that the funds of the country were exhausted or had been embezzled by the "managers. . . . In either case you surely can continue no longer in their service with honour or advantage. Yet you have hitherto been their supporters of that cruelty which, with an equal indifference to your, as well as to the labour and blood of others, is devouring a country which, the moment you quit their colours, will be redeemed from their tyranny. But what need of arguments to such as feel infinitely more misery than language can express? I therefore only add my promise of the most affectionate welcome and attention to all who are disposed to join me in the measures necessary to close the scene of our afflictions."

Arnold's "unparalleled piece of assurance," Washington wrote to Congress when he read the *Proclamation*, had, "if possible, added to the detestation" in which the Continental officers and soldiers already held the renegade.[30] Nor were the British and the loyalists too friendly to the convert, though they hoped he might be followed in by many other rebels. "It is a common saying at

New York," one observer wrote, "that the ship must be near sinking when the rats are leaving it."[31] And a British officer, in a letter a few days after Arnold's *Proclamation*, remarked that he was "to raise a regiment of as great scoundrels as himself, if he can find them."[32]

His temptations had little effect. Badly paid and fed and clothed and housed and equipped as the Continental soldiers were, few of them thought they would be better off under a general who, during months when they admired and trusted him, had been ready to sell them to the enemy. On December 11, according to an official return, Arnold had 4 captains, 2 lieutenants, 2 ensigns, 3 sergeants, and 1 drummer to take with him on his raid to Virginia, but only 28 rank and file. Of his captains,[33] some of whom stayed behind to carry on recruiting in New York, Gilbert R. Livingston, a loyalist member of the powerful New York family, may have joined Arnold in simple loyalty to the Crown; Nathan Frink of Connecticut had already served in both rebel and Provincial regiments, and hoped he might organize a revolt in his native state;[34] Thomas Stewart McClelan and Richard Ness and Robert Rollo and Samuel Wogan (of Connecticut) are merely names on a roster. Arnold drew his corps for the most part from the fringes of the armies, hangers-on of either camp.

In New York Arnold tried hard to find the spies he knew Washington had there. Robert Townsend, the most valued of them, wrote to Tallmadge on October 20: "I am happy to think that Arnold does not know my name. However, no person has been taken up on his information."[35] But Arnold may have got some hint that Tallmadge was in charge of Washington's secret service; and it may have been because of this hint that Arnold on the 25th made a written attempt on Tallmadge. "As I know you to be a man of sense," Arnold said, "I am convinced you are by this time fully of opinion that the real interest and happiness of America consists in a reunion with Great Britain. To effect which happy purpose I have taken a commission in the British army, and invite you to join me with as many men as you can bring over with you. If you think proper to embrace my offer, you shall have the same rank you now hold, in the cavalry I am about to raise. I shall make use of no arguments to convince you or to induce you to take a step which I think right. Your own good sense will suggest everything I can say on the subject."[36]

Arnold's letter went out by some unknown agent toward the American lines in Westchester where Tallmadge—devoted to Washington and the patriot cause—was stationed as major of dragoons. But by the time the letter got to his neighbourhood he had gone, on November 23, in command of a party sent to Long Island to destroy stores and forage collected for the British at Oyster Bay. The raid was a complete success. Washington not only allowed the raiders "the little booty" they were able to carry off but also highly commended them to Congress, which officially recognized Tallmadge's "distinguished merit."[37] In the circumstances, Arnold's unknown agent thought and explained in an undated memorandum in the British Headquarters files, it would be wise not to approach Tallmadge yet.

"The gentleman to whom General Arnold's letter was addressed was, at the time it came out into the country, busily engaged in an affair (at a considerable distance from where the letter was deposited); the execution of which has so recommended him to his patrons that it was thought an ill-timed season to deliver it immediately after that affair was accomplished. It was therefore thought most advisable to let the matter rest, till the ardour of that gentleman's spirits do abate or until it's known whether the notice taken of him in consequence of that affair corresponds with his expectations." Little was to be gained by making offers to contented rebels. Nor did Arnold's letter, when it finally reached Tallmadge on the following January 28, have the least effect. He sent a copy to Washington the same day. "I am equally a stranger to the channel through which it was conveyed, the reason why it was so long on its way, or the motives which induced the traitor to address himself thus particularly to me. I have determined to treat the author with the contempt his conduct merits, by not answering his letter, unless your Excellency should advise a different measure."[38] Long afterwards Tallmadge remembered that he had at first "felt somewhat mortified that my patriotism could be even suspected by this consummate villain. I took the letter, however, immediately to General Washington, who consoled me abundantly on the occasion."[39]

VI

Peggy Arnold, leaving Robinson's on September 27 with her child and with the sympathetic blessings of Washington, Varick, Hamilton, and Lafayette (the youngest and most chivalrous of them all), was at Kakiat on the 28th. "Mr. Reed," Major Franks wrote that day to Varick, "is the only man who would take us in at this place or give our horses anything to eat. . . . We got here, I very wet, Mrs. Arnold, thank God, in tolerable spirits; and I have hopes to get them home without any return of her distress in so violent a degree. She expresses her gratitude to you in lively terms and requests you make her acknowledgments to his Excellency, to the Marquis, and to Hamilton, and indeed to all the gentlemen for their great politeness and humanity. To the Marquis, Eustis, and Hamilton she will ever be warmly grateful."[40]

She was probably the next night at Paramus, where she found in Mrs. Prevost another person who would entertain the wife and son of a traitor. But the journey was a painful one, even though Peggy was generally thought the guiltless victim of her husband's crime. Philadelphia, when she arrived there on October 2 or 3, was full of what had come to light on the seizure of Arnold's papers. The *Pennsylvania Packet* on September 30 accused his wife of somehow sharing in the plot. This was what came of paying so little attention to women as possible conspirators. "We should have despised and banished from social intercourse every character, whether male or female, which could be so lost to virtue, decency, and humanity as to revel with the murderers and plunderers of their countrymen. Behold the consequence. Colonel André, under the mask of friendship and former acquaintance at Mischianzas and balls, opens a correspondence in August 1779 with Mrs. Arnold which has doubtless been improved on his part." But even the *Packet*, reading André's discreet offer to shop for Peggy in New York, supposed no more than that this had led to a correspondence with Arnold. Nobody then suspected that Arnold had himself made the overtures to Clinton so long before, or that Peggy had known about them from the first.

Her cousin and brother-in-law Edward Burd wrote on October 5: "The popular clamour is high." André's letter had been "con-

strued into the beginning of a correspondence since improved to
this horrid issue. The family say there has been no other letter
received by her either before or since. . . . But the letter is an
unfortunate one, coming from the very man who, I will not say
corrupted Arnold (because I believe him capable of the worst
actions a man can commit), but who was connected with him in
the horrid plots. The impossibility of so delicate and timorous a
girl as poor Peggy being in the least privy or concerned in so bold
and adventurous a plan is great, and it is not possible she should
have engaged in such a wicked one." Burd was as much convinced
as Washington of Peggy's innocence.

"A girl of the most refined feelings, of the most affectionate
disposition and dotingly fond of her husband, must be affected in
a very extraordinary manner upon such an unhappy event. She
keeps her room and is almost continually on the bed. Her peace
of mind seems to me entirely destroyed. There is also a letter of
hers to General Arnold found among her papers, giving an
account of her being at a concert of the [French] minister's, in
which she is free in her observations upon several of the ladies
there and which has given them much offense. I do not know who
the ladies are, but . . . it seems rather hard that these observations, which are intended merely for the eye of a husband, should
be made public and criticized upon with severity."[41]

Burd thought that "if Mrs. Arnold should be sent off to her
base husband, it will be a heart-breaking thing. I am not without
hopes she will be permitted to stay." But on the 27th the supreme
executive council of Pennsylvania, having decided there was danger she might correspond with Arnold in New York, resolved:
"That the said Margaret Arnold depart this state within fourteen
days from the date hereof, and that she do not return again during
the continuance of the present war."[42] Her father took her across
New Jersey to the British post at Paulus Hook, and on November
18 the *Royal Gazette* announced: "On Tuesday last [the 14th]
arrived in town the lady and son of Brigadier General Arnold."
They were quartered in a house in Broadway next door to Clinton's Headquarters.

Another refugee lady in New York, who paid Peggy a morning
visit soon after she came in, reported to Philadelphia some time

that month or the next: "Peggy Arnold is not so much admired here for her beauty as one might have expected. All allow she has great sweetness in her countenance, but wants animation, sprightliness, and that fire in her eyes which are so captivating in Captain Lloyd's wife. But . . . they have met with every attention indeed, much more than they could have promised themselves; and the very genteel appointment which he (General Arnold) holds in the service, joined to a very large present which I am told he has received, is fully sufficient for every demand in genteel life."[43]

Arnold's sister Hannah had been permitted to leave Philadelphia before Peggy, and to take her nephew Henry, Arnold's youngest son by his first wife, to Connecticut. The two elder brothers were probably soon sent north from their school in Maryland, to their aunt rather than to their father. But Benedict on November 30, then not yet thirteen years old, was allowed a commission as ensign in the 16th regiment of the British army.[44] Richard and Henry had to wait till October 1781, when they were just past twelve and nine, to be commissioned lieutenants of cavalry in Arnold's American Legion. Henry had, his father later said, "enlisted and delivered at the headquarters of the said Legion, 15 light horsemen," though it does not appear that the boy ever left Connecticut, being, as Arnold put it, "detained a prisoner for near two years among the Americans."[45] Such generous arrangements were possible in the king's service, and these were additional rewards to a rebel who had returned to his duty.

VII

Clinton, reporting on October 30 that he had paid Arnold "the sum of £6315 sterling as a compensation for the losses he informs me he has sustained by coming over to us," admitted that this might seem large, in view of the failure of the plan. But—and here Clinton paraphrased Germain's own words—"your lordship having intimated to me in your secret letter of the 27th September, 1779 that the gaining over some of the most respectable members of the Congress, or officers of influence and reputation among their troops, would next to the destruction of Washington's army be the speediest means of subduing the rebellion and restoring the tranquillity of America, I was encouraged to make the attempt. And I have no doubt that this expense, as your lordship has been pleased to observe, will be cheerfully submitted to."

Since the payment made Arnold after he came in did not include the £210 which his agent Samuel Wallis had been given in July, the traitor got, in cash down, £525 for expenses besides the £6000 compensation which Clinton had authorized in advance and André had promised Arnold at their midnight meeting. The bulk of the money went to London in the form of an order for £5000 on the bankers to the Court, and was invested for £7000 in the funds, at 72¼. A letter from Arnold's broker in January was intercepted and published in American and English newspapers.[46] Franklin, learning in Paris what the price of treason had been, observed in a letter to Lafayette: "Judas sold only one man, Arnold 3,000,000. Judas got for his one man 30 pieces of silver, Arnold not a halfpenny a head. A miserable bargainer."[47]

The bargain, in the long run, was not so miserable as Franklin understood. Arnold valued his house and goods in Philadelphia and his house and farm in Connecticut, all of which were at once confiscated, at more than the amount he received from the British; and he claimed other losses as well. But he certainly was in debt and could think himself worth £6000 in hard money only by counting his most speculative prospects as positive assets. He had been willing to change sides for £10,000 indemnification and £500 annuity for life, in case the scheme miscarried. And though he never ceased complaining about the greatness of his losses and sacrifices and the insufficiency of his rewards, the British actually paid, to him and to his family, more than he had asked for.

Beginning at once, there was his pay as colonel of cavalry, which was about £450 a year, and which after the war became half that for the rest of his life.[48] His further pay as Provincial brigadier (about £200) would customarily have ceased when he went to England in December 1781. But on August 8, 1783, Lord North himself wrote to Sir Guy Carleton, Clinton's successor in the North American command, that "the king allows you to continue Brigadier General Arnold to this time the same emoluments as you have done to other officers of his rank who have continued in America."[49] And though from the peace on Arnold had only a colonel's half pay, his wife and children were already sharing in his rewards.

It is not certain how soon the elder boys began to be paid. But since Arnold in February 1784, complaining that Henry (now over eleven) had so far had nothing, did not speak of the others, they had presumably been provided for. Benedict was promoted lieutenant in July 1783 and had at least half pay till he went on active service against the French in the West Indies, where he died of wounds in October 1795. Richard and Henry, who remained with their aunt in America, drew half pay whether in Canada or in the United States until their deaths: Henry in New York in 1826, Richard in Canada in 1847.[50] Half pay for the two younger was about £75 a year, and Benedict's as much or more. The three had among them something like £225. This, together with their father's half pay, during his lifetime almost made up the £500 annuity Arnold had said he needed for the support of his family. And the half pay of the sons who outlived him went on for nearly half a century longer than any annuity he could have been granted.

Arnold's wife was more amply rewarded than her husband or any of his children. "Our will and pleasure is," the king's warrant informed the paymaster of pensions on March 19, 1782, "and we do hereby direct, authorize, and command, that an annuity or yearly pension of £500 be established and paid by you unto Margaret Arnold, wife of our trusty and well-beloved Brigadier General Benedict Arnold, to commence from the day of the date hereof and continue during our pleasure."[51] She had, as Clinton noted in a memorandum, "obtained for her services, which were very meritorious, £350 per annum."[52] Clinton was not so mistaken about the figure as it appears. Less commissions and fees her pension netted her annually about £360. But besides the pension for Margaret Arnold there was—after July 1783—another of £100 for each of her children. She had had a second son while she was in New York, and from 1783 to 1794 had three more and two daughters, of whom one girl and one boy died in infancy. The five survivors, in time, got £80 net each, or £400.[53]

Half pay totalling £450 (with possible deductions) and pensions finally totalling £1000 (£760 net) gave the increasing Arnold family a yearly income that increased to about £1200, which in the eighteenth century was the equivalent of three or four times as much in the twentieth (roughly $18,000–24,000). And there was the compensation of £6000 (roughly equivalent to $90,000–120,000). No other American officer made as much money out of the war as Arnold did.

Arnold was not satisfied. Drawing up his list of losses for the commissioners on loyalist claims, appointed by Parliament in July 1783, he put in some remarkable items.[54] He had lost £5000, he claimed, by the confiscation of his estate on the Schuylkill. (But through his father-in-law he privately bought it back for less, and in July 1785 believed that land in America must fall off in price.[55]) The house in New Haven, which in June 1780 Arnold said had cost £1800 and he would sell for £1000, he told the commissioners had cost £3000 and was well worth £1800. He declared Connecticut owed him £1125 for depreciation in pay, though his accounts with the state had never been audited; and that Congress owed him £2531, though the treasury auditors had found him overdrawn in his account with the public. If he had remained in the American army to the end of the war he would have been entitled, he said, to £4050 in lieu of half pay for his services and half pay for his disabled leg. Perhaps, he seemed to hint, the British might pay him what he would have earned by fighting them, not merely what he had earned by joining them.

And he had given up further American rewards. He was, he wrote, "also entitled to a considerable quantity of lands promised by the states and Congress, supposed to be worth at a moderate computation £5000 sterling, with other emoluments and advantages which would have arisen to him as third in command in the American army." On a wild chance Arnold put down a preposterous claim. He had been, he said, offered the command in South Carolina which afterwards was given to Greene. Greene, Arnold was informed, "has been rewarded by the states of the Carolinas and Virginia with the sum of £20,000 for his services which would probably" have come to Arnold if he had accepted the southern command. Arnold may have been misinformed about Greene, who had been obliged to expend on his army most of the 10,000 guineas voted him by South Carolina. But Congress had not instructed Washington to choose a successor to Gates in South Carolina till after Arnold's flight, and Greene had been Washington's first choice for the post.[56] Arnold's final claim was based on a rumour and a lie.

Even Arnold seems to have been convinced that he had asked too much of the commissioners, and on April 26, 1785 he himself closed the affair by a letter. "As I have in great measure received (by the hands of Sir Henry Clinton) a compensation for the loss of my personal estate, and as Mrs. Arnold has a pension for life of about £360 which is in some measure, though not a full, compensation for the loss of my real estate, for risks run, and services rendered; yet I have upon duly considering the great expense which I shall probably incur by remaining in London to prosecute a further claim, the loss of time and difficulty attending it, thought proper to withdraw my claim for any further compensation. I have therefore to request that you will be so good as to give orders that my memorial, estimates, and certificates given into your office may be returned to me."[57] They were returned, but somebody in the office took and kept copies of them, as if documents of such enterprising greed must somehow be preserved.

Anticlimaxes

Afterplots

WASHINGTON, on September 27 informing Rochambeau that Arnold had escaped to the British, felt "equal
regret and mortification; but traitors," he observed, "are the
growth of every country, and in a revolution of the present nature
it is more to be wondered at that the catalogue is so small than
that there have been found a few."[1] Though it soon was evident
that Arnold had kept his plot to himself, Washington ordered
certain necessary investigations. Joshua Hett Smith, brought to
trial at Tappan the day after André, was on October 26 acquitted
of the charge of complicity with Arnold. Varick, granted a court
of inquiry at West Point on November 2, was unanimously found,
with Washington's full approval, to have been "unimpeachable"
in his conduct. Franks, who testified at the hearing, made a statement, but was himself exonerated on December 8.[2] Washington
refused to suspect Schuyler or Robert R. Livingston, who had
urged that Arnold be given the West Point command.[3]

Some papers, now missing, came from some unknown source
to Washington and seemed to indicate that General St. Clair,
assigned to West Point on October 1, was involved in treachery.
Colonel Henry Lee, stationed with his dragoons on the lines in
New Jersey, reported on the 13th that there was no proof whatever, and Washington was satisfied.[4] He and Lee believed that a
British emissary named Brown had pretended to have a message
for St. Clair in order to disturb Washington's confidence in another of his generals. But it is not impossible that St. Clair had
really been the object of an attempted offer. Clinton told Chief
Justice Smith on September 28 that there were others "like-
minded with Arnold," and he might have recalled an episode of
the past February.

St. Clair, born in Scotland, had written by a flag to the British Major Charles Lunn, presumably on military business, and had spoken of the loyalist John Small, major of the Royal Highland Emigrants, with whom, according to Lunn, St. Clair hoped to open a correspondence. Small, who was attached to the British general staff, wrote from Headquarters in New York to St. Clair, then at Springfield, New Jersey.[5] "Civil wars," Small wrote, "have ever been the flaw, the malediction, the scourge of human nature. . . . The uniform wish therefore of every truly benevolent friend to mankind must surely be temperately to restore harmony and happiness where they once subsisted, to heal the baneful effects and rankling wounds of wrathful disunion and discord, to bring back parents and children, kindred and friends to the state where God and nature placed them, in tranquil and cordial union and mutual confidence and dependence." Small was, he said, loyal to the best interests of the whole of America, though he was in arms against a part of it. While he hesitated to enter into political discussion, he could not help thinking that St. Clair and he, formerly so intimate, might still be of the same sentiments. If that were so, he would be glad to meet St. Clair half-way.

There is no answer from St. Clair in the British Headquarters files, and probably none came. Nor is there any particular reason to assume, as Small did, that St. Clair ever had a private reconciliation in mind. But here at least was another American major general who had sent a friendly letter to a British officer. Might St. Clair not now, Clinton could speculate, be willing to take Arnold's place in the conspiracy for the surrender of West Point? Lee's guess that the emissary was sent out only to confuse the Americans is no better than the conjecture that he was sent in the hope of reaching St. Clair and influencing him.

Washington made further use of Lee in a scheme to kidnap Arnold, with the "express stipulation" and "pointed injunction" that he must be taken alive. "No circumstance whatever," Washington wrote to Lee on the 20th, "shall obtain my consent to his being put to death. The idea which would accompany such an event would be that ruffians had been hired to assassinate him. My aim is to make a public example of him." That being understood, Washington was willing to leave the rest to Lee's management.[6] Lee, who was twenty-four, arranged that a young Virginia sergeant major of cavalry, John Champe, should desert, get away to New York, enlist in Arnold's Legion, and with the help of two unsuspected patriots in the town capture Arnold some night and take him by boat to the Jersey shore. When Lee wrote his spirited narrative of the undertaking long afterwards[7] he had forgotten so much—and remembered so much incorrectly—that he produced something close to historical fiction.[8] But Champe did desert on the 20th, and on the 23rd was interviewed by someone in the office of the British adjutant general who entered in the Information of Deserters and Others: "John Champe, sergeant major in Major Lee's corps, deserted from Passaic Falls last Thursday night." He gave ready answers about Lee, Lafayette, and "the soldiery very much dissatisfied with the French."[9]

Champe met Arnold "accidentally on the street," was assigned to Arnold's Legion, and laid his plans. According to Lee, Champe soon learned that Arnold was accustomed "to return home about twelve every night, and that previous to going to bed he always visited the garden. During this visit the conspirators were to seize him and, being prepared with a gag, intended to have applied the same instantly. . . . Champe had taken off several of the palings" of the garden fence, "and replaced them, so that with care and without noise he could readily open his way to the adjoining alley. Into this alley he meant to have conveyed his prisoner, aided by his companion. . . . His other associate was with the boat prepared at one of the wharves on the Hudson river, to receive the party. Champe and his friend intended to have placed themselves each under Arnold's shoulder, and to have thus borne him through the most unfrequented alleys and streets to the boat; representing Arnold, in case of being questioned, as a drunken soldier whom they were conveying to the guard-house."

This stealthy design came to nothing, for the reason, as Lee remembered it, that Champe, the day before the night set for the kidnapping, was sent with the rest of Arnold's deserters on board a transport, and did not set foot on land again till the expedition reached Virginia. And Arnold never knew that one of the converted heroes he had welcomed into the Legion watched his goings and comings in the dark and plotted to drag him, gagged and kicking, by shabby ways to a traitor's shabby death.

The hard anger that could make Washington go to such lengths in a plot to get Arnold back and hang him was felt by most of the Continental officers and soldiers, and by the patriot public in general. An effigy of Arnold was carted through the streets of Philadelphia on September 30, and afterwards burned; and similar demonstrations took place in Boston, Providence, and elsewhere.[10] With terrific execration went an upburst of gratitude for what seemed the providential accident which had brought the conspiracy to light. No event in the course of the whole Revolution did so much to intensify patriotic sentiment. After Arnold few patriots could continue to hold in their minds a lingering image of the war as a conflict between political parties. This was between nations, and Arnold had not merely gone over from Whig to Tory but had betrayed—or tried to betray—his country. It was treason, for there was a state to be treasonable to. Arnold as traitor helped fix a powerful new image of the United States in the minds of its people.

The loyalists did not feel the change. If Arnold had come in, other rebel leaders might follow. A deserter on November 26 told the British that the American soldiers had heard "General Greene is gone over to Lord Cornwallis with 700 men. They say they will join General Arnold here the first opportunity."[11] Silas Deane, it was rumoured in New York, had given up France for England. And on December 21st William Smith in his journal commented on what seemed to him encouraging prospects.[12]

Clinton had asked Smith "as to the propriety of giving Arnold a command. I replied that it was prudent as to the rebels, because no American could be ashamed to declare his conversion to him." Every rebel American, in fact, would furiously have denied that he could ever be in agreement with Arnold. Smith had hopes of Schuyler. The *Royal Gazette* of the 18th had published some intercepted American letters. One of them was from Arthur Lee, recently returned from France, who had just been elected to Congress and was already abusing James Duane, member from New York. Lee did not name Duane, and Smith thought Schuyler was referred to. Elizabeth Schuyler had recently been married to Alexander Hamilton. "If Schuyler is with us," Smith reflected, "he may give his daughter to Hamilton to gain a sway over Washington or be in the military plot with him to surrender America back to great Britain and become Monks themselves." Smith need not have known that Arnold had called himself General Monk in his first overtures to Clinton. New York was full of talk of another Monk who might give America back a king. Or possibly Schuyler might "use his sway to ruin both Washington and the Congress; and this seems most probable." But it seemed too good to be true. Smith was "anxious to be satisfied whether Schuyler is the man Lee refers to. Perhaps Duane."

There was even, Smith let himself hope, a chance that Washington might return to his sovereign. Before Smith joined the British in New York he had once talked with John Cochran, "Washington's physician and confidant. . . . I hinted my confidence that these commotions would not separate us from Great Britain; that Washington would one day bring about the reunion and be rewarded with an Irish peerage. I have no doubt of his repeating it to him, nor but that the idea was flattering to his vanity. His wrath at Arnold may be for outrunning him in that race." Here is the unapproachable masterpiece of loyalist guessing: that Washington hated Arnold because Arnold had done first what Washington intended to do.

II

The failure of Arnold's plan did not check such ventures as much as has been thought. While André was still alive at Tappan, William Heron on October 1 wrote to Oliver DeLancey, soon to be André's successor. Heron, it will be recalled, had gone to Arnold's headquarters in August for a flag with which to enter New York on what he said was business, and had at Arnold's urging consented to carry a letter to André; but had instead delivered it to General Parsons of the Connecticut line. This, Heron told DeLancey, was a "precaution which I may say I was providentially influenced to make use of," and thanks to it he "yet retained the confidence of those in high office, consequently can be useful." Whatever his motive may actually have been, he implied to DeLancey that he had turned the letter over to the

Americans in order to convince them of his patriotic zeal. The capture of André had caused difficulties. Heron understood that André, "being deficient in point of fortitude," had given away the secrets of "those whom he knew to be engaged in the same cause with himself. Such conduct in a person of his rank makes those of your friends here shudder and, in their present fright, conclude themselves in danger by holding any correspondence with any person short of the commander-in-chief."

Heron, who fooled every one except possibly himself, was a double-dealer bred by the divided times.[13] Though he had been outwardly an active patriot, a member of the Connecticut legislature, he seems in the dark year 1780 to have determined to come to a secret understanding with the British for the sake of his own security if they should win the war. With DeLancey's help Heron got permission to send a ship through the blockade to his native Ireland, for his own profit. He seems to have obtained this favour by promising to furnish American political and military intelligence and to take British offers to Parsons. "I can know his whole soul," Heron assured DeLancey on December 16, "and hope to improve it to the advantage of the royal cause." Arnold could tell them what kind of man Parsons was. "He is," Heron wrote on March 11, "a person possessed of a low Jesuitical cunning, but far from being a great character. He is in needy circumstances, consequently avaricious."

Parsons, on the American lines above New York, could be very valuable to the British. Like many other American officers, he thought Congress inefficient and the states unenterprising and himself neglected. But he thought of Heron as his own spy and seems to have been unaware of Heron's double-dealing. Heron had, Parsons told Washington after the whole Parsons-Heron episode was over, "as unmeaning a countenance as any person in my acquaintance. . . . An officer in the department of the [British] adjutant general is a countryman and very intimate acquaintance of Mr. Heron, through which channel he has been able frequently to obtain important and very interesting intelligence."[14]

Heron, playing each side against the other, could get a flag from Parsons because Parsons expected the spy to bring back information, and could be favoured by the British because they understood that Parsons, through Heron as intermediary, might be won over. On April 24 Heron, then in New York, wrote DeLancey at length about the response Parsons had made to Heron's discreet overtures. According to Heron, Parsons had said he was "disposed to reconciliation and . . . would use his influence and lend his aid to promote it." But perhaps he ought in honour to give up his American commission before he took his new stand; and certainly "he must have a reasonable and meet compensation for his commission, it being all he had to depend on."

DeLancey the next day noted, in a memorandum, that Heron had promised to get indispensable details about West Point from Parsons. "He is to let me know what Parsons's wish is, how we can serve him, and the methods he means to point out himself. He [Heron] is to tell him he can no way serve us so well as continuing in the army; that the higher his command, the more material service he can render. He is to promise him great rewards for any services he may do us. He is to hold up the idea of Monk to him, and that we expect from his services an end to the war. That during the time he continues in their army he shall have a handsome support, and should he be obliged to fly, to remind him of the example and situation of Arnold." Arnold, DeLancey took it for granted, was to be envied and might be imitated by any sensible rebel.[15]

On the 26th Heron wrote again to DeLancey. He had not yet procured for Parsons the oranges, tamarinds, lemons, and pineapples that had been "the ostensible business for which the flag was granted." It might be, Heron thought, tactful if the fruit could be sent to Parsons "gratuitously, to evince the attention paid to him in the smallest matters." Heron himself was finding his work expensive and would like an advance up to £200. "This will be sufficient to carry me through the summer. Of course I shall make no further applications of this kind till such time as I can render essential service."

On June 20 Heron, again in New York, had another conversation with DeLancey.[16] "Is it your opinion," DeLancey asked, "that General Parsons will enter so heartily as to make us hope he will take an open, determined step in our favour? Should that be the case, you can hold up the situation of General Arnold and say it is in his power to place himself in one equally conspicuous; and as he must lose his present property for a time, the commander-in-chief will, for every man he puts in our possession, pay 3 guineas; or, should he choose it, he [Clinton] will specify the sum that shall be paid on such an event as we shall wish taking place." Clinton had offered Arnold only 2 guineas a head, and had not set a price till Arnold had demanded it. "In the meantime, should he [Parsons] exert himself to give us intelligence, he need only name the recompense, and most punctual attention shall be paid to it." DeLancey assured Heron that "gratitude will prompt us to keep pace, in our recompense to you, with the rewards given to our friend."

Heron had, he said, no authority to say that Parsons "will give up any post or men committed to his care. This in my opinion must depend upon future contingencies, and the adverse turn their affairs are like to take; for, were he sure that independence would take place, his prospects as a general officer would be so great from the country that they would outweigh every other consideration. I have frequently held up Arnold to his view, who (I observed) acquired the esteem, the countenance, and protection of the commander-in-chief, the applause of his brother-officers, and would, in the end, of the nation in general, together with honour and emoluments instead of contempt." But Heron was sure that Parsons would not make a move till he knew what payment he might look forward to. "Whatever you are willing to give shall be my business to safe convey."

On July 15 Heron wrote once more to DeLancey, enclosing a letter to Heron from Parsons, then in camp on the Hudson.[17] Parsons said nothing in his letter that he might not honestly have written to a trusted friend who was also a Connecticut official. But Heron told DeLancey that the information in it was intended for the British, as a sample of what Parsons could furnish. Moreover, Heron said, Parsons wished that if his son William, who had been captured at sea, should be brought into New York, "some provision may be made for him in the British navy, to serve in Europe during the present contest. This is a fact which will enable you [DeLancey] to judge of him for yourself. . . . Our friend manifested a wish that a cask of wine may be sent; however, I gave him not the least encouragement."

A letter from Parsons to his son in Boston, dated near Dobbs Ferry on the 21st, was intercepted by the British and seemed to DeLancey to confirm Heron's assertion that Parsons would like to see his son in the royal navy.[18] What Parsons actually said was: "I have expectations, of which I am not yet certain, of doing something for you [which] will either make you easy at home or at [least] give you the best prospects at sea. I hope in two or three days to be able to decide with certainty. If Mr. Broome [a Connecticut shipowner] will provide for you it will be best, if you are determined to go to sea, as his employ will be certain and enduring. In that case you can come home on a visit at least before you sail. I think your experience will give you, now, some place above that of a common sailor. Mate of a merchantman you can obtain, or some office in a ship-of-war if you insist on going there. I will inform you of some prospects if I see you, which I cannot in a letter."[19]

If DeLancey had not been already told by Heron that Parsons hoped to see his son in the British navy, this letter would have meant to DeLancey that Parsons was referring to an American ship-of-war, as he almost certainly was. But in the circumstances, DeLancey took Heron's word as to Parson's attitude. On July 23 Heron acknowledged £100 sent out for Parsons, but complained of the small amount. "I fear he'll think I have been shuffling with him. . . . When I saw him last I engaged that he should (agreeably to your directions) receive 500 for every one of his dispatches that would be of material consequence." DeLancey on the 31st replied that "we can only be authorized to pay large sums for such information as can be taken advantage of." Parsons had told the British little they did not know. "Our friend knows the secrets of the cabinet and should let us know them, and put us on guard against any enterprise."

There is no evidence that DeLancey sent the additional £400 Heron asked for, or that Parsons ever got—or knew about—the money sent to Heron. And though Heron went on scheming till as late as March 4, 1782,[20] he seems to have brought in nothing more from Parsons which DeLancey would pay Heron for.

Parsons, often disgruntled and resentful, never showed himself disloyal or treacherous. Heron did not profit from his commercial venture. He and his ship were captured by a band of loyalists late in July 1781, and he was for some time a prisoner of war in New York. This was good for his reputation as a patriot.

As the British saw in Parsons a possible Monk to restore the Crown in America, so did they in John Sullivan, though they must have known that he had scorned the overtures of the loyalist Peter Livius in June 1777. Sullivan's health had been so much impaired by the hardships of his expedition against the Six Nations that in November 1779 he resigned from the army. But New Hampshire sent him in September 1780 to Congress where he served with his accustomed vigour. Letters between Sullivan and the president of New Hampshire, intercepted by the British and published in the *Royal Gazette* in New York on December 18 and April 25, 1781, made it known that Sullivan was in serious need of money. La Luzerne, the French minister, sent him an unsolicited loan, realistically expecting that the British might take advantage of his poverty to try to win him from a cause in which he had lost his fortune to one in which he might prosper. The minister considered it his duty to forestall any British move to corrupt the leaders of France's ally.[21]

The British did take that advantage. Sullivan's brother Captain Daniel Sullivan, captured at Sullivan, Maine, in February 1781, was at the end of April a prisoner in New York. A proscribed New Hampshire loyalist also in New York, Captain Stephen Holland of the Prince of Wales regiment, devised a scheme for approaching General Sullivan by sending his brother on parole to Philadelphia to apply for an exchange. There was a plausible excuse for Captain Sullivan's going, and a reasonable chance that General Sullivan might hesitate to send his brother back to a harsh prison. DeLancey consented to the scheme, and Holland wrote a letter which is now first made known.

"When you recollect the friendship that has long subsisted between us I am convinced you will not doubt the sincerity of my intentions; that I most sincerely wish, in friendship to my country and to both countries, that an honourable and lasting reconciliation may take place between Great Britain and this country. . . . Though I have been treated as an enemy to my country by many, I flatter myself you neither view nor would willingly treat me in that light." Holland possibly knew that Sullivan was not in sympathy with the extreme measures taken against the loyalists by some of the states. And Holland assumed that Sullivan might share the common loyalist opinion of some of the rebel leaders. "You know the characters and ambitious views of many who are now in power in this country. Notwithstanding all their pretensions to public spirit, their real ends in view are their own private emolument." Holland repeated in familiar language the familiar arguments for a union with Great Britain as much better for America than an alliance with France.

"I have ventured to represent and name you, my friend, to a person in power here. I ventured to assure him (forgive me if I have gone too far) that you wish a reconciliation, that you will exert yourself to effect this great event. I have represented you as a gentleman of the first abilities and integrity in the government where you live [New Hampshire]. Much, I think, is expected from you in this matter, which I in my conscience believe to be the cause of your country. Pray save the further effusion of the blood of your countrymen. Step forth and let negotiations originate in our province. And I sincerely wish you may have the honour as well as pleasure of restoring peace and happiness to your country."

Holland assured Sullivan that "this shall be kept an inviolable secret, and that no injury can arise to you from this quarter, but many and great advantages." If Sullivan would send "a line by any person you can put confidence in," Holland would be "more explicit in my next. The bearer"—whom Holland nowhere named —"will inform you of many things which I have mentioned to him. If they should meet with your approbation you may be assured everything here will be performed to your satisfaction."

With this careful but unmistakable letter Captain Sullivan went to Philadelphia, returned, and made a report to DeLancey and Holland on May 17.[22] In Captain Sullivan's extravagant, flustered words, General Sullivan "read the letter not less than thirty times. It put him in great confusion and made him shed tears. He said he wished he had received it sooner. He desired

Mr. Sullivan not to forget to say he would do everything in his power to comply with the letter. He said above a hundred times he wished from his heart to bring about a reconciliation. . . . The general said he would ride a hundred miles to have an hour's conversation with Mr. Holland." But though General Sullivan had written an answer "consisting of a whole sheet of paper," he had changed his mind about sending it, for fear it would endanger his brother's life, Captain Sullivan said.

In all this there can have been nothing to convince Holland and DeLancey. And General Sullivan, who consulted La Luzerne, said he had thrown Holland's letter into the fire and rejected the overtures. "I have," Sullivan told La Luzerne, "preserved silence about this matter toward Congress, partly in order not to compromise my brother, partly in order not to make a parade of my own disinterestedness, and partly because I thought it hazardous to announce with too much positiveness to my colleagues that the enemy was seeking a traitor amongst us and that his reward was ready. But I thought to confide to you these particulars, in order to put you on your guard against the enemy's intrigues, even in the very bosom of Congress." There were two unnamed members of Congress who Sullivan thought might be tempted; and La Luzerne agreed with him that it was possible.

Sullivan made what La Luzerne thought "a very strange proposition: to pretend to lend an ear to the overtures that had been made to him, and to send a trusty man to New York to ask of General Clinton a plan of reconciliation; adding that he had been unwilling to use his brother's services, fearing his attachment to the cause of independence. 'I see,' he told me, 'many advantages in thus sounding the disposition of the English, in order to find out what their scheme of corruption may be, and to learn how far they intend to go in their concessions.' And he named to me four members of Congress to whom he proposed to confide his project before putting it into execution—all of them being men of established integrity." La Luzerne disapproved of the risky enterprise, and Sullivan seems never to have undertaken it. It was only, of course, another version of the ruse practised by Schuyler four years before, when he had, after taking counsel with the officers at Ticonderoga, answered Livius's letter to

Sullivan with a letter which pretended to be from Sullivan and aimed to trick secrets out of Burgoyne. Sullivan had then feared that the ruse might miscarry, but he had not objected to it in principle. And he now had reason to be concerned about his brother. Congress, if it suspected Captain Sullivan of wavering motives, would not exchange him. He might be treated with consideration in New York so long as the British thought there was any hope of influencing General Sullivan.

On June 12 Captain Sullivan was again in Philadelphia,[23] with another letter from Holland dated the 9th. "Anxious to profit by the influence you possess," Holland said, "I am induced to request an answer from you to the letter I sent you before. The friendly manner you received it in, and the hopes given by your brother, have opened the most flattering prospect. We should regret the loss of it the more when we consider how much you have in your power and that our wish can only be effected by one in your situation. I communicated the expectation your brother gave me, to the person I mentioned to you, in whose full confidence I am at present; and he has urged me to write to you in the strongest manner. Let me, my dear Sir, conjure you, by the friendship that has subsisted between us, to set yourself seriously to work about so laudable a task. And recollect that in accomplishing it you will equal the great Monk.

"For God's sake, for the sake of your family, say you will assist. I have too much reliance on your honour to doubt it. And reflect in how exalted a station a grateful nation will put the man most instrumental in restoring it to peace and happiness. Your own terms, when you name them, shall be scrupulously adhered to. That no danger may arise from our communication, it is only trusted to your brother, and the greatest pains taken to conceal anything he may carry. His conduct ensures him the protection it deserves, and we shall only make him instrumental till we hear from you and have your advice in what manner to act."

In spite of his poverty, in spite of his concern for his brother, General Sullivan did not follow the course of Monk—or Arnold. For the sake of his brother he kept the negotiations secret, and after his brother's death two or three months later Sullivan was grateful to Holland who "assisted in obtaining his exchange; but while the flagship was in waiting for him a sudden disorder seized him and put an end to his life. Colonel Holland"—Holland had been a colonel in the New Hampshire militia—"attended to his interment and gave me the first intelligence of his death."[24] Such gratitude can mean only that Sullivan was so deeply attached to his brother as to remember Holland's services (however interested they may have been) rather than his proposals. But that attachment had not weakened in Sullivan his strong loyalty to the cause he was enlisted in.

III

Clinton, fixing his hopes on the plan to buy West Point, had for several months paid less than his usual attention to other prospects. After the collapse of his major design he still believed that Ethan Allen and his Vermonters might at any time join the British, and that Rankin and his Pennsylvania loyalists might rise against the rebels. Allen told a British emissary from Canada that he would have no part in any "damned Arnold plan to sell his country and his own honour by betraying the trust reposed in him."[25] But Vermont claimed to be an independent republic, though unrecognized by Congress as even a separate state, and through some of its leaders was carrying on discreet negotiations with Governor Haldimand of Canada. Haldimand, who had known nothing of the Arnold scheme,[26] sent a Canadian army up Lake Champlain in October to divert the Americans from their projected attack on New York. Vermont was not invaded, but tenderly treated as neutral.

The Rankin conspiracy came to fresh life at the news of Arnold's failure: not, presumably, because the plan had failed but because Rankin learned that Clinton had meant to act and might mean to again. On October 14 Rankin and his associates in Pennsylvania, Delaware, and Maryland drew up an address to the king and sent it to André's friend Simcoe of the Queen's Rangers, hoping he might carry it to London and be appointed to lead an expedition to the Chesapeake to co-operate with the loyalists in that region. There were now 7000 of them, the address said, who needed only confidence and support to make them highly useful to the royal cause. Applying to Simcoe, they implied that they had more faith in him than in Clinton. Simcoe forwarded the address to Clinton on November 2, commending it and wishing he might be allowed to go to the Chesapeake.[27] Clinton, sending Simcoe to Virginia with Arnold in December, supposed that that might partly meet the requirements of Rankin's followers.

In November the Associated Loyalists, with William Franklin as president, were finally given their commission to make war in armed bands under their own officers. Clinton on the advice of William Smith withheld some of the powers the board asked for. Franklin in letters to Clinton of December 1 and 18 explained the board's desires. "We wished for more extensive powers merely that the operations of the loyalists might be conducted in the future on a larger and more beneficial scale than they have yet been. Hitherto they have chiefly been confined to the exertions of the lower class of refugees. To engage those of superior stations to take an active part likewise, a more liberal plan seemed to us essentially necessary." Many loyalists would come in if they had "any means of supporting themselves without enlisting as soldiers or being a burden to government." This was an official way of saying that the superior loyalists, embittered though they naturally were by rebel treatment of them, would take an active retaliatory part only if they could count on freer methods and bigger plunder than inferior loyalists had been satisfied with.

"We conceive it, indeed, absolutely necessary to that predatory kind of war proposed to be carried on by the associators, that a latitude of command be allowed to their officers, when on excursion, to conduct themselves as circumstances may seem to them to require"—without too much thought of what Headquarters would approve. And the loyalists particularly wanted to deal with their own prisoners. "It is a matter of public notoriety, and has been a subject of grievous complaint, that the colonial loyalists when captured by the rebels have been generally far worse treated than the king's other subjects; and in many instances instead of being considered as prisoners of war have been executed as traitors: a practice which cannot be stopped or prevented but by retaliation. . . . A power to treat the rebel prisoners in every respect neither better nor worse than they treat the loyalists is all that is asked."

The Declaration of the Associated Loyalists, published in the *Royal Gazette* on December 30, announced that all goods taken would be the entire property of the loyalist captors (except when they acted in conjunction with the king's forces) and that all their rebel prisoners would be exchanged only for loyalists operating under the board. From now on the rebels along the Jersey and Connecticut coasts might expect more frequent and more thoroughgoing raids. The ruthless and successful war in South Carolina the past year furnished the northern loyalists an example, and Greene had not yet been long enough in the southern command to make it seem possible that victory might yet turn to the American side.

Loyalists took the lead in the reorganization of the secret service under the new adjutant general, Major Oliver DeLancey. Though he held his commission in the British 17th regiment, he was American-born, member of a powerful New York loyalist family, and son of the Oliver DeLancey who was senior brigadier general of Provincials. Major DeLancey, the loyalist Colonel Beverley Robinson, and Captain George Beckwith, British aide to General Knyphausen, early in 1781 drew up undated Proposals for a Plan of Gaining Intelligence. They would, their Proposals said, "endeavour to open a correspondence with persons of consequence in different parts of the country. . . . All persons employed by us and who produce passes from us or either of us should neither be examined nor detained by any officers at the advanced posts, either in going out or returning. All intelligence received to be regularly entered in a book kept for that purpose." That book, largely in the hand of Beckwith and marked Private Intelligence,[28] still survives, along with a supplementary volume called Information of Deserters and Others not included in Private Intelligence.[29]

The Information of Deserters and Others had apparently been begun while André was adjutant general, and continued after the ominous entry, undated, of what a certain Jeremiah Hopkins had said of the Americans: "They will hang the officer they have in their possession as a spy. They have a report that the officer is

adjutant general to the British army . . . and that General Washington had sent a flag to General Clinton to say that General
Arnold must be etc. etc." And another entry told of the arrival on
January 5 of one of André's late collaborators. "Mr. Joseph Stansbury, from Philadelphia, left it the 28th December, came to the
Philadelphia galley the 31st, and to town last evening; has been
banished from Philadelphia. . . . He was in jail in Philadelphia
for six months, said to be for treasonable practices." Whoever entered this can hardly have suspected that Stansbury had had anything to do with Arnold, as the Philadelphia authorities had not
known.

Many pages in both manuscript volumes are given to reports
on the mutiny of the Pennsylvania line which broke out at Morristown on January 1 and which seemed to the hopeful British—
as to fearful Americans—to mean that the whole rebellion might
collapse.

What happened was that about 2400 non-commissioned officers
and men, in winter quarters under the command of Anthony
Wayne, on the evening of New Year's day suddenly rose and got
control of the camp. They had as good grievances as mutineers
ever had. They had not been paid for a year; they had had the
poorest food and worse clothing; and they had come to believe
that those among them who had enlisted for three years or for the
duration of the war were all to be held if the war lasted longer
than their three years, whether they chose or not. They had
shown, Wayne said, a "more than Roman virtue," but they now
demanded that something be done for them by the country they
served. They elected a representative committee of sergeants,
marched with remarkable discipline to Princeton and then to
Trenton, and waited there till Congress and Pennsylvania met
their demands. They permitted Wayne, whom they admired and
liked, to stay with them. They gave up two emissaries sent from
Clinton, to be hanged as spies on the verdict of a court martial.
According to Wayne, the mutineers had no "idea of turning
Arnolds (as they express it)."[30] As one of the sergeants put it:
"The path we tread is justice, and our footsteps founded upon
honour."[31] Though by the final settlement about half the Pennsylvania line (more than were entitled to their discharge) left the

service, the mutiny did not spread as even Washington was afraid it might do. A smaller disturbance in the New Jersey line later in the month was promptly put down by troops commanded by Robert Howe, who hanged two of the ringleaders.

How grave the matter looked for several days may be seen in letters Washington wrote from Headquarters at New Windsor on the Hudson above West Point. On first receiving the news, at noon on the 3rd, he said he would set out for Morristown and Princeton (on his way to Philadelphia) the next day. But at seven on the morning of the 4th he had been "advised by such of the general officers as I have seen not to leave this post in the present situation of things, temper of the troops, and distress of the garrison for want of flour, clothing, and in short everything." Better, he seems to have reasoned, to stay where his presence would probably check the further spread of mutiny than to go where mutiny already was, and risk appearing there "without the means of enforcing obedience." He could not feel sure that even his troops "were to be depended upon in a serious and spirited attempt to quell others" whose grievances were the same as their own.[32]

If Washington could be so uncertain of the outcome, the British and loyalists in New York had good reason for the sudden hope which came to them on the morning of the 3rd with the news of the mutiny at Morristown. Orders were sent to British and Hessian regiments on Long Island "to hold themselves in readiness to march at a moment's notice," according to the Journal of the affair kept at Headquarters.[33] A more energetic general than Clinton might have crossed at once into New Jersey and attacked the disorganized mutineers, willing either to capture or to kill them. Clinton, hurrying to Staten Island, preferred to wait a day for further information, and then to make a more peaceful effort. On the evening of the 4th "three copies of the following proposals were sent off to the revolters, one by the Raritan river, the others by Newark and Elizabethtown:

"It being reported at New York that the Pennsylvania troops and others, having been defrauded of their pay, clothing, and provisions, are assembled to redress their grievances, and also that notwithstanding the terms of their enlistments are expired they have been forcibly detained in the service where they have suffered every kind of misery and oppression,

"They are now offered to be taken under the protection of the British government, to have their rights restored, free pardon for all former offences, and that pay due to them from the Congress faithfully paid to them, without any expectation of military service (except it may be voluntary), upon laying down their arms and returning to their allegiance. For which purpose, if they will send commissioners to Amboy they will there be met by people empowered to treat with them and faith pledged for their security.

"It is recommended to them for their own safety to move behind South river, and whenever they request it a body of British troops shall protect them.

"It is needless to point out the inability as well as want of inclination in the Congress to relieve them, or to tell them the severities that will be used towards them by the rebel leaders should they think of returning to their former servitude.

"It will be proved to the commissioners they may choose to send that the authority from whence this comes is sufficient to ensure the performance of the above proposals."

The next day six battalions of light infantry and British and Hessian grenadiers were moved from Long Island to Staten Island and cantoned near the Jersey ferries. But instead of ordering them to cross Clinton sent three more copies of the proposals "and a verbal message to the same import to the Pennsylvanians." He believed the mutineers might join the British if they were coaxed, might turn against them if they were threatened. Clinton was thinking not only of these particular mutineers but also of the entire American army. If he marched to Princeton, and the mutinous troops did not come over to him, he would—no matter what damage he might inflict—probably stiffen the resolution of the rebels in general. For the present he would wait to see what effect his proposals had.

Meanwhile, DeLancey tried other schemes. If deserters from West Point could be found who would go to Princeton and say they had deserted on purpose to join the mutiny there, and would come back to report, he would give them as high as 100 guineas each. Or if men of property would go they might have twice as much, "provided they will make use of artifice to find out their intention and turn them to us. The reward of the person that succeeds shall be unlimited."[34] Beckwith notified DeLancey that Christopher Sower would go, but thought the best man for the enterprise would be Samuel Wallis.

Wallis after the flight of Arnold had not been even suspected in Philadelphia, but had continued his secret correspondence through Daniel Coxe in New York. Beckwith thought Wallis "from mercantile ideas will undertake anything of that nature. But he will expect to have a fixed consideration for his trouble at all events, and an additional gratuity in case of succeeding." There was a messenger who could be almost sure to get a letter to him; "and Sower will conceal it in such a manner as to render a cipher useless."[35] Wallis in Philadelphia had already made up his mind that this mutiny would fail.[36] The mutineers, he pointed out, had not gone to the enemy but had let themselves be drawn to Trenton to confer with Congress and Pennsylvania. And Wallis knew that the two British emissaries had been hanged at a crossroads beyond the Delaware opposite Trenton on the 10th.

On the 15th Jonathan Odell, who had deciphered so many of Arnold's letters, reported that John Rattoon, who had carried so many of them, had brought word of the execution. The bearer of the proposals was John Mason (alias sometimes Haynes, sometimes Morris, sometimes Murphy), a sergeant in Major William Odell's Loyal American Rangers. (It is possible that he was the John Mason who in March 1779 had issued his private Warning to Rebels that the loyalists would henceforth hang six rebels for every loyalist so dealt with.) Mason, according to Jonathan Odell, "was guided by a person procured by Rattoon to South river, from there by one [James] Ogden to the camp of the Pennsylvanians."[37] Ogden was held to be equally guilty with Mason, and suffered the same fate. Two other emissaries, so far undetected, were among the Pennsylvanians when this took place. They dropped their proposals in the camp and escaped.

Clinton, at last convinced that the mutineers showed no disposition to join the British, returned from Staten Island to New York and on the 19th ordered the troops back to their Long Island quarters. And though the abortive revolt of the New Jersey line seemed promising for a few days, on the 29th he wrote to Germain that the malcontents had wanted chiefly to be out of military service, not at all to change sides. "Nothing but coercive measures or gross chicane on the part of Congress could have induced [them] to join us."

Arnold, at the first rumours of the affair, wrote to Clinton from Virginia on the 23rd: "I am happy to hear of the revolt of so great a part of Mr. Washington's army. This event, I make no doubt, will be attended with happy consequences. We anxiously wait in expectation of hearing that the malcontents have joined his Majesty's forces in New York." But Arnold had to admit that in Virginia "the country people have not come in in numbers, as expected."

IV

After the settlement of the January mutinies the British secret service was never again so busy, though DeLancey, Beverley Robinson, and Beckwith kept up the Information of Deserters and Others till March 26 and Private Intelligence till July 19. But in those books and in the Headquarters files there are frequent records of treacherous intelligence sent in and stealthy attempts made on promising rebels.

Samuel Wallis, most secretive of all the informers, continued his letters to Daniel Coxe for the benefit of the Associated Loyalists.[38] At the same time, possibly without Coxe's knowledge, Wallis seems to have been in correspondence also with Captain Beckwith. Beckwith, who had met Wallis when he came in to get Arnold's first payment and had recommended him to DeLancey during the excitement over the mutiny at Morristown, sent offers which a Gentleman in Philadelphia acknowledged in an undated letter copied by Beckwith on April 25. "I thank his Excellency," the Gentleman in Philadelphia said, "for his offer of the 200 guineas annually and accept it as a mark of his approbation for my conduct. I also thank him for his further offer of paying me for any essential service which I may render to government." Beckwith on May 15 had received several letters from the Gentleman[39] and had

begun to reward him. "I have paid the 50 guineas to Mr. ——
and I will always attend to your wishes in that respect. I conclude
you are too prudent to draw any bills upon me, for your own
sake." The Gentleman in Philadelphia replied on the 22nd that
he would indeed not give a written order to be negotiated "by any
other than those who already know our connexion, nor would I
wish the knowledge to go further."

Wallis writing to Coxe and the Gentleman writing to Beckwith
might date their letters the same day or on occasion use the same
words for the same news. "The present appearance of crops all
over the middle colonies are as great as they ever were in the
world," the Gentleman informed Beckwith on June 19. And on
the 27th Wallis informed Coxe: "There never was so great an appearance of crops since the settlement of North America as is at
present all over the middle colonies."[40] But on the whole Wallis
wrote to Coxe about finance and shipping, while the Gentleman
in Philadelphia transmitted—in cipher—to Beckwith a good
many secrets of Congress that he could have got only from intimate acquaintance with members.[41]

Presumably because Wallis insisted on it, Beckwith seems to
have deciphered the Gentleman's letters and to have filed only
the copies in his own hand, without any mention whatever of the
Gentleman's name. The Gentleman was cautious at the other
end of the line. He was one of the owners of the Philadelphia
brigantine *Adventure* which was captured and taken into New
York. The British prize master, the Gentleman complained to
Beckwith, had declared in the hearing of the crew that the *Adventure* had been sent out by illicit traders for the purpose of
being taken. Though this was true, it was a dangerous secret. The
news of it, getting back to Philadelphia, had made trouble. "What
the event will be when the hands return, God knows. I fear the
ostensible owners of her will be obliged to go over to you, at
least"—if not imprisoned for forbidden trading. "I stand very clear
of suspicions myself, having always kept a good Whig between
me and those matters."

The Gentleman pointed out that if naval officers were to handle these delicate transactions so crudely, "the encouragement for
people to risk their lives in supplying your garrison with provi-

sions is really bad. If protection and encouragement was given, you might certainly supply your whole army with flour from this quarter. This I apprehend would not only supply you with it cheaper than you get it from Europe, but it would be taking off hundreds of our busy men and bringing them over to your interest. The war in America is now become a mere partisan war; therefore it then remains with you to make use of every political means in your power to bring over to your party as many as possible of the inhabitants."

There can be little doubt that the Gentleman in Philadelphia was sly Samuel Wallis. As there can be no doubt that Wallis was Arnold's agent and sent secret intelligence to the British, neither can there be that he (if he was the Gentleman) had no scruple about making any money he could out of shipping the British army of occupation food with which to carry on the war. But in Philadelphia Wallis went on expertly pretending to be a Whig. So long as Congress should be in power he would stand well with the patriots. If the British forces should put the rebellion down, then he could prove that he had long been a useful loyalist.

While Beckwith collected information from New Jersey and Pennsylvania, Beverley Robinson looked northward, as far as to the Vermont border. In April and May 1780 he had sent Ethan Allen two copies of a letter which did not reach him till July and which had brought no answer. On February 2, 1781 Robinson sent a copy of his former letter, with further assurances.[42] Now, as before, he believed and hoped that Allen and the Vermonters "would willingly assist in uniting America again to Great Britain and restoring that happy constitution we have so wantonly and unadvisedly destroyed. . . . I am inclinable to think that one reason why this unnatural war has continued so long is that all the Americans who wish and think it would be for the interest of the country to have a constitutional and equitable connexion with Great Britain do not communicate their sentiments to each other so often and freely as they ought to do. . . . If you should think it proper to send proposals to me to be laid before the commander-in-chief, I do now give you my word that if they are not accepted of or complied with by him (of which I will inform you), the matter shall be buried in oblivion between us."

But now, more than before, Robinson felt confident that Vermont and Allen desired to join the king's cause. And Robinson could offer assurance that Vermont might be made a "separate government under the king and constitution of England," and its militia put on a Provincial footing, if the Vermonters would "take an active part with us." He would be glad to hear from Allen how the correspondence might be managed and whether it would be better for him to act with the Canadian army against the rebels or with Clinton's.

A loyalist who had escaped from a rebel jail carried the letter by way of Long Island, Bridgeport, and Williamstown to his brother's house, two miles from Allen's at Arlington, and got his brother to deliver it on the 20th.[43] Allen read it and said it called for no reply. The messenger returned to New York. Allen on March 9 wrote to Congress, enclosing the copies of the two letters.[44] "I am confident," he said, "that Congress will not dispute my sincere attachment to the cause of my country." But he declared that Vermont had a right "to agree on terms of cessation of hostilities with Great Britain, provided the United States persist in rejecting her application for union with them." Congress could not expect Vermont to defend the independence of states (New Hampshire and New York) which claimed "full liberty to overturn and ruin the independence of Vermont. . . . I am as resolutely determined to defend the independence of Vermont as Congress are that of the United States; and rather than fail will retire with hardy Green Mountain Boys into the desolate caverns of the mountains and wage war with human nature at large." There, Allen said, he could live on "mouse meat."

Though Allen and a few other Vermont politicians continued their complex horse-trading with Congress and the governor of Canada, and in time may have come to think that an alliance with Great Britain would be more profitable than admission to the United States, they seem never to have gone beyond claims to independence of either country till after the treaty which ended the war. So far as treacherous assistance was concerned, Robinson had no more success with Allen than DeLancey had with either Parsons or Sullivan.

Washington, who watched everything, wrote to Schuyler on

May 14 about the attitude of the "Vermontese," and on February 22 requested Parsons to look out for the rumoured danger of a loyalist uprising in Connecticut.[45] It was reported to Washington that John Connolly, who in the first year of the war had conspired with the royal governor of Virginia and had been long a prisoner but lately exchanged, was conspiring again: this time to enlist the disaffected in the neighbourhood of Fort Pitt and dominate the Pennsylvania border. Washington on April 25 instructed the commandant at Fort Pitt to "secure or remove" all persons near by who could not be trusted.[46] Connolly, who the past November (within a month after his exchange) had laid his plans for a western insurrection before Clinton,[47] was sent by Clinton to Cornwallis in Virginia the following June. "Your lordship," Clinton wrote on the 9th, "is possibly acquainted with Colonel Connolly's sufferings. They have been great, as he can inform your lordship." Cornwallis made little use of Connolly, who was in three months once more a prisoner and was released in March 1782. only on his promise to leave America for England.

The loyalists on the West Branch of the Susquehanna, who had applied to Simcoe as well as to Clinton, were so much suspected in March 1781 that their leader William Rankin was imprisoned, and on his escape had to go for safety to New York. There on April 27 he drew up a set of proposals which still survive in his hand, with a copy by Beverley Robinson and notes by Clinton. It was a plan "for subduing the rebellion in the provinces of Pennsylvania, Maryland, and the lower counties on Delaware and reuniting those provinces to Great Britain." The British were to land 2000 men at Chester or Wilmington and 10,000 stands of arms, and the people of the district "encouraged to rise by companies, with officers chosen by themselves, and authorized to seize magazines, etc., and officers acting under usurped authority." To this Clinton added a cynical stipulation: "Rankin must engage that they would rise." Clinton evidently did not believe they could be counted on, and he would not commit himself.

On April 30 he wrote to General Phillips in Virginia. "I do not now send Colonel Rankin to you (as I at first proposed), but I enclose his proposals. You will see by them that he is not much of an officer. But he appears to be a plain sensible man worth attending to, and Simcoe can explain a thousand things respecting him and his association which I cannot in a letter. . . . Pray let me have General Arnold's and your opinion upon Colonel Rankin's proposal as soon as possible. I confess I am not sanguine."

This letter reached Phillips when he was too ill to deal with it (he died in May). Cornwallis assumed command in Virginia. On May 26 he wrote to Clinton that Arnold would soon return to New York and could deliver his sentiments in person. "Experience has made me less sanguine, and more arrangements seem to me necessary for so important an expedition than appears to occur to General Arnold." Arnold might be willing to risk a desperate raid, but Cornwallis had concluded, after more than a year in the Carolinas, that the British could not afford to go anywhere except "in respectable force. By the vigorous exertions of the present governors of America large bodies of men are soon collected; and I have too often observed that when a storm threatens our friends disappear."

This had been the experience of all the British generals. Germain insisted that if only they would go among the rebels and raise the royal standard, loyalists would come in by companies, regiments, corps, as the superior loyalists in London and New York promised Germain. But the generals did not find it to be true. While there was always in any district some small group of loyalists who said an army of them were ready to rise as soon as they were authorized, they never (except in up-country South Carolina) rose on any encouragement that any commander-in-chief was able or willing to give them. Clinton was no Arnold, eager to take chances. Rankin, who for three years had given all his energies to his plan, saw it come to nothing and except for one futile brief visit to Virginia had to remain idle in New York.

But not quite idle. In September he seems to have asked a friend in Philadelphia (who was just possibly Samuel Wallis) to find out where the secret papers of Congress were kept. The friend replied that they were, he understood, now in the care of the president of Congress. "I have been taking a view of the president's secretaries. They are young, and have so much of the boy about them as to make it very ticklish to meddle with them." The friend gave as his opinion that the rising in the peninsula—of the members of Rankin's association—depended on Cornwallis's fate. If he were to be overcome, "the friends of government will generally so far sink in their spirits as to give up all hopes of ever seeing an agreeable conclusion to the war."[48]

Yet that same month or early the next a belated memorial came to Clinton from "farmers and inhabitants" of Albany county who announced that, "daily most pitifully tossed about by the furious waves of sedition and rebellion," they would be glad "to spill our blood . . . whenever we can see a prospect of being supported by his Majesty's troops." The agent was Samuel Hake, and 70 of them had signed the memorial "for and in behalf of many hundred of his Majesty's faithful and loyal subjects." If Clinton would promise to co-operate with them they would rise on a day set, disarm their rebel neighbours, and move against the rebel works at West Point. Or if Clinton did not wish them to be in arms when he advanced against the fortress, and would give them warning, they would avoid service in the hated rebel militia. "In this case the friends to government are, as nearly the time of such attack as circumstances will permit, to receive the countersign *Eagle* and then skulk."

Another scheme, offered to Clinton at about the same time, was no more effectual though it had the support of George III and Lord North. Silas Deane, at last worn out by the long wrangle with Congress over his accounts, had returned to Paris in July 1780 and gone in February the next year to Antwerp. Apparently while there, probably through Paul Wentworth again, he resumed his negotiations with the British government. "I think it perfectly right," the king wrote to North on March 3, "that Mr. Deane should be so far trusted as to have £3000 in goods for America." Through him at least one of the provinces might "offer to return to their allegiance." The king was willing to try and to let Deane be suitably rewarded.[49]

Instead of going to America on these terms Deane chose to write letters to various Americans in favour of reunion with Great Britain. He wrote—or at any rate dated—them during May and June, in Paris, and sent them to North for his approval. North on July 19 forwarded them to the king. They were "written with so much zeal for a reconciliation that they will, Lord North fears, have too much the air of being written in concert with this country." The king agreed with North and thought the letters "not likely to have the effect as if they bore another aspect." But the originals were sent to Clinton by warship and copies of them by packet, with instructions from North himself.

The letters, North wrote on August 3, had "fallen" into his hands. He did not say how or why. "Perhaps you may think it right to publish all or some of them in America if the colonies are (as very probably they may be) disgusted at the conduct of France and tired of the war. . . . There are probably several persons in New York acquainted with the handwriting of Mr. D. who will be able to verify the letters, if the author should think proper to disown them; which, though he seems to write with great earnestness, he possibly may when he finds that they are intercepted and published." North would not let even Clinton into the full secret of Deane's connivance. "One thing, however, I must earnestly recommend to you: that you do not mention receiving these intercepted letters from me or any person in Great Britain. Leave the readers to guess where they were intercepted. The authenticity of the letters will be apparent, and there is no reason to gratify the impertinent curiosity of any reader as to any other point."[50]

Clinton could hardly suppose that the interception had been altogether accidental. But here were eleven letters written by a formerly conspicuous patriot who was now urging—on Robert Morris, Charles Thomson, Benjamin Tallmadge, and others—unexceptionable, even extreme loyalist arguments. The first of the letters was published in the *Royal Gazette* on October 24—five days after Cornwallis capitulated at Yorktown.

V

Arnold, setting out on his expedition to Virginia in December 1780, appeared to be in circumstances precisely suited to his talents and his motives. He was in a separate command with a positive aim: to conquer rebel territory and damage rebel property. This would allow him not only to distinguish himself in the king's service but also to take revenge on the cause he had deserted and therefore hated. And the expedition was a raid on a scale which promised that he might make a fortune in happy prize money.

But from the first he had a less free hand than he could have wished—or than he knew. Clinton in his instructions on the 14th told Arnold: "Having sent Lieutenant Colonels Dundas and Simcoe, officers of great experience and much in my confidence, with you, I am to desire that you will always consult those gentlemen previous to your undertaking any operation of consequence." But Clinton did not tell Arnold that the same day he gave Thomas Dundas and Simcoe "a blank dormant commission which is only to be made use of in case of the death or incapacity of Brigadier General Arnold to execute the duties of the command which is entrusted to his direction. You are upon no account to make known that you are possessed of such a commission, or open the same, except in the cases above mentioned; and if this should not happen, you are to transmit this commission to me unopened."

While Clinton was taking natural precautions to ensure the command, he was at the same time arranging for British control over Arnold and his loyalist troops. Though Arnold had the British 8th regiment and 100 Hessians, with a detachment of royal artillery, more than half his command were loyalists: besides the handful he had recruited in the American Legion, Simcoe's well-trained Queen's Rangers, Beverley Robinson's Loyal Americans, and 30 of Robinson's Guides and Pioneers. Their grievances were sure to make them vengeful and perhaps disorderly. Clinton, proclaiming the king's peace in Virginia and offering pardon to all rebels who would come in, wanted to carry, as William Smith said, "the olive branch with the sword." Arnold's loyalists must not be permitted to wage war with indiscriminate violence.

The expedition sailed on the 21st, and Arnold on the voyage agreed with the ship commanders that all prize goods taken either in the Virginia rivers or on shore were to be equally divided between the army and the navy.[51] In this there was nothing unusual. Prize money was an accepted part of soldiers' pay during the war, in both armies. For example, Wayne's dashing capture of Stony Point in July 1779 brought his men profit as well as renown. All the military stores there captured were sold and the proceeds, amounting to more that $140,000, divided among "the gallant troops in such manner and proportion as the commander-in-chief shall prescribe."[52] Many of Arnold's loyalists had had property taken from them by the rebels and hoped for compensation in the form of prizes. But Arnold and his men found themselves involved in the perennial conflict of British army and navy claims.

With immense energy Arnold in Virginia overran all resistance and captured or destroyed whole magazines and warehouses of public and private stores. Thomas Jefferson, then governor of the state, offered a reward of 5000 guineas for the capture of Arnold. Washington ordered Lafayette, sent to Virginia to oppose the traitor, to put him summarily to death if he should be captured. Hated by the Americans, Arnold was perhaps envied by some of the British officers for his successes, and certainly censured for his greed. "The love of money, his ruling passion," it was reported in New York, "has been very conspicuous in Virginia."[53] Though no figures are available, Arnold got less prize money than he expected, and fewer rebel penitents coming in to make their peace. He was restive when on post duty at Portsmouth, which he was required to fortify and hold. "A life of inaction," he wrote to Clinton on January 23, "will be very prejudicial to my health." In April he was superseded in the command by William Phillips, who had come from New York with reinforcements. When, during Phillips's illness, the command devolved on Arnold, Dundas suavely wrote to Clinton on May 12 that while there could be no doubt of Arnold's "abilities and inclination . . . yet, Sir, there are many officers who must wish some other general officer had this command." The command passed to Cornwallis, and Arnold was back in New York on June 10. Along with the prizes taken by the expedition he brought his American Legion and Beverley Robinson's Loyal Americans, because the men had deserted so fast in Virginia they could no longer be trusted there.[54]

Arnold's summer was frustration. Though he obtained a major for his Legion, Thomas Menzies of New York, and another captain, Baron de Ottendorf who had deserted from the Americans, the Legion's rank and file on November 1 numbered only 212, with 684 "wanting to complete." On August 1 William Smith noted in his journal: "General Arnold is discouraged. He

despairs from the defect of a spirit of enterprise and indecision"
—in Clinton. "He can get nothing done. He is desirous to go
home"—to England—"to get into other employments. Sir Henry
is all mystery, seems to approve but changes and resolves nothing.
. . . He [Arnold] is chagrined beyond expression. I advised his
making proposals in writing and dissuaded him from quitting
the service."

Arnold particularly urged Clinton to attempt the capture of
West Point, which the two had discussed by letter while Arnold
was still in Virginia.[55] But Clinton on August 24 represented
Arnold as unenterprising. "General Arnold about a month since
called upon me and told me that he had a man ready that would
give us every information relative to the forts" on the Hudson.
"I desired him to employ him, and I told him I was willing to
attempt them by a *coup de main* provided Washington was at
a safe distance. . . . I have often asked that general since whether
he had any news from thence, but he has not said a word to me
upon the subject. I believe it was done that he might write the
minister [Germain], as usual."[56]

On August 28 Margaret Arnold had a second son, and on
September 5 Arnold left New York for another raid: this time
on New London in his native Connecticut. The raid was very
successful and very destructive, though the army, according to
Smith, complained that their loss was greater than the rebels'.[57]
Arnold was still discontented. On November 5, after the surrender of Yorktown, he had a conversation with Clinton, who
afterwards gave a memorandum of it to a secretary.

"The brigadier told his Excellency that he was come to renew
his solicitations for leave to go to Europe. To which the General
made answer that before he could part with an officer of his merit
he must either have a good reason to assign for it or a certainty
of this post's being in no danger of being attacked this winter.
That when the French fleet was certainly gone off the coast, and
all apprehension of that sort subsided, he should with pleasure
comply with his wishes of leave for the winter when a ship
offered. The conversation then turned upon the present state of
affairs, and the brigadier said he by no means despaired of matters
being yet to be recovered. Which the General said he concurred

with him on if administration sent immediately proper reinforcements of troops with an adequate fleet to co-operate with them." Here Clinton complained that the government in London had regularly thwarted him. "The General then said that he thought the brigadier ought not to trust himself in any but a king's ship, and before he went, he would write a letter to desire that he would not return to this country again unless administration sent over ample reinforcements to carry on the service."[58]

Repeating this conversation to Smith, Arnold gave another colour to it. "He artfully told the General he should recommend a reinforcement of 20,000 men and promised to be back in March, though he tells me he never will return until he is in the command." Clinton, by what he said about the government, had "opened himself incautiously to Arnold," who would now take advantage and would intrigue against Clinton in London.[59] Smith, Arnold's chief adviser, furnished him on December 10 with "notes for answers to questions that may be put to him," probably the basis of Arnold's *Thoughts on the American War— by an American.*[60]

On December 15 Arnold, not safe in any ship likely to be taken by the enemy, sailed in the *Robuste* with Cornwallis, who ever since Yorktown had been at bitter odds with Clinton. Arnold's wife and children, another lady from Philadelphia commented, went "in a private ship, as more agreeable for her than a man-of-war. . . . They give for the cabin 300 guineas and then took in what company they chose, chiefly military I believe. I do not hear of any females but her maid."[61]

Sequels

IN SPITE of the king's desperate hopes, and the loyalists' more desperate fears, there was no reasonable prospect, after York-town, that the British government would continue the war. Germain was removed from his post as secretary for the colonies, Clinton replaced by Sir Guy Carleton as commander-in-chief in North America. Parliament on March 5 resolved against further offensive operations, and on the 27th the Whig Rockingham succeeded the Tory North as first minister.

Clinton, commanding in New York till the arrival of Carleton in May 1782, made little use of his secret service, and probably had no such confidence in DeLancey as he had had in André. What was intended to be the fullest statement of André's case had not been published. After Congress in October 1780 printed the *Proceedings . . . respecting Major John André* Clinton authorized the Rev. Charles Inglis, rector of Trinity, to prepare an answer. *The Case of Major John André,* its preface dated November 28, was in press on December 21, and William Smith saw the proofs on January 8. But General Robertson objected to it because of its account of his mission to Dobbs Ferry to confer with General Greene. Others at Headquarters may have objected on other grounds. The pamphlet survives in a single copy, part of it only proof sheets.[1]

André's memory had little need of Inglis's passionate argument, with its intemperate abuse of Washington. The king gave a life pension to André's mother and sisters, conferred a baronetcy on his brother, and caused a monument to the fallen hero to be erected in Westminster Abbey. Both nations have remembered him with regret and affection, though it is in America that legend and ballad and drama and biography have done most to keep his fame alive. Compared with him, Clinton has come to seem dim and remote. After his return to England he fought his battles over again, exchanged pamphlets with Cornwallis about the responsibility for Yorktown, and wrote a history of his American campaigns in two volumes which are still unpublished.[2] In 1794 Clinton was made governor of Gibraltar and died there the year following.

No official statement about Arnold was undertaken by the British, and the single monument ever raised to him by an American—at Saratoga—calls him "the most brilliant soldier of the Continental army" but does not mention his name. Nor did England give him, besides pay and pensions, the emoluments and honours he had looked forward to. Unable to obtain a command in the British army, he was only a half-pay colonel scheming for a larger income. Margaret Arnold, praised for her beauty, came to look— in Sir Thomas Lawrence's portrait of her—like any pretty young woman of fashion; but she too felt the need of money and wrote much about it in her letters.

Arnold was obsessed by a desire to make some large, quick fortune which would satisfy his terrible restlessness and bring security to his family. Without military or official employment, he turned to commerce, was at Halifax in his own brig loaded with his own goods in November 1785, and that winter established himself as merchant-shipper at St. John, New Brunswick. There he bought the first vessel built in the province, to which loyalist refugees had come in hopeful numbers from the United States, and set out for a long cruise to the West Indies and back to London. It was probably at St. John that he found the unknown woman by whom he had the illegitimate son, called John Sage, whom Arnold remembered in his will.[3] Since the will, dated August 30, 1800, spoke of the boy as then "about fourteen years of age," he must have been born about 1786, not ten years earlier between Arnold's two marriages, as has been said.[4]

Arnold returned to England and brought his wife and children to St. John in 1787. His sister Hannah and his elder sons came from Connecticut to join the household. Arnold's Canadian neighbours liked him little better than so many Americans would have done. When his warehouse, insured for £6000, was burned in

July 1788, he was accused of having it set on fire, though he was at the time in London where he had just taken out the insurance. He boldly sued his former partner, who had made the charge, for slander and was awarded nominal damages. The insurance company waived liability, but was compelled to pay. Arnold, who had almost certainly had nothing to do with the fire, was not cleared in local opinion. His wife late in 1789 risked a visit to Philadelphia, but was coldly treated by her former friends. Husband and wife at last decided they must be aliens in America, left Hannah Arnold with the three boys behind them, and took up residence finally in England, in the summer of 1791.

In May 1792 the Earl of Lauderdale, during a debate in the Lords, incidentally referred to Arnold as proverbial for apostasy—which he was. Arnold challenged Lauderdale to a duel unless he would say he had not meant to asperse Arnold's character. Lauderdale was willing to say only that he had not meant to hurt Arnold's feelings. They met on July 1. Arnold fired, but not Lauderdale. After more discussion Lauderdale apologized in the form Arnold insisted on. "A variety of circumstances," Margaret Arnold wrote her father, "combined to make me acquainted with the whole transaction. What I suffered for near a week is not to be described; the suppression of my feelings, lest I should unman the general, almost at last proved too much for me; and for some hours my reason was despaired of. . . . It has been highly gratifying to find the general's conduct so much applauded, which it has been universally, and particularly by a number of the first characters in the kingdom who have called upon him in consequence of it. Nor am I displeased at the great commendations bestowed on my own conduct upon this trying occasion."[5]

It had been of course galling, and perhaps surprising, to Arnold to find that the change of sides for which he had been promised so much in advance had in the outcome brought him distrust and abuse from the people he had joined. He had not foreseen the difference between success and failure in his enterprise, and he found it hard to see why the difference between what he had hoped for and what he got should be so immense, when his losses were as large as they could have been in any case.

Apparently encouraged by the credit his duel gave him in 1792, he wrote again to Clinton on July 23 asking his interest with William Pitt, now prime minister. Clinton consented to do what he could. Arnold rehearsed his services and stated his case to Clinton, who on the whole agreed with him. Margaret Arnold, in a letter to Clinton on November 13, pleaded for his help. She was, she said, "surrounded by a numerous little family without the means of educating them in a style at all equal to what the former part of my life promised." She and her husband had a "scanty income" which was only for their lives. When they died, their children "would be left to want, in a strange country. . . . You will not be surprised that every maternal feeling is awakened, and that I am deeply interested in General Arnold's present application to Mr. Pitt. . . . From your justice I have everything to hope. May I presume to solicit your friendship?" She knew that Clinton was a solicitous father.

Clinton, after making several confused notes on the matter, talked with Pitt and recommended Arnold to the renewed consideration of his Majesty's government, in vain.[6] Arnold could not rest. On the outbreak of another war with France in 1793 he went on a trading voyage to the West Indies, passing among the French as an American named Anderson. He was captured and escaped, performed useful services at Guadeloupe, and made a plan to seize the Spanish islands for the British. Again he was not employed, but he and his family in 1798 were granted 13,800 acres to be chosen from the waste lands of the Crown in Upper Canada. Arnold engaged in privateering and lost more than he gained by it. When he died at Battersea on June 14, 1801 he left optimistic legacies but actual debts which his widow was barely able to pay. Before her death three years later she had, partly through the interest of Cornwallis, put all her children on their way to substantial and reputable places in the British army or the landed gentry of England. One of her sons, James Robertson Arnold, rose to the rank of lieutenant general. One of her great-grandsons, Theodore Stephenson, was a major general in the first World War.[7]

II

Joseph Stansbury, who had carried Arnold's overtures to New York and who knew as much about the plot as anybody in Philadelphia, was arrested and may have been suspected of complicity. But he had been careful. Nothing was proved against him except that he was engaged in forbidden trading with the British.[8] On his own request he was permitted to go within the British lines, where, as has been seen, he arrived early in January, to be followed in a few days by his wife and children.[9] Clinton allowed him quarters, rations, and a stipend of $2 a day as a reward for his loyalty and services. Stansbury went in August 1783 to Nova Scotia, then to England, where he asked compensation of £1000 from the commission on loyalist claims. The commissioners, disallowing his claim because of his pliant conduct in Philadelphia, said: "He seems at no time to have been true to his allegiance, and however you may like the treason it is impossible to approve the traitor. Such men should claim the reward for such service at the time and upon the spot."[10] Back in Philadelphia in November 1785, Stansbury resumed his business in spite of threats from people who remembered his satires, but did not prosper.[11] In 1793 he gave up Philadelphia for New York and spent the rest of his life as secretary of an insurance company.

Jonathan Odell, who handled the Arnold-André correspondence in New York, had been an avowed and active loyalist, and was differently rewarded. Assistant secretary to the Associated Loyalists and to Carleton, Odell went with Carleton to England at the end of 1783. The next year he returned to loyalist New Brunswick in the comfortable post of registrar and clerk of the province with a seat in the council, at £1000 a year. He held his office for twenty-eight years and then turned it over to his son William Franklin Odell who held it for thirty-two. Odell's favourite messenger, John Rattoon, seems never to have been suspected. He lived the rest of his life in Amboy, part of it in the Perth Amboy house formerly occupied by William Franklin as royal governor.

Samuel Wallis, also untouched by suspicion, stayed quiet and safe in Philadelphia till 1782, when he went back to his stone house on the West Branch of the Susquehanna. There besides increasing his estate to about 8000 acres he devoted himself to trading in land, particularly as a representative of the Holland Land Company of Amsterdam. When he died of yellow fever in Philadelphia in 1798 his affairs were in a crisis, and without his management his entire fortune was lost, as so many fortunes were, in that year of financial catastrophe.[12]

Joshua Hett Smith actually deserved his country's thanks for his unintentional share in André's capture and the discovery of Arnold's plot. Instead, Smith after his discharge by a court martial was held, as a suspected Tory, by the New York authorities in the Goshen jail till May 1781 when he escaped and got to Manhattan in June. He lodged for a time with his brother the chief justice and was allowed by Clinton $1 a day, later increased by Carleton to 7 shillings. Joshua Smith recovered some houses belonging to him in New York which had been occupied by the British while he stayed among the patriots, and was not penniless. But though when he went to England late in November 1783 he had not been attainted or his property confiscated, he lost most of his fortune in the confusion caused by his long absence. He was back in South Carolina in 1801 and died obscure in New York in 1818.[13]

Richard Varick, who as Arnold's aide in the Highlands came under suspicion but was cleared, still had to endure some whispers of doubt till May 1781 when he was appointed, by Washington, to be recording secretary at Headquarters, to arrange, classify, and copy all the correspondence and other papers of the Continental army. The Varick Transcripts in 44 folio volumes now in the Library of Congress, on which with several assistants Varick spent more than two years, are an honourable monument to his ability and skill. After the war he became recorder of New York, speaker of the assembly, attorney general, and mayor of New York City from 1789 to 1801; a founder of the American Bible Society and president of the New York Society of the Cincinnati till his death in 1831. David Solebury Franks, Arnold's other aide at West Point, was sent in July 1781 by Robert Morris as confidential courier to Jay in Madrid and Franklin in Paris, and in 1784 by Congress to Paris with the ratification of the peace treaty. For a short time the next year Franks acted as vice consul at

Marseille, but later returned to the United States and in 1789 unsuccessfully applied for the post of consul general in France. He seems to have turned to business and to have been assistant cashier of the Bank of North America in 1791.[14]

Beverley Robinson, a devout loyalist, had been attainted in October 1779, and with him his wife for no reason except that part of the Philipse estate belonged to her, and also his eldest son to whom the estate would descend. "I have this consolation," the elder Robinson wrote to Clinton on August 8, 1782, "that I acted from upright and conscientious principles, in doing my duty to my king and country, and was it to do over again I should take the same part, for no circumstance in life can ever make me forfeit my loyalty to my king nor zeal for the good of my country." But he could hope for no mercy from the angry patriots. Though appointed to the first council of New Brunswick, he never took his seat there but retired to England, where he lived near Bath till his death in 1792. The commission on loyalist claims allowed him £17,000 for the loss of his estate. One of his sons became a lieutenant general in the British army and another commissary general, and both were knighted. Two others settled in New Brunswick, where they founded families still notable in Canada.

Of the secret double-dealers, Metcalf Bowler in Rhode Island, impoverished by the war, saw his daughter married to the Marquis Langfroi who had come with the French allies of the Americans, and after the peace Bowler made himself a name as a horticulturist. The woodwork and paneling of one of the rooms of his Portsmouth house are cherished in the Metropolitan Museum in New York. William Heron of Connecticut was several times elected to the assembly from 1784 to 1796 and lived at Redding and died there in 1819, considered somewhat haughty and reactionary but never suspected of having been a spy for the British.

William Rankin of York, ambitious leader of what promised to be a general loyalist uprising against the rebels in Pennsylvania, Delaware, and Maryland, continued—after his wasted excursion to Virginia—with the British in New York till the final evacuation in November 1783, when he went to England. He was allowed a pension of £120 a year, and the commission on loyalist claims granted him £2320 8s. for the loss of his confiscated estate.[15]

Christopher Sower, Rankin's principal agent, was allowed £1289 for his losses by confiscation, went from England in 1785 to New Brunswick, and there became printer and deputy postmaster general to the province. He returned to the United States in 1799 and died that year at Baltimore. Andrew Fürstner, Rankin's brother-in-law and Sower's most trusted messenger, went to Nova Scotia in 1783 and seems to have had no reward beyond his pay while the war lasted.

Oliver DeLancey, adjutant general after André, in 1794 became barrackmaster general of the British army and general in 1812, and died ten years later. Chief Justice William Smith managed his relations with both sides so astutely that his estate was not confiscated by the Americans, and by the British he was appointed in 1785 to the lucrative office of chief justice of Canada which he held till his death in 1793. His journal, still unpublished, furnishes an invaluable record of loyalist life and intrigue in New York during the British occupation.

William Franklin, president of the Associated Loyalists, came to be deeply involved in the difficulties of those embittered men who carried on a savage guerrilla war with the patriots of Connecticut and New Jersey throughout 1781, with furious reprisals and counter-reprisals and probably with collusion between the armed bands of the two parties at the expense of civilians generally. Not admitting that the states were independent of Great Britain or had any right to deal with loyalists as traitors, the Associated Loyalists particularly resented such conduct. In April 1782 they got Clinton's permission to take Captain Joshua Huddy of the New Jersey militia, who had been captured by the British, out of the provost in New York on the pretext that he was to be exchanged in New Jersey for one of their number held by the Americans. But the party in charge, commanded by Captain Richard Lippincott under discreet verbal orders from the board of the Associated Loyalists, took Huddy on shore in Monmouth county and hanged him to a tree in retaliation for the killing of a loyalist named White in the same county about two weeks before. A "label" pinned on Huddy's dead body warned the rebels. "We, the refugees, having long with grief beheld the cruel murders of our brethren and finding nothing but such measures daily carried into execution, we therefore determine not to suffer without taking vengeance for the numerous cruelties; and thus begin, having made use of Captain Huddy as the first object to present to your view; and we further determine to hang man for man while there is a refugee existing. Up goes Huddy for Philip White."

Washington demanded the surrender of Lippincott and threatened, if this were refused, to hang a British prisoner of war of captain's rank. Clinton, outraged by the deception practised on him by the loyalists, called the hanging "an act of atrocity . . . scarcely to be paralleled in history." Though he did not give Lippincott up, he had him tried for murder by a court of inquiry. The court acquitted Lippincott of the charge of murder, since he had been obeying orders which he supposed the board had a right to give.[16] Clinton deprived the Associated Loyalists of all their powers, and Franklin in August left for England. Because of his steady adherence to the Crown he was awarded £1800 for his loss of property and a life pension of £800. He died in 1813.

Paul Wentworth, chief of the loyalist secret agents in London and Paris, got none of the rewards he had worked for except a seat in Parliament for six weeks in 1780. He retired to his plantation in Surinam in 1790 and died there in three years. John Vardill, the ministry's alert spy in London, disappointed in his desire to return triumphantly to New York as regius professor of theology at King's College, was instead rewarded with a living in Lincolnshire, where he died in 1811. Edward Bancroft, the subtle double-dealer who served Benjamin Franklin but more faithfully served the British, kept his secret. For the sake of his pension he continued to be a British subject after the Revolution and from time to time furnished later ministers advice and information that seemed to indicate his enduring fidelity. He died in England in 1821, and his treachery did not come to light for nearly seventy years.[17]

Silas Deane fared worse than any of them. Claiming to be still faithful to the best interests of America, which he said he had come to think could be served only by reconciliation and reunion with Great Britain, he denied that there was any resemblance or intimacy between him and the traitor Arnold.[18] Hated by the

Americans and unrewarded by the British, Deane lived in poverty, most of the time in Ghent, and died in 1789 on shipboard just as he was setting out for Canada. He had a just grievance against Congress for refusing to settle his accounts and costing him heavy losses. Congress in 1842 made unavailing amends when it voted his heirs $37,000 in belated restitution. As it was then impossible to repay him what was due, so was it to punish him for the treachery about which Congress did not know.

III

It was hardly to be supposed that, at the end of a civil war so fierce as the Revolution had been in America, the defeated loyalists would not be made to suffer. They had despised the rebels and trusted the king. The loyalists could say that they had naturally retaliated because they had been injured. The victorious rebels naturally remembered the retaliations better than the injuries. If the losers had sacrificed lives and been deprived of property, so had the winners. The winners must now make their own way. Let the losers do the same, or look to the British government which had supported them against their compatriots. The Whig ministry during the peace negotiations contended that the Americans should compensate the loyalists for their confiscated property. Benjamin Franklin relentlessly summed up the American attitude in a letter to Richard Oswald, British commissioner, on November 26, 1782.

"Some of those people may have merit in their regard for Britain, and who espoused her cause from affection: these it may become you to reward. But there are many of them who were waverers, and were only determined to engage in it by some occasional circumstances or appearances: these have not much of either merit or demerit. And there are others who have abundance of demerit respecting your country, having by their falsehood and misrepresentations brought on and encouraged the continuance of the war: these, instead of being recompensed, should be punished. . . . Your ministers require that we should receive again into our bosom those who have been our bitterest enemies and restore their properties who have destroyed ours; and this while the wounds they have given us are still bleeding. It is many years since your nation expelled the Stuarts and their adherents and confiscated their estates. Much of your resentment against them may by this time be abated. Yet if we should propose it, and insist on it as an article of our treaty with you, that that family should be recalled and the forfeited estates of their friends restored, would you think us serious in our professions of earnestly desiring peace?"[19]

The British were not willing to fight longer for the sake of the loyalists, and the Americans in the treaty agreed only that Congress would recommend to the states to make restitution to loyalists whose property had been confiscated. As both the American and the British commissioners expected, the states did nothing. The British government, having throughout the war encouraged the loyalists and promised them protection for their services, felt itself under a strong and just obligation. A Parliamentary commission on loyalist claims was appointed in July 1783 and worked on the difficult matter till March 1790. Claims to the number of 5072 were laid before the commissioners, 954 withdrawn or not prosecuted, and 4118 examined, in both England and America. The total of the claims made was £8,026,045, the total of compensations allowed, £3,292,452.[20]

Compensation for loss of property and income could of course not make up for what the war had cost the loyalists in misery and anxiety, bitter exile, and the hard need of beginning life over again outside their native land. There are no accurate figures as to how many persons including women and children left the United States on account of loyalty to the British Empire, but it may have been as high as 100,000, of whom 35,000 may have gone from New York alone.[21] About half the exiles settled in Canada, where they and their descendants were called United Empire Loyalists. The expulsion was so thorough that the next generation of Americans, with few former loyalists as reminders, almost forgot the civil aspects of the war and came to think of it as a war solely against England. The loyalists disappeared from American history, at least from ordinary knowledge of it. Not till the twentieth century was there much effort to understand the sentiments and motives of the loyalists and the share they had had in the Revolution. Public opinion, gradually learning that there were loyalists, has had an instinct to do justice to them and has gone on, lately, to a disposition to exaggerate their virtues and abilities and to see them as romantic heroes.

They were no more romantic than any conservative, losing party in any revolutionary conflict. While many of the loyalists were genuinely devoted, many were timid, many were stupid. The common men among them looked to their accepted leaders, the leaders looked across the Atlantic to their established rulers. To the loyalists the self-reliance of the rebels seemed lawlessness, and the rebels a mob led by demagogues. The indiscipline and violence and corruption of some of the revolutionaries were held to be characteristic of all of them. The loyalists could not learn that the rebels had either ability or honesty. This was an expensive error. The truth is that no loyalist even approached Franklin in intellectual distinction and political understanding, or Washington for power and dignity of command, or Jefferson as a master of written eloquence. The proportion of educated men among the patriots was as large as among the loyalists. The rank and file of patriot soldiers and civilians were much the same people as the loyalist rank and file. There was only one essential quality in which the loyalists surpassed the patriots. That quality was conservatism.

Few loyalists seem ever to have understood that the desire for independence was, as the war went on, deep and passionate, not scheming and wilful. Patriot rhetoric mystified and enraged them. The patriots talked about the rights of man and the liberties of America. Where were the rights and liberties of loyalists, who were men and Americans? If the patriots talked one way and acted another, they must be dishonest. If they were dishonest, they might be won over by promises, threats, or bribes. There were always loyalists ready to serve the British ministry or the British commander-in-chief in America by transmitting offers to patriots who, it was hoped, might leave the rebels or betray them. Loyalists were indispensable messengers or correspondents: Beverley Robinson to Israel Putnam and Ethan Allen; Paul Wentworth to Silas Deane; Jacob Duché to Washington; Peter Livius and Stephen Holland to John Sullivan; Philip Skene to Philip

Schuyler; Joseph Stansbury and Jonathan Odell and Samuel Wallis to Benedict Arnold; William Heron to Samuel Holden Parsons. The ministry did not hesitate to employ means customary in Great Britain for winning friends for the king's policies. The commander-in-chief in America did not hesitate, because it was—and always is—a commander's duty to use such means to weaken the enemy if possible.

Nor did the loyalists, perhaps, ever quite understand why most of the patriots to whom offers were made rejected them firmly if not furiously. Loyalty to the Empire blinded the loyalists to the loyalty to America which, often apparently hopeless and mad, grew and spread among the patriots. There stood Washington and Franklin, like the unshakable towers of a bridge of faith spanning an ocean. Countless other patriots were, within their range, as resolute. Any of them at any time might have made their private peace with the king, through his busy servants. Desertion or treachery, the patriots were told, would bring them lasting honour and immediate rewards instead of the uncertainty and poverty they had otherwise to face. Besides the enemies in the field the patriots had persistent enemies under cover, claiming to be the real friends of America and believing they were. The patriots, this history at last reveals, had to hold out against a whole set of secret temptations which sought them out when they were tired or poor or resentful or despairing, and offered them ease or comfort or satisfaction or hope. The wonder is—as Washington understood—not that some of them were false but that most of them were true to the ragged colours of a perilous cause.

Appendix

(Transcribed and collated from the original manuscripts
in the Clinton Papers by Howard Peckham, Curator of
Manuscripts, William L. Clements Library. The manuscript text is followed literally except that certain missing
letters and words are inserted in square brackets, and that
the superior letters at the end of various words stand uni-
formly alone instead of having beneath them sometimes
periods, sometimes colons, and sometimes blank spaces)

ARNOLD-ANDRÉ CORRESPONDENCE
CLINTON'S NARRATIVE

◗ ◗ ◗

Arnold-André Correspondence

○

1. ANDRÉ TO STANSBURY

(Holograph draft, enclosed in André to Clinton, No. 2)

[May 10, 1779]

Sir

Altho I think we understood each other clearly this morning and nothing was omitted which I cou'd have to say on the Subject; it is, or may be, of too much importance not to take further pains that all may be perfectly well comprehended—

On our part we meet ~~ArnGen~~ Monk's ouvertures with full reliance on his honourable Intentions and disclose to him with the strongest assurances of our Sincerity, that no thought is entertained of abandoning the point we have in view. That on the Contrary powerfull means are expected for accomplishing our end. We likewise assure him that in the very first instance of receiving the Tidings or good offices we expect from him, our liberality will be evinced, that in case any partial but important blow shou'd by his means be Struck or aimed, upon the Strength of just and pointed information & cooperation, rewards equal at least to what Such Service can be estimated at, will be given, But Shou'd the Abilities and Zeal of that able and enterprizing gentleman amount to the Seizing an Obnoxious band of men, to the delivering into our power or enabling us to attack to advantage and by judicious assistance compleatly to defeat ~~our Enemy~~ a numerous body, then woud the generosity of the nation exceed even his own most Sanguine hopes & in the expectation of this he may rely on that *honour* he now trusts in his present advances. Shou'd his manifest Efforts be foiled and after every Zealous attempt, flight be at length necessary the Cause in which he suffers will hold itself bound to indemnify him for his losses and receive him with the honour his conduct deserves. His own judgement will point out the services required, but for his Satisfaction we give the following hints.

Counsels of —— Contents of dispatches from foreign abettors— Original dispatches and papers which might be Seized and sent to us— Channels thro' which such dispatches pass, hints for securing them. Number and position of troops, whence & what reinforcements are expected and when.— influencing persons of rank with the same favourable disposition in their Several commands in different Quarters— Concerting the means of a blow of importance.— fomenting any party which when risen to a height might perhaps easily be drawn into a desire of accomodation rather than submit to an odious Yoke.— Magazines—where any new are forming— To interest himself in procuring an exchange of Prisoners for the *honour* of America.

The other Channel you mention'd to me this morning thro' which a communication was formerly held must be kept unacquainted with this and with Regard to it the same may be said as with Regard to Monk that liberal Acknowledgem^ts will infallibly attend conspicuous Services.

You will leave me a long book similar to yours. Three Numbers make a Word the 1st is the Page the 2^d the Line the third the Word a comma is placed between each word when only the first letter of the line is wanted in order to compose a Word not in the book, the number representing the Word will be ⚡ (Unit with a Stroke across.)

In writings to be discover'd by a process F is fire A acid.

In general information, as to the Complexion of Affairs an Old Womans health may be the Subject.

The Lady might write to me at the Same time with one of her intimates She will guess who I mean, the latter remaining ignorant of interlining & sending the letter. I will write myself to the friend to give occasion for a reply. This will come by ~~any~~ a flag of truce, exchangd officer &^a every ~~one~~ messenger remaining ignorant of what they are charg'd with, The letters may talk of the Meschianza & other nonsense.

You will take your mysterious notes from this letter and burn it or rather leave it Sealed for me with ——

◯

2. André to Clinton

(Holograph letter signed, enclosing draft of André to Stansbury, No. 1)

York Island the 10th May 1779

Sir

The Matter I mention'd this morning to your Excell^y may be so impor-

tant that I have thought on it afresh here, and written the enclosed, as I felt much more forcibly than you coud do the kind of Confusion such Sudden proposals created when one must deliberate and determine at once. The Man must return in order not to be miss'd, Laird has a Sloop & Whale boat at his orders. Capt. Chinniry is desir'd to recommend him to the arm'd Vessel at Princes bay, and a confidential person is to be his Cockswain at night.

I hope Sir you will think a Sufficient foundation is laid and all done which the time wou'd admit of. The enclos'd is just what he has already Verbally and I take the liberty of requesting you to transmit it if it meets with your Excellencys Approbation Not finding myself very Well I in consequence of your indulgence on these occasions came into the Country

I have the honour to be with the utmost respect and fidelity

Sir

Your most obedient
& most humb. Servant
John André

I must trouble y^r Excell^y to Seal the enclosure as well as Mr Odells Note.

◯

3. André to Margaret Chew

(Holograph draft signed, probably written in May, possibly never sent)

A   New York the   1779
Madam

I hardly dare write to you after having neglected your Commissions and not apologized for my transgressions. I wou'd with pleasure have sent you drawings of head dresses had I been as much of a millener here as I was at Philadelphia in meschianza times, but from occupation as well as ill health I have been obliged to abandon the pleasing Study of what relates to the

Ladies; I shoud however be happy to resume it had I the same inducements as when I had the pleasure of frequenting yours and the Shippen Family: I know besides that you have every thing from Paris the Fountain head and therefore have less regret in neglecting your Orders in this particular: I trust I am yet in the memory of the little Society of third & fourth Street and even of the *other peggy* now Mrs Arnold who will I am sure accept of my best respects and with the rest of the Sisterhoods of both Streets peruse not disdainfully this page meant as an assurance of my unabated Esteem for them.

Captn Ridsdale is very well I see him daily and believe his friends at Philadelphia have no Rival in his heart but his violin to which he pays with great Success a constant Courtship. Captn Campbell is still a grenadier and there, not even a Musical Instrument rivals the fair philadelphians. My Brother is now in the same Regiment with these gentlemen: If Col: Harrison Gen: Washingtons Aid de Camp is amongst your acquaintance I beg you woud present my best compliments to him I was never so sorry to disagree with any body. I intended in case of agreement to have subjoined a clause that all hearts on either side shou'd be restored or others sent in exchange, this wou'd have afforded considerable relief to many Swains who still magnetically turn to the banks of the Delaware.— I beg my particular Respects may be presented to Mrs Chew and your well remembered and regarded Sisters, and my best Wishes to your Brother I have the honour to be

Madam
    Your most obedient
        and most humble Servant
            John André

○

4. STANSBURY TO ANDRÉ

(Code letter, keyed probably to long book mentioned in André to Stansbury, No. 1. Decoded copy, here given, in unknown hand. This letter presumably preceded Arnold's letter of May 23)

[May , 1779]
To write with dispatch G[eneral]. A[rnold]. has made use of Bailys Dictionary 21st ed. 8to: London (1770) by R Ware &c This I have paged for him beginning at A an abbre. &c. Each side is numbered and contains 927 pages he adds 1 to each number of the page of the column and of the Line, the first word of which is always used to[o]. Zoroaster will be 928.2.2. and not 927.1.1. Tide is 838.3.2. and not 837.2.1. When he would express a number so (11,000). He depends on me for Convey[ing]. which is dangerous. He goes to Camp next Week, from thence he will write to you directing to Col. Edward Antill to your Care. His Signature will be A G or a name beginning with A. He is now preparing a Letter which I shall send in a day or two.

[Addressed:] John André Esqr
                Monmouth
[Endorsed:] GA. has made use ol Baily's Dict^y

○

5. ARNOLD TO ANDRÉ

(Code letter, keyed to Bailey's Dictionary, 21st edition, 1775. Decoded copy in André's hand)

Our Friend S[tansbury] acquaints me that the proposals made by him in my name are agreeable to S[ir]: H[enry]: C[linton]: and that S[ir]: H[enry]: engages to answer my warmest Expectations for any Services rendered. As I esteem the Interest of America and Great Britain inseparable S[ir]: H[enry]: may depend on my Exertions and Intelligence: It will be impossible to cooperate unless there is a mutual Confidence. S[ir]: H[enry] shall be convinced on every Occasion that his is not misplaced. Gen: W[ashington]: and the Army move to the North River as soon as Forage can be obtained. C[ongress] have given up Ch[s] Town if attempted. They are in want of Arms Ammunition and Men to defend it. 3 or 4 thousand Militia is the most that can be mustered to fight on any Emergency. Seizing papers is impossible. Their Contents can be known from a Member of Congress. 4 Months Since the French Minister required Congress to vest their Agents with powers to negotiate peace with Britain. The time is elapsed in disputing if they shall demand independency with their original Terms or insist on the addition of Newfoundland. No decision, no measure taken to prevent the depreciation of Money, No foreign loan obtained. France refused to become surety, No Encouragement from Spain. The french Fleet has co[nditional] orders to return to this Continent. They depend on great part of their provision from hence A Transport Originally a 64 and a foreign 28 Guns and daily expected here for Provision. I will cooperate when an Opportunity offers and as Life and every thing is at Stake I will expect some Certainty My property here Secure and a revenue equivalent to the risk and service done I cannot promise Success; I will deserve it. Inform me what I may expect, cou'd I know S[ir]. H[enry's]. Intentions he shou'd never be at a loss for Intelligence I shall expect a particular Answer thro our friend S[tansbur]y.

Madam Ar[nold] presents you her particular Compliments.

M— J A——
    May 23[d]
[Addressed:] M— J— A——

◯

6. STANSBURY TO ODELL

(Second paragraph in code, keyed to Blackstone's Commentaries, *as mentioned in first paragraph. Postscript and decoding by Odell)*

Sir

I beg leave to recommend to your Perusal Blackstones Commentaries Page 46. of the 5th Edition Oxford the first Volume will solve the Question.

The confusion of a Town-meeting hath banished me to Moore'stown for preservation. In two letters for the Capt. —— Bayly's Diction[y] 25th Lond: Edit: 8to is used, pageing it right. A, an abbreviation. An *Integer* is added to the pageing collumn and line, and *that* is the *word.*

                        Paliwoledash
Yours is received.
26. 5mo. 79.

[Postscript by decoder:] *Integer,* I presume, means only a *single figure,* as in no case can there be requisite a number larger than 9 to denote the *word* in a line of a Dictionary Column.

                        Yoric.

◯

7. ODELL TO ANDRÉ

(Holograph letter)

                New York May 31. 1779
My Dear Sir,

I am mortified to death—having just received (what I had been so anxiously expecting) a Letter from S[tansbury] and, by a private mark agreed on between us, perceiving it contained an invisible page for you,

I assay'd it by the Fire, when to my inexpressible vexation, I found that the paper, having by some accident got damp on the way, had spread the Solution in such manner as to make the writing all one indistinguishable Blott, out of which not the half of any one line can be made legible. I shall use every diligence to forward a letter to him, and to instruct him how to guard against the like accident in future, and hope it will not be long before I shall receive a return. The ostensible page of this unfortunate letter is dated the 21st Instant, which I take it for granted must have been before he could have received my last, to which I am in hourly expectation of receiving an answer; and as my friend cannot but be aware of the precarious chances in conveying letters, I flatter myself that the Substance of the one I have received will be repeated with additions in the one I expect. The moment I have the good fortune to get it I shall forward it to you; and beg leave to ask whether it would not be proper on your part to instruct me in the channel through which I can most speedily and safely convey my letters to you. For the conveyance of this I took the liberty of applying to Capt: Smith the Secretary, but did not find that he seemed so perfectly possessed as I expected with the means of speedy conveyance.

There is one point of delicacy in my Situation, which I take the liberty to mention— I must not dissemble with you that my Friend uses with me the same Cypher which you fixed on for your own correspondence, and therefore, without your permission, I am doubtful whether it may not be improper for me to *assay* such papers as I have reason to conclude are intended rather for your own perusal than mine. I should not have taken the liberty in the present case, but I

confess that my joy on getting the letter was such that before I had made the reflection, I had already flown to the fire with my paper, and, as it has turned out, I am glad to have spared you the vexation of an useless trouble. As toasted paper becomes too brittle to bear folding, if you think proper to confide so far in my discretion, I shall make it a rule to assay and carefully transcribe such passages as may come to me for your perusal. Though the receit of this letter is unfortunately of no other use, yet in one view it gives me pleasure, as from its date it appears that our friend, though we waited long for its arrival, was not negligent nor tardy in beginning his expected correspondence.

Permit the *Parson* to conclude with his earnest *prayers* for your health, safety and glory; may our General have the happiness, by his triumphs, to make us forget all past misfortunes— I am, as you see *devoutly*

and most affectionately yours.

Jon^n Odell

[Addressed:] On His Majesty's Service
Captn André
Aid de Camp
at Head Quarters

☉

8. STANSBURY TO ODELL

(Copy, with footnotes added by Odell for André's information)

(Copy from S[tansbury] June 4, received the 12th in answer to mine of May 16 sent by Rattoon of South Amboy)

N° 1.

My dear Friend,

Your ingenious letter was duly delivered by the best[1] conveyancer I am acquainted with. On his return I took the liberty of using a[2] certain Gentleman's name to forward some news-papers and letters to you, which I hope that Gentleman will be so good to excuse, as it proceeded from necessity. If that mode of forwarding Advices through[3] that avenue meets with approbation, it may be made the most certain and expeditious of any yet thought on, by means of some proper[4] tokens which our[5] slender friend will settle with the Commander on that[6] Station. As my[7] present Situation cuts me off from my favorite sphere of usefulness, I endeavor'd, in a circuitous manner, to procure a letter from A. G. to forward by this favorite conveyance. From some unknown cause I have received none, probably owing to the shortness of the notice.

---

1. John Rattoon, of South Amboy. 2. Captn André. 3. South Amboy. 4. Signals. 5. Rattoon. 6. Prince's Bay. 7. obliged by the tumults in Phila[a] to conceal himself for a time at Moore's Town in Jersey.

○

9. ODELL TO STANSBURY

(Copy by Odell for André's information)

(Copy to S—— June 9th) [1779]
Dear Sir,

I lately wrote you by express to inform you that yours of May 21. had been injured by some accident of weather, and was *not legible*; if you mean in earnest, and with advantage to carry on the *commercial Plan*, you must not delay the *expected remittances*. Both *your* credit and *mine* will suffer greatly if you do. Let us leave affairs of State to Politicians, while we attend to our little matters of trade and Commerce; for thus our correspondence, though secret, will be harmless, and we shall have no cause to repent our choice. I have yours

from Gravell's, of May 26, and *for the present* desire you to stick to your *Oxford Interpreter*.

Lothario is impatient: convince him of your sincerity, and you may rely upon it, that your most sanguine hopes will be surpassed. Now is the time for profitable speculation, while the multitude are idly debating about the fate of our paper, which we *may* appreciate if we *will*. Adieu,—let me hear from you soon, and to the purpose.

[To André:] I hope soon to get an answer to the above.

J[onathan]. O[dell].

○

10. STANSBURY TO ODELL

(Copy in Odell's hand, with footnotes by Odell for André's information)

(Copy from S—— dated last Wednesday, the [June] 9th [1779] Instant, in answer to mine by express)
N° 2.
Sir,

About three this afternoon, I received your request of a copy of the *invoice* of the *french Cargo* which got damaged in its passage. The Original is either mislaid or destroyed, and as I *have written* you *several letters* lately which must reach your hands, on a similar *commercial* Subject, it is the less necessary. However it is at present out of my reach, as well as the[1] invoice the prices of which you quote in yours just received. You know the antipathy or rather fear which I have of thunder, and I have sought a *temporary* Shelter *here*, where the[2] *tall trees* and *high buildings*, which surround and make my dwelling rather dangerous in stormy weather, are not to be met with. I have some time since forwarded to M[r3] *Andrews* a plan of trade which will, I hope, be to the satisfaction of the concerned. Mr A. G. [Arnold] is at present out of town on *private business*. I shall endeavor to keep up our *mercantile communications*, and interest you in any thing that bids fair to quit cost. I asked your opinion lately on a passage in *Blackstone's commentaries*, whether you perfectly understood me I know not, but should be glad to have you joined me in opinion that my critique on that celebrated Author was at least defensible. I want to have a *Baily's Dictionary*—having left mine in the hurry-scurry of moving last winter twelvemonth. If it is the same edition with yours it will be more to my satisfaction. Naval and military matters are very dry and unsatisfactory to my turn. *Paliwole* will become Pacoli which is shorter and more intelligible.

---

1. The book for decyphering. 2. Committes &c. 3. Capt. André.

◯

11. ODELL TO ANDRÉ

(Holograph letter, enclosing Odell to Stansbury of June 9, and Stansbury to Odell, June 4 and 9)

New York– June 13th 1779.
My Dear Sir,

I inclose you a copy of my last to S[tansbury] dated the 9th instant, which I sent, by way of South Amboy, by the Bearer of a former billet, and a duplicate of the same is gone by Mrs Gordon who accompanies Mrs Chamier to Philad^a Last night I received a few lines by way of South Amboy, of which the inclosed, marked N° 1. is a copy. As you might possibly be unacquainted with some of my friend's hints and references, I subjoin, at the foot of the page, explanatory notes. This day my Express is returned with an answer to mine of June 3^d The inclosed N° 2 is a copy of this Answer. These letters written

from Moore's-town, are not indeed *satisfactory*, but they give me fresh hopes; especially as my friend seems confident that "several letters he has lately written on a similar *commercial* subject *must* reach my hands," among which, though they have not yet found their way hither, I conclude You will find the "plan of trade which, he says, he some time since forwarded to Mr Andrews. I wish the two letters forwarded to you last night may give you pleasure. They were brought by my South Amboy Messenger. If you are not soon coming to town, be so good as to give me a line, and I will have the honor of waiting on you at Head Quarters, as I wish to see you for one half hour.

Health and happiness attend you. I am most truly,

Dear Sir, your respectful
and affectionate Servt
J. Odell

P.S. The day after you did me the honor of a visit here, Captn Smith sent me a blank permit with a note from you inclosing five guineas. I found by this that you had misunderstood my billet (which probably was obscure from haste in writing) as it was not money that I expected or had then occasion for. I did not think myself at liberty to make use of your permit, not having it in my power, for want of time, to show it to you according to your desire, previous to dispatching my mercury: I therefore inclose it, with my thanks for this mark of your confidence in your most obliged &c J.O.

◯

12. ODELL TO ANDRÉ

(Holograph letter, dated by context as June 13)

[June 13, 1779]
Dear Sir,

Tilton and Hulitt, the two young

men for whom I have lately requested Ensign's Commissions in the Militia, are just arrived from Shrewsbury, and will return in two or three days. By them I have the inclosed, which my Friend tells me is a copy of the note lately sent by way of South Amboy, which you have already received. The date of his letter to me is only one day later than the last. He desires me to mention to you, that the three Frigates cruising between Sandy Hook and Delaware Capes which have done considerable mischief, are the Confederation, the Boston and the General Green, and that they are to continue cruising there.

When Tilton returns I shall write by him, repeating the Substance of the letter I have shown you.

I am most sincerely

your affectionate Servt

Jo^n Odell

Sunday Evening

[Addressed:] Captn André

Head Quarters

○

13. ANDRÉ TO ARNOLD

(Holograph draft of a letter which André began to Arnold but which, presumably because of Clinton's objections, was not sent. It must have preceded No. 14 following. André evidently kept the manuscript and added further notes on Americans who he thought might be helpful to the British)

The most essential Services for wresting this Country from Ruin and Oppression wou'd be in revealing the Counsels of its rulers so as to counteract them and in affording an opportunity to defeat the Army.— Generous Terms wou'd follow our Success and ample Rewards and *Honors* woud be the portion of the distinguish'd Characters which wou'd contribute to so great an End.—

The Operation of the former of these Services is slow, but has its importance and must be attended to. Dispatches to & from foreign Courts, Original papers, intimation of Channels thro' which intelligence passes, &^{a} are the objects chiefly to be attended to, but, the most brilliant and effectual blow finally to compleat the overthrow of the present abominable power woud be the destruction of the Army. This may be effected by a grand Stroke or by successive partial but Severe blows— Here follow Hints for both.—

I should stile a partial blow the taking possession of a Considerable Seaport and defeating the Troops assigned to the defense of the province so as to be able to make a progress thro it drive away or disarm the disaffected and by curbing the trade and displaying at the same time our prowess and lenity give a Spring to the just indignation of the Suffering people and induce them to return to their allegiance Could you obtain the Command in Carolina? The rest you must understand?

A Surprise of a considerable body of men, or the means pointed out of ambuscading them, crossing upon their march &^{a} Such a body might be Collected and put in motion in consequence of Operations on our part and the most effectual ones for that purpose you might Suggest Such as our threatening a Magazine, a port in the Sound &^{a}

The intercepting a convoyed fleet to or from france or the West Indies might be effected by means of proper intelligence.—

Magazines or Barracks might be burnt and on certain occasions all the guns of a Fort or field Artillery Spiked.

———

As to a general project against the whole Army, Cou'd any thing take place on the W Side of the North River? We shoud be glad of your Sentiments on that head.—

Here are our Ideas for movements to the Eastward. A Considerable Corps shall ~~possess themselves of Providence or Boston~~ march into N. England.— The Consequence will be that W[ashington]— will cross the North River and hasten to the points attacked He wou'd possibly be preceeded by a picked Corps similar to that in Jersey under Gen: Lee which wou'd have orders to harass, attack, awe the Country &ª Coud you command that Corps, it might be concerted where and when it shou'd be Surprised, defeated, or obliged to capitulate: Complete information might be receivd concerning the Main body, its baggage, its means of Supply &ª Convoys might be intercepted, Magazines burnt, boats on the N. River Seized, & the passage back prevented by a reembarkation of the Corps to the Eastward or by the Co-operation of troops from N. York.— A chain of Connivance must be very artfully laid to multiply difficulties & baffle resources. Under the Circumstances W[ashington]. might be attacked, or be left to disperse from want of Supplies. At such an hour when the most boisterous Spirits were with the Army and every one intent on its fate the Seizing the Congress wou'd decide the Business. You must observe that our Navy wou'd not be idle during this time & that a Small Corps attending a few Ships of War might either be assisting in bringing of[f] the Cong: or in increasing the general Confusion by descents on the Coast

observ[atio]ⁿ

Miff[lin]: woud be the man to remain at Ph[iladelphia]. & Seize the Cong: is he enterprizing?

If added to this Fᵗ Pitt were taken by Exped[ition]. from ~~Detroit~~ Canada in which Th—— & Mons   and Rankin might assist & an Effort defeated which is projecting against detroit, there coud remain no resource

L. might help us as to the Boats & Convoys across the N. River.— We may call upon, the two QʳMʳ from whom we hear by Gen: Tryons Scouts from Emericks Corps.

Schuyler shou'd be encouraged, as the People near albany begin to shew Signs of impatience under their present rulers & as the Indians are threatening in that Quarter. Coud he negotiate the purchase of M'gommery & Clinton, Spike their guns at a certain time?

Rankin shou'd have a Cypher.—& a Word

Houseker a Word

& they shoud point out a house on the frontier by which Brant might by sending the Parole have Communication & arrange his operation *White* might carry this information to Brant Neither wou'd know the other to be concerned.— If a proper plan of this nature cou'd be concerted Gen Haldimᵈ shoud have it explain'd to him that White might be encourag'd

Might it not be advisable to exchange the frenchman who has 200 p Ann[um]: from Governmᵗ & was taken at Fᵗ Chartres to send him to Canada if the posts on the Missisippi are to be repossess'd he was probably a man of some·influence with the Indians.— Is it impossible to do any thing w[it]ʰ *Maxwell?* Mʳ Elliot.— Has *Sinclair* been thought of lately: Hazen may be had, he is artfull and enterprizing he will be a good Creature of —— whom he knows & to whom he has betray'd *us* in Canada. May —— be promis'd prov[incia]ˡ M[ajor].   G[eneral].ˢ Rank? he asks his own Rank in the B[ritis]ʰ Army.

14. ANDRÉ TO ARNOLD

(Holograph draft by André, containing the first British offer to Arnold. To be enciphered and then sent)

(Middle of June) in Cyp: [1779]

I have your Letter of the 23d May: One in Cypher receiv'd before was injured by the damp and not legible. Some Messages thro S[tansbury]. will have shown my wish to hear from you and that in a Tone consonant to the enlarged plan upon which S[ir]: H[enry]: C[linton]: is taught to expect your Concurrence. With the same Candour which you will experience when engaged in any Operation concerted with him H[is]. E[xcellency]. wishes to apprize you that he cannot reveal his Intentions as to the present Campaign nor can he find the necessity of such a Discovery or that a want of a proper degree of Confidence is to be inferred from his not making it. He informs you with the Strictest Truth that the War is to be prosecuted with vigour and that no thought is entertained of giving up the dependency of America, much less of harkening to such a claim as you have been told the Congress affect to debate upon. He begs you to observe that you proposed your Assistance for the delivery of your Country: You must know where the present power is vulnerable and the conspicuous Commands with which you might be vested may enable us at one Shining Stroke from which both Riches & honours woud be derived to accellerate the ruin to which the usurped Authority is verging and to put a Speedy end to the miseries of our fellow Creatures. S[ir]. H[enry]. C[linton].'s Army is now centrically Stationed 50 Miles up the North River A few hours can embark him for any part of the Coast and an irruption into the Country in any direction is equally at his Choice He forbids any but a circuitous Communication between the Southern and eastern provinces. In this Situation whatever may be his designs, he can concur with you in almost any plan you can advise and in which you will cordially cooperate. Join the Army, accept a Command, be Surprized, be cut off— these things may happen in the Course of Manoeuvre, nor you be censured or Suspected a Compleat Service of this Nature involving a Corps of 5 or 6000 Men would be rewarded with twice as many thousand Guineas. The method wou'd be arranged by my meeting You as Flag of Truce or otherwise as soon as you come near us. It is Service of this nature or Intelligence having evidently led to such Strokes which S[ir]. H[enry]. C[linton]. looks for; It is such as these he pledges himself shall be rewarded beyond your warmest Expectations. The Colour of the Times favours them and your Abilities and Firmness justify his hopes of Success. In the mean time your Influence might be generously as well as profitably employed in procuring the Exchange of Gen Burgoynes Army It coud be urged by none with more propriety, nor woud you be Sorry to See this act of Justice superadded to the Shining revolution you may perhaps be instrumental in effecting. [Endorsed:] A

○

15. ARNOLD TO ANDRÉ

(Code letter, keyed to Blackstone's Commentaries, 5th Oxford edition, Volume I. Decoded copy in André's hand)

18th June [1779]

Gen: Sullivan is at Eastown with three Brigades and Some Militia, the whole upwards of 5000 Men going against Detroit and Niagara to destroy the Indian Settlements.

Gen: W[ashington]'s whole Army that went from Rariton was about 5000 men those on the N[orth] River before between 3 & 4000

Congress has done nothing towards obtaining a Loan or appointing Commissioners to negotiate a peace Their time and Attention is taken up in Trifles

No foreign Intelligence has been received for more than a month: Gerard very ill, altered his intention of going, for the present.

[A. G.]

◯

16. STANSBURY TO ANDRÉ

(Holograph letter signed Jonathan Stevens. Most of it in code, keyed to Bailey's Dictionary, 23rd edition, 1773. Remainder decoded by Howard Peckham)

11. 7. 79

Sir.

I delivered Gustavus your letter ——it is not equal to his expectations. He expects to have your promise that he shall be indemnified for any loss he may sustain in case of detection and whether this contest is finished by sword or treaty that ten thousand pounds shall be engaged him for his services, which shall be faithfully devoted to your interest.

I received a letter from Mr Cox requesting an answer to many particulars: what follows I gathered from Gustavus & must be considered as his own.

Washington's army now with him is ten thousand effectives. Could be joined by militia from 4 to 6 or 8 thousand, that depending on where the scene of action lay. Plenty of everything at camp. Supplied from everywhere. Route various accordingly.

No magazines. Sullivan commands 5 thousand regulars, are now sixty miles above Wio[min]g. Detrite [*i.e.* Detroit] the object, usual route. 6 or 8 field pieces. Plenty of provisions carried on 15 hundred pack horses. Whether likely to succeed you must be the best judge. Gates is at Providence with 15 hundred regulars, design to guard that place, has power to call out the militia if wanted. Heath is at Boston. Lincoln has 3 thousand regulars & 5 hundred militia, not likely to collect any army of consequence, the militia do not turn out with alacrity. 23 to 24 thousand the whole force of the Continental Army. I have written fully on the paper money already. There are 10 or 11 frigates from 24 to 36 guns & they will all be cruising soon. Two of them are out to the eastward, two expected from England with a cartel of 6 or 7 hundred prisoners exchanged with France. Four are in or near our ports. The forts in our rivers are in a better state than ever before. No heavy cannon, garrison small, no stores being supplied from this town occasionally. D'E[staing] coming here this summer depends on the British admiral. We know nothing about it. So far Gustavus.

12th I have since conversed with Mr Samuel Wallace who with his friend was extremely useful to General Howe, as mentioned to you at our last interview. If a perfect knowledge of every thing relating to Sullivan's army is an object with the general he will engage to furnish exact accounts thereof every week or fortnight and that his friend shall go with them as a volunteer & furnish him with intelligence to hand through me. All they ask is that their expences should be paid & that in the end if they are thought to have deserved any thing that they may be considered. It being agreeable to your system to reward in proportion to services done I have encouraged the matter, that there may be no time lost. Mr Wallace is a gentleman of large estate in this province and better acquainted with the Indian country than almost any other person. As such he was applied to by the council to furnish a drawing of the country & to assist them in their plan of the Indian expedition. To have refused would have exposed him to sufferings. His drawing was laid by Reed before Washington & the expedition formed on it. He leads them by it to 1 hundred miles SW of Tioga. A corrected copy of this drawing will be ready by return of your next. As it will be large it will require some address to get it through. He cannot believe the whole Continental Army exceeds twelve thousand—assures me that Sullivan has but 25 hundred regulars & about 1 thousand boats, men, drivers, etc., that they expect to meet a large party from Scohari at Tioga the first of August. Tioga is to be fortified & a magazine of stores &c. about 17 hundred cattle making about 3 thousand barrels of beef for S[ullivan's] army were put up so that the greatest part is spoiled & they are living on bacon & livestock. Have at Wyoming 15 hundred barrels of flour. I saw a letter from a chaplain dated thence 2^d which says they shall move in ten days, & that they expect their utmost distance from hence this campaign will not exceed 500 miles.

I am your most obedient Servant

Jona^n Stevens.

[Addressed:] John Anderson Esqr
near
Woodbridge

○

17. ODELL TO ANDRÉ

(Holograph letter, enclosing Stansbury to André of July 11 and Margaret Arnold's shopping list)

Sunday Evening– July 18th 79.

Dear Sir,

This moment by the return of Mercury, who has been detained by some embarassments on his way, I received a packet, with one letter for you which I inclose, and one for a Major Giles at Flat-bush which I also inclose, leaving it to yourself to determine whether it is intended for you—though I confess from what my Friend says of it I suspect it is really intended for the Person to whom it is addressed— But, that you may have the better information concerning the whole of this Packet, I will transcribe such part of my Friend's letter to me as relates to your affair— the letter is dated the 11th Instant, and concludes thus—

"It was on the Evening of the 7th Mr Anderson's favor came to hand, which I immediately delivered to Mrs Moore. A multiplicity of business prevented M^r M[oore]— giving it the requisite attention. I waited on him yesterday morning, found he had made some progress in the account & promised me cash in the Evening, and to send me a sketch that I might draw out a fair account and send Mr Creek home. Instead thereof I received a note from him, that—"he had carefully examined the letter, and found by the laconic Stile and little attention paid to his request, that the Gentleman appear'd very indifferent respecting the matter, he therefore omitted sending me the memo^o he intended in the morning, and wished to see me." We had a long conversation, the result whereof forms the inclosed Letter from me to Mr Anderson, on the 23^d principle (sans integer) which you will be so good as to lend him."

"Mrs Moore requests the inclosed List of Articles for her own use may be procured for her and the account of them and the former sent, and She will pay for the whole with thanks—"

"My best wishes attend you, &c—[""]

In a postscript he says "351.1.2. 57.1.65. [General Arnold] gave me the inclosed Letter to Major Giles, contents to me unknown, he assured me there was nothing in it—"

I find by the above that in the letter to you my Friend has used the D[ictionar]y 23d Ed[itio]n a copy of which I have, and as it differs so considerably from the one I sent you, I fear you will not be able to do without it, and would send it up, but if I mistake not, the copy which you had before was the 23d

It gives me much pain to find my Friend's Friend has misunderstood your letter, and disappointed (I apprehend) your expectations—yet, if I might take the liberty to suggest my own opinion, I could wish you to write once more at least—as it cannot do any harm, and *may* possibly be still worth while. But I am in much greater pain from an apprehension that the late unfortunate Event may be so consequential as to render it difficult for you to find time at present for attending to a *seemingly* fruitless correspondence. I must however beg a line from you as soon as possible, as our Mercury is already suspected of having been here and therefore wishes to return without delay, lest, if long absent, the danger from such Suspicion should be the greater. If you have not time to write, would you approve of my mentioning your being at present out of Town as a reason, and at the same time renew my assurances to my Friend that his Employer may most surely rely upon your being absolutely in earnest on your part to conduct the business proposed in a manner that cannot fail, but through his own groundless hesitation, to surpass his most sanguine expectations?

On the opposite page I have copied

the list which Mrs Moore writes for, which, if you please, you will remit to me with the necessary pass to enable me to send the parcel by the return of my messenger, of whose fidelity I am more fully assured than I can be of almost any other.

I find, from the letter of which I have above given you an extract, that yours having been done in my handwriting, gave suspicion to your Correspondent that his name was known to me. My Friend assured him "that Mr Osborn only knew that a Mr Moore was concerned in the business—" I mention this that, if you should think proper, without seeming to know he had entertained such a suspicion (which I presume respected not you but S[tansbury]—) you might somehow express yourself, whenever you next write, in such a manner as to reassure him on this head. *Possibly* this groundless suspicion may have had some weight in his unreasonable reserve—yet nothing in my Friend's Letter appears to hint at such a thing —but only what I have copied above, respecting the Stile of your letter. Possibly the inclosed may give you fuller information.

Most fervently wishing you health, happiness and glory,

 I am, Dear Sir,
  your most affectionate Servt
   Jonn Odell
Excuse my haste and my blots.

○

18. SHOPPING LIST

(In Arnold's hand, enclosed in Odell to André of July 18)

Articles for Mrs Moore

18 Yds wide or 22 Yds Narrow Pale Pink Mantua
1 ps Broad Pale Pink Ribbon
6 Yds fine Black Sattinet for Shoes

1 p^s Diaper for Napkins
1 p^r Neat Spurrs
1 p^s Clouting Diaper
[Endorsed in both André's and Clinton's hands:]
　　A x
　　Articles wanted to be taken out ——
　　Andre
　　arnold
　　　　&c &c

◐

19. ODELL TO ANDRÉ

(Holograph letter)

　　　　　　New York 21st July 1779
My Dear Sir,
　　The Book I send, covered and sealed—but, as it is very difficult for me to write without it to S[tansbury] —and as it is highly probable that *your* letters in future will be written from that Edition which I before sent to you, I must take the liberty to beg that *this* may be returned to me with your Letter, in order that I may execute the commission properly respecting the queries I am to propose. I am glad to find you are still patient enough to continue the Correspondence—*something* surely may be expected from it, and I am, I confess, still in hopes of something "on a large scale—" otherwise the conduct already shown is utterly unaccountable to me— Be assured, in the mean time, that I can hardly be disappointed in counting upon every thing that can be learned by my Friend, and the reason why his letters to me have hitherto been barren has been my relying upon his *Partner*.
　　All that my Friend means by "sans integer" is that he does not make the addition of an unit to his numbers, as his Partner had done.
　　You will please to observe that if you write to the *Partner*, you must use the Copy which you took with you from hence.
　　I hope, after evacuating Stoney Point, our impertinent neighbours may soon be driven out somewhere else—at least that they do not sleep with impunity after the Coup they have made. But I beg your pardon—it is only my business, in general, to wish, as I do, and hope from my Soul, that Success and glory may crown the measures of our noble Chief and of his brave veterans—
　　Adieu, my Dear Sir,
　　　　I am most sincerely
　　　　　　your affectionate humble Servt
　　　　　　　　Jon^n Odell
The copy I lend you was not to be had here—you will perceive by pretium 60 Dollars, that I have received it by Mercury from S[tansbury]— I have already numbered the pp— Mercury waits till I hear again from you—
[Addressed:] Captn André
　　　　　　Aid de Camp
　　　　　　　　Head Quarters

◐

20. ANDRÉ TO STANSBURY

(Holograph draft of letter concerning Samuel Wallis, prepared to be sent to Stansbury along with André to Arnold, No. 21)

　　To S[tansbury].—
　　　　　　End of July [1779]
Obliged to him for his Exactness and assiduity. Intelligence concerning Sullivan will be acceptable and the drawing we are anxious to receive. Expences of a limited nature shall be paid and as you judge services considered hereafter in proportion to their importance. This kind of Information however has but a very indirect influence here and does not enable us to distress or counteract.

Immediate information of the movements of the Army opposed to us is the main point. Our Compts & thanks to Mr W[allis].—

Joseph Andrews

◯

21. ANDRÉ TO ARNOLD

(Holograph draft, sent to Odell for enciphering along with André to Stansbury, No. 20)

End of July in Cypher [1779] I am sorry any hesitation should Still remain as I think we have Said all that the prudence with which our Liberality must be tempered will admit, I can only add that as such Sums as are held forth must be in some degree accounted for, real Advantage must appear to have arisen from the Expenditure or a generous Effort must have been made.

We are thankfull for the Information transmitted and hope you will continue to give it as frequently as possible. permit me to prescribe a little Exertion. It is the procuring an accurate plan of West Point, with the new roads, New Windsor Constitution &ca An account of what Vessels gun Boats or Gallies are in the North River or may be Shortly built there & the Weight of metal they carry. The Army as Brigaded with the Commandg Officers of Corps in the form commonly called the Order of Battle. Sketches or descriptions of Harbours to the Eastward which might be attacked and where Stores and Shipping might be destroyed.

The only method of compleating conviction on both sides of the generous Intentions of each and making arrangements for important Operations is by a meeting. Wou'd you assume a Command and enable me to see you I am convinced a Conversation of a few minutes would Satisfy you entirely and I trust woud give us equal Cause to be pleased. In any concerted plan which may not be carried into Execution before that time gen: Philips's coming here on parole wou'd be an exceeding good Opportunity for further Explanations. He is S[ir]. H[enry]. C[linton]'s firm friend and a man of Strict honour, but neither to him or any person can we give the Smallest hint without your permission; which we do not mean to ask unless you are perfectly willing to grant it. But above all Sir let us not lose time or contract our Views which on our part have become Sanguine from the extensive Strain of your Overtures and which we cannot think you wou'd on your Side confine to general Intelligence whilst so much greater things may be done and Advantages in proportion as much greater can be reaped.

◯

22. STANSBURY TO ANDRÉ

(Holograph letter, unsigned, in code, keyed to Bailey's Dictionary, 23rd edition. No date, but in answer to André to Arnold, No. 21, sent end of July. Decoded copy in what seems to be André's hand, marked A and Moore)

Sir

I have had an interview with —— [Arnold] who shewed me your Letter, and remarked that it contained no reply to the terms mentioned in my last Tho' he cou'd not doubt your Honour yet there was no Assurance given that his property in this Country should be indemnified from any loss that might attend unfortunate discovery: however sincerely he wished to Serve his Country in accellerating the Settlement of this unhappy Contest, yet he shou'd hold himself unjust to his Family to hazard his all on the Occasion and part with a certainty (potentially at least) for an uncertainty. He hopes to join the army in about 3 weeks when he will if possible contrive an interview. He will make a point of seeing Gen: Philips if he comes here and may perhaps open himself to that gentleman at Same time he depends on your honour that nothing ever transpires to his disadvantage. I wished him to put pen to paper himself but he said he had told me his Sentiments and confided in me to represent them which I have done with Fidelity.

In the Course of the Conversation he asked me if I knew that Sir Henry was going home and Lord C[ornwallis]—— was to have the Command He said he had nothing to communicate at present that could be of Service. He had not the plan of West point [it] being only in Gen: Washingtons hands and the Engineers who made the draught. It had many new Works and he could when there make a drawing of it easily. The number of Men and the Commanding Officers were shifting daily. The Commanding Officer of a Wing to day being ordered perhaps to some post tomorrow: The Harbours &a to the Eastward he thought you must be well acquainted with and also knew where the Vessels Stores &a. lay at Boston Newbury port Salem &a That the Convention had been for 4 Weeks and was yet waiting to carry Mr Girard home who was detained by Congress not having come to any definitive terms to offer G. Britain. That Four Frigates were ordered to cruize off Newfoundland About a thousand Men were on board the Fleet gone against Ponobscott.

I am sensible I have been tedious & have not leizure at this late hour to throw it into better order or smaller compass.
Saturday 3. AM

[Addressed:] John Anderson Esqr
near
Brunswick

◯

23. André to Margaret Arnold

(André seems to have kept no copy of this letter, here quoted from Sargent, André, 220)

Head-Quarters, New York,
the 16th Aug.1779

Madame.—Major Giles is so good as to take charge of this letter, which is meant to solicit your remembrance, and to assure you that my respect for you, and the fair circle in which I had the honour of becoming acquainted with you, remains unimpaired by distance or political broils. It would make me very happy to become useful to you here. You know the Mesquianza made me a complete milliner. Should you not have received supplies for your fullest equipment from that department, I shall be glad to enter into the whole detail of cap-wire, needles, gauze, &c., and, to the best of my abilities, render you in these trifles services from which I hope you would infer a zeal to be further employed. I beg you would present my best respects to your sisters, to the Miss Chews, and to Mrs. Shippen and Mrs. Chew. I have the honour to be, with the greatest regard, Madam, your most obedient and most humble servant,

John André

◯

24. Odell to Stansbury

(Holograph copy, dated probably October 1779. Probably encoded before being sent)

Dear Sir,
yours of Septr *13 & 26* are just received. I am sorry never to have had

it in my power to execute M⁅rs⁆ Moore's commission, for want of a practicable conveyance. It is solely owing to this cause that She has not long since received the parcel in question. She may however still rely on my attention, and that no opportunity shall escape me. your notions concerning the merit and the views of your Friend the Overseer seem to be the same with mine, and I believe we are not alone in our Ideas on this head—for I am desired by our common Friend pd 53 to address myself on this occasion directly to you, and to request (authentic information concerning any points that you may suppose important at this time; and especially accurate accounts of the French Fleet—where are they? what have they done? what do they meditate? what is the real State of affairs to the Southward? and what are the real views of Congress in their present bustle of collecting militia &c. We suspect they mean to amuse us with pretended preparations for an impracticable attempt, in order perhaps to keep us at home. It is of importance that we should know with certainty whether there is any serious plan formed of any *joint* exertions of the French and the Rebels, and if so, what may the plan be, &c *Authentic* information on these points I beg you, if possible, to procure and transmit by the Bearer.) I have confined myself to such articles in the commercial way as are now most in demand, and if they are genuine they will fetch a very good price; but unless they are of the best quality they will not be so readily salable, and by no means turn to so good account. D S has never given me an *proper* Answer; but I think upon the whole he seems to decline your proposal, and I should imagine you had better authorize me to make the same Burlamaqui of S⁅t⁆ Eustatia. I have not yet had time to call on the Cordwainer,

but shall tomorrow. If you approve of it, I propose to invest your money in good Bills of exchange, as the safest way. Please, if possible, to let me have an answer to the inclosed by the return of the Bearer. Farewell.

I am yours &c
J⁅as⁆ Osborne

Copy.

❦

25. MARGARET ARNOLD TO ANDRÉ

(Holograph letter. There is nothing to indicate how it was sent to New York)

M⁅rs⁆ Arnold presents her best respects to Cap⁅t⁆ André, is much obliged to him for his very polite and friendly offer of being serviceable to her. Major Giles was so obliging as to promise to procure what trifles M⁅rs⁆ Arnold wanted in the millinary way, or she would with pleasure have accepted of it. M⁅rs⁆ Arnold begs leave to assure Captain André that her friendship and esteem for him is not impaired by time or accident. The Ladies to whom Cap⁅t⁆ A. wished to be remembered are well, and present their Compliments to him.

Philadelphia. October 13⁅th⁆ 1779.
[Addressed:] Captain André
[Endorsed by André:] M⁅rs⁆ Arnold

❦

26. STANSBURY TO ODELL

(Letter in mixture of code, cipher, French, and English. The secret parts are transcribed by Odell. The last paragraph was in plain text, and the postscript regarding the date was added by Odell. Correct date probably December 3, 1779)

The Army are going into Winter quarters. They have not over four days flour on hand to depend on.

Twenty thousand barrels were to procure but not taken by the French, who, Mr Moore thinks, are gone off. M[oore]— proposes landing troops in Maryland to cut off these Supplies. Fhp [not deciphered] has not enough flour to subsist her Inhabitants, Pensylvania has none to spare. £90 per hundred weight in open market.

Twenty five hundred North Carolina Militia are ordered to Charlestown—it is said they will not turn out more than one thousand. [blank space] is also ordered there with five hundred Regulars, and five hundred N. C. militia are going home from this place under Hogan. Lincoln has one thousand with him, and the utmost he will be able to muster will not make his Garrison to exceed four thousand armed men.

Tell me if you wish to have an useful hand in their Army, and to pay what you find his Services merit?

Exchange is forty four for one— Decemr 1, 1779.

N.B. The scarcity of flour mentioned in my last is from failure of water to work the Mills. Part of the flour from Maryland is on its way hither. There is no official Account at the War-office of the French Fleet. It is supposed to be gone to the West Indies. A few Frigates are said to be in the Chesapeak.

Washington had about nine or ten thousand before Sullivan joined with three thousand, and Gates is going to him with fifteen hundred, making together fourteen thousand. All these, except two thousand, are veterans inlisted during the war. Blankets are scarce with them, one to four men.

Some Insect of your place hath written the President of Congress that the October Packet was arrived, the Contents not transpired, but that your Officers looked very blue.

Gen: Schuyler has moved in Congress that Congress remove from Philadelphia, because they could do no business but it was instantly communicated to you. The questions to be put are, shall they move to the Eastward or Southward? if the latter, Baltimore and Bladensburg are mentioned; if the former, Hartford in Connecticut.

Congress and the Board of War are confident that the present Embarcation is destined for the Southward, as soon as the French leave the Coast.

Congress are preparing their Bills on Holland at six months sight, to make an experiment how they will sell. The sale will determine the Species drawn for. If the bait takes, they will continue fishing—if not they must soon leave off.

A letter dated from Virginia 26. ulto says 1 Ship of 70 Guns & two other armed Vessels were then at Hampton, to get Provisions for the Fleet of our great Ally. others say it is an old 70 cut down to 50 Guns. I doubt not this News. I console myself from this circumstance that the Count has not left us yet, but none of us know where he is, & some think he has too much understanding to tell his intentions even to the Congress itself.

Yours ever

11.3.79 Canon. Pac. Bur. François
Novemr 3d I suspect this date
is erronious—as the first of
Decemr is mentioned above.

◯

27. Odell to André

(Holograph letter)

Wall Street– Decemr 18th 1779
Dear Sir,

I am much indebted to you for your obliging letter, and for your kind offices with His Excellency the Commander in Chief.

My pay, as Chaplain to one of the

Provincial Corps, after the deductions that are made for agency, &c, is about six shillings a day. With this (which is all that I receive at present from Government) and the precarious appointment of Deputy Chaplain to the Royal Fuzileers, I have to defray my own expences here and to support a Wife and three Children at Burlington, where my property has been confiscated by the present usurpation.

When Sir William Howe gave me this appointment, in January 1778, at which time I had been thirteen months an Exile from my family, he was pleased to add, in the way of a contingent gratuity, fifty pounds a year to my Subsistence, which gratuity was paid up to the time of his return to England; and I had an intimation that it was intended to recommend me to Sir Henry Clinton, from whom I flattered myself that I might hope the continuance of this additional allowance: but the intended recommendation was probably forgotten, as a matter of no public moment.

Whatever the Commander in Chief may now determine on this head, whether in my favor or not, it is most sincerely my wish to *merit* His Excellency's patronage by every service in my power: and, however ineffectual my political publications may be, I cannot but hope that, with some assistance, I may yet make my private correspondence essentially useful.

As I happen to be a competent Master of the Spanish Language, I should be glad, in that way too, whenever occasion offers, to be employed in either department of the Army or Navy; and, possibly, The Commander in Chief may be willing to create in my favor an appointment of Spanish Interpreter.

If these tenders of my Services are improper, I beg you to excuse them, and to believe that they proceed at least from honest motives; though I

do not mean to dissemble my hope of serving my own family in serving the Public.

Doctor Seabury is Chaplain to a Provincial Corps and also to His Majesty's Ship Renown: but his family is much more numerous than mine.

I can answer both for him and myself, that we have never entertained so unworthy a Sentiment as to suppose an illiberal tone of Declamation or invective could fail to incur the disapprobation of Sir Henry Clinton; and we shall with pleasure observe the caution which His Excellency has done us the honor to suggest, and which you have been so kind as to intimate.

I sincerely beg your pardon for this long letter, and have the honor to be, Sir,

> your much obliged
> > and most obed^t humble Servant
> > > Jon^n Odell

Major André
[Endorsed:] Decr 18. 79
> Mr Odell

◐

28. Odell to André

(Holograph letter)

> Wall Street—Decem^r 21. 1779

Dear Sir

Accept my thanks for your kindness. Perhaps it may not be improper for me to inform you that, from the time last Winter when the occasional Services of Dr Seabury and myself were proposed to the Commander in Chief, we have taken such opportunities as seemed favorable to employ ourselves in that way, and sundry pieces have been published by us— particularly those under the Signature of Britannicus, and some under different Signatures—and we flatter ourselves that our Essays, especially on the Subject of Continental Money, have not been altogether without effect.

Please to say for us what is proper to the Commander in Chief, in return for his Excellency's favorable intentions towards us.

I have the honor to be
with undissembled
gratitude and esteem
your most obed^t
humble Servt
Jon^n Odell

A parcel, long since requested by S[tansbury]—to be sent for Mrs *Moore*, is now made up, and I hope soon to be able to send it. Shall I charge it to S[tansbury]—or is it, as one before, to be accounted between yourself and your humble Servt?
[Endorsed:] Decem^r 24th [*sic*] 79. Mr Odell.

○

29. KNYPHAUSEN'S NOTES REGARDING ARNOLD

(*These four notes are concerned with Arnold's renewed offers through Stansbury, who about May 1780 went to New York again, to find Knyphausen in command instead of Clinton, and Beckwith acting as aide instead of André. The notes appear to be in Beckwith's hand*)

Mr Moore's offers.

That he will undertake the part in Question, confiding in the former Assurance made to him by His Excellency The Commander in Chief; provided he now obtains from Sir Henry Clinton or General Knyphausen the security as expressed in the enclosed note written by His Friend; this, Mr Moore destines for his Family, or any proportion of it, which he may not be enabled to dispose of; he asks for a small sum of ready money to employ in a particular Channel; he is now

at *Phil–* goes in a few days to Conecticut on his Private affairs, after which, he returns to Camp & remains their in a Military capacity: he particularly desires to have a Conference with an Officer of Confidence: he will take a decisive part in case of an emergency or that a Capital Stroke can be struck; he requests that a particular signiture may be sent to him— that he may be furnished with a Token to prevent any fraud & that a regular mode of communication may be fallen upon; were it not for his Family he declares he would join the Army without making any Terms.

[*Draft*]

Pacoli: 7:

The matter in agitation is of so important a nature, that G[eneral]. K[nyphausen]. does not think himself authorized to give an answer to it in its full extent, & the more so as it is in a great measure already made known to S^r H[enry]. C[linton]: the General will therefore represent the present transaction to Sir H[enry]. the very first opportunity, & in the mean time will be happy in cultivating the Coñection, and in giving Mr Moore, every testimony of his regard. from the pers[uasio]^n he entertains of his rectitude and sincerity, any trifling expenditures which may be made in the channell of communication, previous to a full Answ^r from S. H. C. will be readily reimbursed.

an Off[ice]^r will give you the meeting for which you apply, when ever you can point out the practibility of it, in the mean time two Rings are procured which are exactly alike, for the purposes of communication—and two Pocket Dict[ionarie]^s for a similar Purpose.

General Knyphausen's answer to Mr Moores proposals.

The affair in agitation is of so impor-

tant a nature that General Knyphausen does not think himself authorized to give an answer to it in
its full extent, and the more so, as
the matter is already known to the
Commander in Chief: the General
will therefore take the first opportunity of communicating the transaction to Sir Henry Clinton and in the
mean time will feel happy in cultivating the Coñection, and in giving
Mr Moore every Testimony of his regard, from the persuasion which the
General entertains of his rectitude
and Sincerity: any trifling expenditures which may be made in the Channel of communication, previous to a
full answer from Sir Henry Clinton
will be readily reimbursed: an Officer
will give Mr Moore the meeting which
he solicits, whenever the practability
of it can be pointed out; in the mean
time, two Rings are procured, which
are exactly alike and one of them is
sent to him by his Friend, with whom
a mode of correspondence by Cypher
is likewise settled;
[Endorsed:] Genl Knyphausens answer.

*[The last five words below were added
in Clinton's hand]*

Memo

A Mr Moore had made proposals
to —— [Sir Henry Clinton] previous
to his departure from hence, relative
to himself, the proposals were declined at first from particular circumstances; but offers were then made,
which Mr Moore had now accepted
of, provided that assurances are given
to him of certain indemnifications,
for himself and Family, in cases of
emergency; the Indemnifications required are as follows, first the loss of
his private Fortune £5000 Sterling;
ye Debt due to him by the *community*
£5000 Sterl^g to be made good, or
whatever part is lost, & to have a New
Raised Batt^n here upon the common

Footing—to be supplied with Money
from time to time as circumstances
may require; Mr Moore is now at
P[hiladelphia]. & waits there for a few
days; he intends going to C[onnec-
ticu]t. and to return in Three or
Four Weeks, to Camp—where [he] is
to remain in a Military Line; he
wishes to have a Conference with a
Military Officer— he offers to take
decisive Part in case of an Emergency—or in view of attack on B[os-
to]^n, P[hiladelphi]^a or any other
place; he declared were it not for his
Family, he would without ceremony
have thrown himself into the protection of the Kings Army;

This to go no further here; it may
be communicated to S[ir]. H[enry].
C[linton]. with the particulars of the
Indemnification required; in addition
to promises made him formerly on
which he relies

to fix upon a particular Token,
place of meeting, Cypher & Channel
of Communication; permission for a
few Articles.

❂

30. Arnold to Beckwith

*(Original in code, keyed to a small
dictionary)*

from Mr Moore to Captain Beckwith
Philadelphia June 7th 1780

I have received from The
Commander-in-Chief a Proclamation
in order to have a number of Copies
printed, the purport of which, will
be transmitted to you by J[oseph]:
S[tansbury]: to whom I have communicated it.

The Minister of France this day assured me that the French Troops
destined for Canada amount to Eight
Thousand.

The 8th Inst. I propose going to
Camp, will be at Morris Town the
12th Kings Ferry the 16th & New

Haven the 20th and return to Camp by the 4th of July: If I meet a person in my mensuration who has the *Token* agreed upon, you may expect every intelligence in my power which will probably be of consequence.

When fully authorized by Sir Henry Clinton to treat, I wish to have a conference with one of your Officers in whom we can place a mutual confidence.

The American Army intended to coöperate with the French will probably go up Conecticut River to Number Four and cross the Country to St Johns.

◐

31. STANSBURY TO BECKWITH

(Enclosed with Arnold to Beckwith, No. 30. Washington's proclamation in code accompanied it, with a footnote by Stansbury. The footnote, given below, has been decoded by Howard Peckham without the small dictionary used by Stansbury, and some words must be guessed at)

I have transcribed the above from the original and it must be a profound secret. I send you this day's parcel. No action but that on 17th April in the West Indies—English fleet at Lucie 13th ult. the French off Martinico or on some expedition. The majority of the rebel army under Fayette will be from Connecticut River to Number Four and to St. Johns to make a diversion when the French shall be ready to attack Quebec.

Yours,
Joseph Stansbury

[Addressed:] G. B. Ring
    Executor to the late John Anderson Esq. to the care of James Osborne

◐

32. ARNOLD TO BECKWITH OR ANDRÉ

(Extracts from two letters, dated June 12 and 15, 1780. Extracts apparently in Odell's hand)

Extract from two Letters of Mr Moore.

"Morristown. June 12th—Six "French Ships of the Line, several "Frigates and a number of Trans- "ports with six thousand Troops are "expected at Rhode Island in two or "three weeks to act under General "Washington. It is probable three or "four thousand Rebels will be em- "barked with them and proceed up "the St Laurence to Quebec, while the "Marquis Fayette with two or three "thousand will go from Connecticut "River to St Johns and Montreal. "Governor Trumbull is laying up "flour and Pork at Connecticut River "for the French the Draughts when "completed will make General Wash- "[ington] twenty thousand. But some "States are so dilatory he does not "expect strong reinforcemts before "August."

"10 P.M. Mr M[oore]. expects to "have the command of West Point "offered him on his return. Troops "and Provision wanting there. Only "fifteen hundred. Little Flour, and "none to be had but from Pennsyl- "vania, whence they have required "Ten thousand barrels. Mr M[oore]. "thinks it would be a good Stroke to "get between General Washington "and West Point." 15th June 1780

◐

33. ARNOLD TO BECKWITH OR ANDRÉ

(Extract from letter dated June 16, 1780. Apparently in hand of Odell)

extract of a letter dated Fish-kills— 16th June.

"I called on General Howe at West

Point, which I never saw before—was greatly disappointed both in the works & garrison. There is only fifteen hundred Soldiers, which will not half man the works, but General Clinton's Brigade of twelve hundred Men are ordered to join the garrison and are on their march from Albany. It is hoped they will arrive before the English can make an attack, which it is thought they have in contemplation. This Place has been greatly neglected General Howe tells me there is not ten days provision for the garrison— A quantity is on the way from Connecticut and soon expected, but if the English were to cut off the communication with Pennsylvania they would be distressed for flour which is not to be procured in this part of the Country. It is surprising a Post of so much importance should be so totally neglected. The works appear to me (though well executed) most wretchedly planned to answer the purpose designed, vizt to maintain the Post and stop the passage of the River. The Point is on a low piece of ground comparatively to the chain of Hills which lie back of it. The highest called Rocky Hill which commands all the other works is about half a mile from Fort Putnam, which is strong. on Rocky Hill there is a small redoubt to hold two hundred men and two six pounders pointed on the other works. The wall six foot thick and defenceless on the Back, and I am told the English may land three miles below and have a good road to bring up heavy Cannon to Rocky Hill. This redoubt is wretchedly executed, only seven or ten foot high and might be taken by assault by a handful of men. I am convinced the Boom or chain thrown across the River to stop the Shipping cannot be depended on. A single Ship large and heavy-loaded with a strong wind and tide would break the

Chain— The Committee of Congress have made requisition to the different States, which if complied with will enable us to act offensively this Summer and to some purpose.

○

34. STANSBURY (CARLETON) TO ODELL

(Undated letter from Stansbury, calling himself Carleton. Probably late June or early July 1780)

Dear Sir

I inclose you a copy of a former letter & beg my compliments to Mr Anderson & M l'anneau. I shoud be glad to know what is said to a request I made a little time ago. I remain affectionately yours.

T. C.

[Addressed:] Mr James Osborne

○

35. STANSBURY (CARLETON) TO ODELL

(Holograph letter)

July 7. 1780

Dear Sir

I received your favors acknowledging my first bill of Excha[nge] being honor'd, since which I have not heard from you, tho' I have sent 2 small bills on the Company account. My partner is come to town & has set those matters right that were not clearly enter'd in my last account current, and which you will perceive make a great difference in the general balance. He thinks it strange that no steps are taken on your part to come to a settlement, which rightly consider'd is of consequence to you both. He intended to have wrote you on that head this day, but tho' I left a person waiting all day in town on that account, business would not permit him an hour's leizure.

I got a verbal message about minuit

& shall forward it to you. My best respects wait on Mr Anderson & M^r de l'anneau.

I am

Your obliged humble Servt
Thos Carleton

[Addressed:] James Osborne

○

36. STANSBURY TO BECKWITH OR ANDRÉ

(Original message in code, keyed to a small dictionary. Decoded copy apparently in Odell's hand)

M^r M[oore]. requests a very explicit answer to his letter of June 7th and that some method may be fallen on to obtain an interview with Major General Philips or some other proper officer, as nothing further can be done without it. On the arrival of the French Troops, N. york is the object, if an Army can be raised which is thought equal to the attempt. The Canada expedition is a secondary object in case the other fails. G. Washington will throw a detachment over the North River when the French fleet arrives at Newport, but not before. The Garrisons of Stony P^t and Verplank's have orders to withdraw on the appearance of the Enemy in force, & not risk a defence. There are in each fifty men, one 12 pound^r & two Howit[ze]r The Stores are already removed from them. Two or three Persons in whom you confide as Spies on General Howe are in his pay & often give him important intelligence. He thinks General Philips might come out to negociate an exchange of prisoners, or his own for Lincoln. He begs you would write to him only by such Channels as may be fully depended on. He is to take the command of W[est]. P[oint]. immediately on the fleet's arrival, or at any rate in the course of this month. He has a Drawing of the works on

both sides the River done by the French Engineer, & thinks he could settle matters with a proper officer that you might take it without loss, and also lay down a plan of communication whereby you should be informed of every thing projected at Head Quarters.

July 7, 1780—

○

37. ARNOLD TO ANDRÉ

(Written in a disguised hand)

Sir

A mutual Confidence between us is wanting, the persons we have employed have deceived us, or we have been unfortunate in our negociation, in which on both sides we are deeply Interested; If the first here our Correspondence ought to end, If the second an opportunity offers of redressing any abuse: If the latter a stricter attention and proper regard to the Interests of both parties may remedy the misfortune.

To my letter of the 7th June I have received no answer I then reffered you to our mutual F^rd S[tansbur]^y for the particulars of a Conversation which I thought Interesting, a few days Since I imparted to him some matters of still greater importance; the bearer (in whom a Confidence may be placed) is Charged with others, and is instructed (preliminaries being first settled,) to fix on a plan of safe Conveyance and Opperation.— my Stock in trade (which I have before mentioned) is £10,000 Sterling, with near an equal sum of outstanding debts, an equal sum I expect will be put *into* stock and, the profits arising be *equally divided*.— I have advanced several sums already, and risqued still greater, without any profit, It is now become necessary for me to know the risque I run in

Case of a loss.— I expect you will pay into the hands of the bearer One thousand Guineas to be vested in goods suitable for our market, on receit of which I will transmit to you their full Value in good *French Bills drawn on sight* or at a short time, for other Advances you shall have *good Sterling Bills well indorsed.*

I wish for a personal Confference with Captain *P* or some one of the Co-partnership, (without which it appears difficult to make a proper arrangement.) This I apprehend may very easily be brought about If you have any regard for your own interest, or my savety by no means trust to any Conveyance that is not known and *Approved, or proved,* you may be deceived with *False friends:* mention no names, write me in Cypher and through some medium: a Clear explicit, & Confidential Answer *in Cypher* will enable us to Co-opperate to mutual Advantage; or end this Correspondence to the mutual safety of all Concerned, as I make no doubt the strictest honor will be observed

> I am
> > Sir
> > > your Obedt Hbl Srvt
> > > > J Moore

11th July [1780]
Mr John Anderson
> Mercht

[Addressed:] To
> Mr John Anderson
> > Merchant
> to the Care of James Osborn
> to be left at Mr Odells

◯

38. Arnold to André

(Letter in code, keyed to a small dictionary. Decoded copy in Odell's hand)

I wrote to Captn B[eckwith]— on the 7th of June, that a F[rench]—

fleet and army were expected to act in conjunction with the A[merican] army. At the same time I gave Mr S[tansbury]— a manifesto intended to be published in C[anad]a, and have from time to time communicated to him such intelligence as I thought interesting, which he assures me he has transmitted to you. I have received no answer to my Letter, or any verbal Message— I expect soon to command W. Pt and most seriously wish an interview with some intelligent officer in whom a mutual confidence could be placed. The necessity is evident to arrange and to coöperate— An officer might be taken Prisoner near that Post and permitted to return on parole, or some officer on Parole sent out to effect an exchange.

General W[ashington]— expects on the arrival of the F[rench]— Troops to collect 30,000 Troops to act in conjunction; if not disappointed, N. York is fixed on as the first object; if his numbers are not sufficient for that Object, Can–a– is the second; of which I can inform you in time, as well as of every other design. I have accepted the command at W[est]. P[oint]. as a Post in which I can render the most essential Services, and which will be in my disposal. The mass of the People are heartily tired of the War, and wish to be on their former footing— They are promised great events from this year's exertion— If disappointed—you have only to persevere and the contest will soon be at an end. The present Struggles are like the pangs of a dying man, violent but of a short duration—

As Life and fortune are risked by serving His Majesty, it is necessary that the latter shall be secured as well as the emoluments I give up, and a compensation for Services agreed on, and a Sum advanced for that purpose—which I have mentioned in a letter which accompanies this, which Sir Henry will not, I believe, think unreasonable. I am, Sir,

> your hble Servt
> J. Moore

July 12th 1780

Mr Jno Anderson

P.S. I have great confidence in the Bearer, but beg Sir Henry will threaten him with his resentment in case he abuses the confidence placed in him, which will bring certain ruin on me. The Bearer will bring me 200 Guineas, and pay the remainder to Captn A—— who is requested to receive the deposit for Mr Moore.

[Original addressed:] To Mr John Anderson

> Merchant
> to the Care of James Osborn
> to be left at Mr Odells

○

39. ANDRÉ TO ARNOLD

(Holograph draft, unsigned. Written after receipt of Arnold's June letters, and received by Arnold on July 13)

H[is]. E[xcellency]. S[ir]. H[enry]. C[linton]. is much obliged to you for the usefull Intelligence you have transmitted him It corresponds with other Information and gives him full conviction of your desire to assist him. He had hoped to communicate with you in a very Satisfactory manner but is disappointed. His Excellency hopes you still keep in view the project of essentially cooperating with him. He thinks the having the Command of W. Point would afford the best opportunities for it and would willingly know from you some scheme for effecting a Service of importance there. The General could point out such plausible measures as woud ward off all blame or Suspicion and be very eligible at the Juncture of an Attack

upon Canada An interview between you and a person he [*sic*] absolutely necessary. Your visiting Eliz^h Town or Some place near us, which a flag of Truce could reach and where you might be supposed to be detained by Sickness is the expedient which strikes S^r H[enry]. C[linton]. as a practicable one. The General trusts that in the Same Confidence in which you communicate with him you will rely on his promise that upon effectual cooperation you shall experience the full measure of the national obligation & his Excellency will in the mean time give you in such manner as you may require it an ample Stipend

○

40. ARNOLD TO ANDRÉ

(Letter in code, keyed to a small dictionary. Decoded copy in Odell's hand)

Inclosed in a cover addressed to Mr Anderson.

Two days since I received a letter without date or Signature, informing me that S[ir]. Henry —— was obliged to me for the intelligence communicated, and that he placed a full confidence in the Sincerity of my intentions, &c. &c. On the 13th Instant I addressed a letter to you expressing my Sentiments and expectations, viz, that the following Preliminaries be settled previous to coöperating. First, that S[ir]. Henry secure to me my property, valued at ten thousand pounds Sterling, to be paid to me or my Heirs in case of Loss; and, as soon as that shall happen, —— hundred pounds per annum to be secured to me for life, in lieu of the pay and emoluments I give up, for my Services as they shall deserve— If I point out a plan of cooperation by which S[ir]. H[enry]. shall possess himself of West

Point, the Garrison, &c. &c. &c. twenty thousand pounds Sterling I think will be a cheap purchase for an object of so much importance. At the same time I request a thousand pounds to be paid my Agent— I expect a full and explicit answer— The 20th I set off for West Point. A personal interview with an officer that you can confide in is absolutely necessary to plan matters. In the mean time I shall communicate to our mutual Friend S[tansbur]y all the intelligence in my power, until I have the pleasure of your answer.

Moore

July 15th [1780]
To the line of my letter of the 13th I did not add seven.
[By Odell:] N.B. the postscript only relates to the manner of composing the Cypher in the letter referred to—
[Addressed:] Capt John Anderson
to be left at Mr Odells
Baltimore

◯

41. ANDRÉ TO STANSBURY

(Holograph draft of letter in acknowledgment, apparently, of No. 35 and No. 36, though the references are not all clear. This seems to be the answer mentioned in the first sentence of No. 42. If so, date of No. 41 was July 23)

We have received yours in date of the 7th and are much obliged to you for its import which we give implicit faith to, as to every thing you are so kind as to Communicate. The Comm[ander] in Ch[ief]. will be happy to learn the Mode of forwarding to you the Supplies mentioned both for Mr Moore & yourself. You must not wonder if we take a View of our new arrived foe and if prudence justifies it make some attempt on him   Our main purpose is however the measure

which your Cooperation is to render Successfull Stony Pt will be taken possession of & from thence I shall find some pretence which you will understand for a Meeting not with the person at first wished as you will have learnt the objection to it but with one you know & will Confide in

◯

42. ODELL TO STANSBURY

(Holograph copy, enclosing André to Arnold, No. 43)

Copy to Mr Stevens, July 24th 1780.

Yours of the 7th was answered yesterday; and after that answer was dispatched I received one of the 15th inclosing one of the same date from Mr Moore to Mr Anderson, and another of the 18th from yourself. I have this morning had the honor of a conversation with the Commander in Chief on the Subject. In addition to what is stated in the inclosed for Mr Moore, His Excellency authorizes me to repeat in the strongest terms the assurances so often given to your Partner, that if he is in earnest and will to the extent of his Ability coöperate with us, he *shall* not in any possible event have cause to complain, and essential Services *shall* be even profusely rewarded, far beyond the stipulated indemnification, &c. but indemnification (*as a preliminary*) is what Sir H[enry]: thinks highly unreasonable. However he has not the smallest doubt but that every thing may be settled to mutual satisfaction when the projected interview takes place at W[est]. P[oint]. from whence it is expected Mr M[oore]: will take occasion (upon entering on his C[omman]d there) to correspond with S[ir]. H[enry]. by Flag of truce. Mr Anderson is willing himself to effect the meeting either in the way proposed, or in whatever manner may at the time appear most eligible— As to the Speculation you propose on your own account, His Excellency has no other objection than that the plan is inconvenient especially in the absence of the Admiral— He permits me to assure you that he will do justice to your zeal and assiduity in transacting the business of the House intrusted to your care, and will reward your Services in full proportion to their value & importance.

I am, &c,

Jas Osborne

[Endorsed:] Copy to Mr Stevens— July 24—

◯

43. ANDRÉ TO ARNOLD

(Holograph draft, written probably July 24, 1780. Enclosed in Odell to Stansbury, No. 42. Signature figures stand for Y—— S——, if same small dictionary was used as in preceding letters)

Your Letter of the 15th is arrived, that of the 13th is not yet come to hand. Tho' West Point derives its importance from the nature of the Operations of our Enemy yet shoud we thro your means possess ourselves of 3000 Men and its Artillery and Stores which [with?] the Magazine of Provision for the Army which may probably be there the sum even of 20000 pounds should be paid you. You must not suppose that in Case of detection or failure that your Efforts being known you would be left a Victim; but Services done are the terms on which we promise rewards; in these you see we are profuse; We conceive them proportioned to ye risk. As to an absolute promise of indemnification to the Amount of 10000 Pounds and Annuity of 500 whether Services are performed or not It can

never be made. Your Intelligence we prize and will freely recompense it 200£ shall be lodged in your Agents hands as you desire & 300 more are at your disposal.

297.8.15   244.9.34

◯

44. ODELL TO ANDRÉ

(Holograph letter, enclosing other copies of No. 37 and No. 38 brought by Wallis. All three sent to Beckwith in André's absence)

New York—July 29, 1780

Sir,

In consequence of an intimation by Letter, that, during the absence of the Commr in Chief, all letters from Mr Moore, when decyphered, should be forwarded to Captn Beckwith at Morris House, I opened the inclosed, which were brought yesterday by Mr Wallace, the person mentioned in the letters of the 15th & 18th and the agent to whom, as you will see, Mr Moore desires the 200 guineas may be paid. These letters by Mr Wallace are of prior date [July 11 and 12] to those brought by your messenger, and contain nothing new, the bearer having been dispatched, as far as I can learn, chiefly with a view of ascertaining whether Mr *Stevens* or *your humble Servant* had *faithfully* conducted the correspondence, and as an agent to receive the *first-fruits*— Mr Moore will be convinced that his jealousy of "the persons employed" was utterly groundless, and, when Mr Wallace returns, which he says he must of necessity do without delay, Mr Moore will probably leave "harping on my Daughter," & think the terms contained in your last letter every way equal to what he can in reason expect. Mr W[allis] is confident that he will no longer hesitate, and that, had he known of such an answer as hath been sent, before he came off, it would have saved him the trouble and risk of his journey—

Wishing a new harvest of Glory to our noble Chief and his gallant Train of Myrmidons, I have the honor to be, Sir,

most sincerely your affectionate Servt
            J[onathan] O[dell]
M[ajo]r A[ndré]

○

45. BECKWITH TO ANDRÉ

(Holograph letter, enclosing Odell to André, No. 44)

Head Quarters Morris House
July 30. [1780] Twelve *at Night*

Dr Sir

I enclose to you Two letters from Mr More, with a Third one, from Mr Odell; this last will save me the attempting any further explanation; I also forward to you Wallaces letter to me; although at present very unwell I went to New-York & saw him and in consequence of a letter which Mr Odell produced to me of yours, and Mr Mores application, I paid the Two hundred Guineas & took his receipt; which I hope the Commander in Chief will approve of—

I could not take it upon me, to fix a direct mode of communication by the *Hudson*. I hinted however the idea of fixing upon some particular place— I also wrote Three or four words to Mr More, relative to the sum paid Wallace on his account. I have fixed on a mode of corresponding with the Gentⁿ W[alla]ce hints at & will soon receive letters from him, but the manner is tedious although certain being by Philad^a I am promised the names of the other Wellwishers & think I know one or two of them already.

Major Delancey did promise to write to me, but I have never heard from him.

all is quiet in Jersey. There are in West Point Three Brig^{des} Poores, Clintons & Pattersons; opposite to it upon Nelsons Point are Parsons & Huntingdons Brigades— Glovers at Col. Robinsons house & Nixons at Continental Village— they are chiefly encamped; there is a late Genl Order in the Rebel Army directing all Genl & Field Off^{rs} to wear Black & White Feathers in their hatts—other Off^{rs} to wear Black Cockades with a White Field.

I am
    Dr Sir
        Your most obed^t
            humble Servt
                Geo. Beckwith
                    A.D.C
[Endorsed in André's hand:] Captain Beckwith

○

46. ARNOLD TO MARGARET ARNOLD

(Extract in Odell's hand. Sent by Stansbury to Odell, August 14, and by Odell to André, August 24. Original in code, keyed to a small dictionary)

(Extracts, &c) July 30th General Wash~ has just arrived at Kakigate when he received intelligence that S[ir]. H[enry]. C[linton]. had gone up the Sound with a considerable Force— He went immediately to King's Ferry, and from thence proposed to go to W[est]. P[oint]. to put the Troops there in motion to join this Army who cross the Ferry to-morrow morning. When the whole form a junction I believe we shall have near ten thousand men together, who will probably move towards N.Y. in order to draw the attention of S[ir]. H[enry]. C[linton]. from Rhode Island. I wish our Force and the provision made for it would enable us to attack N.Y. in his absence, and end the dispute. But I am sorry to say I believe it will be unequal to the undertaking, and am very apprehensive for the French Fleet and Army who are in a critical Situation. However another Division of twenty five hundred men and several Ships of the Line were to sail from Brest as soon as Transports could be procured—those provided being blocked up in Havre de Grace. If this Division should arrive soon they will probably make the French Fleet nearly equal, perhaps superior, to the British; and there is some expectation of a reinforcement from the West Indies. So that upon the whole our affairs which do not wear a pleasing aspect at present may soon be greatly changed.

○

47. ARNOLD TO MARGARET ARNOLD

(Extract in Odell's hand. Sent by Stansbury to Odell, August 14, and by Odell to André, August 24)

(Augt 5th) All the continental Troops from W[est]. P[oint]. have joined the main Army. At present there are no Troops there but about fifteen hundred of the Militia of Massachusetts Bay, who are destitute of almost every necessary. They are in want of Tents, provisions, and almost every thing.

(No date) In consequence of S[ir]. H[enry]. C[linton]'s return our Army is ordered to recross the North River at King's Ferry, and will march to Dobbs's Ferry, where the General intends to establish a Post, and build works, which will confine the British within narrower bounds and shorten our communication with New England. The preparations against N.Y. are at present laid aside, as there ap-

pears no prospect of our collecting a force sufficient this Summer, and we are in want of almost every requisite for the purpose.

○

48. STANSBURY TO ODELL

(Copy in Odell's hand, sent to André in Odell's letter of August 24, No. 49, enclosing Arnold to Margaret Arnold, No. 46 and No. 47)

From Mr Stevens to Jasper Overhill– Augt 14, 1780– Rece^d Augt 23^d from John Rattoon

Dear Sir,

Your several favors by Wallace and Rattoon reached my hands the 8th but no opportunity of answering them has presented till this day. I am highly obliged to His E[xcellenc]^y S[ir]. H[enry]. C[linton]. for his generous assurances; yet, presuming on Mr Anderson's friendly assistance, mentioned in a former letter of yours, and believing that it must be, in itself, an acceptable Service to supply the Garrison with Lumber which it wanted, I immediately engaged several for the purpose. The Dolphin (alias the Shelah) J. Shaw master, will sail in this Week, and the Flying-Fish, O. Phillips, on the 20th with sheathing boards &c. The Sloops Hawk, Field, of 80 Tons, and Swallow, Kerr, of 70, will soon follow. I wish Mr Sproat would sell them in the manner proposed in my former Letter.

Mr Moore commands at W[est]. P[oint]. but things are so poorly arranged that your last important Dispatches are yet in *her* hands, no unquestionable Carrier being yet to be met with. When you have opened your communication on the Spot, these delays will be avoided—

From the same to J: Anderson & Co. inclosed with the above to Overhill. [Here follow extracts from Arnold to Margaret Arnold of July 30 and August 5.]

☉

49. ODELL TO ANDRÉ

(Holograph letter, enclosing Stansbury to Odell, No. 48, and Arnold to Margaret Arnold, No. 46 and No. 47)

Dear Sir,

You will observe that the above extracts [July 30 and August 5] are from Letters written *to Mrs Moore*, but with a view of communicating information to *you–* this remark explains the reason of a Stile which would appear extraordinary in letters directly addressed to Mr Anderson. I wish it were possible to open a shorter road of correspondence.

    J[onathan]. O[dell].

Augt 24.

☉

50. STANSBURY (CHARLTON) TO ODELL

(Original letter partly in code. Decoded copy in Odell's hand. Enclosed in Odell to André, No. 54, September 7. Charlton seems to be another version of the name Carleton which Stansbury had used in No. 34 and No. 35)

Extract of a Letter from M. M. dated
    25th

"I believe the army will cross the "N[orth]. R[iver]. this day– there is a "Report that S[ir]. H[enry]. C[linton]. "has embarked a considerable Force– "It is imagined he has some Enter- "prise in contemplation. If he should "draw off a great part of his Force, "G[eneral]. W[ashington]. has a fine "army of twelve thousand Men ready "to make an Attack on N.Y. One "circumstance is indeed rather against "us, owing to the Derangement of

"the Commissary Department. They "have been three Days without a "mouthful of meat, and this Post is "very little better. The commissaries "drive the Cattle provided for us to "the French, who give them a better "price, which will probably create a "jealousy entre eux. Our Army can- "not keep the Field late, unless better "supplied." 6. AM. 19.43.2992.

I received last night the Drawing, which I shall copy immediately and deliver it to Rattoon, if he is prepared to receive it. G[eneral]. W[ashington]. has ordered the Militia to be discharged, having received Advice that the Second Division will not sail before the first of August.— The Rebel Army in S. C. under Gates have been totally defeated— the militia only escaped—

    yours ever
    Thos Charlton

[Addressed:] Jasper Overhill
[Endorsed:] Arnolds information

☉

51. BECKWITH TO ANDRÉ

(Holograph letter)

    Morris House Augt 27^h 1780
Dear Sir

Were I not confident that you regard the substance not the manner of my letters, I would in my present weakly situation, decline writing; but as I hope I am recovering, I am unwilling to throw the correspondencies with which Gen. Knyphausen has honoured me, in to a different channell, and flatter myself, it will not now be requisite— Capt. Sutherland, with whom the Boats crew are at present, it not being prudent to let them come on shore, informs me that General *Harland* Commands at West Point— I take it for granted *Arnold* as I never heard of the other;

I will sift the matter fully and let you know in the course of the day, with other particulars. I am Dr Sir

Your most obed^t humble

Servt

Geo. Beckwith Aid de Camp

[Addressed:] Major André

D: A: G.

Head Quarters

[Endorsed:] Aug. 27, 80. Capt Beckwith

○

52. ARNOLD TO ANDRÉ

(Holograph letter in disguised hand, sent by William Heron and turned by him over to General Parsons who did not recognize it as a treacherous communication. Original in Library of Congress)

August 30th 1780

Sir

On the 24th Ins^t I received a note from you without date, in answer to mine of the 7th July, also a letter from your house of the 24th July, in answer to mine of the 15th, with a note from M^r B—— of the 30th July, with an extract of a letter from M^r J Osborn of the 24th I have paid particular attention to the contents of the several letters. had they arrived earlier, you should have had my answer sooner. a variety of circumstances has prevented my writing you before, I expect to do it very fully in a few days and to procure you an interview with M^r M[oor]e when you will be able to settle your commercial plan I hope agreeable to all parties. M^r M[oor]e assures me that he is still of opinion that his first proposal is by no means unreasonable and makes no doubt when he has a conference with you that you will close with it. He expects when you meet that you

will be fully authorised from your house: that the risques, and profit of the co-partnership may be fully and clearly understood.

A speculation might at this time be easily made to some advantage with *ready money*, but there is not the quantity of goods *at Market*, which your partner seems to suppose, and the number of speculators, below, I think will be against your making an immediate purchase. I apprehend goods will be in greater plenty and much cheaper in the course of the season; both dry & wet are much wanted and in demand at this juncture. some quantities are expected in this part of the Country soon.

M^r M[oor]e flatters himself that in the course of ten days he will have the pleasure of seeing you, He requests me to advise you that he has ordered a draught on you in favour of our mutual friend S[tansbur]y for £300.— which you will charge on acc^t of the tobacco.

I am in behalf of M^r M[oor]e and C^o

Sir

Your Obed^t Hble Servant

Gustavus

Mr John Anderson

Merchant

[Addressed:] Mr John Anderson

Merchant

to the care of James Osborn to be left at the Rev'd Mr Odells

New York.

○

53. ARNOLD TO ANDRÉ

(On September 3 Arnold, as Gustavus, wrote a letter to André, as John Anderson, which André received but which is missing. For the circumstances see page 301 above)

○

54. ODELL TO ANDRÉ

(Holograph letter, signed Jasper Over-hill, enclosing Stansbury (Charlton) to Odell, No. 50)

My Dear Sir,

I have exactly decyphered the above [Charlton's letter of August 25], all but the following viz. 6 AM 19.43.2992, which I suppose is intended to mark the date, but I cannot make it out– If I *should* hit upon [it], I will call and let you know.

Your affectionate Servat

Jasper Overhill

Sunday, 7th Septr

◯

55. ANDRÉ TO SHELDON

(Holograph draft, undated. Copy sent was dated September 7)

Sir

I am told my name is made known to you and that I may hope your indulgence in permitting me to meet a friend near your Outpost. I will endeavour to obtain permission to go out with a flag which will be sent to Dobbs' Ferry on   next at oClock when I should be happy to see Mr G. —— Should I not be allowed to go the Officer who is to command the Escort between whom and myself no distinction need be made can speak on the Affair. Let me entreat you Sir to favour a Matter so interesting to the parties concern'd & which is of so private a nature that the Publick cannot on either side be injur'd by it I shall be happy on my part in doing any Act of Kindness to you in a family or property concern of a similar nature.

I trust I shall not be detain'd but should any old grudge be a cause for it I shall rather risk that, than neglect the business in question or assume a mysterious Character to carry on an innocent affair as friends advise me to come to your Lines by stealth

J Anderson

[Endorsed:] Letter to S ——

◯

56. ARNOLD TO ANDRÉ

(Holograph letter, September 10 and 15. Enclosed in Beckwith to André, No. 59)

Sepr 10. 1780

Dear Sir

I have received a Letter of the 7th Inst with your Signature directed to Colonel Sheldon in which is the following Paragraph

"I will endeavour to obtain permis-"sion to come out with a Flag which "will be sent to Dobbs's Ferry on Mon-"day next the 11th at 12 oClock when "I shall be happy to meet Mr G. "should I not be allowed to go the "Officer who is to Command the Es-"cort between whom and myself no "distinction need be made, can speak "on the Affair.

From the Tennor of your Letter and of this Paragraph in particular, I suspect my Letter to you of the 7th Inst has been interrupted, and the Answer dictated by the Enemy in hopes of drawing you into a Snare, for I Cannot Suppose you would be so imprudent as to trust a British Officer, Commanding a Flag with our private Concerns altho of a Commercial Nature, you must be sensible my Situation will not permit my meeting or having any private Intercourse with such an Officer: you must therefore be Convinced that it will be necessary for you to Come or send some Person you can confide in to Colonel Sheldons quarters, to whom I have wrote requesting him to send a Pilot with you to meet me which He has promised to do, and will perhaps come himself, by no means hint to him or any other Person your intentions in coming out as it may *prevent our Speculation,* which can be of no Consequence to any one but our selves—

If I have been mistaken and the Letter directed to Colonel Sheldon was wrote by you I do by all means advise you to follow the Plan you propose of geting to our Lines by Stealth, If you can do it without danger on your side, I will engage you shall be perfectly safe here

I am

Dr Sir

your Obedt Hble Svt

Mr John Anderson   Gustavus

PS If you send me the Old token Vizt *John Anderson, on a piece of Paper as I shall Gustavus*

G——

Septr 15. 1780

Dear Sir

On the 11th at Noon agreable to your request I attempted to go to Dobbs's Ferry, but was prevented by the Armed Boats of the Enemy who fired several times upon us, and Continued opposite the ferry untill Night, The forgoing Letter was Intended as a Caution to you not to mention your business to Colo Sheldon or any other Person; I have no Confidants I find I have made one too many already, which has prevented Several profitable Speculations, Lieut Colonel Jameson Commands in the lines in the room of Colo Sheldon. If you think proper to pursue your Former Plan, you will be perfectly safe in Coming to his quarters or those of Major Talmadge of his Regiment either of those gentlemen will immediately send an Escort with you to meet me: If you have any objections to this plan, I will send a person in whom you may Confide, by Water to meet you at Dobbs's ferry on Wednesday the 20th Inst between 11 & 12 oClock at Night, who will Conduct you to a place of Safety, where I will meet

you   It will be necessary for you to be disguised, and If the Enemies Boats are there it will favor my Plan as the Person is not Suspected by them,   I[f] I do not hear from you before you may depend upon the Person being punctual at the place before mentioned

My partiner of whom I hinted in a former Letter has £10,000 Cash in hand ready for a Speculation If any should offer which Appears profitable. I have abt £1,000, on hand and Can Collect £1500, more in two or three days,   Add to this I have some *Credit*—from these hints you can Judge of the purchase that can be made,   I cannot be more explicit at present   meet me if possible. you may rest assured, that If there is no danger in passing your Lines, you will be perfect[l]y safe where I propose the meeting of which you shall be informed on Wednesday Evening if you think proper to be at Dobbs's Ferry.

Adieu and be assured of the Friendship of

Gustavus

[Addressed:] Mr John Anderson to the Care of Mr James Osborn to be left at the Rev'd Mr Odells   New York

○

57. CLINTON TO ANDRÉ

(Holograph letter)

Dear Andre

Col. Robinson will probably go with the Flag him self, as you are with him at the Fore-post you may as well be of the party. you will find me on your return at Gen. Kniphausen.

11. Sept

faithful[ly]

yrs H Clinton.

◑

58. Arnold to André(?)

(Holograph note in code, keyed to a small dictionary. Decoded copy in Odell's hand. Date is September 15)

General Washington will be at King's Ferry Sunday Evening next on his way to Hartford, where he is to meet the French Admiral and General. And will lodge at Peak's Kill.

○

59. Beckwith to André

(Holograph letter, enclosing Arnold to André of September 10 and 15, both in No. 56, and possibly also No. 58)

Morris's House Sept. 18th 1780
Eight at Night.

Dr Sir

About an hour ago a Flag of Truce arrived from the General Officer Commanding upon the North River, with the enclosed order and a Packet of letters sealed, and addressed upon the outer Cover to Mr Loring Commissary General of Prisoners; General Knyphausen having thought proper to desire me to open the Packet, I found it enclosed in a second Cover addressed to Colonel Cuyler, upon opening which, there are several letters, which with the Covers, are forwarded to Head Quarters without being examined; and amongst the rest one from Mr More which I enclose and forward by Express.

General Knyphausen judged it expedient after having detained the Original order for the Flag of Truce, to grant to the Countryman a Certificate of his having fulfilled his orders, which Certificate I signed, and it will be delivered to him when he is dismissed tomorrow, possibly some of the letters requiring answers, or if you have any commands for him.

If you have the former orders, granted for similar Flags of Truce,

you will be able to learn, whether it is the same person, who came to the Lines at Kingsbridge, a few days ago.
I am
Dr Sir
Your most obed [torn]
humble Servant
Geo. Beckwith
Aid-deCamp

[Addressed:] *On His Majs Service*
Major André
Adjutant General
Head Quarters
Morris House   Express
[Endorsed:] Capt Beckwith
Septemr 18th 80

○

60. Sutherland to Arnold

(Letter in André's hand, to show that André was on board the Vulture, *but signed by Sutherland. It was sent on September 21. Original in Library of Congress)*

Vulture off Tallers Point Septr
Sir

I consider it as duty to complain of any Violation of the Laws of Arms and I am satisfied that I now do it where I cannot fail to meet redress. It is therefore with reluctance, I give you the Concern to know that a Flag of Truce having been yesterday shewn on Tallers point, I sent a boat towards the Shore presuming some Communication was thereby sollicited. The Boats Crew on approaching, received a fire from several armed men who 'till then had been concealed; fortunately none of my people were hurt, but the treacherous Intentions of those who fired are not vindicated from that Circumstance.

I have the honour to be
Sir
Your most obedient
and most humble Servant
A. Sutherland

Majr Gen: Arnhold

61. ROBINSON TO CLINTON

*(Holograph letter, quoting a letter
from Robinson to Arnold and
Arnold's reply of September 21)*

Vulture off Sinsink
Sepr 24th 1780

S^r

Maj^r Andree acquainted you, last
Thursday Morning of his Arrival on
board the Vulture the Evening before and that no person appeared, on
Wednesday night as was promised in
the Letters I sent you. This disappointment made us greatly at a loss
what step to take next, but on
Wednesday morning a man appeared
on Tallers point with a W^t flag upon
which Capt Sutherland sent a Boat to
take him off; as soon as ye Boat got
near the Shore, the people called to
him to come into the Water & they
would take him up, he answered that
he had 3 or 4 companions on ye hill
Standing Sentry & he would Run up
& Call them, immediately 10 or 12
Armed men came down, Sheltered
themselves behind the Rocks & fired
at ye Boat; the Gun Boat was then
sent to drive them off, they kept up a
fire on ye Boats some hours but did
no kind of mischief or hurt to any of
our people; Maj^r Andree & myself
proposed to Capt Sutherland to send
a flag to Genl Arnold (which he very
readily came into) Remonstrating
ag^t such a Scandulous & unjust behaviour as firing under the Sanction
of a flag,

I took this Opportunity of writing
a second Letter to Arnold, and said
"I have been greatly disappointed in
"not seeing Mr Smith at the time ap-
"pointed, being very anxious to con-
"clude our business w^h is very neces-
"sary should be done without delay,
"And I can now make a final settle-
"ment with him as my partner, upon
"the receipt of the Letter I forwarded
"to him yesterday immediately set off

"from Nyork & arrived here last night;
"If Mr Smith will come here we will
"attend him to any convenient & safe
"place" This Letter & Capt Suther-
lands flag met Arnold at or near
Smiths house, about 12 oClock that
night (Thursday) Mr Smith came on
board with two men, & brought me
the following Letter from Arnold
open. "This will be delivered you by
"Mr Smith who will conduct you to
"a place of safety neither Mr Smith
"or any other person shall be made
"acquainted with your proposals, If
"they (which I doubt not) are of such
"a nature that I can Officially take
"notice of them I shall do it with
"pleasure, If not you shall be per-
"mitted to return immediately, I
"take it for granted Col^o Robinson
"will not propose anything that is
"not for the Interest of the united
"States as well as himself"

I am & signed B Arnold

Mr Smith had a paper from Arnold
in the nature of a flag for himself,
one man & two Servants to go down
by water to Dobb's ferry for ye purpose of forwarding some Letters to
N york on private business He had
a second paper as a pass to bring with
him two Servants and a Gent^t Mr John
Anderson— he had a third small
Scrap of paper on w^h was wrote nothing more then Gustavus to John Anderson

upon considering all these matters
Maj^r Andree thought it was best for
him to go alone as both our names
was not mentioned in anyone of y^e
papers, and it appeared to him (as
indeed it did to me) that Arnold
wis[h]ed to see him, I therefore submitted to be left behind, and Maj^r
Andree went off with Smith, between
12 & 1 oClock Thursday night Smith
told me Arnold would be about one
oClock at a place called ye old Trough
or Road, a little above DeNoyells
with a spare horse to carry him to his

house; And it is with the greatest concern that I must now Acquaint your Excellency that we have not heard the least Account of him since he left the Ship

You will remember Sir that Arnold in his first Letter to me desired the Vulture might continue her Station, at Tallers point for a few days, this induced us to think we might lay there with the greatest Safety & unmolested; But on Thursday night they brought down on Tallers point, one Six P^{dr} & a Howitzer, Intrenched themselves on ye very point & at daylight Fryday morning began a very hot fire on us from both w^h continued two hours, and would have been Longer but Luckily their Magazine blew up,

It was near high water ye tide very Slack & no wind, so that it was impossible, tho' every Exertion was made to get ye Ship out of their reach sooner, Six Shot Hulled us one between wind & water, many others struck ye sails Riging, & boats on deck, two Shells hit us one fell on ye Qu^r deck another near ye main Shrouds, Capt Sutherland is the only person hurt, & he very Slightly on the nose by a Splinter

Capt Sutherland has wrote to Sr George Rodney desiring to have a Gally or some other reinforcement, if it should be necessary for us to continue here any time Longer

I hope to have your Excell^y further instructions what to do, I shall do every thing in my power to come at some Knowledge of Maj^r Andree

I am y^r Excell^{ys} mo^t Ob^t H Ser^t

Bev: Robinson

62. André to Clinton

(Holograph letter)

Tapaan September 29th 1780

Sir

Your Excellency is doubtless already apprized of the manner in which I was taken and possibly of the serious light in which my Conduct is Considered and the rigorous determination that is impending.

Under these Circumstances I have obtained General Washingtons permission to send you this Letter, the object of which is to remove from your Breast any Suspicion that I could imagine I was bound by your Excellencys Orders to expose myself to what has happened. The Events of coming within an Enemys posts and of Changing my dress which led me to my present Situation were contrary to my own Intentions as they were to your Orders; and the circuitous route which I took to return was imposed (perhaps unavoidably) without alternative upon me.

I am perfectly tranquil in mind and prepared for any Fate to which an honest Zeal for my Kings Service may have devoted me.

In addressing myself to your Excellency on this Occasion, the force of all my Obligations to you and of the Attachment and Gratitude I bear you, recurrs to me. With all the Warmth of my heart I give you thanks for your Excellencys profuse kindness to me, and I send you the most earnest Wishes for your Welfare which a faithfull affectionate and respectfull Attendant can frame.

I have a Mother and Three Sisters to whom the value of my Commission would be an object as the loss of Grenada has much affected their income. It is needless to be more explicit on this Subject; I am persuaded of your Excellencys Goodness.

I receive the greatest Attention

from His Excellency General Washington and from every person under whose charge I happen to be placed.

I have the honour to be with the most respectfull Attachment

Your Excellencys
Most obedient and
most humble Servant
John André   Adj Gen

His Excellency
Sir Henry Clinton K. B.

◉

63. HAMILTON TO CLINTON

(Letter in a disguised hand. Initials look as much like A. B. as A. H. The late John C. Fitzpatrick was satisfied that Hamilton was the writer)

Sir,

It has so happened in the course of events, that Major Andrè Adjutant General of your army has fallen into our hands. He was captured in such a way as will according to the laws of war justly affect his life. Though an enemy his virtues and his accomplishments are admired. Perhaps he might be released for General Arnold, delivered up without restriction or condition, which is the prevailing wish. Major Andrè's character and situation seem to demand this of your justice and friendship. Arnold appears to have been the guilty author of the mischief; and ought more properly to be the victim, as there is great reason to believe he meditated a double treachery, and had arranged the interview in such a manner, that if discovered in the first instance, he might have it in his power to sacrifice Major Andrè to his own safety.

I have the honor to be &c
Sept. 30. 80   A H
No time is to be lost
[Addressed:] His Excellency
General Sir Henry Clinton
&ca &ca
New York

[Endorsed in Clinton's hand:]
Hamilton W[ashington's]. aid de Camp
received after A[ndré's] death.

◉

64. DELANCEY TO CLINTON(?)

(Holograph report of intelligence)

The Rebel Hospital is moving from paramus to Morris town—
The Soldiers say they will not trust their generals, nor will they fight—
Major Andrè is at Tapaan Church—
They have Confined a Mr Smith & it is reported Lord Sterling also—
October 1st 1780
[Endorsed:] Int^{gce} Octr 1st

◉

65. CLINTON TO GERMAIN

(Copy initialled by Clinton and corrected in his own hand. Enclosed in Clinton to Germain, October 11)

October ye 3^d 1780.
A Rebel General, not from any Overtures from me, ('tho' they shou'd not have been wanting) offers to return to his Allegiance, and give Prooffs not equivoque of his Sincerity, by betraying troops or Place into my Hands, and afterwards take Service in the Royal Army. He obtains the Command of an important Post, on Purpose as He says to surrender it to me. He desires a Conference with my Adjutant General, thro' whom alone we had conversed. He names a Place in neutral ground, sends a Flag of Truce to receive the Adjutant General, orders Him to change his name and Cloaths, and promises to return Him safe when his Conversation is finished: The Adjutant General, in Consequence of this goes ashore under the Flag sent for Him, does nothing while on Shore but by General Arn-

old's order and Privacy, is dismissed by that General with a Passport from Him beyond their Lines and is taken up three miles on this Side in neutral ground by three militia men, carried back and delivered up To the Enemy: the Report of the Capture is made to General Arnold, He is taken on the Saturday and Arnold does not receive the Report 'till Monday when He flys— In Short all this past where and when Arnold commanded.

H C

[Endorsed:] The Circumstance of the Capture of Major André upon the 23ᵈ Septᵗ 1780.

○

66. CLINTON TO ?

(Written in October 1780, to some un-identified person in England)

I received frequent Proposals from General Arnold that He himself wou'd return to Allegiance, and also that He wou'd turn to such Account his Command as shou'd appear to me most meet. None suited untill Septᵗ 80 when General Arnold, having obtained the Command of West Point, proposed to surrender it with all the depending Troops, Guns, Stores &ca. To ascertain the Identity of the Correspondent, and ensure Success, I permitted that my Adjutant General shou'd accept Mʳ Arnolds Invitation to meet Him, assured by the method proposed by Him that Major André run no Risque. However, after being conveyed to Mʳ Arnold in his own Barge under a Flag of Truce sent by Him, and returning to our Lines authorized by a Pass-port from Him, Major André was taken, tried by a Board of General Officers as a Spy and sentenced death, notwithstanding proof was given that He acted litterally by the orders of the General

then commanding the Post, whose Power and Privacy were unquestionably a Sanction for the Steps taken in Consequence. Convinced of his Security and conscious to justifie his Conduct by following implicitly General Arnold's directions, He changed his name and Cloaths, even took Charge of Papers (for which there was no necessity) and returned by a circuitous Route By Land, all, evidently by his Letter to me since his Capture, against his own Wish, & my positive orders; [*Crossed out:* but of this as Agent I acquit Him, for an Agent, whose Safety is stipulated, is of course passive.] In short every thing serves to prove his Confidence and Opinion of the matter at the Period of Transaction, Yet, since dejected by the Failure of a decisive Stroke, and the Sentence pronounced upon Him, He has been I fear persuaded and so infatuated as to acknowledge Himself a Spy: this the Board, contrary to Justice, Custom, and Humanity, have laid hold of, and upon this Confession, possibly extorted, condemned Him.

○

67. CLINTON TO HIS SISTERS

(Holograph draft, October 4 and 9, 1780)

Octʳ 4ᵗʰ 1780

The inclosed narrative will explain all I can say upon the subject of our late extraordinary Adventure, the whole may be shewn to very particular friends, to the chief of which however I have desired my Aide de Camp Capt. Sᵗ George to do so.

Notwithstanding every argument has been used W[ashington]. will Consider M. André as a Spy, for my own part I have given the affair all the examination I can & I look upon it deserving no such appellation, Unfortunately for Maj[r] André when he was taken or rather questioned I hear he produced his purse and watch this gave suspicion, but had he produced the passport only no body dared to have disputed it in a district where G. Arnold at that time commanded As there could not be any prooffs of his being a spy, they took advantage of a letter of his written in *low* spirits wherein he may imply that he did not go ashore under the sanction of a flag. and upon this and upon no other do they pretend to Condemn him, from good policy & perhaps a little more feeling than is usual for those in my Situation I have never executed a Spy, I have even at W[ashington's]. request permitted some under that description to be exchanged and I have at this instant 8 or 10 Spys and 20 or 30 Conspiraters of the first rank in S. Carolina, all of which hold their lives from my Clemency, I have been very moderate in my corespondance with W[ashington]. on the subject, but I have assured him if M[ajor] A[ndré] whom I regard as *innocent* should suffer the lives of these delinquents must be forfeited, and such a scene must follow as my pen can not describe, As this business will probably be much talked of I shall endeavour in few words to explain my Idea of it and I request you to read it to C. Mellish.

A Rebel General for such he was from motives of conviction 18 months since without any overtures from me offers to return to his allegiance, betray a corps or place into my hands, and afterward take service in the royal Army, I of course accept his offers. he takes the command of a very considerable post on purpose as he tells me to betray it to me, he desires a Conference with my Adj[t] Gen[l] through whom alone he had coresponded with me, he appoints a place of meeting on neutral ground

he desires me to permit my Adj[t] Gen[l] to go I consent & recommend that it may be done with all security to his person. he tells the Ad. Gen. he must take the name of J. Anderson to avoid suspicion that under that name he will send a flag of Truce for him, which he does in all the regular forms, he meets him at the water side, opens the conference delivers papers, *orders* him to change his military coat for a peasants, and obliges [him] to return by a circuitous route thinking that the safest with an escort and passport beyond the rebel post— 6 miles on the other side of which he is taken by 3 militia men. the charge against him is for being a Spy they pretend a prooff and the sentence passed upon him by the Reb[l] Genl[s] is death— the only evidence they have is a low spirited letter of his own, seeming to imply that he went ashore *not* under the protection of a flag, whereas Genl. Arnold himself declares he sent a flag for him— the Cap[t] of the man of War declares the persons who brought it came as a flag and were dismissed as such & Maj[r] Andre when he went into the boat certainly thought himself safe but refused to let another officer go, because he was not mentioned in the pass— the question for C. Mellish is therefore as follows:

a Gen[l] officer commanding in a district invites the Enemys Adj[t] Gen[l] to come to a Conference, sends a Flag of Truce for him, promises safety to his person, during the conference and that he shall be returned in safety to his Gen[l] and all this he promises while he acted as commanding General in one of the Enemys posts. tho all this is declared by Gen. Arnold in a letter to G. Washington, 'tho all this can be proved either by the people of the Flag of Truce or those sent to conduct him beyond the Enemys posts, the board of Gen[l] officers enquiring into the affair do not admit it but condemn him upon a warped expression in a low spirited letter of his own; they treat him with great tenderness & their whole army seems Concerned that he was taken, as they have delayed it so long I do not think they will proceed to extremities but if they do ——

the defection of one of the best Generals they have at this time has thrown them into great Confusion, & will have most important Consequences, but the Circumstance of poor André's Capture throws a damp upon all, upon me greater than I can describe. should he suffer you will easily believe it will be impossible for me to continue to serve, for reasons I need not mention, nay even if they keep him prisoner it will be horrid to live in that eternal suspence, & be obliged to retaliate upon every unfortunate devil of a Spy that comes among us— hitherto I have made good Use of them by employing them double but I must now secure all I can get to answer for poor André Respecting the Coup manquè I do not feel it, tho had it succeeded all agree it would have finished the rebellion immediately, Nothing is to be obtained in war without some risk, in this however arranged as it was there was scarcely in the opinion of all concerned any, he went ashore at the invitation of G. Arnold, and all he did was by order of G. Arnold at a time when he had a right to expect to be obeyed. Why he was not returned to us by water as he went and as was promised by Arnold I know not except that Arnold thought the other route safer, & possibly he might have been right, As I said before I wish our poor friend André had not been a little too much of[f] his guard when the militia questioned him— I did intend as usual dearest Sisters to have written to you both, but I can say

nothing except upon this horrid subject, W[ashington]. seems a moderate man all my friends say he will not incline nor if he did will dare execute the sentence, but till he assures me he will not I shall be in distress, and entre nous I wish I may obtain leave to resign this command or to go home on leave I will make use of neither without Circumstances should turn out such as to make my remaining in the command distressfull to me, Good God what a *Coup manquèe*, to those who do not feel the private losses we have met with, the defection of such a man as Arnold will appear important, I think it is so, & that the Ice once broke many will follow his example but I shall be affraid to undertake them. I am of course in very bad Spirits, the weather bad also, once assured that poor Andre is & will be safe I shall revive & endeavour to improve this otherwise lucky event to the utmost and then if the Spaniards make peace with us by Xmas which I expect the business here may be soon finished, and the very instant it is I depend on my friends to release me from the most irksome command in every respect that ever officer was placed in. I have desired as I suppose you to be at Bath that every necessary hope may be sent to you the object was a great one, as far as depended upon me every precaution was taken, for success to the enterprise & security for those concerned in planning and executing it, particularly the first as appears by poor Andre's own letter to me, for had my orders been attended to of not changing dress or taking papers he could not have been detained— for your sakes I wish the packet was ready to sail but I have done——

I heartily long to see my dearest Children, Father & Sisters, now it cannot be long first, when next we meet I hope it will be never to part again for I am tired of vagabonding, and there are so many mortifications attending my profession that I am heartily tired of it also, for notwithstanding I have always done my duty and by the assistance of Providence have met with great Success, some Circumstances must have hapened in this horrid war distressing to one that is, I had almost said (cursed) with the deeper sensibility of it that I have. my Constitution I thank God still holds out & if I can return to my Country with out any more Shocks to it I may live to enjoy a good old Age at least long enough to see my Children Comfortable introduced into a world however at best of care— watch the moment dearest sisters of accommodation, for at all events the instant military operations are likely to cease I leave this command, & to insure me the power of doing it I ought to have leave always in my pocket, they may be assured I will not make use of it without the best of reasons, for Gods sake write to me more at large, Send your letters down to Falmouth those that go by packet they will be safe at least from the Enemy more so than any other as the mails are always thrown over board, if not write me in Cypher tho this may be tedious you will I am sure find time, give my affectionate Comps to all friends, & remember me kindly to Hornby poor Molloy— & Nelly, say every thing that is most affectionately dutiful to Mrs Carter hug my Children most tenderly, & believe that I feed on the hopes of assuring you in person Dearest Dear Sisters that I am ever affectionately & unalterably yours

H C

Octr 9th

The horrid deed is done W[ashington]. has committed premeditated murder, he must Answer for the dreadfull Consequences I feel beyond words to describe but I cannot reproach myself in the least. The first burst of passion is over, I am calm, and deliberate in my resentment, as you will observe by my Corespondence with W[ashington]. since he is become a murderer & a Jesuit, God grant me patience Make peace with Spain & give me 10000 men more, Once more remember me most affectionately to my good old Father & dearest Children, I do not dispair dearest sisters of apearing before next Xmas Dear in person but I am now faithfully &

affectionately yours H— C

I am still of opinion I should at all times have leave to resign the command, good policy as well as my own feelings may make that necessary and in case of accomodation you may as well expect to see fire and water in peace together as your humble sert with these *miscreants*. therefore for God sake in case I am doomed to finish this business be careful that I am permitted to resign command and Commission the moment tis concluded, for the world could not tempt me to meet any of these infamous miscreants on any other terms than *Extream* Enmity.

○

68. ARNOLD TO CLINTON

(Holograph letter)

New York Octr 18th 1780

Sir

In the Conferrence which I had with Major André, He was so fully Convinced of the reasonableness of my proposal of being allowed Ten thousand pounds Sterling for my Services, Risque, and the loss which I should sustain in Case a discovery of my Plan should oblige me to take Refuge in New York before it could be fully carried into Execution, that he assured me "tho he was Commissioned to promise me Only Six thousand pounds Sterling, He would use his influence and recommend it to Your Excellency to allow the sum I proposed, and from his State of the matter He informed me He had no doubt Your Excellency would accede to the proposal: I beg leave to observe that it is far short of the loss I have sustained, and that no sum of money would have been an inducement to have gone through the danger and Anxiety I have experienced:– Nothing but my Zeal to Serve His Majesty and the Common Cause could have influenced my Conduct, and I have every reason to believe, the Step which I have taken will in its Consequences have the most happy effect; and will tend to promote His Majestys Service more effectually than an expenditure of a like sum could possably have done in any other way.

I am induced with the greatest Chearfulness to submit the matter to Your Excellency, in full Confidence of Your generous intentions, and that you will not think my Claim unreasonable, when you Consider the Sacrafises I have made, and that the sum is a trifling object to the Public tho of Consequence to me, who have a large Family that look up to me for Support & protection.

I have the honor to be with sentiments of the highest respect

Your Excellencys Most
Obedient, & Humble Servt
B Arnold

[Addressed:] His Excellency
Sir Henry Clinton K. B.
Commander in Chief,
&c &c &c

Clinton's Narrative

(Enclosed with Germain to Clinton, October 11, 1780. There are variations between some of the letters here included and the authentic texts given in the Arnold-André Correspondence above)

NARRATIVE

After a Correspondence had been maintained for some time between the Commander in Chief and Major General Arnold, a Meeting was to be held to concert a Plan; and the Adjutant General the Person fixed upon by General Arnold to meet him at Dobbs's Ferry on Monday the 11th September under the feigned Name of John Anderson.

Major André, Adjutant General went with a Flag of Truce according to Appointment, accompanied by Colonel Robinson; but was unhappily prevented from the Interview with General Arnold by some of our Gun Boats in the North River firing upon the Boat, in which the General was coming, and from whom he narrowly escaped.

On Saturday the 16th Colonel Robinson by Order of the Commander in Chief went on board the Vulture Sloop of War, and proceeded up the North River to Tallers Point from whence he sent a Letter to General Putnam inclosed in one to General Arnold as follows,

[69] On board the Vulture off Tallers
Point September 17th 1780.

Sir,

Having heard that General Putnam is at the Highlands on a Visit to you, I have obtained Sir Henry Clinton's leave to come up in this ship to endeavor to have an Interview with him. My reasons for asking it are explained in the enclosed Letter to him.

As I understand you command in the Highlands, and make your Head Quarters at my House, I have taken the liberty of enclosing my Letter to Genl Putnam to you, and beg the favor of you to deliver it. But if he should have returned to Connecticut I beg his Letter may be returned to me. And in that Case I am persuaded (from the humane and generous Character you bear) that could I be so happy as to see you, you would readily grant me the same Request I should make to him. But, for Prudential Reasons, I dare not explain the Matter further until I have some Assurances that it shall be secret if not granted. I did intend, in order to have had your Answer immediately, to have sent this by my Servant James Osborn with a Flag to you, but thinking he might be stopped at Verplanks,

I have sent it to the Officer commanding there, desiring it may be forwarded to you as soon as possible.

I am &c.

(Signed) Beverly Robinson

Major General Arnold

On Tuesday the 19th a Flag of Truce from General Arnold brought the Answer annexed.

[70]

Head Quarters Robinson's House
September 18th 1780.

Sir,

I have received a Letter from you of yesterday's Date, with one for General Putnam; and have consulted with his Excellency General Washington on the Subject of them; who is of Opinion that any Application respecting your private Affairs in this Country ought to be made to the Civil Authority of this State, as they are entirely out of the Line of the Military. However willing I may be to oblige Colonel Robinson on any other Occasion, it is not in my Power to do it in this Instance.

General Putnam left this Place some days since. I have therefore, agreeable to your Request, returned the Letter addressed to him.

If you have any other Proposals to make, and of a public Nature, of which I can officially take Notice, you may depend on it, that the greatest Secrecy shall be observed, if required. As no Person except His Excellency General Washington shall be made acquainted with them

I am Sir, &c

(Signed) B. Arnold

Colonel Beverly Robinson

This Letter enclosed under Seal another to Colonel Robinson, and one directed to Mr John Anderson, both which are transcribed.

[71]

September 18th 1780

Sir,

I parted with his Excellency General Washington this Morning, who advised me to avoid seeing you, as it would occasion Suspicions in the Minds of some People, which might operate to my Injury. His Reasons appear to me well founded; but was I of a different Opinion, I could not with Propriety see you at present. I shall send a Person to Dobbs's Ferry or on board the Vulture on Wednesday Night the 20th Instant, and furnish him with a Boat and Flag of Truce. You may depend on his Secrecy and Honor, and that your Business of whatever nature shall be kept a profound Secret—and if it is a Matter in which I can officially act, I will do every thing in my Power to oblige you, consistent with my Duty. To avoid Censure, this Matter must be conducted with the greatest Secrecy. I think it will be adviseable for the Vulture to remain where she is until the time mentioned. I have enclosed a Letter for a Gentleman in New York from one in the Country on private Business, which I beg the favor of you to forward, and make no doubt he will be permitted to come to the Time mentioned.

I am Sir &c

(Signed) B. Arnold

I expect his Excellency General Washington to lodge here on Saturday Night next, and will lay before him any Matters you may wish to communicate.

B.A.

Colonel Beverly Robinson

[72]

September 15th 1780

Sir, On the 11th at Noon agreeable to your Request I attempted to go to Dobbs's Ferry, but was prevented by the armed Boats of the Enemy who fired upon us; and continued opposite to the Ferry until Sunset.

The foregoing Letter was wrote to caution you not to mention your Business to Colonel Sheldon or any other Person. I have no Confident, I have made one too many already, which has prevented some profitable Speculations.

I will send a Person in whom you can confide by Water to meet you at Dobbs's Ferry at the Landing on the East Side on Wednesday the 20th Inst who will conduct you to a Place of Safety, where I will meet you. It will be necessary for you to be disguised, and if the Enemy's Boats are there, it will favor my Plan, as the Person is not suspected by them. If I do not hear from you before you may depend on the Persons being punctual at the Place above mentioned.

My Partner, of whom I hinted in a former Letter has about £10,000 Cash in Hand ready for a Speculation, if any should offer which appears profitable. I have about £1000 on hand, and can collect £1500 more in two or three Days. Add to this, I have some Credit. From these Hints, you may judge of the Purchase that can be made. I cannot be more explicit at present. Meet me if possible. You may rest assured that if there is no danger in passing your Lines, you will be perfectly safe where I propose a Meeting; of which you shall be informed on Wednesday Evening, if you think proper to be at Dobbs's Ferry. Adieu, and be assured of the Friendship of
Gustavus.

September 18th 1780.

The foregoing I found means to send by a very honest fellow who went to Kingsbridge on the 16th and make no doubt you have received it. But as there is a Possibility of its miscarrying, I send a Copy: and am fully persuaded that the Method I have pointed out to meet you is the best and safest, provided you can obtain leave to come out.

I am yours

Gustavus.

On Receipt of this Letter the Com-mander in Chief agreed to Major Andre's going to Dobbs's Ferry with a Flag of Truce. For which purpose Major André wrote to Capt Sutherland of the Vulture & Colonel Robinson to fall down the River to that Place.

Thus far the Transaction was carried on with the Knowledge of the Commander in Chief, who before Major André's Departure gave him every Caution that Prudence suggested, not to change his Dress as proposed by General Arnold, but to wear his Uniform, and on no Account to take Papers.

On the 21st the Commander in Chief received the two following Letters from Major André.

[73]

On Board the Vulture
21t Septr 1780

Sir,

As the Tide was favorable on my Arrival at the Sloop Yesterday, I determined to be myself the Bearer of your Excellency's Letters as far as the Vulture. I have suffered for it having caught a very bad Cold, and had so violent a Return of a Disorder in my Stomach, which had attacked me a few Days ago, that Capt: Sutherland & Coll Robinson insist on my remaining on board until I am better. I hope to morrow to get down again. I have the Honor &c

(Signed) John André

His Excellency
    Sir H. Clinton.

[74]

On Board the Vulture 21st Septr 1780
Sir

I got on board the Vulture at about 7 O'Clock last Night; and after considering upon the Letters & the Answer given by Colonel Robinson "that he wou'd remain on board and hoped I shou'd be up," we thought it most natural to expect the *Man I sent into the Country* here; and therefore did not think of going to the Ferry.

No Body has appeared. This is the second Excursion I have made without an ostensible Reason, and Colonel Robinson both Times of the Party— A third wou'd infallibly fix Suspicions. I have therefore thought it best to remain here on pretence of Sickness, as my inclosed Letter will feign, and try further Expedients. Yesterday the pretence of a Flag of Truce was made to draw People from the Vulture on Shore. The Boat was fired upon in Violation of the Customs of War. Capt. Sutherland with great Propriety means to send a Flag to complain of this to General Arnold. A Boat from the Vulture had very nearly taken him on the 11th. He was pursued close to the Sloat. I shall favor him with a News Paper containing the Carolina News, which I brought with me from New York, for Anderson to whom it is addressed on board the Vulture.

I have the Honor &c
(Signed) John André

Sir Henry Clinton.

On the 21t a Flag of Truce from General Arnold arrived at the Vulture. The Flag Bearer was Mr Joshua Smith, who produced two Papers signed B: Arnold. One authorizing him to go with a Flag and two Servants for the purpose of forwarding two Letters to New York,—and the other to bring up a Mr John Anderson and a Boy. Mr Smith delivered at the same Time, this Letter to Colonel Robinson.

[75]

September 21st 1780

Sir,

This will be delivered you by Mr Smith who will conduct you to a Place of Safety. Neither Mr Smith or any other Person shall be made acquainted with your Proposals. If they (which I doubt not) are of such a Nature, that I can officially take Notice of them, I shall do it with Pleasure. If not, you shall be permitted to return immediately. I take it for granted, Colonel Robinson will not propose any Thing that is not for the Interest of the United States, as well as himself.

I am Sir, &c
(Signed) B. Arnold

Colo Robinson

Colonel Robinson not being named in the Flag did not attend Major André.

It being determined that Major André alone shou'd go with Mr Smith, and found that there were only two Men to row a very large Boat, it was proposed that one of the Vultures Boats should go armed to tow them; but this was objected to strongly by Mr Smith, and Major André as not consistent with the Character of a Flag of Truce.

Major André went on Shore without changing his Dress, and he declared to Colonel Robinson & Captain Sutherland, that he dared not do it as he had received the Commander in Chief's positive orders to the contrary. It was understood from Mr Smith that General Arnold would meet the Flag on her return to the Landing at Haverstraw, with a spare Horse, and thence to repair to Mr Smith's House at a few Miles from the Shore.

After parting from the Vulture Major André met Genl Arnold, as the Sequel will shew, who dispatched him back by Land under his Pass, & in a Dress assumed by his Order. The Circumstances of Major André's being taken are pointed out in the following Letters from Lieut Colo Jameison to General Arnold and Lieutenant Allen.

[76]

North Castle 23d September 1780.

Sir,

I have sent Lieut Allen with a certain John Anderson taken going into New York. He had a Pass signed with your Name. He had a Parcel of Papers taken from under his Stockings, which I think of a very dangerous Tendency. The Papers I have sent to General Washington. They contain the Number of Men at West Point and its Dependencies; the Number of Cannon &c; the different Pieces of Ground that command each Fort; & what Distance they are from the different Forts; the Situation of each Fort, and which may be set on Fire with Bombs and Carcasses, and which are out of Repair; the Speech of General Washington to the Council of War held the Sixth of this Month; the Situation of our Armies in General &c^a &c^a—

I am with Regard &c
(Signed) John Jameson

Major Genl Arnold.

[77]

North Castle Septr 23^d 1780

Sir

For some Circumstances I have just heard, I have reason to fear that a Party of the Enemy are above; and as I wou'd not have Anderson retaken or get away, I desire that you wou'd proceed to lower Salem with him & deliver him to Captain Hoogland. You will leave the Guard with Captain Hoogland also, except one Man, whom you may take along. You may proceed on to West Point and deliver the Letter to General Arnold. You may also shew him this, that he may know the reason why the Prisoner is not sent on. You will please to return as soon as you can do your Business.

I am in haste
Dr Sir &c
(Signed) John Jameson

Lieutenant Allen.

On Monday the 25th of September General Arnold arrived on board the Vulture. And Colonel Robinson now become first acquainted with Major Andre's being made a Prisoner, wrote to General Washington demanding him as Adjutant General to the British Forces in America, who had gone under the Sanction of a Flag of Truce to General Arnold; to which no Answer was returned.

September 26th General Arnold and Colonel Robinson arrived at New York and reported the Circumstances to the Commander in Chief. Sir Henry Clinton immediately wrote to General Washington demanding the Restoration of his Adjutant General, & inclosed General Arnold's Letter to him upon the Subject, as follow. [78]

New York 26th Septr 1780.

Sir

In Answer to your Excellency's Message respecting your Adjutant General Major André, and desiring my Idea of the reasons why he is detained, being under my Passports; I have the Honor to inform you, Sir, that I apprehend a few Hours must return Major André to your Excellency's Orders, as that Officer is assuredly under the Protection of a Flag of Truce sent by me to him for the purpose of a Conversation, which I requested to hold with him relating to myself, and which I wished to communicate through that Officer, to your Excellency.

I commanded at the Time at West Point, had an undoubted right to send my Flag of Truce for Major André, who came to me under that Protection, and having held my Conversation with him, I delivered him confidential Papers in my own hand writing to deliver to your Excellency. Thinking it much properer he should return by Land, I directed him to make use of the feigned Name of John Anderson; under which he had by my Directions come on Shore; and gave him my Passports to pass my Lines to the White Plains on his way to New York. This Officer therefore cannot fail of being immediately sent to New York, as he was invited to a Conversation with me, for which I sent him a Flag of Truce, and finally gave him Passports for his safe Return to your Excellency. All which I then had a right to do, being in the actual Service of America, under the orders of General Washington and Commanding General at West Point and its Dependencies.

I have the Honor &c
(Signed). B: Arnold

His Excellency
Sir Henry Clinton.

[79]

New York 26th Septr 1780

Sir

Being informed that the King's Adjutant General in America has been stopt under Major General Arnold's Passports, and is detained a Prisoner in your Excellency's Army, I have the Honor to inform you, Sir, that I permitted Major André to go to Major General Arnold at the particular request of that General Officer. You will perceive, Sir, by the inclosed Paper that a Flag of Truce was sent to receive Major André; and Passports granted for his Return. I therefore can have no doubt but your Excellency will immediately direct that this Officer has Permission to return to my Orders at New York.

I have the Honor to be &c
Signed H. Clinton

His Excellency
General Washington.

On the 30th of September the Commander in Chief received the following Letters from General Washington & Major André.
[80] [Here omitted because identical with No. 62 above.]
[81]

Head Quarters September 30th 1780

Sir

In Answer to your Excellency's Letter of the 26th Instant which I have had the Honor to receive, I am to inform you that Major André was taken under such Circumstances as would have justified the most summary Proceedings against him. I determined however to refer his Case to the Examination and Decision of a Board of General Officers; who have, on his free & voluntary Confession and Letters, reported.

First "that he came on Shore from the Vulture Sloop of War in the Night of the 21t Septr last on an Interview with Genl Arnold in a private and secret Manner.

Secondly "That he changed his Dress within our Lines and under a feigned Name, and in a disguised Habit passed our Works at Stoney & Verplanks Points, the Evening of the 22d September last; and was taken the Morning of the 23d of Septr last at Tarry Town in a disguised Habit, being then on his Way to New York, and when taken he had in his Possession several Papers which contained Intelligence for the Enemy." The Board having maturely considered these Facts, do also report to His Excellency General Washington that Major André, Adjutant General to the British Army ought to be considered as a Spy from the Enemy; and that, agreeable to the Law & Usage of Nations, it is their Opinion he ought to suffer Death."

From these Proceedings it is evident Major André was employed in the Execution of Measures very foreign to the Objects of Flags of Truce, and such as they were never meant to authorize or countenance in the most distant Degree, and this Gentleman confessed with the greatest Candor in the Course of his Examination "that it was impossible for him to suppose he came on Shore under the Sanction of a Flag.

I have the Honor &c

(Signed) G. Washington.

His Excellency

Sir Henry Clinton

It appearing from the above Letter that the Board of General Officers had not been informed of the whole Circumstances necessary to enable them to form a just Opinion of Major Andre's Conduct; Sir Henry Clinton thought proper to call a Council of General Officers assisted by several of the Gentlemen of the Council to the Commission to whose Consideration he submitted General Washington's Letter.

After which he resolved that Lieutenant General Robertson, with Mr Elliot the Lieutenant Governor, & Mr Smith the Chief Justice of New York, shou'd proceed to one of the Enemy's Posts, furnished with the necessary Evidence for ascertaining Major Andre's Innocence of being a Spy, and clearing Doubts upon a Question, in which Humanity appeared to be so much concerned. The Intention and Purport of this Deputation, was immediately communicated to General Washington by the following Letter, which was dispatched by the Return of the Flag that brought his of the 30th

[82]

New York 30th Septemr 1780.

Sir,

From your Excellency's Letter of this Date, I am persuaded the Board of General Officers, to whom you referred the Case of Major André, cannot have been rightly informed of all the Circumstances on which a Judgement ought to be formed. I think it of the highest Moment to Humanity that your Excellency should be perfectly apprized of the State of this Matter before you proceed to put that Judgement in Execution.

For this Reason I shall send His Excellency Lieutt General Robertson and two other Gentlemen to give you a true State of Facts, and to declare to you my Sentiments and Resolutions. They will set out to morrow as early as the Wind and Tide will permit, and wait near Dobbs's Ferry for your Permission and safe Conduct to meet your Excellency, or such Persons as you may appoint, to converse with them on this Subject.

I have the honor &c

(Signed) H: Clinton.

P.S. The Honble A. Elliot Esqr Lieut Govr, & the Honble Wm Smith Esqr Chief Justice of this Province will attend

His Excellency Genl Robertson.

His Excellency General Washington.

Accordingly those Gentlemen attended by Colonel Robinson and the Proofs mentioned were off Dobbs's Ferry, within four Miles of the Rebel Camp, the next Day. But General Robertson only, was permitted to land there, where he met General Green, who was sent thither for that Purpose. The Purport of their Conversation is related in the following Letter from General Robertson to the Commander in Chief.

[83]

Off Dobbs Ferry 1st October 1780.

Sir,

On coming to Anchor here I sent Murray on Shore, who soon returned with Notice that General Green was ready to meet me, but would not admit a Conference with the other Gentlemen.

I paid some Compliments to his Character, and expressed the Satisfaction I had in treating with him on the Cause of my Friend, the two Armies and Humanity. He said he could not treat with me as an Officer; that Mr Washington had permitted him to meet me as a Gentleman; but the Case of an acknowledged Spy admitted no official Discussion. I said that a Knowledge of Facts was necessary to direct a General's Judgement. That in whatever Character I was called, I hoped he would represent what I said candidly to Mr Washington.

I laid before him the Facts and Arnold's Assertions of Mr Andre's being under a Flag of Truce, and disguised by his Order. He shewed me a low spirited Letter of Andre's saying that he had not landed under a Flag of Truce, and lamenting his being taken in a mean Disguise. He expresses this in Language that admits it to be criminal. I told him that André stated Facts with Truth, but reasoned ill upon them. That whether a Flag was flying or not was of no moment. He landed and acted as directed by their General. He said they would believe André in preference to Arnold. This argument held long. I told him that you had ever shewn a merciful Disposition, and an Attention to Mr Washington's Requests. That in the Instance of my Name Sake, you had given up a Man evidently a Spy, when he signified his Wish. That I courted an Intercourse and a Return of good Offices. That Andre had your Friendship and good Wishes; and that Mr Washington's Humanity to him would be productive of Acts of the same kind on our Part. That if Green had a Friend or Mr Washington was desirous of the Release of any Man; if he would let me carry home André, I would engage to send such a Man out. He said that there was no treating about Spies. I said no Military Casuist in Europe would call André a Spy; and I would suffer Death myself if Monsieur Rochambault or General Knyphausen would call him by that Name. I added that I depended on General Green's Candour and Humanity to put the Facts I had stated

& the Arguments I had used in their fairest Light to Mr Washington. That I would stay on board all Night, and hoped to carry Mr André, or at least Mr Washington's Word for his Safety, along with me in the Morning.

Green now with a Blush, that shewed the Task was imposed and did not proceed from his own Thought, told me that the Army must be satisfied by seeing Spies executed —but there was one thing would satisfy them—they expected if André was set free, Arnold should be given up. This I answered with a Look only, which threw Green into Confusion. I am persuaded Andre will not be hurt. Believe me

Sir &c
Signed. J. Robertson

His Excellency
Sir Henry Clinton

The Gentlemen in anxious Expectation of a favorable answer from General Washington, continued off the Ferry until the next Day, on the Morning of which the following short Note only came from General Green. [84]

Camp Tapaan October 2d 1780.

Sir,

Agreeable to your Request I communicated to General Washington the Substance of our Conversation in all the Particulars, so far as my Memory served me. It made no Alteration in his Opinion and Determination. I need say no more after what you have already been informed.

I have the honor to be with respect,
Your Excellency's &c
(Signed) Nath Green.

His Excellency
James Robertson Esqr
&c &c &c

Upon receipt of this General Robertson dispatched a full state of the Case immediately to General Washington; and enclosed a Letter to him from General Arnold, justifying the whole of Major Andre's Proceedings, as originating entirely from himself, whilst he commanded in the District where he landed.

[85]

Greyhound Schooner Flag of Truce
2ᵈ Octoʳ 1780

Sir,

A Note I have from Genˡ Green leaves me in doubt, if his Memory has served him to relate to you with Exactness the Substance of the Conversation that had passed between him and myself on the Subject of Major André.

In an Affair of so much Consequence to my Friend, to the two Armies, and Humanity, I would leave no Possibility of a Misunderstanding; and therefore take the Liberty to put in Writing the Substance of what I said to General Green.

I offered to prove by the Evidence of Colonel Robinson, and the Officers of the Vulture, that Major Andre went on Shore at General Arnold's Desire in a Boat sent for him with a Flag of Truce; that he not only came ashore with the Knowledge and under the Protection of the General who commanded in the District, but that he took no Step while on Shore but by the Direction of General Arnold; as will appear by the enclosed Letter from him to your Excellency.

Under these Circumstances I could not, and hoped you would not, consider Major André as a Spy, in Consequence of an improper Phrase in his Letter to you. The Facts he relates correspond with the Evidence I offer, but he admits a Conclusion that does not follow. The Change of Cloaths and name was ordered by General Arnold, under whose Direction he necessarily was while within his Command.

As General Green and I did not agree in Opinion, I wished that disinterested Gentlemen of knowledge in the Law of War and Nations might be asked their Opinion on the Subject; and mentioned Monsʳ Knyphausen and General Rochambeau.

I related that a Captain Robinson had been delivered to Sir Henry Clinton as a Spy, and undoubtedly was such. But it being signified to him that you was desirous this Man should be exchanged, he had ordered him to be exchanged.

I wish that an Intercourse of such Civilities as the Rules of War admit of might take off many of its Horrors. I admitted that Major Andre had a great Share of Sir Henry Clinton's Esteem; and that he would be infinitely obliged by his Liberation; and that if he was permitted to return with me, I would engage to have any Person you would please to name set at Liberty.

I added that Sir Henry had never put any Person to Death for a Breach of the Rules of War; tho he has had, and has now, many in his Power.

Under our present Circumstances much good may arise from Humanity, much ill from the want of it. If that could give any Weight, I beg leave to add that your favorable Treatment of Major André will be a favor I should ever be intent to return to any you hold dear.

My Memory does not retain, with the Exactness I could wish, the Words of the Letter which General Green shewed me from Major André to your Excellency. For Sir Henry Clinton's Satisfaction I beg you will order a Copy of it to be sent to me at New York.

I have the honor to be &c &c
(Signed) J. Robertson

His Excellency
General Washington

[86]

New York 1ˢᵗ October 1780

Sir

The polite Attention shown by

your Excellency and the Gentlemen of your Family to Mrs Arnold when in Distress, demand my grateful Acknowledgements and Thanks, which I beg leave to present.

From your Excellency's Letter to Sir Henry Clinton, I find a Board of General Officers have given it as their Opinion that Major André comes under the Description of a Spy. My good Opinion of the Candor and Justice of these Gentlemen leads me to believe, that if they had been made fully acquainted with every Circumstance respecting Major André they would by no means have considered him in the Light of a Spy, or even of a Prisoner. In Justice to him I think it my Duty to declare, that he came from on Board the Vulture at my particular Request, by a Flag sent on Purpose for him by Joshua Smith Esqr who had Permission to go to Dobbs's Ferry to carry Letters, and for other Purposes not mentioned, and to return. This was done as a Blind to the Spy Boats. Mr Smith at the same time had my positive Directions to go on board the Vulture, and bring on Shore Colonel Robinson or Mr John Anderson, which was the Name I had requested Major André to assume. At the same time I desired Mr Smith to inform him that he should have my protection, and a safe Passport, to return in the same Boat as soon as our Business was completed. As several Accidents intervened to prevent his being sent on board, I gave him my Passport to return by Land. Major André came on Shore in his Uniform (without Disguise) which with much Reluctance at my particular and pressing Instance he exchanged for another Coat. I furnished him with a Horse & a Saddle, & pointed out the Route by which he was to return. And as Commanding Officer in the Department, I had an undoubted

right to transact all these Matters, which if wrong Major André ought by no means to suffer for them.

But if after this just and candid Representation of Major Andre's Case, the Board of General Officers adhere to their former Opinion, I shall suppose it dictated by Passion and Resentment, And if that Gentleman should suffer the Severity of their Sentence, I shall think myself bound by every Tie of Duty and Honor to retaliate on such unhappy Persons of your Army as may fall within my Power—that the respect due to Flags and the Law of Nations may be better understood and observed.

I have further to observe that forty of the principal Inhabitants of South Carolina have justly forfeited their Lives, which have hitherto been spared by the Clemency of His Excellency Sir Henry Clinton; who cannot in Justice extend his Mercy to them any longer, if Major André suffers—which in all Probability will open a Scene of Blood, at which Humanity will revolt.

Suffer me to entreat your Excellency for your own and the Honor of Humanity, and the Love you have of Justice, that you suffer not an unjust Sentence to touch the Life of Major André. But if this warning should be disregarded, and he should suffer, I call Heaven and Earth to witness that your Excellency will be justly answerable for the Torrent of Blood that may be spilt in Consequence.

I have the Honor to be &c
(Signed) Benedict Arnold.

His Excellency
    General Washington

After dispatching these to General Washington, General Robertson left the Ferry about Noon, and returned to New York.

The Commander in Chief being uneasy at not receiving any Answer from General Washington to General Robertson's last Letter, prepared the following one, which was to be accompanied with Captain Sutherland's Narrative of what he knew of the Transaction.

[87]

New York October 4th 1780

Sir,

I conceived I could not better or more fully explain my Sentiments, in answer to your Excellency's Letter of the 30th September, respecting Major André, than by sending Lieutenant General Robertson, to converse if possible with you, Sir, or at least with some confidential Officer from you. I cannot think Lieut General Robertson's Conversation with General Green has entirely answered the Purposes for which I wished the Meeting. Genl Green's Letter of the 2d Instant to General Robertson expresses that he had reported to you, Sir, as far as Memory served, the Discourse that had passed between them, and that it had not produced any Alteration in your Opinion or Determination concerning Major André.

I have, Sir, most carefully reperused your Letter of September 30th, which contains indeed an Opinion of a Board of your General Officers, but in no respect any Opinion or Determination of your Excellency. I must remain therefore altogether at a Loss what they may be, until you are so good to inform me, which I make no doubt of your Excellency's doing immediately. I will, Sir, in the mean time very freely declare my Sentiments upon this Occasion; which positively are, that under no Description Major Andre can be considered as a Spy; nor by any Usage of Nations at War, or the Custom of Armies, can be treated as such. That Officer went at Major General Ar-

nold's Request from me to him, at that Time in the American Service and Commanding Officer at West Point. A Flag of Truce was sent to receive Major André, with which he went on Shore and met Major General Arnold. To this Period he was acting under my immediate Orders as a Military Man. What Happened after was from the entire Direction and positive Orders of Major General Arnold, your Officer Commanding at West Point. And Major André travelled in his Way to N. York with Passports from that American General Officer, who had an undoubted Right to grant them. And here it may be necessary to observe that Major André was stopt upon the Road and on neutral Ground and made a Prisoner two Days prior to Major General Arnold's quitting the American Service at West Point. From all which I have a right to assert that Major André can merely be considered as a Messenger and not as a Spy. He visited no Posts, made no Plans, held no Conversation with any Person except Major General Arnold; and the Papers found upon him were written in that General Officers own Hand Writing; who directed Major André to receive and deliver them to me. From these Circumstances I have no doubt but you, Sir, will see this Matter in the same point of view with me, and will be extremely cautious of producing a Precedent which may render the future Progress of this unfortunate War liable to a Want of that Humanity which I am willing to believe your Excellency possesses and which I have always pursued. I trust, Sir, to your good Sense, and to your Liberality for a speedy Release of Major André, who I am free to own is an Officer I extremely value, and a Gentleman I very sincerely regard.

I inclose to you, Sir, a List of Persons among whom is a Gentleman who acted as the American Lieutenant Governor of South Carolina. A discovered Conspiracy and Correspondence with General Gates's Army have been a reason for removing these Persons from Charlestown to St Augustine. Being desirous to promote the Release of Major André upon any reasonable Terms, I offer you, Sir, this Lieutenant Governor, Mr Gadson, for my Adjutant General, or will make a Military Exchange for him, should you, Sir, prefer it. Lieutenant General Robertson in his Report to me mentions, his having requested from your Excellency a Copy of Major Andre's Letter to You, Sir, upon which seems to be grounded great matter of Charge against him, given as if that Letter might be considered as a Confession of his Guilt as a Spy. I have waited until this Evening with some Impatience for the Copy of the Letter I mention, not doubting but your Excellency would send it to me. I have now to request you will, Sir, do so; and I shall pay to it every due Consideration & give Your Excellency my Answer upon it immediately.

I have the Honor &c

(Signed) H Clinton.

His Excellency

General Washington

[88]

Vulture off Spiken Devil
October 5th 1780

Sir,

The account Colonel Robinson has given your Excellency of our Transactions, during our late Excursion, is so full and just in all its particulars that there is very little left for me to add. But as they have been attended with such fatal consequences to Major André, I hope it will not be held improper if I beg leave to submit my own Observations, on the Subject, at least so far as they relate to his leaving the Vulture, and the Light I then saw him in.

Your Excellency has already been inform'd that on the Night of the 21t Septr a Mr Smith came on board with a Flag of Truce. The Substance of his Order was, for himself and two Servants, to pass to Dobbs's Ferry and back again. He likewise had a written Permission to bring up with him a Mr John Anderson & Boy, and a Letter addressed to Colonel Robinson. All these Papers, Signed, B. Arnold.

Most of these Circumstances I had been previously taught to expect; & I had also been informed, that Major André was the Person understood by John Anderson; and that he was to go on Shore under that Name, to hold a Conference with General Arnold.

Mr Smith's Powers appeared to me of sufficient Authority; and as Major Andre's going under a fictitious Name was at the particular Request of the Officer from whom they were derived; I saw no reason for supposing, he, from that Circumstance forfeited his Claim to the Protection they must otherwise have afforded him. Clear I am that the matter must have appeared in the same Light to him; for had it not, Measures might have been concerted for taking him off whenever he pleased, which he very well knew I at any Time was enabled to accomplish. I am likewise persuaded Mr Smith's Ideas perfectly coincided with ours—for when on the point of setting off, Colonel Robinson observed, that as they had but two Men in a large Boat, they wou'd find some Difficulty in getting on Shore, and proposed that one of our's shou'd tow them some part of the Way; to which he objected, as it might, in Case of falling in with any of their Guard Boats, be deemed an Infringement of the Flag.

On my first learning from Major André that he did not intend going on Shore in his own Name, it immediately occurred to me that an Alteration of Dress might likewise be necessary; and I offered him a plain blue Coat of mine for that Purpose, which he declined accepting as he said, he had the Commander in Chief's Directions to go in his Uniform, & by no means to give up his Character. Adding at the same Time, that he had not the smallest Apprehension on the Occasion, and that he was ready to Attend General Arnold's Summons, when and where he pleased.

The Night the Flag was first expected, he expressed much Anxiety for its' arrival; and all next Day was full of Fears lest any Thing shou'd have happened to prevent its coming. The instant it arrived on the ensuing Night, he started out of Bed and discovered the greatest Impatience to be gone; nor did he in any Instance betray the least doubt of his Safety or Success.

I own I was equally confident nor can I now on the most mature Consideration of Circumstances, find the least reason for altering my Opinion. What therefore could possibly have given Rise to so tragical an Event, as has unhappily befallen Major André, is matter of the utmost Surprise and Concern to me.

I have the Honor &c

(Signed) A Sutherland

His Excellency

Sir Henry Clinton

But the forwarding these Letters was stopt by the Arrival of Major André's Servant & Baggage, with the News of his Master's having been executed in the midst of the Rebel Army at Tapaan on the 2nd October at Noon. In Consequence of which the Commander in Chief issued the following Orders to the Army.

Head Quarters New York 8th Octr 1780

"The Commander in Chief does with infinite Regret inform the Army of the Death of the Adjutant General Major André.

The unfortunate Fate of this Officer calls upon The Commander in Chief to declare his Opinion, that he ever considered Major André as a Gentleman as well as in the Line of his military Profession of the highest Integrity and Honor, and incapable of any base Action or unworthy Conduct.

Major Andre's Death is very severely felt by the Commander in Chief, as it assuredly will by the Army; and must prove a real Loss to his Country and to His Majesty's Service."

On the Evening of the 8th of October the following Letter was received from General Washington, which was answered by The Commander in Chief the next Day.
[89]

Head Quarters 6th October 1780

Sir,

Congress having received Information that there were good Grounds to believe that a Number of respectable Citizens of South Carolina, Prisoners of War by the Capitulation of Charlestown, had been seized upon and confined on board a Ship of War; have directed me to enquire of your Excellency, whether such Arrests and Confinements have been made and for what reasons. You will oblige me by making the Communication as soon as convenient.

I have the Honor to be &c

(Signed) G. Washington

His Excellency

Sir Henry Clinton

[90]

New York 9th October 1780.

Sir,

Persuaded it is for the Interest of

Mankind that a Correspondence shou'd exist between Generals Commanding Adverse Armies; I do, without waiting your Return to applications of an earlier Date made on my part on a Subject very interesting to me, answer without Delay your Letter of the 6th Inst

I have heard the Report you mention, that a Number of Persons under the Capitulation of Charlestown had entered into a Plot for the destruction of the Place where they are protected, and that the Officer Commanding there had found it necessary to interfere. I have this only from common Fame; no formal Report has been made to me on the Subject. But as I am well acquainted with Lord Cornwallis's Humanity, I cannot entertain the least Apprehension that he will stain the Lustre of the King's Arms by Acts of Cruelty. The Friends of those Persons under the Description you give of them need be under no fears for their Safety. Lord Cornwallis is incapable of straining the Laws to take away the Lives or Liberties of the Innocent. If any forced Construction be put upon the Laws by his Lordship, it will be in favor of the Accused; and every Plea their Friends can offer for them will be humanely heard and respected.

I am Sir,

Your most hble Servant

(Signed) H Clinton

Genl Washington.

General Bibliography

This is not a bibliography of the American Revolution in general but only of the phases of it which are dealt with in the present work. Specific authorities are cited in the Chapter References which follow.

Abbatt, William. *The Crisis of the American Revolution.* 1899 (A detailed study of the Arnold-André affair, concerned chiefly with the events of September 20—October 2, 1780, with much attention to persons and places involved and numerous photographs. There is an excellent bibliography)

André, John. *Proceedings of a Board of General Officers, Held by Order of His Excellency Gen. Washington, Commander in Chief of the Army of the United States, Respecting Major John André, Adjutant General of the British Army. September 29, 1780.* 1780

Arnold, Benedict. *Proceedings of a General Court Martial of the Line, Held at Raritan, in the State of New-Jersey, By Order of his Excellency George Washington, Esq. General and Commander in Chief of the Army of the United States of America, For the Trial of Major General Arnold June 1, 1779.* 1780 (Very valuable)

Arnold, Isaac N. *The Life of Benedict Arnold: His Patriotism and His Treason.* 1880 (A standard biography, based on thorough study of all the materials available at the time. The author was a distant relation of Benedict Arnold, but not an apologist for the treason)

Barbé-Marbois, François de. *Complot d'Arnold et de Sir Henry Clinton.* 1816 (Lively but full of conjectures and melodramatic inventions. English version by Robert Walsh in *American Register*, II, 15–63)

Burnett, Edmund C. (editor). *Letters of Members of the Continental Congress.* 8 vols. 1921–36 (Invaluable)

Carlisle, Earl of. *The Manuscripts of the Earl of Carlisle preserved at Castle Howard.* 1897 (Historical Manuscripts Commission, 15th Report)

Case of André] *The Case of Major John André, Adjutant General to the British Army, Who was put to Death by the Rebels, October 2, 1780, Candidly Represented: With Remarks on the Said Case. . . .* New York: Printed by James Rivington. MDCCLXXX (This was put in type but only partly printed and was never published. The one surviving copy is in the John Carter Brown Library at Providence. There is an account of the pamphlet by J. C. Stockbridge in *Magazine of American History*, III, 738–42. The present work, 423, for the first time identifies the author as Charles Inglis and explains the suppression)

Clinton Papers. The public and private papers of Sir Henry Clinton including the files of the British Headquarters in North America for the period of Clinton's command, 1778–82 (210 vols. of loose letters and documents, about 15,000 pieces; 50 vols. of letter books, warrant books, ledgers, military intelligence; Clinton's unpublished history of his American campaigns in 2 vols.; 350 campaign maps. This indispensable manuscript collection is in the William L. Clements Library at the University of Michigan. It has been described by the Director, Randolph G. Adams, in *The Headquarters Papers of the British Army in North America*, 1926, and *British Headquarters Maps and Sketches*, 1928)

Colonial Records. 16 vols. 1838–53 (Includes *Minutes of the Supreme Executive Council of Pennsylvania*)

Continental Congress. *Journals.* Edited by Worthington C. Ford and others. 34 vols. 1904–37

Davis, Matthew L. *Memoirs of Aaron Burr.* 2 vols. 1838

Deane, Silas. *Papers.* 5 vols. 1887–91 (*Collections of the New York Historical Society,* XIX–XXIII)

The Deane Papers. 1930 (*Collections of the Connecticut Historical Society,* XXIII)

Decker, Malcolm. *Benedict Arnold: Son of the Havens.* 1932 (Contains material not in Isaac N. Arnold's biography, and full bibliography to date)

Dictionary of American Biography. Edited by Allen Johnson and Dumas Malone. 20 vols. and Index vol. 1928–37 (Indispensable for all study of American history and biography. For the present work the following entries are important: Ethan Allen, Benedict Arnold, Edward Bancroft, Lieutenant Colonel John Brown, Metcalf Bowler, Joseph Brant, John Butler, Walter N. Butler, Samuel Chase, Benjamin Church, Silas Deane, Jacob Duché, Elizabeth Graeme Ferguson, William Franklin, Joseph Galloway, William Heron, Guy Johnson, Sir John Johnson, Thomas Jones, Charles Lee, Timothy Matlack, Jonathan Odell, Gideon Olmsted, Samuel Holden Parsons, Beverley Robinson, Joseph Reed, Philip Schuyler, Edward Shippen, Chief Justice William Smith, Christopher Sower, Joseph Stansbury, John Sullivan, Benjamin Tallmadge, John Vardill, Richard Varick, Paul Wentworth)

Einstein, Lewis. *Divided Loyalties: Americans in England during the War of Independence.* 1933 (Valuable information about Edward Bancroft, Silas Deane, John Temple, John Vardill, Paul Wentworth, and others)

Force, Peter (editor). *American Archives.* 4th Series, 6 vols., 1837–46. 5th Series, 3 vols., 1848–53 (A magnificent repository of first-hand materials now sometimes overlooked)

Ford, Worthington C. (editor). *The Washington-Duché Letters.* 1890

Franklin, Benjamin. *Writings.* Edited by Albert Henry Smyth. 10 vols. 1905–07

French, Allen. *General Gage's Informers.* 1932 (Best account of Benjamin Church's treachery and of Benjamin Thompson's activities while still among the Americans)

George III. *The Correspondence of King George the Third from 1760 to December 1783.* Edited by Sir John Fortescue. 6 vols. 1927–28

Hamilton, Alexander. *Writings.* Edited by Henry Cabot Lodge. 12 vols. 1904

Information of Deserters and Others not included in Private Intelligence. MS. vol. kept by the British adjutant general's office, October 1780–March 26, 1781 (There are a few entries as early as August but they may have been copied into the volume later. It is in the Emmett Collection, New York Public Library)

Jesse, J. H. *George Selwyn and his Contemporaries.* 4 vols. 1843–44 (Letters dealing with the Carlisle commission of 1778)

Jones, Thomas. *History of New York during the Revolutionary War.* Edited by Edward Floyd de Lancey. 2 vols. 1879 (The only extended history of the Revolution by a loyalist. Intensely partisan but spirited, and supplemented with full notes by the editor)

Leake, Isaac Q. *Memoir of the Life and Times of General John Lamb.* 1857

Lee, Charles. *The Lee Papers.* 4 vols. 1872–1875 (*Collections of the New York Historical Society* for 1871–74)

Lee, Henry. *Memoirs of the War in the Southern Department of the United States.* Revised edition, 1827

Lossing, Benson J. *The Pictorial Field-Book of the Revolution.* 2 vols. 1860 (Valuable for local materials and illustrations)

Loyalist Transcripts. Transcripts of the MS. Books and Papers of the Commission of Enquiry into the Losses and Services of the American Loyalists . . . preserved in the Public Record Office of England. 60 vols. (Contain much material to be found nowhere else; in the New York Public Library)

Moore, Frank (editor). *Diary of the American Revolution.* 2 vols. 1859–60 (Chiefly from contemporary newspapers)

Moore, George H. *The Treason of Charles Lee.* 1860

Naval Records of the American Revolution

1775–1788. Edited by C. H. Lincoln. 1906

Now and Then. 1868— (A magazine issued somewhat irregularly at Muncy, Pennsylvania, concerned with the history and biography of the region; now edited by T. Kenneth Wood)

Pell, John. *Ethan Allen*. 1932 (Supersedes all previous biographies)

Pennsylvania Archives. 12 vols. 1852–56 (Commonly known as 1st Series of *Pennsylvania Archives*)

Pennypacker, Morton. *General Washington's Spies on Long Island and in New York*. 1939 (A good deal of useful material and unsupported conjecture)

Private Intelligence as to the American Army. MS. vol. kept under the direction of Oliver DeLancey, Beverley Robinson, and George Beckwith, January 20–July 19, 1781 (Original vol. in the New York Public Library; printed serially in *Magazine of American History*, X–XII, October 1883–August 1884)

Reed, Joseph. *Remarks on Governor Johnstone's Speech in Parliament with a Collection of all the Letters and Authentic Papers relative to his Proposition*. 1779

Rush, Richard. *Occasional Productions, Political, Diplomatic, and Miscellaneous*. 1860

Sabine, Lorenzo. *Biographical Sketches of Loyalists of the American Revolution*. 2 vols. 1864 (The only general work of the kind, and valuable, though requiring to be supplemented at many points)

Sargent, Winthrop. *The Life and Career of Major John André*. 1861 (Still the principal authority, based on all the information available to Sargent)

(editor). *The Loyal Verses of Joseph Stansbury and Doctor Jonathan Odell relating to the American Revolution*. 1860 (Useful notes)

Scharf, J. Thomas, and Thompson Westcott. *History of Philadelphia 1609–1884*. 3 vols. 1884 (Abundant material commonly neglected by students)

Schuyler, Philip. Schuyler Papers, public and private, in the New York Public Library (These include letter books, military orders, and loose pieces arranged in chronological order, with a Calendar of letters, 1761–1802)

Serle, Ambrose. *American Journal . . . 1776–1778*. Edited by Edward H. Tatum. 1940

Simcoe, John Graves. *Simcoe's Military Journal*. 1844

Smith, Joshua Hett. *An Authentic Narrative of the Causes which led to the Death of Major André*. 1808 (Loose and untrustworthy)

Record of the Trial of Joshua Hett Smith, Esq., for alleged Complicity in the Treason of Benedict Arnold. Edited by Henry B. Dawson. 1866

Smith, William. MS. Journal, sometimes called Historical Memoirs of the Province of New York, or Journal of Public Events. 7 vols. (In the New York Public Library. This is the most valuable known but unpublished Revolutionary journal. Vols. VI and VII throw immense light on the period August 26, 1778 to November 12, 1783 during which Smith was a refugee in New York and a daily observer of events)

Sower, Christopher. MS. Abstract of his representations to Sir Henry Clinton, and the correspondence between them, from December 14, 1778 to May 1, 1780 (Concerned with the conspiracy of William Rankin. Both the Abstract and some of the original letters are in the Clinton Papers)

Sparks, Jared. *The Life and Treason of Benedict Arnold*. 1835 (The earliest account that still has value)

(editor). *Correspondence of the American Revolution: Being Letters of Eminent Men to George Washington*. 4 vols. 1853 (Valuable)

Stevens, Benjamin Franklin. *B. F. Stevens's Facsimiles of Manuscripts in European Archives Relating to America 1773–1783*. 25 vols. 1889–98 (By far the most valuable single work on the Revolution in its European aspects)

Sullivan, John. *Letters and Papers of Major General John Sullivan*. 3 vols. 1930–39 (*Collections of the New Hampshire Historical Society*, XIII–XV)

Journals of the Military Expedition of Major General John Sullivan against the Six Nations of Indians in 1779. Edited by Frederick Cook. 1887

Taylor, J. G. *Some New Light on the Later Life and Last Resting Place of Benedict Arnold and of his Wife Margaret Shippen*. 1931 (Incidentally contains information about Arnold's employment of Joseph Stansbury)

Thacher, James. *A Military Journal during the American Revolution.* 2nd edition, 1827

Van Tyne, Claude Halstead. *The Loyalists in the American Revolution.* 1902 (Based on the Loyalist Transcripts in the New York Public Library, this book did much to contribute to revised opinions regarding the loyalists)

Varick, Richard. *The Varick Court of Inquiry to Investigate the Implication of Colonel Richard Varick (Arnold's Private Secretary) in the Arnold Treason.* Edited by Albert Bushnell Hart. 1907 (Very valuable)

Walker, Lewis Burd. *The Life of Margaret Shippen, Wife of Benedict Arnold.* In *Pennsylvania Magazine of History and Biography,* XXIV (1900)–XXVI (1902) serially (Valuable though generally overlooked by students)

Washington, George. Washington Papers in the Library of Congress (An immense collection of letters to and from Washington, arranged in chronological order. There are printed Calendars of *Correspondence . . . with the Continental Congress,* 1906, and *Correspondence . . .*

with the Officers, 4 vols., 1915, both edited by John C. Fitzpatrick. Completely indispensable)

Writings. Edited by Jared Sparks. 12 vols. 1837 (Valuable for its inclusion of many other letters besides Washington's. Has an important appendix on the treason of Arnold, with many documents, VII, 520–52)

Writings. Edited by John C. Fitzpatrick. 26 vols. 1931–38 (Further vols. are expected to carry on the work, which at present comes down to June 10, 1783. Indispensable)

Watson, John F. *Annals of Philadelphia.* 3 vols. 1900 (Latest revision of an older work which is clumsily arranged but frequently useful)

Wharton, Francis (editor). *Revolutionary Diplomatic Correspondence of the United States.* 6 vols. (Standard work)

Winsor, Justin (editor). *Narrative and Critical History of America.* 8 vols. 1884–1889 (Invaluable, especially for bibliographies and maps. Excellent discussions of Arnold's treason, VI, 447–68, and of the loyalists, VII, 185–214)

Chapter References

References are normally to printed sources, where these exist, rather than to manuscripts. Manuscripts cited in the text without other reference are all in the Clinton Papers. Full titles not given under individual chapters will be found in the General Bibliography. Abbreviations are used as follows: CP = Clinton Papers; LC = Library of Congress; *MAH* = *Magazine of American History;* NYPL = New York Public Library; *PMHB* = *Pennsylvania Magazine of History and Biography;* WLCL = William L. Clements Library; WP = Washington Papers.

CHAPTER 1

1 Stevens, *Facsimiles*, 2048
2 *Minutes of the Committee and of the First Commission for Detecting and Defeating Conspiracies in the State of New York* (2 vols., 1924–25), I, 149
3 Beverley Robinson's report to Sir Henry Clinton, November 13, 1780, CP
4 Franklin, *Writings* (Smyth), VI, 365, 273, 250–51
5 Jefferson, *Writings* (Lipscomb), IV, 28–30; Stevens, *Facsimiles*, 2038
6 Einstein, 406
7 *The Respective Pleas and Arguments of the Mother Country, and of the Colonies distinctly set forth* (1774)
8 4 Force, II, 1851, 1870–71; III, 255, 240–41
9 *New England Chronicle*, November 23, 1775: quoted in Moore, *Diary*, I, 171–73
10 Moore, *Diary*, I, 209
11 Moore, *Diary*, I, 307
12 Winsor, VII, 187
13 *New York City during the Revolution* (1861), 117–38 (gives names of the signers)
14 4 Force, VI, 1406, 1410, 1411, 1084–1086, 1120
15 4 Force, VI, 1152–83
16 5 Force, I, 731, 1550
17 Jones, II, 120–23, 162, 269, 287, 416–17
18 4 Force, V, 511, 1665; 5 Force, I, 1607; Washington, *Writings* (Fitzpatrick), V, 464
19 5 Force, I, 1159–62; II, 1217–19; III, 1579; Moore, *Diary*, II, 157
20 Jones, I, 630
21 Graydon, Alexander, *Memoirs* (1846), 215
22 Jones, II, 27
23 Jones, I, 630–31
24 French, *General Gage's Informers*, gives the best account of Church's treachery
25 French, 181, 167, 154
26 4 Force, III, 1481
27 4 Force, III, 1479–86
28 French, 114–46
29 4 Force, III, 956–58
30 4 Force, III, 1911
31 4 Force, III, 1636–38
32 French, 198–201, 158
33 4 Force, III, 1047–48; IV, 616
34 4 Force, IV, 617; III, 1385, 1661
35 4 Force, IV, 616; J. D. F. Smyth, *A Tour in the United States* (2 vols., 1794), II, 245–55

36 4 Force, III, 1660–62; IV, 892, 508, 1646

37 4 Force, IV, 958–59

38 4 Force, VI, 1667, 1674, 784; 5 Force, I, 1296; III, 777

39 Loyalist Transcripts, LVIII, 51–71

40 *Colonial Records of North Carolina*, X, 190–91, 266; XI, 295, 402; *State Records of North Carolina*, XXI, 854

41 4 Force, 314–52

42 4 Force, IV, 485; V, 1235–36

43 Loyalist Transcripts, LVII, 318–50

CHAPTER 2

1 Moore, *Treason*, 40–69; Moore, *Diary*, I, 360–61

2 Moore, *Treason*, 23

3 Moore, *Treason*, 25

4 *Lee Papers*, I, 184

5 4 Force, II, 1850–51

6 5 Force, II, 1390

7 *Lee Papers*, II, 371

8 Serle, *Journal*, 186–87

9 Baker, W. S., *Exchange of Major General Charles Lee*, *PMHB*, XV, 26–34

10 Moore, *Treason*, 84–90

11 Serle, *Journal*, 165, 178, 190, 200, 206; Moore, *Diary*, I, 413; Scharf and Westcott, I, 389

12 Baker, XV, 26–34; *Lee Papers*, II, 382, 383–89, 390–91

13 Serle, *Journal*, 305–06

14 5 Force, I, 1121

15 5 Force, I, 1621; II, 603

16 *Pennsylvania Evening Post*, October 14, 1777 and later issues

17 *Pennsylvania Ledger*, October 22, 1777

18 Stevens, 2094

19 Warrant, May 15, 1778, CP

20 W. Howe to H. Clinton, May 18, 1778, CP

21 Stevens, 2097

22 Serle, *Journal*, 215–16

23 Ford, *Washington-Duché*, 7–8

24 5 Force, I, 1570; II, 1280, 1405

25 Sabine, I, 291

26 Ford, *Washington-Duché*, 9–25

27 Ford, *Washington-Duché*, 26

28 *PMHB*, XXXIX, 290

29 Loyalist Transcripts, XLIV, 323–26

30 Stevens, 2075

31 Sullivan, *Letters*, I, 355–59

32 Schuyler Papers, Letters and Orders, June 15–16, 1777, NYPL

33 Sparks, *Correspondence*, I, 384

34 Papers of the Continental Congress, No. 153, III, 188–94, LC

35 Schuyler Papers, Letter Books, NYPL

36 Washington, *Writings* (Sparks), IV, 466–68 (note on Amsbury)

37 Sullivan to Washington, June 21, 1777, WP, LC

38 Sullivan, *Letters*, I, 446

39 Thacher, 86

40 Washington, *Writings* (Sparks), III, 535–40

41 Jones, I, 200–03; Lossing, *Field-Book*, I, 137–38; Skenesborough Papers Special in the Museum at Fort Ticonderoga

42 Schuyler, *Proceedings*, 51: *Proceedings of a General Court Martial . . . for the Trial of Major General Philip Schuyler, October 1, 1778* (1778)

43 Sparks, *Correspondence*, II, 514

44 Schuyler Papers, Letter Books, July 20–21, 1777, NYPL; Schuyler to Washington, July 21, 1777, WP, LC

45 Additional Germain Papers, July 19–20, 1777, WLCL

46 Skenesborough Papers Special, June 8, 1784, February 14, 1787, Museum at Fort Ticonderoga; Loyalist Transcripts, XLV, 189–234

47 Moore, *Diary*, I, 512

48 H. B. Livingston to Schuyler, January 3, 12, 1778; Gabriel Ludlow to Schuyler, January 6, 1778: both in Schuyler Papers, NYPL

49 Memoranda by Clinton, December 6, 1785, October 1783, CP

50 George III, IV, 40

CHAPTER 3

1 Stevens, 483

2 Stevens, 315

3 Stevens, 277

4 Franklin, *Writings* (Smyth), VI, 251–252

5 Stevens, 327

6 Stevens, 489

7 Stevens, 1769

8 Stevens, 231

9 Stevens, 234

10 Stevens, 335

11 Stevens, 1833

12 George III, IV, 29–30; see also IV, 189

13 Stevens, 162

14 George III, IV, 50

15 Franklin, *Writings* (Smyth), VII, 107–09
16 George III, IV, 27–29
17 George III, IV, 30, 36
18 Stevens, 347
19 Stevens, 67
20 George III, IV, 44
21 Stevens, 394
22 Stevens, 101
23 Stevens, 378
24 Stevens, 383, 386, 67
25 Stevens, 412
26 George III, IV, 91, 93
27 Stevens, 1062, 1069
28 Stevens, 101, 441
29 Stevens, 440, gives full text of instructions
30 George III, IV, 65
31 Franklin, *Writings* (Smyth), VII, 124
32 George III, IV, 79–81
33 Wharton, II, 523
34 Franklin, *Writings* (Smyth), VIII, 43–46
35 Andrews, Charles M., *A Note on the Franklin-Deane Mission to France*, *Yale University Library Gazette*, II (1928), 53–68
36 Stevens, 411
37 Franklin, *Writings* (Smyth), VII, 141–42
38 Stevens, 68, 69
39 Reed, *Remarks*, 9–12
40 Sparks, *Correspondence*, II, 108–09
41 Stevens, 438
42 Monaghan, Frank, *John Jay: Defender of Liberty* (1935), 53–54
43 Stevens, 487
44 Stevens, 71
45 Stevens, 421, 447
46 Wharton, II, 511; Stevens, 824
47 Wharton, II, 443; III, 7–8
48 Stevens, 419
49 Stevens, 426
50 Stevens, 424, 434
51 Serle, *Journal*, 205
52 *Clare College* (Cambridge, 2 vols., 1928), I, 174
53 Stevens, 835, 836, 837
54 Adams, John, *Works*, III, 178
55 Arthur Lee Papers, July 7, 1778. Harvard College Library
56 Stevens, 421
57 George III, IV, 94
58 Stevens, 1077
59 Stevens, 446
60 Stevens, 499

61 Eden to Clinton, October 10, 1778, CP
62 Stevens, 68
63 Stevens, 72

CHAPTER 4

1 Washington, *Writings* (Fitzpatrick), XI, 277–78
2 Ford, Worthington C. (editor). *The Spurious Letters Attributed to Washington* (1889)
3 Washington, *Writings* (Fitzpatrick), XI, 289
4 Continental Congress, *Journals*, X, 374–83
5 Washington, *Writings* (Fitzpatrick), XI, 309
6 Stevens, 101
7 Stevens, 496
8 Stevens, 101
9 Serle, *Journal*, 294
10 Serle, *Journal*, 295
11 Serle, *Journal*, 297
12 Stevens, 2096, 2097, 2098
13 Serle, *Journal*, 307–08
14 Continental Congress, *Journals*, XI, 575
15 Serle, *Journal*, 309
16 Stevens, 1104
17 Stevens, 1102, 1103
18 Continental Congress, *Journals*, XI, 605–15
19 Jesse, III, 281–82
20 Stevens, 499
21 Serle, *Journal*, 307–10
22 Stevens, 432, 500
23 Stevens, 498; Sparks, *Correspondence*, II, 136–37
24 Stevens, 75
25 Wharton, II, 811
26 Washington, *Writings* (Fitzpatrick), XII, 45–46; Continental Congress, *Journals*, XI, 608–16
27 Stevens, 75
28 Wharton, II, 616–17
29 Washington, *Writings* (Fitzpatrick), XII, 59
30 Reed, *Remarks*, 13–16
31 Stevens, 2046
32 Serle, *Journal*, 309
33 Reed, *Remarks*, 39–58
34 Reed, *Remarks*, 17–21
35 Stevens, 1132
36 Reed, *Remarks*, 36–38
37 Reed, *Remarks*, 38–39
38 Loyalist Transcripts, XLIX, 323–56

39 Stevens, 517
40 Stevens, 500
41 Carlisle, *Manuscripts*, 345, 347
42 Stevens, 1125
43 Continental Congress, *Journals*, XI, 770–76; Burnett, III, 370
44 Stevens, 1132, 1133
45 Carlisle, *Manuscripts*, 360
46 Peckham, Howard (editor), *Dr. Berkenhout's Journal, 1778.* In *PMHB*, LXV (1941), 79–92
47 Burnett, III, 388–89, 398–401; *Colonial Records*, XI, 567, 569–70, 576
48 Sparks, *Correspondence*, II, 96–97
49 Papers of the Continental Congress, No. 83, I, folios 289–90, LC
50 Wharton, III, 7–8, 14–16
51 Carlisle, *Manuscripts*, 356
52 Jesse, III, 340
53 Stevens, 1177
54 Washington, *Writings* (Fitzpatrick), XIII, 20
55 Stevens, 1172
56 Continental Congress, *Journals*, XII, 1015–16
57 Stevens, 1215
58 Stevens, 559
59 George III, IV, 286, 302–04
60 Burnett, III, 398, 516, 541–42, 544–545; Einstein, 72–113
61 Bowdoin-Temple Papers, *Collections of the Massachusetts Historical Society*, 6th Series, IX, 433–36

CHAPTER 5

1 Van Tyne, *Loyalists*, 318–41, for laws against loyalists
2 Stevens, 1121
3 Winsor, VI, 605–84, for detailed account of Indians and border warfare
4 Germain to Clinton, January 23, 1779, CP
5 Return of Provincial forces, August 15, 1779, CP
6 Jones, II, 66–67
7 Hammill's Memorial to Clinton, September 3, November 29, 1779, CP; Hammill's claim for compensation, Loyalist Transcripts, XLI, 511–14
8 Anonymous letter to Parsons, May 5, 1778, WP, LC
9 Proceedings of the court martial held at Fort Schuyler, July 1, 1778, WP, LC

10 Washington, *Writings* (Fitzpatrick), XII, 320
11 Clark, Jane (editor), *Metcalf Bowler as a British Spy*, in *Rhode Island Historical Society Collections*, XXIII (1930), 101–17. Transcripts of original letters in CP
12 Sower, Abstract; also separate letters of particular dates noted in text
13 André to Clinton, March 20, 1779, CP
14 Battwell's claims for compensation, Loyalist Transcripts, LI, 12–19
15 Loyalist Transcripts, XXV, 250–56
16 Washington, *Writings* (Fitzpatrick), XI, 143
17 Loyalist Transcripts, L, 108–22
18 5 Force, II, 6, 31
19 Loyalist Transcripts, L, 410–14
20 William Phillips to Horatio Gates, November 15, 1778, Gates Papers, New York Historical Society
21 William Phillips to Horatio Gates, undated but apparently November 1778, Gates Papers, New York Historical Society
22 William Phillips to Horatio Gates, December 1, 1778: copy in CP with Gates's letter to Clinton, December 8
23 Horatio Gates to William Phillips, December 3, 1778: sent by Phillips to Clinton in letter of December 8 and preserved in CP
24 Horatio Gates to Congress, December 3, 1778: copy in Gates Papers, New York Historical Society; original in Papers of the Continental Congress, No. 154, II, 33, LC
25 William Phillips to Horatio Gates, December 3, 1778: copy sent by Phillips in letter of December 8 to Clinton, CP
26 Continental Congress, *Journals*, XIII, 104
27 Germain to Clinton, September 2, 1778, CP
28 James Chalmers to Clinton, September 12, 1778, CP
29 Stevens, 548, 549
30 Germain to Clinton, March 3, 1779, CP
31 William Tryon to Clinton, June 30, 1779, CP
32 William Eden to Clinton, November 19, 1778; Jonathan Odell to John

André, December 21, 1779: both in CP

33 William Tryon to Clinton, June 30, 1779, CP

34 William Knox to Clinton, January 23, 1779, CP

35 John Mason to Clinton, March 27, 1779; July 5, 1780: both in CP

CHAPTER 6

1 *MAH*, X, 314–17, for Arnold's letter and Johnstone's reply

2 Loyalist Transcripts, hearing on Skene, April 3, 1787, XLV, 222–23

3 Decker, 472

4 Arnold, *Arnold*, 34

5 4 Force, II, 383–84

6 4 Force, II, 485

7 4 Force, II, 555–60, 606

8 4 Force, II, 584–85, 645–46, 735

9 4 Force, II, 808; II, 707; II, 1382–83; II, 186–88

10 4 Force, II, 1596

11 4 Force, II, 1598–99

12 4 Force, II, 1541, 1592–93

13 4 Force, III, 1639, 1650

14 4 Force, II, 557

15 4 Force, IV, 590, 1018

16 Washington, *Writings* (Fitzpatrick), V, 152

17 4 Force, VI, 1107

18 5 Force, II, 303, 532

19 5 Force, I, 630, 649

20 5 Force, II, 933

21 5 Force, II, 982; Franklin, *Writings* (Smyth), VI, 451

22 5 Force, I, 1185–87, 988–89, 1002–03, 1051, 1073, 1268, 1277

23 4 Force, VI, 1038, 1104–05

24 5 Force, I, 1272–75

25 5 Force, I, 1268; II, 295

26 5 Force, II, 224; see also 5 Force, I, 810

27 4 Force, IV, 464, 907–08; 5 Force, I, 1219–20, 1593, 1594; 5 Force, I, 1221; 5 Force, II, 143, 295

28 5 Force, II, 1039, 1080; III, 875

29 5 Force, III, 1158–60, 1042–43

30 5 Force, III, 1343

31 Leake, *Lamb*, 152–53

32 *New England Historical and Genealogical Register*, II (1857), 75–76

33 Washington, *Writings* (Fitzpatrick), VII, 234, 251–52, 353

34 Sparks, *Correspondence*, I, 355–56, 360

35 Smith, J. E. A., *History of Pittsfield*, I (1869), has the fullest account of the Arnold-Brown controversy; see also W. L. Stone, *Life of Joseph Brant* (1838), II, 116–19

36 Washington, *Writings* (Fitzpatrick), VIII, 48

37 Arnold, *Arnold*, 134–35

38 Continental Congress, *Journals*, VII, 371–73

39 Washington, *Writings*, (Fitzpatrick), VIII, 47

40 Continental Congress, *Journals*, VIII, 382

41 *PMHB*, XIII, 357

42 Arnold, *Arnold*, 138

43 Washington, *Writings* (Fitzpatrick), VIII, 377, 427

44 Arnold, *Arnold*, 149

45 Continental Congress, *Journals*, 623–624

46 Burnett, II, 442, 445, 448

47 Sparks, *Correspondence*, II, 518

48 Arnold, *Arnold*, 156–57

49 Sparks, *Correspondence*, II, 519

50 Sparks, *Correspondence*, II, 521

51 Wilkinson, James, *Memoirs* (1816), I, 254–60

52 Washington, *Writings* (Fitzpatrick), X, 324–26

53 Thacher, 103

54 Arnold, *Arnold*, 213

55 Arnold to Washington, March 12, 1778, WP, LC

56 Decker, 285–88

57 *Connecticut Journal*, May 6, 1778

58 Washington, *Writings* (Fitzpatrick), XI, 31, 325–26, 359–60

59 Washington, *Writings* (Fitzpatrick), XI, 466; XII, 84

60 Facsimile of oath in *The Centennial of the United States Military Academy at West Point: 1802–1902* (1904), I, 170–71

CHAPTER 7

1 4 Force, II, 1087

2 Washington, *Writings* (Fitzpatrick), XII, 94–95

3 Continental Congress, *Journals*, XI, 571

4 Arnold, *Proceedings of a General Court Martial*, 10

5 Scharf and Westcott, I, 390; Continental Congress, *Journals*, XIX, 40

6 Continental Congress, *Journals*, XII, 1071

7 *Pennsylvania Packet*, July 6, 1778

8 Burnett, III, 333

9 *Deane Papers* (1930), 136

10 *Deane Papers* (1887–91), V, 280

11 *Deane Papers* (1887–91), V, 213–14

12 Arnold, *Proceedings*, 31; Washington, *Writings* (Fitzpatrick), XII, 161

13 Meng, John J., *Dispatches and Instructions of Conrad Alexandre Gérard: 1778–1780* (1939), 160

14 Washington, *Writings* (Fitzpatrick), XII, 270

15 Continental Congress, *Journals*, 885–886, 905; Meng, 283–84

16 Arnold, *Arnold*, 216–17

17 Continental Congress, *Journals*, XVIII, 871

18 American Art Association Catalogue, June 12, 1932, Sale No. 3941

19 Continental Congress, *Journals*, XI, 779

20 Arnold, *Proceedings*, 8, 19, 27

21 Arnold, *Proceedings*, 8–9, 23–25, 27–28, 31, 42

22 Washington, *Writings* (Fitzpatrick), XIII, 168

23 Arnold, *Proceedings*, 6–7, 15–23, 28–31, 32–39, 49–50, 52

24 *American Clipper*, Vol. 5, No. 3, Catalogue of the American Autograph Shop, Merion Station, Pennsylvania

25 Taylor, *New Light*, 54

26 Carson, H. L., *The Case of the Sloop Active*, *PMHB*, XVI (1892), 385–98

27 Continental Congress, *Journals*, XIII, 86–92

28 1 *Pennsylvania Archives*, IX, 33–34, 178–80

29 Continental Congress, *Journals*, XV, 1194–96

30 Taylor, *New Light*, 53–54

31 *Naval Records*, 311

32 Arnold, *Proceedings*, 12–15

33 *Lee Papers*, III, 250–52

34 *Lee Papers*, III, 270

35 Arnold, *Proceedings*, 50–51

36 American Art Association Catalogue, January 24–25, 1935

37 Loyalist Transcripts, XLV, 222–23: Arnold's testimony, April 3, 1787

38 Arnold to Schuyler, February 8, 1779, Schuyler Papers, Letter Books, NYPL

39 Arnold, *Arnold*, 241

40 Arnold, *Arnold*, 230

41 Walker, *PMHB*, XXIV, 427–29

42 Lossing, *Field-Book*, 97–101

43 Konkle, B. A., *Benjamin Chew* (1932), 180–89

44 Hazard's *Register of Pennsylvania*, XIV, 295–97; manuscript copy of an early date in the Historical Society of Pennsylvania

45 Burnett, III, 452

46 Continental Congress, *Journals*, XII, 1001, 1018

47 Walker, *PMHB*, XXIV, 414

48 Arnold, *Arnold*, 228–29

49 Arnold, *Arnold*, 228

50 Duane, W. (editor), *Letters to Benjamin Franklin* (1859), 84–85

51 Walker, *PMHB*, XXV, 32, 33

52 Walker, *PMHB*, XXV, 35–36, 38, 40

53 Watson, III, 449

54 Arnold, *Proceedings*, 7

55 Arnold, *Proceedings*, 18, 21–22, 33, 50

56 *Pennsylvania Packet*, February 23, 1779

57 *Pennsylvania Packet*, February 16, 1779

58 *Pennsylvania Packet*, February 23, 1779

59 Arnold, *Proceedings*, 243–45, for text of charges

60 Burnett, IV, 93–95

61 Continental Congress, *Journals*, XIII, 188–89, 324–26

62 Arnold, *Proceedings*, 52

63 Continental Congress, *Journals*, XIII, 412–17

64 Arnold, *Proceedings*, 53

65 Washington, *Writings* (Sparks), VI, 518–19; *Writings* (Fitzpatrick), XIV, 450

66 Washington, *Writings* (Sparks), 523

67 Arnold, *Arnold*, 274–80

68 Chastellux, Marquis de, *Travels in North America* (2 vols., 1787), I, 97

69 Stevens, 1059, 1186, 1194, 1209, 1214, 1215; Continental Congress, *Journals*, XII, 1214; XIV, 614; XV, 1373; XVI, 72

70 Clinton to his sisters, October 4, 1780, CP; Appendix, No. 67

71 Arnold, *Arnold*, 183

72 Davis, *Burr*, I, 219

73 1 *Pennsylvania Archives*, IX, 178–80

CHAPTER 8

1 Taylor, *New Light*, 55: Stansbury's statement in support of Arnold's claim for compensation, March 4, 1784

2 Sargent, *Loyal Verses*, 103–04

3 Sargent, *Loyal Verses*, 23
4 Sargent, *Loyal Verses*, 9
5 Phipps, W. Pownoll, *The Life of Colonel Pownoll Phipps* (1894), 88
6 See Appendix for this note (No. 2) and other letters quoted hereafter from the Arnold-André correspondence in CP
7 Sargent, *Loyal Verses*, 40
8 Odell to André, June 13, 1779, Appendix, No. 12
9 Rattoon to Washington, May 22, 1779, WP, LC
10 Whitehead, W. A., *Contributions to the Early History of Perth Amboy* (1866), 233, 235, 239, 240, 278
11 Washington, *Writings* (Fitzpatrick), XV, 207
12 Sargent, *Loyal Verses*, 49

CHAPTER 9

1 Wallis's name is commonly misspelled Wallace in CP
2 Meginness, J. F., *Otzinachson* (1857), 178–79, 187; *Now and Then*, VI, 173–76, 25–54
3 1 *Pennsylvania Archives*, VI, 664–65
4 1 *Pennsylvania Archives*, VII, 41
5 Washington, *Writings* (Fitzpatrick), XIV, 160, 314–18
6 Sullivan, *Journals*, 303
7 André to Rankin, after June 20, 1779, CP
8 Sower, Abstract
9 Sower, Abstract; some added names in Report of Andrew Fürstner, August 1779, CP
10 Sower, Abstract
11 *Archives of Maryland*, XVI, 326, 378, 508; XXI, 70
12 Continental Congress, *Journals*, XI, 765; XII, 1086, 1096, 1200; XIII, 126
13 Stevens, 2076
14 Hamilton, *Works*, I, 201–09
15 Washington, *Writings* (Fitzpatrick), XVI, 333–34
16 Continental Congress, *Journals*, XV, 1103
17 Edward Fox to Congress, September 24, 1779, Papers of the Continental Congress, No. 78, IX, folio 287, LC
18 Continental Congress, *Journals*, XV, 1128, 1343; Edward Fox to Congress, December 2, 1779, Papers of the Continental Congress, No. 78, IX, folio 295, LC
19 Appendix, No. 13
20 Stevens, 997
21 Appendix, No. 14
22 Washington, *Writings* (Fitzpatrick), VI, 45; VII, 141–42; Haussegger's Memorial to Congress, January 9, 1779, Papers of the Continental Congress, No. 41, IV, folio 47, LC
23 *Wisconsin Historical Society Collections*, XVIII, 214; *Illinois Historical Collections*, VIII, 613
24 Account of Expenses, February 21–September 13, CP
25 André to Kemble, September 16, 1779, CP
26 Eden to Clinton, January 23, 1779, CP
27 Jones, I, 315
28 Anonymous letter, January 1782, CP
29 Undated memorandum in André's hand, CP
30 Sabine, II, 171–74
31 Washington, *Writings* (Fitzpatrick), XV, 326–27, 374
32 Clinton to his sisters, October 4, 1780, Appendix, No. 67
33 Stevens, 1013
34 *Vermont Historical Society Collections*, II, 59
35 Stevens, 1034

CHAPTER 10

1 Washington, *Writings* (Sparks), VI, 523–24
2 Washington, *Writings* (Fitzpatrick), XIV, 418; XV, 86, 110, 172
3 Washington, *Writings* (Fitzpatrick), XX, 370
4 Washington, *Writings* (Fitzpatrick), XV, 204–10
5 Washington, *Writings* (Sparks), VI, 527
6 Arnold, *Proceedings*, 40–55
7 *Pennsylvania Packet*, September 30, 1780
8 1 *Pennsylvania Archives*, VII, 223–24
9 Continental Congress, *Journals*, XVI, 161–62
10 Barbé-Marbois, 33–34
11 Washington, *Writings* (Fitzpatrick), XVIII, 225
12 *Deane Papers* (1887–91), IV, 116
13 Continental Congress, *Journals*, XV, 513; 1126, 1134; XVI, 166, 168

14 Washington, *Writings* (Sparks), VI, 530
15 Watson, I, 425–27; *PMHB*, XXV, 157
16 Burnett, IV, 476–77
17 Continental Congress, *Journals*, XV, 1147
18 Sparks, *Correspondence*, II, 411
19 Washington, *Writings* (Fitzpatrick), XVIII, 114–15
20 Washington, *Writings* (Fitzpatrick), XVIII, 174
21 *Naval Records*, 138
22 *Pennsylvania Packet*, September 30, 1780
23 Barbé-Marbois, 136
24 Continental Congress, *Journals*, XVI, 393–96
25 Continental Congress, *Journals*, XVII, 428, 433; Papers of the Continental Congress, No. 136, IV, folios 233–275, LC
26 4 Force, V, 1099
27 Arnold to Schuyler, May 25, 1780, Schuyler Papers, NYPL
28 Arnold, *Arnold*, 263

CHAPTER 11

1 Washington, *Writings* (Fitzpatrick), XVIII, 476
2 Arnold to Washington, June 7, 1780, Gratz Collection, Historical Society of Pennsylvania
3 Burnett, V, 202
4 Burnett, V, 234
5 Washington, *Writings* (Fitzpatrick), XVIII, 483; XIX, 2
6 Washington, *Writings* (Fitzpatrick), XX, 214; Rush, 78–84
7 Robert Howe to Washington, September 26, 1780, WP, LC
8 Hoadly, *Public Records of the State of Connecticut* (1894–1922), III, 21, 62–63
9 Taylor, 54
10 Arnold to Titus Hosmer, August 15, 1780, Tomlinson Collection, NYPL
11 Order dated June 23, 1780, Tomlinson Collection, NYPL
12 Arnold to Enoch Brown, June 25, 1780, Tomlinson Collection, NYPL
13 Arnold to Ebenezer Townsend, August 30, 1780, Tomlinson Collection, NYPL
14 Taylor, 54

15 Arnold to Titus Hosmer, July 8, 1780, Tomlinson Collection, NYPL
16 Robert Howe to Washington, June 30, 1780, WP, LC
17 Stevens, 728; Jones, I, 355–58
18 Stevens, 730
19 Washington, *Writings* (Fitzpatrick), XIX, 91
20 Arnold to Congress, July 17, 1780, Papers of the Continental Congress, No. 162, folio 205, LC
21 Continental Congress, *Journals*, XVII, 649
22 Appendix, No. 48; *Pennsylvania Packet*, November 25, December 2, 1780
23 *Now and Then*, V, 175
24 Washington, *Writings* (Fitzpatrick), XIX, 311–12, 318

CHAPTER 12

1 Rush, 79–85
2 Washington, *Writings* (Fitzpatrick), XIX, 302, 309–11
3 Continental Congress, *Journals*, XII, 917–19; XIV, 782; XVII, 581; Burnett, III, 415–16; IV, 523
4 Arnold, *Arnold*, 218–20
5 Arnold to Robert Howe, August 5, 1780, WP, LC
6 Thacher, 131
7 Varick, *Court*, 82
8 Arnold to Robert Howe, September 12, 1780, WP, LC
9 Lafayette, *Memoirs, Correspondence, and Manuscripts* (3 vols., 1833), I, 254
10 Arnold to Robert Howe, August 5, 1780, WP, LC
11 Robert Howe to Arnold, August 14, 16, 1780, WP, LC
12 Arnold to Robert Howe, August 16, 1780, WP, LC
13 Robert Howe to Washington, September 26, 1780, WP, LC
14 Smith, *Record*, 90–94
15 Joshua Hett Smith to Arnold, August 13, 1780, WP, LC
16 Varick, *Court*, 89–91
17 Arnold to Washington, August 12, 1780, WP, LC
18 Washington, *Writings* (Fitzpatrick), XIX, 370
19 Udny Hay to Arnold, August 15, 1780, WP, LC
20 Arnold to Udny Hay, August 16, 1780, WP, LC
21 Leake, *Lamb*, 251

22 Villefranche to Franks, August 19, 1780, WP, LC

23 Arnold to George Clinton, August 22, 1780, WP, LC

24 Arnold to Timothy Pickering, August 23, 1780, WP, LC

25 Arnold to Caleb Bull, August 15, 1780, American Art Association Catalogue, February 5–6, 1929

26 Caleb Bull to Arnold, August 26, 1780, WP, LC

27 Arnold to Nathaniel Shaw, August 10, WP, LC

28 Jacob Thompson to Arnold, August 22, 1780, WP, LC

29 Arnold to Jacob Thompson, August 28, 31, 1780; Arnold to Jesse Penfield, August 31, 1780: WP, LC

30 Varick to William M. Betts, September 18, 1780, WP, LC

31 Continental Congress, *Journals*, XVII, 725

32 Continental Congress, *Journals*, XVII, 725–27, 772–73

33 Arnold to Parsons, August 27, 1780, WP, LC

34 Arnold to Greene, August 23, WP, LC; Varick, *Court*, 197

35 Varick, *Court*, 158

36 Varick, *Court*, 154

37 Varick, *Court*, 135, 155–56, 184–85

38 Varick, *Court*, 134–35

39 Varick, *Court*, 134, 138, 183–84

40 Jonathan Copp to Arnold, August 21, 1780, WP, LC

41 Parsons to Arnold, August 28, 1780, WP, LC

42 Varick, *Court*, 100–01

43 Stevens, 733

44 Smith, Journal, VI, entry for September 4, 1780

45 Appendix, No. 52

CHAPTER 13

1 Varick, *Court*, 106–07

2 Varick, *Court*, 124, 171

3 Arnold to Francis Barber, September 4, 1780, WP, LC

4 Arnold to Sheldon, September 7, 10, 1780: Washington, *Writings* (Sparks), VII, 522–23

5 Sheldon to Arnold, September 6, 1780, WP, LC

6 Arnold to Sheldon, September 7, 1780

7 Varick, *Court*, 197–98

8 Davis, *Burr*, I, 219–20

9 *Pennsylvania Packet*, September 30, 1780; *PMHB*, LX, 380–81

10 *Pennsylvania Packet*, September 30, 1780

11 Hannah Arnold to Arnold, September 4, 1780, Tomlinson Collection, NYPL

12 George Meade to Arnold, August 24, 1780, WP, LC

13 Walker, *PMHB*, XXV, 163

14 Arnold, *Arnold*, 234

15 Franks to Arnold, August 28, 1780, WP, LC

16 Here reproduced from Arnold's copy, WP, LC

17 Arnold to Samuel Bellows, September 5, 1780, Tomlinson Collection, NYPL

18 Washington, *Writings* (Sparks), VII, 523

19 Appendix, No. 55; Washington, *Writings* (Sparks), VII, 522–23

20 Washington, *Writings* (Sparks), VII, 523–24

21 Appendix, No. 56

22 Sparks, *Correspondence*, III, 81

23 Varick, *Court*, 199–20 (reproduced in facsimile)

24 Washington, *Writings* (Sparks), VII, 82

25 Livingston to Arnold, Arnold to Livingston, September 13, 1780, WP, LC

26 Washington, *Writings* (Sparks), VII, 524–25

27 Originals of the papers taken with André in New York State Library, Albany; printed in Lossing, I, 721–23; Smith, *Record*, 107–15; Abbatt, 16–18; for bibliography of these papers, see Winsor, VI, 457

28 Sparks, *Correspondence*, III, 85–87; Varick, *Court*, 203–05 (facsimile)

29 Appendix, No. 56; No. 72, as edited by Clinton; Washington, *Writings* (Sparks), VII, 527–28

30 Walker, *PMHB*, XXIV, 414

31 Washington, *Writings* (Fitzpatrick), XX, 48

32 Appendix, No. 58

33 Sparks, *Correspondence*, III, 90

34 Varick, *Court*, 124–25, 171–72

35 Appendix, No. 69; Washington, *Writings* (Sparks), VII, 525

36 Lamb's testimony at Smith's trial: Smith, *Record*, 103–04

37 Smith, *Authentic Narrative*, 19–20

38 Varick, *Court*, 170, 177, 178; Smith, *Record*, 104

39 Barbé-Marbois, 100–01

40 Varick, *Court*, 133–34

41 Appendix, No. 70, as edited by Clinton; Washington, *Writings* (Sparks), VII, 526, as sent

42 Appendix, No. 71

43 Smith, Journal, VII, entry for October 11, 1780

44 Washington, *Writings* (Sparks), VII, 526–28

45 Varick, *Court*, 123–24, 140, 170

46 Walker, *PMHB*, XXV, 173

47 Smith, *Record*, 116; Abbatt, 5

48 Smith, *Record*, 17

49 Charles F. Heartman, Auction No. 192, October 2, 1926; Anderson Galleries, Sale No. 2273, May 16, 1928

50 Account of Expenses, February 21–September 13, 1781, CP

51 Tallmadge to Sparks, February 17, 1834, *MAH*, III (1879), 755–56

52 Sargent, *André*, 234–49, gives text of poem printed from André's manuscript with useful notes

53 Appendix, No. 59

54 Clinton to Germain, October 11, 1780, quoted in Sargent, *André*, 256–57

55 Lossing, *Field-Book*, II, 589

CHAPTER 14

1 Smith, *Record*, 6–7

2 Appendix, Nos. 60, 73–74; Washington, *Writings* (Sparks), VII, 529; Sargent, *André*, 349

3 Quoted in Appendix, No. 61

4 Arnold to Eli Leavenworth, September 20, 1780, WP, LC

5 Smith, *Record*, 98–99, 101–03

6 Smith, *Record*, 7–8

7 Smith, *Record*, 11–13

8 Appendix, No. 61

9 Appendix, No. 86; Smith, *Record*, 115

10 André's Statement, Sargent, *André*, 349

11 Appendix, No. 88

12 André at his trial, quoted by Washington to Clinton, September 30, 1780, Appendix, No. 81; André to Washington, September 24, 1780,

Sargent, *André*, 324–26; Washington, *Writings* (Sparks), VII, 531–32

13 Appendix, No. 68

14 Smith, *Authentic Narrative*, 31–32; but see also Smith, *Record*, 75–76

15 Smith, *Record*, 8–9

16 André to Washington, September 24, 1780, Washington, *Writings* (Sparks), VII, 531

17 André's Statement, Sargent, *André*, 349–50

18 Appendix, No. 61

19 Smith, *Record*, 72

20 André's Statement, Sargent, *André*, 350

21 André to Washington, September 24, 1780, Washington, *Writings* (Sparks), VII, 531

22 Sargent, *André*, 298

23 Smith, *Record*, 27, 30, 49, 65, 76

24 Smith, *Authentic Narrative*, 35–37

25 Smith, *Record*, 17–18

26 Smith, *Record*, 43–45

27 Smith, *Authentic Narrative*, 43; Abbatt, 19–20, for topographical details

28 Varick, *Court*, 126–27, 178–79

29 Smith, *Record*, 76; Smith, *Authentic Narrative*, 43–48; Abbatt, 23

30 Continental Congress, *Journals*, XVIII, 1009

31 For details of the capture, Sargent, *André*, 312–30, 461–64; Winsor, VI, 466; Abbatt, 26–32

32 Smith, *Record*, 52–60

33 André's Statement, Sargent, *André*, 350

34 Appendix, No. 76

35 Pennypacker, 112–19

36 Tallmadge to Sparks, November 16, 1833, *MAH*, III (1879), 749; Tallmadge, *Memoir* (1858), 35–36

37 Sparks, *Correspondence*, III, 102

38 Washington, *Writings* (Sparks), VII, 531–32

39 Varick, *Court*, 150

40 Varick, *Court*, 173–77

41 Varick, *Court*, 98

42 Varick, *Court*, 179–80

43 Stevens, 739

44 Varick, *Court*, 130

45 Varick, *Court*, 180–81

46 Varick to Jane Varick, October 1, 1780, Varick, *Court*, 189–93

47 Jones, I, 745–46

48 Varick, *Court*, 142

49 Varick, *Court*, 131

50 Washington, *Writings* (Sparks), VII, 533
51 Hamilton, *Works*, IX, 207–08
52 Davis, *Burr*, I, 219
53 Walker, *PMHB*, XXV, 178–90; Arnold, *Arnold*, 318–20
54 Varick, *Court*, 192–93
55 Washington, *Writings* (Fitzpatrick), XX, 84–88
56 Major William North, manuscript (1823), School of the Fine Arts, Yale University
57 Washington, *Writings* (Sparks), VII, 533–34
58 Stevens, 739, has account of flight by Andrew Elliott probably furnished him by Arnold

CHAPTER 15

1 Tallmadge to Sparks, *MAH*, III, 750
2 Hamilton, *Writings*, IX, 219
3 Washington, *Writings* (Fitzpatrick), XX, 101
4 Here quoted from original manuscript, September 29, 1780, WP, LC; printed the same year at Philadelphia, accurately reprinted in Sargent, *André*, 346–56; for André's written Statement, see Sargent, *André*, 349–50, and Washington, *Writings* (Sparks), VII, 535–36
5 Smith, Journal, VI, various entries as noted in text above
6 Arnold to Clinton, September 26, 1780, Appendix, No. 78
7 Clinton to Washington, September 26, 1780, Appendix, No. 79
8 Washington, *Correspondence . . . with the Officers*, II, 1554
9 Washington to Clinton, September 30, 1780, Appendix, No. 81
10 André to Clinton, September 29, Appendix, No. 80
11 Ogden, Aaron, *Autobiography*, in *Proceedings of the New Jersey Historical Society*, 2nd Series, XII, 23–25; Sparks, *Arnold*, 267–70; Sargent, *André*, 366–67
12 Hamilton to John Laurens, undated, and to Elizabeth Schuyler, October 2, 1780, Hamilton, *Writings*, IX, 222, 209
13 Hamilton to Clinton, September 30, Appendix, No. 63
14 Simcoe, *Military Journal*, 294

15 Ogden, *Autobiography*, XII, 23–25
16 Robertson to Clinton, October 1, Appendix, No. 83
17 Greene to Robertson, October 2, Appendix, No. 84
18 Robertson to Washington, October 2, Appendix, No. 85
19 Arnold to Washington, October 1, Appendix, No. 86
20 Washington, *Writings* (Fitzpatrick), XX, 131
21 For details of the execution, Sargent, *André*, 392–99; Abbatt, 69–76
22 Washington, *Writings* (Fitzpatrick), XX, 173
23 Arnold to Clinton, October 18, Appendix, No. 68
24 Stevens, 739
25 Reprinted, Arnold, *Arnold*, 330–32, from Arnold's manuscript
26 Arnold to Germain, October 28, 1780, CP
27 Jones, II, 210–12; Fox, Dixon Ryan, *Yankees and Yorkers* (1940), 162–63
28 Arnold, *Arnold*, 332–34
29 Scharf and Westcott, I, 413
30 Washington, *Writings* (Fitzpatrick), XX, 264
31 Moore, *Diary*, II, 344
32 Quoted in Channing, Edward, *A History of the United States*, III (1912), 307
33 *Collections of the New Brunswick Historical Society*, No. 5 (St. John, New Brunswick, Canada, 1904), for valuable list of loyalist officers; Sabine, *Loyalists*, alphabetical entries
34 Henry Van Dyck to Oliver De-Lancey, January 7, 1781, CP
35 Pennypacker, 186, from WP, LC, October 20, 1780
36 Arnold to Tallmadge, October 25, 1780, WP, LC; Pennypacker, 196–197
37 Washington, *Writings* (Fitzpatrick), XX, 335–36, 416–17, 420, 472–73; Continental Congress, *Journals*, XVIII, 1122
38 Pennypacker, 196–97
39 Tallmadge to Jared Sparks, February 17, 1834, *MAH*, III, 754
40 Franks to Varick, September 28, 1780, Tomlinson Collection, NYPL
41 Edward Burd to Jasper Yeates, October 5, 1780, *PMHB*, XL, 380–81

42 *Colonial Records*, XII, 520
43 Walker, *PMHB*, XXV, 162–63
44 *A List of the Officers of the Army*, printed by the British War Office, April 28, 1783
45 Arnold to Viscount Sydney, February 15, 1784, CP
46 *Pennsylvania Packet*, July 21, 1781; reprinted, *MAH*, II, 55–56
47 Franklin, *Writings* (Smyth), VIII, 251
48 For schedule of Provincial pay, *Collections of the New Brunswick Historical Society*, No. 5, 221
49 North to Carleton, August 8, 1783, Shelburne Papers, WLCL
50 Arnold, *Arnold*, 404–05
51 Arnold, *Arnold*, 363
52 Clinton's notes on his conversation with William Pitt about Arnold, November 14, 1792, CP
53 Arnold, *Arnold*, 363, 401, 413
54 Taylor, 51–54
55 Margaret Arnold to Edward Shippen, July 17, 1785, *PMHB*, XXV, 452
56 Continental Congress, *Journals*, XVIII, 906; Washington, *Writings* (Fitzpatrick), XX, 181–82
57 Taylor, 53

CHAPTER 16

1 Washington, *Writings* (Fitzpatrick), XX, 97
2 Washington, *Writings* (Fitzpatrick), XX, 442
3 Washington, *Writings* (Fitzpatrick), XX, 213–15
4 Lee, *Memoirs*, 271, 281; Washington, *Writings* (Fitzpatrick), XX, 178; Washington, *Writings* (Sparks), VII, 544–45
5 Charles Lunn to John Small, undated but about February 13–15, 1780; John Small to Arthur St. Clair, February 16, 1780: both in CP
6 Washington, *Writings* (Fitzpatrick), XX, 223
7 Lee, *Memoirs*, 270–84
8 Compare Washington, *Writings* (Sparks), VII, 545–49; Washington, *Writings* (Fitzpatrick), XX, 178, 223–24
9 Information of Deserters, October 23, 1780
10 Moore, *Diary*, II, 327–28, 333, 337

11 Information of Deserters, November 26, 1780
12 Smith, Journal, VII, December 21, 1780
13 *MAH*, X, 416–17; Heron, William, in *Dictionary of National Biography*
14 Parsons to Washington, April 6, 1782, *MAH*, XX, 293–94
15 *MAH*, XI, 64–65
16 *MAH*, XI, 347–51
17 Both letters in *MAH*, XII, 163–67
18 DeLancey to Heron, July 31, 1781, CP
19 Parsons to William Parsons, July 21, 1781, CP
20 *MAH*, XX, 329–32
21 La Luzerne to Vergennes, May 13, 1781, *MAH*, XI, 158–60
22 *MAH*, XI, 156–57
23 *MAH*, XI, 538–39; Holland to Sullivan, June 9, 1781, CP
24 Sullivan, *Papers*, III, 344
25 Pell, 199
26 Haldimand to Clinton, November 15, 1780, CP
27 Simcoe to Clinton, November 2, 1780, CP
28 Printed in *MAH*, X (October 1883) —XII (August 1884)
29 Manuscript volume in Emmett Collection, NYPL
30 Washington, *Writings* (Fitzpatrick), XXI, 88
31 Stillé, Charles J., *Major General Anthony Wayne* (1893), 259
32 Washington, *Writings* (Fitzpatrick), XXI, 57–58, 104
33 Journal, January 3–21, 1781, CP
34 DeLancey to John Stapleton, January 14, 1781, CP
35 Beckwith to DeLancey, January 14, 1781, CP
36 Samuel Wallis to Daniel Coxe, January 13, 1781, CP
37 Memorandum on Odell's information, January 15, 1781, CP
38 Wallis to Coxe, January 13, 1781, CP; January 25, *MAH*, X, 497; February 3, 9, CP; May 22, *MAH*, XI, 161; June 27, *MAH*, XI, 542–44
39 Gentleman in Philadelphia to Beckwith, April 21, 23, May 4, 1781, *MAH*, XI, 68–69
40 *MAH*, XI, 443, 543
41 Gentleman in Philadelphia to Beck-

with, June 19, 27, *MAH*, XI, 440–44; July 24, CP

42 *Vermont Historical Society Collections*, II, 59–61, 92–93; Pell, 192–94, 210

43 *MAH*, X, 505

44 *Vermont Historical Society Collections*, II, 104–06

45 Washington, *Writings* (Fitzpatrick), XXII, 81–82; XXI, 275–76, 355–356; Sparks, *Correspondence*, III, 26–63

46 Washington, *Writings* (Fitzpatrick), XXI, 501–04

47 John Connolly to Clinton, November 25, 1780, CP

48 Letter dated only September 1781, in answer to Mr. Alexander (Rankin's pseudonym), CP

49 George III, V, 200

50 North to Clinton, August 3, 1781, CP

51 Arnold to Commodore Thomas Symmes, February 5, 1781, CP

52 Washington, *Writings* (Fitzpatrick), XVI, 63

53 Mackenzie, Frederick, *Diary* (1930), II, 540

54 Cornwallis to Clinton, May 26, 1781, CP; William Smith to William Tryon, June 3, 1781, Germain Papers, WLCL

55 Arnold to Clinton, April 16, 1781, CP

56 Clinton's journal in manuscript volume No. 2, Government Orders, 38th Regt., CP

57 Smith, Journal, September 13, 1781

58 Memorandum of a Conversation . . . between the Commander-in-Chief and B. General Arnold, November 5, 1781, CP

59 Smith, Journal, November 8, 1781

60 Arnold, *Arnold*, 419–27

61 *PMHB*, XXV, 163

CHAPTER 17

1 General Bibliography

2 CP

3 *PMHB*, XXVI, 467–68

4 Arnold, *Arnold*, 392–93

5 Arnold, *Arnold*, 383

6 For this correspondence see the following letters and notes in CP: Arnold to Clinton, July 23, 1792; Clinton to Arnold, August 2; Arnold to Clinton, October 17; Pitt to Clinton, November 10; Margaret Arnold to Clinton, November 13; Arnold to Clinton, November 14; various notes made by Clinton during November; Arnold to Clinton, December 3; an undated statement by Arnold regarding his services, possibly sent by Clinton to Pitt on November 17

7 Arnold, *Arnold*, 406–17; Decker, 458

8 Scharf and Westcott, I, 412

9 *Colonial Records*, XII, 554, 568, 573, 594

10 Taylor, 18

11 Sargent, *Loyal Verses*, 101

12 *Now and Then*, VI, 250–54

13 *MAH*, VI, 279–82

14 *Publications of the Jewish American Historical Society*, I, 76–86; IV, 81–87; X, 101–08

15 Loyalist Transcripts, XXV, 250–56

16 Mayo, Katherine, *General Washington's Dilemma* (1938) gives a full account of the Huddy episode

17 Einstein, for later lives of Wentworth, Vardill, Bancroft, and Deane

18 Deane to Benjamin Franklin, *Deane Papers* (1887–91), V, 213–14

19 Franklin, *Writings* (Smyth), VIII, 625–26

20 Winsor, VII, 211–12; Jones, II, 645–663; Sabine, I, 104–13

21 Bradley, A. G., *The United Empire Loyalists* (1932), 108; *The American Revolution in New York* (1926), 222

Index